Hellman
and
Hammett

Hellman
and
Hammett

The Legendary Passion of Lillian Hellman and Dashiell Hammett

JOAN MELLEN

HarperCollins*Publishers*

The author acknowledges that permission to include quotations from certain writings of Lillian Hellman and Dashiell Hammett has been granted by the Literary Property Trustees under the Will of Lillian Hellman. Grateful acknowledgment is also made to the following: Harry Ransom Humanities Research Center at the University of Texas at Austin; Shirah Kober Zeller for permission to quote from the letters and diaries of Arthur Kober and Maggie Kober, Warner Bros. Archives, School of Cinema-Television, University of Southern California; Josephine Marshall; Richard Moody and the Lilly Library, Indiana University, for the manuscript of *Lillian Hellman, Playwright* with marginal notations.

HarperCollins books may be purchased for educational, business, or sales promotional use. For information please write: Special Markets Department, HarperCollins Publishers, Inc., 10 East 53rd Street, New York, NY 10022.

FIRST EDITION

Designed by Alma Hochhauser Orenstein

Photo inserts designed by Barbara DuPree Knowles

ISBN 0-06-018339-X

96 97 98 99 00 ❖/RRD 10 9 8 7 6 5 4 3 2 1

For Ralph Schoenman,
as always, and
for Dorothea Straus and Alvin Sargent,
with gratitude

Because no battle is ever won he said. They are not even fought. The field only reveals to man his own folly and despair, and victory is an illusion of philosophers and fools.

WILLIAM FAULKNER,
THE SOUND AND THE FURY

We are the vanguard, but of what?

ISAAC BABEL,
1920 DIARY

Contents

Photographs follow pages 204 and 396.

Preface

The legend of Lillian Hellman and Dashiell Hammett has scarcely been penetrated. Hammett's intractable silence was followed by Lillian Hellman's four volumes of memoirs, which turned out to be more fantasy, psychic obfuscation and inversion than autobiography. The uniqueness of their relationship, the depth of their love—and hatred—for each other has yet to be explored.

Did anyone actually ever see them together? Gore Vidal is said to have quipped viciously. Because Hellman inflated what she meant to Hammett, some have concluded, incorrectly, that it was of small consequence. Yet down the thirty years of their connection she was Hammett's closest friend. If he was unable to be all that she demanded out of her insatiable need, if he refused to fulfill her romantic fantasies, he gave her a very great deal.

He also needed her, depended on her, and longed for more from her, facts which she sometimes chose to ignore out of her profound disappointment that he did not partake of some medieval notion of courtly love. She yearned for a noble knight errant who would love her for herself despite her plainness and tried to make one out of an ex-Pinkerton operative turned mystery writer, an alcoholic man terrified of feelings. Lillian the master chef had created a recipe for violent conflict and certain pain for herself, even as there was a stoical nobility about Hammett, a selflessness that partook of its own grandeur.

The San Francisco-based Hammett cult has long hated Lillian Hellman, believing it had to be her fault that shortly after they met he stopped writing. It seemed clear to the private-eye world that Hellman stole Hammett's talents to build her career. Was it she who was greedy, he self-sacrificing? Or was he a bearer of heartbreak, a perpetual fount of rejection inspiring perpetual yearning? Yet even as he never loved anyone as much as he did her, their relationship seems a Faustian bargain, with both of them settling for something less than what life might offer.

After her death, Lillian's friends remained curious about the truth behind what Philip Rahv called the Tristan and Isolde legend she made of herself and Hammett. "What was there between those two?" Blair Clark, whom Lillian selected in the early sixties as Hammett's romantic replacement in her life, pondered into the nineties, as he suggested to me the concept of this book.

When seen together, each stands in relief; she becomes more than herself, and he does too. They were more and less than married. He supported, encouraged, and edited her work as few husbands could—or would. She nurtured, took care of him as consistently as a woman who was not a wife might be expected to do. He was generous, but often less than compassionate toward her, less than kind. If for the most part he was emotionally faithful, he was never sexually so.

She was kind to him, emotionally faithful in spite of her own best interests, and not sexually faithful, because he made it impossible for her to be. She had frequented the same speakeasies, drank to keep up with the men, but she did not become Dorothy Parker. She taught herself to be a woman of discipline who would not let herself go. For better or worse, she gave a damn. Cooking, gardening, entertaining, writing—she gave her all. At the risk of sounding foolish, she invoked "standards." Meanwhile they hurt each other badly, he first, but she when he was most vulnerable.

They were two halves of a couple, heeding no one else's definition of what a man and woman might be to each other. They made traditional expectations of couplehood, of marriage, seem provincial, adolescent, and lacking in spirit. They belonged, if not to the twenty-first century, then to the raucous eighteenth. They continued to capture people's imaginations even after both of them were dead.

How each behaved during the tribulations of McCarthyism has never been told.

It has been difficult to discover their story because they were too proud and too independent and too private to expose the actual nature of their relationship. He kept no papers in a lifetime of attempting to obliterate himself. Nor, unlike her, would he substitute legend for the real thing. "He had an absolute contempt for lies," Lillian Hellman wrote of

Dashiell Hammett. "You didn't owe anybody a lie. It was undignified and you only hurt yourself in the end. In the end it was a way of life."

She was addicted to lying from childhood on, a malady she periodically attempted to cure; he abhorred it but saw that one could not easily get through life without lying. But sometimes, even Dash knew, lying was necessary just to make life bearable. "Tomorrow, if there's no more news than there is today," he wrote Lily in October of 1944 from the Aleutian Islands, "I may make up some fancy lies for you. I don't want to go on with letters like this and have you think that I'm leading a dull, empty and eventless life."

A foremost literary fabulator of her generation, Lillian Hellman invented her life, so that by the end even she was uncertain about what had been true. She had also long been ready to shed the illusion that there was actuality to the stories she told in her memoirs. Talking of the marriage of her parents, in 1982, two years before her death, she told screenwriter Alvin Sargent, "It's a real memory. I didn't make it up. It really happened." So she would distinguish the story she was about to tell from all those she had with such conviction presented as true but rather had been merely woven from threads of the real.

The biographer stumbles through a minefield.

I wrote this book because although I met her only five or six times in the last two years of her life, Lillian Hellman had a powerful effect on me. Often in the perilous crossings between men and women I found myself wondering: what would Lily do? And it always comes back to me. She would act; she would throw her hat into the ring, take a stand, present herself, draw on her strengths: wit, great intelligence, perseverance, and the inspiration and courage she had learned from Hammett, who had taught her to trust no authority, to do her damnedest to outsmart a cynical and corrupt society.

In her lifetime Lillian Hellman did her best either to thwart or to control any biographies written of Dashiell Hammett. To both Diane Johnson writing of Hammett and Alvin Sargent writing a Hellman-Hammett screenplay called *Two Lives,* she insisted that nothing in their work deviate from the account she gave in her published memoirs. With letters written to her friends requesting that they not talk to writers, she made certain that no unauthorized biography of herself would appear in her lifetime. She also attempted to thwart those written after her death by destroying her letters, many of which she had successfully retrieved from their recipients.

This book is the first to make use of Lillian Hellman's papers, as well as those of Dashiell Hammett deposited with her archives at the Harry Ransom Humanities Research Center of the University of Texas. With new material available, another biographical impression of these people may thrust light into some dark corners.

I wish to thank Blair Clark, for introducing me to Lillian Hellman, for inviting me to her Christmas Day party in 1983 at the Tuileries, for co-hosting a dinner for her with me, and for arranging several other occasions with Miss Hellman. Twice I cooked for her. The first time she sampled graciously the biographer's crawfish bisque, which could not possibly have met her standard. She stopped only at the New Orleans fig cake. "I don't eat cake!" she said loudly and defiantly. The second time she instructed me on where to buy fresh geese (at Schaller & Weber, in Manhattan's Yorktown).

For his generosity from the start, truly an *acte gratuit,* and his confidence in me and this project, I am deeply grateful to Peter Feibleman. Without his approval, many of the people I interviewed would have been reluctant to share their memories of Lillian Hellman with me. His generosity, his trust, his largesse came from an openness of spirit, and a belief in freedom of biographical inquiry, for he demanded to see no line of this text before publication. His approach was a model for all those heirs to literary property who would jealousy guard the words of our subjects in the hope that their view might be represented in someone else's pages. My thanks as well go to Richard Poirier and to William Abrahams for their similar trust.

To Rita Wade, Lillian's right hand for twenty years, I am indebted in so many ways there isn't space to enumerate them.

A heartfelt thank-you goes as well to Josephine Hammett Marshall, for patience in sharing with me her memories of her father. Pearl London, the widow of Lillian Hellman's lawyer Ephraim London, has been extraordinarily helpful to me as well. Special thanks go to Jack Bjoze for his unstinting efforts in locating old friends and acquaintances of my subjects. For her unstinting generosity and patience I would also like especially to thank Mrs. Helen Rosen.

For their generosity I would like to thank literary agent Don Congdon, and Ben Camardi of the Harold Matson Company, Inc.

I am pleased and grateful to be a part of the confederacy of biographers, that generous band of people so often willing to share their research with those who come after. To Richard Layman, who worked on his biography of Dashiell Hammett against impossible odds and who opened his files to me, I am grateful and in awe of this degree of unselfishness. I wish to thank as well Carl Rollyson, who behaved always as colleague rather than competitor. Diane Johnson was generous with her insights. William Abrahams kindly gave me copies of Dashiell Hammett's letters to Lillian Hellman from the Aleutian Islands. Alvin Sargent, writer of the film *Julia*, who worked closely with Miss Hellman on a screenplay about Hellman and Hammett, was an immediate and generous support. His encouragement helped me through the last stages of my writing, his kindness consistent to the end.

Thank you also, Fred Gardner, for sharing interviews done with Lillian Hellman in the 1960s. Dorothy Herrmann shared her S. J. Perelman research tapes and valuable advice. Thank you, Carole Klein, biographer of Aline Bernstein, Lillian Hellman's set designer. Among this splendid confederacy I would also like to thank Martin Gottfried for talking to me about Jed Harris, and William Wright, Lillian Hellman biographer, for taking that detour to Hardscrabble Farm. Marion Meade, Dorothy Parker's biographer, shared many insights and offered gracious assistance. Jay Martin, Nathanael West's biographer, contributed material about Lillian and Pep West. Thank you, Louise Collins of WHWH radio, Princeton, for sharing your tape of Muriel Gardiner. Film director Edward M. Zwick sent his Harvard senior thesis on *Watch on the Rhine* and its biographical implications. Thank you, Peter Manso, author of *Mailer: His Life and Times*, for a frank conversation.

Both the biography seminar at New York University, headed by Fred Karl, Ken Silverman, and Brenda Wineapple, and the Women Writing Women's Lives seminar at the City University of New York, which invited me in the autumn of 1994 to present some of the ideas garnered from the research for this book, have been welcoming, encouraging, inspiring, sustaining.

Unlike Lillian Hellman's more loyal band, Dashiell Hammett's friends often sold his letters to them. For helping me to track down some of this material, I owe a large debt of gratitude to another friendly confederacy, that of rare-book dealers. Thank you, Otto Penzler, of the Mysterious Press and the Mystery Bookshop in New York, for setting me forth on this trail. Thank you as well to John Schulman of Caliban Bookshop in Pittsburgh and Jeffrey H. Marks of Jeffrey H. Marks Rare Books in Rochester, New York. Jim Pepper and Peter Stern of Pepper and Stern Books, in Santa Barbara and Boston, were very kind.

Special thanks for the graciousness and courtesy of Mr. George Lowry, president of the Swann Gallery in New York City, which often handles significant literary properties.

I am very grateful to all those people who were willing to talk with me about Lillian Hellman, that unfinished woman, and Dashiell Hammett, that most silent of men: Renata Adler, William Alfred, Eugene R. Anderson, Linda Anderson, Sam Aronson, Eliot Asinof, Michael Avallone, Helen Benedict, Howard S. Benedict, Burton Bernstein, Nina Bernstein, Shirley Bernstein, Walter Bernstein, the late Becky Bernstien, Lenora Berson,

Simon Michael Bessie, Jack Bjoze, Kathleen Brady, the late Harold Brod-
key, Heywood Hale Broun, Robert Brustein, McGeorge Bundy, Lynn
Chaleff, Jean Chelnov, Frances Cheney, Virginia Bloomgarden Chilewich,
Robert Colodny, the late Joan Cook, Jean Dalrymple, Edgar Dannenberg,
Annabel Davis-Goff, Inge Dean, Richard de Combray, Midge Decter,
Irene Diamond, William Doering, Roger Donald, Harriette Dorsen, Nor-
man Dorsen, Isadore Englander, Barbara Epstein, Jason Epstein, Emil
Erdelsky, Rose Evans, Howard Fast, Jules Feiffer, Frederick V. Field,
Franklin Folsom, the late Joe Fox, Blair Fuller, Diana Fuller, Martha Gell-
horn, Si Gerson, Madeline Gilford, Stephen Gillers, Robert Giroux,
William Glackin, Ruth Goetz, Muriel Alexander Golden, Richard Good-
win, Stephen Greene, Albert Hackett, Emily Hahn, David Hammett,
Leslie Hanscom, Kitty Carlisle Hart, Dr. Philip D'Arcy Hart, Helen Har-
vey, Charles Haydon, Shirley Hazzard, Grace Hechinger, Fred Hills, Robin
Hogan, the late Irving Howe, the late Alice Hunter, Julius Jacobson, Phyl-
lis Jacobson, J. J. Joseph, the late Mary Kaufman, Miriam Dickey Kinsey,
Goldie Kleiner, Catherine Kober, David V. Koch, Sarah Jane Kramarsky,
Nancy Kramer, Emmy Kronenberger, Robert Lantz, Jonathan La Pook,
Ring Lardner, Jr., Elena Levin, the late Harry Levin, Mildred Loftus,
William Luce, Norman Mailer, Stephen Marcus, the late John Marquand,
Robert Meiklejohn, the late John Melby, Howard Meyer, Belle Moldevan,
Honor Moore, Kathleen Harriman Mortimer, Patricia Neal, William
Nolan, Paul O'Dwyer, Lynda Palevsky, Max Palevsky, Jim Peck, Austin
Pendleton, Arthur Penn, Otto Penzler, Anne Peretz, Martin Peretz,
William Phillips, Mina Towbin Pingar, Norman Podhoretz, Richard
Poirier, Miriam Procter, Marilyn Raab, Sophie Raab, Victor Rabinowitz,
Maurice Rapf, Adele Ritt, Flora Roberts, Gaby Rodgers, Mary Rolfe, Dr.
John Rosen, Richard Roth, Judy Ruben, Lucy Ruskin, Victor Samrock,
Dorothy Samuels, Judith Firth Sanger, Sydney Schiffer, Lola Shumlin,
Robert Silvers, William M. Sloane, Abe Smorodin, E. E. Spitzer, Lee
Brown Spitzer, Maureen Stapleton, the late Francis Steegmuller, Dorothea
Straus, Lucy Strunsky, Rose Styron, Telford Taylor, Evelyn Teichmann,
Jamie Bernstein Thomas, Albert Todd, A. Robert Towbin, Diana Trilling,
Jerome Weidman, Dina Weinstein, James Weinstein, Lisa Weinstein,
Paula Weinstein, Milton Wexler, Nancy Wexler, Charlee Wilbur, Richard
Wilbur, the late Eleanor Wolff, Jane Fish Yowaiski, and Fred Zinnemann.

Biographers are dependent on the kindness of librarians, obviously.
Thank you very much: Dr. Tom Staley, and Cathy Henderson at the
Harry Ransom Humanities Research Center of the University of Texas at
Austin, and to Barbara Smith-LaBorde, who was always there, gracious
and supportive, and to Pat Fox. Without you this book could not have
been written.

Thank you, Stuart Ng, the curator of the Warner Brothers Archives at the Doheny Library of the University of Southern California. Thank you, Bernard R. Crystal at Columbia University and Fay Thompson of the Library of the American Academy of Motion Picture Arts and Sciences. Thank you, John Curry and Clay Bauske at the Harry S. Truman Library. Thank you, Harry Miller at the State Historical Society in Madison, Wisconsin. Thank you, Michael Ryan at the University of Pennsylvania Van Pelt library. Thank you, Saundra Taylor at the Lilly Library at Indiana University in Bloomington, Indiana. Thank you, Edward Skipworth of Rutgers University Libraries, R. Russell Maylone, curator at the Northwestern University Library, Special Collections Department. Thank you, Margaret Roman, troubleshooter at the Freedom of Information office of the Department of State. And thank you to Linda Kloss at the Freedom of Information office of the Federal Bureau of Investigation. Thank you too, Roy Dunn at KERA/KDTN Dallas, Texas. My thanks go as well to Yale University Library, Amherst College, the Archives of American Art of the Smithsonian Institution, the University of Michigan, the Huntington Library, the Copley Library in Boston, and the University of Washington library.

Finally, as always, special thanks to Hope Suloff at the Mercer County Library, Hopewell Branch, in New Jersey.

It was most gracious of Ellen Hodor to provide a tour of Hardscrabble Farm, and of Anthony Perry for accompanying me there and to Dashiell Hammett's cottage in Katonah.

Gretchen Ambach was a fine assistant during the early stages of this project.

To my editor, Gladys Carr, vice president and associate publisher at HarperCollins, a legend herself, I am grateful. My thanks goes as well to Cynthia Barrett and to Elyssa Altman, but especially to Deirdre O'Brien for her constant nurturing support.

To my hardworking and generous agent, the superb Jane Gelfman, a sterling authors' advocate, I am more than grateful.

This book was copyedited by the incomparable John P. Lynch. His intelligence, grace, and elegance have been a beacon for me in the writing of biography.

Prologue

"In spite of her chic, highly polished expensive exterior, she was all marshmallow inside. She could no more face the raised voice than the raised hand. Sam, who liked her and wished he could love her, at once felt like a dog."

JEROME WEIDMAN, *THE SOUND OF BOW BELLS*.

She sits in her bedroom across the floor from where he lies awake in what had once been her workroom, her office. Since breathing is so difficult, no matter the hour he will be sitting up reading. He has been living with her for just over two years and his face has grown sadder every day. Finally she cannot help herself. She enters his room.

"It's tough, been tough these last four or five years," he admits. And he cries with one tear. She sits down on his bed.

"Tell me," she urges, "do you want to talk about it?" She yearns for him to open himself to her; she hopes he will at last speak of what they have been to each other, something he has been avoiding assiduously since his return from the Aleutian Islands in 1945.

"No," he tells her angrily, "my only chance is not to think about it."

She had expected, wanted a scene. Vaguely she had hoped for the tears that would have been healing for her; she longed for at least gratitude, if not an admission of love. But she is given nothing but ill nature. In these last years she has very often grown angry with his ill nature. It doesn't explain much to say there was a lack of oxygen to his brain and thus the ill nature.

Why me? Lily torments herself. Why is he cruel and unforgiving only with me? Facing herself alone, she knows she has often promised herself his death and she has been angry.

In these last years he has punished her for that anger. Now he seems, a few minutes later, to have forgotten his outburst. Frequently in this time she has thought he was irrational. But, she thinks, maybe the forgetfulness wasn't that, but only an attempt to come closer. Now, as he lies dying, she waits for a sign, an affirmation that he does love her and always has.

He has few visitors. One is the grown daughter of Lily's long-ago husband, Arthur Kober. It cheers him up. He wants it, and she is as jealous today as she was all those long years ago when she discovered that there would be women, always there would be women. He is frail, barely able to walk now, to get out of bed, yet she suspects that a last sexual surge is there, and she is appalled to discover that she is subject to the same old fantasies about him and another woman that she used to have. Once he told her he had not always been excited by women he esteemed. "Too much is not good," he said. If she needed to torment, to hurt herself, she had those thirty years ago chosen a man who would see to it that she was hurt to his last breath.

Lily watches. He grabs at the young woman, at his other women visitors; he feels urges he never expresses toward her, and once again she feels the old jealousy and the old what she calls moral crap about don't harm, don't touch, don't seduce. She knows she is being foolish. It is sad and it is a last try. The ladies know it and respond to it and are pleased. They don't believe they are being harmed.

On another day he talks to her of his unfinished story "Tulip." He says he can't work, has never liked writers who didn't know what they were doing, and now he doesn't know what he is doing.

"Maybe because the book comes from another period," she ventures. She is as afraid to talk to him about his writing as she has always been. Afraid and hating it, always afraid and hating it. He speaks of two other books. She is torn with pity and love and hatred, and she is bored by the struggle.

Something had gone wrong a long time ago. She wondered whether it was because it was not a grand passion. Their old friend Jerome Weidman wrote in his roman à clef, *The Sound of Bow Bells*, whose main characters are the two of them, that he had "wished he could love her," but never could because "in the game of love the cheaply won victory moved many things, but never the heart." Or, Weidman had speculated, it might have been that he had felt "through the warmth of her embrace as a woman the chill of her superiority as an artist."

"Deep down I don't *really* have you," Weidman's Lily laments.

She is tortured still by his evasion.

One afternoon he staggers into her bedroom. He is not entirely coherent. Why is it happening, why is it happening? he says. We must try . . . something . . . I can't.

"It's because you were mean to me," she says.

He is angry now. "That wasn't what I was talking about," he tells her harshly, and they don't go on with it. Lily knows she seems very self-centered, as if she expected a dying man to be something else. Yet how much of all this isn't true? His behavior in his last days seems a summation of the paltriness of what they had.

It has been years since they have really talked, or known each other. She thinks she did her best but she also knows now, and it makes her sad, that it wasn't a very good best.

And still it rankles. With other people, she remembers, there was warmth and need. Maybe even in these last weeks with his visitors there was a sexual need, or a need for a mother. But not with her.

Throughout their long thirty years she was "frightened of being hit, frightened of the humiliation, frightened of his superiority." She wishes her old psychiatrist Gregory Zilboorg were still living. She feels very shallow and frightened. He had some kind of love in his life, much of it duty maybe, and it seems now as if she will have none.

Childless women do not grow up, she thinks. It becomes their custom to pretend that they are like the young, and are the children of people their own age. In their own eyes they're closer to the children of their friends than are the friends. Some virginity still remains, some burdens lessened.

She is tortured that she is not being taken into his last secrets. Is she being rejected or is it the old crap that everybody has rejected her? Sometimes she thinks he wanted to be good friends, and often she knows that he did not. Didn't trust her, didn't believe in her final kindness. He has called her "hard-eyed," and it stings and it will always sting.

She wishes she could go back and begin it with him all over again.

PART ONE

Samuel Dashiell Hammett
Meets
Lillian Florence Hellman Kober

1

"Who's That Man?"

"If a man has a past that he wants to forget, he can easiest drug his mind against memory through his body, with sensuality if not with narcotics."

THE DAIN CURSE

"I wanted blond curls and great blue eyes, tiny nose, rosebud mouth . . . you can see that I didn't get any of what I wanted."

LILLIAN HELLMAN

On November 22, 1930, they were both in Hollywood married to other people. She was out for the evening with Lee Gershwin, a queen bee herself, whose house was always filled with people. Outside you could hear the sound of the racket hitting the ball on the tennis courts, inside the shuffling of cards. Every Sunday was open house. Lillian had met Lee in Paris in 1928. Her husband was Ira and her brother-in-law was George. Oscar Levant was often in attendance playing the piano.

Lee and Dotty Parker and Lillian were all twenties women with an appetite for life. They shared an acerbic wit. Lively and fast-talking New York Jewish women, they smoked and they drank, and it didn't matter that they weren't beauties. Keeping up with the men, manipulating always, they demanded sexual freedom and they got it. Pragmatists, they knew how to cut their losses. If getting their way meant lying, they would lie. "That little area in her throat would throb when she was about to lie," Lee observed of Lillian, breaking into peals of laughter. "You always knew when she was lying."

That night of November 22 was producer Darryl Zanuck's party. The Gershwins were his guests at a movie premiere and their guests were Lillian, a script reader at M-G-M, and her far better-known husband, would-be playwright Arthur Kober, now drawing a weekly salary from Paramount as a scriptwriter.

Lillian Hellman at twenty had already been so resolute and independent a spirit that Kober doubted from the start whether he could hold her. He was short and round and soft-looking, not unlike Lillian's father, Max Hellman—a dark little butterball whose appearance was very Semitic. He had emigrated at the age of three from Austria-Hungary and was more at home in Yiddish than in English. His forte was humor, his style modeled on that of Ring Lardner.

Kober adored young Lillian Hellman; the room lit up for him when she appeared. He was diffident. She knew how to make him feel good about himself. On their first date they went on a carriage ride through Central Park. Lillian wore a new hat. Considering herself a homely woman, she did everything she could to transcend that disadvantage. Beautiful clothes were one important way. In the middle of the ride, Kober seized the hat and threw it into the bushes. Then he leaped out of the carriage, ostensibly to find the hat. Later he told her he only had to urinate. The hat was lost forever.

Lillian kept herself slim and tight; at five feet three inches she weighed one hundred and five pounds. She dyed her thick brown hair reddish blond, then sometimes red, sometimes blond. All the while, she knew that no matter what she did she wasn't going to be pretty, with her prow of a nose, which even her teenaged beau, up-and-coming critic and man of letters Louis Kronenberger, said made him think of Gilbert Stuart's painting of George Washington. It didn't help that she had thin lips and large ears. Nor, alas, was her figure prepossessing: she had broad shoulders and large, full breasts; she was heavy-chested and narrow-hipped, with no rear end at all. But she did her best to display her shapely legs and small, dainty feet, and her greenish-gray eyes were clear.

Always she was elegant, deploying hats and veils; her hair, of course, was perfectly coiffed. Lillian's shoes were never scuffed, and she wore very good gloves. As a young woman she did not falter when she saw something she wanted. After she dropped out of New York University in her junior year, Lillian worked for the legendary publisher Horace Liveright as a copywriter in the advertising department and then as a manuscript reader. Soon she aborted Kober's child without telling him. Six months later they were married.

Marriage for a flaming youth in 1925 represented not domestic bondage but freedom. Only a married woman had the liberty to go about as she pleased. It was a license to live as she wished, without inhibition, one denied to the single woman, who was condemned to remain under parental discipline. Lillian's mother, Julia Newhouse Hellman, preferred that she marry Kronenberger.

Lillian Florence Hellman was born in the parish of New Orleans on June 20, 1905. Her mother was a Newhouse, from Demopolis, Alabama, a member of a rich family presided over by matriarch Sophie Marx Newhouse. Lillian's father, Max, was of the lower middle class, in trade. He had graduated from being a bookkeeper to opening his own business. If the Newhouses, the Marxes, and the Hellmans were all German Jews of the 1840s migration, by the time Lillian was born strong class distinctions inextricably separated them. The Newhouses were so assimilated in their Alabama town that they were not specifically Jewish. They were not interested in sending their children to college and their questions were invariably: how did the store do that year? what piece of real estate did you pick up? "My mother's family used to have fun cutting each other's throats," Lillian was to say of them.

Her childhood was spent half in New York and half in New Orleans, where the family lived at a succession of boardinghouses operated by Max's sisters Jenny and Hannah. A feeling of social inferiority plagued her as soon as she became aware of the gulf between the circumstances of her family and those of the Newhouses.

The Hellman boardinghouses were located in the Uptown residential section of New Orleans, "on the fringe of the Garden district." The first, deeded in Max Hellman's name, was at 1718 Prytania Street. This was a big Victorian two-story clapboard house with upper and lower porches, surrounded by leafy trees. Moving frequently in the same neighborhood, the aunts took in boarders also at a house on St. Charles, at Valence, on other nearby streets, only to wind up in a small house on General Pershing. The first move came when Lily was seven and they moved to 4631 Prytania, with its stained-glass attic window and surrounding oaks. There was no fig tree that Lillian Hellman later said she climbed only to fall and break her nose.

From her earliest days Lillian was confronted by the contrast between rich and poor, and how the rich used their power to humiliate those weaker—namely, her poor father, whom she adored and who was no match for the supercilious Newhouses. Sophie Marx had brought her own money to her Newhouse marriage. Her family had been speculators and bankers and shopkeepers in dry goods. Max Hellman had a shoe business, the Hellman Shoe Company, which existed only by virtue of his wife's dowry. He went bankrupt when Lillian was six years old, and from then until she was about ten, she said, the family was quite poor. Max then became a traveling salesman in haberdashery, working for others.

As an adult, Lillian liked to tell the story of a friend who looked up one of her Newhouse aunts in Demopolis. "I'm a friend of your niece's," he began when the old woman came to the door. "Which niece?" she asked suspiciously. When he named Lillian Hellman, the aunt slammed the door in his face. "We don't like her" was Miss Newhouse's parting thrust.

Little Lily felt as if the Newhouses were looking down not only at her father but at her. From childhood she felt as if she were an outsider, an observer of life's feast condemned to exclusion. It was plain to Lillian's friends later that she felt bruised by having had to live in the aunts' tawdry boardinghouse, at having to take meals alongside the paying guests. It was a humiliation that her family didn't have their own house, that her mother did not make a home for her in New Orleans. The shabby lower-middle-class surroundings in which her childhood was spent infuriated her, gave rise to an anger she cultivated all her life. "I was uncontrollable," Lillian Hellman was to remember herself as a child.

Another early defining moment occurred one day when, as a very little girl, Lillian looked in the mirror. She registered that, unlike the pretty children, she didn't have deep blue eyes, blond naturally curly hair, a tiny nose, and a rosebud mouth. Beauty is not only power, it is necessary, she realized. Lily learned early that she would never have that power. She would never be the beauty who thinks she has done enough by merely walking into a room.

From the time Lillian was six, the family lived for six months each year in New York, where Lillian was placed in public school. The Hellman apartment was on Manhattan's Upper West Side, on Ninety-fifth Street between Riverside Drive and West End Avenue. This less fashionable residential area Lillian would never inhabit from the time she became a theater celebrity in 1934 to the end of her life. The Hellman apartment was plain, its furnishings in sharp contrast to those of the nearby Newhouse abode with its fine china and antiques. Lillian was ashamed to invite friends to her home because Julia provided none of the nurture of domesticity. The stuffing peeked from the furniture. Can it be repaired? she would plead.

"If you like," Julia Newhouse said mildly, surprised. It would never have occurred to her. As soon as she was able, Lillian Hellman established herself at the best East Side New York addresses, filling her homes with splendid if conventional furnishings, always in fine, expensive taste.

Julia Hellman was fey, distracted, and docile, obsessed with visiting churches. Lillian was to describe her as the wife in her play *Toys in the Attic:* "kind of sadly whacky, not crazy, but fey, and disjointed, and sweet, and lost." Julia was a mousy little woman for whom Lillian had little respect because her husband habitually cheated on her. "She was a very naive woman," Lillian Hellman was to say.

Nor did Julia Newhouse Hellman ever provide a mother's nurture. "I didn't have a mother," Lillian reflected bitterly years later. From her earliest years it was a source of simmering rage, inducing an anger comparable only to her dismay over her plain looks. "I was mean to her," Lily later confessed.

A fighter from the start, a child with a strong intelligence, Lillian invented the myth that her wet nurse, a large black woman named Sophronia, who was with the Hellmans only briefly, was the real nurturing figure in her life. Sophronia was the only woman she loved. "I was desperately in love with her," an aged Lillian Hellman was to declare. What Lillian admired about Sophronia was that she "was an absolute controller," that she would not allow the fiery-tempered little girl to get away with anything. "I was a cutup," Lillian later admitted. She believed that if Sophronia had stayed to discipline her, if she had been around to say "nix" to the child's antics, she might have become a different woman.

In Lillian's later years Sophronia was transmuted into the woman who saw through her and, unlike her parents, tolerated no nonsense. She served also one of Lily's theatrical personae, Lily the Southern belle shielded by the warm, large, comforting black woman. It was also the emblem of her Southern identity. An enlarged photograph of Sophronia holding a tiny, impish Lillian was to adorn the drawing rooms of Lillian Hellman's mature life, as Sophronia's talismanic line served her as a motto: "Don't go through life making trouble for people," precisely what she was compelled to do. In reality, Sophronia knew her only as a baby, and Lillian certainly passed through life making trouble.

By the age of four Lillian was both a rebel and a nuisance, the essential pattern of her life well in evidence. Max Hellman, out on the road selling and in New Orleans as well, enjoyed his chippies, his "girlies," and Lily discovered that fact. She became permanently angry, furious that she had to share her father, ever distraught about his infidelities, which she viewed, narcissistically, as betrayals of herself.

Filled "with pity and contempt" for her mother, no less than anger at her father, whom she perceived as having betrayed her, Lillian vowed never to become a passive and whining creature like her mother, a woman cringing under the shelter of convention. She compared her mother to a feather getting in her face, a woman so inconsequential she couldn't sit on a couch without floating away. She was a woman without substance or worldly competence. Lily would model herself instead on her father, soon learning that Max "was often angry when I was most like him."

As a spoiled only child, and one angry at her mother for having placed her amid the lower middle class, for not having protected her, Lillian focused on her father as the parent whose love was worth having. With relative ease she seduced her father away from both her mother and his chippies. She won him as well from his sisters Jenny and Hannah. "As an only child you never have enough of anything," Lillian Hellman was later to realize. "Because you're so spoiled all the time, and a lot has led to wishing for more."

Lillian was in love with her father, and if in her later memoir *An Unfinished Woman* she described the short, plump, homely Max as goodlooking, "a handsome man, witty, high-tempered, proud," it was because for the fiercely competitive Lillian the Oedipal prize had to be one worth having. Transparent jealousy consumed her in overt displays of Oedipal passion. "You're jealous of your mama and you ought to get over that before it's too late," her aunt Jenny felt compelled to tell her.

"Mama nags," said little Lillian self-righteously. "Papa understands."

"You and your papa!" her aunt would remark with periodic scorn.

The world found short, fat, unmannerly Max Hellman, with his garrulous talk of the stock market and his fondness for eating off other people's plates, unattractive. To the dismay of fellow diners, he would reach into their food, demanding "a schmeer of that and a schmeer of this," a habit in which Lillian Hellman herself would as an adult occasionally indulge. But Lillian took her cue from the primal scene: his sisters Jenny and Hannah were in love with him "since the day he was in his cradle"; Lillian's mother professed to have "been in love with him since the day she first laid eyes." Lily easily defeated mild Julia in the Oedipal war. Her mother, feminine women, were easily bested, Lillian discovered. Her father and her masculine aunt Jenny were the ones who had "interesting things to say," and the "opinions by which the other two," her mother and her aunt Hannah, "would abide."

That Max Hellman sought his share of "girlies," disappearing with regularity, intensified his appeal to Lillian, who discovered when she was fourteen that he was sleeping with a sexy resident of the aunts' boardinghouse. Lillian watched as Max kissed the giggling, faded woman. Then they got into a cab together and drove off. Lillian, who later wrote that the experience led her to throw herself from a tree in the backyard, breaking her already prominent nose, was filled with inevitable anxiety about her value as a woman, no less than with anger at a rejection she experienced as if it had happened to her and which she had somehow to overcome.

The root of her neurosis, Lillian herself came to acknowledge, lay in her relationship with her father. Nor was she ever able to forgive him for what she interpreted as his neglect. Greedy with longing, Lillian wanted all of his attention, a quixotic quest certain to fail. Meanwhile she continued to scorn her mother for putting up with Max's philandering.

What also infuriated defiant Lillian was that her father's infidelity caused her to lose not only him but her mother as well, because she could no longer look at Julia in the same way. By being demeaned, her mother became devalued. Her mother was also her rival, and, like his chippies, simultaneously took Max from little Lillian. So Lillian Hellman would write in a letter years later to "Dear Papa" which she sent off as a joke to Arthur W. A. Cowan, her friend at the turn of the 1960s. "No, I cannot forgive you," Lillian writes.

Her father's "evil," she wrote to Cowan, was revealed to her at the age of six when she awakened on a Sunday afternoon "hungry for the love of my mother" only to find that Max had taken Julia for a walk. "I ran from the house, not believing, tricked, crying, broken, knowing that never again could there be trust, never again in all the years to come." It was, she writes, an act for which she never forgave her father. The letter is remarkable in the honesty of its self-revelation. Unlike her later fictionalized memoirs, there is here no sentimentalized black icon, the all-knowing Sophronia, her mammy of later mythology. There is only a black servant named Fanny, disgusted with the spoiled Lillian.

"Shut up, you stinker!" Fanny reprimands.

Her "Dear Papa" letter to Cowan closes with typical Miss Hellman hauteur. "I am leaving a ticket for you for this Monday night in my name at the box office, no charge." Through the theater, she strove with distinction to secure a place of power and invulnerability where no one could hurt her.

Lily both identified with her spurned mother and competed with her to win her father's love for herself. She both fell in love with her father and resented him for the betrayal of her mother. Then she was to transfer those feelings to herself, becoming simultaneously self-indulgent and narcissistic. Willing to use any strategy to win a man's love, she hated herself for being unworthy of fidelity.

Lily, a quick study, perceived she would need power to conquer attention, to command affection not to be voluntarily hers. The love, approval, and deference for which she hungered would not be derived from her appearance, the sole avenue through which women could obtain affirmation in the culture and era in which she was born and raised. She became defiant. To make up for her deficiency she would fight without limits.

In classic projection she arrived at a strategy. She decided to make her father her model. It would be she who did the betraying, rather than remaining the one who was betrayed. All the while, the petit bourgeois tawdriness of her father's family so appalled her that she would place into an aunt's mouth a fundamental truth about her own snobbery: "worry about yourself and why you like very thin people who have money."

These emotions were fueled throughout the years of her youth by the Alabama Newhouses, her mother's rapacious family, as she was to portray them in *The Little Foxes*. They compounded her sense of inadequacy and made her feel like a poor relation. She hated them for it, loathed their lack of elegance even as she wanted their power. Their furnishings, once the Newhouse clan moved to New York, were "dull," she decided. The Newhouses had no taste.

Having grown up without limits, Lillian entered adolescence never hesitating to act out her rebellions. At fourteen, dating a boy in his second year at Columbia, who was nineteen, she announced to him that she had "left home." He was to "come and look after me." This romantic fantasy was soon shattered as the boy, looking, as she later admitted, "protective and very bored," promptly brought her home. Julia Hellman was, predictably, "in tears from grief and worry."

"Are you all right, baby?" Julia wanted to know, "baby" being the name by which both her mother and her father addressed her as long as they lived. Lillian seized the moment to stage what may have been the first of her fake heart attacks.

At Wadleigh High and New York University, and at Columbia summer sessions, she was an indifferent student. Her grades at Wadleigh for 1921 and 1922 were B's, with a solitary 95 in grammar. Lily did appear in a play at Wadleigh in 1922, as the villainess in *Miss Gorringe's Necklace*. Unable to leave the stage after her final exit because the door stuck, she rejoined the cast and invented a series of "showy remarks" for herself before the drama coach could get her off the stage. So her career as an actress concluded.

Emerging into young womanhood, Lillian chronicled her coming of age. She was "rather weak and inclined to be dramatic," she wrote in

1922 at the age of sixteen. She was already conscious enough politically to perceive the contradiction between her professed beliefs and the manner in which she lived. "How can I be socialistic without having yet reached middle classdom?" she asked herself. She embraced violation of the Eighteenth Amendment as a matter of course. Like any self-respecting flaming youth for whom the twenties offered freedom and license, she smoked, drank, and was eager for sexual intercourse without legal sanction.

At seventeen, Lillian had both an inflated and an accurate assessment of her character. "I am a seeker of the truth," she confided to her diary. "I arrive at conclusions and then dissect them." Already she knew she was in no danger of becoming an intellectual. "My mind is not well-ordered," she recognized, "and I am essentially artificial in my struggle for the truth. For instance, what is written here was probably influenced by the fact that at least I can imagine someone reading it."

Men would and did hurt her. When she managed to develop an intense relationship with a man, she remained conscious that "I cannot arouse such emotion often." Not yet out of her teens, she was plagued by her lack of power as a woman; that she was plain, even "ugly," not only infuriated her but broke her heart. When people said "Lillian has lovely hair," she was thrown into a rage. She found that it was generally women who made her feel miserable about herself, not men.

Young Lillian Hellman honed her lifelong strategy. She would ignore her deficiencies to the point where many who knew her were convinced she thought herself a beautiful woman. She approached men with steely resolve as if she were beautiful. Under the force of her personality, determination, and will, some did succumb.

She resolved to believe in herself, ever to make the best of what she had. She would compensate with grit and relentless will; she would wrest advantage, an edge. "I will assuredly forget all that which is not flattering to me," she wrote in her diary in April of 1924 when she was eighteen years old. She meant it. If secretly she felt "uncertain," and even "noodle-headed," as she later described herself, she would conceal it from the world.

Sex would be her trump card, sex followed by contrived desire. She would conquer and swiftly place herself under a man's sway; she would be taught by men. "Always—always when I write here it is under his influence," she wrote on October 28, 1924, perhaps of Kober, or of another of her beaux. She trained herself to be calculating. She would try not to ask of a man what he was unable to give. If a man had only physical favors to offer, she taught herself to be "satisfied with the physical . . . it is better to realize it than to fool myself into believing something else.

This way it is like eating a meal. I tried to make it like eating a banquet." She sought to secure more by compartmentalizing relations, never seeking everything from one individual.

It may have been to Kober that she was referring when on December 24th, about a year before their marriage, she acknowledged, ever convinced she could not be desired for herself, "I can't have the complete Don Juan because then I'd suspect something, so I am growing quite content with a substitution." Kober was not the man she desired passionately, but one with whom she would make do. "He seems to think I'm quite wonderful. My God! The number of people I've managed to fool! Perhaps I shall make a success of my life this way."

Lillian Hellman was not yet twenty years old, but knew she remained the spoiled little girl who had dominated her childhood scene. She had become a woman who freely acknowledged her own "childish nature." "I am such a damned egotist, such a born actress," she admitted to her diary. She knew already that she wanted to be a writer. She ruled out poetry because she had "no fine feelings."

After she married Arthur Kober in 1925, one wag remarked that the ink wasn't dry on the marriage certificate before she was unfaithful. She chose someone who would allow her to live as if she were not married, a person from whom she could keep secrets, who would permit her to get away with it, a man who would give her the money to live apart from him. "She could have had him for breakfast," her friend Talli Wyler said years later. Yet Lillian thought Arthur Kober had a "great future" and would help her to get ahead in the literary world. A fellow press agent named Leo Friedman, who had worked with Kober in the Shubert office in New York, thought Lillian married Arthur because "she thought he had a promising future as a playwright."

Sex between them was far from good. Already experienced, Lillian enjoyed cunnilingus, which Kober called a "going down" episode. He had to be told by a psychiatrist, after they were no longer together, that "there is nothing wrong with the act if it's a prelude to the natural one." Many more years later Lillian "wondered if he was gay."

They went to Europe together, but she abandoned him to travel alone to Italy in search of her own pleasure. "Things seem so unarranged for me, so terribly in need of clearing up and settling for good and all," she wrote her friend Helen Berlin Schneider. The separation from Kober had proven "not so wise." Yet in the winter of 1928–29 she was in Rochester arranging publicity for a stock company, while playing poker with the men, as she had long liked to do, as she had before with Arthur Kober's press agent cronies.

Despite his ready wit, Arthur Kober was actually depressive and tormented, a man plagued by such insecurity that he couldn't resist making himself the butt of his own jokes. He was unable to take himself seriously no matter how hard he tried. He had ambitions, and he was a good press agent, representing Marc Connelly's *Green Pastures*. When he was called to Hollywood during that gold rush frenzy of seeking writers to do screenplays, he went like a shot. Lillian stayed in New York and had an affair with David Cort, later to become foreign editor of *Life* magazine.

Lillian had published only a few short pieces; Kober remained the rising star of the pair. But their fortunes were beginning to be reversed. He was dependent on her for editorial advice. She had, after all, worked for Horace Liveright. From California, where he had relocated without her, Kober mailed his *New Yorker* stories to Lillian in New York to edit before they were submitted to his agent. As time passed, she was not at all certain she wanted to live with him. "I think if she can be kept busy she'll be very happy," he wrote his mother optimistically, as he awaited Lillian's decision on whether to join him.

"If I don't find something, she's going to leave me," he worriedly told Sam Marx, who was in charge of the script readers at M-G-M. Kober got her a job at M-G-M when she was in New York, hoping she would come, and aware that his marriage was in trouble.

Finally arriving in Hollywood in October 1930, Lillian was restless immediately. She loathed Hollywood, as she had hated Kober's New York press agent crowd. She informed Kober that she was happy to be with him again, a declaration he suspected was "flattery." But she went off to look at houses and "gaped at Gary Cooper, Ruth Chatterton and others."

At M-G-M, Sam Marx at first thought Lillian Kober a rather nice, homely young woman, "a thin, bony slip of a girl," who was also smart. He gave her the job and paid her fifty dollars a week to write story synopses culled from books, magazines, and newspapers. Bright, fiercely intelligent, Lillian completed her work quickly. Then she began to assess how she and her fellow workers were being treated by M-G-M. It was clear to her that unless they organized, their situation would never improve. Soon Marx registered that Lillian was in a state of perpetual indignation, full of causes. She was like a child swinging a baseball bat in a Fifth Avenue toy shop, Marx thought, with all the joy that contained. Marx at once stepped in, and obstreperous, troublemaking Mrs. Kober was fired for trying to start a union.

The night of November 22 was still young. After the movie, Zanuck wanted to continue the party. Their next stop was Bing Crosby's opening at the Roosevelt Hotel, across the street from the theater. They would,

Zanuck insisted, take a limousine to the hotel rather than walk. When Lee Gershwin objected, it seemed so pretentious, Zanuck retorted, "Walking isn't done here. We drive." With great aplomb he ushered them to a table directly in front of the stage.

The lights dimmed. Then, just as the spotlight came up on Crosby, a leanly handsome bone-thin man over six feet tall, with a surprising shock of white hair framing an angular face and muddy-brown eyes, passed their table on his way to the men's room. His nose was slightly twisted, the imperfection granting him a distinctive look. His features were sharply honed, as if with a sculpting blade. His hands were long and graceful.

"Who's that man?" Lillian demanded at once of Lee Gershwin.

Gershwin had no idea. She turned to Zanuck, but he didn't know either. Who was this dapper, elegant figure, dressed in pinstripes, yet so masculine. Someone else might have looked gaudy, like a dandy, in clothes like that, but not this man. As he sauntered by, he seemed an expensive person, this sexy man with a cigarette dangling from his lips, a drink in his hand. Only "the flatness of his chest hinted at any constitutional weakness." Zanuck turned to another of the party, who recognized Dashiell Hammett.

Dashiell Hammett was a famous writer, the master of the detective genre, which he had transformed into searing social criticism. He was the inventor of the hard-boiled hero. On this evening in November 1930, he was the author of three brilliant, hugely successful novels. *Red Harvest* and *The Dain Curse* had been published in 1929, the third, *The Maltese Falcon,* last February. A new novel, *The Glass Key,* was awaiting April publication.

The literary and social world had at once acknowledged his achievement. The high-toned *Town & Country* applauded Hammett for his "development of the American tongue," and called him "an amalgamation of Mr. Hemingway, the Mr. Burnett who wrote 'Little Caesar' and . . . Ring Lardner in his prize-fighting aspect." A *Black Mask* advertisement asked under his photograph, "Do You Know This Man?" and then supplied the answer: "He is the greatest living writer of detective stories." The El Paso *Times* in March had declared that Dashiell Hammett was on his way to becoming "the outstanding writer of our day in the field of detective fiction." Already, however, he longed to break free of the genre.

That year Hammett was summoned to Hollywood from New York by David O. Selznick. "His vogue is on the rise," Selznick had noticed. In a weekend Hammett produced for Selznick a seven-page handwritten story treatment called "After School," which would become Rouben Mamoulian's *City Streets*. Money flowed to his door in these, his high-living years, and he was paid $5,000. Someone else actually did the script. He lived initially at the Roosevelt Hotel and later at the Hollywood Knickerbocker.

He wrote another film treatment at the Hollywood Knickerbocker called "The Ungallant," its subject a detective rescuing a Russian princess. Vanity and a certain self-indulgence are in evidence, as his dashing persona is increasingly compensatory. This self-portrait of Hammett in 1930 is of a man whose "outstanding qualities are his physical fitness and his utter self-assurance." He hates to be lied to, and calls himself "a professional rescuer of princesses in trouble, a sort of modern Sir Galahad for profit." He is also a "gentleman" in small things from table manners to language. He is proud to "have no feelings above an animal's, no sensitiveness, no consideration for others." A Hammett man, he expects nothing from anybody.

As had the New York critics, so Hollywood embraced Hammett, a cool yet colorful figure, not only a writer but a former Pinkerton detective.

Samuel Dashiell Hammett was born on May 27, 1894, in his grandfather's house on the Hammett family farm called Hopewell and Aim. It was located in the rural backwater of St. Marys County in southern Maryland between the Potomac and the Patuxent River sixty miles southeast of Washington D.C. Amid gently rolling hills and rich dark earth, tobacco and corn were grown. Plantations dating from the seventeenth century dotted the landscape. His first ancestor had emigrated to America in 1630 on the ship *The Ark and Dove*. Young Samuel Dashiell Hammett was baptized a Catholic in St. Nicholas Church by one Reverend Giroud, a Jesuit.

Living in that three-story, two-hundred-year-old white frame farmhouse which had been assembled with wooden pegs were Dash's grandfather, Samuel Hammett, who worked two hundred acres of tobacco land at Jarboesville, and his much younger wife and children as well as his son, Dash's father, Richard, his wife, and their daughter, Aronia Rebecca, called Reba. Anne Bond Dashiell was of Huguenot ancestry but had converted to Catholicism when she married Richard Hammett. Her family motto was "Neither early nor late." Later Dash would joke that there were on his mother's side sixteen army men of France named De Chiell who never saw a battle.

Richard Hammett, a reluctant farmer and would-be politician, was over six feet three inches tall. He weighed more than two hundred pounds and had dark black eyes and prematurely snow-white hair. He was fond of dressing in formal attire, and his niece Jane Fish once remarked that he looked like the governor of Maryland himself. Richard Hammett dabbled in local ward-heeling politics sufficiently to become a postmaster and a justice of the peace.

He was a Democrat, but in 1898, two years after McKinley had defeated William Jennings Bryan in the general election, he changed his affiliation to Republican in the hope of garnering money to run for Congress. The ploy failed; as his younger son, Richard, was later to put it, he was run out of St. Marys County, "more or less on a rail."

Hammett moved his family to Philadelphia, and finally to the western part of Baltimore. Dashiell Hammett grew up at 212 North Stricker Street in a three-story row house near Franklin Square opposite the Baltimore Orphan Asylum. The family struggled against hard times as they moved in with Annie's mother, Mrs. Dashiell. It was a working-class neighborhood where most of the people, like Mrs. Dashiell, took in boarders. If black families didn't reside on that street, they lived nearby. The road was cobbled, unpaved, and filled up with water, and the children waded there in the summer. The privy was in the yard. House flies abounded. A smithy shoed horses in the neighborhood, where there were as yet few automobiles. Peanut vendors visited the street every day, roasting chestnuts in the fall. The hokey-pokey man sold two-inch squares of ice cream wrapped in tissue.

Richard Hammett took any job he could get: salesman, bus conductor, foreman in a lock factory, and guard employed by the Safe Deposit and Trust Company. In later years his son scoffed: "The Hammetts were an interesting family because no one had done anything outstanding."

Young Dashiell Hammett "was not an exceptional child," his brother Richard later remembered. Nor was Richard Hammett, Sr., to acquiesce in any positive views of his son. Young Dashiell was "not a particularly remarkable child except for being quite stubborn at times," he said. A tall, gangly boy with dark red hair, Dashiell Hammett was a loner, with little interest in his younger brother and harboring considerable contempt for his father. He loved to read, frequenting the Pratt Library branch, as did H. L. Mencken, who lived six blocks to the south.

With neighborhood boys he played leapfrog, shinny, ball-in-the-hat, and home-sheep-run. In competitive sports, he could be violent, suddenly out of control, as in one hockey game when he hit a friend with his stick, producing a bleeding cut over an eye. Hating restrictions of any kind, he enjoyed summer trips back to the isolated Hammett farm in St. Marys County because there he could go barefoot or fish in the lake a few steps behind the house and in the rivers. He traveled by steamboat, accompanied sometimes by his grandmother, Mrs. Dashiell.

Fiercely intelligent, fiercely proud, Dashiell even once upbraided his mother's best friend because she had misspelled the name Hammett on a postcard. His behavior suggests a belief that somehow he had been mistakenly thrust into the wrong family, the wrong environment, one in which he would never be understood, one which he would have to escape later if not sooner.

Early on Dash retreated into himself, establishing a lifelong habit. Silence and secrecy were his defenses, even as his reserve was misinterpreted as shyness. He was long and lanky; a local teenager remembered him as "the ugliest boy I ever saw in my life." His dazzling good looks were not to come until later.

Of formal education, Dashiell Hammett had only what he called "a fraction of a year" of high school at the Baltimore Polytechnic Institute, where the smart kids went. At thirteen he quit to go to work. His grades that one year, 1908, were mediocre: a 78 average with a 75 and an 82 in American literature. Never a man to make excuses for himself, Hammett let people believe that he quit school to help the family. Richard Hammett had fallen ill and, as Dash's brother later reported, Dash as the oldest son "was elected to pick up the pieces." Indeed he took his father's place at the age of thirteen supervising street peddlers called "Arabs" who sold seafood door to door.

Yet it also seems apparent that Dash's mother, Annie, did not wish him to quit school. Relatives knew he seldom brought money home. Instead he bought gifts for the mother he adored, or used his money to disappear, beginning another lifelong habit. "I was kind of excited about going out and being a man," he later told his daughter, Josephine. "But I knew I was missing school." His biographers wrote that he dropped out of school in "a failed attempt to rescue a family business from bankruptcy."

His choice was more ambiguous than that. Even in grade school he had preferred to teach himself, reading long into the night. He hated the discipline, this indifferent student supremely sure of himself. School was too slow for him, and he soon felt he knew as much as his teachers. Dashiell Hammett needed to be self-taught, and his father's impending bankruptcy may well have allowed him the excuse to flee classrooms which did not inspire.

What he really thought no one knew. He did wish his mother would leave his womanizing, drinking father, whom he distrusted. As Lillian preferred her father, so Dash loved and remained devoted to Annie, and once he told his cousin Effie indignantly that he would never treat a woman the way his father abused his mother. In particular, Dash hated that his mother, who was tubercular and coughed incessantly, had to go out to work as a private nurse despite her poor health. He blamed his ineffectual father, who repelled him with his delusions of grandeur and failed dreams. When his mother insisted, Dashiell even attended church, although he preferred to spend his time reading.

His mother, no stranger to pain, counseled him: "all men are no good." Then she added, if you couldn't keep your husband with love, do it with sex. She told him that a woman who wasn't good in the kitchen wouldn't be much good in any of the other rooms either, words he would remember all his life. Meanwhile as Annie failed to succeed with her own advice, Richard Hammett caroused, consorting with beauticians, whom he seemed to favor, drinking heavily.

Scarcely in his teens, Dash went out to work: first as a newsboy, then as a messenger for the B&O Railroad, as a freight clerk, as a clerk for stockbrokers noting market transactions on a chalkboard, it didn't matter. Often Annie had to struggle to awaken him in the morning so that he would get to work on time. Often he was fired.

He went out into the world with scant formal education, no prospects, no one to support his efforts. There was no one he could trust but his mother, no one to care what happened to him. This extraordinarily intelligent boy in whom no one took an interest, who had to do everything for himself, soon developed the pattern of a lifetime. He became secretive. It was no one's business why he did anything or how he became what he was, and that would later include his own child. So in 1934 he described that moment when he left school. "I can loaf longer and better than anybody I know," Dash wrote. "I quit school when I was thirteen because I wanted to loaf." Even after his death his brother had to admit he was "an enigma, even to those who knew him best."

From early adolescence, his habits were those of the working-class male of his era. "Dashiell was a wild one," his sister Reba was to remember. Men smoked cigarettes, one after another. They drank. Dash smoked and he drank. Annie smelled her son's handkerchiefs and knew. He gambled at dice, at cards, on the horses, on the fights. He hung out at the local pool hall as soon as he was in long pants. So he internalized his father's behavior as that appropriate to a man even as he developed within himself a self-loathing for becoming what he despised. The rejection of his father which characterized his youth became rejection of himself. Alcohol anesthetized, for a time. It was never sufficient.

There were two kinds of women: the saintly, good women like his mother, Annie, and the whores who were sexually exciting as the decent women were not. To the good women, he was always the gentleman; once when he was in his late teens he even tipped his hat to a much younger relative. But good women were no fun in bed. In 1914 when he was twenty Dash contracted his first case of gonorrhea. To arouse this man, Lillian Florence would have to affect the slut, the free woman. The times cooperated. She was to come of age in the twenties when women were shedding Victorian restraints.

Dash began to frequent the Baltimore waterfront, where he met socialists. "I don't like his friends," his father blustered. "I don't like the company he keeps." Bitter arguments between father and son ensued, even as Dash continued to live at home.

As for working-class men then and now, opportunities remained elusive. In 1918 he enlisted in the Army for want of anything better to do. On the examinations he scored the second highest in IQ of all those who had been interviewed. He took some pride in that. On his application he left the space for "religion" blank. His hair was now prematurely snow white, like that of his father.

Soon Dash was a medical sergeant; an accident with an ambulance led him never to drive an automobile again. In that planetary epidemic, one of the legacies of World War I, he contracted Spanish influenza, followed by bronchial pneumonia which released a long-latent tuberculosis. Yet he had to struggle for his disability pay and his war pension. As no one had ever given him anything in his life, so the authorities hounded him. He grew bitter, alienated from power. By the time he met Lillian Hellman, Dashiell Hammett was persuaded of the innate callousness of capitalism, its barbarism. He was to remain a naif, a provincial whose instincts were those of that boy who had to bang in solitude against the doors of learning. When he moved to San Francisco, the public library became his university. Always he remained unpretentious and down-to-earth, as his greatest disciple, Raymond Chandler, would remark, "quite unspoiled."

He worked for eight years as a Pinkerton, until February 1921, as his secretive nature served him well. He was assigned to the Anaconda strike which broke the IWW, the International Workers of the World, the infamy of his role haunting him for years. He worked as well on the Fatty Arbuckle case, in which the actor was accused of a vicious sexual assault with a bottle. As Hammett was to put it, "in trying to convict him everybody framed everybody else."

He sat down at the kitchen table and became a writer. Having become immersed in detective stories, he told himself, "I can do better than that." So he began.

Dashiell Hammett's gallantly stoical detectives, the Op, and Sam Spade were his alter egos exuding the masculine style of the day: no sentimental talk, no illusions, no romantic tenderness. They were tough-talking, hard-boiled, ascetic, and inaccessible to women; only a woman who emulated men and was one of the boys could be trusted. But even such women were offered only the ephemeral encounter.

"In 1917, in Washington, D.C.," Hammett wrote in his sardonic way in 1923, "I met a young woman who did not remark that my work must be very interesting." Dorothy Parker was to write that she fell in love with Sam Spade, "so hard-boiled you could roll him on the White House lawn," with his "clear eye for the ways of hard women." Women in life were drawn to the silent, sensual Hammett too, seemingly so kindly and chivalrous. He never overtly asked anything of people, which made them all the more eager to please him, pursue him, and seek his approval. He made it clear that he was sexually available. It was apparent that he liked women, liked sex. But coupled with his sexiness was an aura announcing that he could not be possessed. It was of course a sexual pose that concealed his own need.

His writing was like his person: direct, blunt, brutally honest, and rudely impatient with pretension. Sentimentality and disguise characterized the powerful and those sycophantic upon them. Hammett had vanishingly little patience or need for either. From his solitary outpost in San Francisco, he had revolutionized the genre.

When his editor at Knopf objected to the "to bed" and the homosexual parts of *The Maltese Falcon,* Hammett wrote, "I should like to have them as they are, especially since you say they would be all right perhaps in an ordinary novel. It seems to me that the only thing that can be said against their use in a detective novel is that nobody has tried it yet. I'd like to try it." He lived as he wrote, a writer with nothing to lose, defiant in this assertion of freedom.

He was, as Hammett described himself in *Black Mask* magazine in 1924, "long and lean and grayheaded, and very lazy. I have no ambition at all in the usual sense of the word." Once in New York he appeared at the offices of *Cosmopolitan* magazine with a half-completed story, asking for a thousand-dollar advance to finish it by Monday. Monday arrived and passed with neither story nor Hammett. A search revealed him to be neither at home nor at any of his haunts. When he was located finally, he was "a bit boiled," with the half-story rolled up under his arm and the advance spent in bars and on bottles. "Three times I have been mistaken for a Prohibition agent, but never had any trouble clearing myself," Hammett wrote in "From the Memoirs of a Private Detective," published in *Smart Set* in 1923. He was an alcoholic long before Lillian Hellman met him.

Remaining a man of working-class origins with the habits of his class, Hammett quickly developed a taste for living high and well. There were the binges in which he indulged in alcohol and women, deliberately contriving to be devoid of money as the binge played itself out. When he worked, he assumed the trained discipline of the writer, eschewing his habitual pleasures. Otherwise he was addicted to drink and to chippies. His silence, his aloofness, his air of inaccessibility, his startling intelligence and extraordinary good looks combined to make him attractive to women, as his father had been before him. Drenched in feelings of inferiority long imbibed from a culture that devalued them, many women of Hammett's day preferred men who confirmed their self-loathing with indifference and worse.

Some thought his behavior was the consequence of his tuberculosis. His mother, Annie, was to die of tuberculosis and he had fallen victim to it as well. To conceal his frailty, his vulnerability and weakness, he affected that aura of inaccessibility. His behavior was so unpredictable, so self-destructive, that his Hollywood friend Nunnally Johnson attributed his recklessness to Hammett's "assumption that he had no expectation of being alive much beyond Thursday."

Dashiell Hammett had married Josephine Dolan, his Army nurse, on July 7, 1921. As with Lillian, marriage carried no imperative of fidelity. He believed that marriage was an absurdity, and he had married only to spare the woman the humiliation of bearing an illegitimate child. His detective hero, the Op, or Continental Op, was a "monster . . . without any human foolishness like love in him," and such toughness, in his view, is what allows him to survive. Hammett had not fared well at the hands of the nuclear family, and he had no taste for domesticity.

If Lillian was unfaithful to Kober from the start, Dash married a woman who was neither bookish, nor ambitious, nor even bright, resembling him only in that she too never made it past the eighth grade. Josephine Dolan was a public health nurse when he had been a patient at a lung hospital in Tacoma, Washington. She was a small-boned woman whose dark hair had a reddish cast. She had blue eyes and fair skin, and a full bosom. She was also thin and had bad teeth. Josephine, called Jose, was an orphan who had suffered a horrendous childhood, being locked in the cellar for long periods, and made to work as a servant by the unfeeling relatives who had taken her in.

They made love in a canyon across the desert, under the stars. It was "merry," as Hammett described it in one of his stories, "ribald," although Jose, an uneducated Catholic girl, did not like the dirty words. Their lovemaking "was a thing of rough and tumble athletics and jokes and gay repartee and cursing." "Neither of us"—Hammett was careful to be explicit—"ever said anything about seriously loving the other." He added in another autobiographical story: "It seemed as if one of us had said 'I love you,' the next instant it would have been a lie."

There being little to keep them together, they separated. When he received a letter from her from Montana, telling him that she was pregnant, he responded gallantly. Jose did not lie to him. The child was not his.

She had been kind to him, he said later, explaining his reasons for marrying a woman pregnant with another man's child. She had cared for him when he was sick with tuberculosis. He repaid her by marrying her when she was in trouble. Why not, he reasoned, help the vulnerable little nurse who had violated her strong Catholic inhibitions by having sex with him. He understood her shame and her pain. He had once been a Catholic too.

Hammett was a kindly man. Jose asked for his help; he responded. That she did not lie to him made it seem even more the right thing to do. At once he accepted Mary Jane, born in 1921, as his daughter, and even wrote a sketch of her for *Smart Set*, which he signed "Mary Jo Hammett." For the most part, he kept Jose's secret; Mary Jane would die without knowing he was not her natural father. The name Hammett means "the keeper and tender of flocks," in its Norman French origins. Samuel Dashiell Hammett lived up to it, if not to the Hammett family motto, "Faithful in everything."

Dash's mother, Annie, was not easily reconciled to this marriage. "This is going to kill me," she said. She knew that Jose had changed the date on their marriage license to conceal that she got married because she was pregnant; the Hammetts forgave her because she was ashamed. Hammett himself as late as the 1948 edition of *Who's Who in America* listed his wedding date as December 27, 1920; the real date was July 6, 1921. For Richard T. Hammett, Dashiell's wife, a nurse like his mother, was a "fine lady." Lillian, however, he was to regard as another of the "bad women" his son favored.

Chivalry defined Hammett in the early days of his life with Jose. He had rushed home to fetch the baby clothes she had forgotten to bring to the hospital; he cooked for her and the children, for he would have a daughter of his own, Josephine, born in 1926. He drank, gambled, and spent his money on clothes. Out of duty and obligation, he had married a woman he didn't love; he lived as he pleased, disappearing at will.

Everything was a secret with Dash, Jose lamented. His close-mouthed furtiveness reflected his days as a Pinkerton detective protecting business from labor, scabs from those on strike. In 1926 he took a job writing advertising copy for Albert Samuels' jewelry store. His adolescent habit of disappearing on binges continued. One day he reappeared and old man Samuels forgivingly took him to lunch. Hammett wore a heavy bright red plaid lumberjack shirt and a multicolored knit tie. He smoked cigarettes as rapidly as he could light them.

The typist who worked on his advertisements, Peggy O'Toole, claimed she never saw Dashiell Hammett take a drink. But then as later, Dash lived by a personal code which prevented drinking on the job. He did make love to Peggy, who some thought was the model for Brigid O'Shaughnessy in *The Maltese Falcon.*

Jose remained both in awe and grateful to him. She pitied Hammett and hoped that he would return so that she could take care of him. When he was a Pinkerton detective, a suspect bounced a brick off his head. Hemorrhaging, he refused to see a doctor, but just sat in a chair or lay in bed for a few days. Stoical, he was determined to be tough and fatalistic about the punishment he perhaps deserved. But he didn't need her.

They parted for the first time in 1923. By 1926 he was living on his own. In 1927, still alone, he was spitting blood. He was two years away from success.

In 1930 Hammett borrowed a thousand dollars from Albert Samuels and went to New York, where he completed his last great novel, *The Glass Key.* He lived that April 1930 at 155 East Thirtieth Street in New York.

Now, in November 1930, Hammett was living at the Ambassador Hotel. One day his little girl Jo wet her pants and he put her in a great big bed naked while drunken people paraded in and out of the room. The year he met the fast-talking, sharp-witted, short, full-busted, feisty, willful woman with the red hair, he earned the most he ever would, well over $100,000. He had a black chauffeur named Jones. He had endured another of his periodic bouts with gonorrhea and the previous July had a severe flare-up of his chronic tuberculosis.

The man who recognized him as Dashiell Hammett informed Lee Gershwin, who turned to advise Lillian. Someone else had already told her. Before Lee could utter a word, Lillian was up and out of her seat. Hammett was slow as he made his way across the floor heading for the men's room. She had time.

Without a word to the Gershwins, Lillian went right up to the tall, handsome, white-haired man and grabbed his arm. All the while she was talking, holding on to his arm, walking along with him to the men's room. Already drunk, he was bemused. He allowed the redheaded woman to accost him.

She continued to walk along with him on his way to the toilet. From the table Lee Gershwin, herself no shrinking violet, watched in amazement. "That's how fast she was," Gershwin would say cattily but in admiration.

Lily laughed her deep infectious laugh. Bright men were drawn to her, and Hammett experienced her as a whiff of smelling salts—startling the senses while clearing the head. He perceived something of himself in this young woman. She induced him to see *her*, rather than her *appearance*. What stirred him was her remarkable energy and her intelligence. She came not to seek favor but to engage him. A shock of mutual recognition passed between them.

They soon repaired to the parking lot to be alone in the back seat of her car. They went off as much to discover more of each other as to yield to the excitement of initial attraction. In that defiant instant it mattered little to either of them that Hammett was married and the father of one child, the legal father of two, nor that Hellman languished in a lackluster marriage. These legal entanglements made them only temporary hostages to convention.

They continued talking, she in her sexy, husky voice, he in his cultivated accent, with a slightly nasal tenor. He told her he was getting over a five-day drunk. Indeed, his face looked "rumpled," his "very tall thin figure was tired and sagged." T. S. Eliot was mentioned. Hammett had never met a woman who could command language, who knew about art, life, politics, men and women, Hollywood, New York. They talked until daylight.

He registered at once that she was a woman to whom you could say anything. Hammett liked outrageous, unpredictable people, like his great-uncle who one day, having failed to get up in time for church, rubbed red pepper in his eyes to teach himself a lesson. Lillian, he saw, was also a person of excess. He found her antics funny and her persona exotic, exciting, sexy, and defiant.

He took to bed this fierce woman who was, for all this, anxious to please, the same way he took other women to bed. There was for him only one way to take a woman to bed, for the moment, unspoiled by any promises of where he might choose to be on the morrow.

PART TWO

Dash as Mentor

2

Better Than Pretty

"As a little girl I dreamed of being a beauty, but I wasn't a beauty, so what was there to do about it?"

LILLIAN HELLMAN

H e remained amused by her, more even than by his favorite lover, Nell Martin, a self-styled adventuress and pulp novelist. Nell, a former actress and taxi driver, was, for Hammett, a good companion. She was independent, and "one of the boys."

But in Lily he saw a woman whom he could really like. As he got to know her, she continued to be funny, brash, fast-talking, both smart and highly intelligent. That she was a New York Jewish woman made her seem exotic. Lily told him she was psychic and that too he liked about her.

Lily had entered his life, but he saw no reason to break with Nell Martin.

Lily liked that he was a famous writer. This was important to her. She also responded to his style, for it evoked something for which she yearned. She was short, and Jewish, as were Kober and her father. If the Hellmans, German as opposed to Eastern European Jews, were Europeanized, Hammett was their American opposite: cool, inaccessible, and unyielding. He was tall, thin, and silent, the antithesis of fat voluble Jewish men such as her father and Kober who had peopled her life. They were given to emotional display, qualities she felt were vulgar and of which, like many Jews, she felt ashamed. At this level, she had internalized the values of Anglo-Saxon culture, judged her own background as wanting, and was the aspiring Aryan.

It was deeply appealing for Lillian Hellman that Dashiell Hammett was "born of early settlers," a type she would forever pursue. Indeed, she soon discovered, the first Hammett ancestor who migrated to America in 1630 had settled in the county which was the home of George Washington's grandmother, Anne Pope. That the original American Hammett may have been a thief transported from England, or, at best, an indentured servant, hardly of aristocratic stock, did not mitigate the hold of his ancestry on Lillian, an assimilated Jew who nonetheless felt herself to be outside the dominant culture. What counted for Lillian was the vintage. Nor were Dash's origins any less authentically American on his mother's side. James DaShiell came to America in 1665, settling in Maryland. The family pronunciation of the name was "Da-sheel," and ever after Lillian insisted that Dash's name be pronounced with the accent on the second syllable.

Beyond all this, Hammett was "elegant to look at." His manner exuded a certain silent strength. Male sexuality, then, was defined by tough-minded, hard-boiled asceticism combined with cool self-sufficiency; indeed Dashiell Hammett had contributed to the enthronement of the austere style in the culture. Men who were men drank, chain-smoked, ignored pain, and allowed nothing to come between them and their principles. No effete writer, or Hollywood hanger-on, he was the real thing.

In his Pinkerton days Hammett had rolled his own cigarettes. He had gone up to Butte, Montana, to do what had to be done for the mining companies against the Wobblies, the International Workers of the World. So soon he told her about himself. One night, as Lily sat on a bed next to him, he confided in her about his Pinkerton days. Pinkertons worked for mining companies; Pinkertons tracked down union men. Later, she would write that he told her that Anaconda Copper offered him five thousand dollars to kill a union organizer. She heard "the anger under the calm voice, the bitterness under the laughter."

"He couldn't have made such an offer unless you had been strike-breaking for Pinkerton," Lillian volunteered, an aggressive remark to make to a new lover, its boldness revealing she had not yet grown afraid of him.

"That's about right," he said. He would have other women, and he would drink himself into oblivion, and he had a politically checkered past. He knew she would be repelled. She thought: I don't want to be with this man. She walked back from the living room to the bedroom to tell him that for this reason and more she did not want to be with him. He was ready for her.

"Yes, ma'am," Hammett said. "Why do you think I told you?"

Strikebreaker or not, she had found the man perfectly right for her. Perversely recapitulating the pain she had felt when she saw that she was no beauty and never would be, she cast her lot with a man whom she could never wholly please, but to whom even the beauty for which she craved wouldn't have been sufficient. Swiftly she invented their relationship as "a grand passion, in the real old-fashioned sense." It was a form of self-deception as well as a posture for the outside world.

That she wasn't conventionally beautiful turned out not to matter at all. "You have one of the most beautiful Renaissance faces I ever saw," he said. He showed her a tiny picture of his mother, Annie, and claimed that Lily resembled her. Lily saw no resemblance.

His approval mattered greatly. "It was responsible for the way I carried myself, the way I walked," she was to remember of their first days together. The Lily whose cousin Bethe had told her she was "unattractive," which "meant you wouldn't ever get married," was now being given a second chance.

The insecurity, of course, could never quite melt away. Years later when Karl Menninger met her with Hammett, she told him wistfully, "I'm the kind of woman that people can never quite remember." Menninger, ironically, admired young Lillian Hellman as frank, free of pretentiousness, and a woman of taste.

Lily told Dash early on that she wanted to be a writer; he took her seriously. "It is not easy to convince men that you can do anything complex," Lily knew. It was part of the honor and pride in which Hammett took his craft that he should help people become writers. It never entered his head that because she was a woman she was not a worthy pupil.

From the start, knowing in her heart it was no grand passion for him, it was important to Lillian that Dashiell Hammett was a man who could help her become a writer. He would be the "cool teacher" for whom her character Julie in *Days to Come* was to yearn. Lillian Hellman had published only a few inconsequential stories when she met Dashiell Hammett. She was twenty-five years old and did not believe she could achieve success on her own.

She spent much of her time now associating with people who knew more than she did, avoiding the mistake of spending too much time with people who were inferior. Hammett was a very famous older writer. He even taught her Pinkerton things, such as to lay a rose on her suitcase, and a thread over its stem in hotel rooms so that she would know whether the maid had been in her suitcase.

It didn't go smoothly for Lily and Dash after that first meeting. They met again a few weeks later, and she discovered the other side of him. Drunk, he would become viciously cruel, alternating between cutting, demeaning remarks and open violence. "Doesn't it remind you of when we were both still menstruating," he said in a loud voice to an aging actress seated next to him at a dinner when she spilled tomato sauce down her dress. Drunk, Hammett liked to make other people suffer, particularly women. It revealed that behind the cool exterior was a fear and loathing of women, a terror of rejection. Later Dotty Parker told Lillian that Dash Hammett was a cruel man.

"Is he?" Lily answered.

They met again at a party. Before long they got into a loud argument. Lily said something. Suddenly, to everyone's horror, he punched her in the jaw hard enough to knock her down. An acquaintance of hers named Eddie Mayer rushed over to commiserate.

"You don't know the half of it," Lily said, bravado her defense. "I can't bear even to be *touched!*" People reported seeing her with eyes blacked and face battered. For all her defiance, she acquiesced no less than did passive women. From the beginning she knew he could be cruel, and learned he was not someone with whom to trifle or to whom she could speak without considering his special sense of privacy. It was an unequal interaction marked by intimidation, her bravado aside.

So it began. The violence was always there as a threat should she step out of line or say too much. It excited her at first, and it kept her for the most part under his sway. Later she wrote of the first time they went to bed. She had brought up her cousin Bethe. "You can tell me if you have to, but I can't say I would have chosen this time," Hammett remarked with languor. "Come back to bed," she pictured him telling her. He was no romantic and he wanted things his way.

That Hammett tolerated no pretentiousness was his gift to her and his best lesson. She liked that about him. With Kober, she could do no wrong. Hammett always let her know when she had gone too far. If she had grown up testing the limits and had succeeded in all but obliterating her mother from the primal family scene, the spoiled only child had met her match.

Lily was still Lily Kober. Even after she met Dashiell Hammett she and Arthur continued to be considered "adorable," a "fun-loving couple, given to pranks and jokes" at parties. Lily liked to shoot craps with the men and fancied herself a great poker player although she never knew when to deal or when to bet. Once in New York she had dragged Kober's fellow press agent and friend Howard Benedict to a contract bridge game. "We'll take 'em on," she proclaimed even as neither of them knew anything about this new game. Lillian and Howard won a hefty $700 and sailed out of the room laughing.

When Benedict beat her at craps one night, she told him, "You're not going to get off that cheap," and insisted he buy her a pair of pajamas to take along on her trip to Europe. At once Benedict went out and bought her an expensive pair of silk pajamas.

Lillian and Arthur at Hollywood parties did a little stunt. "Lily! Let's do our trick," Kober would cry out, and then crouch down as Lillian climbed on his back. As he straightened up, she would raise one arm, brandishing an imaginary torch, demanding that the other guests decipher the charade. "The statue of Liberty!" someone would call out, and Lillian could climb down. At one party, Charlie Chaplin was doing a dance, only for Kober suddenly to get up and start his particular little dance. Chaplin swiftly withdrew.

But at the heart of Kober's hail-fellow-well-met extroversion was a deep sense of insecurity. Self-doubting, Kober hated the way he spoke. He affected a pathetic English accent so that people could rarely catch the names when he introduced them to others. He liked to talk about his writing, forever seeking advice from others. "What do you think I should do here?" he'd ask. People said he was driving them nuts.

Before long Lily stopped going home directly from her job at M-G-M. She arranged as often as she could "chance" meetings for a drink with Hammett. When she arrived home, invariably she would quarrel with Kober, whose diffidence now irritated her to distraction. Kober was despondent, fearing failure, fearing he would run out of money. He threatened to kill himself by putting his head in the oven. Lily scoffed at all this and held him in a certain contempt. She ceased coming home every day, and the places where she had her trysts with Hammett became less public.

Kober had lost her—as a wife if not as a permanent participant in his life. Lacking in self-esteem, he took it as inevitable, and refused to speak of her with bitterness. Later Lillian revealed she had told Kober, "I think I'd rather live with Hammett," and Kober said, in effect, "O.K." In fact, as Lillian continued with David Cort, and then began to live with Dash, Kober was crushed. If, at first, for the sake of her parents she pretended that she and Dash were not living together, that charade ended quickly. As for David Cort, he considered his rival to be not Kober, but Hammett, whose advent marked the end of their passionate affair.

Cort was in love with her, this bright woman with her infectious laugh and a charisma for very bright men. Later he would say that she was "ultimately the worst thing that has ever happened to me, costing me a near-breakdown, the summoning up of more courage than I thought I had, and five years of psychoanalysis." Only in later years was he able to see their affair as "the classic 'love story' of pre-Depression New York emancipated morality." Lillian, looking back, saw them as "lost kids, maybe, bewildered, sometimes mean to each other, but not bad," and, "in love."

Before long, Lillian was turning up at parties in the company of *both* Kober and Hammett. Friends invariably sympathized with the gentle, self-effacing Kober, whose transparent pain was so pathetic. "Oh, Lillian, be kind to him," Lee Gershwin chided her. "He's such a sweet man."

"I don't want a sweet man," Lillian retorted.

Everyone knew, and as one onlooker observed, "it was not Lillian's nature to be secretive." Jose, like the adoring little woman in Hammett's story "Ruffian's Wife," kept house, took care of the two little girls, and waited for his sporadic visits. Dependent, subservient, asking little of life, Jose pretended Dash remained her husband because a paper said it was so. She thought he'd get sick and come home for good.

Often when he did appear at her house, he was drunk, sarcastic, and emotional, and would vent his rage at Jose and her daughter Mary. Hammett's own daughter, Josephine, of whom he was always fond, had to look on in horror. Sometimes he would cry, becoming a maudlin drunk, the antithesis of the repressive tight-lipped persona he usually affected. He never again slept with Jose, so that Josephine never thought of her parents as being in any sense married. As soon as she was old enough Josephine became angry and thought: Why doesn't she do something? She has a trade! But Dash had told Jose, "If you take care of the children, I will always take care of you." It was this pledge that she lived by, even when he didn't keep his promise.

Lily remained a romantic and would be all her life. A woman of her time even as she grew in self-sufficiency, she remained addicted to romantic fantasy, with herself as heroine, her Southern origins making her Scarlett to Dash's Rhett. Yet Hammett was not going to be faithful to her. Being faithful to any woman was inconceivable. "Try to figure out which part of what I told you is the truth," Dinah Brand tells the Op in *Red Harvest*. Men lie in Hammett's books too, even the Op, who observes that "like a lot of people, I looked most honest when I was lying." But women were more dangerous because they were better at deception.

Fearing infidelity, as her father had been unfaithful to her mother, Lily had chosen the quintessentially unfaithful man. It was an attempt to re-create the primal experience hoping it would turn out differently. Of course, it could not. There came a moment when she was ashamed of the contempt she had felt for her mother as a woman who allowed herself to be deceived. She wished to apologize, but could not. She was proud, obsessionally so, and vain about it.

Hammett tried to induce her to distrust the word "love." Of such talk, which implied permanence, he was instantly suspicious. You couldn't ask him anything, let alone demand protestations of affection. If she "did not learn the suspicion of such talk from Hammett," from their earliest moments the word "love" was to have little currency with them. "He expected nothing from anybody," Lillian discovered, while she "expected too much." Even as she had begun to teach herself to imitate him, the boundaries of their conflict had been drawn. She internalized his values and became her own tormentor.

Often he retreated into silence, as if he knew that a man who keeps silent retains power. Meanwhile he showered her with presents, spending every penny he had. She came to suspect that it was less generosity than a compulsion to strip himself of the accoutrements of the privilege which he had found he could not do without: the butler, the chauffeur, the grandest suite at the best hotel.

Because it meant so much to her, he did try to tell her in his own way that he loved her. He wrote on a restaurant menu: "Sweetheart—I love you! There is in the whole history of femininity no member of what we more or less laughingly call 'the sex' to . . . " Then he had to stop, unable to complete the sentence; it was against his nature. "What the hell! I love you!" he granted. He did love her in his way. She would have liked more words. She studied him and knew what she must do without.

Hammett, obsessed by lying women, took up with a woman who lied to him from the start, a woman who was addicted to lying. She was twenty-seven, she lied, adding two years to her actual age. She feared he might not take her seriously if she was too much younger. Soon he discovered that she had a lover, David Cort. Moreover, her sexual relationship with Kober also continued.

"You weren't made to be a liar," Dash told Lily one day. "When did it happen to you?"

"Nobody's ever thought I was a liar," she retorted disingenuously.

"Nobody but me," he answered, undaunted.

*   *   *

In Hammett's novels, women use their sexuality to make their lies stick, which makes them attractive, a lesson Lillian imbibed. "I like to lie," Julie says in her *Days to Come,* lying being a means to survival. Lee Gershwin would notice: "She would lie about anything—a man, a woman, it could be anything—for what we used to call 'a pretty good story.'" Lillian wanted to be fun. Lying was a form of entertaining people. Mostly it had to do with survival. When you had stretched the limits too far, lying provided a safety net, an avenue of escape. If she lied, it was not in her nature to be secretive. Hammett made do with that.

Lily's veracity did not matter. One could not love a woman without qualification no matter the mix of vices and virtues. "Maybe you love me and maybe I love you," Sam Spade tells Brigid O'Shaughnessy in those famous lines. Even the indefinite "maybe" is qualified. "I don't know what that amounts to. Does anybody ever?"

The most elusive of men, a man who did not let down his guard for anyone, and especially did not trust women, had come into battle with the most trying of women. A man with enormous contempt for lying took on a woman who cultivated the lie. He called her "sister"; she called him "Dashie" and indulged in baby talk. Far from minding, he bought her toys out of the Sears catalogue, or from a variety store that carried windup toys made in the Orient. He bought her Japanese dolls.

Hammett attempted to set the tone. He chose the tables and the food. She thought he was using his age to make the rules. Despite his flagrant infidelities, he attempted to impose a double standard. One day shortly after they met, he demanded, "Can you stop juggling oranges?"

"I don't know what you mean," she said.

"Yes, you do," he insisted. "So stop it or I won't be around to watch."

"You mean I haven't made up my mind about you and have been juggling you and other people?" she asked tentatively. Fearing that she might lose him, she was contrite. "I'm sorry. Maybe it will take time to cure myself, but I'll try." Then she teased him about his snoring. She tried to gain an edge.

"Maybe it will take time for *you.* But for me it will take no longer than tomorrow morning," he threatened.

Hollywood abounded with starlets, and Hammett, before whom women melted, had his pick. Women found him irresistible because he appeared kindly and chivalrous and clearly meant no harm, even if he was profoundly unreliable. If he would never again live with Jose as a husband, neither would he cohabit exclusively with Lillian. Nor would he give up Nell Martin, to whom he remained on terms close enough for her to dedicate to him her 1933 novel *Lovers Should Marry.* Lillian mocked Nell's books, risking Dash's anger. At least she writes and gets them published, he said, throwing her idleness in her face.

There were no limits to his sensuality, except those imposed by drenching alcoholism and cyclic battles with gonorrhea, which cramped his style. Not surprisingly, Hammett turned the heads of women who *matched* him in sexual appeal. One of them was a starlet named Elise De Viane, slim, elegant, and exotic, with ashen pale skin, and silky dresses. The advent of Lillian did not put an end to this relationship either. On one occasion he took Elise on a shopping trip for a present for Jose, with the little girls tagging along. Elise was elegant, exotic, very slender.

"Don't tell Mama," Mary whispered to little Josephine. Dash bought Jose a lamp on that outing.

One night, only months after he met Lillian, Dash invited Elise to his hotel room for dinner. Later she called the police. After dinner, she claimed, he had raped her and beat her. She sued him for $35,000 in damages in Superior Court. He would not defend himself. Pretty women were too easy to have. They were also, for the most part, fawning where he was concerned and less than a challenge. What aroused an immediate response in Dash was Lily's intense energy. She was vital and determined. She conveyed an appetite for daring, risks be damned. In that, she was like him.

There was something unspoken but profound which also bound them; already frail, and with intimations that he would not write again, he saw in her the energy to carry on what he had been, not only as a writer but in his style, persona, politics, and his very substance. Simultaneously, Lillian had discovered a persona she could take as her own. He answered a search as to whom she might be, and she began to imitate him—his tough talk and his bravado. Lillian gave off an air of defiance that transcended not merely the stereotype for *women.* She tested limits most people accepted as both given and unalterable; this posture matched his own contempt for flattery and the timidity of those who feared or submitted to authority.

In Lillian, he met a woman already capable of pushing willfulness as far as it would go, a spoiled child furious that she could not compete as a Southern woman must devote her life to doing. Without beauty, such women were doomed. This cultural dictate and her need to surmount it liberated Lily to live as did Hammett—to try anything.

What drew them to each other at first was that both were willing to live without restraints, to see what would happen. He was a man who made absolutely no connection between morality and sex. Nick in *The*

Thin Man calls young Dorothy Wynant "a pretty little thing." She's only a child, her mother, Mimi, protests.

"What's that got to do with what?" Nick asks. This was Hammett. Sex was for the taking, wherever and from whomever, as desire dictated. Life was short, fragile, and absurd. He would take his pleasure where he could.

Out of unresolved need to confirm a devalued sense of herself as a woman, compounded by her limited capacity for happiness, Lily craved Hammett's darker, more dangerous sexuality. She got it, but on his terms. One night, both of them drunk, he got her into a taxi with another woman and said he wanted her to come home with him so he could watch the two of them together. He said it interested him to see how far she would go. She accepted lesbian experiences to amuse Hammett, although since she was, as always, the less attractive, the ugly one, it was rough on her.

One night they were in a cab on the way to one of these lesbian encounters. Hammett's woman of the night put her hand on Lillian's knee. Lillian suddenly ordered the driver to stop the cab and she got out. It was over. Years later Lillian said she put a stop to these threesomes, all having sex together, for fear of liking them too much. It was a way of restoring her dignity while being simultaneously outrageous.

He had virtually stopped writing, although it appeared only that he had merely postponed the completion of his novel *The Thin Man* so that its publication would not coincide with that of *The Glass Key*. Life hung heavy on his hands. Yet his works were just beginning to sell to the movies, and to radio. He wrote a comic strip. Money began to pour in just as he approached the moment when all writing would cease.

His first help was financial and social. He took her to dinner with Charlie Chaplin and Paulette Goddard. Lily had no money of her own and he supported her in style. He left money on a bureau which she could dip into as needed. They never mentioned that she was living on his money. That she was being supported by a man didn't bother her. She knew: "Independent natures aren't worried about dependency. It's a ridiculous thing to worry about anyway, because you're dependent on some things all your life." Nonetheless, for these early years when his money freed her to discover who she might be, she was always to be grateful to him. "He fed me," she would say. "You never forget somebody for that. You never forget that."

Lillian also knew: "If you have worked, living on other people's money isn't a solution." She was, for all her submissiveness to him, craving independence, as a matter of pride and common sense and dignity;

she wanted to live on her own money. It was obvious to her that it was a matter of personal integrity that she do so.

Sober, he was a hermit. Drunk, he moved restlessly from one night-club to another, seeking people, Lillian was to remember, with whom he grew bored immediately. He seemed willing to stay up for any reason, as if he needed noise. They never danced together.

"Let's hit the Trocadero" he would say. They hung out at the Brown Derby and at the Trocadero in Hollywood. When they began to spend time in New York, their haunt was a speakeasy called Tony's on Fifty-second Street, which was what Lily was to call a "kind of literary joint."

They loved to sit and have drinks at Tony's. Lillian, younger than all the others, was the only one who wasn't famous. She hungered to be. She drank to keep up with Hammett; she became alcoholic. Dash was what Lily was to call "a good, true drunk." Sometimes he stumbled home and vomited in the street. Sometimes he stumbled home without vomiting. Sometimes he got a taxicab. Sometimes he got into a mild argument. Sometimes it was all very pleasant and he went on to another place. When he got home, he complained that he couldn't keep Lily awake; sometimes he pinched her in an attempt.

One night at Tony's James Thurber threw a glass of whiskey at Lillian. Hammett became her male protector, a fine thing for a Southern woman, or one who fancied herself *au fond* in the role of the belle. Hammett pushed Thurber against a wall; Thurber picked up a glass from another table and threw it, aiming at Hammett, only to miss and hit the waiter. If Hammett could be cruel and violent with her, as Dotty Parker had warned, it was sexually exciting when he directed that cruelty toward others.

They also had fun together. He took delight in the absurd, and telephoned her once from a wild party at Jean Harlow's house to tell her how Harlow had rung the bell for the butler and said, "Open the window, James, and leave in a tiny air." He liked to go to trashy movies and took her and Max to Tarzan. She kept asking him to give her a synopsis. "Isn't it sad," Max Hellman asked, "to have a daughter who can't follow the plot of a Tarzan picture?" Dash was amused by Max when he sprinkled perfume on his dirty laundry so the laundress wouldn't have to smell it.

Dash took Lily to the Brown Derby so often that years later she thought they had met there. She did remember, or perhaps invented, drawing on the emotional trajectory of those years, a Hollywood Boulevard hustler who purported to be an American Indian. The man shook down Hammett for having arrested an Indian in his Pinkerton days.

"How much do you want?" she reported Hammett asking, wasting no time. He pleaded only for silence.

"He's proud, isn't he?" Lily asked him.

"No," Hammett told her, "he's a Negro pretending to be an Indian. He's a no-good stinker."

"Then why did you give him the money?"

"Because no-good stinkers get hungry too."

He introduced her to his daughters. Jo was four years old, Mary nearly ten. The advent of Lillian meant to Jo that her father had married again. Lillian was never nurturing toward the child, and little Jo thought she always seemed angry, like a pressure cooker about to explode. She was scary and fierce.

Dash liked to take the girls to stores, where he would buy them presents. Lillian was often rude to the clerks. Once in the riding shop at the Beverly Wiltshire as Jo was getting riding clothes, and Lily came in, the clerk asked, "Ma'am, would you like to sit and wait?" "No," she snapped, "I'm not going to sit there!" Dash was amused. Lillian was polite to the girls, but they felt she wished they would just get lost.

Before long she tried to induce the girls to take her side against their mother. Josephine later decided the rivalry between Lillian and her mother was like Godzilla up against Mickey Mouse.

"Josephine, you're very religious, aren't you?" Lillian asked when Jo was about eight. The child squirmed uncomfortably.

Hammett came to the rescue of his child. "Well, Jo feels that there is nothing wrong with being religious. If it turns out that there is a God, then she's that much further ahead of the game." Lillian felt awkward, and derived no pleasure from these visits. Once she said "goddamn" in front of little Jo, adding, "Excuse me, Josephine," in a mocking tone. The children soon accepted her as a fixture in their father's life; he explained nothing. But Mary hated Lillian. Knowing Mary was not his natural daughter, Lillian resented her in particular.

Lillian's was a jealous nature. She was jealous of his past, and begged for details about the women he had known, including a girl he had mentioned who lived across the hall on Pine Street. Dash laughed and said, "She lived across the hall in [sic] Pine Street and was silly."

"Tell me more about that. How much did you like her and how?" She wanted to know how it had been in bed with other women.

Hammett yawned. "Finish your drink and go to sleep," he told her. Even then Lily would not let the matter drop. She was on one of her "find-out kicks."

"O.K., be stubborn about the girls. So tell me about your grandmother and what you looked like as a baby." She begged for normalcy, for the illusion of their being an ordinary couple who shared all the details of their lives before the loved one had entered the scene, the better to exorcise experiences in which she had taken no part. Impatiently, Hammett brushed aside her compulsive queries.

"I was a very fat baby. My grandmother went to the movies every afternoon. She was very fond of a movie star called Wallace Reid."

If her jealousy extended its tentacles to his past, it encroached ferociously on the present. She loved Dash with a driven need. His open promiscuity perpetually wounded her. It produced in her what he would call her "mean" jealousy and he told her she had the meanest jealousy of all. Sexual jealousy would remain with Lillian her entire life. Later she admitted to being "jealous of women who took advantage of men, because I didn't know how to do it."

Lily was jealous of all his women, even ones for whom he felt but a twinge of desire on which he had no intention or opportunity to act. She was jealous of anyone he liked at all, even if sexuality did not enter into it. She was intensely jealous of poor passive Jose, who never interfered, who remained in the background of his life.

Lily also got jealous when it soon became apparent that if he called her "baby," "sweetheart," or "darling," they were the terms of endearment he used for all the women in his life. Later he also called her Lilishka and Lillibelle and Lilly-pie. It was never enough. Like any woman pained by her appearance, she took sexual rejection hard.

She was jealous of great beauties with whom she knew she could not compete. She was jealous of him for bringing other women home, and he was adamant that she have nothing to say about it. She vented the anger she had cultivated from childhood when she had stamped her foot and gotten her way each time. She knew the charming flirtatious voice he used on the ladies, "half in plea, half in contempt," and she hated him and them for it. Hammett told her, amused, that her power was in her rage.

Her looks remained a permanent source of distress, no matter that he told her she was beautiful, for she had always thought of herself as ugly. He told her she was "better than pretty," a phrase she used in two of her plays, *Days to Come* and *The Autumn Garden*. The metaphor for her intense fear that she might not measure up as a woman, she was to write late in her life, was her fear that she exuded a nasty vaginal odor.

"How do I smell to you? Nice or bad?" she asked Hammett.

Hammett would not be trapped. "I can't describe smells and I'm not going to try. Freud said something about that. You are off on one of your kicks and I'm sleepy." In the early days her need for his approval was insatiable.

The outward accoutrements of style she could do something about. Her clothes were elegant, tailored to perfection, products of Bergdorf's. Hammett liked that. He enjoyed fine clothes himself, and he liked beautiful garments on women; his Dinah Brand "looked like a lot of money in a big gray fur coat." He admired Lily with her Eastern aura. She was not a provincial woman, or a California woman.

Early on, Lily assessed what she had with Hammett. He expected her to accept his womanizing, and so she learned to do it. She was hurt, appalled, furious. She wanted to be cherished, but there was no way she could extract sexual loyalty from him.

She flirted with other men. She learned to compensate with coyness. She stimulated and tested. She placed before men the obligation to measure themselves and aroused in them the need to prove they were worthy. Later one of her lovers was to observe that Lillian knew how to make a man feel he had bestowed on her a great gift merely by entering the room. She taught herself to convey vulnerability, frailty, and produce a need in a man to nurture her. She could provoke, and she could gain attention through her strength.

They existed as a couple even when he was in the arms of other women and she, alternately humiliated and jealous, focused her attention on others. Their bond was tested perpetually and from the start. Lillian became a harder woman. In self-defense, as in her yearning for the man she could not have, she became him, a she-Hammett. So she attempted to retrieve her dignity and her equality within the relationship, no matter that he seemed bent on not caring "what he did or spoiled." She already had his respect, as much as he could grant any woman. But she needed to maintain her own. "In every relationship there's a winner and a loser," she'd say years later. "But the winner ought to be careful." He was the winner and he wasn't careful. She had reacted with fire to his infidelities, so that later he would throw up his hands, apparently in play, but ruefully: "All I ever wanted was a docile woman and look what I got!"

She knew, too, that her emotional survival required that she forge a separate sexual life; there was no alternative but to respond to his loveless philandering with a series of hasty sexual encounters. As Hammett revealed, he could discover an endless supply of chippies; the she-Hammett would match his whoring with open involvements of her own. She would assume her own form of machismo; she would match him in the sexual stakes. He taunted her; she responded to his chronic, heartless, and driven sexual betrayals with every weapon in her arsenal.

She hated the whores; she hated the drunks. But, fearing him, she learned to hold her tongue. He was her future. So began their Faustian bargain.

3

She-Hammett

"I had found somebody who stood by himself, who was himself."

LILLIAN HELLMAN

"There's a woman with hair on her chest."

THE THIN MAN

She was studying Hammett continuously now. He was blunt, direct, liberated from adjectives. He had made a fetish of being unpretentious by writing almost exclusively within the genre of the detective story. These were her early times of watching the methods and mysteries of his personality.

He would make an open pass at a woman at a party; Lillian began to imitate him, accosting a man, declaring, "Let's fuck." It was an outcry of despair as much as a seizing of sexual freedom, let alone lust. Hammett continued to drink hard and she kept up with him. He smoked nonstop and so she became a chain smoker.

He enjoyed mischief, a pastime in which she learned to be adept. When he saw how much she liked clothes, he steered salesmen to her door. She lived consciously in the Hammett manner. One of the boys, she played poker.

They argued volubly in public. "It bothered other people. It didn't bother us," Lily said in later years in her clipped, tough, macho, Hammett-like cadences. Nor to outsiders did she seem to be trying to impress him.

Drunk a good deal of the time now, he was "capable of walking out at any minute of the day and night and not returning." Unable to stop herself, knowing it was futile, Lily remonstrated. She kept on trying to get him to stop drinking. He kept his silence, the silence by which he retained the power to elude her.

Pushed beyond endurance, she would issue ultimata: he must stop drinking and he must cease having sex with the other women. Couldn't he see how he was tormenting her? To neither of these pleas would he yield. He forced her to learn to leave him first, his foolproof means of having things his way.

On March 4, 1931, a little more than three months after they met, Lily fled to New York. Indeed the ploy seemed to have worked. Dash waited for her to call until ten o'clock, hoping she had missed her train. In New York she registered at the St. Moritz on the Park.

He wrote a letter. Only in letters did he risk expressing his feelings. He could affect need in letters, since distance negated any implications of dependency, commitment, or capitulation. He was a man terrified of looking into himself, of coming face to face with unresolved childhood pain. With his taciturn manner, he made certain no one else caught a glimpse of that hurt either.

Lily immediately sent him a telegram. Minutes after it arrived, Arthur Kober appeared at Hammett's and hung around for a few hours. Hammett promised to take him to the fights. Kober was hardly a threat. Even in the presence of men who, unlike Kober, were objects of Lily's romantic fantasies, Hammett maintained cool distance.

Hammett immediately wrote Lily that he had begun a "thousand-stanza narrative verse," a love poem dedicated to her, selecting for his own persona the sobriquet of one of his many fictional detectives, Elfinstone:

> *In San Francisco, Elfinstone*
> *Fell in with a red-haired slut*
> *Whose eyes were bright as the devil's own*
> *With green-eyed greed, whose jaw was cut*
> *Wolfishly. Her body was lean and tough as a whip.*
> *With little of breast and little of hip,*
> *And her voice was thin and hard as her lip,*
> *And her lip was as hard as bone.*

In one odd respect his paean to their lust disguised Lily. She was not "little," but ample of breast. So he took from her the one feature that the culture found desirable in women.

They were mentioned frequently in the gossip columns. He reported that there "were no unusual idiocies in the Persons column for tomorrow." He urged her to describe her impressions of "the subway, greed for gold, Central Park, and Anna Held. Maybe you'd better wire me—prepaid—about her." Held was a sexy actress of the demimondaine, the kind millionaires took to the Waldorf. He had always to remind her of his attraction to other women lest she mistake his apparent feeling for any promise of constancy.

In his dry, unsentimental manner, he wrote, "The emptiness I thought was hunger for chow mein turned out to be for you, so maybe a cup of beef tea. . . ." Only when she was absent did he admit that he wanted her. It was to be the pattern of a lifetime.

In New York, Lily was on her own. A free woman, she went out every night. All the while, she was assessing her situation. It was in these early years that Lillian Hellman decided, consciously, that if she could not have Hammett, she would become him. She would behave exactly as he did, even as she would teach herself to write in his style. Only thus could she avoid the danger of becoming merely the wallflower, the homely woman ever grateful, waiting for him to beckon her to his temporarily unoccupied bed.

She must burn no bridges. From the St. Moritz she wrote Arthur Kober that she still loved him. Convinced she fared best with Hammett when he was not entirely sure of her, she continued the juggling he despised, since it was a measure of her control he could not command. She sought to maintain their relationship while leaving open all her other options. She pretended to the world—and to poor Kober—that her marriage was far from over, no matter that she was Hammett's lover and all the gossip columns reported it.

From New York that spring of 1931 she wrote to Kober, who had in one of their fights about Hammett threatened to divorce her. She wrote not only as if their marriage would continue, but that they might still have children together. Treating Kober as Hammett handled her, she refused to accept a defensive posture. She responded to Kober's complaint that she had not written by insisting that she had written twice as many letters as he had.

Soliciting his compassion, which was always available to her because he was a kindly man, she told Kober that after getting "the curse," she "cried like hell for almost two solid hours." It was "lousy" and "unjust." It was not surprising, she consoled him, that she did not conceive a child immediately, given "so long a period of birth control." She had just traveled across the country, climbing into upper berths, as if such physical "effort" were relevant.

"Please don't feel bad," she begged, "we can try again. Maybe even, it is better this way. Write me that you don't mind overmuch and cheer me up. It alters no promises I made you & I hope you understand that—if you don't and are still entertaining the idea of a divorce now is your time to get it on the record." She was unhappy, "ashamed," she wrote. Her failure to conceive was also, of course, a challenge to her sense of herself as a woman: "I always thought I was a super-creator of babies." It was an index of female strength too. "I feel lousy about getting the curse," she repeated. "I'm an old weakling."

She urged Kober to "please love me," and told him, "I miss you an awful lot, but I take it out a little by talking about you constantly." Although these were the early, more halcyon days with Hammett, there is no reference to any trouble he might have caused the Kober marriage.

"I love you very much," Lily wrote Kober yet again. "Certainly, I'm coming back & if you want me sooner I'll leave right away. I really love you & I hope we are going to stay married the rest of our lives." She wrote him three letters that week.

Jose tracked down Arthur Kober in Hollywood. Was he planning to divorce Lillian? she asked.

"No, no, no," he said consolingly. It was a mere passing thing between Lillian and Hammett. He and Lil were still a couple. Jose had nothing to worry about.

With the culture of the lower middle class behind him, Dash brought to his relation with Lily the predictable double standard. Even as he offered no promise of fidelity, he pumped their friend Laura Perelman, who with her writer husband, Sid (S.J.), and Kober formed his Hollywood circle. Laura had been circumspect about Lily's behavior in New York, Dash reported. She had given Lillian so "respectable a tint" that he at once "suspected" her "of the loosest sort of conduct." He had, after all, "previously received reports about you."

"Ts! Ts! Ts! Just a she-Hammett!" he half-complained mockingly.

He tried to entice her back by announcing that he had stopped drinking. "This is my seventh day on the wagon," he boasted. He might come around on this major point of disagreement if only she fell in with his terms of engagement. That gave him the right to his final sentence: "When are you coming home?"

He had made no promises, and would offer none now; nonetheless he wanted her back. "So you're not coming home, eh?" he wrote. "I suppose it doesn't make any difference if I have to go on practically masturbating." He threatened her with his infidelity, thereby acknowledging that nothing had or would change: "God knows I'm doing my best to keep celibacy from rearing its ugly head in Hollywood," he was soon reporting to her. All that delayed him from resuming his whoring was another case of the clap. "Something's got to be done to keep the gals moderately content while I'm out of order," he said. Then he added: "I have been more or less faithful to you."

Lily returned to Hollywood to find Dash in the throes of repeated alcoholic binges. In despair, he announced that he planned to kill himself. He had left the Knickerbocker Hotel, where they had been decent to him, for the Roosevelt. Now he threatened to free himself from the chains of an existence that did neither him nor anyone else any good. He wasn't writing. He was a distant father, an elusive lover, and no husband at all. He was plagued by the emptiness of a life devoid of convictions.

Dash had made no secret of his plans. An unknown man called to inform Jose that her husband was threatening to take his life. She packed the children into a cab and headed for the Roosevelt Hotel. The children were told to sit down and wait on the carpeted stairway while Jose investigated. She was not able even to see Hammett. Someone told her he was all right; it was a false alarm. She retreated meekly and took the children home.

Lillian was not about to take anyone else's word for how he was. To Lillian, he did open the door. Seeing her there, he felt ashamed of himself.

"Why, for heaven's sake?" Lily demanded.

"I'm a clown," he told her. But he still lacked a reason to go on living, and had no answer as to how life might be lived without the bottle.

In the fall of 1931, all but broke, Dash went to New York to finish *The Thin Man*. He put up at the Hotel Elysée and pursued the pleasures of a man of his class. He paid fifty cents for a seat in Madison Square Garden, where he enjoyed "the fights." As soon as his finances improved, he became a regular at "21." The alcohol with which he medicated himself functioned as a depressant. Introspection was not an option. It had been fifteen months since he wrote his last short story.

In a reprise of his suicide threat, he wrote Lily a poem that spoke to his emotional nihilism:

* * *

STATEMENT

Too many have lived
As we live
For our lives to be
Proof of our living.

Too many have died
As we die
For their deaths to be
Proof of our dying.

Unable to sustain any attempt at cool distance, she could not remain apart from him for long. Lily returned to New York and joined him at the Elysée. In November and early December he sat up all night talking with novelist William Faulkner. Breakfast meant opening another bottle. Most of the time the two men ignored Lily, Hammett's girlfriend. Occasionally, from the stupor of their alcoholic haze, they addressed her. Sometimes, while they talked and drank into the night, she fell asleep on the sofa. Hammett was jealous of Faulkner, calling *Sanctuary* "overrated," even as he enjoyed the companionship of a writer toward whom he could not feel superior. For Hemingway, whose spare, laconic prose style he was said to have imitated, he professed no use at all: "Hemingway sees himself as Hercules astride a woman," Dash told Lily.

The best-known incident of that autumn occurred when Alfred Knopf threw Hammett out of a formal party which he and Faulkner had crashed wearing tweed suits. It was a conscious act of contempt by Hammett, who always knew the difference, as he had Ned Beaumont formulate it in *The Glass Key:* "never wear silk socks with tweeds." Indifferent to what his publisher thought, Hammett passed out in broad sight of Knopf's disapproving guests.

At a cocktail party given by William Rose Benét, Dash and Lily met brilliant Dorothy Parker, who had given Hammett such an effusive *New Yorker* review the previous April. As Lily watched jealously, Parker fell to her knees and kissed Hammett's hand. She had already fallen in love with Sam Spade, and now here he was in the flesh. Hammett was embarrassed. Already half drunk, he "simpered."

That night at dinner Lily accused him "of liking ladies who kissed his hand." Jealous always, and with cause, she was particularly irritated when women prostrated themselves before him. They followed him to his bed without his even having to ask.

"You're crazy," Hammett told her.

"I'm not going to live with a man who allows women to kneel in admiration." Her quarrels with him, whatever the ostensible cause, grew out of her deep-seated anger that he forever betrayed her with other women.

"I 'allowed' no such thing," Hammett protested. "I didn't like it, but if you want to leave right now, I will not detain you."

Unwilling to back down, yet frightened that she had gone too far, Lily tried to save face.

"I'll go as soon as I've finished my steak."

A few months later, in the midst of another fight about his women, she brought up Dorothy Parker and how she had kissed his hand.

"If you ever remind me of that incident again, you won't live to finish another steak," Hammett said then. As always, he combined the tough-guy, macho manner with a cool, elegant exterior. The incipient violence, his cruelty, and his utter inaccessibility allowed her to know it could be over at any time. It was all not only demeaning but sexually arousing. Meanwhile Hammett developed an aversion to Parker.

At first he said he didn't want to be around Parker because he couldn't argue with her. "She cries," he said disdainfully. But what really appalled him, he claimed, was that she savaged her friends as soon as they left the room, exposing thereby her essential moral carelessness and inconsequentiality. "Did you ever meet such a shit," was a typical punctuation to a friend's departure. He may have seen in Parker's alcoholism, her willful self-destructiveness, a reflection of his own. In these early days, and into the 1950s, however, Hammett's putative revulsion for Parker's style, which Lily much recounted, did not prevent him from seeing her, and even seeking her out, socially and as a political comrade.

Kober came to New York and so they became a threesome. At one gin mill a man made a nasty remark. Confident of the help he could expect from the tough ex-Pinkerton, Kober said, "If you'd like to settle this thing, come outside." Hammett said nothing, but Kober was certain that at the very least he carried a long blade in his cane.

Outside, Dash went down on the first blow; short, pudgy Kober then quickly succumbed. Tough Dash hadn't even managed to put up his hands, Kober was astounded to discover. It was, in fact, Kober who had to help Dash up. When he was on his feet, all Dash could say was "Where are we going now?" He was too drunk even to register what had occurred.

At Hammett's insistence, on December 8, 1931, Dash and Lily attended Horace Liveright's marriage reception (the bride was an actress named Elise Bartlett), despite the fact that, Lily was to report in *An Unfinished Woman*, Hammett didn't like him very much. Although these were his heavy drinking days, Hammett, in Lillian's account, remained sober, a silent figure seated on the couch, waiting until midnight for the bridegroom to celebrate a marriage which was to last only a few months. These were their best times, when he taught her overtly how to behave and how to be.

Liveright arrived, rumpled. At once Hammett rose to his feet.

"You don't have to rise to greet me. Nobody does anymore," Liveright told him.

"Don't tell her things like that. I'm having enough trouble keeping her respectful" was Hammett's reply.

Hammett objected when she decided to take five hundred dollars from the bureau where he left his money and give it to Liveright, now ill and broke.

"He won't want money from you, have a little sense," Hammett advises. Lillian had worked for Liveright in the twenties; now, as Hammett's woman, she seemed prosperous while he suffered hard times. "Find somebody else to take it to him," Hammett urges.

"That's foolish," Lily replies. At this, she has Hammett do what he must often have done. He says, "O.K., do what you want." Having made his point, he retreats. Reconsidering, Lily chooses publisher Dick Simon to deliver the money. By the time he could get it done, however, it was September 1933 and Liveright was dead.

The hero of the episode is Hammett, compassionate toward Liveright, respectful of his last shred of dignity. Such unerring instruction denotes a man worthy of any amount of grief, the real point of the story. Yet there was also a side of Hammett jealous of the men who had been in Lillian's life, a jealousy he manifested indirectly but with a sharp tongue. When a young mystery writer asked him for permission to use a murder device he had mentioned, Hammett shook his head. "Sorry, I might want to use it someday to kill Horace Liveright." He made that remark with such intensity that no one in the room laughed.

Late in 1931 Hammett revealed his hopes for his own writing future. He wanted to write a play. Only after that would he go back to writing "straight" novels. He had no great admiration for what he had done in the detective genre: *The Dain Curse* was "a silly story," *The Maltese Falcon* "too manufactured." *The Glass Key*, easily his best, was "not so bad." Only that his money had run out kept him working on the long-delayed *The Thin Man*. But his heart was never in that work, and it was to be his weakest and most self-indulgent.

*   *   *

By December 1931 there could no longer be any doubt that Lily's marriage was over. Lillian allowed Kober to believe it was he who wanted the divorce. She was not leaving. He was "letting her go." "I guess it's a pretty silly thing I'm doing," he wrote his mother back in the Bronx. They had taken "sabbatical leaves, vacations from each other," over the past years, both before and after the advent of Hammett. "I don't think I'll ever love any girl as much as I have her," Kober confessed. Whatever he believed, or allowed himself to know, he informed his family: "Lillian is all cut up about the divorce. She is still very much in love with me."

Although it was Lillian who had found another man who represented, unlike her other lovers, more than an interlude, Kober blamed himself. He attributed his failure to keep his wife to his temperament. His personality had caused the two of them to become "emotionally upset, so terribly distraught." He blamed himself as well for their failure to have a family. "Lillian wanted children, was crazy about them," he convinced himself. He desired children too, but he feared not having a job, he feared the responsibility. He wanted to travel "and a family would stop me."

In fact, Lillian's infidelity with Hammett had led to bitter, noisy quarrels until the two could no longer live together. It was a marriage, Kober would conclude, doomed by "her restlessness, her personal satisfactions." She had been "thoughtless, restless, idle." Although Kober was a short, fat Jewish man, like her father, Lillian hadn't wanted to marry her father; she wanted to be him. Now she had taken for herself in Hammett a new model. She had lived as Kober's wife exactly as Max Hellman had done with his "girlies." If now she was asking fidelity of Hammett, it was not because the habit of domestic commitment had ever been hers.

Lillian and Arthur visited Max and Julia Hellman to announce that their marriage was over. Julia already hated Hammett. She saw her only child living in sin, having left a husband Julia liked enormously; Lillian had sacrificed safety to involve herself with a drunk who spent everything he made. When the Hellmans expressed their alarm, Lillian and Arthur kissed and hugged each other. They were still "passionately" fond of each other, they said. Marriage, however, "confined" them.

In court, Lillian preferred "charges of cruelty," collapsing in laughter at the preposterousness of Kober's taking the blame. Meanwhile he would dream of her abortions, and of her infidelities with David Cort, and with Hammett, labeling himself a "cuckold." Only in one respect did Arthur Kober reveal his bitterness: he was not about to give Dashiell Hammett any credit for Lillian Hellman's emergence as a playwright. "Her success as a playwright," he wrote later in his memoirs, "only proves what can be done once one is free of matrimonial shackles."

"What is she going to do when she comes home at night?" innocent Mrs. Kober wondered. "Say, 'Hello, my beautiful apartment'?"

Chivalrously, years later Lillian said, "If he noticed that I had divorced him, he never brought it up."

Soon Kober began to see other women, and he thought of remarrying. Prospective brides, however, were brought to meet Lily, who invariably said, "No, no, she's not the right girl for you." The women caught on. When he said, "I want you to meet Lily," they knew it was the end.

When Lillian finally began to write her first play, it was not by herself, but with a collaborator, her old friend Louis Kronenberger, the very beau her mother had preferred. They decided to write a satiric play set in the eighteenth-century and called it *The Dear Queen*. With distant echoes of the encroaching formula proletcult, it had the aristocrats discover that it was not the bourgeoisie which was really free, but the peasantry.

They worked upstairs; Dash sat downstairs, seemingly unperturbed by jealousy. Later he said he knew exactly how *The Dear Queen* was written: Louis would write his joke and burst into hysterical laughter. Lillian would then write her joke and compete with hysterical laughter of her own. Dash said he knew who had just written a given line because they would never laugh at each other's jokes. As he had affected affability with Kober, so he appeared to welcome Kronenberger. The resentment Hammett felt, however, emerged when he inscribed *The Maltese Falcon* to the miserly Kronenberger: "with dollar bills between the pages to lure him through it."

By May 1932 Lily and Dash were still living together in New York. When, in June, Elise De Viane's case came up in a Los Angeles court, the defendant was not present. De Viane was awarded $2,500 for having been "bruised and battered in resisting the asserted fervid love makings of Dashiell Hammett." He had gotten off easy.

They moved from the Hotel Elysée to the Biltmore, where, that May, they again enjoyed the company of William Faulkner. They argued about Thomas Mann, as Lily dozed on the couch. A letter from Blanche Knopf arrived: expecting *The Thin Man* "next week."

Lily went to New Orleans. When Dash returned to the Biltmore that day, he expected "to find some such message as 'Mrs. Kober, who missed her train, phoned.'" There was no word. He never wanted her so much as when she was absent.

He sent her a wire. "There wasn't anything here," he wrote, "but a bed you'd never slept in." He signed off: "I love you, mugg!" He was frightened that she would take advantage if he allowed her to know he needed her, or that he would thereby lose his hold over her. His loneliness allowed him to overcome such fears.

The next day, May 5, he termed "the second day of the hegira." She had wired him; he sent her a telegram designed to catch her in Atlanta. Only then would he sit down to "work on the masterpiece." The intensity of his need for her was apparent: "The missing of you is terrific!" he wrote. "Huey Long called up this morning to ask when you'd reach New Orleans," he teased. "I stalled him. Was that all right?" He joked that he was "living here on Lenox Avenue with a woman named Magda Kelmfuss," counting on Lily's jealousy.

He was jealous of her too. "While I'm at it," he insisted, "I don't believe there's any General Pershing Street in New Orleans or anywhere else." This letter was signed "Much love from I and Magda, Mr. Hammett." A postscript combined pleading with taunts. She was to "watch out for strangers on those late trains. Them fellers are likely to take you for a Yankee and not respect you. Maybe you'd better use your accent— and be taken for Anna May Wong." Her pretensions at being a Southerner amused him.

They had had a quarrel. "If I pay any attention to what you said this will be the last letter I can send south," he warned. Why must she spoil what they had with demands he could never fulfill? It was the motif of their first decade together. "Why don't you keep your silly mouf shut?" he reproved her. He was gentle. These were the early days. The sex between them was still good. It was only later that she would complain about his sexual coldness and he would put her off with lines like "What do you mean I'm cold? Last time I checked I was 98.6."

Now he spoke ardently. "Mr. Hammett when interviewed," he wrote, "said, 'a bed without Lily ain't no bed.'" He signed that letter "with love of the lewdest sort."

Out of money, Dash and Lily moved from the Biltmore to the Pierre to the Diplomat's Suite at the Sutton Club Hotel on East Fifty-sixth Street, run by aspiring novelist Nathanael (Pep) West, brother of Laura Perelman; Lily had known Pep in her Liveright days. Hammett had no choice now but to complete his novel.

Jose wrote to Alfred A. Knopf complaining that Hammett had sent her only one hundred dollars during the past seven months. "I feel as though he is not getting my letters—someone is holding them back," she whined, implicitly accusing Lillian of driving a wedge between her and Hammett. "I know he loves his family." Jose asked if there was some way she could cash Hammett's royalty checks which had been inadvertently mailed to her address. Her daughters didn't have enough to eat.

Dash and Lily arrived at the Sutton Club Hotel in late September. The three rooms of their suite were small, the food often slightly spoiled. Lily hung out with Pep West. Sometimes she swam in the pool. If she looked for a job, she didn't succeed.

Then she watched in amazement as the drinking stopped. There were no more parties. Dash went ten days or two weeks without going for a walk for fear something might be lost. She watched as he took pride in the neatness of each typed page. He seemed not to need her at all now.

Feeling rejected, she enlisted her new persona of the she-Hammett. One night she made it clear to Pep West that she wanted to sleep with him. West was engaged to a model named Alice Shepard. Yet with her sharp sense of people's vulnerabilities, Lillian sensed that Pep could be had. Too proud to be even Dashiell Hammett's victim, she had to demonstrate her independence as well as her allure.

One night Pep drove Alice to Grand Central Station. Lily went along. Alice perceived Lillian's intent, but there was nothing she could do. Pep dropped her off as she made her way home to Westchester. Lillian remained in the car. As soon as she got home, Alice began to telephone Pep. He did not pick up the receiver.

Bluntly, Lillian made her overture. Pep shrugged his shoulders; Pep took her to bed. I did it because she asked me and men are not taught how to turn a woman down, Pep pleaded later.

It wasn't the most exciting sexual encounter West had known, but it sufficed. Sex for these supposedly flaming youths had more to do with power and manipulation than with pleasure. Lillian later acknowledged that "those of us who grew up in the twenties were very informed and liberated about sex—but we really didn't know what to do with it." She had many encounters, but lacked a genuine easiness about sex. For Lillian there was always far more at stake. If beauty yielded admirers, she would contrive so many admirers that beauty would lose its advantage.

Lily and Dash remained in the orbit of the Perelman family. In November, Lil, Laura, and West drove out to Bucks County to visit writer Josephine Herbst and John Herrmann. Dash was absent. Whatever lingering feeling Lily had for him, it was over between her and Nathanael West.

Dropping off Pep in Frenchtown, Lily and Laura drove back to New York. A spark from Laura's cigarette flew into Lily's lap and she hit a telephone pole. They seemed to be friends, if Lillian could ever really trust a tall, languorous young woman with "lustrous hair, large sensual blue eyes, and an aquiline nose."

In her brief affair with Pep West, Lily had let Dash know he could not control her, and she had bested a beauty. His clear-eyed cynicism demanded that he grant her the same freedom he assumed as his right. He rather enjoyed her in the role of the she-Hammett, registering it as the sincerest form of flattery. But if he accepted the company of Kober and Kronenberger, whom he did not take seriously, Hammett was not so forgiving of Pep West. He repaid Pep in the manner of a man scorned.

Hammett seized every opportunity to humiliate West. At one of his Hollywood parties, Hammett intervened just as West had struck up a conversation. "Leave him alone. He hasn't got a pot to piss in," Hammett warned the woman, to West's mortification. Another time Hammett pretended he didn't understand West's question, calling out in a loud voice, "I haven't any money to lend you now, but call me next week and I'll lend you some."

Later Pep told people he never liked Lillian, and that his sister Laura, who was to figure nastily in Lillian's relationship with Dashiell Hammett, disliked her as well. Among the aspects of Lillian's character that appalled Laura was the deep shame she felt for her parents, particularly her father, whom she regarded as a low-class Jewish merchant.

4

The Literary Grift

"I haven't had a dry shoulder since your career began."
DASHIELL HAMMETT

"Look at me. Empty. Finished. It's all gone. She's got it all now."
JEROME WEIDMAN, *THE SOUND OF BOW BELLS*

In "On the Way," published in March 1932 in *Harper's Bazaar*, Hammett portrayed himself as Kipper, a disenchanted screenwriter and "a long, raw-boned man," as Hammett was. His writer girlfriend, Gladys, has just received a movie contract for "Laughing Masks," the title of a 1923 Hammett story. As Lillian was already in the process of assuming Dashiell's identity, so, no longer of much value to himself, he decides to participate in his own literary demise. He will give up to her all he was, all he had. Meanwhile he would remain elusive, leaving her perpetually unsure of him. The trajectory of their relationship was set.

Gladys-Lillian, an intelligent woman, knows that for Kipper's help she must make the effort worthwhile. Coy, feminine, she curls up on his lap, wriggling her "back against his body." She is certainly grateful.

"You're as much a part of it as I am. You gave me something that—"

Hammett distrusted sentimental talk; Kipper cuts her off. His sense of fairness decrees that he not blame Lily for what had been his own idea, her emergence as a writer at the moment of his decline. His eyes do not avoid hers, although he would like to turn away. With his empty hand Kipper pats Gladys' shoulder. He speaks "awkwardly."

"Nonsense. You always had things—just a little trouble knowing what to do with them."

Early on Hammett anticipated their coming reversal of fortunes. Kipper has run out of money. Gladys, newly enriched, longs to be generous to him. "You carried me long enough," she tells him. She's "insulted" that he will not allow her to help him. She tries to make him believe that there is still work for him, writing "sea pictures." But by 1932 Hammett, still to publish *The Thin Man* and some lesser works, suspected the truth.

At this moment of Gladys-Lillian's first success, Kipper is restless. Now that he has given her a career and a future, he is anxious to leave her, to "leave town." He does not envision domestic partnership. Whatever joys they had in bed were far from enough to bind them. He was an alcoholic; his capacities, his appetites were waning.

You "can get along all right now you've got a foot on the ladder," he says, his "lean face . . . stony." Before Lillian Hellman had even begun her first play Hammett was writing as if his function in her life was completed.

On this, their last night together, they go out on the town with a Hollywood director named Tom, who has his eye on Gladys; Hammett reveals that whatever sexual liberties he took, he was jealous when, as a she-Hammett, Lily paid him back in kind. Kipper-Hammett slugs the man.

Then Kipper bids Gladys farewell. "It's been swell. I hope it's been as swell for you as for me."

"It's been as swell," Gladys replies. Using his speech was her safest means of talking to him. Always she would fear him, fear his violence, his cruelty as he lashed out at her. No less did she fear his indifference.

Then, suddenly, quixotically, Gladys requests that Kipper marry her before he departs.

"I know that wouldn't hold you," she grants, "wouldn't bring you back." No matter the terms, she wants him.

Gladys admits that she's not pregnant; she will not lie. "I just would like it," she says. "Maybe I'm bats, but I would like it. I wouldn't ask you if you were staying . . . but you're going and maybe you wouldn't mind . . . whatever you say, I won't ask you again." Lillian, of course, would ask Dash again. Perhaps he wrote this in 1932 hoping she would not.

Gladys gives Kipper until the next day to reply. She wants him to decide when he's sober. But it takes only five blocks of driving before he provides his answer.

Kipper's face is again "stony" as he tells her, "It's a go." He puts his arm around her and pulls her over against his chest, even as he informs her it would be the same tomorrow. He will marry her. But he will not change his wandering ways.

"I'll do anything you say. I'll stay if you say so."

And then Gladys-Lillian falters. She will not have him marry her because it doesn't matter. A lifelong romantic, Lily wanted a man who wanted her, needed her, for whom she came first and whose passion remained as if in a first love. She wanted a committed man who trusted her, and who would not disappear. That Dashiell Hammett would never be for Lillian Hellman.

"I want you to do what you want to do," Gladys whispers desperately, overreaching.

In her confusion she has opened to him his avenue of escape. Kipper's lower lip twitches so that he must pinch it between his teeth. He stares through the window at streetlights. His answer is Hammett's own.

"I want to go."

As good a poker player as Lily was, she has lost. Because she had great strength of character and was a woman who knew how to cut her losses, she recovers instantly. Lily takes her defeat gracefully. She puts a hand on his cheek, and holds it there.

"I know, darling, I know," Gladys tells Kipper. It is all she can do.

In life it was not over. She would take advantage of his generosity to writers, to her, and she would finally learn her craft. He could not give her what a man could give a woman—protection, fidelity, domestic habit, the certainty of his companionship. Chivalrously, in compensation, he gave her the best he had, which was his art.

It wasn't easy for Hammett. At times he felt ambivalent as her star rose and his declined. She perceived that "the toughness of his criticism, the coldness of his praise, gave him a certain pleasure." Resentment came with the package and it lasted as long as he lived.

But he knew as well that he needed to rid himself of the creative enterprise in which he had so unstintingly spent himself in the twenties. It served his need to stand as mentor, disciplinarian, stern teacher, permanent observer. From the start he endorsed the transference of his identity to her.

Writing, his seeing her through, became her way of keeping him, something he wanted on some level no less than she did, although to the day of his death he would not admit it. "I worked better if Hammett was in the room," she said, although rarely as the years passed were they to live together for any considerable period of time. She took what he gave

her, which was generous and considerable; he gave her "the deep pleasure of continuing interest."

Hammett did settle down and finish *The Thin Man*. But self-indulgent, tired writing revealed that he was merely going through the
motions. He gave Lillian half the manuscript and told her she was Nora.
When she seemed overly pleased, he laughed and said she was also
Dorothy and Mimi, one a "silly girl," the other a villainess, and both liars.
Ever after she chose to praise this book for picturing the two of them as
"an affectionate pair of people . . . who amused each other and got
along."

Unlike the Op, unlike Sam Spade, unlike the original hero, John
Guild, Nick Charles is married. He is Hammett after his move to Hollywood, lazy and idle, and retired. In what would have been unheard of for
these predecessors, Nick, forty-one to Hammett's forty, lives on his wife's
money. Like Hammett, he is also an alcoholic. "My glass is empty," he
says on the first page. That he wakes up feeling "terrible" one morning he
attributes to his having gone to bed sober.

Hammett depicts how he initiated Lillian into the hard-drinking life.
Nick wakes up in the middle of the night for a drink, offering Nora one
as well. She declines. A moment later, to ingratiate herself with him, she
asks him to get out of bed to make her a drink too. Unsure of him, to
make herself indispensable, she participates in his alcoholism.

Married or not, Nick is also unfaithful to Nora. The night before the
action opens he wandered off at a party with a redhead. "She just wanted
to show me some French etchings," he dares to explain. Nora has no
comeback. All she can do, as Lillian did, is become one of the boys, talking dirty. Shocking his publisher, she asks Nick whether he had "an erection" in his wrestling match with Mimi Jorgensen.

In self-defense, a she-Hammett now out of necessity, Nora finds
other women's husbands attractive, as Lillian did. "Mind eating alone?"
Nora asks Nick. "Larry asked me to go see the new Osgood Perkins show
with him." In an attempt to keep Hammett's attention, Lillian yielded to
her own philandering impulses while Hammett encouraged her to do just
that. Mimi complains of Nick as Lillian did in these years of Dashiell:
"You're the damnedest evasive man," while Mimi's daughter Dorothy tells
him, "I never know when you're lying." There is no point to sexual
fidelity, Hammett implies in *The Thin Man,* and elsewhere, because no
one can be trusted and everyone's motives are suspect. Nick doesn't even
always know himself when he is lying. "Were you telling the truth when
you said Wynant didn't kill [Julia Wolf]?" Nora asks. "I don't know. My
guess is I was," Nick replies.

Within these terms, Hammett admired Lillian, creating even a "Hell-man Avenue" in his story "Nightshade." He dedicated *The Thin Man* "To Lillian," and told reporters that summer of 1934, "Nick's wife in *The Thin Man* is real." "There's a woman with hair on her chest," a copper says of Nora, who is also called "a mighty smart woman." Nora also carries Lillian's cadences of tough-talking speech, which she had learned from Hammett: "I know bullets bounce off you. You don't have to prove it to me," she says.

The Thin Man was Hammett's apologia to Lillian for all he was putting her through. "Let's stick around awhile," Nick tells Nora at the end. Often it was, as Nora puts it, "pretty unsatisfactory." But it was better than what most people had, Lillian Hellman would insist of her relationship with Dashiell Hammett. As for *The Thin Man*, it depicted "one of the few marriages in modern literature where the man and woman like each other and have a fine time together."

Hammett's aversion to introspection made him unsuited to transcend the detective genre. Meanwhile the moral relativism carried to its extreme, the dead end his characters confront in *The Thin Man*, suggest why Hammett stopped writing. Sam Spade had been the apotheosis of that vision, a man who gives up the woman he loves for a principle, that the death of one's partner does not go unavenged, even as that partner was worthless and unsavory. As Heywood Hale Broun puts it, Spade endured the agony of having to live up to his code of honor. He fulfills the demand of honor but it almost destroys him.

Nick Charles, however, is a tired man, beyond principle. Broun notes: "He is an amoral, ugly man who lives off his wife's money." In that philosophical journey from the Op, through Spade to Nick Charles, "there isn't anything more to write." The despair that suffused Hammett's own life had invaded his work and out of respect for the craft he was to write little else.

By 1933 Lillian Hellman had been a hanger-on in Dashiell Hammett's life for more than two years. She was his girlfriend, his financial dependent. If she affected the persona of the she-Hammett, as a famous man's moll she could not be her own woman. In these years before her first play was produced, her only job was as a reader for Herman Shumlin, the theatrical producer, whom she met at a party given by the Ira Gershwins. Shumlin was tall, loud, pompous, humorless, shaved his head every day, and exuded a certain sexy male authority. He paid her fifteen dollars a week.

The drinking, the sexual rejection, the nights wasted among the famous had palled for so intelligent a woman. Lily had long known she wanted to be a writer. She also wanted to be famous. But by herself she had not been able to accomplish much: a few short stories and some book reviews for Irita Van Doren at the *Herald Tribune* book section; in a review of *Mosquitoes* she predicted William Faulkner would go on to write another excellent book, and some short stories, but to no great acclaim! Looking over one of her short stories in which a woman drops her fork on her plate to signal her realization that she is not in love, Lily realized that her future did not lie in fiction. She had just about given up, deciding that she "was not going to be any good and that I wasn't going to be bad."

Her time had come, and Hammett stepped in. She looked to him to show her where to go. Seeing that she had lost heart, he teased her; he "annoyed me back into writing, baited me back into writing," she was to remember. "And then watched for as long as he lived."

That this feisty veteran of the John Reed Club and noisy would-be union organizer needed a man's guidance to become a writer reflects the abiding contradiction within which most women of Lillian Hellman's generation struggled. Born in 1905, still the Victorian era, she was as much the daughter of fey, dependent Julia Newhouse as she was a new woman. She had grown up in a world where even female flaming youths looked up to men, valued them more, and believed that men could point the way. That she saw herself as her mother's daughter is reflected in how often she used her mother's name for her characters. As she had attempted to appropriate her mother's place in the Oedipal scene, so in her second play, *Days to Come,* she calls the protagonist, a woman bearing many resemblances to the playwright—Julie. When she decided to invent a friend who was more admirable than she, she named her Julia too.

With autobiographical forthrightness, Lily admitted in *Days to Come* that she had required a man to facilitate her effort to discover "something to want, or to think," a man "to show me the way." She was one of those people "who had to learn from other people." She needed, as she put it years later in her memoir *An Unfinished Woman,* "a teacher, a cool teacher, who would not be impressed or disturbed by a strange and difficult girl." Dashiell Hammett was that man. Wisely, and for all his intransigence, Lily had chosen a man who was willing to lend himself to nurturing her efforts. He was a man who was successful enough, who had achieved enough, not to be so obsessed with his own efforts as to refuse her his concentration.

*   *   *

When Lily started writing plays, Hammett would even type them up for her. It was a symbol of how he would do anything to help her. He poured his craft into her. He treated her and her work exactly as he would have treated his own had he continued to write. He was ruthlessly honest. It was, she perceived "as if one lie would muck up his world." He was critical of her, but "the rules didn't apply the other way." After 1934 it was dangerous for her even to refer to his having stopped writing.

"Now you've begun to write. Now we can count you in," he finally said one day. She perceived there was no one who cared as much about writing as he did. He had offered a window into his meticulous method in *The Glass Key.* As Ned Beaumont, who is not a writer, sits revising a letter, "I shall some day be able to more clearly show my gratitude" becomes "be able some day to show my gratitude more clearly." Dash believed in her. If Lily knew that "it is not easy to convince men that you can do anything complex," she did not have that problem with Hammett.

She studied him, and she became him. She would never be one of the sweet ones, the chippies offering inebriated Hammett consolation. She would be the one hard as bone, who would be a writer to make him proud of her.

She couldn't control his behavior, but she could appropriate some of what was his: his hard-boiled, pure, and unencumbered prose style, the breezy machismo, the ruthless banishment of sentimentality, of irrelevancies, the lucid talk between characters that drove to the heart of the matter. The "well-made play," for which Lillian Hellman became the best-known woman playwright of the century, was born of her embodiment of Hammett's cool, lean style. But her moral sense was her own: Hammett came early to the view that life was absurd, capitalism so entrenched that nothing much made any sense. Nothing was more meaningful than a black bird sending people scurrying to the far corners of the earth. Lily added the promise of moral rigor.

And so, at this moment before her first success and his last, she transcended the female role of uselessness, of being decorative, vulnerable, available, and dependent. Simultaneously, he rejected the pressures of the male role: to perform, succeed, command. As she had already taken on his habits—the hard drinking and sexual promiscuity—he renounced the dominance that comes with being the successful half of the couple. Late in 1931 he had said that he wanted to write a play, and then "straight" novels, and that he needed a new environment, Europe for a year or two, to do it. Lacking the will, he stayed home. He had written his last novel. He had set too severe a limit on the degree of intimacy he was willing to allow his reader to have with him and it finished him as a writer. All that was left was for him to hand on his creative gift to her.

Meanwhile Lillian, all energy, gathered her strength to take up what would have been his life. For the moment Hammett remained the accomplished writer. He was only thirty-nine years old, a youngish man, if one worn out by lung disease and alcoholism. But it was she who would write a play, she who would become him.

First, he ordered her to stop writing about herself. He had her write an exercise against introspection, against relying on her own life history, against those stories she was writing about herself. Hammett decided she would do better with a foundation in fact.

It was May 1933 when Hammett discovered, in a book called *Bad Companions,* the story of the Drumsheugh case of two teachers ruined because one of their pupils accuses them of being lesbians. Hammett recognized at once the daring character of the material. As author William Roughead puts it: "These two gentlewomen had conceived for one another an inordinate affection, which they did not scruple wantonly to display in the very presence of their pupils."

By no means having accepted that his writing days were over, Hammett was searching for material to follow *The Thin Man,* and his first thought was to use the story himself. The lie the little girl tells is Hammett material, as lies were so often the barometer of his characters' integrity from *The Maltese Falcon* to *The Thin Man.* It seemed the perfect material for that play he had announced in 1931 that he wanted to write. But Lily needed her start, and did not seem capable of generating material herself.

In the lying child Miss Jane Cumming, Hammett saw Lillian as that spoiled, willful only child she had been. Mary, as she was named, after the Hammett child Lily disliked, seems the child-Lillian, devoid of discipline, a breaker of the rules, who lies to get her own way, and who is acutely "conscious of the disadvantages from which she suffered in competition with her fair companions." In that disappointed child who would ruin her teachers, Dash saw Lily's reflection. This was a story she should tell. So Dashiell Hammett in a singular act of generosity gave Lillian Hellman the gift of the plot he had discovered.

Lily picked up William Roughead's *Bad Companions,* and she began, making her outlines and showing them to him. He was patient. From the start she felt there was no malice in his criticism. She had become his cause. She recognized that "he was chancing the whole relationship on the fact that he wanted [her] to be some good." He would tell her the truth, hoping she was "good enough to fix things." As Lily, the she-Hammett, was becoming him, the material soon came to seem as much hers as his.

On this, her first play Hammett was a stern taskmaster. He began by attacking everything she had written up to that point. When he first read what she had done, he said the whole idea was a mistake and apologized for offering it. But he made her believe it would be worth her while to try again. On one draft of what would become *The Children's Hour* she wrote: "he spared me nothing."

"If this isn't any good, I'll never write again. I may even kill myself," she threatened. She hoped her flaring temper might intimidate him into telling her that the play was finished, satisfactory. This strategy, however, proved to be a dismal failure. As Lily worked on *The Children's Hour* every day at a fishing camp in the Florida Keys, Dash taught her to take an unsentimental attitude toward writing. To her agonies, he would reply, "Don't be a writer. Nobody asked you to be a writer. This is what it costs. This is what you have to do. If you can't take it, don't do it." Lily the romantic learned to divorce writing from romance.

"If you never write again, what difference will it make?" he told her with heat. "If you aren't going to be any good, you should stop writing anyway. Go back now and try again." But he also told her he thought she "would be all right some day." That, she said, was "the nicest compliment I have ever had."

Now they were truly co-conspirators. He wanted her to become what he had been, and so he taught her his style of bare-boned lucidity, that style he had developed independently of Hemingway. Spareness of language granted force to complex ideas.

For three years she had listened to his voice. Now she assumed it in a strange, symbiotic ritual, absorbing his sensibility along with his life force. As he shaped her, their roles were reversed. Alone with Hammett in a virtual cocoon in Florida that spring and summer of 1933, she created herself by becoming him. Dashiell Hammett transferred to Lillian Hellman his creative enterprise; her abiding restlessness, which amused and exasperated him, was channeled into her writing. Her energy depleted his own for good. She assumed his voice, and her writing became a surrogate for his. The way she carried herself, the way she would pose for photographs, were also now imitations of him.

Meanwhile even as she assimilated Hammett's language, she assumed her own direction. If he infused in her the confidence to persist, it was she who transferred it to the medium of drama. For whatever his avowed intention of writing a play, he never wrote for the theater.

Relentlessly, he told her how bad the first draft was, and then how bad the second was, and the fifth, and the sixth. (In 1935, however, while the play was still running, she told the press he had read only the fourth draft, when he made his suggestions. The young playwright under-standably did not want to assign too much credit to a mentor.)

He suggested changes. One of the catalytic figures in her original conception was Judge Amory Potter, lying little Mary's uncle, who comes for dinner on the night she makes her accusations against her teachers. When her grandmother, Mrs. Amelia Tilford, cannot resist asking Mary exactly what she heard in "Miss Karen's room," the judge at once expresses his outrage: "Amelia!" His presence suggests he would have nipped the catastrophe in the bud: "I heard nothing more than the talk of an hysterical overwrought child who was home sick and who had acci-dentally heard some family quarrels that she didn't understand," he says.

Unlike the maid Agatha, who also does not fall for Mary's lies, the judge was a figure of authority. "That's swift punishment," he objects as Mrs. Tilford talks of removing all the children from the school at once. When she says—as if by virtue of her class she had appointed herself judge and jury to punish Karen and Martha, the schoolteachers—there are things that are "criminal and horrible" that "should be stopped—by society," he demands, ironically, "Are you society, Amelia?"

"I don't give a damn what you'd do," she replies, affirming the arro-gance of her class. Her fury, Hellman-like, seemed to Hammett inconsis-tent with her genteel exterior.

Hammett perceived that the lying Mary had to be able to get away with her calumny. The presence of the judge as the voice of reason would prevent that, and place the audience at once on his side. Sus-pense, the fuel for the forward motion of the plot, would be lost. Judge Potter's presence removes the inexorable downward slide to disaster for the two teachers, for he also demands an inquiry the audience would also demand: "there's a chance for a mistake." The tragic denouement was in danger of being rendered superfluous.

"Has it occurred to you that they may not be guilty? For God's sake, Amelia, put that thing [the telephone] down," the judge says. The audi-ence needed a sense of things out of control; the judge's insistence, "You must hear them first," would have prevented that.

In suggesting that Lily remove Judge Potter from the play, Hammett also permitted the character of Mrs. Tilford more ambiguity. Judge Pot-ter's dialogue had made Mrs. Tilford a sinister rather than a foolish char-acter, which was inconsistent with the ending, and took the focus off Mary's evil. The audience, Hammett saw, had to perceive Martha and Karen as completely vulnerable.

In Lillian's early versions Judge Potter also reappears accompanying a penitent Mrs. Tilford at the end to fix what cannot be fixed and to "make all arrangements" for the public apology and payment of the damage suit.

Finally, reading the fourth version, Hammett frowned upon the judge with a destroying frown and he was gone.

Hammett also suggested other important changes. He argued that a scene should be written showing the irate mothers descending upon the school to remove their children after Mrs. Tilford had bruited the scandal about.

Lillian wrote a speech of Martha's directed to her aunt, Lily Mortar:

"Spite? Couldn't you possibly reserve your fancied snubs for another day. I've been working since six o'clock this morning."

In pencil, Dash changed Martha's speech to: "Oh don't let's have any more of this today. I'm tired. I've been working since 6 o'clock." His suggestions were always for greater simplicity:

There is no record of what Hammett thought about the changed ending; the original is much tougher; Karen does not accept the offers of help from Judge Potter and Mrs. Tilford, and the language is far stronger. "Go home to your Mary, your viper, and watch her grow," she says bitterly, a line excised. In the final version Karen raises her hand in a conciliatory farewell to Mrs. Tilford, a gesture of forgiveness undermining the stark truth of the original.

That summer of 1933 Dash took a house by himself in Huntington, Long Island. Lily remained in New York, spending a few days a week on Long Island with him. She made gumbos. Her men were always to be the beneficiaries of her nurturing cuisine. Hammett was a rough example of his class. He hated salads. "Feed the lettuce to the cow, then let me eat the cow," he said.

One day she asked Hammett to make the bed.

"What's the point? It just gets unmade," he said. "He's so irritating," she remarked. He laughed. Lillian settled back into the role of catering to men and allowing them privileges she would never grant a woman.

Hammett's competitive side that resented her working with such determination while he remained unable to write at all reasserted itself. He signed a contract to be "assistant" to producer Hunt Stromberg and returned to Hollywood.

In the fall of 1933 Lillian was in New York with a first draft of *The Children's Hour.* Hammett in Hollywood awaited the filming of *The Glass Key; The Maltese Falcon* had already been filmed. If he had turned the "literary grift" over to her, financially he was doing better than well. He announced that he was working on a novel which was "not a mystery story."

For the early winter of 1934, on the eve of the publication of *The*

Thin Man, Hammett set himself up at the Lombardy Hotel on Fifty-sixth Street. He pored obsessively over his reviews. Most were positive, paying homage to Hammett the icon. Isaac Anderson in the New York *Times Book Review* insisted that Hammett was "at the top of his form." In the daily *Times* John Chamberlain enumerated the qualities for which Hammett had long been praised: "his hard-boiled lingo . . . the speed and execution of his plots . . . the realism of his characters . . . his Hemingwayese and Little Caesaritis . . . his ability to knock 'em all dead." Will Cuppy, writing in the New York *Herald Tribune,* claimed that Hammett had "come through with a new hard-boiled opus worthy to stand beside the best of his other works," a book "better than we fans had a right to hope for."

Only T. S. Matthews, writing in *The New Republic,* in a review entitled "Mr. Hammett Goes Coasting," noted correctly that *The Thin Man* was "a less excitingly fresh performance than, say, *The Maltese Falcon.*" In *Esquire,* Edwin Balmer remarked that the publisher's tease in the advertisements regarding "a five-word question," Nora's wondering whether Nick had an erection, was "a cheap way to stir up excitement."

In interviews Dash spoke of himself as a married man with two children.

In the early spring of 1934 Dash and Lily tried living together once more at their Florida Keys sanctuary. Lily was still revising *The Children's Hour.* Hammett talked of trying "to finish my next book."

It was Lily herself who saw to it that *The Children's Hour* was produced. One day, still working as his reader, she put her own play on Herman Shumlin's desk and told him, "This is the best one I've read." She had not depended on Hammett to speak for her. While Lillian paced, Shumlin read. He was skeptical about whether he could get away with the lesbian theme on Broadway. It was the force of the writing no less than the playwright's personality that made him agree. Meanwhile Hammett remained at the Long Island house.

During the summer of 1934, Lily spent only a few days a week with Dash out on Long Island. In June, often by herself in New York, she continued her revisions of *The Children's Hour.* Moving between Huntington and New York, she spent many nights with Louis Kronenberger concocting plot changes for the moribund *The Dear Queen,* of which she was "sick." She considered going away with Louis for a week, just the two of them, to "work steadily on the play." One evening she and a friend named Mani, an ardent Communist, "screamed at each other for several hours." With Hammett unreliable and spending more time away from her now, Lillian "juggled" her men. Once the casting began, she remained in New

York. The name she typed on her drafts of *The Children's Hour* was "Lillian Hellman Kober."

Julia Newhouse watched disapprovingly as her divorced daughter visited "unmarried gentlemen." Lillian felt the pressure of her disapproval even as she did as she pleased. She wrote Kober she never felt "quite free to move around the way I might want to," since all had "to be accounted for to Mama." Lily had lived freely for years, yet she felt sorely her mother's censorious eye.

Lillian did not go to Europe in 1934, as she said she did in her story "Julia," published in *Pentimento* years later. She wrote that Hammett gave her money to go to Europe to finish *The Children's Hour,* but it was not so. She was not in Austria during the February events of 1934 to visit a friend named Julia in a hospital. "I've told a lot of lies," Lily later confessed to her friend Blair Fuller. Then, with a smile, she added, "Haven't you?"

Indeed in lying, in the willful child Mary who lies to get her way, who fakes a heart attack, who will not listen, Lillian Hellman in her first play pictured herself as a child. Even then, she had known, the best lies are founded on a degree of truth, for Martha does have homosexual feelings for Karen. There is also an apologia about lying as Joe, Karen's intended, Dr. Joseph Cardin, says that, given a second chance, he would always have told the truth. So autobiographical was *The Children's Hour* that there are even "TL's" between the children, those "trade lasts" in which people must come up with compliments they have heard about each other, a game which amused Lily to the end of her life.

In its passions, *The Children's Hour* is hers. In the simplicity of its style lies Hammett's restraining hand. His assistance extended beyond helping her with the text. It was to Hammett that Alfred Knopf wrote in reply to his having received Lillian's script. "The play is grand," he responded before the play had opened. "Shall I send you or rather Lillian a contract or what?"

In September 1934 Lily placed the completed text of *The Children's Hour* on Herman Shumlin's desk. So she entered the theater world in her own right, a world she had known since Kober's days of working for the Shuberts. During rehearsals the spoiled child who had been Dashiell Hammett's protégée at once asserted herself.

Her battles with Shumlin became legendary. One resulted from Mrs. Rose Shumlin's insistence that the lisp of Evelyn, one of the children, should come out. Lillian threatened to take the matter to the Dramatists Guild. "Lisp, lisp, lisp and Thomas Wolfe," Lillian wrote in her diary, the latter a reference to set designer Aline Bernstein, who was Wolfe's mistress, and whom, Lillian made it apparent, she did not like. Herman Shumlin consoled Bernstein. Lillian didn't like her because she didn't like beautiful women, Shumlin explained.

Several actresses refused to play in *The Children's Hour* for fear of being branded as lesbians, and one of the Pulitzer judges was to refuse even to see it. Max Hellman teased his naive wife, informing her that there would be a toilet right there in the middle of the stage and wasn't that vulgar of "baby"? Lillian Hellman was on her way and on her own terms.

PART THREE

The Arrival of Miss Hellman

5

The Tops off Bottles: 1934-35

"There's never been a time in my life I wouldn't have swapped art for
real life if I had the choice."

LILLIAN HELLMAN

"Love is casual—that's the way it should be."

THE CHILDREN'S HOUR

*T*he *Children's Hour* opened in New York on November 20,
1934. Less than a month earlier, on October 26, Hammett had
returned to Hollywood by train, ostensibly to write a film
sequel to *The Thin Man*. M-G-M hired him at $2,000 a week
for ten weeks. If he was leaving Lily at the most important moment of
her life, just as her first play was about to open, he let her know it was
not because he did not love her. From Kansas City, en route to Hollywood, he sent her a wire: "SO FAR SO GOOD ONLY AM MISSING OF YOU
PLENTY LOVE NICKY." When the train stopped at Albuquerque, he sent
another message: "HAVE NOT GOT USED TO BEING WITHOUT YOU YET WHAT
SHALL I DO LOVE.

Whenever he had the option, Hammett pursued luxury. Now he put
up at the Beverly Wilshire, a high-rise apartment hotel in Beverly Hills
between El Camino Drive and Rodeo Drive. Dash chose a penthouse
apartment with six bedrooms at a cost of $2,000 a month. Servants
tended to his needs.

He passed his first day in Hollywood "pleasantly," at the "picture-galleries," he wrote Lillian. At first the arrangement with M-G-M even seemed to be to his liking. "I think it's going to be all right. I like the people thus far and have a comfortable office," he reported. He enjoyed the fuss made over him at M-G-M because of the success of *The Thin Man;* still at heart the working-class boy whose nose had been pressed against the glass of privilege, he was impressed when Joan Crawford and Clark Gable were brought over to be introduced to him.

He wrote Lily that he missed her "awfully," and thought lazily that "it would be so thoroughly nice being back here if you were only along." All he could do was hope "the rehearsals are going smoothly and I hope you are being a good girl." He closed by telling her, "I love you v. m."

At those rehearsals, "a very quiet and reserved presence," Lily wore one of her hats, willing her own style as Hammett's clothes brought him an effortless elegance. She had hats with veils that came down over her nose splattered with velvet spots, hats which gave her a jaunty look and pulled the attention of the viewer away from her less than perfect features.

Before long Hammett's rooms became the outpost of the harlots whose sexual company alone pleased him, coming as it did with no responsibility to care. One woman who had a fling with him at that time broke it off because she couldn't stand being in the company of all the whores. These were the years when in his rough working-class way he would ask virtually every good-looking woman he met to go to bed with him. Many took him on.

He could easily afford his pleasures. In 1934 he had already earned $80,000. He had given his name to a syndicated comic strip called "Secret Agent X-9"; M-G-M had bought the rights to *The Thin Man* for $21,000. Nick Charles had retired from battling the world of calumny thanks to his wife's fortune: Hammett was now slowly, unconsciously, distancing himself from writing with the help of Hollywood money for past work.

He did little work on the treatment for *After the Thin Man.* Albert Hackett, who with his wife and partner, Frances Goodrich, wrote the screenplay for the first *Thin Man* movie, thought he was "a bewildering kind of person; everything just washed over him." The mistake the Hacketts made was in believing that Dash was going to be in any way helpful to them. When Frances finally asked him what he thought, Dash said, "Well, I don't know," or "Uh-hmm." So little was he wedded to seeing the novel produced with fidelity on the screen, however, that he always was in favor of their cutting. "You don't have to have that scene," he would say. When a scene went, Dash seemed satisfied. "It just cluttered up the thing," he said once.

Then he would go off on one of his "awful drunks" or just disappear. A man who believed his days were numbered did not stay home in the evenings. In Hollywood in the thirties Hammett was drunk most of the time and, people came to know, an absolute monster, a beast, when he was drunk. A Jekyll and Hyde personality, he could be gentle and sensitive, even saintly, when he was sober. But when he was drunk, he was mean, far meaner than the she-Hammett would ever be.

A dinner at the home of Herbert Asbury, critic and aspiring screenwriter, and a Hammett admirer, where the cocktails were too weak for him, was followed by town-roaming until five in the morning with Mrs. Joel Sayre. Sayre maître had been present at the dinner, Dash added. It had all been innocent, Dash demonically reported to Lily. After all, he did get up at ten the next morning to work on his *Thin Man* treatment. Then he felt compelled to add: "but still loving and missing you very much all the time." He insisted: "And I do and I do and I do! Want to make something of it?" He had been gone less than a week.

Lillian had continued to beg him to stop drinking. He reported his progress to her. He had indeed gone on the wagon, only to go "back on the booze pretty heavily." Within a week of his return, he was sick for two days. Lily also continued to beg him to give up the other women. "I've been faithful enough to you," he wrote her with his customary qualification. Habitually he promised to give up drinking and he promised to give up chippies. But he could do neither.

Nor did Hammett mind facing the consequences of his errant ways. Starlet Elise De Viane, who had won a judgment against him, resurfaced, and Dash told Lily, "my pay-check is sewed up." Three hundred dollars a week would be taken out of his check for nine weeks. "But I'm stuck for it so I suppose there's no use bellyaching," he wrote.

M-G-M soon discovered he was disappearing every two days. They fired him and rehired him, more than once. They assigned to him a secretary named Mildred Lewis, who appeared at his house to encourage him to work and spent long hours there.

"I love you something awful," he wrote Lily four years after they met, "and days are years till I see you again." He closed another letter: "I love you and miss you and love you and miss you and not much else." Yet even as he expressed both his affection and his interest in the progress of *The Children's Hour*, he also demanded, irrationally, in contradiction to all those hours he spent bringing her to this moment, that she choose him over the career he had given her, that she put him first. Even as he had demonstrated repeatedly that he was not a man about to be domesticated, he revealed his need that she should be there in Hollywood to take care of him.

"Too hangovery to go out to the studio," he wrote Lily on the first of November, addressing her as "angel," as Sam Spade might do, and with the self-absorption of the alcoholic. "And god help me you'd better come on out and take care of me." He closed with a plea that she choose him over what he suspected would be a brilliant career. In capital letters he added: "BUT ALL THE TIME I'M LOVING YOU VERY MUCH PLEASE."

Twenty days before the opening of *The Children's Hour* he wrote as if this momentous event were not imminent, as if indeed he felt considerable ambivalence about this writing life of hers ascending as his was taking a spiral downward. It was Lillian who now made the Faustian bargain demanded of any woman writer of her time for whom the doors to literary credibility would not be opened without great sacrifice.

If Lily had the choice to become Scarlett O'Hara, if she thought she could hold him, she might have decided differently. But she would never be a sexually appealing woman, and for sex Dash obviously did not prefer her. He had made no secret of that. Lily chose the career.

Hammett did not go East for the opening of *The Children's Hour*. In part, he wanted her to succeed on her own and not as the girlfriend of the famous writer Dashiell Hammett. Simultaneously, even as he issued paeans to their love, he was setting a limit. He would not be there by her side at the most crucial moments of her life; he would not be there to support her and defend her in fair days or in foul. At some level he felt both threatened and competitive. He was having so much trouble finishing *The Thin Man* script that it was clear to him that he was not far from becoming unable to write at all. Yet here was Lily on the threshold of literary acclaim with a hard-hitting play based on an idea which had originally been his. He had asked her to come out and take care of him and she had not done it. She would henceforth be responsible for whatever happened to them.

Hers was to be a substantial consolation prize: at the age of twenty-nine, Lillian Hellman had a fabulously successful play on Broadway (it ran for 691 performances), the very play her famous writer lover had thought about writing himself. Disappointed that he would not share this moment with her, feeling very much alone, she took her pain out on herself and got drunk. She was drunk often in this decade, as she and Kober and Hammett went drinking together, as the times encouraged heavy drinking and chain smoking. Among their crowd, Laura Perelman was often drunk, as was Sid.

In New York, short of money, Lily stayed once more at the Hotel Elysée on Fifty-fourth Street. Her hotel bill had grown huge. Hammett had promised to send her money as soon as he got to Hollywood. Then, in his alcoholic haze, he had forgotten about it. It didn't matter.

It was to the Elysée that the congratulatory messages were addressed. *The Children's Hour* was a smash hit, and telegrams poured in: "It is really a swell play Darling a really swell play," Pep West wrote her. Lee and Ira Gershwin wrote, "A girl who can make Lee Shubert cry deserves the Nobel Prize." Laura and Sid Perelman wrote, in advance of the opening, "We hope it's a boy love and kisses."

But there was no telegram from Hammett that opening night. Lillian, a new hat on her head, stood at the back of the theater by herself, extremely nervous. Later she wrote that she sent the wardrobe woman out for a bottle of brandy and got so drunk she had to go outside and vomit. Yet at the end of the play Robert Benchley patted her arm approvingly as he left the theater. Then she knew.

There was an opening-night party filled with strangers and celebrities, among them Lord Zuckerman from England. By the end of the evening the little nobody, as one guest put it, who had suddenly become Cinderella, could be found lying passed out on the floor in front of the elevator.

But if at the moment of her first triumph, which he had made possible, Hammett wasn't there, he was there in spirit. For she seized this moment of her triumph publicly to become him. In her sharp, hard-edged spare dialogue, nothing extraneous or sentimental, she had assumed his style. In her hard drinking, his preferred means of pushing down feeling, she behaved like him, getting drunk with strangers. The she-Hammett conducted herself with such bravado that when a newspaper reporter called on her a few days later he found her in a tailored suit and in so Hammett-like a mood that he wrote, "She's the kind of girl who can take the tops off bottles with her teeth!"

That her pain in his absence was severe is revealed in an incident Lillian Hellman later invented as an emblem of her emotional disarray at Hammett's defection. Making no reference to any disappointment she might have felt at his absence, in her memoir *Pentimento* she portrayed herself awakening the morning after the opening of *The Children's Hour* and suddenly remembering that she "should have telephoned Hammett to tell him the play was a hit."

Although he was at the Beverly Wilshire, she placed him at a house rented from film comedian Harold Lloyd. A woman answers the telephone and identifies herself as Mr. Hammett's secretary. "What a strange hour to be calling," she tells poor Lily. It is two more days before Lillian realizes that he had no secretary, Hellman's later acknowledgment that Hammett had never bothered to tell her about Mildred Lewis, who often stayed overnight and may well have answered Hammett's telephone. In her fantasy revenge Lily hops the next plane for Los Angeles, arrives at night, manages to get herself to the Pacific Palisades. With sheer bodily force she smashes Harold Lloyd's basement soda fountain. Then she returns to the airport and flies "back to New York on a late night plane," as if the airlines in the mid-1930s ran on 1970s schedules.

The story is an emblem of her jealousy, a summation of her pain over all those occasions when she came face to face with Hammett's women. Releasing her anger, smashing his property, relieves her humiliation and restores a dignity she believed at the time she had lost.

The Children's Hour enjoyed a twenty-one-month run, earning the author $125,000. Lillian went out and bought herself a mink coat and garnered a new admirer, her producer, Herman Shumlin, who fell in love with her. "Dear, sweet, gorgeous, lovely, darling Lillian," he wrote her in December.

At once, even as she claimed the field, Lillian Hellman rejected the label "woman playwright." [Her female competitors in the thirties were to include the now forgotten Zona Gale (*Miss Lulu Bett*), Zoë Akins (*The Old Maid*), Rachel Crothers (*When Ladies Meet, Susan and God*), and Clare Boothe, later Luce (*The Women*)]. Her temperature would always rise, press agent Richard Maney noted, whenever she was called "one of our leading women playwrights." The reverse was no less true. "Lillian Hellman would be sore as hell if I said she had a mind like a man," Howard Lindsay, co-author of *Life With Father* and *State of the Union*, wrote of her in 1947. "She can think and reason like a man . . . she has, to my mind, no superior in the playwriting field, man or woman." Such was her reputation at the height of her powers.

Lillian Hellman restored the morality play to the twentieth-century theater. Her plays exuded such power, zeal, and urgency of conviction that harsh Jed Harris, a Broadway icon himself, called her America's "most virile" playwright. Having more in common with such later playwrights as Tennessee Williams and Arthur Miller than with political writers like Clifford Odets, Hellman explored how greed, lying, and self-deception destroy individuals and families and societies alike. Often she was compared by critics to Ibsen. *The Autumn Garden* (1951), some noted, suggested a resemblance to Chekhov, as she had in fact consciously set out to write her own version of *The Cherry Orchard*, depicting the same kind of people, but in a society that was not declining.

Simultaneously Hellman crafted the well-made play, bound by unities of time and action. Following Chekhov's warning, a pistol which appears in Hellman's first act has been fired by the third, as, literally, in

Watch on the Rhine (1941). This play was to prepare the West for the coming sacrifices of war. Each of her plays was a social document no less than being compelling theater.

Hellman belonged to an era when a writer could enlist with confidence themes of good and evil, certain that the difference between the two would be readily apparent to audiences. Hers was the era of American theater stretching from the Depression through the rise of fascism, the Spanish Civil War, World War II, and its McCarthyite aftermath; within these parameters she did her best work. Her perspective was international even as her best plays, with the major exception of *The Searching Wind* (1944), were set in America. *The Searching Wind* was, she thought, her closest attempt at a political play, with its theme of "nice, well born people who, with good intentions, helped to sell out a world."

She approached theater in the classic sense of its being by definition artificial. In her plots she employed with relish coincidence, artifice, the return of long-lost relatives, people being hoisted by their own petards. In the later age of postmodernism, which eschewed plot and professed to scoff at character revelation as an end in itself, insisting upon the relativity of all moral issues, she became old-fashioned to some. Lillian Hellman admitted even to using "tricks" for purposes of stagecraft; in *Watch on the Rhine* she has Kurt Muller ask his wife to bring the children downstairs for their farewell instead of his going up to them. Aware that plot empowered by character alone moves action forward, she welcomed, as Richard Moody put it in his book about her work, "awkward, embarrassing and unyielding confrontations."

Her dialogue, as Harold Clurman, who was to direct *The Autumn Garden,* noted, was "astringent." "Cynicism is an unpleasant way of saying the truth," Ben says in *The Little Foxes.* The villainous Teck tells Muller in *Watch on the Rhine:* "You have the understanding heart. It will get in your way some day." And here is Mrs. Ellis in *The Autumn Garden* speaking of growing old: "A room of one's own isn't nearly enough. A house, or, best, an island of one's own." Lillian Hellman retained a suspicion of sentimentality, although even she had to admit that the focus on twelve-year-old Brodo in *Watch on the Rhine* "harmed" the play "by many sentimental minutes."

Her other great strength was atmosphere, those strong morally accusing settings. "I see things happening in a room, or in a garden," she said. So we have: the Farrelly house in Washington, D.C., in *Watch on the Rhine,* the "Deep South" stronghold of the Hubbards in *The Little Foxes,* its Alabama counterpart in *Another Part of the Forest* (1947), and the resort near New Orleans in *The Autumn Garden,* all scrupulously presented.

The well-made play, she believed, was one "whose effects are contrived, whose threads are knit tighter than the threads in life." Referring to one of her weakest efforts, *Toys in the Attic* (1960), Robert Brustein was to write that "her work is constructed with all the rigidity and tensile strength of a steel girder." With her best work, this would be a great strength.

She wrote for a general audience that came to Broadway to enjoy the discoveries and climaxes her plays offered and the satisfaction of seeing evil exposed. Later Brustein would place her among those playwrights "limited by their realism." Yet in art realism tends to reassert itself after periods of experimentation and the returns are not yet in with respect to Lillian Hellman as a playwright.

At her best, as in *The Little Foxes,* arguably her finest work, Hellman offered a strong point of view without didacticism. She focused on the internal moral curve of a character, allowing "external probabilities" to enter only as an aid to character development. It was their tone of urgency, the insistence that attention be paid, that underscored her plays as she explored: the imperative of not betraying the self, the unnecessary tragedy of life wasted, the quest for dignity, the value of pride. She perceived the moral violence in us all, the rapacity beneath surface charm, and how lack of confidence can do irreparable damage. Speaking of *The Children's Hour,* she said she hated in that play both "complete worldliness and high minded innocence," calling them "parallel sins." Equally she despised "thoughtless passivity" and "thoughtless action."

Her plays thrived on those confrontations between morally outraged characters and those who behave without limits. People are ruined, come to naught, are destroyed spiritually, financially, and physically. Accused of melodrama early on, Lillian Hellman rejected what she called its "corrupted modern meaning." Melodrama, she said, was "violence for no purpose, to point no moral." That never happened in her plays. "If you believe that man can solve his own problems and is at nobody's mercy," she argued, "then you will probably write melodrama." Hers wasn't the melodrama of the pulps, but tragedy without moral logic, with no justice dispensed at the end.

She winced at the pejorative meaning of the term, and when in their weekly list of Broadway shows *Time* magazine described *Toys in the Attic* as a "melodrama about the doomed conspiracy of three women to regain their control over an engaging leech, well acted by Jason Robards, Jr.," she asked Kermit Bloomgarden to demand that they alter their language. ("I think we should do something about this," were her words.) Yet the melodrama of *The Little Foxes* made some of Lillian's show business friends smile. It was like an old Jewish melodrama with Regina withholding the medicine, thought Irene Lee, the brilliant story editor at Warners.

"I am a moral writer," Hellman declared, and this sometimes led her astray, as when she ended *The Children's Hour,* not with Martha's suicide, as she admitted she should have done, but with a final summing-up, a foray into explanation she would rarely repeat. In 1974, from London, critic Clive James would conclude that her plays remained "bold efforts, indicative social documents . . . problem plays whose problems are no longer secrets, for which in some measure we have her to thank." And it was to be so.

Six days after the opening of *The Children's Hour,* Kober, drinking with the Perelmans, stated his case. Unable to take Hammett seriously as a romantic rival, he revealed that he had not given up hope that he might resume the role of being the most important man in Lily's life: "I do miss Lillian more than I will admit." Simultaneously, he envied her success. The next day he confided to his diary, "Perhaps it's Lil's success which makes me feel that I can hardly look for a similar reception."

Hammett continued to carouse in his Beverly Wilshire suite. Alone with her success in New York, Lillian was learning how to enjoy life as the famous playwright Lillian Hellman, single woman. She was at the theater one night at the end of the third act to watch the confession scene, where Martha admits she loves Karen. The audience was hushed. Anne Revere began to say, "I have loved you the way they said . . ." Suddenly a drunk in the audience called out, "Oh, who gives a shit!" Lillian burst into laughter. Lillian laughed so hard she had to rush to the ladies' room.

If, although they had been divorced for three years, Kober was not ready to view Lillian's connection with Dashiell Hammett as permanent, the success of *The Children's Hour* made clear to him where she would place her loyalty. She dedicated *The Children's Hour:* "For D. Hammett with Thanks." From then on she believed that she could not write a play without his help. No matter how deeply against her nature the compromise of sacrificing the possibility of an equal and loving committed partnership with a man might be, whatever the price her need of Hammett exacted, she would pay it for the sake of her future success. "Love is casual, that's the way it should be," she had written in *The Children's Hour,* a view only a she-Hammett could accept. Lily would spend the rest of her life teaching herself to believe it.

A letter from Lillian to Kober on December 11 let him know how he stood. Dashiell Hammett was the man in her life; Kober would never again be that man for her. At the basis of her decision, Lily explained to

Arthur, was "her gratitude toward Dash." At last Kober had to face the truth, to see "how I'm completely and entirely out of the scheme—which is as well, but why I was allowed to dangle, why I wasn't sawed off, why I tortured and wracked myself these many months is unexplained." It was only the success of *The Children's Hour* which determined the path she would take.

Other writers noticed an enormous difference in Lillian Hellman before the success of *The Children's Hour* and after. Before, she was more tentative. "Didn't you go to PS 6?" she asked playwright Ruth Goetz at one party. Lillian had remembered seeing her at the school at 109th Street near Amsterdam Avenue. She was silent when Goetz explained that her father had put her into private school soon after. But after the opening of *The Children's Hour,* Lillian behaved as if a great writer had come to town. Even her friend Howard Bay, who became her set designer, had to admit: she took herself as a celebrity too seriously. She was proud that she had made it in a man's world, that even Moss Hart had sent "Lillian Kober" a congratulatory telegram, as had Blanche Knopf and Carl Van Vechten. Dash, incapable of taking celebrities or celebrity seriously, called Hart "Miss Moss Heart." A man of his class retaining its view of what maleness entailed, Hammett "didn't like homosexuality when he noticed it," or thought he did.

It was a closed circle Lillian had entered. The glamour of the theatrical world was laced not only with heavy drinking and smoking and exquisite clothes but also with ever-replenished fountains of gossip, the more malicious the better. Lee Gershwin could always be counted upon for entertainments no less than easy opinions as she told Lillian she thought Irene Lee resembled her and that might be the reason Arthur Kober liked Lee, "because she can't see any other reason."

Kober believed that Lily should at once begin another play, not come to Hollywood to join "the vast army of hacks, the frustrated futzy-boys who waste it talking about it." But Lillian couldn't stay away, not with Hammett on the loose.

As soon as *The Children's Hour* was launched, Lily returned to Hollywood to write movies for Samuel Goldwyn for $2,500 a week. Goldwyn admired her, was intimidated by her, and he relied on her. Her talents as a she-Hammett worked well with Goldwyn, as Hammett himself was later to explain to Margaret Case Harriman, who was interviewing people for a Lillian Hellman profile for *The New Yorker:* "her success with Goldwyn springs from a mutual gift they have for causing people to vanish by not looking at them. When Sam doesn't look at you, you cease to exist. Lillian solves that by just not looking at *him.*"

She arrived in Hollywood on December 18. At the Beverly Wilshire, Lillian contributed half the rent, $1,000 a month, and endured the periodic residence of the chippies from whom, even in her presence, Dash could not be weaned. At Christmas she could be reached as "Lillian Kober," care of Dashiell Hammett's suite at the Beverly Wilshire Hotel, even as she rarely called herself by her married name in New York during her married life.

Kober was glad to see her, becoming all at once "gay & animated" again. Two days later he took her to the Brown Derby for lunch as she persuaded him "how silly it is for me to make an obsession of her." Kober gave her the issue of *Vanity Fair* that nominated her for the "Hall of Fame, 1935": "Because she is author of *The Children's Hour,* one of the most literate, sensitive, and human dramas in the contemporary theatre; because she is only twenty-nine, writes a fine prose, and plays what is credibly reported as a wicked game of poker."

As she had in her letter, now in person Lily reiterated to Kober how important Dashiell Hammett was and would be in her life. She spoke of the "strong tie between her and Ham." Kober finally had to face the inevitable: that "D. has firm hold—a sentimental one perhaps."

In the early months of 1935 Hammett and Hellman and Kober often formed a threesome. One night Kober joined Lily and Dash for a drink at the Trocadero, where all three sat commenting on "awful people present."

This was the heady time of Hammett's most lavish, most munificent present-giving; the money the studios lavished on him burned guilt into his working-class soul, and he got rid of it as soon as it arrived. Dash showered Lillian with gifts, a mink coat, a broadtail coat, an enormous broadtail stole, jewels. Meanwhile, Kober noticed, a now rich Lillian never picked up a check, as if this was not what a "girl" did. Ever insecure as a woman, she must have manifestations of the devotion of men, and the spending of money was convenient and sufficient proof.

Once a week she met Kober for dinner, and often for lunch as well, still "juggling." Even as Kober had been cut loose, been told in no uncertain terms that Hammett was the man in her life, they could still fall into bed together. "Most enjoyable" was Kober's reaction to one such encounter. Yet as soon as she was gone, he realized that he actually received little sexual satisfaction with Lillian. He even wondered whether he would have sought consolation elsewhere were he still married to her. Arthur Kober would remain in love with Lillian Hellman for the rest of his life. But in his private moments, he decided that it was not particularly gratifying to be in bed with her.

The sex with Hammett was no more satisfying. "Something had gone wrong," Lily reflected in later years. "Had felt the reason was because it was not grand passion." So she endured sexual rejection, and remained with him, masochistically, even though he still sometimes frightened her. She was "frightened of being hit, frightened of the humiliation, frightened of the superiority." She became him, a hard-talking, no-nonsense, sometimes cruel woman, in part as a defense against him, in part as a reaction to the way he treated her. Always she feared his sharp tongue, his scorn, and his fists; always she found him "forbidding."

Hammett kept his power over her by his silence, and by his flirtations with other women. They would go out to dinner. To arouse his attention, she would raise hell about the food, or the service. Nothing was right. He would look sweet and enjoy it, getting what he wanted without having to ask; the waitress would invariably look to see what he wanted before he even asked for it. Lillian would accuse him of flirting with the waitress. Just to annoy her, he *would* flirt.

Hammett finally wrote a treatment for a *Thin Man* sequel involving a dope theme, only for M-G-M to declare it was a subject they wouldn't touch. Hammett did manage to produce two *After the Thin Man* sequel treatments, one dated January 8, 1935, of 34 pages, the other September 17, of 115 pages. But in the years to come it was with Lillian that the film successors to *The Thin Man* would be negotiated, she who handled Hammett's affairs.

Lillian knew she must keep on working, if only to fill the void Hammett created between them whenever they seemed to be drawing close. After writing *The Dark Angel* for Goldwyn, desperate to write another play, in the spring of 1935 she spent a few weeks in Ohio researching a play about the war between labor and management.

The success of *The Children's Hour,* no less than the infusion of Hollywood money, brought Lily wealth and fame. These she coveted and enjoyed. But she remained unhappy. Once more she thought she would find some peace if Hammett were to marry her. She asked him, and he refused her. He was still married; his wife was Catholic; she would never divorce him.

He moved to a big house at 325 Bel Air Road accompanied by his butler, Jones, and his male lover. He couldn't write. Lying in bed, he would call his secretary, Mildred Lewis, to come upstairs and lie with him, promising that nothing would happen. Then she lay down and he put his arms around her and held her. Lewis did not find the experience enjoyable, chaste as it was. Nor was her husband amused when Hammett sent so many flowers to their apartment.

Lillian's picture was on the piano, but she was not always in residence. Hammett threw lavish parties. He got a girl pregnant. Albert

Hackett was about to send her some money on Dash's behalf only for Dash to instruct him to "ask her to describe the chandelier."

He ran after a girl called Sis, and told Lily that if you wanted to get anywhere with Sis, you had to sleep with her mama first, since Sis and her mama shared men. Later Lily, in a summary of Hammett's girls, described this Sis as "too doped up to talk much," a girl with a dog accompanied by "her vigorous green-blonde mother," a girl who slapped Lillian's face when she tried to talk to her.

Certainly he didn't hide his chippies from Lillian. She was miserable, "very unhappy these days," Kober noted in his diary. There were days when Dash could not be found. He wasn't at the Bel Air house; he wasn't anywhere anyone could discover. There were many days she hoped he would call to see how she was and he didn't.

One night, granted courage by huge doses of alcohol, she derided him once more for his alcoholism, for the whores. Taking the high moral road, she accused him of being unjust, of being careless and selfish, of insisting that he get his own way always without considering her feelings, and of being sharp with her, but never with himself. When she looked at him, he was grinding a burning cigarette into his cheek.

"What are you doing?" she demanded, horrified.

"Keeping myself from doing it to you," Dash answered. What made it all worse was that the sex between them had dwindled, indeed scarcely existed now. "I don't think anything in the world goes faster than, say, sexual passion," she knew. Yet she yearned for him still.

Such incidents led Lily shrewdly to assess her situation. Even as she was "still very upset with Hammett," she "knew a change between us had to be faced." One day at lunch she spoke to Kober "of status of her arrangement with Dash," as Kober put it. Lily admitted that there were new terms, a new agreement between her and Hammett. Lily seemed ready to relinquish her romantic fantasy. By early 1935 her hope that he would be the man in her life was reduced to an "arrangement."

He would be there to help her with her plays, and, indeed, as she went on writing, he would sit with her, occasionally giving her an outline of how a scene should go. Or he would talk it out with her. "No, it shouldn't be like that," people heard Dash say. He would keep it human, they thought, since Lillian had very little sense of what human beings were like.

But he would live exactly as he pleased, and if she wanted him in her life, she must take him as he was. She would not deceive herself into believing she could ever win him over to her completely. She would never succeed in persuading him to choose her over his careless life.

Yet despite their quarrels, despite all her announcements that she had given him up, they remained a couple. She gave him Kober's *Thunder over the Bronx* anthology, reporting to Kober that he "was very excited about it and said that when they were all together in one book, they seemed so much more than the humorous pieces that they were in *The New Yorker,* and that the people not only talked right, but thought so right and with never a mis-step . . . He was very impressed with it." What Dash said was gospel.

He still tried to please her. When Gertrude Stein came to Hollywood in April 1935 the one person she wanted to meet was Dashiell Hammett. Hammett in turn would not accept the invitation of Stein's hostess, Lillian Ehrman, unless he could bring someone to the dinner. That person was Lillian.

Whether or not she knew about the success of *The Children's Hour,* Stein ignored Lillian, focusing her attention on Hammett. Stein wanted to know why, like so many male writers in the twentieth century, he could only write about himself, "strong or weak or mysterious or passionate or drunk or controlled," but always himself, while women writers could invent many kinds of women.

Hammett said he saw what she meant. He told Stein, in Stein's memory, that "the men have no confidence and so they have to make themselves . . . more beautiful more intriguing more everything and they cannot make any other man because they have to hold on to themselves not having any confidence."

Gertrude Stein did not direct a word to Lillian. Nor did Lillian sign the guest book that night, although Hammett, Charlie Chaplin, Gertrude Stein, and Alice Toklas did.

6

Retaliations

Consciously now Lily examined the few options Dash had left to her. She could search for a man who would offer himself more completely. She might marry again. But then she would lose Dash for good.

It wasn't only that she believed that her continued success as a playwright depended upon his helping her with the plays. He had gotten under her skin so completely that she would never be free of him. Always she longed for him, the man who was unattainable. Nor would he free her by letting her go. Never would he entirely disappear. With anger, she called him "arrogant," as indeed he had set the terms. Sex she would pursue with others, even as she would remain available to him should he want her, and should the state of his increasingly precarious genital health permit. But she would try to loosen some of his hold on her, if only for her emotional sanity. So Lillian refined their Faustian bargain.

Meanwhile she confided to Kober that she wanted to be unattached, the better "to take advantage of her position." She now behaved as if every man in a room found her sexually attractive, and some did. In an era in which women still waited for men to declare themselves, Lily conquered in an open field.

She began by sleeping with Kober more often. When Kober went off for a weekend with some woman, Lil seemed upset, so possessive was she even of men she did not want exclusively herself. Meanwhile Kober was disappointed when he entered a room only to find Lily once more with Dash. Suddenly she was "quite far away from me," and he felt tired and low.

They formed a circle in Hollywood, a distinct clique: Lily and Dash and Kober, the Perelmans, the Hacketts, Dorothy Parker, Budd Schulberg, Lee and Ira Gershwin. John O'Hara took to calling them the "Hammett-Hellman-Perelman-Kober group," bitterly noting that they had no time either for F. Scott Fitzgerald or, later, for himself. He did note "with some sardonic pleasure that they're having trouble convincing people that Pep West was better than Fitzgerald AND Jonathan Swift."

They frequently drank themselves sick, Dash habitually, Lily to keep up. Drunk, Dash invariably became cruel and got into fights, including one with Mrs. Ed Robinson, whom he took pleasure in calling a "horse's ass."

When Herman Shumlin came to town to direct *These Three,* an adaptation of *The Children's Hour,* and his first film effort, he joined the group. Lil and Dash and Herman and Kober were a frequent combination that spring of 1935.

One day Dash found himself flat broke. He asked Lily, rich now, for money; willingly she gave him $5,000. A week later he told her he was broke again. She demanded to know what he had done with the money.

Furious she should dare ask, dare behave as if he were accountable to her, he hit her. "I went to a whorehouse, found a pretty girl and gave it to her," he said viciously. This was not a man to whom you could put questions. His emotional dark corners could not be penetrated, not by her and not by anyone. He was especially nasty when anyone dared cross these boundaries.

"You son of a bitch," she raged, and she pummeled him with her fists, and then he hit her back even harder. Now there was nothing for her to do but leave. She finished the screenplay for *These Three* and made plans to go to New York. She asked their mutual friend Laura Perelman to look after Dash. What Lillian did not know was that Laura was in love with Dash.

If she had hoped Dash would pursue her to New York, that did not happen. With a heavy heart Lily did what she had to do for her own survival. She began in earnest a romantic life without him.

It was June 1935. Her plane encountered a storm and set down in the middle of the desert just outside Albuquerque. Amid blowing dust and wind the sun was just slipping below the horizon. Walking over the tarmac from the plane to the adobe depot, Lily began to chat with another passenger about the delay. She talked quickly, just as nearly five years before she had begun talking at Bing Crosby's opening to that tall, slender man on his way to the toilet.

This man thought the blond woman had an interesting face. "She was very handsome, ugly but handsome," he would say later. He admired her elegant costume, her perfectly coiffed hair. He "found her attractive." He asked if the delay annoyed her.

"Not particularly," said the feisty woman. "I'm on my way home from Hollywood." She had faced the outer limits of her relationship with Dashiell Hammett. From now on home would be New York, no matter where he was.

She told the man she was a playwright.

"Oh, have you written any plays?" he wanted to know. Hardly a rube from the provinces, he had at the age of twenty-five been appointed managing editor of *The New Yorker,* and was now managing editor of *Fortune* magazine. But she had never heard of him either.

It soon became apparent that the storm would hover perilously over the neighborhood. They must remain overnight in Albuquerque. The man bought her a drink. They shared the artificial moment of intimacy. She told him about the fight she had with Hammett, how he had given $5,000 to a chippy, how she had attacked him, and he had hit her back. He confided that he had a tubercular wife with whom he could not have sexual intercourse. They both had a great deal to drink.

They went to the restaurant to wait for their room assignments. When the number of her room was announced, it was she who whispered, "Come, darling," she who made the first move, as Lillian had done before and increasingly would do. A romantic, Lily enlisted her gift for creating adventures. For the man, it was "the gayest [adventure] he had ever known."

He felt for Lily a violent physical attraction, so violent he would later remember they neglected to close their hotel-room door, so that at one point they noticed an astonished hotel employee watching them in bed. Years later Ralph Macallister Ingersoll remembered the effect Lillian Hellman had on him, the sexuality she generated: "the least little gesture she made, the shake of her head, the turn of her wrist, was infinitely more attractive than the most alluring movement any other woman could make with all of her, and the trappings of a state costume and a spotlight thrown in." Her touch was "like the caress of a flame which did not burn but whose whole vitality went into healing and making well. He knew that he was as alive as any human being could be alive." Lillian Hellman knew how to make love, and how to receive it, Ingersoll later recalled, and that night she poured all her yearning for Hammett into a man who would be the first in a long line of mostly tall, mostly Anglo-Saxon substitutes.

In the morning, Ingersoll was certain he was in love. He would leave his wife and marry Lillian. "Living an emotionally unfaithful life with Tommy is unthinkable," he said self-righteously. Lillian, fed up with Hammett, reconsidering her decision not to marry anyone else, let Ingersoll believe she might agree. Their intimacy established, she told Ingersoll that Hammett had virtually written *The Children's Hour,* steering her line by line.

In New York, Lillian proceeded with life as an unattached woman. Honing the Hammett style, she went immediately to Kober's Fire Island weekend house, where with great bravado she started the day with a breakfast of clams. "Such Hammett *mishigos,*" Kober noted disapprovingly.

Back in Hollywood, perhaps having learned about Lillian and Ingersoll, or perhaps merely sensing her alienation, Hammett retaliated. One night in July at another of the wild parties he threw at his big Bel Air house, he called for some Chinese prostitutes from Madame Lee Francis', where he was a regular.

As Hammett revealed in "Dead Yellow Women," first published in *Black Mask* in 1925, he had a taste for the beauty of Asian women. Of Hsiu Hsiu, less than four and a half feet in height, he writes that "her face was a tiny oval of painted beauty . . . her red flower of a mouth shaped a smile that made all the other smiles I could remember look like leers." When he was in the East, Hammett frequented Harlem brothels in search of black or Asian women. Subscribing to a racist stereotype, he believed that they were duplicitous, a trait which increased their sexual appeal.

Before the night of this party Dash had been on what they called in those times "a tear." That night, on one of his worst benders, he went beyond his customary trafficking with prostitutes. He paid Lillian back mercilessly.

Among his guests were the Hacketts and Sid and Laura Perelman. In the midst of the revels, a drunken Hammett sent one of the call girls he had hired to a bathroom to disrobe. Then he lured Sid up to that bathroom.

Sid has been absent a very long time, Hammett remarked, inspiring Laura to conduct a search upstairs. Soon she opened the door. Soon she caught Sid and the whore flagrante delicto.

On Independence Day, both of them tight, Dash took off with an enraged Laura Perelman, who not only was attracted to him but by now had developed strong feelings. Long jealous of Lillian's sexual liaison with her brother, Pep West, Laura felt she owed her no particular loyalty. For Dash the notion of sexual fidelity was entirely alien.

It was a Friday. They rented a car and drove to San Francisco. As soon as they arrived, however, Dash was ill; Laura didn't know what to do for him. It was hardly the weeklong romantic adventure she had envisioned.

But they did make love, even as, between the sheets, Dash told Laura how close he was to Lillian; it didn't seem anomalous even to Laura that he should do so. At their moments of deepest estrangement, when it might seem Lily and Dash were utterly lost to each other, it still was not yet so. But the whores and chippies whom Lillian could feel superior to were one thing and Laura Perelman, beautiful Laura, their friend, was another. The liaison between Dashiell Hammett and Laura Perelman drove a far deeper wedge into Lily and Dash's relationship than his drunken philandering had ever done.

There were immediate consequences. Distraught, Sid called Lillian in a panic. He couldn't find Laura anywhere and Dash was missing too. Had Lillian heard anything? Was it possible that Dash and Laura were together? Lily and Dash were planning to get married, Sid told Kober. What was this all about? The friends gathered—Nathanael West, Arthur Kober, Irene Lee. There was tremendous tension in the air, and also jokes, because it was all so horrendous. Whatever the men felt, Irene Lee was not sympathetic toward Lillian, whose insecurities allowed her to admit few pretty women into her inner circle.

Kober, however, was indignant on Lillian's behalf. It was "absolutely cheap and despicable." He compared the "heartache" Lily felt at Dash's defection with what he felt when Hammett entered her life, "and I'm sorry for her, too," he noted in his diary. Loving Lily still, he felt no joy in it. Worse, Dash was "loudly proud of it too." He made no effort to conceal the escapade. Soon the whole world knew.

But when he did not hear from Lily, who kept her silence, neither phoning nor writing, Hammett became anxious and worried. For as she was assuming his persona, his identity, he was increasingly becoming emotionally dependent on her, a process he was neither to face nor to acknowledge. Meanwhile it could hardly have pleased Lillian to receive a letter from Laura herself advising her, "If you love him as much as he does you I would go to him immediately or at least phone him."

Ignoring Laura, heartsick, Lily plunged into imitating Hammett, never more than at this moment of his deepest, most egregious betrayal. Usually tight with her money, now, her defenses in a shambles, she exhibited "the Hammett influence . . . in the careless, sweeping way in which her money is thrown around," Kober noticed. That she had been with Ingersoll in no way compared with Hammett's sleeping with one of their closest friends.

In disarray, Lillian remained in New York, dreading the idea of a return to Hollywood. When poor Rose Shumlin, Herman's wife, made some "foolish arguments" during a discussion about Communism, a frequent topic of conversation in their set now, Lil angrily snapped at her.

Laura Perelman remained obsessed with Dashiell Hammett. On July 27, back at the farm in Bucks County, Pennsylvania, she wrote him that she had "started and torn up three letters to you in the last ten minutes." She could not let go. She wanted to know how he felt, whether "everything is alright with the studio," and "whether you and Lil have smoothed it out." Laura offered even to see Lillian. She had such "warm feelings" about Hammett that she would do anything he asked. (Shamelessly, she gave him an address in Manhattan where he could reach her.)

Finally there came a day when Lily confronted Dash in full rage over Laura Perelman.

Why hadn't he told her? she demanded. It was one thing to savor whores, another to run off with their mutual friend. He had hurt her many times before, but never as much as this.

He kept the truth from her, Dash told Lillian, "because he'd given Laura his word not to tell anybody." That was all he had to say. He wouldn't discuss it further. He had been silent out of "loyalty to Laura," Hammett repeated. It was always worse when he did answer one of her charges.

Whatever her new relationship with Ingersoll meant to her, and from the start Ingersoll knew she was crazy about Hammett, "hooked," it did not lessen the pain Lily felt over Hammett's defection with Laura Perelman. She threatened never to speak to Laura Perelman again. She didn't speak to Sid, the messenger of the awful tidings, for a year. Meanwhile, Pep West, who hated Hammett, was close to his sister, and had bedded Lillian, was beside himself.

For the rest of her life Lily remained angry with Dash for his interlude with Laura Perelman. Forty years later, she told her close friend Peter Feibleman: "I could kill him for that . . . even now, after all this time . . . I could still kill him . . . I wish he were alive so I could kill him."

Hammett had shed himself of all entrapments, cast off illusions about "love," taught himself not to pursue dead ends, would not enlist in the future. Shedding everything, miscalculating, he had left himself with too little. He hadn't enough flesh on his bones or enough fiber in his soul to make an independent life. The brief affair with Laura Perelman and its aftermath wearied him and hastened his decline. Meanwhile Lillian, a fierce she-Hammett, threw herself into a plenitude of sexual liaisons to get back at him, show him she didn't need him.

By September, Lillian was ready to tell Kober about her "new boyfriend." His name was Ralph Ingersoll, "married & of course a goy— or it wouldn't be Lil," Kober reflected. She spent the summer and autumn of 1935 in New York, sleeping with both Kober and Ingersoll, and lecturing at New York University. She furnished a new apartment, a duplex at 14 East Seventy-fifth Street, with prints of Picassos and a grand piano which George Gershwin played. Acting as a gracious and generous and nurturing hostess, she filled her rooms with celebrities. Her companion was a large apricot poodle named Jumbo.

Meanwhile, Ingersoll's wife asked him not to go to Reno for the divorce until he made sure of his feelings for Lillian. Having bought time, she became an invalid again. As soon as he told Lillian there would be a delay, Mrs. Ingersoll's pulmonary lesions miraculously disappeared.

Yet even as he had retreated from commitment at the penultimate moment, Ingersoll remained enamored. Even as at the deepest level he held himself apart, he enjoyed Lily's rages "into which she could be worked with the drop of a cliché." They even, he, like Hammett, thought, had a comic quality. But if she made him angry, she would not allow him to stay angry. Soon she would be flirting. She pretended to be a little girl pretending to be a serious woman, one moment "fluttery feminine," the next a person of strong opinions. Together again on the New Mexican desert they saw in the New Year 1936.

Finally Lillian saw that he was using his wife's health to postpone marriage, and she finished with him sentimentally. For later he did leave his sick wife, whose illness had always repelled him. "I can't stand to be around sickness," he had told his wife when her illness surfaced just after they married. All the years Tommy Ingersoll had justified his aversion to her sickness, telling friends, "He's not like other people. He's so sensitive." Had he wanted to marry Lillian, he would have.

During the summer and autumn of 1935 as she remained in New York, and Hammett remained in Hollywood, Lily showed others her work in progress. She also read the drafts of Kober's play *Having Wonderful Time*.

Julia Hellman died on November 30. It was Kober, not Hammett, who was there to take care of Max and help Lily with the funeral arrangements. The chapel was filled with Newhouses, Kober noted, with "tremendous beaks," although Julia Newhouse was buried in what Kober called a "goyish cemetery." As soon as her mother died, Lillian discovered something about herself: she was no longer in love with her father. Still, she began to wear her mother's wedding ring.

With Lily in New York, Dash deteriorated even further. He didn't show up at meetings scheduled by Hunt Stromberg, his boss. Work was not delivered on time. Sometimes he disappeared completely. Lawsuits were filed against him for nonpayment of his debts, and settled by default judgments. His chauffeur, Jones, continued to drive him around in a rented limousine.

In January 1936 Dash finally boarded a train for New York. But he had not been invited to stay with Lillian at her duplex. Instead he went to the Plaza. When he was sick, and couldn't pay his bill, he was asked to leave. His old flame Nell Martin cared for him at her place. It was at this time that, weakened as he was by lung disease, venereal disease, and alcoholism, Dash began a relationship with Pru Whitfield, the wife of *Black Mask* writer Raoul Whitfield, who had himself fallen ill with tuberculosis.

Before long Dash was watching the snow fall from a room in the Private Pavilion of Lenox Hill Hospital. He wrote his daughter, Jo, he wasn't going back to the Plaza because "the service is too lousy." There was no question of Dash's moving in with Lily, with whom he had quarreled. Leaving the hospital, he settled at the Madison, an elegant, residential hotel with a walnut-paneled lobby and supercilious, protective clerks.

Lily and Dash renewed their tenuous connection. He needed her, but never would admit it. She needed him, but shielded herself with as many men as she could accommodate, none of them meaning much to her. When they saw each other, they argued, loudly. She told him he didn't appreciate her or her dog; she pointed out what he owed her. Finally he told her to shut up about it since he'd supported her for several years.

They went to the theater to see Clifford Odets' *Awake and Sing.* Hammett was drunk, Lily restless in his increasingly censorious company. Afterward, when she told him that she liked the play, and why didn't he, he said: "Because I don't think writers who cry about not having had a bicycle when they were kiddies are ever going to amount to much." So he justified himself, he who kept his feelings buried, washed away from consciousness with alcohol but never complaining about the deprivations of his youth, or his illness.

Lily occupied herself with her trust fund, which had gone from her grandmother to her mother. Now that her mother was dead the distribution had to be changed. She was already a tough trader, and in her contract with Herman Shumlin for her next play, *Days to Come,* it was stipulated that whenever his name appeared in an advertisement, hers must appear as well.

That winter of 1936 she continued to sleep with Ingersoll. In March, they traveled to Cuba, where they went fishing. There were loud screaming matches over politics, over his evasion of commitment to her. Once in anger she told him she had secretly aborted his child. At the time he mistakenly thought he was sterile and didn't believe her. Once she yelled that he was "an anti-Semitic son of a bitch."

When they finally met, Hammett decided he had no use for Ingersoll. He neither liked nor trusted naive, unworldly men, knowing what trouble they could cause out of their fear and ignorance. Nor did Ingersoll like Hammett, believing he "could be a very cruel man." As for Ingersoll's sexual liaison with Lily, Hammett kept aloof from that, and tolerated Ingersoll's presence to prove it. Ingersoll viewed Hammett as a rival, but one who raised in him no resentment or hostility: "He was too totally detached on the level of personal emotions."

Bored, Hammett went to a dog show and to the fights. He collected matchbooks from New York watering places, which he sent back to California to his daughter, Jo. Nights were for brothel-crawling in Harlem.

He was supposed to be writing a new book for Knopf. In May, Blanche Knopf wrote, "Anxious to know how the book goes and whether you will have it ready in the summer." At the end of July, back from Europe, she wrote again, believing "that you must be about finishing your book." When might she see it? But so completely had Lillian absorbed his identity that it was not his own work but hers which occupied the center of Dashiell Hammett's life. He wrote to Jo, urging her to see a movie called *These Three,* in which there was a little girl who "looks . . . quite a bit like you." Even when they were apart he remained in Lillian's sphere.

At last he decided that hiring a secretary whom he must keep busy might help him to write again, and he placed an advertisement in the New York *Times.* A twenty-nine-year-old Wellesley graduate named Eleanor Wolff, who had studied at the Sorbonne, called at ten-thirty one morning. It was as if she had awakened the dead. It turned out that Hammett hardly ever got up before noon.

When she arrived for her appointment, he immediately asked what she would like for lunch and what to drink. He himself would not be drinking. He was on the wagon.

"I had a drink downstairs to fortify myself," Wolff told him.

"Well, you can certainly manage another," he replied—like most alcoholics, compulsively drawing others into his disease. She asked for a martini; Hammett ordered two.

"I thought you told me you were on the wagon," she murmured.

"Well, the service is so slow here," he answered, he had assumed she would want another. Hammett ate nothing. During the spring of 1936 when Eleanor Wolff worked for Dashiell Hammett, spending full days with him at his hotel, she never saw him eat solid food.

He told her he needed someone to dictate to in case he got any ideas. It appeared that he had had a quarrel with Lillian, and had decided he would shut himself up, isolate himself in the Madison, seeing no one.

Wolff sat on one side of the room with her pencil and paper in hand and Hammett sat on the other. At three o'clock, he said, "Well, I guess that's enough work for one day."

On the second day he was reading the newspaper when she arrived. "Hello," he said, and kept on reading. Soon he fell asleep. She settled down to George Santayana's *The Last Puritan,* then practiced her shorthand. Around four he awoke and said, "Well, let's call it a day."

As she put on her coat, Wolff could not help saying, "I'm afraid I'm not a very loud voice of conscience, but I don't dare to be."

"Oh, I want a very soft, low, scarcely audible one," Hammett said.

On the third day she hurried into the Madison five minutes late to announce herself. But Hammett had left a note for her at the desk. It read: "Dear Miss Wolff—I feel too lousy to work today—thank God. See you tomorrow. D.H."

The next day was Friday. He telephoned her at home around eleven. "Don't bother coming today," he told her. "Let's keep it a virgin week!"

On the following Monday when she arrived, he was dressed in a sweater and coat and a bright red-and-yellow tie. Surely, Wolff thought, the energetic costume was a sign that work was to begin. Indeed Hammett told her he had a letter to write. With her pencil and her shorthand book, she waited.

"It's too short for that," he said. Then he dictated his letter: "Dear Everitt, I like the anthology idea. Give me a ring any day this week and we'll get together. Sincerely yours, Dashiell Hammett." Then he lay down on the couch. When she brought him the letter addressed to C. Raymond Everitt of Little, Brown & Company, he waved it away. "Don't you want to sign it?" she asked.

"You sign it," he said.

For the rest of the afternoon, she sat reading in an armchair. He remained on the couch until he said he supposed they wouldn't do any more work that afternoon. "It's payday," he said, handing her a fifty-dollar bill. She asked him to give her only half. She hadn't done any work all week.

"It wasn't your fault, was it?" he answered. "No, if you want half when you don't work, you'll want double when you do."

Soon she began to find him in bed when she arrived. "Come in," he beckoned her from the bedroom the first time. So she went into his bedroom and sat in a chair with her shorthand book. "What's new?" he asked. He seemed low, weary. He ordered breakfast, looked with discouragement at his orange juice, drank it, turned over, and went back to sleep. After a while he awoke and poured his chocolate. On his third waking, he looked at the chocolate in despair but drank it. The cream of wheat he disregarded. Then he lit a cigarette. He looked clean and tidy in his pajamas. He didn't cough or sneeze, didn't even seem to need a shave, and his room had no morning-bedroom smell at all.

"You know who my favorite poet is?" he said one day. "Laura Riding. She wrote me a poem once on the corruption of the body. It had nothing to do with the corruption of the body, but it was a swell poem. You know, she lived with Robert Graves for years."

His tone turned gay. "Robert Graves wrote me the funniest beginning of a letter that I've ever had. It started, 'Life has been very different since Laura jumped out of a fourth-story window.' A policeman seems to have picked her up and brought her in all mangled. But Graves said, 'She'll be as right as rain in a month.' She's still a cripple. Graves ended the letter with something I never quite understood. He said, 'I was with her at the time, but it was not against me that she did it.' I never knew whether he meant not against his protest or not against his inclinations."

When the telephone rang, Wolff answered it. Hammett told her he didn't want to speak to anyone. "Tell them I'm all tied up in bed," he said once. The only person for whom he would come to the telephone was Lillian Hellman. Then there came over him a sense of excitement. Then he would speak to Lily in a very low voice.

The telephone rang. Wolff took it in the other room. It was not the one person Hammett would always speak to. Knowing her part, Wolff immediately said, "Mr. Hammett cannot come to the telephone. Can I take a message."

"Tell Mr. Hammett that all we want is to give him some money for work he's already done. He's promised to send over some short stories for us to syndicate for radio. It's a matter of a few thousand dollars for him and all we want is to have him send them over."

His gray hair was very short then, almost a crew cut. The barber arrived and remained in the bedroom for an hour. A few minutes later Hammett appeared.

"Well, that's something accomplished!" he said with his rueful smile. Then he dropped exhausted into the nearest armchair. When Wolff told him about the phone message, he replied, "You wouldn't think it'd be so hard, would you? All I have to do is get hold of the stuff and choose which ones to send 'em." But the stories were at Lillian's apartment, and that posed a problem. "D'you think those people could be induced to send for them themselves?" Wolff ventured.

"Oh . . . ," Hammett said, and waved the subject wearily away. It was obvious that he held his idleness in contempt, yet could do little about it. She opened the mail—there wasn't much. Most of the time he said, "Dump it! Dump it!"

On another day he remained in bed and she sat reading until dusk. Around six, Hammett emerged, dressed and ready to go out.

"What are you doing?" he asked. "Saving on the light bill, or studying to be an owl?" "Studying" was a favorite word of his.

There was never anything to dictate, and so he began to send her to the New York Public Library at Forty-second Street. One day he told her to look up "Methods of American private detective agencies." He also wanted to know about Billy the Kid, about Tombstone, about Robin Hood, about "a year with a whaler." Another subject was labor spies and industrial espionage. He asked for histories of the Pinkertons, "how Allan Pinkerton thwarted the first plot to assassinate Lincoln."

One book by Allan Pinkerton he wanted was *Strikers, Communists, Tramps and Detectives.* Another volume was called *Two Evilisms: Pinkertonism & Anarchism,* "by a cowboy detective who knows, as he spent twenty-two years in the inner circle of Pinkerton's Detective Agency." He wanted to know about strikes and lockouts, and union organizing and blacklisting, and about the sin of spying on workers. The Pullman strike. The Homestead strike.

He also had Wolff write to the Department of State and the Treasury Department and the Library of Congress to inquire about the rumor that some of the Louisiana Purchase money was sunk off the Georgia coast in a shipwreck and that attempts had been made to salvage it. She wrote to the University of Georgia, to Louisiana State University. No one had heard of the story. But a man named Carl Holm did send her a telegram: "Am about to join final expedition for possible recovery. Willing to relinquish all data for fifty percent of gross proceeds."

Suddenly, for several weeks Hammett didn't pay Wolff. Then one day he told her he'd gone off the wagon. "I got restless around three o'clock, so I went around to the Stork Club," he confessed.

"You take this check to the bank and cash it," he ordered her. Then he gave her all her back salary and told her he was going to Russia, where he would be doing research for his next book. He gave her fifty dollars extra as a goodbye present. She never saw him again.

That late spring of 1936, Hammett was bound not for Russia but to doctors for a series of injections to clear up his gonorrhea. He told Lily about the sitz baths and rectal irrigations and how humiliating they were. Things were "not very cheerful with her," Kober noted in his diary. Terrified that Hammett had given her a venereal disease, she remained in a white heat of anger.

In June 1936, in despair, needing "to get away from it all," Lily reluctantly sailed for Havana by herself. Nobody goes to Cuba in June, Kober thought. It was Max, Kober, Shumlin, and Louis Kronenberger who saw her off amid, in Kober's eyes, "a horrible banana-eating crowd." Although he was in New York, Hammett was conspicuously absent.

Hammett wrote: "I'm missing you terribly. Last night I almost phoned Rhinelander 4-4108 just to hear it ring, but that seemed a little too silly." She was already gone. Hammett read *Variety* and mailed Lily tidbits of gossip. "Well, where else am I going to get news if I don't go out?" he wrote, anticipating her complaint about secondhand gossip. Revealing no jealousy, he was "awfully glad you like Havana and are having a good time."

As always too, he let her know that, take him as he was, he remained in her life. "I've been practicing looking like Corey Ford," he wrote, "so you've got that to come home to." He also reminded her that he was profoundly true to her—in his fashion. "I love you, as you may remember," he closed.

7

Roosevelt Bohemians

"Don't kid yourselves that there's any law in Poisonville except what
you make for yourself."

RED HARVEST

By the close of 1935, and into 1936, Dashiell Hammett, a man
better than his afflictions, was finding a life devoid of purpose
increasingly intolerable. Unable to deceive himself any longer
that the discipline of writing would form the cartilage of his life,
he turned instead to politics. An admirer of Marx and Engels, long a bitter opponent of capitalist society, Hammett responded to the call of the
American Communist Party.

In the wake of the Depression, Lillian Hellman and Dashiell Hammett had joined those who rejected the capitalist parties controlled by
those whose class interests were incompatible with redress of the economic injustices permeating American society. But the party to which
Hellman and Hammett were drawn had already purged those who had
been committed to testing democratically how a movement for revolutionary change might be built in America.

Instead, it had become a crude transmission belt for Stalin's dictates,
a carbon copy of his authoritarian rule. Conveniently, however, for Hammett, this most American of sensibilities, it was the very moment when,
under orders from the Comintern, the Party was discarding its revolutionary ideology, abandoning the ideals of Communism and socialism

and the class struggle, and instead proclaiming its Americanism, its patriotism, its New Dealism, and its antifascism.

In 1935 and 1936 the Comintern declared the Popular Front, which required every foreign Communist Party to subordinate itself to bourgeois parties, for Communists in America, for example, to behave as if they were enthusiastic members of the Democratic Party. Radical energy was channeled into the New Deal, abandoning the idea of building a socialist movement. Patriotism was the order of the day as the Party focused on its leader Earl Browder's "colonial and pioneer stock," an ideology reflected in Lillian Hellman's later praise of Hammett as coming of "early settlers."

Even antifascism in these years before Hitler invaded the Soviet Union meant support for Franklin Roosevelt—and lobbying for the interests of Stalin's Soviet Union, the "first workers' state," which at that very moment was a revolution being betrayed. *New Masses* described the Third American Writers Congress in typical Popular Front vernacular: "These writers are united in their determination to defend our tradition of democratic culture."

Out of submission to Stalin's agenda in the years before 1939, fascism had to be opposed as a military threat to the Soviet state. The Party's task was to enlist America and the Western democracies on Russia's behalf. There was to be no more talk of American imperialism. There was to be no talk of militant union activity by the Communist Party or, in these Depression years, of injustice apart from the terms set by the New Deal. Class collaboration was the order of the day. While, to destroy opposition in the Soviet Union, Stalin unleashed purges, in America the Communist Party leadership became obsessed with whether its members might not be influenced by Leon Trotsky.

Dashiell Hammett, a man of considerable intelligence, fell prey to uncritical acceptance of all this and more.

Hammett had long known better than to put any faith in reforming American society through conventional political parties. When he was a country boy of the lower middle classes, no one had made his way easier. No one had taken any notice of him, this exceedingly bright boy who had been permitted to leave school at thirteen. There had been no one to help him or to care whether he lived or died.

As an adult, he was infused with compassion, and became a man with too much integrity not to aspire to justice for other people. His life continued to be difficult as authority hounded him. Throughout the twenties he pleaded for his war pension. As his tuberculosis raged, he was in constant danger of drowning in his own blood. In the pay of the mine owners, Pinkertons killed Wobblies. Forever after, Hammett felt tainted by having served them.

Before he ever joined the Party, Hammett in his novels and stories had offered a radical critique of American capitalism. In *Red Harvest* (1929), his first novel, Hammett originally called America "Poisonville," whose facade concealed the fact that capitalists, police, and thugs were in symbiotic control of the country. In his even earlier story "The Gutting of Couffignal" (1925), the bandits are ruthless White Russians who kill whoever gets in their way as they seek indiscriminate revenge for the confiscation of their property and their loss of luxury. The story opens on a bank being blown up, as, with his exquisite economy, Hammett in a single image summarized a society in anguish. In "Fly Paper (1929)," a wayward daughter of the rich gets into serious trouble once she perceives the perfidy of her family. In Hammett's works, as he came to create the atmosphere and mood which were to define the genre ever after, violence arrives without warning.

From his first stories Hammett expressed his revulsion for the violence, murder, and mayhem endemic to capitalism. He perceived it as a system in its death throes, containing inexorably within itself the seeds of its own destruction. He portrayed the misery of its victims, those caught in the path of its fox fire. Society under capitalism is in chaos, and the pretense of social civility is a joke. Reformist apologists for such a system are as bad as the capitalists themselves. In *Red Harvest*, Quint calls the capitalist and reformer Willsson, Jr., "a lousy liberal." That Willsson, Jr., dies before he can enact any reforms is no great loss for the place he finally named Personville. Hammett introduced a social consciousness to the detective story form that was unrelenting, uncompromising, and thorough.

The claustrophic mood of Dashiell Hammett's four great novels, *Red Harvest, The Dain Curse, The Maltese Falcon,* and *The Glass Key,* flows from the moral and artistic premise that all are guilty and there is no exit from the brutal social order. In *Shadow Man,* his biography of Hammett, Richard Layman points out that a hard-boiled detective movement already existed by 1925—Hammett did not entirely invent that genre. However, no writer before him had offered so intense and unrelenting a vision of the corruption of America's social institutions; his metaphors defy sentimentality as his prose takes on the razor edge Hammett insists is required for survival in his United States of America. In what was called the "murder mystery" genre his only rival was the now long-forgotten S. S. Van Dine.

Although a profound political vision permeates Hammett's fiction, always it is mediated through art, as language is carved to express his vision. Never a pulp writer, although he wrote for the pulps, not only *Black Mask* but *Action Stories, Argosy–All Story, True Detective Mysteries,* and others, Hammett honed his prose. "To write of washing machines in terms of yachts is not to be too literary," he wrote in a 1926 article for *Western Advertising* called "The Advertisement IS Literature." "It is to be not sufficiently literary. The disproportionately florid, the gaudy, have worse reputation in literature than ever they have had in advertising."

Before he published his first novel, Hammett had perfected his style, his goals of "simplicity and clarity," which he knew were "the most elusive and difficult of literary accomplishments." Hammett wrote: "The needlessly involved sentence, the clouded image, are not literary." Then he quoted Anatole France on the nature of "the most beautiful sentence." The answer would be Hammett's own: "The shortest!"

Hemingway simultaneously produced a lean prose, which he offered in somewhat more benign settings. Hammett alone, without ever didactically saying so, produced works in which the reader feels himself to be tottering on the brink of Armageddon. "Everybody has something to conceal," Hammett asserts through his defining character, the man with a code, Sam Spade, in *The Maltese Falcon,* and "most things in San Francisco can be bought, or taken." Of the District Attorney, since government in Hammett's oeuvre yields to no one in its perfidy, Spade says, "I don't know that he ever deliberately framed anybody he believed innocent, but I can't imagine him letting himself believe them innocent if he could scrape up or twist into shape proof of their guilt."

It was such perceptions that inspired those whom Hammett influenced, from Raymond Chandler to Robert B. Parker, whose private eye, Spenser, is a direct descendant of Sam Spade. The most recent beneficiary of Hammett's vision is the founder of cyberpunk fiction, William Gibson, author of *Neuromancer* (1984), who found in Hammett an "American naturalism but cranked up, very intense, almost surreal." Gibson has said that "Hammett may have been the guy who turned me on to the idea of *superspecificity,* which is largely lacking in most SF description." What Larry McCaffery calls Gibson's "futuristic slang, the street talk, the technical and professional jargon," were inspired by Hammett's vivid prose.

Chandler wrote of how Hammett had revolutionized the genre, taking "murder out of the Venetian vase and dropp[ing] it in the alley." Murder was now no longer an affair of "the upper classes, the week-end house party and the vicar's rose garden," but had been restored "to the people who commit it for reasons, not just to provide a corpse." From Hammett, Chandler admitted, he learned how to transform "a physical observation into something that reveals character." As for who influenced

Hammett as he evolved his detective stories, he told Lillian Hellman that he learned to tell a detective story "chiefly from reading Henry James and a great deal from Dostoevsky."

"It is doubtful if even Ernest Hemingway has ever written more effective dialogue than may be found within the pages of this extraordinary tale of gunmen, gin and gangsters," Herbert Asbury began his *Bookman* review of *Red Harvest*. "Better than Hemingway!" declared Knopf's advertisement for *The Maltese Falcon* in *The World* of March 10, 1930. "I believe I have discovered a new technique in the writing of murder-mystery stories and a new technician," William Curtis exulted in his review of *The Maltese Falcon* in *Town & Country*. Only the fact that Hammett had "never been in Paris, has never played around with the Little Review group," accounted for his not having attracted "respectful attention from the proper sources." "There is nothing like these books in the whole range of detective fiction," Donald Douglas wrote in *The New Republic*. Hammett's work bore the "absolute distinction of real art."

Into this universe, in twenty-six of his stories, as well as in *Red Harvest* and *The Dain Curse*, Hammett thrust the Op, whom he described once as "a little man going forward day after day through mud and blood and death and deceit—as callous and brutal and cynical as necessary—towards a dim goal, with nothing to push or pull him towards it except he's been hired to reach it." He created the antihero whose entire mode of being was a measure of the era he inhabited. Richard Layman has put it best: "the archetypal hard-boiled detective, who embodies that complex blend of responsibility, nobility, cynicism, and frustration, was created by Hammett."

By the late twenties labor has been beaten down in Poisonville. Government is in the pocket of the mob. The police are so corrupt that the Op can't leave the all-powerful capitalist Elihu Willsson alone with them. The crooks "own the courts, and, besides, the courts are too slow for us now."

The degenerate capitalist of *Red Harvest* eventually does become "sick" of the butchering, but only because it's "no good for business." "Hired gunmen, strikebreakers, national guardsmen and even parts of the regular army" are mobilized against the Wobblies. The author, as distinct from his alter ego, the Op, dissembles only once: from the list of the types hired to break the strike against the Personville Mining Corporation he omits the Pinkertons.

Hammett reveals little confidence that the victims have the ability to be authors of their own emancipation. All the Op can do is enlist Poisonville's methods to clean up Poisonville. By the second page of *Red*

Harvest he finds himself lying. By the end he admits that he may have murdered his lover, Dinah Brand, one of the many dangerous women who confound and arouse the Hammett hero. No better than any man, another mark of the Hammett hero, the Op discovers his only bulwark against the slide toward entropy is self-control. "I was tempted to tell him what I thought of him," the Op says of Leggett in *The Dain Curse,* "but there was no profit in that."

In *The Glass Key* (1931), Hammett's last serious novel, a vast and sinister conspiracy permeates society: the newspaperman's mortgages are held by the State Central, which is owned by the gangster's candidate for the Senate. To own a newspaper, one must bow to the hegemony of the powerful, and spread corruption: banks, press, gangsters, and politicians conspire under the direction of robber barons; all line their pockets greedily.

A senator kills his own son rather than risk losing an election. In the defining metaphor the key opens a magical cottage filled with life's bounty, only for slithering snakes to emerge. "We couldn't lock the snakes in and they came out all over us," dreams Janet Henry. Evil cannot be contained in capitalist society; the glass key shatters. If in Hammett's fiction plot takes supremacy over depth of character portrayal, the author's decision has been inevitable from the start. His characters must survive in an environment which leaves them little opportunity to delve inward. Some have been born into Depression America. Hammett's earlier stories reveal that pre-Depression America was no better.

Identifying with the suffering of others, Hammett read Marx and Engels. He supported the unions. Later he would join the fronts, sign the petitions. Hammett, who never affected any interest in Russia, a place he was never to visit, was more comfortable when the American replaced the red flag at Party rallies and "The Star-Spangled Banner" supplanted the "Internationale." Self-educated, a provincial, he responded to the legitimacy of the Communist party, a legitimacy not enjoyed by its left alternatives. He suffered the intellectual blindness of the self-educated, the gaps in logic he had not been trained to avoid. He had also been corrupted by Hollywood to enjoy fine living, and the Communism of the Popular Front did nothing to discourage that.

Seizing enthusiastically on the opportunity to share an enterprise with Dash, with whom her relationship was becoming ever more tenuous, and ready to cut her conscience to fit the fashion of the Popular Front, Lily joined him. In Hollywood both became members of a special group of the Communist Party that was so loosely organized as not to be a regular Party "branch." Because its members were all well-known writers and movie people, the secrecy of their membership had to be preserved.

The Party used them principally for fund-raising and for the prestige they bestowed upon its front organizations. Indeed few in the Party ever knew with certainty whether Hellman, or even Hammett, who was so obviously available to the Party and who followed so precisely all the twists and turns of its line as it issued from Moscow, was actually a member. Their close friend Dorothy Parker, no "dues-cheater" herself, did openly send a check every month to the Communist Party.

Lillian attended the Tenth National Convention of the Communist Party, held in New York City in June 1938. That year she too joined the Party.

The new Party line emerging from Moscow in the mid-thirties was antiradical, only vaguely socialist, and encouraging of members who liked to live well. The Popular Front, with its overtures to the ruling class rather than to workers, was to the taste of Communists like Hellman and Hammett. In contrast was Mike Gold, who, until the Popular Front, made a show of not putting up curtains in his apartment, out of a feeling that people dedicated to opposing injustice should live simply.

Hammett, with his butler and chauffeur, with his dandified appearance and exquisite clothes and "live for today" mentality, would have seemed anomalous to Communists and working-class activists of the twenties. Now there need be no talk of revolution or of sharing the wealth. Amid paeans to Americanism, Lillian could display her mink coat.She had no sense of a politics which embodied the obliteration of the distinction between the haves and the have-nots. The dichotomy between her professed views and her style of life would be blatant all her life.

It suited Lily even more than it did Hammett that her period of Communist activity was that of the Popular Front. Stalin's decree that American Communists support the New Deal and his line that capitalism was no longer in the process of decay and American democracy no longer a facade with real power concentrated outside its institutions, were convenient. She could be "radical" and yet never alienated from power.

As her friend Norman Mailer would later put it, Lillian was always an "establishmentarian." "She substituted the Soviet establishment for the American because she had more entrée there." She knew high Soviet officials and generals—and what she liked was power. Certainly the fact that the Communist Party had so much more power, money, and cachet, and yet was allied with the first socialist state, accounted for Hellman's and Hammett's placing their allegiance there rather than with the struggling, critical alternatives on the socialist left. Because Stalin had proclaimed "socialism in one country," rejecting the task of building a socialist movement in America, parlor radicals like Hellman and Hammett were absolved of the necessity of creating a revolutionary movement. Lily and Dash both could be, as Benjamin Gitlow put it in *I Confess,* his book about American Communism, "Roosevelt Bohemians."

There was a dinner at Lillian's apartment in New York. One of the guests was James T. Farrell, who, like Pep West, had already endorsed the Party's call for a Comintern-sponsored Congress of American Revolutionary Writers, which had met at the New School for Social Research in New York in April 1935. The purpose of this undertaking was to draw non-Communists into an activity controlled and organized by the Party. All the signers and members, however, were Party people.

The guest of honor at Lillian's 1936 dinner was V. J. Jerome, a member of the Central Committee of the Communist Party, whose responsibility was cultural affairs. Hammett, whom the FBI at least a year earlier was investigating as a "Red," was pleasant, mostly silent, and agreeable. V. J. Jerome's decision to be present at Lillian's dinner reveals that Hellman and Hammett were already Party faithful.

By 1936 Hellman and Hammett were one both in their perception of the barbarism of American capitalism and in their acceptance of the American Communist Party. As Lillian was to put it, from "Hammett's belief that he was living in a corrupt society . . . he came to the conclusion that nothing less than a revolution could wipe out the corruption." Meanwhile, as he waited for the revolution he did little to organize, he turned to drink as the only place where he could find "a world that was rosy, cheerful, and full of fellowship and peace on earth."

He also drank to forget his past, as Lillian discovered when she confronted him about his Pinkerton days. "If a man has a past that he wants to forget," the villain Fitzstephan says in *The Dain Curse,* "he can easiest drug his mind against memory through his body, with sensuality if not with narcotics." Throughout the thirties Hammett did both.

The Communist Party, Hammett was too intelligent not to perceive, was far from perfect. But it seemed to him the only game in town. He had long yielded to the rationalization that only moral relativism made sense in a corrupt society. "I'd rather lie to him than have him think I'm lying," Nick tells Nora, speaking of a cohort in *The Thin Man.* Nick admits, "I'm suspicious of everybody."

As early as *Red Harvest* Hammett knew as well that the corruption would rub off on anyone, a radical included. In *Red Harvest* the IWW member Quint is another liar. "Anybody that brings any ethics to Poisonville is going to get them all rusty," the Op learns. "Play with murder enough and it gets you one of two ways. It makes you sick, or you get to like it."

By the end, the Op is in danger of becoming unhinged, "blood-simple," as he puts it. Hammett held out no hope that the Communists would be any less immune to evil than the Op, and so he refused stalwartly to speak out against their flagrant betrayals of their presumptive ideal. In loyalty to them he found a bulwark against emptiness, and he was to remain publicly under the discipline of the Communist Party for the rest of his active life.

He didn't bother to ask questions, not about Stalin's order that the German Communist Party not oppose Hitler, not about Spain, the purge trials of Bolshevik leaders, or the earlier betrayal of the Chinese Communists as Stalin supported the Kuomintang and Chiang Kai-shek. Nor is Hammett on record as having demurred when Stalin purged many foreign Communist leaders who deviated from his policies. He did not blink in 1940 when Stalin hired at last an effective agent to murder Leon Trotsky. Dashiell Hammett could be counted on to defend everything the Party said, everything it did. Lillian went along, having found a means of sharing life with him, ingratiating herself as she could not as a wife, as the mother of his child, although she would later admit only to attending a few Party meetings with Hammett, in "an ugly Spanish house in Hollywood; one or two in New York."

About writing, however, Hammett was incapable of being less than honest. For the literature of the proletcult he had only contempt. Richard Wright was "a blackface Cliff Odets who never had any roller skates either," and later Howard Fast's *Freedom Road* may have been "on the right side, but oversimplified to death." Yet, as a member of the Communist Party at large, Dashiell Hammett did exactly as he was told.

For the veteran Pinkerton it became a question of any port in a storm. Dashiell Hammett entered his commitment to the Party wholeheartedly and completely. He was monogamous in politics as he could not be sexually. The year 1936 was a heavy drinking time, another promiscuous period. It was also the moment when he was faced with his inability to write. But he had found another way to validate his existence.

His evasion of introspection, his unwillingness to confront feelings that would have liberated him from the detective story genre, had also led him to Party allegiance. He blinded himself, not because he had illusions about Stalin, but so as not to be vulnerable to his own lost child-hood. On some level he was in mortal dread of insatiable, long-repressed emotional needs from which he was perpetually in flight. He fled father-hood, so that his daughters scarcely knew him. Soon he would engineer a humiliating scene which would ensure that he and Lily would not be united by blood and he would not again become a father.

Fortunately for the Communist Party, Hammett made his vows to them early, just before the Moscow purge trials and the betrayals in Spain. After the pact with Hitler, it became clear even to the deluded that the state interests of the Soviet Union were the Party's sole agenda. Hammett lacked the emotional space to consider that the revolution for which he hoped might have been more likely if a less hypocritical, more truly socialist, political organization had been created. He seems not to have understood that a society like Stalin's, where there was no right to criticize, no independent trade unions and no right to strike, no right to hold a meeting or publish a newspaper, and where opponents were tor-tured and shot, could hardly be a model to which American working peo-ple might be expected to aspire. Nor did he ever consider that the Com-munist Party which he had embraced might be the gravedigger of the revolution he sought.

Dashiell Hammett hated the capitalist nightmare. Then out of the nihilism of his life, out of having lived as if each moment might be his last, this man with a consuming passion for justice faltered. He stopped writing virtually in tandem with his confounding of Stalinism with a socialist ideal of justice.

Expecting little of life, of other people, he turned that sensibility to a lack of expectation toward the people with whose cause he identified. In the face of Stalin's flagrant betrayal of the socialist ideal, Dashiell Ham-mett retreated behind his own precarious sense of integrity. He lived in denial, drinking to escape his feelings of worthlessness, denying through acquiescence in an organization where the disparity between professed belief and actual practice strained credulity. He did, of course, experi-ence doubts. Once he told Lillian, as she was to recall his words, "Oh, this is very temporary. When I find something better, I'll change to it. But I haven't found anything better. You can be quite sure when I find it, I'll change to it." But he lacked the energy and the will to discover the anti-Stalinist alternatives that did exist.

From the time Dashiell Hammett took these vows to the Party, he signed his name endorsing every turn of Soviet policy. He willed himself to remain unperturbed by the fact that American Party policies were determined entirely by decisions made in Moscow. He supported the verdict of the purge trials in April 1938, a signatory to the petition "Leading Artists, Educators Support Soviet Trial Verdict," as did Lillian. American liberal philosopher John Dewey's investigation into the murderous hounding of Leon Trotsky was met by the Party's hysterical "Open Letter to American Liberals," which Hammett signed, warning people not to help Dewey because his investigation gave "support to fascist forces."

Hammett became one of the ten-member initiating committee of a group which labeled Dewey a "fascist agent of Leon Trotsky"; Dewey's crime was that he had formed an independent commission which would examine the evidence behind the charges against Leon Trotsky and the left opposition to Stalin, featured in the confessions of the purge trials.

Hammett penned a petition on August 14, 1939, denying the rumored possibility of common ground between the Soviet Union and Nazi Germany—this nine days before the Hitler-Stalin pact. It was only "fascists" and "reactionaries" who could concoct the "fantastic falsehood that the U.S.S.R. and the totalitarian states are basically alike," he declared. Lillian went along, showing, as she had during all those poker games, that she was one of the boys, and would show herself an even more devoted camp follower than he, as if this might win his approval. He signed more petitions than she did, a source of joking competition between them when McCarthyism struck. Their names appeared together often enough on Party-sponsored initiatives. "You're a good man," Sam Spade tells his secretary, Effie, the one decent woman in *The Maltese Falcon*. She was as much Lily's model as Nora Charles.

Lillian had already expressed strong sympathy with the working class in her plays. In *The Children's Hour* a class argument is made to Mrs. Tilford: the "honest work" of teachers Karen and Martha will be defended in a libel suit. Her new play, *Days to Come,* was an attempt to dramatize the struggle between labor and capital. Lillian talked Communism, even as she dressed in one of her many furs, "a gift," Kober noted of one such garment at the beginning of 1935, "from the rich Mr. Ham."

In 1929, as a girl, she had joined a John Reed Club in New York, a group under the control of Earl Browder and the Communist Party. Before the ideology of the Popular Front completely smothered the Communist movement, she campaigned for the passage of the Wagner Act, affirming the right of employees to engage in collective bargaining, and prohibiting employers from discriminating against union members. Out of her fervent sense of justice, she had tried to create a union at M-G-M. At parties now she was outspokenly political; Kober, who still hung on her every word, reported to his diary: "Lil who has just found the cause speaks like expert & like all those eloquent dogmatists will not allow anyone else to think or listen to what is being said." She never studied the writings of Karl Marx, however.

Rather, her politics now took the pattern of matching Hammett's, keeping close to him through the exercise of her passion for justice. It was another step in the process of becoming him, assuming his identity. As long as her style of life need not change, she was prepared to be a member of the Communist Party. Yet Party faithful soon discovered that if Hammett could always be counted upon when they needed anything, Hellman had to be approached gingerly, carefully. She was never entirely "reliable."

As the she-Hammett, however, Lillian Hellman became even more single-minded, more zealous than Dashiell Hammett in her support of Stalin and Stalin's Russia. Such was her nature, her vociferous temperament. "For many years," Hammett wrote her later, "you've thought it cowardice not to take pretty definite sides on people and things without bothering very much about the question of whether any pretty definite sides existed to be taken." It was Lillian who was the watchdog of Party orthodoxy. After a private screening of Communist John Howard Lawson's film about Spain, *Blockade,* she demanded, "Whose side was it on?"

Unlike Lillian, it wasn't always easy for Dashiell Hammett to adhere to Party discipline. His daughter, Jo, found him in tears one day. He had learned that the Party had taken a stand and he would be forced to turn his back on someone. The man had approached him about doing something, but the Party jettisoned the idea. Hammett was expected to follow the Party line rather than his own convictions, and he did, although he believed the man to be right.

Much later, Lillian described him as one of those "turning toward radical political solutions . . . with me trailing behind, worried often about what didn't worry him, inhibited by what he ignored." But it wasn't so. No more honest was her use of the term "radical" for Communist. In later years she called Hammett a "committed radical" rather than a Communist Party member, which he was.

Their political life, a joint life, had begun. "Lil talks revolution," Kober wrote in his diary for May 6, 1935. She joined the League of Women Shoppers in New York, along with Ruth Goetz. It was a Communist Party front: the women put themselves at the disposal of groups trying to organize, like laundry workers or houseworkers. Women working for starvation wages brought them their complaints and they took action.

Lillian was a member of the board of directors, which was composed of prominent women, who would appear in a delegation before an employer. Dressed in their best mink coats, they would personally present the complaint of the women workers who were trying to form a union. Some of the women, like Goetz and journalist Rebecca Drucker (later Becky Bernstien), went to jail. But not Lillian, who, unlike other directors, did not attend meetings, did not participate in actions. Rather, Lillian played only a public role, speaking from platforms, always in furs.

Politically Hammett set their tone. He objected to her reading the Hearst papers' syndicated "Li'l Abner," which he called "a fascist comic strip." How could she accept the image it projected of people? He called it "a low-down mess," so condescending was it to the ordinary person. He was violent on the subject.

Lily obeyed. When she found herself turning to the muddled denizens of Dogpatch, she stopped herself, inhibited by his authority, wanting always his approval. Later she was to claim she didn't know what he was talking about, although, she insisted, he "turned out to be right." But after his death everything he said, everything he did was nothing short of gospel.

He gave her Engels to read. She tried, but had no interest. Politics were a matter of temperament and one's sense of justice. Lillian attempted no political arguments worthy of mention. Her point of view was moral, not political. Nor was the social life Lillian increasingly sought to Dash's liking, and from the start he was not keen about appearing at Lillian's shows.

Conflict broke out in Spain. From July through October 1935, Stalin sent no help to the struggling Loyalists. He still hoped that England and France, with whom he had an alliance, would fight Hitler for him; a socialist revolution in Spain would jeopardize that goal and he set out to abort it even if it meant the victory of Franco. Socialism in a single country meant socialism nowhere else.

Dutifully Spanish Communists followed this policy, appealing to workers not to seize property, not to strike, to submit their press to censorship. They demanded the liquidation of the workers' militias and began their own systematic campaign against POUM [Partido Obrero de Unificación Marxista], and the anarchists. Simultaneously they announced that they were "motivated exclusively by a desire to defend the democratic republic."

POUM members were called "fascist spies" and were thrown into jail. Trade unions were broken. "Trotskyists" were massacred. Returning Communist Party members who had taken seriously the struggle against fascism in Spain were told they were to be honored in Moscow. Upon their arrival, they were murdered. Soon the Communist Party in America would begin recruiting for the International Brigades. Americans would fight under the command of Spanish Communists, oblivious and in denial of how the revolution in Spain, and with it hope of a Loyalist victory, was being betrayed.

By June 1936, Lillian herself was urging Earl Browder, the head of the Communist Party, of whom she was already a confidante, to go to Hollywood, a fertile field for funds.

8

The Baby Years

"I drank a lot in those days, partly because I was still confused by the fact that people's feelings and talk and actions didn't have much to do with one another."

"TULIP"

"CAUTION TO TRAVELERS"
Hold it lightly if you'd carry it long,
Nor bind too tightly what you'd bind strong,
Heavy the thing mightily gripped,
The too-tight string is soonest slipped.

DASHIELL HAMMETT

"Woman waiting, heartbroken, for years. Then the two men show up on same day."

"MEMORANDA," LILLIAN HELLMAN'S DIARY

In the early summer of 1936, Dashiell Hammett went not to Russia, but to Hollywood with Lillian. From a suite at the Beverly Wilshire, they prepared on behalf of the Screen Writers Guild to do battle with Warners, Goldwyn, and Louis B. Mayer. Sexy, chain-smoking Lillian Hellman, wearing a big picture hat, perched on the desk of young M-G-M screenwriter Maurice Rapf. He had intended to join anyway. Now nothing could keep him away from the meeting that night.

Hammett did most of the talking. But Party member Rapf soon realized he would not see either Hellman or Hammett at fund-raising events, nor at Party meetings. Hammett did appear at "fraction" meetings attended by some non-CPers. Only later did he surface at Communist Party fund-raisers.

To the Screen Writers Guild, Hammett and Hellman brought the ideology of the Popular Front. They urged the Guild to endorse Democratic Party candidates. Alarmed at this reformism, Rapf complained to Hammett, who remained distant, evasive, and unwilling to challenge the Party line.

I have no reason to condemn him, Lily confided to the Hacketts regarding Hammett's continuing promiscuity. We're both doing the same thing. As carelessly nihilistic as he, as Dash courted venereal disease, Lily became pregnant with other men's babies. "I've done it again!" Lily laughed as Lee Gershwin accompanied her to one more illegal abortion. More often bitter, she went to war with other women, who triggered her insecurity.

Dash disapproved. Later he chastised her. People "had to be loveable or hateful, and they, of course, had to feel the same way about you." Hammett assumed ambivalence. "It's doubtful that anybody ever loves or hates anybody anyhow," he believed, "though of course they may love or hate the *idea* of them. For the rest, we get along on loving, liking, hating, disliking or being indifferent to this or that part of them."

Lily's insecurity extended to her work. "I feel blue and lousy and worthless and I'm getting panic stricken about the short time left," she confessed to Kober. It was summer. *Days to Come* was scheduled to open in December. Never too depressed to be a hard trader about her work, she refused to cut royalties for the San Francisco run of *The Children's Hour.* Annoyed, Shumlin dubbed her "a beggar on horseback."

She returned East and rented a cottage on Tavern Island near Norwalk, Connecticut, that summer of 1936. In July, Dash headed for Lenox Hill Hospital and more gonorrhea treatments. "Stop it! You're frying his brains!" Lily protested. The carelessness of a nurse left him with a deep hole in his leg.

Weak as he was, as soon as he arrived at Tavern Island, Lillian wanted him to read her current draft of *Days to Come.* Later she insisted this play was to have been a joint collaboration only for "contrary activities of both parties" to "void the enterprise." In fact, now painfully thin, Dash was too sick even to read. With a cursory glance at the manuscript, he pronounced the play excellent and turned to Ping-Pong and badminton. He was drinking as heavily as ever.

Still he retained the power to unnerve her. Later she wrote of how she returned to the cottage one day by boat only to catch sight of him standing on the dock: It was "the handsomest sight I ever saw, that line of a man, the knife for a nose, and the sheet went out of my hand and the wind went out of my sail." Lily remained the masochistic little girl for whom an inaccessible man, one who could never fully accept her and whom she feared, remained her fantasy. Such was Hammett, this tall slim figure in white set against the sparkling sunlight.

In *Days to Come*, although Lillian later claimed it was a friend of theirs, Hammett seems the model for the militant union organizer, Leo Whalen. "All his movements . . . show calmness, and are the movements of a man who knows he can take care of himself," Lily wrote. Whalen even talks like Hammett: "The world is a bad place and you're a bad boy," he tells Firth, the stereotypic workingman.

The play Hammett wearily pronounced as "fine" and "good" was not fine. Evading its ostensible subjects, a strike, anti-union calumny, and the battle against scabs, it pours its energy into the yearning of Mrs. Julie Rodman, the capitalist factory owner's wife, for Whalen. "Do you think I'm pretty?" she demands as if it were Lily addressing Dash. "Better than pretty," he replies. "You'd be fun." *Days to Come* is finally about Julie's desperate need for love.

"One of the things that brings people like you and me together is the understanding that there won't be any talk about it at the end," Julie promises Whalen in the first draft, as Lillian attempted to ingratiate herself with Hammett by becoming his emotional alter ego. "I hope you will talk. I like to listen," she pleads. "I always wanted somebody to show me the way."

It was sheer autobiography. As Leo evades Julie, so Dash did Lily. Between the lines, she had depicted the impasse in their relationship, pleading that they find their way back to each other. The conflict between workers and capitalists, the melodrama of the strike, receded into the background.

When Ralph Ingersoll arrived at Tavern Island on September 27, ready for a reprise of his affair with Lillian, he discovered Hammett once more at the virtual head of the table. They seemed to have reconciled and to be in such harmony that Hammett evinced no jealousy at the appearance of an ostensible rival. Nor did he waste any words on Ingersoll, who dubbed him "the most silent man I ever knew."

Even as the conversation was "gay, witty, and relaxed," Ingersoll despaired. Amid a menage of Kober, Shumlin, and Hammett, the passage to Lillian's bed was sealed. As usual, the talk was of Communism and socialism. Ingersoll pleased no one as he insisted he wished "to take the best of capitalism and Communism while avoiding their faults." At one point he stole off and paddled away in a canoe. He would demonstrate his superior manhood to Lillian by founding his own newspaper, Ingersoll decided.

Back in New York during the autumn of 1936, Dash headed every night for "21," where he table-hopped, greeting people even tolerant Kober pronounced "awful." Lily sat beside him, blue and disappointed. Kober saw "how much she leans on Dash in her writing and how disappointed she is at his drunkenness."

A policeman stood often outside "21." One night as Lily and Dash emerged, Dash grabbed the policeman's gun out of its holster. Then, according to Lillian, he shot blindly down the street. Finally Lily managed to wrest the gun away from the weakened, drunk Hammett, a man who needed a caretaker now more than a lover.

There was no respite. On October 4, Kober arrived to find Dash already in his cups. Together they headed for Yankee Stadium, although Dash insisted they stop for beer along the way. Sliding drunkenly into his seat, Hammett muttered about Lou Gehrig. The afternoon proved disappointing; his favorite player, rookie Joe DiMaggio, didn't do much. After the game, Hammett was back at "21."

Lily continued to demand his help, and five days later she was seated beside him discussing her revisions. "Here is collaboration!" even Kober had to note. Saturday night she held them all close: Kober, Shumlin, and Dash dining at her place on snails and pepper steak. It was a farewell dinner for Dash, who had rented a mansion at fashionable 90 Cleveland Lane in the west end of Princeton. He could write again if only he could escape from those drinking nights at "21," Dash declared. Accompanying him to Princeton was Jones, his black chauffeur-butler from Hollywood days, and a dog called Baby, after Lillian's childhood name.

Hired by Princeton University to give a seminar in creative writing, Dash entertained his students at home, sitting in a corner with a bottle of whiskey between his legs. Emaciated, worn, shaky on his feet, he made a show of not caring whether Lily visited or not.

Lily came, her *Days to Come* revisions in hand. Dash obliged. The writing should be more spare, he thought. Leo Whalen makes a tendentious speech: "And whether you make the best brush in America or the worst, I think your rent's the same, and the grocer's not reducing his prices for your art. Why don't you work for nothing and admire yourself? You can eat fine on that." Dash winced and grabbed a blue pencil. Lily had included a flirtatious scene between Julie Rodman and Whalen in which he tells her not to feel sorry for him, and she replies she wasn't. It was obviously about Lily and Dash. Hammett excised it all.

Lillian's politics were sophomoric, her attempts at naturalism overblown. Julie says, "Then you didn't hate. Not the poor anyway. You loved them." Her Whalen answers, "Any man who loves the poor is either a fool or a hypocrite. Do you think you can love the smell that comes from dirty skin, or the scum on dishes, or the holes in the floor with the bugs coming through or the women all sick and flabby?" Dash reduced Whalen's speech to "Love them? No. Do you think you can love the smell that comes from dirty skin or the scum on dishes, or the holes in the floor with the bugs coming through?" The next line, an addition—"or the meanness and the cowardice that comes with poverty"—is pure Hammett.

She tried to write like Hammett—awkwardly. Whalen tells Firth, "I told you that you weren't tough enough to take what he could give you." Dash edited the line down to "Didn't I tell you not to fight?" Lillian's Whalen says, "You thought he was good, and that mixed you up. Now you think he's bad, and you're still mixed up." Dash deleted the whole speech. Believing that only with his editing could she write a viable play, she traveled back and forth to Princeton. By November 9, she had a sharper text.

When she was gone, Dash entertained other women, particularly Pru Whitfield, whom he called Madame, as he did Lillian. Unlike Lillian, Pru was a beauty, and years later he was to remember her "pretty body in fine silks spun by pedigreed silk-worms that are fed on nothing but nectar and ambrosia." He demanded information on her "pre-Hammett past."

Pru could also be feisty, and one night she gave him a black eye. Hammett retained his contempt for women. "Oh, Pru," he explained. "So she always wants attention. So she always wants to screw. So, is she sexy? No. She just thinks you can't fuck her without paying attention to her. So I took a paper to bed and did a crossword over her shoulder while I screwed her. So she hit me." As always with Hammett, sex was divorced from sentiment.

Lillian's friend Lois Jacoby visited Dash in Princeton. Prettier than Lily, with short, bobbed black hair, Lois thought she might try Dash in bed. That he held back, Lois thought, made him all the more seductive. But Dash refused her and Lois became angry.

Lily had told her how the sex between them didn't work because of his drinking, Lois informed Dash. It was sick, his relation to her, and his drinking spoiled everything. "You who are such an attractive man. . . ." Lois went on.

Suddenly Dash rushed into the kitchen, grabbed a knife, and was holding it at Lois' throat. Later she reported to friends that he had almost killed her.

On December 4, two weeks away from opening night, Kober, attending a rehearsal of *Days to Come,* was alarmed. There were bad moments in the second act, while the third was uneven and much too long. Two days later he ran into Dash, drunk at "21." Dash had not been to any rehearsals. With the help of playwright Marc Connelly, Kober ambushed Hammett and conveyed him home, where Hammett proceeded to read the entire third act out loud. The final curtain, Dash decreed, had "to be fixed." In his condition he was unable to make any other suggestions. Lillian seemed oblivious, finding time with Dotty Parker to "fall to & tear the Perelmans to pieces." Still she raged over how Laura had betrayed her by sleeping with Dash.

Predictably, *Days to Come* failed. The audience laughed when Julie Rodman told Leo Whalen she loved him. As soon as the curtain came down, Hammett and Kober flew backstage. They located Lily in the alley behind the theater, "weeping hysterically on Herman's shoulder." It's a flop, she cried. Then she sent Kober and Hammett away.

A pall quickly settled over the guests at the opening-night party held at Ralph Ingersoll's Fifth Avenue apartment. Lily arrived late, stormed past the guests, flinging off her mink coat. She ran into Ingersoll's bedroom, and slammed the door. When she finally emerged, she found Dash chatting at the bar with James T. Farrell.

"Dash, didn't you tell me last week that *Days to Come* was the best script you ever read?" she demanded for all to hear. Hammett remained silent.

"You son of a bitch!" she screamed. "You said it was good."

"I did indeed," Hammett finally said as he took up his cape and headed for the door. "But I saw it at the Vanderbilt tonight and I've changed my mind."

It seemed to Lillian then that he had revealed a certain satisfaction in her failure, that she was not to reach his level of success after all. It was almost as if he were "very happy" that *Days to Come* had failed so miserably, and vindicated that she had gone no further.

Lillian soon returned to political work, fund-raising for the film *The Spanish Earth,* to be directed by Joris Ivens and written by Ernest Hemingway. The Party had declared POUM a "Trotskyist" organization of fascists as Stalin ordered the murder of POUM leader Andrés Nin. Lillian didn't notice. Nor did Dash.

He wrote her from Princeton, wondering what kind of hangover she was suffering from, as if no breach had occurred between them. "I'll have to go to work as soon as I've finished this," he said, preposterously, perhaps ironically. But he might walk into town first. In another letter, he addressed her as "Lilushka," joking over their mutual vows to Stalin's Russia. As always in letters, he was liberal with protestations of his love. "I love you and miss you," he wrote.

In despair, sending her poodle Jumbo to Princeton, Lillian set off on a cruise. He had almost come to see her off, Dash wrote, only it would have been impossible to find her. "You're so little and the boat's so big," he said sadly. He reported "a phone call from Prue [sic]," which could hardly have pleased her.

Late in January 1937 Lillian spoke at Edwin Seaver's New School writing course. The classroom was packed. She had just launched into her lecture when suddenly she stopped.

"I'm not going to continue until that tall thin man sits down!" she said severely.

Shocked silence followed. Dashiell Hammett cast his eyes upward, then headed to the rear, where he joined other latecomers reduced to sitting on the aisle steps. Soon the room was abuzz as those in the know explained Lillian Hellman's playfulness to those not in the know.

For all her bravado, however, Lily was at a low ebb. She had "leaned heavily on Dash," she told Kober. The result had been disaster and she decided to take a year off to learn her craft. Off she went to Hollywood to write *Dead End* for Samuel Goldwyn.

Dash attended the opening night of Kober's hit, *Having Wonderful Time,* and even had a drink afterward with Ralph Ingersoll. "A sweet guy, but dull," Dash pronounced his former rival as he wrote Lillian the "thoughts of a middle-aged and slightly tight guy sitting around alone at home on a rainy Sunday night." So he pleaded once more for her understanding. "I love you and miss you," he wrote once more. André Malraux, a man "like a soft hawk," visited him in Princeton. Dash liked Malraux better than Lillian's friend Archibald MacLeish, "who is a stuffed shirt if ever I saw one."

In Hollywood, Lillian happily signed the Communist Party "Open Letter to American Liberals" opposing asylum in America for Leon Trotsky. She also crossed a picket line of the scenic artists at the Goldwyn studios. "They're dopes!" she explained scornfully to her old boss, Sam Marx. "I came up to the picket line and asked if I could go through and they just said, 'sure.'" She was also grumpy when Franklin Folsom its executive secretary, asked her for a fifty-dollar loan for the League of American Writers. "All right," Lillian said grudgingly, "but I want my money back in two weeks!"

"She doesn't like you," Dash explained later to Folsom, who had to repay the debt out of his twenty-five-dollar-a-week salary. "She says you act as if you were her conscience."

By the middle of March, Dash gloomily faced his last weekend in Princeton. His dog Baby had died, as had Jumbo. Kober "wonder[ed] at Lillian and the sad things that happen to her animals." Dash's Cleveland Lane house was a shambles with an enormous hole burned in the expensive living-room rug. His Princeton landlord was suing him for back rent. Wearily Hammett made his way back to Hollywood.

Lily and Dash lived together in Hollywood from April to August 1937, a long time for them. Lillian had negotiated with producer Hunt Stromberg for Hammett's $40,000 fee for a "Third Thin Man," an original story," while she hoped Goldwyn would buy *The Grapes of Wrath* for her. But the "gloom and sordidness of the background and the people plus a pro-Communist indication" were not for him. "Let Zanuck make a mess of it," Goldwyn said foolishly after Fox bought the property for the great John Ford, who went on to create a masterpiece.

Working for the Screen Writers Guild, with both being elected to the board, kept Lily and Dash close, as did their living together at the six-bedroom, six-bathroom Royal Siamese suite at the Beverly Wilshire. "I've decided to live flamboyantly!" Dash announced to the Hacketts, flush with his Hunt Stromberg money, itching to see it disappear.

Even with Lillian in residence, he kept up with his chippies. He did try to appease Lillian with notes now, if not letters. "My dearest Miss Hellman," he wrote one afternoon while she napped. "I should be more than pleased to have you visit me on the roof when God pleases to end your, I hope restful, sleep." Mocking her constant need for reassurance, he closed by calling himself her "humble and obedient servant." He went on the wagon. Their sexual life resumed.

Although Dash and Lily did not attend the June meeting at which the Hollywood cell of the Communist Party was formed officially, on Party orders they did participate in its many Hollywood fronts. Among them were the Anti-Nazi League and the Western Writers Congress. Hammett sent five hundred dollars to the Abraham Lincoln Brigade. What he really wanted was to go to Spain and join the International Brigades. But he was not free to do as he pleased. He had first to ask the Party for permission. For a while it seemed as if they might agree.

"They're thinking of sending me to Spain," he told Jose. But the Party decided that Hammett, still a very famous writer, was more valuable to them here as a showpiece.

"Lil & Dash very domestic," Kober observed. He was startled to hear Dash refer to whorehouses in front of his little girl, Josephine. Meanwhile Ring Lardner, Jr. was shocked to note that Kober sometimes spent the night with Lily and Dash. Yet they seemed more than ever a couple. Together they attended the memorial service for George Gershwin and went out to dinner at Kober's, where the other guests were Dorothy Parker and her husband, Alan Campbell, and F. Scott Fitzgerald.

Lily became pregnant with Dash's child. At once he said he was glad, delighted. He was sweet as he told her he wanted her to have the child. They would be a family. It was not too late. Lily at once renewed her demand that he ask Jose for a divorce, even as she remained skeptical that his Catholic wife would agree. "She'll never divorce you," Lily told Dash, assuming defeat.

"I'll tell her to," Dash said.

He went off to the little house where Jose lived with her two daughters. Dash ordered the girls out of the room. He wanted them to sit in the kitchen so that they wouldn't hear. He was, however, certain of the outcome. He had rescued Jose from a double shame; he had both married her and accepted as his own another man's child. Now she could deny him nothing.

All was going well. It seemed to Lily that Dash wanted her, wanted them to be together. One day, in a mood of celebration, on impulse she bought a bouquet of flowers and returned to the Beverly Wilshire. And there she found him, shamelessly in bed with one of his "great many ladies," as she was later to put it. Even her being pregnant did not bind Hammett to her sexually. Nothing ever would.

Worse, he had staged this demonstration to make the point that nothing had changed. The renewal of sex between them, her becoming pregnant, had not domesticated him. He knew her, knew she would be so angry when she found him with his chippie that there would be no baby, no marriage. Lillian was a proud woman. She would not allow him to publicly humiliate her; she would not live quietly as a victim, like Jose. Nor would she be saddled with the responsibility of a baby while sharing its father with other women.

Up to now, Dash had set the terms. Now Lily decided there would be no baby for them. Lily chose not to bear Dashiell Hammett's child, as she headed once more for the abortionist. Later she rationalized. "How was I going to support them?" she would say, explaining why she had no children, no matter that the abortions came in her flush years. Money was never the issue. It was about loyalty and a way of life into which she could not introduce a child.

Heartsick, depressed, Lily now confided in her closest friend, Arthur Kober, about "Dash's change of feelings." Kober, as always, sympathized. "Poor kid," he chronicled the moment, "doesn't know what to do."

What Lily knew she would not do was let Dashiell Hammett go. For literary no less than social purposes, she wanted him by her side, the better to face the world. Together they continued to attend Screen Writers Guild meetings, behaving, one night, "very much like quarreling married people." When she had to attend parties at Samuel Goldwyn's, Lily wanted to be on the arm of a handsome man.

Then she traveled, as she always did when he betrayed her. There was a theater arts festival in Moscow. She wanted to see the Russian theater, she announced. "No, you don't," Hammett told her. He knew she didn't even like the theater any longer.

Even as he scrupulously obeyed the Party's Moscow-directed orders, Dash had no interest in viewing the "first Socialist state" up close. Lily scoffed and later wrote he was "contemptuous of the Soviet Union in the same hick sense that many Americans are contemptuous of foreigners." If Stalin was not to his taste, however, Hammett never admitted it.

Lillian Hellman sailed for Europe in August 1937 on the *Normandie*. Bitter still over Hammett's latest betrayal, the she-Hammett flirted so outrageously with poor, ambiguously heterosexual Alan Campbell that she made Dotty Parker, who adored her, visibly unhappy. "We young people ..." Lily chattered, referring to herself and Alan, who was eleven years Dotty's junior. Lily, now thirty-two years old, was twelve years younger than Dorothy Parker.

There was no romantic encounter with Hemingway, who supposedly came to her Paris hotel room clutching the proofs of *To Have and Have Not* in quest of her judgment. Hemingway did call on Dotty one evening before dinner. Instead he found Lillian, who made her overture. Lily was short, Hemingway tall, and she missed. Her lipstick formed a landscape on his collar. Like a horse bolting from a burning stable, Hemingway, knowing Martha Gellhorn awaited, made his retreat.

Throughout this trip Lillian was a she-Hammett in action, offering herself to men recklessly. Then she went to Spain. Later she described herself broadcasting in the midst of an air raid which in fact never took place the night she said it did. Martha Gellhorn, her knapsack on her back, lacking the "good boots" Lillian described her as sporting, watched indignantly. Gellhorn decided Lillian Hellman with her bleached-blond hair was a frivolous woman, irritable all the time. Knowing nothing of Hammett's latest perfidy, Gellhorn and Hemingway attributed Lillian's temper to physical fear.

As for the true nature of the struggle against fascism in Spain, neither Hemingway, Gellhorn, nor Hellman had anything illuminating to contribute. There wasn't a George Orwell among them. Lillian was to be the most dishonest, as she later pictured herself in *An Unfinished Woman* "half" listening to "the fights among the anarchists and Communists and Socialists; who is on what side today and who wasn't yesterday." Party apologists would not want to know. Dashiell Hammett at least had the good grace never to write about Spain.

It was supposedly during this trip that Lillian said she transported money to a friend named Julia, an antifascist socialist working in the underground in Austria. Lillian Hellman, of course, had no such childhood friend, nor had she ever met Muriel Gardiner, the only American woman fitting the description of Julia, and whose story Lillian appropriated for her own purposes.

The fantasy printed years later as "Julia" in *Pentimento*, however, is replete with autobiographical resonances. Julia, who bore the name of Lillian's mother, was Lillian as she would have liked to be: a courageous militant who did not need a Dashiell Hammett to validate her existence or edit her work. Unlike Lillian as she viewed herself, Julia is beautiful, brave, brilliant. Moreover, unlike, in this one respect, her real-life model Muriel Gardiner, Julia had borne a child out of wedlock, even as Lillian regretted having lacked the courage to have done, borne Dashiell Hammett's baby, no matter his intransigence.

In "Julia," the heroine's baby, named Lilly, has disappeared. It was, of course, Hellman's own baby, baby Lily, who cannot be found because she has been aborted. Years later when Lillian saw the film *Julia* with its scenes of her supposed search for Julia's baby, she whispered to screenwriter Alvin Sargent, "It never happened. I didn't go back for any baby." Indeed, how could she have? Within the truth of the psychic map Lillian Hellman drew in "Julia," the baby, conceived by her and Dash, was dead. In terms of the authentic story Lillian was telling, she could not picture herself looking for the baby she herself had destroyed.

Still later, in *Three*, the one-volume collection of her memoirs, Lillian added that Julia's daughter had been killed by the Germans. Far from having been aborted, the Hellman-Hammett baby was now a martyr of the Nazis. As Lily and Dash had both been "premature antifascists," supporting Moscow's alliance with the Western powers which preceded Stalin's pact with Hitler, no more noble fate could have been granted their child.

*   *   *

Back in Hollywood, Dash stayed on the wagon, his penitence for the death of their baby. He also "worried over his fragile lungs." He was elected chairman of the Motion Picture Artists Committee of the Screen Writers Guild, another Communist grouping. At a symposium in December on whether writers should "mix in politics," Dash spoke in a folksy, Popular Frontish way: "As soon as producers convince themselves liberalism or radicalism are real b.o., they will go for progressive-minded films hook, line and sinker."

Dash wrote to Lily as if nothing terrible had happened. She remained Lilushka, Party stalwart. "I was divorced in Nogales, Sonora, Mexico, on the 26th of last month," he added amid gossip. Jose had kept her promise, pleading "unkind treatment . . . without justification" and "threats and grave injuries to such an extent that their living together became impossible."

From Spain, Lily retreated to the physical comforts of London's Berkeley Hotel, where her friend Dr. Philip D'Arcy Hart was astonished to discover that Lillian, who had been visibly pregnant the last time he saw her, was no longer. Her return to New York was celebrated at "21," where Ralph Ingersoll joined the company and Lily whispered to Kober that she had been one of Hemingway's girls, and was "very bitter over him." At a party that December she quarreled with Mary McCarthy, who "grew heated" over the murder of POUM leader Andrés Nin. So their enmity began.

When she did not write to Hammett in Hollywood, he complained. It was he who was unwilling to let her go now. "My Lily is a postage stamp miser," he pleaded. He wrote *Another Thin Man,* in which their baby would live, a prodigy who reads the newspaper at the age of one and plays the piano by the time he is two. "Nobody ever invented a more insufferably smug pair of characters," Dash now thought of this cloying "new fable of how Nick loved Nora and Nora loved Nick."

He had spent Christmas alone, Dash wrote, offering Lily this proof that he was true, "brooding over nothing." He closed mildly: "wish you were here." Evading as always what he felt most deeply, Dash made no reference to their lost child. He did let her know he had gone ten months without a drink. Unappeased, Lily headed for Florida.

Frantic now for contact with her, Dash kept up the correspondence. "Did I forget to tell you that the John Brights' Christmas card was a picture of a Spanish loyalist bayonet charge, with the greeting 'Viva'?" he wrote in January 1938. Politics remained the link between them. Stalin had decreed, as Philip Rahv put it in *Partisan Review,* that in Party rhetoric "the international class struggle, bag and baggage, had been exported to one country: Spain." American Communists followed suit.

Early that January, Lily mounted a podium in New York's Union Square to address what a cynical Kober called a "tea-party" of the faithful on Spain. A few days later, with the Campbells and Kronenberger in tow, she attended a banquet for a man blinded in the Spanish Civil War. Her social life and her political life were one. Bacon and eggs followed one meeting, her meals always "great weight makers," poor Kober protested. On February 13, she spoke at a benefit for the Abraham Lincoln Brigade, "well-spoken, direct and honest," Kober described her. This was her way and would always be.

"The ideal democratic state," Lily insisted, is Russia.

She wrote little, began no new play. She tried a short story and showed it to Kober. But even he found it "childish as far as style, manner, construction is concerned."

"Very depressed," she headed back to Los Angeles, stopping in New Orleans on the way. Ingratiatingly seductive on paper, Dash sent a wire: "It is raining here but only on the streets where they don't know you are coming. Dotty expects you for dinner and I love you."

Hollywood offered more Screen Writers Guild activity. Lily was bored by meetings. Dash thought they should consider themselves a trade union rather than a professional society. Lily and Dash together joined Donald Ogden Stewart to call on Nate Witt, executive secretary of the National Labor Relations Board, as they worked for the legitimacy of their Guild. To Witt, Lily seemed "immersed in the minutiae." But Hammett "was the most politically astute" of all the writers he met in Hollywood.

Dash threw a party on the day the NLRB ruled for the incorporation of the Screen Writers Guild over its company union competitor. Now they had to sign up members, people who had worked as of June 4. In a famous story, Lily suddenly emerged from one of the many rooms of Dash's palatial suite where she had been talking to an M-G-M writer. "Well, if I get Talbot Jennings to join this thing," Lily said, speaking like the she-Hammett Dash had forced her to be, "somebody's got to pay for the abortion."

Dash and Lily both dutifully supported one Communist Party initiative after another. Lily sponsored a League of American Writers campaign to send supplies to the Loyalists and joined the Theatre Arts Committee, the Medical Bureau, and the North American Committee to Aid Spanish Democracy. Both signed an appeal, sponsored by the American Friends of Spanish Democracy, to President Roosevelt to lift the arms embargo on the Spanish government, to no avail. Dash joined the editorial council of *Equality* magazine.

No petition they signed was more virulent, however, than one which appeared at the end of April in support of the Moscow trials "of the Trot-skyite-Buckharnite [sic] traitors," as *The Daily Worker* put it. Stalin had forced confessions of treason from the leading figures of the Bolshevik movement, then executed these heroes. Many Party sympathizers reconsidered their loyalty to Stalin's version of socialism as news of these show trials appeared prominently in the international press. Lily and Dash, however, approved the killings, which the Party declared prevented "the fascists from strangling the rights of the people."

In the spring of 1938, among Hammett's duties was ensuring that members paid their weekly dues of fifteen dollars, his Party membership now increasingly public. *Hollywood Now,* the Communist newspaper, described him that April as "no mere figurehead or 'big name' but an active worker who pitches in with time, money and energy." Less accurate was its claim that Hammett "labors hard for his own art."

Peripatetic as always, Lily was ready to move back East. She met Dash at the Gershwins' one afternoon just before her departure. Dash had a going-away present for her, a black steel geometrically shaped brooch with a large pearl embedded in it. It was hardly valuable enough to elicit her approval.

"Did it cost more than five hundred dollars?" she demanded.

"Yes, but not so much as six hundred," Hammett retorted, meeting her rudeness with corresponding vulgarity. Later he rubbed it in: since she hadn't argued, he decided to classify her in his mind as "a five-hun-dred-dollar girl." Direct challenges never worked with Hammett. Lily remained the carbon copy, he the original.

Alone in Hollywood, he made the gossip columns. He was so close to his political ally Dotty Parker that when he didn't appear at one of her parties, someone asked where he was. "Hammett is in his room at the Beverly Wilshire, contemplating his novel," Dotty said. He in turn spoke of Parker as someone who "carries brass knuckles—on her tongue."

After fourteen months without a drink, Hammett found himself sexually impotent. He awakened on May 14 feeling "weak, frightened and panicky." At once he telephoned Lillian in New York. Hanging up, he took a shot of scotch. Later that day he wrote to Lily. It was "the first I'd had since when was it, and it didn't do me any good." The letter began as a paragraph, then dwindled to a single line of type streaming down the page. "Just about what little imagination I've got is used up," he concluded, "and so love Dash." Once more he had turned to her to take care of him. This was his side of the Faustian bargain as he increasingly asked that she be not lover, not companion, not wife, but nurturing caretaker, preferably without his having to ask.

He called down to the Beverly Wilshire shop for several bottles and drank himself into a form of paralysis. It wasn't long before he could scarcely move. He crawled into bed. He was too weak to answer the telephone.

Alarmed, Frances Goodrich went to the Beverly Wilshire. Observing his condition, she called at once for reinforcements, Albert Hackett and Philip Dunne, a comrade. "Hammett's feeble blue eyelids looked like those of a bird," Dunne was to remember.

As destitute as he longed to be, Hammett couldn't pay his $8,000 hotel bill. The Hacketts took charge. They decided to ship him to Lillian in New York. First they had to locate a doctor willing to sign a statement so that the airline would permit him to fly. "He can die here as quickly as on a plane," the doctor said. Lillian sounded "terrified." But she agreed to meet the plane with an ambulance.

Hammett drank on the flight all the way to New York. At what was by now his second home, Lenox Hill Hospital, doctors determined he had "a definite fear of insanity." Emaciated, he had lost twenty-five pounds in the past three months. He suffered from low blood pressure, low blood sugar, and high cholesterol, not surprisingly. Impotent, he had, again, gonorrhea. His heart, they discovered, was unusually small.

Fellow Communist Donald Ogden Stewart was Hammett's first visitor. He brought with him one lily.

Lillian fell once more into a depression. The "Dash business," Kober thought, "got her down." It was during this time that Lily later wrote she went to London to retrieve "Julia's" body, an event that could not conceivably have taken place.

When Hammett was released, seven pounds heavier, he went to live not with Lily, but at the Plaza Hotel. By the end of June he had gained twenty pounds. Anyone who asked was told he was working on a new book. Its title would be either *My Brother Felix* or *There Was a Young Man*. Of titles, Hammett was never in short supply.

9

Hammett and *The Little Foxes*

"Often I hated him for what he said."

LILLIAN HELLMAN

I n New York that May 1938, surrounded by her admirers, Ingersoll, Kober, and Archibald MacLeish, and a new poodle named Salud, Lily was deep at work on a new play. Its subject would be her own Jewish bourgeois Southern family.

In pre-World War II, anti-Semitic America, it was inconceivable that any playwright, Jewish herself or not, could carry a work to Broadway with its characters explicitly defined as Jews. Wealthy assimilated German Jews were terrified of calling attention to their Jewishness, even in America.

Lillian Hellman, whose aim was to succeed within the mainstream, would not have considered denying herself the rewards only received wisdom brought. Her writing was never peripheral to the approved culture, which is why many would conclude that she was not at heart a political woman at all, and that her Communism had more to do with gaining Hammett's approval than with her own convictions. They ignored that by the late thirties she had long been unable to differentiate between the two.

It was not to Dashiell Hammett but to Arthur Kober that she read aloud her first act. Kober thought it was "partly about her family and partly not." She was closer to Kober than ever. They now had two topics of conversation: the new play and "Lil and Dash" and the future of their relationship.

Idly, Lily suggested to Kober that they remarry. Both of them, he believed, were momentarily tempted. One Sunday morning Lily was even to appear at Kober's apartment and crawl into his bed, "like the old days when we used to play so crazily together," Kober recorded, his erotic feeling for her intact. That day they were interrupted by Dash, as he and Lily took off for a political meeting.

It was plain that Lillian feared that were she to marry anyone, she would lose Dash's help, which she needed desperately now that she felt she was defined by the failure of *Days to Come* rather than by the success of *The Children's Hour.*

Having tasted that success, Lily was determined that it would not elude her again. "Both of us want help," Kober knew, "and I know I can't do much for her." Lily admitted she needed Dash to work on her plays and that she feared she would never succeed again without him. Although she longed and would always long for the security and pleasure of a man by her side who was genuinely committed to her, she chose consciously to sacrifice this need. Instead she would hold close to Hammett. So she renewed her end of their Faustian bargain.

A recovered Hammett began to help Lillian with the new play, which was to be called *The Little Foxes.* That summer of 1938 Hammett, pleased to be a star among stars, joined the Elbow Room, an eating and drinking club whose members included the Goldwyns, Ralph Bellamy, Gary Cooper, the Hacketts, and Moss Hart. Lily and Dash and Dotty all refused offers to write the screen adaptation of Clare Boothe's *The Women.*

Lily and Dash worked in earnest on *The Little Foxes* on Tavern Island, with Lily, by her calculation, having already written four versions of the first act by July 16. One Sunday, she announced to her two houseguests, Shumlin and Hammett, that she had a second act. She offered to read it aloud. "Churlishly," as she later described the moment, they refused. She left the manuscript with them and retired in a huff.

In the morning, Shumlin left for New York. He might or might not return, he said cryptically. It wasn't a good sign, however, that he took his dog with him.

That Sunday night Hammett took the manuscript to bed with him. In the morning Lily found a note under her door. "It's too hot to return to the city," Hammett wrote. "Me, now I go to bed. Me say nothing so velly wrong with play." Then, according to two versions Lily gave, he objected to Lillian's handling of the black servants as a low-comedy chorus in darky dialect. "If only Miss Lillian could write 'em and not be so busy with chit-chat," he suggested. In Lillian's other memory of that note he was more adamant:"Missy write blackamoor chit-chat. Missy better stop writing blackamoor chit-chat." There were also very encouraging words: "The script is getting warmer," Dash said. "It will be a good play someday, I hope, but tear it up now and start all over again."

Then he did go to New York in time to support a Party-inspired Peace Parade of the American League for Peace and Democracy. *The Daily Worker* duly listed his name alongside those of Malcolm Cowley, Leo Huberman, Freda Kirchwey, Ring Lardner, Jr., and Donald Ogden Stewart.

Lillian was to "go back to work." Instead she went swimming, a life-long favorite pastime. Later she insisted she had thought during that swim of drowning herself. But it could not have been so. If she was self-destructive, bringing contradictory needs to her relationships with men, then juggling and compartmentalizing, toward her work she was both ambitious and scrupulously disciplined.

Hammett later suggested another major change in *The Little Foxes*, one involving the ending. In her third act, Lillian had included a detail from the real life of her Newhouse grandmother, the model for Regina. As her husband had lain dying, she rode around the town on a horse; only after he died did she return. In the play, while Horace dies, Lillian wanted to have the sound of horse's hooves going round and round the house. Hammett vetoed the idea.

"It doesn't work," he told her in his blunt way. "You'll have to think of something else."

"It really happened," Lillian defended herself.

"Do I have to tell you the difference between truth and artistic truth?" Hammett demanded. "This is a play. If it doesn't work in the play, it doesn't matter if it really happened or not."

In the final version, instead of Regina's creating an enormous racket while her husband dies, she remains perfectly still. Horace asks for his medicine. Regina less melodramatically murders him by doing nothing.

If he could not give her himself, Hammett gave Lily first her success with *The Children's Hour* and then renewed accomplishment with *The Little Foxes*. Scrupulously and with unstinting generosity, he rewrote, edited, mulled over every word of the text. She would deposit a manuscript with him, murmuring, "I hope *this* satisfies you." Then she would steal away, always frightened of what he might say.

She later reported that even after a ninth draft, he told her, "Well, you're on your way. Now start all over again." By now she deeply resented his imperious tone. "I never hated anyone so much in my life," she remembered. Because many years later the harshness of his criticism still pained her, and because at the time it felt as if he must not care for her or he could not speak to her like that, she added: "It took bravery and great affection to chance saying such things."

For Hammett, there was no other way. "Get it," he wrote impatiently all over one of the drafts of *The Little Foxes,* omitting the question mark to make his impatience a trifle more palatable. He was rough and unrelenting in marking what he thought was "wrong," determined as she that there not be another flop. The fiasco of *Days to Come* was not forgotten for a moment by either of them.

An entire notebook is composed mainly of his suggestions and her reactions to them. Under his name on one page she wrote: "Negroes see that being employed in the factory will bring level down and then white trash will blame negro." Under "Dash" for Act I, Lily listed: "homecoming, talk about deal, has cash in his pocket, family come, supp. half through act, business conference & he is happy they are all at each other's throats."

There is a draft of the play covered over with Hammett's suggestions. Ben says, "what greed is Man's," and Regina says, "let us take Mr. Marshall to the station and kiss your fine plans goodbye." In the margin, Hammett writes: "this is wrong; she should be triumphant, Ben defeated. It is when they return that she should tell him about cutting in."

Lily had the black servant Addie say, "Once Mr. Ben get an idea, there it stay, no matter what happens to nobody else. You know no white man in this town going to work next to a nigger." Charlotte answers her: "Yes they will. For a little while. Then one day there'll be a fight and down on South Street there will be a riot." To Lily, it seemed politically correct. She liked the idea of the ordinary people, the black servants, speaking the messages of the author. But in the margin in pencil beside these speeches, Hammett wrote: "not good enough."

It was Dash who had the fine ear for colloquial speech, one better than Hemingway's. Lily had Leo say, "didn't you see them bonds?" Hammett accelerated, writing onto the text: "didn't you even notice them?" Lily had Ben say, "Leo is going to lend us the money." Hammett intensified the moment, adding, "Hear that Oscar?" Oscar says, "all we know is that you came along and helped us out." In pencil Hammett wrote: "wrong speech. The Oscar speech begins with 'Ben means it ain't our business where you got the money.'"

When Oscar says, "did you come across the square dressed that way, my dear Birdie?" Hammett had to add, "please go home." But in parentheses, designed to shake Lily out of complacent writing, shame her into going beyond herself and doing better, he wrote impatiently: "(fear—get it.)" Sentimentally Lily had Ben say, "never leave a meal unfinished. There are too many poor people who need the food." However Hammett may have followed the Popular Front politically, he was not about to allow its rhetoric to invade his craft. Beside this paean to the poor he just wrote: "wrong."

"Get line right," Dash orders Lily, as if by now, having years of his tutelage, the she-Hammett ought to have known better than to make certain fundamental errors. At other places, with more patience, he showed her how to make the correction. Ben says, "now somebody ask me how I know the deal is set." Hammett rewrote the line: "Now somebody ask me what I mean." Ben says, "I wanted more than his signature. And what is more than a gentleman's signature?" Hammett rewrote: I "already had his signature. But we've all done business with men whose vow over a glass was better than a bond and it don't hurt to have both."

On long yellow legal sheets, under the heading "Dash," Lily reproduced more of his suggestions. Sometimes they're elliptical; often they're far-reaching:

- lines aren't from a dying man.
- Birdie's scene went too far.
- Lines with Horace about playing together.
- Beginning of play.
- Horace-Regina.
- Come to bed with me—from Regina.
- Cut Regina-Horace scene about bonds.
- Opening: too plainly stated. "We are not aristocrats." Word middle class. Cut in first act between Ben-Regina. Take Zan off stage. Oscar.
- Girl saying "what am I going to do."
- No "hate" from Birdie in 3rd act.
- Horace-Regina scene too long.
- Last scene too long.
- "That's the reason I know I'd find it." I should have known that's what you think. Too much laughter.

On still another draft, Dash marked his initials, DH, beside each of his suggestions. This time he seems focused on emotional mood, pacing, diction, clarity. Addie tells Miss Birdie she looks "young." Dash writes: "don't understand. DH." Birdie and Alexandra play the piano; Leo rises, sees his father and Ben are watching him and puts down the bottle. Hammett thought: "too fast in here."

Birdie breaks into Ben's paean to the old great days as opposed to the present when you can't get "niggers to lift their fingers." Dash wanted her to "interrupt earlier," because otherwise it was "confusing." He thought Marshall should be "more amused" when he says of their deal, "it ain't my business to find out *why* you want it."

Not only was Dash better with dialogue but he had a finer sense, a more subtle appreciation of human character. Ben looks at Oscar and says, "I can't believe that God wants the strong to parade their strength, but I don't mind doing it, if it's got to be done." Dash cautioned: "no snarl." When Ben becomes irritated that Regina does not understand he is trying to keep Oscar quiet, Dash added a stage direction: "cross, press her shoulder."

It was Hammett's idea too that the dialogue between Birdie and Alexandra on the matter of her marrying Leo be handled "so tensely that you can't understand them." He rejected Alexandra's coy disclaimer, "I wouldn't marry, Aunt Birdie. I've never even thought about it," as "wrong." At the close of the first act, he didn't want Birdie to turn: "if possible." "Watch," he wrote beside the instruction "quickly, as if anxious to keep Alexandra from coming close."

In the second act, Horace "walks stiffly, as if it were an enormous effort, and carefully, as if he were unsure of his balance." Dash sought to tone down the melodrama. "Horace's walk is too much," he wrote. Oscar orders Birdie to go home; Hammett wrote in parentheses again, "(Fear. Get it.)" Regina tells Horace, "you shall tell me everything you thought— some day." This too was "wrong." It was up to Lily to figure out why something was "wrong." He forced her to find the courage to throw back her head and tackle the next set of his objections.

No moment in the play was too insignificant to merit scrutiny by Hammett's critical eye. Dash wanted Horace to "hold medicine for water," a foreshadowing device. When Lillian shortened one of Addie's speeches, eliminating at least some of the "blackamoor chit-chat" by removing "I don't know what they believe. They ain't thinking folk," Dash wrote: "better." Lily also cut a long reminiscing speech of Addie's about "old Joe Keys, a good nigger out by Senateville."

"Possum" became "squirrel" in the servant Cal's talk. Where Lillian had him say "I didn't say nothing about anything," Hammett made it "I didn't say nothing about nothing." He also had Cal repeat a second "Grits didn't hold the heat!" Lily had Addie ask Alexandra to command the servant Belle, "tell her to bring the water very hot." "Awful," Hammett wrote. The line disappeared. Addie used the phrase "g'wan be." "Wrong," Hammett decreed. Addie thereafter said "going to be."

There are also speeches Hammett wrote, such as Alexandra's in the third act: "You know, like today. Just us. We sit around and try to pretend nothing's happened. We try to pretend we're not here. We make believe we're just by ourselves some place else. But it doesn't seem to work." (The final version is only lightly edited: "You know, we sit around and try to pretend nothing's happened. We try to pretend we are not here. We make believe we are just by ourselves some place else, and it doesn't seem to work.") Hammett also wrote a speech amplifying Alexandra's character: "Oh are they *all* here? Why do they always have to be here. I was hoping Papa wouldn't have to see anybody—that it would be nice for him and quiet."

Always Hammett could create an edge. Lillian had Regina say, "Mr. Marshall is still trying to console me." Hammett made it: " Mr. Marshall, I think you're trying to console me." The drinking man also wrote the line for Marshall: "no one ever had their first taste of a better port." Sometimes it was only a word. Birdie claims they were good to their "blacks." Hammett made it "people." Lily didn't know where to cut, and often Hammett did it for her. Ben's "And then came the war. And ride off our fine gentlemen and leave the cotton, *and* the women, to rot" became "But when the war comes, these fine gentlemen ride off. . . ." Marshall said sententiously: "Now if you gentlemen are trying to convince me that you're the right people for the deal, you are wasting your time. I'm already convinced. I was convinced six months ago when you first came to me. I wouldn't have come down here if I hadn't been convinced." Hammett seized his pencil and crossed it all out, leaving only "you don't now convince me that you're the right people for the deal. I wouldn't be here if you hadn't convinced me six months ago."

Lily wrote the autobiographical line "God forgives those who invent what they need." As they fantasize about what they will do with their new money, Regina tells Ben, "You will be rich and the rich should be eccentric." This speech became "you will be rich and the rich don't have to be subtle." In later years Lillian Hellman's frequent lines about "the rich" echo what had been a Hammett locution, as his work on *The Little Foxes* reveals.

Hammett wanted the ending sharply condensed. Originally Lily saved for the ending Addie's blackamoor reminiscence: "There was people who ate the earth . . . that's the Hubbards. Mama used to say it was like in the bible with the locusts. They get awful big and rich, people like that. The earth makes 'em fat." It was to be the centerpiece, the truth spoken by the common folk. At Hammett's suggestion, Lily moved the speech to early in the third act, and rewrote, sharpening the insights: "They got mightily well off cheating niggers. Well, there are people who eat the earth and eat all the people on it like the bible with the locusts. . . ."

Hammett urged Lily to end not on the dialogue between Addie and

Alexandra, but on the confrontation between Regina and her daughter. It was his idea that Regina ask Alexandra to sleep in her room, only for her to call herself foolish. Lillian moved the dialogue to the play's last moment, so that the final line is "Are you afraid, Mama?"

Into September, Hammett was offering suggestions. Regina's "antebellum tales" became "ancient family tales." "Dinner" becomes "supper," "carriage" becomes "buggy." Kober thought there was too much talk of bonds, too much melodrama from Oscar. But the majority of changes came from Hammett. It must also be said, however, that a new note had entered their relationship, and Lily did not always accept his suggestions. Regina accuses her husband, Horace, of contracting his illness from his fancy women (as Hammett had contracted so many venereal ailments from his own). Lil wrote in the margin: "Can this come out? Dash thinks it should." The accusation remained.

By November 5, Lily had yet another complete draft ready. That fall Dash and Lily resumed their political life in New York. On November 21 they attended a mass rally against Nazism at Madison Square Garden, at which both Dash and Vito Marcantonio were featured speakers. It was to be Lily's idea of political life: large rallies at which the political elite addressed the faithful. Meanwhile Communists broke up Trotskyist meetings, offering the spurious argument that "they are demonstrations against the Soviet Union of the same type as monarchist and socialist demonstrations." Hellman and Hammett were defenders of the civil liberties only of those with whom they agreed.

Openly now before Hammett, Lily pursued an affair with Herman Shumlin. She had already appealed to Sam Goldwyn to give Shumlin a contract to direct movies. As Hammett helped her, she was to help the men in her life further their careers, so binding them to her. Lily was so obvious in her pursuit of the married Shumlin that at a party given by set designer Aline Bernstein, everyone was aware of "poor Rose" Shumlin playing "the lady with the broken heart, glass in hand," as Kober put it. At Kober's Fire Island rental cottage that past summer, in Hammett's absence, Lily had perched on Shumlin's lap, crooning baby talk, while Rose hovered nearby in misery.

By now it was obvious that Lily had Shumlin in the palm of her hand, and people like Irene Lee, who, according to Arthur Kober, twice asked him to marry her, found it terrible to watch. Dash, however, evinced no jealousy. When Lily and Shumlin shouted at each other at *Little Foxes* rehearsals, flaunting their intense attraction, he just rolled his eyes to the ceiling in disdain.

It was not Dash but Kober who was jealous of Shumlin. One night Kober even said "something cheap about Lil" to columnist Leonard Lyons and rued his words all evening. On Thanksgiving, Kober arrived at Lil's only to find Max and Herman already there. Louis was due later. Hammett was nowhere to be found. Lillian served her favorite dish: goose.

Talk was of the profile of Clifford Odets that Kronenberger planned to do for *Time* magazine. Among the issues debated over dinner was whether André Malraux was a revolutionary or counterrevolutionary. The novel under discussion was *Man's Hope.* Malraux had spoken at the 1935 Writers' International Congress for the Defense of Culture, along with many comrades. "The cultural heritage does not transmit itself, but must be conquered," he said. But lacking the revolutionary ardor of *Man's Fate,* the later *Man's Hope,* with, as then Trotskyist Irving Howe put it, "its contrived and shabby rationale for the brutalities of Stalinism in Loyalist Spain," was "meretricious."

Lily's focus was on the play, on her collaboration with Dash, on the help Shumlin and even Kober gave her as well. On November 30, Kober arrived at her apartment ready to discuss more changes in *The Little Foxes.* This time Dash had arrived ahead of him. Dash was already slightly tipsy and was showing no sign that he was about to stop drinking.

Off they all went to Fifty-ninth Street and the Plaza, one of their redoubts. Dash claimed he was celebrating his liberation from Knopf. Henceforth he would be a Random House author! People enjoyed his company in these years, and in his *Evening Journal* column "The Voice of New York," Louis Sobol wrote, "There is none whose conversational companionship I prefer more than Dashiell Hammett's."

Dash went off to pick up poet Muriel Rukeyser, and then they all went to "21." By now, Dash had become "very silly and loose in his talk." Soon he became maudlin. Close to tears, he called himself "an old man." He was forty-four years old.

Disgusted, Lily collected Kober and took him home to continue the discussion of *The Little Foxes.* But, as always, Lily's conversation came back to Dash and his conduct. Using her favorite word, Lily called it "deplorable." The telephone rang. Lillian ignored it. She knew who the caller was. It was Herman Shumlin. That November 1938 he had finally left Rose in the hope of marrying Lillian.

On December 4, Lillian cooked a goose for Max, and Louis Kronenberger and Kober. Amid high talk, Kronenberger analyzed *The Little Foxes.* Kober professed himself to be embarrassed that Lillian "leans so heavily on him." Kober thought play reading required more experience than Louis had. Social life was about making contacts, being seen and furthering one's work—or it was on behalf of the cause. People came to Lillian with political questions and she sometimes brought them to Dash, who was in a position to take them up. Rarely alone of an evening, she went to Bennett Cerf's, where an admiring throng listened to John Strachey field questions from Heywood Broun and Rockwell Kent. Dick Watts talked about China. The guests included not only Lily and Dash, but Dotty and Alan, Kober, and Clifford Odets.

Lillian maneuvered to hold the men close. When Kober said he wanted to get married, Lillian discouraged him. He "ought to do it at a high moment and not when I'm low and it an 'out,'" she told him. Kober invested $2,500 in *The Little Foxes*. Shumlin and Kronenberger enjoyed her company and were always available. Drunk now so much of the time, Dash was ready to relinquish his advising function even as Lillian had to find physical affection from others. Meanwhile, during rehearsals Lillian and Herman would get into a box and shout at each other. Onstage, Tallulah Bankhead would stop and yell at them, "Come out of there!" Shumlin generally took his temper out on managers and set designers, not on the actors.

As the opening of *The Little Foxes* approached, Dash seemed drunker and more obstreperous in public than ever. One night at "21" he arrived drunk and soon was chiding Edla Benjamin, Aline Bernstein's daughter, who had inadvertently sat down in Lily's seat. It was as if he dreaded the coming reaffirmation of Lily as a writer, even as he had made that success possible with his own unstinting effort. But her triumphs now had simultaneously become rebukes of him, the master craftsman who no longer wrote. Increasingly he disappeared for days at a time.

The Little Foxes opened on February 15, 1939, and was a great success. Glorying in her triumph, Lily carried the mink skins designed for a new coat she had ordered to a cocktail party held in her honor. Dash accompanied her to several performances of *The Little Foxes* during its long run. One night they ran into Howard Sternau, Hammett's old friend, whom he had once bailed out of a crap game, and a girlfriend. The woman began to tell Lillian how deeply moved she was by the play. Tongue-tied in the presence of an indomitable Miss Hellman, she felt herself grow more awkward by the minute. But then there was kindly Dashiell Hammett, guiding her through the ordeal, something Lily would not do for a pretty young woman then or later.

Lillian Hellman's circle now embraced the highest echelons of the theater community: Dorothy Parker and Alan Campbell and Albert Hackett and Frances Goodrich of course, but also Beatrice and Moss Hart, Sara and Gerald Murphy, John Emery, Ruth McKenney, Leland Hayward and George Kaufman, whose message regarding *The Little Foxes* was succinct: "That's telling them." Openings were accompanied by telegrams, which also arrived after the play had been seen. Opening-night parties were de rigueur. Lillian relished it all. Always, too, she heard from Jenny and Hannah, the aunts who approved of her, as well as Daddy, who wrote: "I am so proud of you."

Her head wasn't entirely turned, however; she kept close by a small notebook in which she recorded the royalty records of *The Little Foxes*. Lillian stayed at New York's elegant Plaza Hotel across from Central Park, where she received reporters one morning wearing a greenish-blue tweed skirt and a bold plaid jacket and announced that she preferred tea in the morning to coffee.

There hadn't been much sex between Dash and Lily for years. The end came finally during a car ride. It was a flaring of desire Dash had not felt for her in a long time. Half sloshed already, he offered himself. "Let's go home and mix a pitcher of martinis and take it to bed like we used to," Dash proposed. He put his hand on her knee in the old way.

Lily considered. There were some people she wanted to see, a party she needed to attend. He was drunk. Her old grievances surfaced.

At that moment the social engagement, which might further her career, seemed more useful, a more reasonable way to spend the evening. The years of chippies, flaunted in her face, the overtures to other women in her presence, the threesomes during which she was the ugly one no one would prefer, the humiliation of his whore putting her hand on Lillian's knee in a cab, Laura Perelman, the abortion of their child—all had taken their toll. Something inside of Lily had chilled against him. If she had only a limited capacity for happiness, he had withered what they did have. Lily said no to him, meaning no for that time.

But Dash experienced her rejection as a rebuke of his drinking, another moment when she dared interfere, criticize. Surprised, and at once belligerent, as so often he was when drunk, Dash removed his hand from her knee. Such rebukes never went unpunished; later he was even to decide to leave the Army on the day a young lieutenant, appalled by his drinking, had asked, "Do you really think you are doing right for this unit and the country? Would you say this is the way to behave?" Confronted by his disarray, Dash responded in a way beyond all proportion, just as Lily would when someone accused her of lying.

Dash vowed never to make love to Lily again, a promise to himself he kept. She had a whole new set of priorities now, priorities which he found shallow and which did not interest him. On this night her choice of a petty social encounter over him seemed like disloyalty. It also gave him an opportunity to distance himself he may long have sought. By aborting his child it was she who had rejected him, and in the profoundest way possible.

He had not rebuked her, nor would he now. But he was paying her back in kind. Certainly Lily hadn't meant for their sexual lives to end forever, and in the years to come would happily have gone to bed with him again. But something inside him had chilled against her, and there was to be no reprieve.

"Thank God the sex had stopped," Lily later told her friend Renata Adler. That had been her first reaction. Later she wished it otherwise.

The success of *The Little Foxes* brought Lily little happiness. Celebrity, the notoriety she courted, even on that night she had denied Hammett sex, only made an old chasm yawn more widely. If her life was to be about work, that game plan had failed miserably. She began to drink more than ever.

But alone as she was, she would not yield to despair, no Dorothy Parker she. Lily saw she was "miserable and drunk" and decided to do something about it. Soon she was seeing one of the most prominent Freudian psychoanalysts of the day, a Russian Jew named Gregory Zilboorg, whose exotic background, he told people, included his having served in the provisional government of Alexander Kerensky as secretary to the Minister of Labor. His being a veteran of the Red Army was a better credential.

That he had analyzed George Gershwin without perceiving that his problem was a brain tumor did not give Lillian pause. That at a time when the average fee for psychoanalysis might be four dollars an hour, and Zilboorg charged seventy-five, did not deter rich Lillian either. That he pursued social life with his prominent patients, Lillian and Ralph Ingersoll and Herman Shumlin among them, seemed acceptable too.

Zilboorg told Lily she was an alcoholic and refused to accept her denials. He told her she didn't have the stamina of Hammett as far as drinking went, and later she would say that he did cure her of heavy drinking. That she continued to drink, hardly evincing recovery, was apparent. The other malady of Lily's he hoped to cure was her chronic lying. Zilboorg fretted as well about her anti-Semitic remarks, the deprecatory way with a curling lip she spoke of other Jews.

Dash made sardonic remarks. He did not like the short, dark, slightly menacing psychoanalyst. Once more he rolled his eyes skyward. Lily shared so many of the details of their sessions, Hammett quipped, that he learned more about himself from Zilboorg's treatment of Lily than she ever learned about herself. Indeed, others agreed that the only thing Zilboorg cured her of was "a good deal of her money."

If Hammett was skeptical of Zilboorg, the psychoanalyst disapproved of Lily's relationship with Dash and told her so. As she had told Kober so often, Lily insisted once more that she needed Hammett. The success of *The Little Foxes* proved that.

But Zilboorg told her it was not so. She should get married, have children. The relationship with Hammett could bring her only pain. She must free herself, find a man who could love her and who would allow her to love him. The Faustian bargain might yet be broken, Zilboorg urged.

PART FOUR

Reversals

10

Hardscrabble Days: 1939–42

"I knew why men go off and live in caves by themselves. And I didn't blame them!"

"Dead Yellow Women"

"Lily, I'm too old for that stuff."

Dashiell Hammett

I n May 1939, Lily bought Hardscrabble Farm, a rambling house built in 1810 on 130 acres in Pleasantville, New York. Its crowning jewel was an eight-acre flowing man-made spring-fed lake with three islands. It was an isolated sylvan paradise, unspoiled and rural then. The woods were full of deer and other creatures. Yet the previous owner had created bridal paths and a riding ring, an elaborate Japanese rock garden, orchards, vegetable gardens, and a grape arbor. There were also a six-room caretaker's cottage, two guesthouses, a game house where the Ping-Pong table was set up opposite the long mahogany bar and piano, a stone smokehouse, and stable. Lily paid $37,000 of *Little Foxes* money and took a mortgage. By January 1942 she had paid it off.

The house with its five fireplaces was weathered and cozy. Lily at once made it a place where she could express her best self. She grew vegetables in summer, priding herself on her white asparagus, swam and fished in the lake, ice-skated in winter. It was the place where she could at last share a domestic life with Hammett, the man who in one of life's many ironies was no longer her lover. "I was running a boarding house," she would remember, as if in this too she was recapitulating her childhood experience. "It wasn't entertaining people; it was just an old boarding house."

Lillian was glad to put some distance between herself and the incestuous, ego-fraught environment of the New York theater. Even as she savored her celebrity, it was never an easy fit. No matter that it was the scene of her sturdiest accomplishments, by now Lily hated the phoniness of the theater, the backbiting, the vulgarity of audiences, the compromises inherent in collaboration, both in theater and in cinema. So she expressed her weariness with its pomposity in a poem to Herman Shumlin:

> We are now in a theatre.
> It is a world of glamour,
> Taste, charm, learning shit.
> I do not like it.

Her solution was to appear at the theater in her best mink, a cigarette in hand, watching a rehearsal and giving everyone, as theater manager Victor Samrock put it, the "jimjams."

Now, at Hardscrabble Farm, her own domain, she could entertain those theater people she enjoyed. Lillian Hellman brought the world of the New York theater to her in Pleasantville. Sometimes she invited the entire cast of a play. But the so-called excitement of the New York theater world held little charm for her and none for Hammett. Social life meant Hardscrabble Farm now, or the political involvements which took up an enormous part of her time in the late thirties and forties.

With boundless energy she devoted herself to her farm. Immediately she painted the dark-shingled house white. Then she had an addition built. Two stories, it had a downstairs workroom with its own wood-burning fireplace. Its separate entrance opened out onto a stonework terrace, facing the lawns, close to the Japanese rock garden with its meditating grove. The walls of Lily's study were paneled in dark rich wood with carved moldings, and there was a little library up two steps. A spiral staircase led upstairs to her private bedroom.

Both study and bedroom were decorated in "a riot of colors, wallpaper and rugs full of flowers." A chair was a rich red velvet; the sofa was green satin. Lily's bed was covered in peppermint green. It was all, Kober admiringly thought, "audacious and aggressive and so like Lil."

Upstairs, a door separated Lillian's wing from the rest of the house. Dash's bedroom, the original master bedroom with its own bathroom and long deep tub, was at the opposite end of the hall. In the cedar closet adjacent to Dash's bedroom, Lillian pasted instructions for the servants. One read: "blue trim and pink sheets for Miss Hellman's & Mr. Hammett's rooms."

Outside she planted one thousand twelve-inch pine trees, destined to become a virtual forest; she raised chickens in little cages in the basement of the main house and sold the eggs.

If Zilboorg couldn't keep her demons at bay, activity might. Lily bought turtle traps and cooked turtle soup, made sausages, head cheese, blood sausage, and liverwurst, soaked hams in brine in a bathtub in the cellar, raised poodles, grew roses. She kept cows and killed their calves for the meat, savoring the livers. She hired a farmer named Fred Herrmann. There were also a cook and a butler.

At night the dogs barked; at dawn the roosters crowed. She helped Fred Herrmann milk the cows; she worked long hours in the vegetable garden, where she could often be found. Dash excelled in trapping frogs at the lake and managed the turtle traps. In the woods they picked wild raspberries.

Hammett was always to be a presence at Hardscrabble Farm, the place always available to him even in her absence. There they continued to enact their Faustian bargain, she taking care of him in exchange for his work on the plays. He had virtually rewritten *The Little Foxes*; now she provided him with a refuge. He saw his life as apart from hers now. When he spoke of moving out to the country, it was as "I," not "we."

They were not a couple. "It's beginning to look as if I'm not going to be able to move to the country this summer," he wrote Jo. When Lily posted a sign outside her workroom forbidding anyone to enter without knocking, and held a Christmas court-martial, those indicted included "Mr. Samuel Dashiell Hammett, former eccentric," who joined, among the guilty, Kober, Kronenberger, and Max Hellman. He was one among many in her life now.

Sometimes guests saw him come into her workroom with manuscript pages in his hand, which he would hand to her, then, wordlessly, depart. Sometimes he sat in the living room and listened to a baseball game on the radio. He might yell through the dining room to her study, where she would sit pretending to be working. Often Dash played Ping-Pong with Kober in the game house; when he was sober, Dash won.

They settled into being what they were. She did his Christmas shopping for him. He painted what needed painting around the farm. He picked vegetables or flowers on her orders. Fiercely she tore open the mail every day, including his. Fond of Lily in his tolerant, paternalistic way, he indulged her. He understood her and treated her as if she were a naughty child. Occasionally she crawled into his bed, kissed the back of his neck, but dared go no further. He would not make love to her. He had never suffered a *coup de foudre* over her, and need not make the genital effort now.

Dash wished he could live at Hardscrabble Farm like a hermit, reading, walking in the woods, shooting an occasional rabbit or a bird they might roast for dinner over apple wood in the fireplace. But Lily wanted guests, and there were many, mostly men, although Kronenberger brought his new wife, Emmy, and Lois Jacoby wormed her way in. Dorothy Parker came rarely because Lily had decided she "hated" Alan Campbell. Henry E. Sigerist came to dinner, only to admire Lily in a flowing white robe, bare legs, and sandals. She offered a "very refined dinner with excellent wines and conversation like fireworks."

On a typical Saturday in midafternoon Lily would tell her guests she had to work. She told the maid, Irene, to call her in time to dress for dinner in case she dozed off. Then she went into her study or upstairs to the bedroom, where she lay down and shut her eyes, so that people might think she was asleep. When she came down and the guests asked how the work went, Lily would answer, "It stinks!" Dash laughed: they would think she was being modest, not knowing that she had not done anything whatsoever to be modest about.

Lily invited her lovers to the farm; Dash took women where he found them, and once in the Hardscrabble years young Jim Weinstein, Lily's friend Bobbie's son, walked in on Dash having sexual intercourse with a woman on a Ping-Pong table at their Stamford, Connecticut, house.

Promiscuity was another path out of her depression, and Lily perfected her talents. She became the plain-featured, slightly dumpy woman who, behaving as if she were Scarlett O'Hara, turned out to be "a very good lay," as one recipient of her favors later reported to Westchester neighbor Helen Rosen.

Lily was now the lover of her producer, Herman Shumlin. He was a man with a "perpetual fear of failure," Kober decided. He was also manly and virile, with a deep voice, a man who behaved as if he enjoyed women. Shumlin would look right into a woman's eyes, and was not afraid of a woman being right. He was also a far better lover than Hammett ever was, Lillian had to conclude. Lily found the sex with Herman so passionate, the best she was ever to have in her life, that she believed their sexual connection alone would keep them together.

He was also a difficult man, who suffered from migraines, and could evince a violent temper. Herman Shumlin was a man tempestuous in his opinions, but a progressive with the right politics for Lily and Dash. He was also deeply in love with Lillian. Lily in turn dedicated *Watch on the Rhine,* her next play, to Shumlin "with thanks and affection" and wrote him love poems. A portion of one reads:

> *Herman-Sherman, this hymn I cast*
> *Is a hymn of pocket, of vest and of pant*
> *A hymn of passion, of desire and hate*
> *A hymn of love, of hair, of barren pate*
> *A hymn I say to you and to hirr*
> *A hymn in a word—Eugsirr . . .*

Of course they fought, angry lovers fighting over artistic and personal questions, unable to separate the two. She was the writer, he the director, and their strong egos clashed. She was not faithful to him. But if he looked at another woman, she went wild.

Hammett, as always, pretended not to notice anything. He said nothing, until one day, Lillian was to report, she told him she had decided not to marry Herman. The dialogue is as she reported it.

"*Marry? You* decided? There was never a chance you'd marry him."

"It was about to happen. We set the day and the place. I thought you knew that." Perhaps she could still make him care, elicit tenderness, proof.

"You needn't have worried," Hammett told her coolly. "I would never have allowed it."

Lily was pleased, even as she had lashed out, calling him "arrogant." Then Hammett told her, "It was no good. It would never have been any good. The day it is good for you, I'll allow it."

Their symbiosis extended to the details of everyday life. Lily called in a loan she had made to Lois Jacoby, and Lois, trying blackmail, threatened to report her to the income-tax people. Lily dispatched Dash. "How could you do a thing like that?" he demanded. "You know what you are? A stool pigeon, giving your friend over to the cops!" Dash terrified Lois Jacoby into keeping her mouth shut. "Nobody will ever have anything to do with you again," he told her, "you'll be beyond the pale."

"God knows who he gets in Harlem," Lois remarked bitterly to their mutual friend, writer Jerome Weidman. Still it chafed that Dash had not taken her to bed that weekend in Princeton. Later she wrote to Dash: "I'm thinking of writing a play. Since I have been around here and seen the jerks who do it, I think I must be a sucker not even to try." Her jealousy of Lily did not abate.

While Hammett settled in at Hardscrabble Farm, the columnists continued to report his absence from the literary life. "It should be easy to remember a name like Dashiell Hammett, now, shouldn't it?" Marshall Maslin (a.k.a. the Browser) had written. "He wrote 'The Thin Man' and that was the last of him. The Browser is very much annoyed at him and forgets his name frequently." Always impeccably dressed, his skin pink and white as if he just emerged from the shower, Hammett took long solitary walks with his .22. He went ice-fishing on the lake in winter and read widely, from "How to Make Turtle Traps" to a study of the retina of the eye, to how to play chess, to Icelandic sagas, to Marx and Engels.

When he was in residence, Dash sat at the head of the table, but he seemed not so much host as a permanent houseguest. At those increasingly few times he deigned to join her guests, he was the intellectual guiding force. To some, he seemed as if he were Lillian's father, amused by a precocious daughter. They did not touch each other in the presence of others. Mostly he stayed in his big bedroom overlooking the gardens reading. Occasionally she would intrude—once, she was to remember, to ask which flight she should take.

"Come back in an hour," Dash ordered.

"The three-thirty flight," he told her when she returned. She laughed, swore, and was grateful for the rare demonstration of affection. His teasing denied her pretensions. One day he found her with a book of literary criticism. Dash called it one of her "carrying books," books that were "good only for balancing herself as she climbed the stairs to bed." Well aware of how fastidious a housekeeper she was, he provoked her:

"I was almost raped by a hummingbird," he told her. "I was peeing in the rock garden and the hummingbird swooped down."

"You mean you did that outside? It's disgusting!" Lillian rose to the bait.

"What does it hurt?" Hammett countered.

He accused her of being a sucker for the Irish, and knowing she was ambivalent about being a Jew, told her she should have been born one. When she agreed, he turned his face away in mock horror. Nor did he let her get away with using anger as a sport, a weapon of manipulation. "Now let's get in there and use some of that famous anger judiciously, huh?" he once said. When her activity became too frenetic—the cooking, the sausage making, smoking the hams—he told her, "Please sit down, will you?" Peevishly he told her, "For Christ's sake, sit down for two minutes and give my eyes a rest."

Banter kept away the demons. Her poor sense of direction amused him, so he drew a map of Hardscrabble Farm, showing how the house was west of the woods. A guest in his hearing apologized for interrupting her train of thought.

"She hasn't got a train of thought," Hammett said. "She's thinking about whether that chair should be over here or over there." Lily burst out laughing. Staying awake late into the night also kept away the dark forces, and once she got into a "ragging tone" over a book she was reading. Dash said he didn't mind, "because it was the first time in our life together I had been willing to stay awake past ten o'clock."

He saw through her baby talk, saw she often did it to conceal a lie, or some other mischief. "Now, Lily, what really happened?" he would demand. Then she tried to climb onto his lap and talk baby talk until he would growl and tell her, "Lily, grow up!" Once in a better mood, on a car trip, he probably did pay her five dollars an hour not to talk baby talk, eventually handing over, as she said, forty dollars. Nor did he enjoy those TLs she had put in *The Children's Hour*. "Keep your damn TLs to yourself," Dash said. He distrusted flattery, needed no one's approval.

Dash preferred the company of unpretentious people, and of children. One day he sat on the stone steps taking farmer Fred Herrmann's son through his catechism. Ten-year-old Peter Feibleman, the child of Lillian's friends, visited and told Dash he wanted to be a writer, and Hammett looked at him as if he really saw him and smiled. Dash liked Max Hellman.

Otherwise he kept to himself, so that when on Thanksgiving Louis Kronenberger brought his wife-to-be, Emmy, to Hardscrabble, Hammett was in bed. They all trooped upstairs to see him. He had been on a three-day bender and looked frail, "bad." But he smiled good-naturedly at them all. Later Emmy was shocked when Lillian pointed to a picture of her mother and declared, "I was mean to her." Emmy was further shocked when Lillian referred to someone as talking "like an overeducated Negro."

Buying Hardscrabble Farm did not, of course, free Lily of her "unhappy nature." By January 1940, Kober noticed she was "always on point of tears." Herman had become "too difficult and irrational." Dash was "too weak and too tortured" to do her much good.

Obsessed by Lillian, whom he still worshipped, Kober saw a psychiatrist, who connected "the quarrel between Dash & Lil with the quarrels of my parents." Quiet harmony did not reign at Hardscrabble Farm and even easygoing Kober became "jittery with Dash's high spirits, Lil's profanity." In New York, one night Kober invited them both. Dash did not show up until after dinner, and it was "apparent he has been drinking again—a continuation of his mood of other nite," Kober recorded. In despair, Lily sat there "nibbl[ing] on Slivowitz."

During the spring of 1940, Dash, "out of sorts," made no attempt to write. He sat under a sunlamp until his face turned red. He contracted pleurisy. He slipped off the wagon. Lil worked in her Hardscrabble study on the screenplay for *The Little Foxes*.

Disillusioned with Shumlin, Lily took on Charles Wertenbaker, who wrote on business for *Time* magazine, and was "an extraordinarily good-looking Virginian," another goy. When he brushed her off, it was, Kober sympathized, "a blow to her pride." Ever loyal to Lily, hating to see her in pain, Kober told his psychiatrist that Wertenbaker was "a louse, stinker & finally a shit."

Lily moved on to Ken Crawford, who worked on Ingersoll's *PM* as chief of the Washington bureau; his politics were considerably less liberal than Lily's, but she didn't mind. In her ruffles and bows, with her weekend lovers Lily seemed to be impersonating a pretty woman. Her insecurities as a woman were always apparent.

One May afternoon Lily and Dash entertained Kober and his new girlfriend, rich, darkly handsome Margaret Frohnknecht, who was nursing unrequited passion for Bennett Cerf. She was tall and attractive, with sparkling dark eyes and a mop of dark curly hair; her family were very rich Jews, whose box at the opera was invariably filled with glittering celebrities; Maggie's sister had married the renowned conductor Erich Leinsdorf. Soon she and Kober were engaged. Maggie was to turn out to be a spoiled woman, nice, but rather silly and entirely incompetent as a housekeeper. She would pose no threat and Lily approved.

That summer of 1940 Dash stayed away from Hardscrabble Farm. Kober escaped the gnats in the guesthouse to sleep in his empty bed. When Dash did appear, he looked "very bad tho puts up a bold front," Kober wrote. Dash had promised to read Kober's new play and then did not, but Lily never criticized him. Dash had other work to do, like writing articles, Lily said.

Dash was in no shape to do anything. If people dared ask what he was working on, he replied that he was working on something but couldn't remember what it was. Lily would just walk away then. Sometimes she admitted to people that he was "just hopeless." Periodically he disappeared completely.

Increasingly he spurned Lily's guests and quietly returned to New York. Ambassador Maxim and Ivy Litvinov came, for by now Lily befriended Soviet higher-ups. When Litvinov referred to Turgenev and Pushkin as handsome men, Lillian laughed and said, "As handsome as Dash?" As Mrs. Litvinov looked him over, Hammett squirmed, crossed and recrossed his long legs, and a blush worked its way out of his open collar and across his face. It wasn't often that he subjected himself to such scenes.

On the second night of that weekend he did not appear for dinner. Lillian went up to his bedroom, where she found him reading. "Why?" she demanded.

"Because Ivy Litvinov is the biggest waste of time since the Parcheesi board," Dash said.

Writer Leane Zugsmith came and Dash complained to Lily that if she did not stop typing over his head, he was going to leave the house, because it made him feel bad as a writer. It was one of his rare admissions of the agony he experienced at not writing. To interviewer Margaret Case Harriman, working on her profile for *The New Yorker,* Lillian admitted she was "concerned" because Hammett hadn't written a book since *The Thin Man.* "She is violently interested in the one he is working on now," Harriman reported. Once more Lily had covered for him.

Howard Fast visited, and Lillian told him emphatically that Hammett's novels were important social documents, not mere detective stories, as Fast implied. Hammett sat on a sofa with a glass in his hand, pale as a ghost, silent.

Hammett did like Jerome Weidman and his new wife, Peggy, injecting Yiddish words into his conversation for their benefit. Once he called Hemingway a "smuck."

"I think you mean schmuck," Peggy said.

"I mean he's a horse's ass," Hammett said.

"In that case the proper word is putz," Lillian settled the matter. Weidman saw that Dash's "presence diluted hers," so that she seemed less harsh, more human.

Hammett was fond of Weidman, so that when one night Howard Fast made some disparaging remarks about him, Hammett was furious.

"If you had a hat, I would hand it to you," Hammett said. "As it is, I'm reduced either to telling you to get out of here or taking you by the seat of your pants and throwing you out. Don't ever show up around here again."

"Wasn't that a terrible thing for Dash to have done?" Lily asked the Weidmans in all innocence.

A year after Hammett's death, Weidman published a roman à clef, *The Sound of Bow Bells,* about Lily and Dash as he remembered them at Hardscrabble Farm. Dash, called Sam, doesn't love Rebecca-Lily sexually, the way he does other women, but wishes he could. He is a man who believes "to make a woman truly happy it was essential on occasion to cross her." Weidman believed that Dash could no longer love Lily because she had so far outstripped him as a writer: his Sam feels "through the warmth of her embrace as a woman the chill of her superiority as an artist."

Weidman's Dash believes Lily stole his creative gift and jealousy churns in his heart. But Sam is paralyzed as a writer, not because he has given away his gift to Rebecca, but because he is "afraid to reveal himself to the reader." He writes mystery stories so that he won't be subjected to the critical examination serious novelists face. It was as if he were saying, "I'm not taking myself seriously, why should you?"

During these Hardscrabble years, neither Dash nor Lily flourished under the terms of their arrangement. One September day Dash appeared looking so "badly" that Kober decided his "beer binge is doing him no good." He did tell Kober how much he liked Lillian's new play, *Watch on the Rhine*. He would not discuss Kober's own play.

Dash attended Kober and Maggie's wedding, at which Lillian was matron of honor ("If I can't be maid of honor, I'll be maître d'hôtel," Lily quipped); soon Lillian's picture would be displayed in the Kober marital bedroom. A few weeks later, Kober confessed to "my own erotic dreams again & this time Lil the object of my affections."

By April 1941, even Max had to report to Kober that Lillian looked "bad": "I preach to her to go away & rest, but no go & bangs on—busy gal & God bless her." In her heart Lillian knew. Work was all she had.

In July, Dash's daughters, Mary and Jo, came for a visit. Dash took them to his hotel, which was his home. Since his rooms were hardly big enough, they put up at Lillian's. He took them to the Stork Club, where they saw rich European exiles flashing their diamonds; he took them to the theater. Then they went off to Hardscrabble Farm, where Mary and Jo stayed in a guest cottage.

Mary, nineteen, the daughter who was not his, was a wild girl. She drank. She was promiscuous. She lied. "How long has your sister been like this?" Dash asked fifteen-year-old Jo. Peg Zilboorg, a frequent visitor with her husband, Gregory, thought it hurt Hammett that his daughters had taken their mother's part. His tone was a combination of "gentle apology" and sarcasm that his daughters were so unworldly. Lillian disliked Mary more than ever.

One day, Jo couldn't find the bathroom in the main house and stumbled by accident into Lillian's bedroom. Lily was in bed. Dash sat on one side of the bed holding her hand. He looked at Jo.

"What are you doing here?" he demanded, his voice harsh and reproving. Then he said coldly, "The bathroom is at the other end of the hall." Later he explained that Lil had cramps, wasn't coming down to dinner.

Lily was relieved when Mary and Jo returned to California.

*   *   *

On a typical Sunday at Hardscrabble Farm now, Lily and Dash would start out reading the papers. Soon the drinking would begin and they would drink steadily all day. A fight might erupt, perhaps about Roosevelt, whose part Lily would take. Dash got dressed.

Lily knew: he was off to one of the Harlem whorehouses where black and Oriental girls helped him attain what pleasure he could at this time of the waning of his sexual powers. Often he could be spotted at the Plantation Club, which had replaced the old Cotton Club as "the hottest of the uptown sepian spots."

"You want to get back to town to your floozie," Lillian accused. Then Dash was out the door.

Lily consoled herself with a new lover, *New Yorker* writer St. Clair McKelway, a balding man whose cool, reddish-blond looks and little mustache appealed to her. McKelway was tall and thin, witty and charming, with a bit of a swagger that reminded some of an aviator in the Royal Air Force. It was said there wasn't a woman he didn't fuck. But he was intelligent, a good writer, if also a colossal drunk. Lily chose men not for their capacity to care about her, but for their aesthetic value, how well they might appear beside the woman she wished she resembled. Lillian said she liked McKelway's name, as she liked the names of her WASP lovers.

McKelway now became the recipient of her babytalk. One afternoon a crowd went down to the lake for a picnic, only for McKelway and Lily to swim off to one of the islands, as often Lily would shed her clothes and swim out to the float stark naked.

"You look happy," Emmy Kronenberger said when Lily returned.

"He couldn't get it up!" Lillian replied scornfully. But, as always, she tried harder than other women and years later McKelway remembered a nurturing Lillian taking care of a group of *New Yorker* drunks at Hardscrabble Farm.

The first weekend of December 1941 found Dash acting as host. Lil was in bed, and so Dash took the Kobers on a tramp through the woods. On December 7, Maggie and Dash were fiddling with the radio in Lillian's bedroom when the news that Japan had bombed Pearl Harbor came.

In January 1942 Lil had decided to let Dash write the picture version of *Watch on the Rhine*. The Hardscrabble entertainments continued. Guests were greeted by the butler, Felix. More exuberant than usual, Dash announced he was writing a one-hour mystery show for Herman. He was less than convincing.

That February, another romantic fantasy was punctured as Lily discovered McKelway was no longer interested in her. "My feeling is that

McKelway has wandered from home," Kober wrote. Lil was "very unhappy." Worse, the she-Hammett confided to Kober that she had "crabs." As she had gone to Europe when Hammett defected in 1937, now she headed for Nassau.

It depressed her even more when Kober and Maggie had a baby, whom they named Cathy. "Lil so envious," Kober noted after she and Dotty went to the hospital to see the baby. "I really believe she'd give everything else she had to be happily married and have child." Lily was made little Cathy's godmother. In years to come Cathy saw that in the extended family of Lily and Dash, Arthur and Maggie and herself, it was Lillian who was the patriarch, whom even her father talked of as if she were a man.

Lily was left to live out the arrangement she had made with Dash. The turtle that would not die, later immortalized by Lily in a chapter of *Pentimento,* was an emblem of how she wanted to remember their relationship during these, the Hardscrabble years. In 1940 at the wild lake in their first spring, Hammett traps a huge, fierce snapping turtle, which refuses to die, either by ax or by rifle. Bleeding and battered, it staggers out of the kitchen. Its indefatigable spirit leads Lily to ask Dash, "How does one define life?" Lily would allow the turtle to evade the soup pot, believing it has earned its life. Hammett, as always, rejects metaphysics: "Lily, I'm too old for that stuff." By the end, after promising to bury *her,* even as he refuses to bury the turtle, he has secretly painted a tombstone.

The fable, written, of course, after Dashiell Hammett's death, pointed to a truth, but one other than what Lily intended her readers to perceive. They were now in it for life, Zilboorg's advice notwithstanding. As the wounded, bloodied turtle would not die, so their Faustian bargain would remain intact. They had passed beyond the romance they never had to the companionship of an old marriage. He would look after, not her, but her work, for as long as he could; her part was to look after him, see to his comfort, nourish his solitude, and, finally, bury *him.*

11

The Communist Couple

"Maybe you had to be a socialist to get the best hats."

Judith Firth Sanger

During these Hardscrabble years, as it had in Hollywood, politics bound them. They were a Communist couple in New York and in Pleasantville. If sometimes he would correct her social history in the presence of other people, and she would grow fierce in opposition, they shared a fundamental compliance with the postures of the Communist Party.

She had so become him, this she-Hammett, that someone as close to her as Ralph Ingersoll thought that she was much more radical than Hammett. It was she who was the friend of Earl Browder and V. J. Jerome and everyone knew it. She was the romantic, emotional and idealistic. He was the realistic one, looking at the revolution as something in progress, and refusing to be distracted by its excesses. Stalin's Soviet Union was also a state where the revolution was established and to its power Hammett could turn over responsibility for theory and practice; from its legitimacy he could derive a sense of potency, making his radical activity less marginal.

As he didn't expect much of life for himself, so as the years passed he surrendered any serious interest in rectitude from either the Communist Party at home or the Soviet Union which dictated its policies. As a result, Hammett continued to seem impervious to Stalin's desecration of the ideals and the core values of the Russian revolution. He called himself a Marxist, but this translated to little more than allowing the Party to use him. He expressed no doubts.

The alcoholic haze, flamboyant living, evasion of introspection, unwillingness to confront his own pain, and the excruciating loss of his craft—all these numbed his sensibility and enabled him to blind himself. He was a man who feared emotional need and, paradoxically, who dreaded dependence, from which he was in perpetual flight. He had fled fatherhood so that his deserted daughters scarcely knew him. He had engineered a humiliating scene the better to subject a vulnerable and pregnant Lillian to a trauma sufficient to oblige her to cease demanding an emotional commitment he would never grant.

Now in a wild miscalculation he continued to believe Stalinism could embody a quest for justice. Thus did he choose his safe haven as he subjected himself to all its macabre twists and turns. "He had the politics of a baby," William Phillips, co-editor of *Partisan Review* and now an anti-Stalinist, observed. He was not engaged in reflection about political choices, but merely in parroting a "superficial Party line." Drunk much of the time in the years before America's entry into the war, Dash didn't have to think. One night, when he went out with Spanish Civil War veteran Edwin Rolfe, Rolfe's wife, Mary, observed that Eddie came home drunker than he had ever been before.

Yet Hammett remained better than these Party cohorts. He had neither illusion nor serious expectation that the Party could or would develop any kind of revolution in America. "Now I'm going to get up and type a long letter to Herbert Biberman on the state of the nation," he wrote Lily in March 1939, "and how to keep Viewing the Future through rose-colored testicles."

In *An Unfinished Woman,* Lily wrote, disingenuously, "Hammett and I had not shared the same convictions." Behind that sophism is that Hammett abhorred the spectacle of socialists living like the rich. He was now more at ease setting up housekeeping in New York at modest 14 West Ninth Street. Lily lived uptown in an elegant rented apartment in the Henry Clewes mansion on Eighty-second Street.

Dash was now giving away whatever money he had. Lily never allowed politics to impede how she aspired to live. Later, working for the Independent Citizens League with rented offices at the Astor they could scarcely afford, Lily, ever on a diet, regularly ordered expensive room-service lunches of hard-boiled egg, lettuce, and tea.

Unlike Hammett, who didn't care what those in the social whirl thought of how he lived, Hellman had a well-developed sense of her own importance; her pride transcended her political activity. She contributed a manuscript of *The Little Foxes* to the Exiled Writers Committee auction on behalf of anti-Nazi writers in need of rescue—on the condition that Franklin Folsom promise to bid two hundred dollars if no other bid went that high; Lily would later reimburse him. The auctioneer was a tipsy Kober, who ranted on: "Lillian's a wunnerful woman, a wunnerful woman." Luckily two hundred dollars was bid, preserving Lillian's amour propre. Folsom also asked her to help him bail Comintern agent Otto Katz out of Ellis Island. Lily had met Katz (a.k.a. André Simone) in Paris, and it was he who had urged her to visit Spain.

"I haven't got it," Lily barked. "But if you come to my apartment at midnight, you'll have your money."

At midnight, the maid opened the door. Lillian was nowhere to be seen. In the living room Folsom observed dirty glasses, the aftermath of a party. The maid went over to the fireplace mantel, where an envelope with Franklin Folsom's name sat. Inside was the cash.

Their political styles differed as well. Hammett behaved like an open Party member. Lily's Communism, Trotskyist Irving Howe later observed, was in essence "a kind of platonic affiliation." Sometimes when there was every reason to expect her signature on a Party-inspired petition, it wasn't there. She did not sign a Hammett-authored telegram of January 22, 1939, to Secretary of State Cordell Hull from "Artists of Hollywood" urging the repeal of the embargo on Spain. At a party, one of Lily's friends insisted she was not even sympathetic to the Party. "Isn't that true, Lillian?" she asked, turning to Miss Hellman. Lily demurred, however, replying, "Well. . . ." She would say no more. She would not openly dissociate herself from Hammett's cause.

Ever trying to ensure herself a place in his life, Hammett's daughter Jo wrote him that she was willing to join the Communists too. Like Lily, Jo felt if she could not truly have her father—as no one could—she might emulate him and thereby attract his attention. "All the Communists I know would be very glad to have you," Dash wrote her graciously. "They feel that as a rule they don't get enough royalty."

During political discussions at the farm, Dash and Lily formed a united front. What he said was gospel; when he talked about *The Little Foxes* as a conflict between "aristocracy and the middle class," Lily decided it must be so. During the period of the Hitler-Stalin pact, pace the Party, they became ardent pacifists, discarding their antifascism as warmongering and opposing the "imperialist war" in Europe. With their coterie of Kober, Shumlin, and Ingersoll, they defended Stalin. "You don't trust Stalin," Ingersoll accused his lover, novelist Laura Hobson. "I do." At Hardscrabble Farm there could be no other view.

*   *   *

The Soviet Union invaded Finland in November 1939. At once Lily and Dash signed an open letter to President Roosevelt sponsored by the American Council on Soviet Relations demanding a U.S. declaration of war against Finland. Then in January 1940 when all theaters were asked to offer a night's receipts in a benefit for aid to Finland, Lily and Herman refused to allow *The Little Foxes* to be involved. Tallulah Bankhead protested and created an uproar in the press, one Lily never forgot, so that later she invented the charge that Tallulah refused to do a benefit for Spain. In fact, neither Hellman nor Shumlin had ever asked the cast to do a benefit for the Loyalists.

With the Hearst press reveling in the scandal, Lily was obliged to respond. "I don't believe in that fine, lovable little Republic of Finland that everybody gets so weepy about," she declared. "I've been there, and it looks like a pro-Nazi little republic to me." She made it all up as she went along, aided by Shumlin's press agent, Richard Maney. She had never been to Finland.

Much time was spent at Hardscrabble Farm devising a strategy with which to respond to Tallulah's criticism, her "cutting up about giving benefit for Finland," as Kober put it. "I feel enraged at this drunken, foul-mouthed degenerate bitch & I think of letters to write & things to say denouncing her," Kober fulminated. The Stalinists and their periphery reacted rabidly to left or liberal challenges to their pro-Soviet politics. Those who would separate socialism and political challenge to capitalism from the Stalinist model, they savaged as spies, sellouts, or hired hands in a classic case of projection.

Shumlin considered canceling the Washington bookings of *The Little Foxes,* on the ground of the theater's refusal to admit blacks, in "an attempt to spike Tallulah's Finnish fins," as Kober described it. Hammett, "out of sorts," left Lily and Shumlin to manage the brouhaha. Finally Lillian wrote an article for the New York *Times:* "Theatrical benefits for Finnish relief would give a dangerous impetus to war spirit in this country," she said. Stalin and Hitler had assured peace; opposition to fascism was no longer acceptable.

It was in this period that Ralph Ingersoll started his newspaper *PM*. It was to be a "new kind of newspaper," its credo "against people who push other people around in this country or abroad." With America's best writers, it would expose "fraud and deceit and greed and cruelty." Politically, its stand on capitalism was based on "what degree of private property is in the greatest interests of the greatest number."

Participants from the start, engaged with Ingersoll in the early stages of *PM*, Lily and Dash remained in each other's orbit. Ingersoll attributed the impetus for his starting the paper to "Lil," who had "challenged all my ideas and put me under pressure to do something on my own."

Early on, Ingersoll invited Hammett to his Connecticut house for a weekend to discuss *PM*. It was just the two of them. Ingersoll found the experience infuriating. "He never opened his mouth," Ingersoll recalled. "He just sat there five, six hours at a time, not saying anything."

But then Dash did become involved. While Lily wrote letters asking people to support the new enterprise, and worked on the dummy issue, Hammett, ensconced in a room at the Plaza, interviewed applicants to work on the paper. It was a secret operation because the writers were elsewhere employed. He sought to hire, Ingersoll concluded, as many Communists as he could. It was true; Hammett did not hire many people, but of those he did, three were Party members; others were "dues-cheaters," Stalinists who remained formally outside the Party but accepted its discipline.

Both Lily and Dash worked on the thirty-two-page dummy issue, which included a book review by Hammett and an essay by Hellman called "What Movie." Lily thought of ways to politicize standard journalism. In a memo to Ingersoll, she proposed that instead of printing conventional reviews of films, *PM* should address the issue of "the financial set-up of movie companies. Do they interlock, and if they do, does it influence the pictures they make? When movie people claim that business is bad, what do they mean by it?" Lillian also wanted to reveal that Sam Goldwyn believed that no Jew should produce so radical a novel as *The Grapes of Wrath*, the real reason he let Darryl Zanuck buy the property.

When Lily saw the dummy issue, she was appalled at Ingersoll's "broken promises."

"You can't bring this out. It's just too bad to bring out," she told him. "Wait a month, two weeks, postpone it." Ingersoll was upset. Dash intervened. "The man is already a hysteric," he told Lily. "You'll make him crack completely." Zilboorg, who was treating Ingersoll, was called down to the office.

Hammett sat in the newsroom editing *PM*'s copy, a task he performed for a year. He would put a sentence or two into proper English while hysteria erupted around him. He helped Ingersoll with the first editorials.

Ingersoll's nerves became even more frayed when right-wing pickets turned up outside *PM*'s offices. Now he feared the Communist taint would render the paper stillborn. Among the rumors circulating was one that Hellman and Hammett really controlled *PM*. One night at the Stork

Club with Ingersoll, Lily, unable to restrain herself, called him a "son of a bitch." Lily let him know that "they" had denounced him.

"Who exactly are 'they'?" Ingersoll demanded.

"None of your business," Lily said.

"If you don't want to tell me, I don't want to know," Ingersoll told her. But it was clear to him. "They" meant the Communist Party.

The crisis erupted in July 1940. An unsigned handbill was distributed to New York newspapers listing twenty-four supposed Communist Party members and supporters on the staff of *PM*. Ingersoll told Hammett that he planned to devote the entire "Press" section to a story called "Volunteer Gestapo," printing photographs of the twenty-four denounced writers. He would also publish the handbill and a signed editorial condemning the charges.

Hammett tried to dissuade him. Ingersoll could hurt the people exposed, he pleaded. But when Hammett arrived home, he received a call from Ingersoll. He was planning to go ahead. "Incidentally, Dash," Ingersoll said, "things are pretty hot down here right now on this Red issue. Maybe you'd better stay away from the shop for a month or so until it cools off."

Ingersoll believed Hammett's presence alone confirmed Party involvement, and, rather than defend the right of radicals to write and publish, he wanted to distance himself. The root of the problem was the refusal of Party types to acknowledge their politics and defend them cogently. Only thus could assaults on civil liberties be countered. But the defense of Stalin's police state was not easily reconciled with invocations of freedom for dissent. It was an impediment which allowed the witch hunt of the forties and fifties to flourish.

Now, in a thirteen-page confidential memo to *PM* investors, subtitled "Rumors of Radicalism on *PM*," Ingersoll repudiated by name both Hellman and Hammett. On the issue of Hammett's having done the hiring, he said most of the people Hammett interviewed were not hired. Although Ingersoll insisted that it would not have made any difference if they had been employed, his submission to Red-baiting was clear. To the best of his knowledge, Ingersoll tried to reassure his stockholders, no member of *PM*'s staff is "an organizational member of the party, taking orders from 14th St. (or Moscow)."

Lillian felt that Ingersoll was saying, in effect, that Hellman and Hammett are Reds, but they're my friends, and as old friends they'd been brought in to work with writers. He had, in Kober's estimation, struck "at friends to hide his terror."

Hammett had no use for Ingersoll now. The memo, he thought, was "a real fingering job." Later remembering his days on *PM*, Hammett summed up the amateur enterprise and the staff as a "net-full of zanies."

No longer lovers, Lily and Dash remained, in the years before America's entry into the War, companions and comrades. When he was in New York, time hung heavy on Hammett's hands. He picked up a script Shumlin had rejected, and told him he'd be "sending back a fortune." Dash enlisted Lillian. "You must be crazy," she told Shumlin, who went on to produce the play—James Thurber's *The Male Animal.*

One day Shumlin introduced Lillian to Jack Bjoze, executive secretary of the Friends of the Abraham Lincoln Brigade. Bjoze wanted Lillian to sponsor an appeal-for-funds letter for returning wounded veterans.

Dash was waiting downstairs. The three walked to Child's for a drink and Hammett gave Bjoze $150. With sadness in his voice, he said he was sorry he hadn't gone to Spain. Lillian agreed to sign the appeal letter. One drink and the meeting was over.

Invocations of the Spanish Civil War could still keep them together. They attended the premiere of "Return to Life," a benefit for Spain. Both supported all the Party fronts devoted to Spain: Friends of the Abraham Lincoln Brigade, the Spanish Refugee Relief Campaign, the American Rescue Ship Mission, the Joint Anti-Fascist Refugee Committee, American Friends of Spanish Democracy, and the North American Spanish Aid Committee.

Together in June 1939, Lily and Dash sponsored the third call of the League of American Writers. The League never actually requested of its members an endorsement of Stalin or his government, claiming to be a democratic independent organization of writers free of Party control. In practice, as Philip Rahv noted in *Partisan Review,* it would "not tolerate the active participation of anyone who is not ready to defend every policy of Stalin."

At a Party fraction meeting before the Third Congress, Party secretary Earl Browder declared himself pleased with the turnout: "It is among the writers particularly that the Party made its first big advance in influence in the broad cultural field." Party members among the writers must speak out in support of President Roosevelt and the Democratic Party, he told them. They must also combat the "disruptive ideology" of the non-Stalinist left, specifically the Trotskyists with their "destructive and wrecking influence."

Both having been made League directors in July, with Lily a vice president, Lily and Dash signed the August 14 declaration declaring it a "fantastic falsehood that the USSR and the totalitarian states are basically alike." Anyone who made the comparison was a "fascist" and a "reactionary." On August 23, Stalin signed his nonaggression pact with Hitler. It was a tactical maneuver, Lily quickly explained to Ring Lardner, Jr., voicing the Party's early rationale; it was necessary for the Soviet Union to defend itself now that the British and French weren't coming through with their own alliance with Stalin—in which case opposition to colonialism would have become as unacceptable as opposition to fascism now became with the Hitler pact.

Stalin decreed that antifascist activity should cease and Party faithful should work for peace. Lily, dubbing herself "the greatest meeting-goer in the country," now worked beside Clifford Odets on antiwar resolutions from the offices of the League of American Writers. *New Masses* began at once, as Kober chronicled, to "lash out at Roosevelt's new defense measures." By January 1940, Hellman and Hammett and Kober were active in the Keep America Out of War Committee of the League of American Writers.

Both Lily and Dash had been on the editorial council of *Equality* magazine, which was dedicated to combating anti-Semitism—and fascism. As late as September 1940 Lily gave a benefit for *Equality* at Hardscrabble Farm, which Paul Robeson and other Party celebrities attended. The magazine was discontinued by the Party later in the year in keeping with Stalin's policies.

Apart from denouncing antifascism, Communists were to turn their attention to domestic matters. In February 1940, Hammett conducted a study group in Lily's New York apartment. Both signed the leaflet "In Defense of Civil Rights," which condemned the government for indicting Earl Browder and Sam Darcy, state chairman of the Pennsylvania Communist Party, who faced imprisonment for a California voting registration infraction in 1934. "Serious efforts are being made to silence and suppress the Communist Party, in violation of the Bill of Rights," the leaflet read. The text declared: "We are not Communists."

In May 1941 a woman named Dr. Ettie Stettheimer wrote a letter to Dashiell Hammett objecting to the League's antiwar posture. Perplexed by the League's persistent determination to denounce the fight against fascism, she accused Hammett of being disinterested in defending democracy, of cynical indifference to "whether or not you will become Nazi slaves." The letter was published in the *New Leader*.

There is no record of a Hammett response. But Suzanne La Follette, daughter of the populist leader, seeing the letter, set Dr. Stettheimer straight. "Before the Hitler-Stalin pact they were all for collective security of the democracies against fascism," she explained. "And my dear girl," La Follette could not resist adding, "the guy you picked out to complain to is one of the most notorious of Party stooges.

"The name of Dashiell Hammett has been signed to every public statement in praise of Soviet policy, from that which tried to break up the American Committee for the Defense of Leon Trotsky through that which justified the Russian terror down to that just before the Stalin-Hitler pact, which called the American Committee for Cultural Freedom fascist ... from his record it seems no exaggeration to say that Mr. Dashiell Hammett will sign his name to *anything* provided it be something the Communist Party wants signed." At a historical moment when millions organized in industrial unions, Hammett opposed any independent political expression, any challenge to the Democratic Party. Indeed Hammett remained in the forefront of those who behaved as satraps for Stalin, behavior which in its cynicism undermined the possibility of an authentic socialist, revolutionary movement rising out of the ashes of the Depression.

That year Dash and Lily were supporters of Communist longshoreman Harry Bridges, who was facing a deportation trial.

Yet Stalin's rapprochement with Hitler or not, they were both concerned with the fate of the Jews. Hammett signed a letter put out by the Jewish People's Committee protesting the treatment of Jewish refugees by Great Britain and requesting that Britain allow Jews to go to Palestine. They did not support, however, the admitting of Jewish refugees to Britain—or to the United States.

Lily spoke in January 1940 at a Book and Author lunch sponsored by the American Booksellers Association and the New York *Herald Tribune*.

"I am a writer and I am also a Jew," she told an audience numbering nearly two thousand. "I also want to be able to go on saying that I am a Jew without being afraid of being called names or end in a prison camp or be forbidden to walk down the street at night."

Notwithstanding this, privately her ambivalence about her Jewish identity remained and would intensify in the years to come. Being Jewish, she sometimes seemed to suggest, was a joke the universe had played on her. It robbed her of the acceptability she craved, reduced her edge, even as she never considered plastic surgery on her prominent nose, and never denied that she was Jewish. Years later when "Julia" was made into a film, she quarreled angrily with director Fred Zinnemann, demanding that the character based on herself and played by Jane Fonda be made explicitly Jewish. Yet right after the war, she criticized the German Jews for not having done enough to save themselves. Dash and Max ganged up on her then.

"You don't know what you're talking about," Dash said.

Hammett signed a call by prominent liberals calling for an investigation of the violation of the Constitution by the notorious Dies committee, which had inaugurated the witch hunt in America.

Meanwhile Dash alone involved himself in open Party activity. He joined a 1940 campaign to keep the Communist Party on the New York State ballot. He became head of the Committee on Free Elections, chairing one meeting for Election Rights on October 9, 1940. One speaker after another got up to proclaim how many signatures they had garnered for Communist Party candidates. Suddenly a man named Hamilton got up to speak.

"The Communist Party protests the denial of civil rights against themselves," he said. "But at the same time it organizes movements to deny civil liberties and election rights to the Socialist Party."

Hisses issued from all four corners of the room.

"Mr. Hamilton," said Chairman Hammett, quieting everyone down, "has violated the spirit and purpose of this meeting. Only antidemocratic elements could benefit by disrupting this rally."

It was, of course, true. The Communists kept, as William Phillips described it, a "blacklist" of people on the left who had broken with the official Communist movement. Phillips had been writing reviews regularly for *The Nation* until one day an embarrassed Margaret Marshall, the magazine's literary editor, told him and Philip Rahv that she had been given orders not to print any "Trotskyites," a designation which covered not only the intelligentsia that identified with Trotsky's defense of Marxism but also any non-Party socialists or radicals.

Marshall had been both a friend and a non-Communist, which was how Phillips discovered the truth. *New Masses* had proudly proclaimed that the 1939 Third American Congress, unlike the 1937 meeting, was a "truly literary conference," thanks to the "expulsion of the disruptive Trotskyists." Opponents on the left were excluded, their views held in contempt.

Lily and Dash were both active in initiating fronts, securing a number of names, and then receding into the background. In one case, Lily enlisted New York governor Herbert H. Lehman to attend an October 1941 dinner-forum on "Europe Today," of which she and Ernest Hemingway were sponsors. When Lehman discovered that the sponsoring organizations were all directed by the Party, he declined to attend.

Lily was self-righteous in confronting Lehman. She was "deeply shocked" that he had withdrawn his support. "I do not ask the politics of any people if I am certain enough that they are giving aid where it is needed and deserved," she insisted. She didn't care, she proclaimed piously, "what their color, what their church." Then she sought to exploit the fortuitous fact of Lehman's being a Jew, declaring, "Of all the peoples in the world, I think, we should be the last to hold back help."

Lehman was not appeased. He detested Nazism and fascism no less than she, he told her. That was the basis of his objection. Stalin, who stood behind all of the sponsoring groups, was "a partner of the Axis powers" and had collaborated with and condoned Nazism. Indeed, the NKVD and the Gestapo were at this very moment sharing files and hunting down opponents of Nazism across Europe.

Dutifully Lily and Dash both signed the Call of the Fourth Congress of the League of American Writers in April 1941. Its motto was: "Keep America Out of War." The war in Europe was denounced once more as a "brutal, shameless struggle for the redivision of empires." If the capitalist powers were competing with Germany for colonial spoils, as in World War I, the Party advocated only support for the Hitler-Stalin pact, which meant no resistance either to fascism, to the "redivision of empires," or, indeed, to capitalism anywhere.

Lily contributed two hundred dollars to the financing of the Congress with the understanding that she would be repaid immediately "from the money coming in from the Congress." So Hellman and Hammett kept faith with Stalin. They opposed equally lend-lease to Britain and conscription in the United States. Hammett spoke bitterly at a public meeting opposing "the new and greater American national defense effort against civil liberties."

Both appeared at the June meeting, at which Hammett was elected president of the League. Then Lily went off to Hollywood. It was a Sunday afternoon in Bel Air when she walked into the house of Sidney and Beatrice Buchman, the very Sidney Buchman who later took a valiant position against the House Un-American Activities Committee. Buchman was to assert that he was willing to describe his own politics but never those of others. It was a position which preceded her own stance, and Lily simply pretended she had never heard of it.

Lily walked slowly, as she always did. She was dressed all in white. It was difficult to tell whether she was angry or self-mocking as she said dramatically, "The Motherland has been attacked!"

Indeed, on June 22, 1941, Hitler invaded the Soviet Union. Suddenly their politics changed. Lily and Dash immediately signed the League of American Writers call to "all Creative Workers" for "'full support to Great Britain and the Soviet Union in their struggle for the demolition of fascism.'" Hammett signed letters to the members of the League of American Writers soliciting expressions of support "for the Soviet fight against the Nazi invasion" to help "the morale of the Soviet people which has evoked universal admiration." Soon they were both demanding that America open a Second Front so that the Soviet Union might be defended against Hitler's brutal attack. No longer were Churchill and Roosevelt considered to be fighting Hitler for the spoils of imperial control.

The Communists in the Screen Writers Guild ended their support for a minimum wage for writers (only to be outvoted). Helping Russia took precedence over everything. There were to be no labor struggles in America, not even for workers, like screenwriters, who had nothing to do with the national defense.

That year President Roosevelt signed into law the Smith Act, rendering illegal "teaching and advocating the overthrow of the United States government by force and violence." It was the organization of the Teamsters that was targeted by the Smith Act, designed to imprison opponents of a no-strike pledge. The Trotskyist support of labor leader A. Philip Randolph and a march on Washington for better living conditions threatened the subordination of the Congress of Industrial Organizations (CIO) to the Democratic Party. In December, Trotskyists active in the Teamsters union were imprisoned in Minneapolis for violating the Smith Act; their "crime" had been socialist opposition to the war, the very position the Communists had taken during the period of the pact.

Hellman and Hammett remained silent as the Smith Act was turned against their ideological opponents on the left. Yet Hammett signed a letter opposing the prison sentence of Sam Darcy, who had been prosecuted because he was a Communist, and another defending Morris Schappes, a teacher fired for his Communist beliefs. Later, ironically, Dash himself would go to jail for refusing to testify in a Smith Act case, amid the hue and cry of outraged Stalinists who wrapped themselves in robes of virtue as they were hounded by Senator McCarthy, as if they hadn't themselves acquiesced in the very repressive legislation now turned against them.

"It is unconstitutional to persecute a man for his beliefs, political or religious," read a hypocritical League leaflet. Lily and Dash were never willing to extend that principle to those with whom they disagreed, another of their positions that marked the end of any hope that the Party could lead a credible radical movement in America.

Stalin's assassination of Trotsky and his family went unremarked by Lily and Dash. So too did Stalin's overt anti-Semitism, although they long knew he had passed over Benjamin Gitlow as general secretary of the American Communist Party, preferring Earl Browder, because he did not want a Jew in that position.

The Communist couple persisted in their activities. As chairman of the Exiled Writers Committee, Hammett signed Party-authored letters requesting financial support for antifascist figures, now in good repute wih the Party. Lily, always eager to ingratiate herself with him, would rush into the fray, and then express anger at Hammett. He was infuriating, so "un-angry" a man, Lily said. Something would happen and he would just sit there. Then she would take action, do anything, get involved noisily, just to show him.

12

Hellman Edits Hammett

"Anger is protest."

WATCH ON THE RHINE

In Lillian Hellman's *Watch on the Rhine* (1941), Kurt Muller, a leader in the anti-Nazi underground, brings his wife, Sara, and their three children from Europe to the safe haven of Washington, D.C. The year is 1940. A houseguest of Mrs. Fanny Farrelly, Sara's mother, is one Teck, a Romanian count and Nazi spy, who soon attempts to blackmail Muller by revealing his identity. By the end, Muller has killed Teck and returned to Germany to fight the fascists, sacrificing his own family happiness for the greater good. "In every town and every village and every mud hut in the world," Lily wrote, "there is always a man who loves children and who will fight to make a good world for them." Liberals like Fanny Farrelly, and those in the audience, now know the value of "radicals" like Kurt Muller.

The Communist Party still could not count on Lillian, as they could on Dash. The sanctity of her work came first and she went forward with the antifascist *Watch on the Rhine* during the period of the Hitler-Stalin pact. She had written her story of Kurt Muller, based on Comintern agent Otto Katz, before the agreement; indeed the completed first draft is dated August 15, 1939, a week before the announcement of the Molotov-Ribbentrop nonaggression alliance. Lillian would not revise or put aside this work which called openly for involvement in the struggle against Hitler, no matter that Stalin was soon to decree that Communists now concern themselves not with antifascist struggle, but with peace. "Are you a radical?" Kurt's mother-in-law, Fanny, asks him in Popular Front parlance when "radical" meant "Communist."

"You would have to tell me what that word means to you, Madame," he replies coyly. Fanny at once readjusts: "Perhaps we all have private definitions. We are all anti-Fascists, for example."

Party hacks seized their pens to attack this politically incorrect play. *The Daily Worker,* unwilling openly to admit Lillian Hellman had violated Party directives by encouraging the antifascist struggle at this inopportune moment, faulted her for not mentioning the working class as the leaders in the struggle for a better world. Worse, she failed to indicate "that a land of socialism has already established the permanent new life of peace and freedom." "Peace," of course, was the buzzword.

In *New Masses,* afraid to attack the formidable Miss Hellman directly, fellow Communist Alvah Bessie argued that the play had already been "misused by those who would like to whip us or cajole us into imperialist war under the banner of fighting fascism in Germany." Lillian had fallen into "a network of fallacy, both dramatic and political." It was no longer possible to be "anti-nazi, and nothing more," he wrote, echoing *The Daily Worker.*

After the war, appalled, Albert Maltz wrote an article called "What Shall We Ask of Writers?" for the same *New Masses,* in which he cited Lillian Hellman's "magnificent play" as an example of art which Communists reviewed not for itself, but for whether it adhered to the Party line. Within two weeks Howard Fast had accused him of "liquidation, not only of Marxist creative writing—but of all creative writing which bases itself on progressive currents in America," while Joseph North attacked him for his "anti-Marxist position." Poor Maltz, victim of a literary purge, at once recanted. His article had been "a one-sided, non-dialectical treatment of *complex* issues," he wrote two months later. Might he not be forgiven? As for the "bourgeois" reviewers and critics, *Watch on the Rhine* received the New York Drama Critics Circle Award for 1941.

Although in September 1940, Dashiell Hammett told Kober he liked the play, his enthusiasm clearly waned during the period when the Party was uneasy with this Hellman work. Most unusual for him, he did not come to rehearsals, where he might have been witness to the ludicrous spectacle of Paul Lukas, who played Kurt Muller, bickering with a twelve-year-old actor, who took to rubbing garlic into his hair in retaliation. The man sitting there one day massaging Lily's sore foot was not Dash, but her doctor, Abe Abeloff. During *Watch on the Rhine,* Hammett stayed away from Herman's offices as well. Dash did go to Baltimore for the out-of-town opening, and did sit up all night arguing with Lily about where the curtain should come down in one of the acts. But it was not a happy trip for him.

Nor on April 1, 1941, when the play opened, was Dash at Sardi's to wait with Lily for the reviews, a transgression for which she had not forgiven him twenty years after his death. Finally he let her know his objection: "You ruined a great play by too much sentimentalism," Dash told her. "Antifascist sentimentalism." After all, it was two months after the opening of *Watch on the Rhine,* in June, that Hammett, as the new president of the League of American Writers, was still condemning "this criminal war." Lily's new play had proven to be an embarrassment.

The Boston chapter of the Joint Anti-Fascist Refugee Committee knew well how the Party felt about *Watch on the Rhine,* and when someone proposed that a copy of the limited edition be raffled off at a fundraiser, the objection was raised that it was not "sufficiently desirable." But at that June meeting of the League of American Writers in New York, *Watch on the Rhine* won a prize in drama. Its line was not correct, but the Party could ill afford to lose the goodwill of so influential a figure as Lillian Hellman.

Indeed, apart from her play, she had followed Party policy, working with Clifford Odets on those antiwar resolutions. Lily had revealed her bifurcated personality as she moved between contradictions with ease, feeling no compulsion to reconcile opposing ideas or emotions. It damaged her credibility as a political intellectual, but it made her a shrewd survivor. Of course, when Hitler invaded the Soviet Union on June 22, all was forgiven. *Watch on the Rhine* became a Party *cri de coeur.*

But before the invasion, and reacting to Hammett's and the Party's strong disapproval, Lily refused to talk about *Watch on the Rhine* in public. When the New York *Times* asked about the circumstances of its development, Lily was evasive. It was "too long and involved a story, one which would prove uninteresting." She had broken the bond of shared political loyalty with Hammett, one of the few bonds remaining to them, and she was uneasy. Even in the first anthology of her plays, she is silent about *Watch on the Rhine.* "Only eleven months have gone by since it was finished," she explained weakly, "and this is not time enough for me to see it clearly." In private life, however, she remained herself. Her birthday was two days before the Hitler invasion; friends had long been in possession of their telegrams: "A birthday present for Lillian Hellman is a blow against fascism."

It was not Dash, but Herman Shumlin who accompanied her to Washington for the "command performance" of the play. Lillian, full of outrageous fun, enjoying her role as one of America's leading playwrights, wanted John Lodge, who played David Farrelly, and was a naval reserve officer, to carry a sword to the party and she actually located one at the Shubert warehouse. That madcap facet of her personality, the relish for mischief, Hammett no longer shared.

Herman Shumlin was banished to another table, but Lily sat next to President Roosevelt, who had a question for her. Having been briefed by informant Morris Ernst, certain that it could not have been after the Hitler-Stalin pact, he wanted to know exactly when *Watch on the Rhine* was written. It was begun in 1938, Lillian told him, and finished and in rehearsal early in 1941. Roosevelt said "uh, huh," and nodded. Obviously she had time to alter her text since it had not opened before the pact, and yet she had not. Lillian passed a test that mattered to her, that of being acceptable to those in high places.

Lily did not hold Dash's reservations about *Watch on the Rhine* against him. In December 1942, she discussed with Kober and Shumlin, who was to direct the film version, whether Dash might not be enlisted to write the screenplay. He was idle, depressed. He was drinking, and she was worried about him.

Producer Hal Wallis wanted Lillian to write it herself, Hammett's reputation for "slowness" having preceded him. But Lillian was adamant as she enlisted Herman to reassure Wallis that Dash was up to the task. She would now encourage and edit his writing, make him a writer again, do for him what he had once done for her.

With the Soviet Union at war with Germany, Dash could take on this assignment in good conscience. For a fee of $30,000, he agreed to write under the supervision of Lillian and Herman. When Dash asked for ten weeks to write the script, Wallis nervously insisted that it could easily be done in six or seven. Underlining how deeply their roles had been reversed, it was understood by all that Lily would be in control of the script. Wallis assumed she would come out to Hollywood to polish the script before filming began. He paid her $11,500.

He couldn't begin for two or three weeks because he had "some work" that needed to be finished, Dash said, but would "get script out in record time," and the treatment in two weeks. With Wallis on tenterhooks, Dash slowly began. Alone at Hardscrabble Farm, he wrote laboriously, in pencil. Finally Lillian and Shumlin read Dash's thirty-two-page treatment and sent it off to an already distressed Wallis.

Hammett's biggest contributions were the exteriors, geographical settings which could not have been put on the stage. He added an immigration station on the U.S. border with Mexico, train scenes as the Muller family makes its way east to Washington, a sightseeing trip around Washington, and a scene at the German embassy, where the villain Teck discovers how to blackmail the antifascist Muller. He even added a rowing scene on a little lake similar to the one at Hardscrabble Farm. "The pond covers some 3 or 4 acres," Hammett wrote, "with a small, flat, bushy island near the center." A vegetable-planting scene, which goes on far too long, ends on the older Muller son Joshua's asking one of the servants to teach him how to play baseball. Hammett, who enjoyed children, gives them much more screen time; Lily abruptly ushers them offstage. Hammett also added a scene taking place after the play ends. Kurt Muller is in a German city awaiting his next move while his children remain in America playing baseball.

Wallis liked the treatment, but had reservations. Anticipating objections from the Hays office, which decreed that a character cannot commit murder and go unpunished, he wanted Teck to goad Muller into shooting him. He was also uneasy about the open ending, in which the viewer would not learn whether Kurt has been successful in his anti-Nazi mission. Lillian and Herman discussed the film's last scene with Wallis. The producer thought Joshua should decide to carry on where his father left off, instead of hunting for his baseball glove, as Hammett had it.

Hammett, however, objected to Teck's bringing on the showdown. "Shumlin agrees with you and Hellman with me," he wrote Wallis. "So we decided to try it my way first." Ever mindful of his feelings, Lily would not take anyone's part against him. She agreed that Kurt should bring on the denouement himself. Hammett was willing to add a scene in which Joshua decides to join the resistance.

After five more weeks, Hammett had sent Wallis only twenty-two pages. Another week passed. Only six more pages reached Hollywood. Knowing Lillian would not act against Dash, Wallis considered hiring another writer. "Would suggest you talk to Shumlin and let him handle Hammett," Wallis scrawled at the bottom of a March 13 letter to Jacob Wilk, a Warners employee in New York he enlisted to give Hammett "a gentle goosing." Meanwhile in Hollywood, Jack Warner urged Wallis to wait one more week "before putting the screws on Dashiell Hammett." Even when Hammett sent nineteen more pages with a note: "the complete job will be in your hands on schedule," Wallis remained skeptical.

After St. Clair McKelway's treason, Lily fled to Nassau. Shumlin took over as go-between, praising Hammett's handling of the embassy scene. But Hammett had hurt his back, which "set him back a couple of days," he reported to Wallis stalling for time. Shumlin was kindly and protective, treating Dash as a family member. "I know that Dash has kept steadily at the story," he reassured Wallis. "He has hardly gone away from the house in the country where he is living and working."

Finally Hammett wired Wallis: "If I don't break a leg will finish script this week." It was April 13. "Done," Hammett wired Wallis on April 23. "Wonderful. Thanks," a relieved Wallis wired back.

Even as he wanted Lillian out in Hollywood at once for the "polishing job," Wallis tried to get out of paying her expenses. "Don't indicate that we expect to pay expenses as I have feeling Hellman would like to be here with Shumlin while picture being prepared," he wired Wilk. Lillian's most difficult task, however, was neither circumventing Wallis' petty financial chicanery nor even getting Sam Goldwyn's permission to work on the script, since she was still under contract. Rather, it was outsmarting the Hays office.

Hammett had censored himself, keeping Kurt's politics vague, removing Lillian's stage reference to Karl Marx. Kurt Muller could be given no connection to the Communist movement. His politics had to be exclusively antifascist. But there were still objections.

Predictably, Joseph I. Breen, Hays's right-hand man, came back with opposition to Muller's unpunished murder of Teck. No matter that Teck was a fascist, the murder rendered the film "unacceptable." There was also "suggestive" dialogue between young David and Teck's wife, Marthe, and a "display of liquor and drinking . . . not necessary to either plot or characterization." "Please avoid," a worried Breen wrote Jack Warner, "any showing of, or reference to, a toilet."

Breen insisted Kurt could kill Teck only if it is clear he would have been assassinated had Teck remained free to report him. But Kurt had to be killed by the Nazis anyway. He could not "go off scot-free" even for murdering a Nazi.

By 1942 Lily had long been a she-Hammett, knowing that to outsmart the world, you had to take the offensive posture. First, she threatened that should Breen and his boss, Will Hays, persist in demanding that Kurt be punished, she would write a piece about Hays office censorship. Then she wrote a scathing letter to Breen. It was "scandalous," she said with full indignation, that "we, who are a country at war with Nazis, need to say that a man must himself be killed if he kills a Nazi." It was as if "any of our soldiers who kills a German must pay for the killing with his own life." It was "immoral thinking," "dangerous doctrine," and "deeply shocking."

As for the adultery between David Farrelly and Marthe, the woman was married to "a Nazi and a villain." Lily easily dismissed the problem of the liquor cabinet: "it is not drinking to have a drink." She would not dignify Breen's uneasiness with the toilet by even referring to it.

Fearing that "Miss Hellman . . . will attempt to 'try the case in the newspapers,'" the Hays office backed down on every one of its objections. A woman alone in Hollywood, Lily drew on feistiness and courage, her sense of justice, her belief in her work.

More difficult was the editing and rewriting she had to do on Hammett's self-indulgent, loose, and baggy script. Lily kept silent, but Kober confided to his diary: "I suspect that Lil has changed a lot of stuff Dash put in movie version of play." In 1952 she was to tell the House Un-American Activities Committee that she had "edited" his screenplay. In fact, she made more changes on his work than he had done on all her plays put together. Uneasy with how extensively she had to amend his work, which revealed the tendentious writing of a man no longer a writer, she said much later, "He did it as a favor to me. He wasn't crazy about doing it . . . it certainly was very difficult; at times I was very angry . . . and he, I guess, must have been quite angry as well. But we worked it out." About the specifics she revealed nothing.

Later they inscribed copies of the published version of *Watch on the Rhine* to each other. "To Lillian Hellman from an ardent but critical reader—D.H.," he wrote cryptically. "For Dash, who knew all about it and knows it comes with love, Lily," was her more effusive and heartfelt rejoinder.

That May 1942, despite talk about her and Dash going to Hollywood together, Lily traveled alone. Settled at the luxurious Beverly Hills Hotel, she did eighty pages of rewriting in one week. The enormous task took her only a month. Hammett's script, handwritten in pencil, was dated April 23; Hellman's typewritten version was dated May 20, and read: "Screen Play by Lillian Hellman." The film's actual credits read: "Screen Play by Dashiell Hammett, Additional Scenes and Dialogue by Lillian Hellman." It was more than generous. In these years she was as careful of his fragile ego as of his fragile health.

Dashiell Hammett's screenplay for *Watch on the Rhine* so lacked the rigor of his early novels that he seemed a different writer entirely. As writers, they had by now completely exchanged roles. Just as once he had urged her to cut excess, she now had to do that for him. He was no longer her "cool teacher," but her pale shadow.

Nor, although he had worked in films too, could he render the play cinematic. Lillian eliminated many of his cuts, substituting pans within a long take, the style Orson Welles a year earlier had brought to *Citizen Kane,* revolutionizing the language of the American film. Hammett was clearly out of touch.

Dashiell Hammett's plodding, languorous script for *Watch on the Rhine* reflects the indolent mood of a writer who believes he has all the time in the world. The emotional nihilism that suffused his life had led him to sentimental writing, interminable scenes, sententious speechmaking, and flabby dialogue. David Farrelly says of his returning sister Sara, the heroine, that he is "afraid she won't like me, I guess." Hammett felt compelled to add, "I always liked her so awfully much." Hammett has Kurt tell Sara, "And you are happy? That is good." She replies, "Happy? That's too little a word. And what are you?" Kurt now answers, "I am happy. That is what a vacation is for." Lily retained a scant one line. Kurt tells Sara, "Your face is most happy." She even removed vestiges of Hammett's hard-boiled detective story diction. Hammett calls the baby belonging to an Italian couple traveling on the same train a "little cut-throat." Lily deleted this.

Absent from Hammett's work is a sense of pacing, of narrative drive. With an urgency that had once been so vital a part of *his* prose, Lillian began at once to crosscut scenes of the Farrelly family household with those of the Muller family en route by train to Washington, the better to move the action forward.

Nowhere does Hammett's new insecurity as a writer become more obvious than in that long train sequence which opens the film, and which was entirely his idea. Hammett's substitution of Communist Party life for writing is reflected in this sequence in uncharacteristic polemicizing about the rich and poor. The youngest Muller child, Bodo, is shocked to discover so much poverty. "Perhaps it is my fault," precocious Bodo says in Hammett's script, "that when you talked about houses in the United States of America I did not imagine them to be as those I have seen from this train." Hammett had his mother, Sara, add, "There are too many houses like that here." Lillian cut the entire exchange.

Hammett also had Bodo say, "I know that chauvinism is wrong." Lily cut that too. Nor was she easy with Hammett's Popular Front rhetoric, paeans to American history that Hammett included in a spoken catalogue of the tourist attractions of Washington, D.C. Lily expunged it all.

Hammett had written a long confessional speech for an Italian passenger. It began: "I know it's wrong to sometimes be ashamed of being Italian. It's just sometimes it gets me, see—sometimes when they do those things. . . ." Hammett's attack on American chauvinism continues over three pages: "But all peoples, I think, have had their black times, when their worst men lead them—and when all but the worst have shame that they are of the same race . . . but that shame—it is no good. It is too easy. It is not of any value. You have shame—you try to forget. You try to shut your eyes to what gives you shame. Or you say you can do nothing about it. Or you tell yourselves those things are not so evil."

The speech reflects not only Hammett's new self-indulgence as a writer but his own shame at no longer writing, no less than his aversion to facing himself, which had led him into so extreme an alcoholism. Cutting all this autobiography to the bone, Lily wrote one succinct summary line for the Italian's scene: "Hitler alone is not what is wrong." Her clarity is what one would have expected of Hammett. But by the time World War II was upon them, she had imbibed all the craft he had to offer. As a writer, she had become him—and more.

Wedded to the unwieldy notion of the train as melting pot and microcosm for America, Hammett couldn't find his way out of the sequence. Compulsively, he added a gum-chewing Armenian and a blond Scandinavian in a weather-stained coat. Hammett has Kurt further explain that it is not only Hitler and Nazism that are wrong, "but all fascist doing and thinking, by no matter what name you call it; and all the things that bring it into existence."

Working without a plan, Hammett committed the error of prematurely mentioning the underground leader Max Freidank, captured back in Germany, whose imprisonment will be the impetus for the film's culminating drama. He is a "mensch," Kurt says of Freidank, as Hammett so enjoyed exercising the Yiddish words he picked up from Lillian and her friends. "He is not so big when you look at him first—but you will hear," Kurt says. Coming so early in the film, the description of Freidank lacks point.

Lily applied her blue pencil. She cut the early references to Freidank and concluded the train sequence with an exchange one would have expected of Hammett before she had assumed his identity.

"What do you do? I mean, what's your trade?" the Italian asks Kurt Muller.

"I? I fight against Fascism. That is my trade," Kurt says succinctly in a powerful example of the she-Hammett's writing.

Ignoring dramatic imperatives, writing as if the denouement might just as well wait, Hammett indulged himself in biographical satire of Lily's foibles through the character of Sara's mother, Fanny Farrelly. He has Fanny reply in response to her servant Joseph's complaint about an unnecessary bell, "That's what I put it there for. I like to disturb folks." This was his picture of Lily. Dash also has Fanny assume a Lillianesque sense of her own importance. The servant Anise tells Fanny people may be giving their Romanian guests credit because "tradesmen take into consideration that they are guests of Madame Joshua Farrelly." So Dash himself often called Lily "madame." Lily added a "perhaps" to the revision.

Dash had long been amused by Lily's penchant for rearranging the furniture at Hardscrabble Farm, a trait he imparted to Fanny. Lily removed it. He also laughed at Lily's endless curiosity and has Fanny say of her servant, "It's true, you're a snooper. I rather admire it. It shows an interest in life." So he allowed Lily to defend herself. In Hammett's script, Fanny later asks her husband's former law partner to bring his wife to dinner, then mutters under her breath, "Not soon—in about five or six years." Irrelevant to the plot, it was Dash's mocking joke about Lily's aversion to other women. Dash made Fanny a silly woman purely to ridicule Lily's more exasperating traits. In her revision, Lily turned Fanny into a serious person.

Even in the type of scene which had once been Hammett's forte, where violence lurks beneath the surface of everyday life, Hammett falters. To a scene between Teck and his wife, Marthe, which ends with Teck saying, "I think not. I would not like that," Hammett felt compelled to add, "Do not make any arrangements, Marthe. I may not allow you to carry them through." Lillian cut the old-fashioned melodramatic threat and ended the confrontation with "I think not."

Hammett suffused his script with references to his favorite sport, baseball. He has Sara remember how she played baseball as a child: "I was pretty good at it for a girl—at least that's the way I remember it." It was as if Hammett has lost the old rhythm of his prose. Lily cut, although baseball remains an emblem of Americanism in this patriotic 1942 work. However, Lily's quasi-Marxist line spoken by the wise child Bodo—"Baseball players are among the most exploited people in this country"—never made it to the final cut.

It had been Lillian's idea for the film to eliminate Fanny's upholsterer and substitute a rich, idle friend named Mellie. But she still had to cut the scene Hammett wrote for Mellie by pages. Hammett was literal in his depiction of their shopping trip, guiding them through a jewelry shop, a department store, and a candy emporium. Lily simply put the women in Mellie's limousine and surrounded them with their purchases. Hammett had also included byplay about Mellie's wearing unbecoming organdie dresses, a hidden reference to Lily and her frilly evening costumes. Lillian dealt with the motif in one sharp line Fanny directs to Mellie: "I never understood why you need so many evening dresses. Do you lead a secret life—at your age?"

In another of his poor dramatic decisions, Hammett had Fanny get rid of Mellie and then ride off home in her friend's limousine. Granting Fanny more spunk, less passivity, Lily had Fanny leave Mellie behind in the car with the packages. Fanny jumps out to evade her gossiping friend and heads on foot for her son David's office. Hammett went on to add ponderous details of office business. Lily saw that the plot had better return quickly to the Teck-Muller conflict. Teck isn't "good-natured" at all, Fanny says, drawing us back to the central theme.

It was Lily, not Dash, who made drama of the political conflict between fascist and antifascist. Hammett had Teck ask about Muller, "Is he a Jew?" But Lillian added a discussion about refugees in which David demands of Teck, who, disingenuously, has called himself a refugee from Europe, "From what Europe?" Teck answers, too casually, "Just Europe." All the pointed moments were hers.

Far the better dramatist now, Lily knew that she had to keep the battle between fascist Teck and antifascist Muller in the foreground. Hammett became lost in a comic bathroom scene in which the two Muller sons discover the wonders of American plumbing, hence the Hays office alarm about an on-screen toilet. Delaying in bringing protagonist and antagonist together, Hammett had followed the bathroom scene with another of his longueurs, a scene between Babette, the Muller daughter, and the servant, Anise, who rambles on about how she brushed Sara's hair when she was a child. In her revision Lillian moved rapidly into a quarrel between Teck and his disaffected wife, Marthe. "Let these people alone," Marthe tells him. At this moment Lillian has Kurt look out the window and spy Teck on the lawn.

Neither Hellman nor Hammett wrote credible love scenes. But Lily did better. Kurt spies Sara in her new dress. In Hammett's version, Kurt tells his wife, "Mostly now I think of beauty, I think, m-m-m, looks pretty good. Maybe I could make an impression on her." Sara laughs and they kiss. In Lillian's rewrite, Kurt says, "It makes you have tears. It also makes me have tears." Hammett had closed the scene on "I think only with pride how beautiful is my Sara." Lily was not afraid to continue the scene with Sara in Kurt's arms. Lily's Kurt says, "If you had not married me so many years ago, would you have married me today? I am so tired and so shabby and you are so. . . ." Sara adds, reflecting Lily's own autobiographical message to the elusive Hammett, "I would have married you any day in my life."

It was only after the romantic scene between Kurt and Sara that Hammett got around to introducing Kurt and Teck to each other. Then, postponing the substantive moment yet again, Hammett interpolated a lengthy kitchen scene in which servants debate the similarities between doughnuts and partridges. It was the very "blackamoor chit-chat" for which Dash had chastised Lily in her early draft of *The Little Foxes*.

So little concerned was Hammett with the gathering action that he even included a shot of a page of one of the dead Joshua Farrelly's books: "There is in our social organizations an institutional inertia, and in our social philosophies a tradition of rigidity. Unless there is a speeding up of social invention or a slowing down of mechanical invention, grave maladjustments are certain to result." Even Hammett must have known the moment was hopelessly didactic; he has little Bodo yawn and turn the page. If Hammett had forgotten that he was writing a film rather than a political pamphlet, Lily had not. She cut it all. A similar moment occurs in Hammett's montage of newspaper headlines, which include "Norman Thomas Again Head of Socialist Ticket." That shot may well have reflected Hammett's otherwise unacknowledged skepticism about the Communist Party's insistence that Communists support only Roosevelt and the Democratic Party.

Lily told people that Hammett's finest additions to her play were the scenes at the German embassy. There was no German embassy scene or card-playing scene in the play, she kept reminding her friends. "He's put in one scene that I'd have given anything to have written. Do you remember the villain talking about a poker party in the German embassy? Well, he's written in that poker party. And it's marvelous." Keeping silent about how much revision she had to do, Lily awarded Dash whatever credit she could.

Indeed, in the scene at the Germany embassy, Hammett did well with the dialogue between the Nazis and their cohorts. One calls another a pale man, wondering whether he is a member of the secret police: "Perhaps he's even writing a book." Hammett had one of them describe Hitler as a "funny Leader with a funny mustache. His name used to be Schicklgruber and he was a paper-hanger. That, too, is funny, yes. And we have divided the world into two parts. Those like you [Teck] who want to work for us. And those who lie awake trembling and hating us because they are afraid of us." All this is Hammett at his best.

Yet Lillian's lines remained the stronger. "Our Herr Hitler violates their morality in the morning, but by evening they have recovered and are here in the Embassy for dinner," she wrote. It was Lily who brought Teck back into focus as the commanding Nazi guesses that "at the moment you are a man who has nothing to sell." It was Lily who pulled even Hammett's best scene together.

Hammett had omitted these lines from the play: "Anger is protest. And so you must direct it to the proper channels and then harness it for the good of other men." Lillian returned the concept, rendering it as film dialogue. Bodo tells his mother: "You must not get angry. Anger is protest and should only be used for the good of one's fellow men." Hammett, however, drew the important distinction between justifiable and mindless violence. Bodo argues that while "it is not right to shoot upon people," neither "is it right to grow fat on poor people." In a play designed to persuade Americans of the inevitability of the coming war, the line expresses the film's wholehearted endorsement of Kurt Muller's murder of the fascist Teck.

Lillian tightened the denouement, linking Kurt Muller's return to Germany with the plan to gain resistance leader Max Freidank's freedom. Removing still more of Hammett's sententious philosophizing ("We don't like to remember, do we, that they came in on the shoulders of some of the most powerful men in the world"), she brings the action to a swift climax. Lillian alone utilized the money in the Farrelly house safe as the means of getting rid of Teck. Hammett deployed the money only to reveal David's conversion to the cause; he offers it to Kurt as the Farrelly contribution to the struggle against fascism. Lillian's idea was far more dramatic.

In the final confrontation between Kurt and Teck, Kurt tells the Nazi, "Please do not describe me to myself again." In Hammett's ponderous scene, Kurt takes the time to add another long speech, ending, "Well, Count de Brancovis [Teck], where has this led us?" More follows: "There are those who give the orders, then there are those who are half in half hoping to come in. They are made to do the dishes, clean the boots. Frequently they come in high places and wish now only to survive." Lillian cut everything that slowed the pace.

Hammett wrote instructions for the murder scene, which Lillian at once excised ("The ensuing battle should be short but vicious. Kurt must make it brief because he is sick—making up in sudden violence what he lacks in stamina"). It was as if Hammett were, again, writing about his own condition. Lily also cut more dialogue. Dash wrote: "If fascists would raise us in darkness they should not be surprised that we grow to see like cats . . . and you silly trifling fool—with your shabby debts. . . ." Lily condensed: "You are a fool. You play with men's lives in order to have money to live in worthlessness."

The most Hammett-like line, the one which closes this crucial scene, was written not by Dash, but by Lily. Kurt says, "I have seen many men die. I give you advice. It is easier without words. They will not now do you good. You will be better without them." That most silent of men had so given over his writing enterprise to the she-Hammett that she wrote as if she were the silent man herself. It was Dash, however, who wrote Kurt's farewell to his sons, not in the original play: "When the time comes train yourself in mind and body. Your day is not so distant . . . the world goes bad."

The stage play's last line had gone to Fanny, addressing her son, David: "I'm not put together with flour paste. And neither are you—I am happy to learn." Neither Hammett nor Hellman was satisfied with that for the film. Hammett took us to a shabbily furnished room in an unspecified German city where Kurt, "worn and gaunt," sits at a table straightening a pile of German money he hopes to use to free Max. He places his Luger on top of the pile.

Two months have passed. Kurt waits to discover whether he will be able to free Max or will join him in prison. With the sound of two pairs of heavy boots, it remains unclear whether the Germans have come to accept the bribe or to arrest Kurt Muller. Lily kept Dash's inconclusive scene in Germany, but it never made the final cut. A dissolve returns us to the Farrelly living room.

After a tendentious scene in which the children babble in dou-bletalk, Hammett and Hellman, both following Hal Wallis' suggestion, close on a shot of Joshua, who holds a map and a steamship folder. He is about to join his father and the anti-Nazi resistance. As American wartime films so often expressed the need for people to join the good fight, Lily and Dash collaborated on a film in which mother must part with son for the greater good of humankind.

By the time the film version of *Watch on the Rhine* opened in September 1943, *New Masses* had forgiven Lillian for the apostasy of writing an antifascist work during the period of the Hitler-Stalin pact. The adaptation of a play which they had once angrily condemned was praised as an "artistic expression of the ideals and aspirations of the best people in our time—the fighters in the ranks of anti-fascism."

PART FIVE

Dash at War,
Lily at Home

13

The Woman Alone

"Woman pursuing can be oppressive."

LILLIAN HELLMAN, *DIARY*

I n March 1942, in the midst of writing his screenplay for *Watch on the Rhine,* Hammett returned his $5,000 advance to Bennett Cerf. For several years he had been reassuring Cerf, who hoped to publish in the fall of 1939, that he was "plugging away at" a new novel. When no manuscript was forthcoming, Cerf had pursued him. "A. No, I'm not drunk," Hammett replied. "B. No, I'm not on my way to Hollywood. C. No, I never decided to work on something else." Now Hammett admitted defeat. Officially, he would no longer pretend that he was a writer.

Unable to write himself, he remained capable of sporadic attention to Lily's work. At five in the morning one summer Sunday in 1942 at Hardscrabble Farm, Jerome Weidman tiptoed down to the kitchen to make coffee. The voices he heard in the living room were those of Lily and Dash arguing about a problem in the screenplay of Lily's latest effort, *The North Star.* To Weidman, so "cold, hard, impersonal" were their tones that they might have been a "couple of workmen calling off measurements to each other as they prepared to cover a basement floor with linoleum."

Dash made a suggestion. The she-Hammett was skeptical, maintaining that her way was better. Hammett told her she was rejecting his suggestion for the wrong reasons. She must listen again. No, Lillian persisted. Her firmness, Weidman thought, was "exactly like his." In matters of writing Hammett no longer possessed his former authority with Lillian Hellman.

Well aware of how profoundly depressed he was over his inability to write, Lily had taken to praising Dash to others. She covered for him and proclaimed his continued superiority as a writer. Later that same Sunday, in the kitchen, Weidman solicited some Hollywood gossip. Lily seized one more opportunity to elevate Hammett. "Dash never lies about Orson Welles," Lily insisted. Whether out of her own perpetual insecurity or her desire to save face for him, she maintained that she was unable to write a screenplay without the help of Dashiell Hammett.

"I do the scene the way I hear the people talking in my head," Lillian told Weidman. "Then Dash puts in the dissolves and the fades and the jump cuts and all the rest of that Hollywood shit." Weidman professed many years later in his memoir to remember Lily's words. But just as there could have been no "jump cuts," a technique of the French New Wave of the 1960s, in a 1942 script, so the notion that Hammett was still the master educating his pupil had ceased to be true. Far from having exhausted himself giving away his craft to her, Hammett had, rather, reached a dead end as a writer.

One night in September 1942 Dash disappeared. Several days passed. Lily assumed he was on one of his drunks and had gone whoring in Harlem. Finally, Dash telephoned. He had enlisted in the Army, he announced. It was a fait accompli.

Dashiell Hammett had discovered one more way of tormenting Lily, of demonstrating that she had no real claim on him. On September 17, the day he enlisted, the address he gave the Army as his residence was not his Ninth Street abode, the Plaza Hotel, Hardscrabble Farm, or Lily's uptown apartment. The address Dash listed was that of Jose, his divorced wife in California. The message was to Lily, not to Jose. He also wrote that he was a divorced man, for all of Jose's later claims that their Mexican divorce was invalid.

Hammett enlisted in the Army in the aftermath of his admission to Random House that he would not be writing a novel for them anytime soon and in the wake of Lily's extensive rewrite of the script for *Watch on the Rhine*. In their complex interaction, his need for her far transcended her need for him. It was a dependence he found intolerable, and he had discovered another way to escape it.

For nearly a decade he had found a substitute for writing in Party activity. The Party was encouraging the war effort now that the United

States and that country Lily called "the Motherland" were allies against Hitler. Far from being an anomalous choice for Dashiell Hammett, despite his age and uncertain health, the Army seemed his only option.

"You can't go," Lily pouted at dinner one night as Dash awaited one more physical. She had begun a new play, even as *The North Star* remained in need of revision. "Who's going to tell me to tear up each version?" Lily demanded, concerning the play that was to become *The Searching Wind*. "Who's going to tell me it's no good?"

Dash acquiesced in the fiction that his presence was necessary to her writing.

"You send it to me," Dash told her. "I'll be somewhere."

"You'll be in a hospital," Lily countered. "How can you train with men twenty years younger than you are? You won't even stay in the hospital very long, because they'll find out you're crazy and you'll be in a loony bin." At nearly six feet two inches tall, while weighing a scant 141 pounds, Dash was an unlikely recruit.

"Don't worry about me," Dash told her. "Just take my word for it. The day I enlisted in the Army was the happiest day of my life."

"Well, it wasn't the happiest day of mine," Lily retorted. Hammett laughed. Overhearing all this, Jerome Weidman concluded she took his enlisting as a matter of her personal deprivation.

Hammett thought he'd better put on some weight before the Army physical. He spent three days at Hardscrabble Farm making himself, as Lily put it, "almost sick with milk and pudding and potatoes, trying to gain a pound." Sympathetic to his need for some center to his life, she found him "touching about it, like a child."

"I hope to God they take him," she wrote the Kobers. "I never saw anybody want anything so much. I don't know if they will, he must be badly underweight for one thing, but it means so much to him that I am praying for him."

At Fort Monmouth, New Jersey, the Army doctor decided to allow Dashiell Hammett into the armed forces. He called Dash "the tall, spare American type that can stand anything." Later Dash made a joke of the examination. He had told the doctor he had been underweight when he had enlisted in the last war and they had still let him in.

"All right, then," Dash quoted the doctor. "We'll let you in this time. But don't come back still underweight during the next war and expect to get in!"

Seductively apologizing, chanting, "Hammett's yellow! Hammett's yellow!" Dash left Lily the task of packing up his Hardscrabble possessions. Like a partner in an old marriage, she was soon to become his banker and his shopper. He gave her his Abercrombie credit card, and began to send precise instructions. One of Lily's first assignments was to purchase a pair of "low brown shoes . . . the size is ten and one-half, C, and I'd like the plainest pair they have, no straps or other nonsense and either tipless toes, or very plain tips."

Dash, characteristically, spent his last night as a civilian not with Lily, but at a bar on Charles Street in Manhattan with another woman. They were joined by Franklin Folsom, still executive secretary of the League of American Writers. When Folsom expressed his amazement that Dash had been accepted by the Army doctors, Dash replied, "I've had so many X-rays of my chest that I know how to stand in front of the camera so that the scars on my lungs are hidden." Folsom wondered whether Dash might not have used the money he gave away so freely to bribe an X-ray technician into overlooking his TB lesions.

Folsom was attempting to raise money for a Win the War Writers Congress. Instantly Hammett wrote out a check for one thousand dollars. He was proud, Hammett said drunkenly, to be able to write the check without his hand shaking. The Win the War Writers Congress was never held, but Hammett's money was not returned.

Hammett's companion that night was an attractive woman in her forties. Their talk was highly erotic. Hammett said he had a formula for getting rid of a woman he didn't want to take to bed. He would tell her he had a different venereal disease from the one she had, making sex between them impossible.

Dash adjusted quickly to life at Fort Monmouth. He enjoyed the Army, eating, he claimed, "like a wolf," and sleeping "like a log." He favored the company of unpretentious people and was friendly with lowly recruits. A young lieutenant came bumbling up to him one day and thanked him because, he said, Hammett's books had "given him back his self-respect at a time when he had got himself in a very bad hole."

"That's probably the nicest thing anybody could say to a writer," Dash told him.

A soldier named Robert Boltwood quoted a passage from the Bible to Dash one night. Dash bet Lily fifty dollars that she could not identify it. Boltwood wound up with a copy of *The Complete Dashiell Hammett*, inscribed: "With thanks for having made my days less empty." Boltwood also received a copy of Lillian's *Four Plays* with the admonition: "It is more profitable for you to read the Bible."

Lily reported to Kober that Dash hoped to be "in the African landing force." She remained skeptical—and fearful. "I think it's going to be harder than he realizes, but that's his business and he must have known about it from the last time." Maternal, she worried about his health. He indulged her, promising to "bundle up in great coat and muffler . . . woolen socks and gloves" and to return early from a dinner out in Red Bank. But soon on weekends he was arranging for one of the soldiers to drive him to his favorite Harlem whorehouse, where he would remain until Sunday night. Lily did not hear from him then.

Although they had long ceased to be lovers, Lily felt bereft without him at Hardscrabble Farm. "I've been lonely here," she admitted to Kober, "but it's better here and better to be lonely here." Hammett's defection depressed her. "I have five cows," she wrote Kober, "three pregnant; everything here is pregnant, except me, and I wish I was." Hammett's departure was also exacerbated by her final rupture with Herman Shumlin.

After two very bad days, Lily decided she could "no longer manage it. In some strange way, the fights and the confusions and the foolishness now seem to me a step backwards, and a step so far backwards that I no longer want to chance it." Kober had hoped Herman would ask Lily to marry him; Kober believed Shumlin would "never be happy with anyone else or at least not as happy as with Lil."

Yet over the past year their relationship had deteriorated badly. "I know it isn't right now," Lily wrote Kober, "and it is, in its way, good to know the truth." Dash, who had never approved of this alliance, called Herman and Lillian "as a pair . . . a closed book." Later Dash would tell Lily, "You never made any recognizable pattern for me . . . I never could see *what* sense you made or *whether* you made any." Clearly Lillian had never told him of Shumlin's exciting sexuality.

In December, Lily went to Hollywood to work on *The North Star.* "I know you're gone," Dash wrote her, "but I suppose I'll first really miss you when I can't phone you in the morning. Maybe I'll phone anyway just to keep my hand in." He closed one of these letters: "I love a girl like you."

Lily dreaded going to Hollywood to tangle with Goldwyn and director Lewis Milestone over *The North Star.* A cigarette in one hand, a drink in the other, she went off to do battle. Hal Wallis took her to see *This Is the Army.* "I liked him, liked the show fairly well, and had a pleasant evening," Lily confided to Kober.

One day Lily encountered former Warner story editor Irene Lee, now working for Goldwyn. Lily drew herself up in hauteur worthy of Queen Victoria.

"It has been brought to my attention that you said . . . ," Lillian began. Hal Wallis had confided in Lee that Lily was in hot sexual pursuit of him but he was not interested, and Lee had told Kober. Kober, of course, had reported it all to Lillian.

"I will not tolerate this," Lillian told Lee.

"Lillian, I will say what I want, when I want, and how I want," Lee replied. "And you can do whatever you wish about it." She never had any difficulty with Lillian Hellman after that.

As soon as she was out of his ken, Dash missed Lily. She did not write to him from California. "You're a low character," he chastised her. He hated the idea of her being out there. "Haven't you been out in that place long enough?" he complained on January 8. "Are you afraid to come home or something? Have you fallen in love with an actor? Have you lost your return ticket? Won't Irene Lee let you leave yet?"

He couldn't even bring himself to spend a weekend in her absence at Hardscrabble Farm. After one of his nights at "21," he stayed over at her New York apartment. "It is nice waking up there Sunday mornings," he reported, "as you could find out for yourself if you only gave it a trial. Maybe I can show you how to do it." The old seductive tones returned. But as his finding it "awfully nice" to wake up in her New York apartment on a Sunday morning seemed too close to dependency and domestic commitment, Hammett turned it into a joke: "In some ways it's more comfortable than the barracks."

Far from having fallen in love with an actor, in Hollywood Lillian was deep in conflict with Milestone. Appalled by the alterations he made in her script, she accused him of "disrespect." Lillian had sent Milestone a four-page single-spaced letter outlining her objections to his changes even before she went out to California. There was no notion of the auteur theory or cult of the director in those days, certainly not for Lillian Hellman, who demanded prerogatives as the screenwriter. "What I have to say will not be altered," Lillian had declared before she left for the coast. When Goldwyn sent her a telegram, "I LOVE YOU TOO MUCH TO DO ANYTHING YOU FEEL SO STRONGLY AGAINST," Lillian had replied, "AND I LOVE YOU TOO MUCH TO TELL YOU ABOUT IT IN A TELEGRAM."

Lillian had her new secretary, Nancy Bragdon, send a copy of the script of *The North Star* to Dash at Fort Monmouth. "Dear cutie and good writer," Dash wrote, "last night I read the script and I kind of guess it's kind of all right." This was as much praise as he could muster for this least credible of all her screen efforts. "Maybe you're going to have to cut the early parts a little—as who doesn't . . . ," he had to admit, "but you've done what you set out to do, and what's wrong with that? The desired documentary effect comes over nicely. It's nice and warm and human and moving. And so are you." He closed that evasive letter: "Love, A Rookie."

If what she required was moral support, Dash was glad to supply that. But no longer would he scrutinize a text with the attention he had brought to his reading of *The Little Foxes*. He no longer possessed either the stake or the intense interest he had in her earlier work. As her revisions of his script for *Watch on the Rhine* had made apparent to both of them, he had little more to teach her about screenwriting.

Before she had left for California, Lillian had her lawyer, Wolf Schwabacher, a close friend of Muriel Gardiner, the hidden model for "Julia," negotiate her expenses with Samuel Goldwyn. She stalled for three more weeks, and then she left.

Soon Lily was seated in a Goldwyn screening room watching a rough cut of *The North Star*. Forty minutes into the screening, Lily began to cry.

"Shut up, shut up, shut up," Goldwyn yelled. "How dare you cry!"

"Don't tell me when to cry!" Lily retorted. "You've turned it into junk."

Whatever saving graces of realism she had included in this preposterous story of a Soviet village suffering a Nazi invasion and defending itself with a little guerrilla band of neighbors, they were now gone. Mengele-like doctors drain the blood of innocent and pure Soviet children in a preposterous scene. "No people in the world were ever as happy or as clean as they are in *The North Star*," Lily told Goldwyn. "And I don't have to remind you that I had nothing to do with that." In that rough cut, she even discovered nail polish on the toes of one of the Soviet girls. "Is this an oversight or a new joke?" Lily demanded.

Never a passive victim, the she-Hammett at once contacted the Screen Writers Guild in an attempt to remove her name from the advertisements of *The North Star*. Hammett kept his distance throughout her struggle with Goldwyn, and only late in 1943 did he offer her some sympathy over "what they've done to *The North Star*." He used the moment to lecture her in the old, now obsolete way.

"*Now* you know about Hollywood," Dash said unnecessarily. She should take comfort, he told her, in the importance of what the picture argues, "however bitched up." He had no problem with the sentimental, pro-Soviet politics of *The North Star*, and because the film so obviously expressed his own political persuasions, Lily dedicated it to him. Appalled, Goldwyn later said, "When Stalin got depressed, he ran that picture." The New York *Mirror*, a Hearst paper, wrote that "had Stalin paid for the making of this film, it could not have been more offensive to American audiences." However, such was Lillian Hellman's standing in Hollywood in those days, and so powerful were the Party people in the industry, that she was nominated for an Academy Award for best original screenplay.

While Dash was writing her letters signed "Graybeard" and "Whitey," suggesting his relief that nothing should be asked of him either as a writer or as a man, Lily was attempting to break free of her contract with Goldwyn. She refused a film called *Bid for Happiness*, inspiring Goldwyn to insist that she do some other film for him. Lily then accused Goldwyn of attempting "to trick me and to injure me," since *Bid for Happiness* had been "junk."

"I hope you paid for it in Confederate money," Lily told him.

Lily decided to offer Goldwyn $10,000 for her contract. "I can't afford much more than that," she fibbed. She threatened him with a lawsuit on the ground that *Bid for Happiness* had not been a proper submission. Not one to be bullied, Goldwyn insisted on $50,000 in exchange for her freedom. They settled on $27,500 as Schwabacher completed the negotiations. Then Lily went on to squabble with Schwabacher about his bills.

Still Lily was not writing to Dash. "There was no letter from you at noon," he wrote accusingly on January 13. "Now isn't that a pretty way to act? It would serve you right if I didn't even look to see if I had any mail this afternoon."

Lily was due to return from California on January 26. "I'll put coins in phones like mad all day until I get hold of you," Dash promised. "Don't go away from the phone!" Upon Lily's return, Maggie Kober reported to Dash that she had looked "more radiant" than Maggie had ever seen her. "Keep some of that radiance for me Monday night," Dash said when he was about to see Lily at last.

On the following Wednesday, he asked her if she would be "so kindly" as to "have a little just-you-and-me dinner at 5 East 82nd Street," her new address. He signed that letter "Love, the Ancient Warrior." From the Hardscrabble years on, he preferred that it be just the two of them; it was she who needed the world, not he, and she who had inadvertently ended their sexual relationship by refusing him just one of those "you-and-me" evenings.

Not that Dash had turned celibate by choice. In January and in March 1943 there are records of his having checked into the Plaza Hotel, where he entertained women beyond Lillian's scrutinizing eye. He reminded Lily often that he remained sexually free. Even in a letter devoted to instructions about setting turtle traps he added that he was going to New York for a ball game—and to see if any old friends had daughters. It was, however, mostly bravado. By now Dashiell Hammett had not much more use for his sexual freedom than he had for his writing craft.

Lily took up with the rich real estate heir George Backer, soon to be the ex-husband of Dorothy Schiff, of whose family newspaper, the New

York *Post,* he was president until their breakup in 1942. The short, curly-haired Backer was immensely charming, and romantic-looking, with his dark hair and hazel eyes. He was addicted to elegant English tailoring, a dandy like Dash. He was also a popular man-about-town and was rich enough to dine with movie stars. Lillian described Backer as a man "of whom I am very fond. But he is mixed up." She had to add, "I don't have to say that—I undoubtedly wouldn't be having dinner with him if he wasn't." It was for her a familiar story. Lily, the insecure little girl who had become the insecure woman, repeatedly pursued men who could not love her, endlessly recapitulating her early childhood pain.

One night, after sex, as he lay back in bed with a cigarette, Backer noticed that Lillian was no longer in the room. That was all right with him. He continued to smoke his cigarette. Soon he began to think about getting dressed and going home.

Suddenly Lillian appeared in the doorway. Lillian threw him a bathrobe. "Supper is served!" she announced. It was now five hours since they had eaten. Backer decided he wouldn't mind having something to eat. He donned the bathrobe and entered Lily's elegant dining room. There he sat down to what he was to call the best meal of his life.

Later Backer summed it up: whatever you say about Lillian, there was no woman like her. He spoke of how "unbelievably seductive" she had been, and how he had "one of the damnedest breakfasts I've ever had in my life." Another lover reported that getting into bed had been slightly difficult because he did not find her sexually attractive. But once the lights were out, "it was just unbelievable . . . anything went . . . anything . . . it was terrific!"

As they continued together during the war, Lillian considered whether she might not marry George Backer. He was rich and prominent. Why not marry George Backer? He sensed her need, however, became frightened, and fled.

Such experiences made Lily bitter. After Backer remarried in 1945, his new wife a Macy's heiress, Lily meanspiritedly took to telling a nasty story about him and his first wife, Dolly Schiff. Backer and Dolly had arrived at Alexander Woollcott's estate on one of the Thousand Islands, where they encountered George Kaufman. Kaufman's wife, Bea, had had an affair with Backer. "Where did you meet that cunt?" Kaufman asked Backer, according to Lillian. And Backer had to reply, "We got married yesterday!"

It was psychologically difficult for Lillian to write in Hammett's absence. "I'm sick of all writing," she complained. In a letter to Maggie and Arthur, she said, "I hate like hell to write anything, and as the years go by that gets worse." As the she-Hammett, she seemed almost to assume Dash's writing paralysis. "Every day I return and sit on the couch, every day nothing happens," Lily lamented.

She was too disciplined, too ambitious, and she had staked too much of her life on her career to yield too long to idleness. Far from giving up, she was hard at work on the new play. As always, as if by reflex, she turned to Hammett for support, even as he was now too honest to pretend that he could be of much help. She feared she had nothing more to say, she told him. Hammett encouraged her to believe that she was far from through.

"If you had any memory—or I'd saved such letters as you may have written me while you had previous work in progress," he reminded her, "you'd know that your present dithers over the play are only the normal bellyaching of La Hellman at work. You still think you dashed those other plays off without a fear, a groan or a sigh; but you didn't sister: I haven't had a dry shoulder since your career began, and I was an amphibian long before the Army and Navy ever heard of combined operations."

They could still be at their best tough-talking, him teasing, cajoling, calling her "sister," the way a twenties gangster addressed his moll. In many letters Dash still addressed her as Lilishka. Lovers no longer, they would be comrades forever.

That winter Dash wrote Lily a penciled newsletter from Fort Monmouth called "What's News." Under "financial," he admitted having made someone a twenty-five-dollar loan, even as he knew she would disapprove. Under "fashion," he reassured her that he wore his galoshes, although they made his feet "too hot." He did it "for my lover who is far, far away." Under "travel," he announced that he was planning to go to New York for dinner on Monday "with a little playwright I know there." His editorial stated: "Enough women don't write enough soldiers enough letters." Under "personal," he told Lily that his "ex-spouse" was about to have an operation. Not for years had he thought of Jose as his wife. Lily functioned throughout the war as a wife as he chronicled to her what he ate, how he slept, and whether and when his "prick" was examined.

Throughout the war years, Lilishka remained immersed in the politics they both had shared. She spoke in October 1942 at an Artists Front to Win the War meeting, advocating the immediate opening of a Second Front. At a Russian War Relief dinner, she had contributed a thousand dollars. February 1943 found her a sponsor of a dinner celebrating the twenty-fifth anniversary of the Red Army. Four days later she and Herman Shumlin shared the platform at a Russian War Relief benefit rally in Brooklyn.

In June 1943 she was an honorary co-chairman welcoming a delegation of Russian writers and artists which included Itzik Feffer, the Jewish poet soon to perish in Stalin's camps. September found her at Hunter College on Park Avenue in New York City leading a group discussion on racism in the armed forces on behalf of the Citizens' Emergency Conference for Inter-Racial Unity. In December 1943 she attended with Earl Browder a gathering honoring Georgi Dimitrov, the former head of the Comintern. In April 1944, *The Searching Wind* was previewed in a benefit for the American-Soviet Medical Society.

Seeing no need to reconcile her Communist politics with her steady accumulation of a fortune, Lillian devoted a good deal of time to consolidating her financial holdings. Careful about authorizing productions of her plays, she refused Rabbi Julian B. Feibelman, a distant cousin of Peter Feibleman, who would figure importantly in her life, the right to do a reading of *Watch on the Rhine.* "The only way a playwright has of earning a living is to have a paying public come into a theater," Lillian wrote.

Lawyers and accountants handled her money. Stanley M. Isaacs dealt for Lily with the Internal Revenue Service; he contended that her buyout deal from Hal Wallis on *Watch on the Rhine* should not be conceived of as "ordinary income," but as the sale of a capital asset. He also supervised her income from the Sophie Newhouse Trust.

She set up entities such as Crescent Productions, to deal with her share of *The North Star.* Arthur Kober at once became a shareholder, as did Dash, who paid $562.50 for 5.625 shares, the stock to remain in Lillian's name. She would provide Dash with his dividends. Hopeless about money, Dash gave her his power of attorney and the charge of his checking account. Lily was now also receiving his royalty checks from Knopf. "Please buy bonds when the account gets too much in it," Dash instructed.

In March 1943 Dashiell Hammett entered the Army hospital at Fort Monmouth suffering from bronchitis, acute, and laryngitis, acute, periodontoclasia, and dental caries. Peculiarly, it was his teeth that proved the greatest problem. To ensure his being sent overseas, Dash decided to have all his teeth pulled, a few at a time. He didn't see Lily for a few weeks; then he phoned that he was "well and cheerful," although more teeth were gone.

One Saturday night Dash arrived at "21," where Lily was waiting for him. When she first saw him, she cried out, so ghastly did he appear without a single tooth in his mouth! Dash cheerfully ordered soft-boiled eggs.

"Very horrible," Lily said later. Then, because he didn't seem overly upset, neither was she. "He goes straight along in an incredible fashion," she told the Kobers. "Hammett, he's a character."

"I love you," Dash had written Lily from Fort Monmouth back in February. With no idea of the more frigid climate he was shortly to endure, he signed that particular letter "The Cold Corporal."

14

Love Letters from the Front

"Do you want me to tell you about Hammett? . . . You may have to put up with him for many more years—it'll be thirteen in November—and I don't want you to have the comfort of too many illusions."

DASHIELL HAMMETT

o you suppose I'm in love with the Army?" Dash wrote Lily. Gleefully glad to be in the Army, he was like a boy let out of school. Letters could serve as a substitute for his being writer, lover, father, companion. Meanwhile Lillian had settled into her own pattern, a series of sexual affairs, and the illusion of loving a man without the diurnal devotions and sacrifices of real life.

Hammett had become the man in the background of her life who saved her from the risk of learning to love another. Now, by mail, the two communicated as husband and wife in an intimacy they had not shared for years. As always, in letters he could convey his profound feeling, and express his very strong need of her.

In her letters, Lily poured out the minute details of her ailments, and her anxieties about her writing. He teased, and worried. She decided she was suffering from tobacco poisoning; he wrote he was glad she was going to a doctor rather than a hairdresser, needling her about her vanity, her always dyed and perfect coiffures.

Absence made him fond. By May 1943 he felt it was once more "a long time since I have seen you." He embroidered: "What do you look like? Do you appreciate music and flowers? What are your hobbies? Would you like to correspond with one of our soldier boys in a New Jersey camp? He is a dandy fellow. His hobby is Jewish playwrights." He could not imagine his life without her in it and tried to reassure her. "Hold tightly on to my love," he signed off.

June found him at Camp Shenango, in Transfer, Pennsylvania, where the subversives were dumped in barbed-wire-enclosed stockades, indicating that the Army had been suspicious of him from the start. When Eleanor Roosevelt objected, they were dispersed, seemingly to be shipped to arenas of combat. From Seattle, he sounded the old note: he would look up friends he had known twenty-three years earlier to see if they "now have presentable grown daughters, or, anyhow, daughters." But even as he once more ostensibly denied her his fidelity, a moot point now, he was cross when she broke her promise of not writing to him twice a week. Lily replied she had written "a lot of letters." He retorted, "You haven't exactly clogged up the mail lanes."

They were not yet done with each other and never would be. All the old quarrels surfaced. In July he wrote he had not had a drink since the day before he left Camp Shenango; it had been one day short of two weeks.

"So I'm an alcoholic, eh?" he demanded. "Do you want to apologize for anything?" He clung to the belief that since he could stop drinking for weeks or even months at a time, he was not alcoholic. Lily, who drank every day herself, was in no position to know better.

His solace from boredom in Seattle was talking to Lily on the telephone. "I felt better after talking to you last night," he wrote her, "if this keeps up it'll probably drive me to trying to write stories—and that's one of the dangers—faint as it was—I came into the Army to avoid." He wrote as if only she appreciated the pain connected to the loss of his craft.

He was far older than even the officers and it made him feel "elderly." From Seattle, although he could just as easily have written this sentiment, he sent a wire: "I am a dull old man without any news." He compiled for Lily a list of aphorisms, beginning with "Just as every woman thinks any woman five years older is a hag, so every man thinks any man five years older must be growing feeble." The twelfth and last was "I love you."

Writing to her, he rediscovered her. He ate too much, "and I've still got at least one more meal to go today," he reported. Then, suddenly, he realized how much they had come to resemble each other: "I sound like you."

Their photographs crisscrossed the continent. He looked "very intelligent and mean," Lily wrote upon receiving one. "I choose to think you meant 'soldierly,' for it seems to me they are qualities one would want in a fighting man," he laughed. He looked like "an aging tulip tree," Lily wrote in response to another, and he took the simile for the title of his last piece of writing.

"I could use more photos of you too," he requested. When she wrote that she had included a photograph in the envelope and none appeared, he joked, "I imagine Bonwit Teller were pretty surprised at getting a snapshot instead of a check," a barb at her compulsive shopping. Jealous as always of her activity which did not include him, he imagined her having pictures taken "for the press, for foyer display, for anti-defamation league publications, but never one for me." He resorted to tough talk: "what's humanitarian or even plain low-down kike-ethical about that?"

Lily wrote as if he were the absent husband at war who had left her with the chores. Where could she buy wire turtle traps? she asked. He sent instructions on how to bait hooks for turtles. He reminded her that by September the fish in Hardscrabble pond weren't "very cooperative," although they started every season off "like wolves." There were only two usable fly rods at the farm.

He had enlisted to fight in the war against fascism. "Men were going places and I wasn't going any place," he had complained. He was disappointed, restless. Then, in August, several weeks passed without Lily's having heard from him. She was alarmed. "Dash has landed somewhere, but I am unable to figure out where," she wrote Maggie.

Instead of being shipped to a theater of war, however, Dashiell Hammett was stationed in the Aleutian Islands. The Japanese were gone and the Aleutians were now another dumping ground for subversives the Army wanted to keep far from combat. With Hammett were other radicals, like Robert Colodny, who had fought in Spain, and militant Trotskyist Irving Howe.

The men who came to know him soon learned that the famous writer among them took no pleasure in what he had wrought. At their first meeting Hammett was chilly to young Eliot Asinof, later to write *Eight Men Out,* suspecting that he wanted only to meet the great man. When Asinof asked Hammett to talk about *The Maltese Falcon* after a screening, Dash declined. "That's a part of my life that's all over," he said. But Hammett always responded kindly to aspiring writers in search of guidance. When Asinof later wrote an article about the corruption of officers smuggling booze and then awaited Dash's approval, Hammett told him, offering fine advice for any writer, "Lieutenant, everyone knows what. Why don't you try to find out why?" Asinof never forgot it.

By October, Lily still didn't know where he was. "It'll teach you patience, maybe," he wrote, "and, perhaps, something about that world in which women wait at home while their menfolks range afield or in ships." Even as he thrived on her concern, he pretended it was unwarranted. So he urged her "not to worry about anything connected with a man named Hammett be he dentist, undertaker or lord high executioner."

Before long she learned that not only was he on Adak Island in the Aleutians but a contented Hammett loved this wet, windy, muddy landscape. "If it weren't for you there wouldn't be anything I really miss up here," he decided. One day he thought it would have been nice to have been born on the Aleutians. Then he had to laugh at himself and remind Lily of their mutual disapproval of "Cliff Odets," whose plays were always about how he didn't have skates when he was a boy, who continued to whine about his disadvantaged youth.

From the Aleutians, embellishing the motif he had begun earlier, Dash wrote Lily creating imagery of himself as husband at war and she as wife waiting at the hearth for his return. He trudged through the mud to send her a radiogram, hoping it would catch her in Pleasantville the next day: "nothing's too good for the little woman." It obviously pleased him to sound as if he were a husband.

He wrote as if they had grown so like each other as to become interchangeable entities. He was to be photographed for *Yank*, an idea he liked. "Or do you want to make out you're different?" he demanded.

From the start, she either organized his business back home or supervised it. He arranged "to send the ex-wife and youngsters $100 a week, mailed in a check once a month by the bank," but Lily had to know about it. He enlisted her to send a poodle to a little girl, who, he teased, was "small and dark and elfin-pixyish exquisite" and whom he even thought of marrying if . . . young as she is, she has the sort of feminine mind with which I'm likely to get myself involved." His teasing could be merciless, and even emerged in letters to others. In one to Maggie, he called Lillian "Madame Helsinki."

"Whether and what I should invest in the forthcoming A. Kober show," he wrote, she must decide. She was editing the introduction and overseeing the Lawrence E. Spivak editions of his works, edited by "Ellery Queen." Hammett felt guilty about the time she was spending: "editing little tasties out of Ellery Queen is all anybody should be expected to do for anybody," he wrote. "Going to lunch with Spivak isn't to be expected of you. Commerce should exact only so much from the parties involved."

When she wrote she was "borrowing" money from his account, he

Sophronia's enlarged photograph holding a tiny, impish Lillian was to adorn the drawing rooms of Lillian's adult life.

Julia Newhouse Hellman: "I was mean to her."

(Unless otherwise noted, all photographs are from the Lillian Hellman Archives.)

Max, Lillian and Julia Hellman at Niagara Falls. Lillian is seven. "Mama nags. Papa understands."

Max Hellman (*center*) on the SOU.RY. Special: "A handsome man, witty, high-tempered, proud." (On the back Julia Hellman had written: "Willie Caudle, Uncle Albert Lob, a Christian Scientist, and Your Daddy.")

Lillian at fourteen: "Rather weak and inclined to be dramatic."

Lillian and Julia Hellman: "Fey, and disjointed, and sweet, and lost."

Lillian as a young woman, with friend, Atlantic City: she did her best to display her shapely legs and small dainty feet.

The young Lillian with an unidentified gentleman: "In every relationship there's a winner and a loser."

Dashiell Hammett, c. 1920: "He was a wild one." (*Courtesy of Josephine Marshall and Alvin Sargent*)

Lillian Hellman the year she met Dashiell Hammett: "I am such a damned egotist, such a born actress."

Arthur Kober, Lillian's only husband: "If he noticed that I had divorced him, he never brought it up."

Josephine Dolan, Dash's only wife, before their marriage: "Neither of us ever said anything about seriously loving the other." (*Courtesy of Josephine Marshall*)

Josephine Hammett with baby Jo and Mary, c. 1926: The child was not his. (*Courtesy of Josephine Marshall*)

Dashiell Hammett in 1929: "Long and lean and gray-headed, and very lazy." (*Photography Collections, Humanities Research Center, University of Texas*)

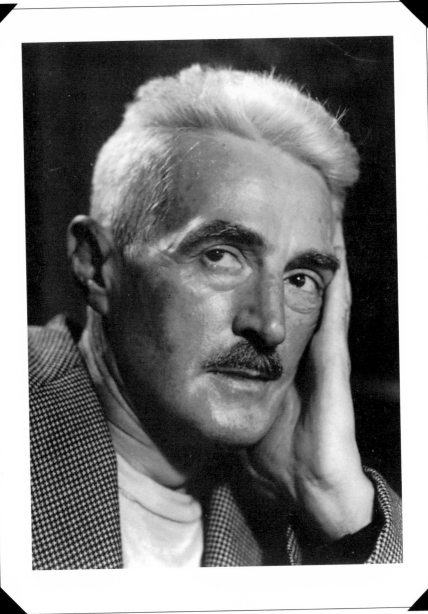

Dashiell Hammett: "Elegant to look at."

Lillian in the 1930s:
"Better than pretty."

Louis Kronenberger, Mrs. Samuel Kamsley, Lily, Dash, Huntington, Long Island, 1933. Mrs. Kamsley's businessman husband, Sam, a friend of Lillian's, snapped the picture. *(Courtesy of Emmy Kronenberger)*

Lily at the gate, Hollywood, 1935 or 1936.

Lillian Hellman and Dashiell Hammett. On the back of this photograph, Lily wrote: "Dash took this of me."

Bucks County, on the Perelman farm: Robert Coates, Dashiell Hammett, Nathanael West, Laura Perelman, Sidney Perelman. Laura was in love with Dash.

Lillian on the Perelman farm: "He'd given Laura his word not to tell anybody."

Lillian at the moment of her success: "Ts! Ts! Ts! Just a she-Hammett!"

Lillian as a theater celebrity: hats gave her a jaunty look and pulled the attention of the viewer away from her less than perfect features.

Herman Shumlin with Lillian Hellman: "Herman-Sherman, this hymn I cast… / A hymn of passion, of desire and hate / A hymn of love, of hair, of barren pate…."

George Backer in the late 1930s: "one of the damnedest breakfasts I've ever had in my life." (*Courtesy of Mrs. Werner H. Kramarsky*)

Lillian in the forties: "Now, Lily, what really happened?"

Lillian Hellman and Dorothy Parker: "Dressed in their best mink coats."

"Of course there's a great deal of good in Dotty, darling, which is one of the reasons I don't like her, maybe the chief one." Hammett with Dorothy Parker at an anti-Nazi rally, late thirties. (*Photography Collections, Humanities Research Center, University of Texas*)

Lillian during her first decade with Hammett: "Her voice was thin and hard as her lip, / And her lip was as hard as bone."

Lillian, Herman Shumlin, and Hal Wallis in Hollywood reading the script of
Watch on the Rhine (1941): "It has been brought to my attention that you
said...." (*Photo courtesy of Warner Bros.*)

Lily and Dash at "21," 1941: "How much she leans on Dash in her writing and
how disappointed she is at his drunkenness." (*George Karger:* Life *magazine*)

Lily and Dash with James
Benet, early 1940s. "I preach
to her to go away & rest, but
no go & bangs on—busy gal &
God bless her."

Lily and Dash at Hardscrabble Farm. c. 1950.

Hardscrabble Farm: Lily's two-story study with
its private entrance is at the right. "A riot of
colors, wallpaper and rugs full of flowers."
(*Photograph by Joan Mellen*)

Lillian's aunt Hannah Hellman: in love with him "Since the day he was in his cradle."

Josephine Hammett as a teenager: "I love you, darling, deeply and completely."

A birthday photograph sent to Jo, c. 1940. *(Courtesy of Josephine Marshall)*

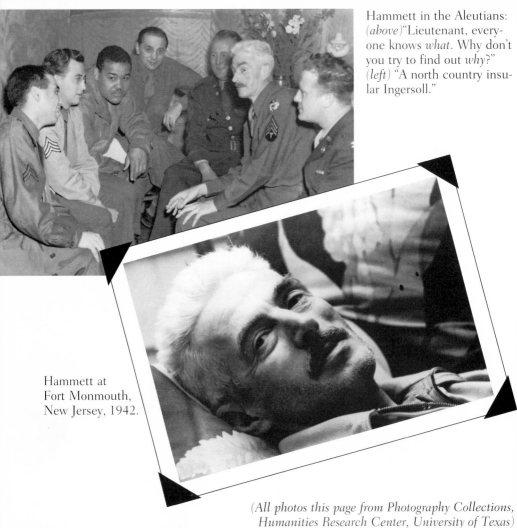

Hammett in the Aleutians:
(above)"Lieutenant, everyone knows *what*. Why don't
you try to find out *why*?"
(*left*) "A north country insular Ingersoll."

Hammett at
Fort Monmouth,
New Jersey, 1942.

told her to charge it as repayment of loans she had made to him. Above all, she was in charge of purchases. She sent a gold chain on which he hung his dog tags; "light, strong, and naturally expensive," he had ordered. He wanted a dozen pairs of "light weight wool-mixture socks either gray or white," the mixture holding up better than wool, "which I would otherwise prefer as more expensive."

Lily was unstinting. Pipes came from Dunhill's. She chose a chamois-faced hood from Abercrombie's, which delighted him. "Thank you, darling, you are kind, generous, brilliant, rich and young," he wrote. She sent gourmet delicacies from a fancy shop called Martin's: rum cakes, maple sugar, chocolate, grapefruit peel, canned lobster, caviar, smoked turkey, pâté de foie, anchovies. "You are a generous girl as well as a good one," he repeated. "Maybe you are simply everything." He hoped to let her "continue picking out food for me throughout many a coming year." It was one more means of letting her know he hoped they would be together for the long haul.

Hammett shared her packages with his fellow soldiers, and they all knew of the relationship. Lillian was now writing the social commentary he could no longer accomplish himself, he told Robert Colodny. Dash gave Colodny his inscribed copy of the published script of *The North Star*. It read: "For Dashberger, Who is too far away; who is always too far away if he isn't in the next chair." Dash did his best to alleviate the bad feeling she had about the film. Having not yet seen it, he wrote Lily he liked reading *The North Star*. It was "a simple, compact, neat and moving piece of work and you are all right, you are, and in many ways, you have my approval, you have."

Money meant a great deal to her as she remembered being a Newhouse poor relation. Dash knew her well and joked he would keep his pay, his "$2 \times \$78.20 - 2 \times \$11.40$," so she couldn't get her "pretty but niggardly little hands on it." Lily determined to make Dash money now and she didn't always inform him of her schemes. He learned that *The Thin Man* was back on the radio.

"What goes on?" he demanded of Lily, knowing she must be behind it. "I hope the cutie-pie hasn't been hiding things from the old corporal. Don't let's have any nonsense of that sort—or I will take my trade to some other financial manager." When she wrote she was taking "a firm stand on money matters," that alarmed him. "Lady," he answered, "I didn't join the Army to get rich: it had something to do with fighting fascism." He must have been annoyed with her on the day he told fellow soldier William Glackin that at one time Lillian Hellman had been his "secretary." Then he had been her "play doctor." Now they were "very good friends." He had kept a straight face.

Lily ignored his protests and worked on a sale of some Hammett stories to Warner Brothers. He asked how much it would make him, and accused her of "trying to make a miser of me." He pictured himself writing sums of money on slips of paper and fondling them. The trouble was he was unable "to get the proper erotic reaction out of it." Perhaps, he concluded, the amounts were not correct.

They shared their reading tastes. She suggested *Wuthering Heights.* He teased: "Does that mean I should try some of those other pompous hacks you've tried to foist on me?" But he admitted, "You were right this time and I was wrong, but that proves nothing—purely an isolated instance." By the time he finished *Wuthering Heights,* his judgment was less sanguine: "I'm not sure the book isn't a rather shameful waste of some good characters."

Lily preferred the classics. "Crawl back in your kennel, Proust," Dash growled, lest she claim another victory, "and take Melville with you." He preferred Graham Greene. He read *Das Kapital* for the third time.

She had missed his birthday, May 27. Now he made a telling request. "You are a very rich woman, and this next play will only make you richer," he reminded her. "You say you love me, but you haven't yet given me the birthday present due last May." What he wanted from her was "to have some very nice little thing to hold on to." Only Lily truly understood him. "You will understand this," he wrote her, "not because I have made it clear, but because you will understand it." He wanted to feel as if he were her husband. What he wanted was a symbol of their bond.

"I want a ring," Dash said. Nor was it to be just any ring. "I would prefer that the mounting be platinum," he instructed, as a groom might his bride, "but I'll leave the details to you. All I ask is that the ring be sturdy, beautiful and valuable. I don't want any Japanese hacking off my finger to get at some trifling bauble." He also wanted "something engraved inside the band."

Lily wrote at once telling him she was glad he had asked for a ring. "I'm glad you're glad I asked for the ring and I'm glad you're glad to send it," he answered.

Dash loved the ring Lily sent. "I keep looking at the ring first instead of at my watch when I want to see the time," he joked. In that letter he wrote, cryptically, that he was "thinking things over" and "coming to conclusions." He wasn't ready for announcements, or declarations. He told her only she would probably find him "a changed man and it's not for me to say if for better or for worse." He implied that he was ready to be for her what he had failed to be in the past. Meanwhile he waxed on about his ring: "I'm far too attached to the ring to consider separating myself from it even temporarily for any reason whatever," he wrote, "and I can't understand how I got along without one all these years." No husband could have written a wife with greater affection.

He still sounded his old themes. He teased her about his having decided to live with an "Aleut squaw," along with his pet blue fox Sasha, only to confess he had seen only four women since July (it was now October) and none to speak to. He tried to make Lily understand that his taste for the lowlife in women meant nothing. Nor were her affairs of concern to him; he urged her to send his best to once and present lovers, like Ken Crawford, "I hope his health is on the upgrade," and to St. Clair McKelway.

Her work remained a constant theme of their correspondence. Whatever conflict their collaboration on *Watch on the Rhine* had wrought, generously he overcame his hurt. "The Variety Man liked 'Watch on the Rhine,'" he noted, "alright, alright, and I hope he is right." Before long he was trying to get 16-millimeter prints for an Army training program.

By November, Lily was deluging him with her doubts about *The Searching Wind*, the first play she would write in his absence. "Write it now and begin to worry along about the second or third rewriting," Dash advised. Her report had sounded "exactly like a girl named Lillian Hellman I used to know, when she was writing a new play." He encouraged her to use the title *The Searching Wind* so she must stop "dilly-dallying about it." She must not "worry too much." He retained his authority with her about work.

Rarely did he mention his own efforts at writing, although when he rewrote Robert Colodny's text for *The Battle of the Aleutians,* an Army-sponsored pamphlet for the soldiers, he was proud that the local Army folk thought it "hot stuff." Colodny's version was all ideology; Hammett's rewrite substituted action and history. Colodny said the war was a clash of ideologies. "Ideologies don't win wars, bullets win wars," Hammett retorted. All that remained of Colodny's text, according to Bill Glackin, were the captions.

Much of Hammett's time was taken up with writing letters, not only to Lillian but to Pru Whitfied, who received seventy-five letters during these years, to Maggie Kober, to his daughters, Jo and Mary, to his ex-spouse, Jose, to Lillian's secretary, Nancy Bragdon, and even to Lois Jacoby and Leane Zugsmith. He mentioned Pru in his letters to Lillian, but not Lillian in those to Pru.

He wrote to Max, to Jed Harris, to Herman Shumlin, to Louis Kronenberger and to Emmy. He was fond and mocking about eccentric Max. "It's nice that your old man should like and have a high opinion of me," Dash wrote Lily. "If his employment should ever become a problem, I am sure we can get him a job as an Army psychiatrist."

Dash also wrote to his own unpleasant father, for whom he was buying an artificial leg. He had never forgiven his father not only for his indifference to him in his childhood and his unkindnesses to his mother but for a time in San Francisco when Dash had asked to borrow some money and his father had turned him down. His family's utter unworldliness amused and half shamed him. His brother Dick had taken a picture "with Annabella the Movie Star," he wrote. "Now you know about my family. Aren't you glad we never married?" That they had come close to marrying bound them too.

As any couple would, Lily and Dash shared their ailments. Proudly she told him she had lost weight; he replied she should take care of "what's left of yourself." She feared a bladder infection, then had to report it had been a false alarm. "You've always been healthy as a horse," he told her, "and always will be except perhaps for a little biliousness now and then from overeating, you pig."

Hammett thrived in Alaska, no matter that the fierce Aleutian winds drove tiny frozen pellets into your face. He took "tundra-hopping" in stride, discovering muscles he said he'd forgotten. Some mornings, he admitted, he felt more like eighty than forty-nine. Yet he succumbed neither to cough nor to sniffle, remaining "as healthy as so many Hellmans." He sympathized when she had to go to the dentist: "that tittying around is no fun." He boasted of having taken "the easy way out, having them all out, and the bone whittled down in practically one fell swoop."

He needed to imagine her well and waiting for him. When the hospital threatened, he wrote, "I don't like it and won't like anything connected with it until I hear that you are all through with it and all right." His stay in the Aleutians would be "spoil[ed]," he wrote, if he had "to sit around and worry about what you are up to."

He knew her foibles, was amused, and wouldn't allow her to get away with them. When he sent Mary fifty dollars for her birthday, he cautioned Lily not to conclude Mary had forged his signature when she spotted the canceled check. It was another secret they shared, the daughter who was not his natural daughter could not be trusted.

Almost as soon as he arrived in Alaska, Hammett began to imagine returning to Hardscrabble Farm after the war. He joked, given his relative idleness in the Aleutians, that he would be "entitled to years of complete rest after the war is over." He enumerated all the things he would refuse to do, the things Lily had required of him: "starting with not helping you rearrange the living room furniture! And not painting anything! And never picking vegetables or flowers!"

The passing seasons reminded him of Hardscrabble Farm, his home. In October, he remembered the leaves on the ground "and fat and edible gray squirrels scampering through them." He remembered Lily's cooking: "I'd like to be eating one of your gumbos tonight," he wrote, "but I don't guess you can get it cooked and delivered up here in time. Oh, well, no hard feelings. I know you just didn't happen to think of it in time—probably working too hard on the play." Once more he joked about priorities, her not putting him first, which had so maddened him that one night he had exacted the cruelest punishment.

As once she had longed for his approval and affection, now, in one more reversal of roles, he longed for hers. "He didn't have you," he wrote of some man, "and I do." One of her letters he found so "extra-special double-portion triple-ply nice" that he said he felt like courting her all over again. He wished he could do something about it, but he couldn't now say, "Gee, I'd like to see her!" He couldn't phone her "for a date. And I can't go send you some flowers that would get to you right away. And there's not much use of my promising I'll never complain about your twisting your hair, is there? You'd know I meant a lot by that, but you wouldn't believe I'd stick to it."

As he wore her ring, so he wrote her love letters. Writing daily, he admitted, "It's obvious that I'm writing this because I want to talk to you, which makes it a kind of love letter, only I'm too old to write love letters." He studied his picture in *Yank* and thought he looked like "God's older brother, the one that always stuck up for Him, but never thought the Kid had enough gumption to make His mark in the world." He definitely didn't "look like the type that ought to be writing love letters." Indirectly, obliquely, he poured forth reassurances: "So even if I love you and miss you and you have got beautiful wrists I'll have to just let it go at that."

He knew her, knew she was so insecure that no assurances could suffice. "No temper now!" he ordered. "Leave us be adult. And leave us have no caustic remarks about the goyim." But he also genuinely wished to satisfy her need. "I will go so far, however, as to say you are a sweetheart, I mean even in addition to the wrists." She had complained over the years that she wanted a man who wrote poems to her. Once more Dash tried his hand:

LOVE POEM

I am silly
About Lily.
Without Lily,
I am silly
Willy-nilly.

He demanded that she wire him her new number and gave her copious instructions about receiving his telephone calls. "Now all you've got to do is get home so we can go to it," he wrote, the sexual innuendo another reassurance. The joke on Adak Island became that Hammett received more radiograms from Lillian Hellman than the commanding general, Harry Thompson, got during the entire war.

Thanksgiving of 1943 marked the thirteenth anniversary of their acquaintance. Hammett did not allow the day to pass unmarked. "Yes, Ma'am, it's thirteen years just about this day," he wrote Lily. "And that's nice, that is, and I thank you, I do. They have been fine grand years and you are a fine grand woman and for all I know I must have been a fine grand man to have deserved them and you." As with the ring, and his talk of "thinking things over" and "coming to conclusions," once more he promised her a future. "And, with such a start," he waxed on, "think of, not only the next thirteen but the ones after that! A lot of very great poetry has been written about much less, and I mean that." He was telling her what she had so longed to hear: there had never been anyone else and there never would be.

He was quite adamant as well about her remaining free for whatever role he would play in her life. "I think, however, it would be better all around if you did not marry anybody, but stuck to me," he advised. Once more he sounded the new reassuring note, the suggestion that his whoring days had come to an end. "I have a warm, if small heart," he wrote, echoing that old medical report from Lenox Hill, "and it may be assumed that I've sown my wild oats."

When Christmas of 1943 drew near, Dash sent Lily his Christmas shopping list, acknowledging that this was "the first time I've had any excuse except laziness for foisting the job on you." Lily in turn foisted the job on her secretary, Nancy Bragdon. Her own gift she was to purchase herself, "whatever takes the Hellman eye—and I hope I'll see it before too long." His new motif became wanting to know "what I'm giving you for Christmas." Later it became "now do you want to tell me what I gave you for Christmas?" When he finally learned she planned to buy a coat, he urged her to "buy an extravagant one so that when you tell people I gave it to you for Christmas they will say, 'Ah, that Hammett! He certainly treats his women well!' "

She entered Lenox Hill hospital that December; he wrote her two letters in one day. When he didn't hear from her, he complained. "It seems a long, long time since I've heard from you," he wrote on December 18, "and it is . . . I tell myself not to worry; but I *haven't* heard from you since before you went to the hospital—and you know how fidgety us old men are—and I *do* worry. So make me stop it by writing me that you are all right."

"This will be the second Christmas in a row that we haven't shared," he noted. "That could become a bad habit." It was another allusion to his hope that they might share a life together after the war. On December 28 he marked another anniversary. It was "six months ago tonight" that he had said goodbye to her. "That's kind of a long time to be without seeing you," he wrote now, "and I don't know that—except for a war—I would for a moment consider it practicable."

Ten minutes before the New Year 1944 Dashiell Hammett was lying in his bunk writing to his "dear Lilishka." The flame of their affection persisted as he settled down to another year and then some amid the wind and the mud of the Aleutian chain.

15

Hammett of the North, Big Brother of Nanook

"So it must be love that sets me down at the typewriter like this
when I could be dragging my skinny legs down Pneumonia Gulch
towards my hut and bunk."

DASHIELL HAMMETT

At the close of 1943 Dashiell Hammett was made editor of *The
Adakian*, a four-page newspaper for the troops on the Aleutian
Islands to keep up their morale, connect them to life back
home, and make existence more bearable (there were three cartoons in each issue). There were to be eleven on the staff; Hammett quietly found three African-Americans, an artist, a mimeograph production
man, and an engineer. Soon the snowbanked hut they all lived in and,
inevitably, the mess hall as well were integrated without Hammett's having uttered a word about it.

Calling himself "a north country insular Ingersoll," he talked more
about William Randolph Hearst than Earl Browder. He trained a staff of
would-be journalists, including Asinof and Bernard Kalb, and as an elder
(and famous) brother dispensed advice. "A woman would be nice, but
not getting any doesn't cause your teeth or hair to fall out" is the oft-
quoted Hammett line. He kept a bottle of scotch under his bed. One
night someone brought in a copy of *Time* magazine in which a French

critic had named Hammett among the ten most influential American writers of all time. Sam, as the men called him, just grinned. He seemed pleased.

Information was scarce. Dash asked Lily to send daily airmail packages of newspapers and magazines, everything from the Sunday New York *Times* to Communist Claud Cockburn's *This Week* out of London. He wanted both *Variety* and *New Masses*. He asked Nancy Bragdon to forward all his subscriptions, even the Museum of Natural History magazine, to Alaska. "Lillian will no doubt be unpleasant about this," he predicted, "so you'd better buy her a subscription on my account." He considered asking Lillian to return the Nikon he had given her.

Hammett ordered Bragdon to "involve Lily heavily in all this." She must not allow Lily "to suppress those [items] she thinks might have a bad influence on me." He told Lily herself to "stick your pretty little nose into the matter now and then so that I will have—at no cost to myself— the advantage of your sagacity" about world affairs. Lily must inform him of "what's cooking in the national mind, and what people say and print about the origins of the war, the conduct of the war, and what's going to happen at home and abroad after the war." The essence of their relationship was collaboration; now it had taken a new turn. He expected of her the generosity he had offered. When in her next letter she seemed "remote," he was troubled.

Isolated in the Aleutians, he wrote as if nothing had changed, although it is clear he was less connected to her work emotionally. He reported he had heard *The North Star* was "a worthy effort though probably propaganda." Busy with *The Adakian,* he had missed the screenings.

He remained solicitous of her health, and he ordered her "not to sit up late in smoky rooms. You are to avoid committee meetings and other rat-races where flu germs are rife . . . if you do those things I will continue to love you." When in February 1944 she fell and hurt her back, he was upset and called her a "clumsy ox." He also continued to reassure her of his devotion: "I don't love nobody no better than you." "As usual, there were qualifications: "I love you to the extent that it is in me to love any of my fellows right now—only I do you," he wrote.

When Peggy Herrmann, Lillian's farmer's wife, thanked him for her Christmas present, adding, "Miss Hellman thinks you are wonderful," he was pleased. "My instinct was always right in trying to make you do my yule shopping for me," he wrote triumphantly, "so that is established precedent from now on out; be I at home or abroad!"

He wrote far more frequently than she did. When she was silent, he complained. She pleaded that she was deep in the casting and rehearsals of *The Searching Wind*. If she continued using her playwrighting as an excuse for not writing to him, he threatened playfully, she would "be cut off with a phrase in my memoirs."

It was their old quarrel about priorities. Writing to him was most important, he insisted. "After all, what are money and fame and admiration of thousands?" He showed one of her letters to his *Adakian* assistant Bill Glackin, then wrote Lily he was "one of your admirers," although should she wish to marry him, her name would be "Mrs. Glackin, which in itself should be no mean inducement." He needled her about her periodic determinations to marry; irony sustained them.

Their attitudes about money were a persistent source of disagreement. "It is only money and what is there is yours," he told her, like a husband. But he also needed to control her possessiveness. He ordered her "not to sulk" about his having sent mystery writer Raoul Whitfield $500 when he was discharged from the hospital. She was "not to mislead the bank with hints that my check may be a forgery." She was to "be brave and kind and—mind your own business."

Family matters he still shared only with her. "Maybe it didn't fit his dancing pumps," he wrote sardonically when his father was dissatisfied with the new artificial leg Hammett had bought him. He had not heard for fifteen years from his brother Richard, who was with Standard "Oil-ing." Richard's politics were laughable. "His mental processes are those of the true Hammett," Dash wrote Lily, "uncorrupted by any glimpse of the world as it is." Mary wrote asking for advice about "how much love in a romantic sense is needed to make a go of marriage" and "how much difference in age is wise." Hammett shared the absurdity with Lily: "Lucky, lucky girl to have such a father!"

How much money went to Jose and her daughters was also something he discussed with Lily. Jo was about to enter UCLA. He considered raising "the western Hammett family allowance. I might just as well face the fact that they're three adults now and can no longer be fed on Nestle's food." He asked Lily's advice: "Should I double it?"

Like a child, hating still his connection with Jose and the girls, Lily remained silent for a month. Dash broached the subject again: "Now, emboldened by your silence, I clear my throat again and ask you will you do whatever's necessary to induce the good old County Trust Company to send them—meaning those Hammetts—their millions at the rate of $200 a week instead of at the lower rate hitherto obtaining? Thank you, Ma'am."

Foremost on Lillian's mind was her new play. He tried to reconcile her to working without him. "I hope the play is coming along better than if I was on hand to get into quarrels with you about it," he wrote, "and that therefore you are devoting to sheer writing those periods you used to take out for sulking because I was hampering your art or objecting to a glittering generality, which, it's possible, is the same thing."

She was not appeased, and pictured herself "writing a lot of dull shit, long and rambling"; she sensed the play was disappointing, "flat and long." Finally, out of patience, he told her, "You give it what you've got and do what you think best, and then you take your chances."

When she was silent, he inquired: "Does it go forward with running or a crawl?" Two days later he added: "If it can't go on till September, what of it?" He tried to bolster her confidence. She was "America's foremost playwright" and he was proud of her. She was "the finest of all playwrights," he had told a soldier at the Special Service Office who asked about "Lillian Hellman."

He did everything he could to reconcile her to working on this play without him. "You're practically breaking my heart with your letters about the play," he relented. "I think we're going to have to make a rule that you're not to tackle any work when I'm not around to spur, quiet, goad, pacify and tease you, according to what's needed at the moment. It is obvious that you're not capable of handling yourself." Nor did he want anyone to take over this function in her life. "I hope you are not paying too much attention to what people—I still distrust everybody's advice but my own—tell you about what you are writing."

He did alter some of the dialogue. "Your instinct is right," he replied to one of her queries, "you can't have a character say, 'Everything can't be put in words.' That's as bad as, 'it's just like in a book,' 'these thing's just happen—you can't explain them,' or, as everybody has written at one time or another, 'I don't know—it's all so crazy.'" So Lily's writing lessons went on, although Dash had to read in Leonard Lyons' column that she had torn up two acts and was starting over.

As insecure as ever about her work, Lily desperately wanted him to go over her final draft. "Until it gets here and I've reported on it you've nothing to worry about, so you're to stop your fidgeting," he wrote. "It will give Zilboorg a bad name."

One month before *The Searching Wind* was scheduled to open, Hammett at last received his copy of the play. Reading it before breakfast, he saw that it was a weak effort. It was "polite comedy," Hammett thought, although this was not what Lillian intended in a play about the tragedy of a decent man who opposed fascism, then destroys himself by not choosing as his life partner a woman of character and commitment.

Gently, Dash praised her for "a defter touch than in any of your other plays." Never less than honest, he added that "it doesn't seem to me that you make your points." He softened the blow by remarking that it might be in the "nature of light comedy that its points aren't so much made as revealed in passing." At once he saw that the flashbacks, the action hopping back and forth from Mussolini's entrance into Rome to the present, didn't work. The historical scenes were best, but they were subordinated to the love triangle between the diplomat Alexander Hazen, his frivolous wife, Emily, and Cassie, the woman of character he mistakenly renounces.

The ending became "anti-climactical," so much so that the final speech is given to Sam, the son of Alex and Emily. Only that Montgomery Clift played Sam, and that the character sounds like Hammett, saved that ending. Sam has lost his leg in the War. "I don't like losing it all. I'm scared—but everybody's welcome to it as long as it means a little something and helps bring us out someplace," he says in quasi-Hammett cadences. His indignation at those who believe that "nothing anybody can do makes any difference, so why do it?" is also Hammett-like.

"Catching these characters now here, now there, doesn't give me a chance to know, to *feel* them and what they do to one another," Dash said. The "essential frivolity that fucked things up . . . isn't *shown*." Her people were "essentially characterless characters"; in particular the two woman lacked "any bite to them."

Dash apologized for so thoroughgoing a critique so late. It was March 15, and the play would open on April 12. He had come "to the whole thing not only cold but with practically no time to have let it sink in or to have thought it over." Lily must not consider his comments "anything like considered judgment." It was "in ways the most interesting play you've done, and it's got swell stuff in it." Then he signed his letter "SDH (who does not always know as much about everything as he acts like he does and who hopes the play gets its points over in a manner that'll make this letter sound like the work of a smart-aleck)."

Writing again on March 21, he called himself "still a cluck" regarding what she should do about the play. He wished he could devote a solid day to it. Whatever financial investment she wanted to make in the play in his name was "fine and pleasing to me." He had given her "a free hand in the matter of my Broadway investments." All he could do was hope that the play would be "a coming honor to the American stage," that it "come out right for you." He wished her "a long and opulent run and all the good things in the world forever and ever." Then he resorted to his merciless teasing. "I know one has to put up with a lot from folk in your profession," he wrote, "but just the same, it seems to me you're going a little too far . . . when you send me 'loge' instead of love. Let's have no more of this talking shop."

Writing to Herman Shumlin, he was more blunt. He imagined the progress of *The Searching Wind* as "a blood-flecked froth of casting and what not for a forthcoming Hellman charade." To Maggie Kober, he said, "I suppose the die is more or less cast with Lily's play. Do you want me to make a *mot* about its dying?" Maggie wanted to bet him one hundred dollars that *The Searching Wind* would win the Pulitzer Prize, but Hammett declined. "That's a bad play," Lily herself was to say about *The Searching Wind* years later.

Lily took the play to Wilmington and to Baltimore. To please Herman, she packed a picnic of two salamis, smoked salmon, two roast ducks, and a lemon meringue pie. The salamis, which had been placed on the windowsill, fell out of Herman's hotel-room window as he was arguing on the telephone with one of the engineers. Everyone laughed but Herman, who ordered the engineer to go out into the dark to retrieve them. Nervously, Virginia, the wife of stage manager Kermit Bloomgarden, knocked the lemon meringue pie off the table. Shumlin scooped it up. After the duck was taken away, without any humor he turned and said, "Why don't you serve the pie, Ginny?" It was Lillian's—and Kermit Bloomgarden's—last play with Herman Shumlin.

Dash had thumbtacked above his desk a picture of Lillian and the cast in rehearsal. "It's not very flattering of you," he had to admit, "but I like it. You look very solid and purposeful." He instructed Nancy Bragdon to send Lillian flowers from him on opening night. "I'm walking the floor till I hear what's what," he wrote on April 1, as if she were delivering the baby they almost had together.

He needn't have worried. *The Searching Wind* ran for more than 300 performances. The "news about the play is marvelous," Dash wrote as soon as he knew. Meanwhile Lily had resumed her social life, and was attending, along with Earl Browder, the forty-sixth birthday party of Paul Robeson.

Pleased as he was, Hammett used the success of this play to attempt to cut Lily loose from her emotional need of him, her disarray over his absence. At first he was gentle. "I just go around muttering 'fine, darling, fine, fine, fine!' and grin into my mustache," he reported. There was also a "lesson" to be learned, he told his "fine buxom cutie."

"You are a big girl now and you write your own plays the way you want them and you do not necessarily give a damn for the opinions of Tom, Dick and Dashie unless they happen to coincide with your own." He was both good-humored and stern. "No matter how close to you T, D or D may be, and no matter how hard they try to think in terms of your play, you must always bear in mind that what they're actually fooling around with is some slightly different idea of their own, which may be all right, but with which you have no business involving yourself." He anticipated her rejoinder that she was too close to her own work.

"So maybe sometimes you *are* too close to what you are trying to do and it *doesn't* quite come off," Dash told her. "So what?" His prose grew sententious, but he was determined to both set her free and shed the responsibility. "So you've certainly inched yourself closer to being able to do what you want to do than if you had let yourself be talked into doing something you didn't want to do because it would come off. And when—as now—you've done what you want to do and it has come off, why you've made a sap of the author of that stuff about not eating your cake and having it too and you are of the elite . . . with hemstitching!"

"What are you going to do now that your opus has been launched so nicely?" he wrote. "Go away somewhere for a while? Or stay around for the resultant dancing in the salons? Or bury yourself in the Thoreauisms of Hardscrabble Farm?"

It was clear to him that Lily had come to the end of something in the theater. He urged her to "make good your threat to write a novel next." The theater, he believed, "is for folks who like actresses and want people to know they're making loads of money. It's much more refined with us novelists." The irony was obvious; Lily, of course, did love people to know she was making money. She considered writing a novel, using the figure of New York *World* editor, bon vivant, and socialite Herbert Bayard Swope. "That gives you no exclusive right to him," Dash warned. "He is public domain stuff if I ever saw any." Dash sent her a program: "Sleep, write, sleep, write—it's as perfect a program as you'll ever find."

None of these letters in which he attempted to extricate himself worked. Lily was now "out of sorts." He told her it hadn't been easier with her earlier plays, "that the strong of heart never remember how badly off they've been at one time or another, which is what leads you, for instance, to the eventual belief that each of the past plays wrote itself." Undeterred, Lily insisted that he promise to continue as her play doctor, her adviser. "I may not be able to do you much good in a hurry," he relented, "but if I can take my time, maybe." Again he reminded her she was a "big girl," that he was "inclined to think you're ripe to go on ahead and play your string out in your own way and to hell with the no-matter-how-well-meaning-or-even-shrewd counsel of no-matter-whom."

"Should I do anything about my income tax?" Dash asked Lillian's secretary, Nancy. "My very vague notion was that soldiers overseas can postpone everything until some four months after they get back home." He would pay his taxes when the war was over. Meanwhile Knopf sent $2,319.59 in royalties for 1943.

His letters to Lily continued jolly, witty, loving, and constant. He promised to "continue to love you until your negligence makes it whatever your negligence makes it." However she thought she needed his writing help, the balance had shifted. Still they gossiped. Lillian wrote she decided John Huston might be "queer," welcome news to Hammett, who never liked that director's version of *The Maltese Falcon.*

Lily had defended Dorothy Parker. "Of course there's a great deal of good in Dotty, darling," Dash replied, "which is one of the reasons I don't like her, maybe the chief one." Being fond of her was fine, so long as "it doesn't lead you into thinking she's ever actually going to do anything worthy of her—and not just through sentimentality or for the applause of the part of society she wants to be petted by at the moment."

By February 1944, after scarcely two months, and not having done much writing himself, Dash was already "bored" with the mechanics of getting out *The Adakian.* In May, he turned fifty, and requested "something like gold paper and platinum shears to cut paper dolls with." In its hilarious birthday tribute published in the newspaper, his staff listed as his most famous work, written when he was seventeen, "The Gefulte Fish." To their delight, he often asked Jewish soldiers to help him brush up "on his Yiddishisms."

His gums had shrunk and the Army-issued false teeth no longer remained firmly in place. "I guess I'll go around clicking like a dice game on a cement floor until the war's over," he wrote Lily. "If I had any sense, I would stay away forever so that you could build up a kind of dream picture of me without ever coming up against old bubble-pricker reality, but I haven't got sense enough, so do not throw away the clothes and things I left around the house."

Hammett wrote often to Pru Whitfield in the spring of 1944, calling her "Madame" just as he did Lillian. He also hung her picture on the wall over his desk. "What did Caligula have that I haven't got—if you keep sex out of it?" he demanded. Unlike those to Lillian, his letters to Pru invariably made some reference to sex. There was rarely this sensuality in his many letters to Lily. "Tonight I need a soothing hand and I wish yours were around," he wrote Pru.

It was as if once more he sensed Lily slipping away from him, preoccupied with career, social necessities, her own involvements. In self-defense he had tried to let her know now that as a writer she must proceed alone. Now he told Pru he remembered that she was "very exciting—and annoying." He encouraged the correspondence. "I would like to see more of the poetry," he wrote Pru, "don't you remember that I was always in favor of it?" Terms of endearment went to others as well, like Maggie Kober, to whom he closed one letter with "that does not mean that I do not love you." Maggie, indeed, adored him.

*　　　*　　　*

All other connections sooner or later paled, however, before his involvement with Lillian. Only to Lily could he write, "I do not like your friend André Gide's comment on *Red Harvest* . . . and I wish the old fairy would keep his lecherous tongue to himself and his ilk." His horror of homosexuality could only conceal fear of his own repressed desires. "Writing people besides you doesn't become any easier with practice," Dash told Lillian, "though it seems to me that by the time you're fifty you should have perfected a smooth patter that would fill pages satisfactorily without your having to think about what you're saying."

Maggie bombarded him with trivial letters about her servants and money. "I guess the smaller your world the gladder you are to have *anything* happen in it," Dash wrote Lily, sympathetic with poor Maggie, who was now suffering from multiple sclerosis. He called her "really—technically—crazy." He was not fond of middle-class women, he said, and was ready to admit that Lillian might "be an intellectual." But this gave her no license to enter into "any Marxian discussions on this point."

When she had a falling-out with Louis Kronenberger, Dash took her part. "It has been a long time since there was any reason for anybody supposing that he was heading in any direction at all in any field whatever and, even if you're moving at a snail's pace, it takes a loud voice and very sharp ears to carry on any kind of intercourse with one who's lying down," Dash thought. Lily remained his "number one cutie." If she wanted to make a fuss about something, he wrote, "what I say is, Lily is a cutie and if she wants to make a fuss, why then let her make a fuss to her heart's content." When she fired her maid Irene, he said, "It's likely a good idea to change domestics once in a while anyhow, just as you do wallpaper."

He thought of her as frail, feminine, touching. "I guess I'd like you to live in a tissue-paper world," he wrote. "I suppose I will go to my grave thinking of you as frail." If his letters were not erotic, they did recall intimacies. "In cold weather you sleep with your buttocks sticking out from under the covers," he remembered fondly.

Again in the spring of 1944 he considered what he might do with himself once the war was over. He knew better than to consider writing a serious option. He pondered entering politics, as in "office-holding." He developed the fantasy without imagining that he might be a target of the anti-Communist brigades already in force, even as only a few months later some people from *Yank* were to visit bearing "Joe McCarthy's regards." "Would Madam speak to me when I was, say, a City Council member in Detroit, for instance, or a legislator in California?" he wanted to know.

A strong side of him longed to be useful. He contemplated living wherever the "best pickings" were for "an earnest left winger who was willing to spend a year or two digging in." Once more it was as if he had all the time in the world. Soon the bubble burst; soon he admitted he wanted only to "loaf—and I mean really loaf, not just idle around the way I used to."

He repeated that he would be returning to her. "I've probably only got fifteen or twenty years of youth left," he added, "and it seems needlessly spendthrift to waste them away from you. So you may definitely expect me back."

Lily took his political fantasy seriously and decided he should pursue his politics right there in Westchester County, where Hardscrabble Farm was located. Dash demurred. It was "populated by people I don't understand," he said. He liked working people, simple and unpretentious. He considered Michigan, Nebraska for the shooting and the fishing. "I'm trusting you to put your mind to it," Dash told Lily.

At Easter he had Nancy buy "bales of flowers" for herself, for Maggie, and of course for Lily, who also received a poem:

EASTER VERSE

(For L.H.)
That Christ has risen
And this be true:
You've been good for me
And I for you.

—D.H.

He had written Lily that she would find him "a changed man," that he had come to "conclusions." But his attitude toward sex had not changed since "the very early days." He admitted that he "could give in to a temptation if it played its cards right," although at the moment "there is no way to implement it." He told Pru he had changed his mind about his grandfather, who in his seventies had remarried and "begun turning out a new crop of uncles for me." Hammett thought now "maybe he wasn't as batty as he seemed to me then." The "saloons and the whorehouses" of the mainland beckoned, Dash wrote Lily.

Just as Dash was concluding that nothing had changed after all, Lillian received an invitation from VOKS, the union of movie and theater workers, to visit the Soviet Union. With government approval, she accepted, thinking she might visit Dash in Alaska on her way. "Go easy on those plans, darling," he wrote, "you're scaring me." August was a long way off. Shouldn't she wait for his leave, when they might meet in Seattle, and go down to Los Angeles and then East, "or wherever we felt like going"?

Still she handled his business matters. "I trust you're going ahead and using your best judgments," he wrote when she referred to disposing of the Sam Spade stories, "which is what you are supposed to do and why the power of attorney was given you." Formally, he thanked her "for taking care of the family money." Lily was entrusted to get the *Adakian* cartoons into the hands of Viking Press "with an introduction by that well-known ex-writer."

She created a stock corporation for the manufacture of motion pictures and the production of stage plays and called it Dashiell Pictures, Inc. Its first task was to handle the sale of the film rights of *The Searching Wind* to Hal Wallis. When she wrote Dash the name was a dubious honor, he replied that he was flattered. "And I don't like its being referred to as a dubious honor," he objected. Business matters continued to elude him. He didn't remember whether he had put any money in *The Little Foxes,* "but if you can't trust the Shumlin books what can you trust?"

The troops attended a screening of *Watch on the Rhine.* "I was quite proud," Dash told Lily simply.

Her birthday was always a major event for the spoiled only child. The day after D-Day, the Second Front having been opened at last, Dash wrote urging Lily to buy herself "a very gaudy" present "so that people will look at it and say, 'That Hammett—he spoils his women!'" He wished he could spend her birthday at Hardscrabble Farm with her. Then came a dig at her twisted sense of priorities; he imagined she would have spent with him only "the early part of it before you had to dash off to [Bea Kaufman's]."

It seemed as if their intimacy would continue indefinitely. He asked her to send him more poetry since he had enjoyed the Everyman editions of Milton and Donne so much. She inquired whether it was safe to pick the turtles up by their tails. She must not tow them "across the lake by the hook." A burlap sack was preferable. It seemed she could always consult him politically. He was too tough-minded to take Henry Wallace seriously. "I love him as much as you do," he wrote when Roosevelt dropped Wallace from the 1944 presidential campaign, "but you simply can't make a politician out of him." When Lily reported attending a rousing Wallace rally in Madison Square Garden, Dash wrote indulgently that he was "glad for you and glad for him. I think both of you are the kind of people who should be encouraged." His irony was unmistakable.

She wanted his advice about buying a house at 63 East Eighty-second Street. In fact, in an hour she had made her decision and agreed on the price, $33,000. More proof of Dash's complete lack of business acumen was his impression "that the high rent area wouldn't be a good buy near the end of a war." Tastefully Lily decorated her new town house in eighteenth-century English style. There was a brown velvet sofa, and in the dining room a red satin Victorian couch which had been in *The Little Foxes*. A mahogany highboy had once appeared in *The Children's Hour*. In 1944 Lily earned $134,358.30, more than a million dollars in 1990s money.

The last week of June marked "one long year" since Dash had seen Lily. "I'll say that's too long if you will," he bargained. "Try to be worthy of the love of one such as I," he closed another letter. He missed her. If it had been a "mighty fine year," he still "could have used a little more Hellman in it, but then think of the poor people who never had *any* Hellman."

During the summer of 1944, as Lily worked on the logistics of her visit to the Soviet Union, Dash embroidered on missing her. "To me, of course," he wrote on July 31, "it's absurd that anybody should miss anything but you." She had told him of her involvement with a "handsome Russian colonel." Confident his word would carry, as it always had, he responded as he had to her affair with Shumlin: "I'm sure I don't approve."

When he heard she had dazzled a cocktail party wearing black satin and a hat the color of her hair, he was pleased and wrote he had "a very satisfactory dream about you." Another night he dreamed of a yellow cat belonging to Lily: "Besides being witty, she was very pretty, and sexy too . . . I hope you will not get rid of her before I come home." This was the side of her he wanted.

"I'm interested in the details of your inner and outer life, though, and your sidewise life if you have one," he wrote. He sent her his letters of commendation for writing *The Battle of the Aleutians*. "Darling," Dash instructed, "just put these in the archives. You needn't keep a candle burning before them." The "ex-writer" was defensive now about his writing. "It is no 'War and Peace' you understand," he added, "and it was meant primarily for the troops up here, so you are not to quarrel with its rather severe tone of understatement. That was my own idea."

Dashiell Hammett never discouraged Lillian Hellman from seizing her opportunities. "You would be an idiot to let *anything* stand in your way," he told her, urging her to go to the Soviet Union. When she argued that all trips were "escapes," he disagreed. "You've got no right to classify all trips as escapes. That's just as bad—and almost exactly the same—as only using trips as escapes."

In April she had been denied a passport to go to England to work with Alexander Korda on a film version of *War and Peace* on the ground that she was "one of the key figures in the Communist Party in the New York area." But her New Deal connections helped now. When the passport obstacle was removed, Dash was thrilled. "I'm tickled to death that your travel plans are shaping up so well and am keeping all my fingers, my legs and my eyes crossed for you," he told her.

Before she departed for Moscow, Dash ordered her to have her portrait painted. "Strict orders, to be carried out to the letter and with absolutely no use of what you perhaps call your own best judgement: *You are to have Luis Quintanilla paint you for me.* I have spoken." In his mind nothing had and nothing would change. "I should like to find you the same simple country maid who was content to sip brandy strained through marajuana," Dash wrote, "or however the hell you spell it."

16

Lily Is Loved

"I am in love with you and always will be."

JOHN MELBY

"It's awful nice to hear your voice again, sister!"

DASHIELL HAMMETT

L ate in August 1944, Dashiell Hammett was at last liberated from Adak Island. Promoted to sergeant, he was sent on an island-hopping assignment as part of an Information and Education program to lecture bored, disgruntled troops on the importance of their serving their country by remaining out of combat in Alaska. "Thank God I've always led a sheltered life and thus have never had to come up against the sharp corners of reality which seem to bother so many people," Dash said sardonically. A soldier told him, "You don't remember me, but I met you at Lillian Hellman's home several years ago. Remember the May Company strike meeting?" Their shared history followed him.

Pru warned him "against the local fleshpots," sending him a lock of her hair and the news that she made a belt out of one of his old ties. "It's nice to think of something belonging to me wrapped around you," he wrote in the old chivalrous tones which gave away nothing. Neither Pru nor Lily had any effect now on his wildly profligate behavior.

Hammett found in Fort Richardson "saloons, stores, restaurants, taxis, cement sidewalks—boy, oh boy! this is high life!" Traveling from Attu to Kodiak to Fairbanks and Nome, to Whittier, to Anchorage (a one-street town then), and Fort Richardson, he hit every fleshpot, drinking heavily. In one bar, he gently removed a glass from a woman drinking a martini, and threw it over the bar, where it crashed at the bartender's feet. "Mix baby a Dashiell Hammett special!" he ordered. Into a brandy snifter the bartender then poured all manner of liquors. Missing the extra-long, narrow tub in his personal bathroom at Hardscrabble Farm, he enjoyed his first bath since he left home.

Lily received ironic reports. He told her not to believe the reason he had not written was that "he was shacked up with a native woman on the outskirts of Anchorage." He also felt compelled to write Lily about a birthday party he attended for one of the USO girls in the "Kiss and Tell" company. "You know me and actresses," he said, "I just can't stay away." He feared his partner wasn't much of an actress, "but then I guess they seldom are." They were "little play-girls." When his actress, Lee Brown, took an interest in Bill Glackin, Hammett became jealous. "You could have talked to any of the other thousands of GIs," he told her, upset that she had chosen his assistant over him. (To Brown, Hammett seemed an old man whose dental plate rattled, hardly an attractive sexual partner.)

With Lillian about to take off for Moscow, Dash instinctively began to focus more on Pru, as if some sixth sense told him to anticipate a dramatic alteration in their relationship. Now he wanted to know from Pru rather than from Lily "where you go and what you wear and eat and drink; what time you go to bed and when you get up." He threatened to send her a questionnaire "so I'll have my fingers on your past as well as your present. I mean your pre-Hammett past." He thought it would be "indelicate" to pry into her life either before he met her or since the last time they saw each other. He bought Pru an ivory necklace made from walrus tusks. He was drinking heavily. His worst periods of alcoholism coincided with Lillian's absence or with those more and more frequent times when he feared he had lost her.

Still, he kept track of Lily's progress toward Moscow. When her transport was delayed, he imagined her distress. "I'm worrying about your worrying, though god knows why," he wrote in early September. "You have been fretting about uncertainties for years and it hasn't done you any damage that I can't fix up." He worried that she now had the grippe, that she didn't know how to take care of herself, but only "how to be snippy giving other people advice on how to take care of his or herself." Other people might find her formidable, a bitch on wheels. To Dash, she remained "a silly little woman to whom nobody ought to pay any attention, as I wouldn't if I didn't love you."

Lily bought herself new luggage, had her hair permanent-waved and dyed an amber color, and set out for California. After visiting the Kobers, she boarded a train for Seattle, leaving on October 14 for Fairbanks.

Hammett lost track of where she was. "It would be nice to think you were far to the north of here right now," he wrote her on October 11, "between me and the pole star . . . winging your way to Moscow at last." He wrote a similar letter on the sixteenth, picturing himself looking at the North Star and imagining her on the plane carrying her from Fairbanks to Russia. Hammett postponed his furlough. He didn't "see much sense to trying to get back home before you do anyway."

In Fairbanks, Lily had been taken up by Miriam Dickey, a woman dubbed the "key to Fairbanks," and secretary to Austin E. (Cap) Lathrop, the richest industrialist in western Alaska. Unable to find a hotel, Lily slept on Dickey's couch as one night stretched to a week and the Russian plane was delayed. She flirted with Cap, talked of Dash. On the sixteenth she sent Dash a wire. Couldn't he get a "day off" and meet her in Fairbanks?

Dash was way out on Attu; her wire reached him only when he returned to Adak on the twenty-third. He showed it to the young soldiers, laughing at Lily's writing as if all he had to do was commandeer a plane to meet her a thousand miles out in the Pacific. But in his reply of October fifth, he had let her down gently. It would take three days to make the round trip "if everything went like clock work." He was "over a thousand miles from that part of the country and still headed west, so there's no use. It was a nice idea though, baby, and I would've made a stab at it." Never one to take no for an answer, she persisted, so he had to tell her he would not be anywhere near Fairbanks for at least a month. She would "probably go stark raving mad" if she had to wait. Meanwhile he would "look kind of wistfully at the North Star."

Obsessed with her whereabouts, on October 26 he wrote again, hoping "your Russian bomber has already picked you up and that you're looking down on Moscow just about now." He sensed their loss of connection, feared that they would not be able to write to each other. "From now on I'll be writing to you in a kind of semi-vacuum," he complained, "not knowing whether you're yet off to the other side of the world." He wondered how long she would be gone; she had not told him, nor was he told by her secretary where he should send mail. He thought it "kind of whacky . . . to be writing you, in Moscow by now, from Alaska by way of New York." He was especially lonely for her now that he did not know where she was. He hoped she was "having the best of times." When he returned to Adak he had been so drunk the men had to carry him into his Quonset hut.

In a letter on November 5 he described himself as "he who wishes he were with you in Moscow this Sunday night where you are no doubt flirting with handsome colonels in chic white uniforms, and why aren't they at the front?" He knew her well; he feared the worst. Losing connection with her troubled him greatly. "Even though I know it's unavoidable," Dash wrote, "I can't help missing the letters from you which don't come these days, and probably won't be coming for many a day. I don't know how long you'll be gone, but maybe it'll lure you home earlier if I tell you that telephone communication is now to be had between here and the states."

He had urged her to go to Russia, but as soon as she was gone, he wanted her back. He was alarmed, even before he had cause to be. He even offered a bribe. If she would "give him a hint at her possible return date," he would decide "when I want to try to get my long over-due 30-day furlough." There was no sense in his returning home "while you are off in foreign parts." However often he wrote to Pru Whitfield, her availability was not of sufficient appeal for him to return home on furlough.

When by the third week of November he had still heard nothing from Lily, he was deeply upset. "This is a long dry spell, my darling," he wrote on November 18, "and does my disposition no appreciable good at all." On the twenty-fourth he wrote, "I've still had no word from you since your wire while you were waiting to take off." The sight of Russian planes taking off pleased him, however. "It's kind of nice seeing the Russians take the Russian planes through here," he said. Regarding their politics, he clung to his invincible innocence.

By November 24 Dash still had no word beyond the original wire Lily had sent from Fairbanks. By now he had met Miriam Dickey, who learned from Nancy Bragdon that Lily had arrived in Moscow, "for which I'm thanking the appropriate gods," he wrote. His information about Lily was coming to him at third hand. Listening to Dash talk about Lily, Miriam Dickey concluded she was the love of his life; he did not mention his children, only her. Those two people have to get back together, Dickey concluded. They're in love with each other.

At a cocktail party at Dickey's, however, Dash encountered a young woman, just thirty, pretty, petite, brown-haired, who told him she was researching a book about early aviation in Alaska. Jean Potter asked him to read her manuscript, which he did in one sitting while she went off to the hairdresser. He told her it was "fine," "breathtaking." It might even have seemed as if he were starting all over again with Lily, he the mentor, she the eager pupil. "Your hands are small and delicate and Lillian's are big," Hammett crooned as he offered to go over the manuscript with her line by line.

He talked to Potter about Lillian. They were swimming at a beach once, Dash said. Lily suddenly told him, "You know, I have very good-looking feet." This was typical of her. He had just looked at her and said, "You know, *I* have very good-looking feet. I never noticed it before." So he had punctured her vanity.

It wasn't long before Hammett let Potter know he was sexually attracted to her. She returned the feeling. Alas, Hammett had to tell her, he would have liked to make love to her, but he was incapable of the sexual act. He called her sometime after that, and talked romantically, even lewdly, so that Potter had to say, "Look, Hammett, I'm going to have to hang up. Please, will you hang up!" He was obviously very drunk.

When he returned from his lecture tour, the men of *The Adakian* had moved to a much bigger hut, with a chest full of food from the commissary, hot plates for cooking, and an eight-foot-long table where "Sam" would lie on his back, prop his head up against a package of paper, and read for a few hours. No longer editing *The Adakian,* he made notes on 3-by-5 cards, supposedly for a novel about a guy who gets drafted and sent to the Aleutians. He said he preferred "the pre-writing period when all is grand and vast and majestic," and wrote Pru he didn't think "anybody's actually panting for a Hammett book." He had lost his confidence. Later he denied he had ever intended to write a novel. He had thought of doing it only "in terms of *if* I stayed on the island," he explained to Lily.

Even as he feared his words were vanishing into a vacuum, he continued to write to Lily. When a book she had recommended, *A Walk in the Sun,* arrived, he wrote, "Maybe I'm lucky in love," adding he hoped "you and Moscow are doing all right by one another."

Flying from Fairbanks with a Soviet Army pilot at the controls, Lily's plane encountered a snowstorm in the depths of Siberia. The pilot set down in the deep snow in a town called Stantsia Zima, or Winter Junction. Lily emerged from the plane swathed in furs. Out of relief that they had survived, Lily and the Soviet pilot fell into each other's arms in mad passion.

Right there out in the open, they succumbed, making love to each other amid the wind and snow and ice. A young schoolboy, twelve years old, came walking down the road. Then he stopped, transfixed as he watched the undulating couple obliviously in the throes of sexual intercourse. Years later when Lily met Yevgeny Yevtushenko, he realized that the woman in furs had been she, Lillian Hellman, the first American ever to have set foot in the town of Stantsia Zima and doing it in her particular style.

When her plane landed in Moscow, a short man with a high sloping forehead, ears with pricked tips, a balding leonine head too big for his body framed by cloud-like tufts of hair and small, delicate hands and feet was waiting for her at the airport. She was tired and ill. Within an hour it seemed as if the warmth and wit of Sergei Eisenstein, with his twinkling blue eyes and his irony, his whimsical smile, and his brilliant mind, had cured her grippe and wiped out any trepidations she had about this trip. He spoke English, replete with American slang. He was the most international man she had ever met, and, of course, one of the greatest artists of the century. There was also a sadness about him, for these were hard times for Eisenstein. For years he had been under heavy surveillance. Stalin had spared his life, but at so great a price that he would be dead in four years at the age of fifty.

Lily had reached Moscow early in November, but Dash remained out of communication. He wrote to Nancy Bragdon on December 1: "By the way nobody has as much as hinted to me how long Lillian's going to be away. Is it a secret?" Christmas came and went. Bragdon discouraged him from writing to Russia: "It's unlikely any of the letters will get to Moscow before the addressee has left." Lillian would be back in January.

In Moscow, where the people seemed hungry and every house in want of repair, Lily tried to regain contact with her Soviet pilot lover, only to be told first that he was away on duty and later that he had been killed in action. In making love to her he had committed a forbidden act, and the KGB may have exacted suitable punishment.

Moscow seemed tired, cold, and shabby to Lillian and before long she came down with pneumonia. She was unhappy with her spare and chilly hotel room at the National, no matter that it was right on Red Square, facing St. Basil's Cathedral, built in the sixteenth century for Ivan the Terrible. Soon she moved into the much more comfortable Spaso House, the residence of the American embassy. Ambassador Harriman was away in America and George Kennan had to wire for permission. The residence had its own fuel problems in frozen Moscow and they were dependent on the functioning of two heaters which exploded periodically. Lily wore her red bathrobe to keep warm. "Let's heckle Lillian on her politics," Kennan encouraged his cohorts one night. Lily proved to be his match, as she talked with self-proclaimed authority about Spain.

"I think I'm dining with more generals than any woman since Catherine the Great," Lillian said, enjoying her proximity to the higher-ups. So they drank toasts to President Roosevelt, to the Red Army, and to Lily's own health. Russian men, she decided, had a "very attractive quality; they are men who know they are men and like all such act with simplicity and tenderness." It was another romantic fantasy, the plain little girl transported to the ball with a whole room "of handsome gentlemen & in uniforms," a dream she had at the age of thirteen now come true.

Lillian enjoyed hobnobbing with "Russian diplomats in black uniforms with gold braid, and many medals & decorations on everybody." Her loyalty was to the state which she and Hammett had defended through barbarous years. Now she wrote in her diary of "the deep reverence & respect that even intellectuals have for Stalin." Lily had no use for the minor diplomats and foreign journalists and American fur buyers swarming at the Metropole Hotel close to the walls of the Kremlin and the site of international intrigue.

She was, however, at once ill at ease with the prevailing and inescapable anti-Semitism. She was made to feel, she wrote in her diary, "like the Jewish shopkeeper during a pogrom rumor." Sergei Eisenstein, whom she saw frequently, wanted to know whether she was married to Hammett. He himself had a "wife" who was not a wife.

Lillian Hellman was now thirty-nine years old, her hair dyed that reddish-blond color. Still the romantic, she craved a man who would cherish her as a woman as Hammett was no longer capable of doing. She confided to Kathleen Harriman that she had married Kober too young, that she hadn't really wanted to settle down.

On the evening of November 11 Lily was at dinner at Spaso House. At the table was a man she had not seen before, a diplomat attached to the embassy, who had only just returned from a trip to Murmansk. The man disapproved of her mockery of the canapés, which were made of peanut butter, a delicacy for these provincial Americans sated with caviar. "You're not going on about peanut butter!" Lily laughed at him. No, she definitely did not like him, Lily thought.

John Melby was a third secretary attached to the American embassy, a married man with two small sons, but separated from his wife. He was thirty years old, tall and thin and Anglo-Saxon; his mother's family, the Geers, had been original settlers of Connecticut. Melby had an ageless look about him with a long facial scar and half of his face partly paralyzed as the result of an accident; he could smile only with one side of his face. He was a dour man, Harriman's perspicacious secretary, Robert Meiklejohn, thought. Kathleen Harriman didn't think Melby was at all sexy.

On Christmas morning, Lily, dressed in oversized pajamas, entered Melby's bedroom. She had a frightened look on her face. She needed his help, she told him. He was flattered, although her problem was merely a hangover.

One night soon after, they sat on opposite sides of the fire, Lily in the black satin Hammett had admired. Melby told her he loved her. He brought her upstairs and took her in his arms. He caressed her breasts. But still he held back, did not make love to her.

There was a party at which gypsies sang "Los Cuatro Generales." Melby was jealous when General Russ Deane, Harriman's military adviser, made a pass at Lily. She quickly drank two full glasses of scotch. Melby had to undress her and put her to bed.

At times Lily repaired to her room at the National Hotel, room 209. One afternoon at dusk she was dressing. Outside there was a white glow from the snow. She wore a purple suit, a strand of gold beads, and brown pumps. Today she was irritated when Melby appeared. "Don't take me so casually," she told him.

Suddenly Melby was making love to a woman as he never before had. For the first time in his puritanical sexual life, he "went down on" a woman. Lily, he found, was full of "the strange exciting odor of the curse," so that he could not have her completely. That she had the curse during their first time, he told her later, meant that for him she would "always be life and creation." When they returned to Spaso House, it seemed to John Melby that he smelled so strongly of her body that all the world must know it.

Soon Lily was telling John Melby that it was all over between her and Dashiell Hammett. Soon he was telling her that his wife hadn't wanted him on their wedding night. ("You're safe!" a relieved Kathleen Harriman told her father, who was at once relieved too. Lily's reputation as a predatory woman had preceded her. Ave had feared she would go after him. Later Lillian was to refer to Harriman as "the Great Thinker.")

John Melby told Lillian Hellman that he had not even been a man until he met her. She replied that for her it was as if he were her first beau. Everything about her pleased him, the way she pulled and twisted her hair, the way she made the typewriter bounce around on the table when she was at work. They met in Meiklejohn's room, which had the only kerosene heater and was the only warm place. She stopped writing to Hammett; she felt like a young woman again.

When Melby showered her with gifts, she felt both "pleased" and "puzzled." There remained that part of Lily which could not believe that she was loved for herself. She told Melby he had brought her "all of security and pleasantness and warmth." He replied that no woman could bring a man any greater gift than that of peace of mind and body and she had brought him both. She went to sleep with her back up against his and when they awoke her head was on his shoulder. Everything had to be different from the way it had been with Hammett. She did not talk baby talk with John Melby.

He asked her to marry him. At once she expressed what he called "bitter doubts and discouragements," and referred to his "cold Anglo-Saxon way." Once more she felt her familiar masochistic yearning for men who withheld themselves. Like Hammett, Melby recognized that she needed reassurances and that her plainness was at the root of her lack of self-esteem and insecurity. "My beauteous one, I love you," he said. He told her he loved her warm husky voice, her infectious laugh. As with Hammett, she didn't believe him.

Together they drove around Moscow in the big black Buick he had shipped for him across Siberia, Lily happy in her big heavy fur coat. Lily spent more time shopping than in social observation. Always she was fun as she and Melby and Kathleen Harriman made toast on the electric floor heater and got into food fights.

Together they attended a screening of *The Little Foxes*. Together they went shopping in the commissary, where she took what Melby called "a piece of canned crap" and, using a "reluctant burner," created a dish "eminently edible." They went to a Prokofiev concert, he keeping on his warm red mittens. Afterward they ate cold Spam sandwiches. If it was bitter cold, they were always warm before they went to sleep. Later she would remember Melby sitting on her bedroom radiator in his brown suit, and that she was so cold she wore heavy woolen underwear, pajamas, a sweater, and socks to bed.

Lily told Melby she was not a Communist and had made no application to visit the front. Nor was she eager to go when her translator, Raya Orlova, announced that she had been granted that rare privilege. There she was treated as a tourist, entertained by a juggler and an acrobat, served tea, and given a pistol-shaped cigarette lighter for a souvenir. "It looked like a scene from War & Peace with horses & men," she thought, having no idea of how close they were to the fighting. She did write to Hammett now. Back on Adak, he read part of her letter out loud to his fellow soldiers with such a sense of excitement that, as Bernard Kalb was to remember, they were lifted "out of our Aleutian stagnancy and placed . . . at the front lines."

There was some talk of her returning to Moscow as a cultural attaché, an idea sponsored by Archibald MacLeish, then Assistant Secretary of State for Cultural Affairs. Lily declined. "If I stay here for any length of time I'll get to be as anti-Russian as the rest of you," she said. When she returned to America, sometimes she said Stalin had told her he was too busy to see her and sometimes she said that his secretary had called—he would see her—but she didn't want to bother a great man who was so busy during a war; it wasn't fair to him. Sometimes she said she had the appointment, only for it to be canceled.

She gave a farewell party for the artists she had met who had entertained her, along with members of the Russian casts of *The Little Foxes* and *Watch on the Rhine,* and the Russians dressed for the occasion, wearing jewelry to which they had access from a huge warehouse of furs and jewels and clothes confiscated from the old nobility. (Millionaire Averell Harriman was allowed to buy a present for his wife from this treasure trove of the Czars: Harriman looked at some ruby pieces. One was $45, the other $55. He chose the one for $45.)

Lily never gave a bad party. The rugs were pulled back, the Russians danced the tango and the rumba, and the liquor flowed freely. The only embarrassing incident came when the woman who played the lead in *Watch on the Rhine* tried hard to get Kathleen Harriman to dance with her.

At last came Lily's final night with Melby. "I was bad tired; now I am good tired," she said, contented after their sex. On January 18, he took her to the airport. He sat there quietly, staring at her. She said she was sorry to go. For her it had not been an *amour fou;* she was beyond that, and had long sought not to love a man, but to be validated, approved, admired. But he was "a nice man, a dignified man," and it had been "good for me." Melby stood and watched as the plane disappeared into the snow.

Lily now traveled to Baku, Teheran, Cairo, and finally to London, where she arrived on January 29, and where she remained until February 23. There was a big, fancy party at Claridges for William Wyler, which shocked her friend Philip D'Arcy Hart since the war was still on. Lily recounted her experiences in the Soviet Union.

Believing Lily had been due to arrive in London on January 10, Dash wrote another letter reflecting his insecurity. "I guess it's about time that I started seeing you have something worth coming home to," he began. "It's strange writing to you again after all this time—though it's going to be both strange and wonderful hearing from you again—so if I should sound a little distant or something at first it's because I don't want you to think me—by now comparatively a stranger—too fresh."

Awkwardly, he thanks her for the "swell" Christmas gifts, assuming those that came from Abercrombie's had to be from her. There had been no card. He confessed that he had almost "snapped up" his overdue furlough, then decided to "gamble on my chance of getting it after your return." Never had he been so out of touch with her, so unaware of her actual mood. Once more he wrote he was on the wagon and "surprised to find I can have a good time staying sober." Even that failed to draw a response from Lily.

Still having heard nothing from her, on February 25 he wrote hoping she was "speeding over the Atlantic in a generally westward direction." As if nothing were wrong, as always he shared his reading experiences. He had read a book about Poland called *Story of a Secret State*. "I tell you, sister," Dash wrote in his old style, "the gentry can be trusted to save our world." Jealousy had always worked; he tried that. On the same day he wrote another letter, informing her that in the course of his having helped Jean Potter edit her book on early Alaskan fliers he had "become very fond of Jean." Then he discussed whether they should wait for his furlough to settle the matter of her Christmas present. He was alarmed.

Back in Moscow, Melby dreamed that Lily had become pregnant. He thought "it would be wonderful." He wanted marriage and he wanted her children; he begged her to "try to love me, not just a little, but a great deal." Although she had sent a note from Teheran, saying she missed him "too much," Lily had held back this time, and that excited her lover as eager availability never could.

One morning, Melby woke up muttering, "Baby, God made your cunt just for me to fuck and if it has ever been used otherwise, that is abuse because God made it just for me." She had released in him strong and abiding passion, and he loved her for it. Now he needed her, he said, "to look after me, asleep or awake," which is of course what Dash had always wanted as well.

When still Lily didn't write, not once from London, Dash became angry. In a letter to Maggie Kober, he called her "a bastard." He wrote plaintively to Nancy Bragdon: "She's been gone so long that I've no clear notion that she'll ever come back." Nancy had better warn Lily "that she'd better fix up very good reasons for not having written me from London." In his dismay, he kept writing to Pru, sometimes two letters in one day. When Pru asked his advice about whether to marry a man she described as a "conventional, strait-laced stuffed shirt—who thinks PM, the administration and everything about Russia, etc. stinkin', lousy and untouchable," he urged her to remain free.

Finally, on February 27, Dash received a wire from Nancy: "HELLMAN COMING HOME TUESDAY ARE YOU ALL RIGHT SPEAK." He wrote Lily that same day: "Mighty glad of it even if I'm not there to welcome you." When Lily still remained silent, he kept on writing. "No-news Hammett, they call me," he wrote her on March 1. "I hope Nancy warned you that I was going to expect some sort of explanation why you didn't write me all the time you were in England. It seems to me if Cockburn could keep in touch with me. . . ." On March 9, he turned on the radio and heard her being interviewed, "talking just like life and sounding fine and stirring and better than music to my old ears." His yearning is unmistakable. "It's awful nice to hear your voice again, sister!"

"I'm still without a letter," he wrote her the next day. She had been home for ten days and still hadn't written. "I haven't been blaming you. I only blame you for not having written from England, and probably wouldn't even do that if Cockburn's paper hadn't kept coming through on time to remind me of what you weren't doing." That same day he wrote Maggie: "I guess I'll never understand women." On March 13, he wrote Lily again: "I remember you. You're the tart-tongued problematic woman in *Time* this week and I bet you're having fun . . . I still haven't—except for your wire . . . heard from you since your return and am doing my best not to attribute it to anything." It had been five months. He wrote her as well that day of a "small dark distant political cloud" which had appeared on his "political horizon," courtesy of the Chicago *Tribune*, prophecy of turbulence to come.

Two letters arrived from Lillian on March 15, the first he had heard from her since October. "It was awful nice being on your mailing list again," he wrote sarcastically. The reference to Potter had worked; Lily included a disparaging reference to the young woman. "I know what you mean about Potter, who can be a very foolish woman," Dash agreed, "but . . . I got to kind of like her very much . . . which may or may not be Alaska." Lily and Dash both could make people believe they liked them, and then speak devastatingly about them behind their backs. Bill Glackin thought of Dash as a "second father," but Dash wrote Lily, "I don't especially like him—by which I mean I've not much warmth toward him—but he's a good boy."

He depicted himself to Bragdon as coolly picking up "the frayed ends" of his correspondence with Lily. When Lily wrote of an exchange with "La Bankhead," he told her he "mildly disapproved." He was now reading Lenin's *Theoretical Principles of Marxism*, Vol. 11 in the *Selected Works*. He wrote Lily that he was thinking of writing a novel, "for which I've got a kind of feel if not exactly any clear idea." He blamed his idleness and lack of resolve on Alaska, and said, "It's hard to convince me that I haven't all the time in the world ahead of me for practically anything I wish to do." He was a childish man at times.

John Melby returned to America in April, flying immediately to San Francisco for the peace conference. He purchased a copy of *The Maltese Falcon*, writing Lily that Hammett used the word "utterly . . . as often as a Spaso lunchtable argument on how to chip ice from the driveway." The ending, in which Spade asserts the precedence of the principle of avenging his partner's death over love, was "strange." Although Lily had insisted it was over between her and Dash, he couldn't resist a few gibes at his rival. "What I want to know is what was Hammett so bitter about when he wrote it," Melby asked. If Hammett was a worldly American provincial, Lily had now chosen an unworldly variety. In one letter after another Melby referred to "our children."

Ensconced in her house on Eighty-second Street with its cool green walls and red chairs and red sofa, Lily was depressed in the absence of her new lover. "Right now, I think it would be nice to get to know you," she wrote Melby. She had lunch with Kathleen Harriman, then shared her impressions with John. Harriman looked "bad; dried and older than she should look. Maybe she should just sleep with her Pa and get it over with," Lily wrote meanspiritedly. Melby did not approve. As opposed to humor, he later concluded, Lily's wit was always at someone's expense and invariably cruel.

Having been told nothing of Melby, Dash kept on writing, commiserating with Lily over the "pretty pickle" she had gotten into with the Russian colonel. He discussed her efforts to get Viking to publish the *Adakian* cartoons. Then, in the habit of a husband, he complained of the red blotches on his face, signs of an old vitamin A deficiency. Finances still bound them as well. "That bank account shall be treated as sacred and I only wish I had millions in it for you to draw on."

They gossiped about Maggie Kober. Lily had complained he had "encouraged Maggie a little in the eccentric princess stuff"; Dash pleaded that "she had got a fine start before I knew her, aping her mother, the batty duchess." From Fort Richardson, he wondered when he should phone Lily: "what days of the week are best and what part of the day . . . morning, afternoon or night? And where . . . Pleasantville or New York? RSVP."

Still she planned to enlist his help in her work. She had an idea for a new play; Dash approved: "The Little Foxes folk back in reconstruction days should be a very satisfactory setup for a play. It's a nice—theatrically nice—period and with a few exceptions only the worst things have been done with it." When she made disparaging remarks about her film script in progress for *The Searching Wind,* he fulfilled his old function, brushing aside her doubts: "I do not pay too much attention to your complaints about what you'd done. I remember you," he wrote. Hammett told her that Hal Wallis' liking it should be enough.

From a literary perspective things were not going well; Harold Ross asked her to return a $1,000 advance from *The New Yorker* for her piece on her trip to Russia, concluding that it was no more than "a good little piece on your emotions and what you think about things." Only *Collier's* would take it.

In June, Lily and Kober and Dotty spent a weekend at the George S. Kaufmans'. Their hostess's cooking was pronounced "dreck" before they even arrived. The guests at Lillian's birthday party that week were reviewed: "Mrs. Averell Harriman's feathers were completely plucked, and her skin along with them. Mr. Jimmy Sheehan got a thorough roasting, and J. Raymond Walsh, the news commentator, was praised, but it was revealed that he is a fairy." The purpose of the weekend was a burying of the hatchet between Dotty and the Kaufmans. Yet that Sunday morning *The New York Times Book Review* included a Parker statement referring to Kaufman and Hart's "nasty little play *The Man Who Came to Dinner*" and quipping that in their writing about Alexander Woollcott they "went for the obnoxious." Dotty gasped. Lillian grabbed the book review section and rolled it up, ordering Dotty to take it up to her room and bury it in her suitcase.

George arrived for breakfast late. Attempting to avoid a scene, Kober started a gin rummy game the minute he came down. But Kaufman wanted the newspapers. Looking over the *Times,* he announced, "My favorite part is missing." When Lillian looked at him with fear in her eyes, he added, "The real estate section."

"It's probably up in Dotty's room, locked in her suitcase," Lillian said. Such was the glamour of life amid the world of the New York theater.

Although Lily had resumed sending delicacies from Martin's, and agitating Dash by neglecting to inform him of a royalty fight over book reprints, they wrote to each other only sporadically now. In May, Hammett announced he might stay in the Army after the war since it would "still represent the heart and guts of American manhood or something and I belong with it." He did not indulge in dreams of returning to Hardscrabble Farm.

"Try to pretend you're not sorry you ever met up with such an old fool," Dash pleaded at the end of June 1945.

PART SIX

The Crucifixion of
Dashiell Hammett

17

The Postwar

"Lillian is my right foot and I'm her left hand."

DASHIELL HAMMETT

Under a streetlight Lily waited for John Melby. Then, as soon as she saw him, she ran into his arms. The summer of 1945 was to be their summer as she spirited him away to Hardscrabble Farm, where he met the Zilboorgs and the Kronenbergers, Shumlin, Archie MacLeish, and Paul Robeson. In the expectation that Hammett might return on his long-delayed furlough, she rented a house in East Hampton; she was indignant, if undeterred, when her first rental choice was denied her after the owner learned she was Jewish. With Melby, she spent many days on "lovely Sammy's beach." Mrs. Christian Herter, Sr., greeted John Melby on behalf of Lillian's crowd: "So you're the young mystery man from Moscow!"

Lily settled down to work on the script for *The Searching Wind*, sexual comfort not interfering with steady work. Only the accident of goose bones splintering in her throat and necessitating a hospital stay delayed her. Then it was Shumlin who was shaken by her close call. "I can't begin to tell you the terrible first feeling I had when losing you," he wrote. "You know how we Jewish people dramatize our emotions, but it really was a very sinking sensation." No longer either lovers or collaborators, they remained close.

From John Melby, her young lover, Lily demanded constant attention, as if he must make up for long deprivation. Hammett never danced with her, not once. Melby did, but then Lily protested as they danced, "You don't really love me, because you don't hold me tightly enough." When she wore a new blue suit and he didn't notice, she became testy. She wanted to hold hands in public, then dubbed herself "a silly woman" for feeling such a need. Out of some shame of her middle-class Jewishness, she chose those cool Anglo-Saxon men whose feelings had been iced over, then complained of their lack of effusiveness. She had a "warm Mediterranean nature," she explained to Melby, while "he was cold." If Hammett seemed a childish man, so Lily seemed always, in her own words, an "unfinished woman."

Always she offered imaginative sexuality. Back in New York, one day Melby walked up the stairs at 63 East Eighty-second Street, and there was Lillian standing in the doorway, stark naked but for a pair of mules and, Melby thought, an appealing look on her face.

Meanwhile Hammett's vague notion of remaining in the Army after his furlough disappeared. One day he was reprimanded for drinking by a young officer. Reproved for how badly he represented his country, he felt the shame he always did when he was criticized. At once he applied for his discharge. In late August he left Anchorage; by September 6 he was in New York. On his separation and honorable discharge paper he gave as his permanent address not Jose's, as he had when he entered the Army, but Hardscrabble Road, Pleasantville, New York.

Hammett headed first for Lillian's house on Eighty-second Street. There in the hallway he encountered John Melby, in residence. They went into the living room and chatted about innocuous subjects. But Hammett was not pleased. His clothes, his books, were in her house. The moment was deeply awkward.

It will take a day or two for him to retrieve his possessions and find a place of his own, Lily explained to Melby. She requested that he move out for a few days. Melby spent two nights at the Plaza. When he returned, Hammett had checked into the Hotel Roosevelt on Madison Avenue.

Guilty ever after about how quickly she shunted Hammett out of her life as soon as he returned from the Army, Lillian began to say that it was Hammett who had not come home to her. Rather, he had instantly disappeared as soon as he returned, as she enlisted the truth of his habit of disappearing in earlier years in a self-serving fabrication. One day, as she spun the tale, she learned he had shacked up with a rich, non-Jewish socialite. The day was rainy. Lily turned up at the socialite's Fifth Avenue apartment and immediately spied Hammett sitting in the study with a martini in his hand. When she demanded that he leave with her, he obeyed.

In September 1945, as Hammett returned from the Army, it was he who was rejected and Lily who drove the wedge between them, betraying the returning veteran. Until she had gone to Moscow, he had worn her ring, dreamt of her gumbos and her domestic nurture. Now, driven by a loneliness he dared not acknowledge, Hammett descended into three years of alcoholic trauma which nearly cost him his life. The whores returned. Any woman would do.

Lee Brown, who had been on that Aleutian Islands USO tour, sent Hammett a clipping. Soon he wrote her a long chatty letter which included a reference to "Lillian Hellman" and how taken she was with the glamorous journalist Claud Cockburn. He told Brown he hoped *she* would not be similarly taken in by a mere pretty face. That September in New York, Hammett asked Lee for a date. He was still famous enough to attract a beautiful young woman and she agreed to meet him at the Stork Club.

When Brown arrived, Hammett was sitting with another woman. She was a writer down on her luck, Hammett explained as he handed the woman some money. "That's what old friends are for." People in uniform came up to his table to greet him, and he obviously savored the attention. It was nearly eleven before the other woman left. Now drunk and incoherent, Dash took Lee up to Harlem. "You know, you're really okay, you're not like other women, politically your ideas are okay," he told her. That she had befriended Robert Colodny in Alaska pleased him. He was too drunk to dance, and his sexual overtures, his slobbering, repelled her.

"Don't leave. Stay with me," Hammett pleaded when at one in the morning Lee said she wanted to go home. "Let's spend the rest of the night together." She found a taxi and sped off.

Sometime later he saw Ed Spitzer, whom he had known in Alaska. Would you like to be president of the New York Civil Rights Congress? Spitzer asked him. In New York City they were working to make the educational system more democratic. Hammett agreed without bothering to ask any of the details. Before long Spitzer and Lee Brown married. In New York State, Hammett registered as a member of the American Labor Party.

At loose ends, Hammett inquired of Herman about Sheffield Island, off the coast of Maine, which cost only "a fat $160,000." Shumlin tried to help him by giving him the proofs of a novel he was considering for a movie. Lily worried about him, pitied him, even as Melby encouraged her to distance herself. "When something is finished," he said, "it is over and trying to hang on to some part, except in distant fashion, is only to befuddle and cause new trouble." Despairing for Dash, however, Lily let him know both the farm and her New York house were open to him.

One night he invited Jean Potter over to Lillian's apartment. Opening the refrigerator in search of something for them to eat, he could find only pigs' feet.

"Lillian is my right foot and I'm her left hand," Hammett said then. They didn't quite fit together, never had and never would, but neither was complete without the other. So Lily and Dash had settled into the uneasy postwar years unable to part yet with neither expecting much of the other.

Dash continued in a bad way and one night Potter met him at a bar only to find him holding a large hunting knife. Disturbed, she got up and walked out. Potter dedicated *The Flying North* to Dashiell Hammett for his confidence in the concept of her book. "What's this 'concept'?" he demanded. Then sardonically he asked, "I don't know how fortunate it is for me saying this book is good, suppose it fails?" Meanwhile Lillian hovered, telephoning Potter's apartment when she didn't know where Hammett was, making herself a presence in this new relationship. It was a late-middle-age parody of Hammett's old taste for threesomes.

Potter was distressed when Hammett presented her with a diamond-and-ruby watch from Tiffany's for her birthday. She refused to accept it.

"Give it to Ethel if you can't accept it," Hammett insisted, referring to Potter's black maid. "I spent twenty minutes choosing it and I'm not going to take it back." Potter had run out of money, and when Macmillan would not contract for a new book, Hammett wrote her out a check for $5,000. On her first attempt to repay him, he replied, "Why are you always acting as if I'm dunning you about that silly dreck?" He was talking like Lily now.

Before long Potter became engaged to be married. When she showed Hammett her ring, he was sulky. "That's kind of cute," he said. When she departed for Europe in November 1946, she telephoned him at Hardscrabble Farm. "Just a minute," he said, "Lillian wants to say goodbye." They had never met, but Lily was not above establishing her place. It seemed to Jean that Hammett was glad she was going off to be married; he hadn't wanted a connection with any other woman after all.

John Melby's ambition was to be Secretary of State. When he was posted to China in the autumn of 1945, although he loved Lily there was no chance of his declining the assignment. "I'll go with you," she said. Then they decided that he would ask for a different posting, or she would join him later. She saw him off at the airport wearing a new black hat with a big brim, dressed all in black and brown. Then she wrote to

Philip D'Arcy Hart wondering how she could get a visa to China. "Who am I to be able to get you into China?" Hart replied.

To Melby, Lily wrote letters full of longing in which she told him she wanted to share a home with him. He called himself a "goddamned fool" for leaving, even as he suspected she would never give up her literary life to follow him to outposts of the foreign service. By November she was writing a memo to Spyros Skouras outlining a plan for a National Repertory Theater, "a true art theatre," to encourage America's "few serious, first rate playwrights."

Yet Melby's departure left a deep emotional void. "I've been bad angry for weeks," she wrote him. "I get angry when I get most neurotic and then I pay hard for it." Still a patient of Gregory Zilboorg's (she paid him $3,220 in 1946 alone), she saw herself as "full of hidden nastiness and resentments, depressed about everything." She doubted whether Melby could really return in less than a year or two; she wrote him she was "not even sure that you really want to, not knowing what I would say or do if you did come." No more now than with Ingersoll or Shumlin or any of the others did she see herself as ready to cast her lot with a man other than Hammett. Trying to help, Zilboorg himself wrote to Melby to say he thought John and Lillian "were happy together and would be."

Once more Lily tried her hand at a short story. She did not show this effort to Dash, but mailed it to Melby. Melby had said, jealously, "You never told me whether Dash ever found a place to live or whether he still bunks with you." In fact, Dash had rented an apartment at 15 East Sixty-sixth Street. Lily reported that she was relieved. They had a pleasant dinner, and "all the strain is gone, thank God."

On Christmas Eve 1945 Lillian went out by herself for a walk with the dogs in the beautiful heavy snow. The evening was very cold and clear, the trees standing out against the snow. Christmas Day found Dash at the table of Hardscrabble Farm along with Max, the Kobers (father and daughter, Cathy, now, with Maggie suffering the tortures of multiple sclerosis out in California), the Durants, and the Weidmans. Melby continued to write every day. His parents and his brother visited her. She was able to approve of Max's forthcoming marriage as something nice for a lonely old man; she was letting go at last.

Lillian had resumed the social life at Hardscrabble Farm she had begun in 1939. At one dinner at her table she had George Kaufman, his daughter, Moss Hart, George Backer, and Barbara O'Neil, who played Cassie in *The Searching Wind*. Conversation was pleasant. But when Backer offered his "educated version of Marxism" to Moss Hart, Lillian snapped. She had had enough of liberals on committees in the past few weeks, she explained in a letter to Melby, and she took out her annoyance on George. Hammett's absence was not noted. The Warburgs, the Zilboorgs, the Kobers, the Kronenbergers, Dotty, who pleased her when she didn't bore her—Lillian spent her time with the old crowd.

Lillian the celebrity was often invited out, and deferred to, in these years. She attended a lunch given by Pearl Buck for a Chinese playwright. In what Lillian described as her "pleasant lady club manner," Buck wondered if her guests wouldn't like to "ask the Chinks some questions." The Chinese playwright had used the phrase "art used as a weapon." Now James T. Farrell launched into what Lillian called "a violent and dull attack on something he called Stalinist art, and then into Irish art and revolution."

Some guests were appalled, Lillian thought, while "the two little foreigners looked terrified." Then Buck turned to her and asked what she thought. It was as decadent a discussion as I ever listened to, Lillian said. Nor did she understand why the Irish had to get their problem onto every agenda. With that she took her leave. It was an argument, Lillian said later, "that could be taking place in the home of an Iranian freshman who has only the week before discovered it isn't sanitary to drink the water you shit in, and that very week read a few books."

During the week before New Year's 1946 two New York cocktail parties beckoned. But Lillian did not allow her depression to dictate her calendar this time. "Of the larger number of people I know in New York, and the small number I think I like," she wrote John Melby, "fewer and fewer mean a whole evening to me now. If once I did too much with people, now, I suppose, I do too little."

In February 1946 the superintendent of his new building asked Hammett if he needed a housekeeper.

"She's colored," he said apologetically.

"I don't care if she's navy blue. Send her up," Hammett told him gruffly. Rose Evans soon learned of Dashiell Hammett's connection to Lillian Hellman. But Miss Hellman neither came to the apartment very often nor called on the telephone. One day she did turn up without prior announcement. Hammett was in his usual position, lying on his back on the couch suffering from a hangover.

"Oh, I see you got that chair fixed," Lillian remarked.

"Me and Mr. Hammett fixed it," Rose intervened.

"You asked *him* to fix it?" Lillian demanded indignantly.

"He broke it," Rose had the temerity to reply. To Rose, Hammett seemed to enjoy seeing Lillian Hellman put in her place. Sometimes when she called, Rose would say, "I'll see if Mr. Hammett is here." If he gave her a stare, Rose knew he didn't want to talk to her. "You're an awful liar," Lillian told her one day. Most of the time when Lillian came, Rose would walk out of the room. And once Dash gave her a china animal Lillian had given him, entrusting her not ever to tell Miss Hellman.

Much more than a housekeeper, Rose Evans became a loyal friend and protector of Dashiell Hammett. When the whores got too close, Rose shielded him, to the point that one of them called her "a black bitch." It was Rose who urged him now to be closer to his family, the children in California as well as to his sister, brother, and father. She sensed that Lillian didn't like that very much, but, from California, Jose wrote her a thank-you note.

Now that she was in contact with his family, Dash confided to Rose Evans that Mary was not his biological daughter.

Rarely did Lily mention Dash in her letters to Melby. They shared news of China, agreeing that it was inevitable that the Communists would defeat Chiang. Lily found it "odd and interesting that so many people come out of China knowing the truth and never seem to make it clear to other people here." That this view was politically dangerous she did not yet perceive.

When she did mention Hammett, it was as an object of her compassion. They had dinner in New York one night and it was apparent that he had "obviously been on a long and debilitating bat." She took him back to Hardscrabble Farm with her. "I would like to think it would be to do him good," she admitted to Melby. "The truth is I don't like to be alone there as much as I used to like it." They needed each other, even as each would rarely admit it. On another occasion she "talked Dash into riding back" to Hardscrabble with her, and they "had a pleasant, friendly few days." On yet another day Dash turned up with two friends. "No three drunks were going to keep me up," Lily said, and went to bed.

On one evening in New York she intended to eat with Dash and then go home to work on *Another Part of the Forest,* only for him to become "quite drunk and sad." Then she couldn't leave him. He continued to come often to Hardscrabble Farm and had stationery printed: "D. HAMMETT/Hardscrabble Farm/Pleasantville, N.Y." Lily admitted it was "pleasant" for her, "except for the times when I feel guilty. I don't know why I feel guilty, but I do." It pained her that her success had coincided with so monumental a decline as his had been. It seemed as if his helping her so profoundly had left him little for himself, that her assuming so much of his identity had left him a shell of a man. Then he had been confronted by her love for Melby.

It was Lillian Hellman and not Dashiell Hammett who in 1946 was inducted into the American Institute of Arts and Letters. The occasion was diminished for her by an anti-Russian speech by Senator Fulbright, but redeemed when Van Wyck Brooks said hers were "the best plays written since Ibsen." Lily felt like a little girl of eight "decorated for winning the spelling-bee."

Once more she gave Dash her "monthly lecture," which she knew was "as worthless as the night I must have given it fifteen years ago." It was very sad, she wrote Melby, for her "to see him drink this way, with no work, and very little happiness in it." She remained "very devoted to Dash, deeply devoted, and I wish I could see him happy and settled and sure of some kind of future." He was "a wonderful human being . . . a fine, fine guy made of honorable stuff."

Lily felt loved by John Melby (one day in March 1946 she went into New York and found six letters from him waiting for her). She was also working well. So she could not help but find it "heartbreaking" to see Hammett's talent going to waste. No longer asking anything of their relationship, Lily could feel genuine friendship for Dash now. She felt "more sad that so much that is so wonderful, should be neurotically handicapped in working or in living . . . and I only hope to God he will live to fulfill himself." Yet she doubted whether Hammett would have another chance. "It makes me sad to know it," Lily said.

Still Dash talked about writing a novel. Now his hero was an artist named Helm who just came out of the Army and has been on a drunk since his discharge; he also announced a short story about two men discharged from the Eighth Air Force, one of whom wants the other to marry his sister so they can hang around on the farm together and shoot ducks. He liked the sister well enough but she reminds him of another girl down South and he decides to go down South to see *her*. Women remained expendable, no matter that Lily for fifteen years had demonstrated that women came in more varieties than "madonna" and "whore." Yet Lily herself saw women as devalued. When Kitty Carlisle complained that her new husband Moss Hart's working at home cut her out of giving ladies' lunches, Lily was incredulous. "You're crazy," Lily told her, "ladies' lunches are the worst form of entertaining!"

His face skeletal, Hammett once more made politics his raison d'être. He never got over the insidious role he had played as a Pinkerton, and one night at Hardscrabble Farm he told theater manager Victor Samrock how he had once been hired in Nevada by a maintenance company to spy on a troublemaking trade unionist. Then, years later, he had met that very trade unionist at Lillian's, where he had come to ask for a contribution. Hammett's name now began to appear on Civil Rights

Congress publications. He signed a statement for Gerhardt Eisler, the German Communist, and called upon Mayor O'Dwyer to stop police violence against the Negro people. But it was clear to many that he was capable of no more than offering his name.

At Cornell, where he was to address a student group, he was so drunk that Jim Weinstein wrote a fake telegram conveying his regrets. But drunk as he was, Hammett suddenly remembered the meeting and insisted that they get there. They arrived just as the telegram was about to be read. Hammett could offer no more than three coherent sentences to the assembled students.

Moving through an alcoholic haze, he would drunkenly pull a roll of bills out of his pocket for this cause or that. At one fund-raiser he took out a big roll of hundreds and offered it to fellow radical Belle Moldevan. "Take what you want," he insisted, all but forcing the money on her. Moldevan refused. She feared when he was sober the next morning he might wonder where all those hundreds went.

"Hey, you with the knockers!" Hammett called out to one of the fund-raisers at a Party event in Philadelphia. People liked him and forgave his lewdness. He was just a nice man who liked pretty girls. "Who'll give five thousand dollars?" the fund-raiser called out, and Hammett raised his hand. "Who'll give two thousand?" Hammett's hand went up again. "Who'll give a thousand?" and there was Hammett, dead drunk, hand up.

He also began to teach a course in mystery writing at the Communist-sponsored Jefferson School of Social Science. Classes were held in a decrepit building near Union Square. His theme was "the possibility of the detective story as a progressive medium in literature." To his student Samm Baker Sinclair he seemed "a dispirited guy holding himself up as if by a coat hanger." Sinclair read a story one night, a burlesque of advertising, and when he had finished, Hammett stood up, gave a mock shiver, and said, "Brrr, that story is so tough it scares me." The student was less than impressed and hardly enlightened.

When he brought Fred Dannay (one of the Ellery Queens) to class one night, the students had a glimpse of what a real teacher was. "Most days I see no point in getting up in the morning," Dash told Sinclair one night over a drink. The playwright Arthur Miller has observed that in these postwar years Hammett greeted everything new "with a supercilious grin, as though the past were just around the corner and the present not a serious matter."

One of Hammett's students was a small, dark, voluptuous woman with blue eyes and black hair named Marjorie May. Soon she had attached herself to him; soon she became a fixture in his life, and he began to introduce her as "my secretary." Lillian telephoned, making sure May knew where Hammett's loyalties lay, as she had with Jean Potter. Among friends, she sniffed. May was not worth her attention.

May began to tell people Dashiell Hammett loved her, although he never actually told her so. If he came into town from Hardscrabble Farm and wanted to see her, she was always available; he dropped in and out of her life as it suited him. For whatever sexual gratification he could get, Hammett still preferred Harlem.

During the fall of 1945 and much of 1946 Lily longed for and missed John Melby. "I want to be with you," she had written him back in December 1945. "I feel safer and better about myself."

Lily was appalled by the film version of *The Searching Wind* directed by William Dieterle. It was "plot-muddled and far too talky," as well as "horribly directed, German heavy-footed." Manny Farber, writing in *The New Republic,* in a review headlined "Hellman's Movietone News," wrote that "Miss Hellman's characterization generally leads to people with Wheaties in their blood."

She longed for Melby to "come back and make me better and console me." Lily turned as well to Melby for her political education, as she wondered whether "Marx ever wrote about revolution in one country," a sign that, if only in her love letters, she might have some doubt about Stalin.

As Melby asked about Dash, so Dash one evening in May 1946, only "slightly tight," wanted to know what place Melby now had in Lillian's life. He asked, Lillian reported, "with the greatest affection and good taste." He said he liked Melby and thought he and Lily were "very nice together." Dash used the word "decent" in relation to the man now most important to Lily. Like so many, Melby needed Hammett's approval. "To be thought well of by him is, I think, something of a compliment," he wrote back.

Hoping Melby would return for the summer of 1946 and they could go to East Hampton again, she bought new summer clothes. But he remained helpless to leave his post in China. One night Herman took Lily on an all-night cruise and it seemed as if he was trying to recapture his former position with her. Dash just shook his head. It was as if he was saying that whatever Lily did was all right with him.

The dogwoods bloomed at Hardscrabble Farm, the asparagus multiplied. Lillian planted strawberries. In New York she called on Dorothy Parker, only to meet at her place "a gent who is now her lover, maybe thirteen years old, maybe fourteen, drunk and silly, and cheap-faced." Marion Meade, Parker's biographer, identifies the thirteen- or fourteen-year-old as aspiring writer Ross Evans, who had been at officer candidate school during the war with Alan Campbell. He was in his thirties; Parker was fifty-three. Evans collaborated with Parker on a play called *The Coast of Illyria*. Later she took him to Hollywood, where they did several screenplays together. The evening left Lily depressed. Seeing *Born Yesterday* with Kober, starring "a girl I always thought would be a good actress," Judy Holliday, was more pleasant.

Restless that summer, she decided to go to Cape Cod, leaving Hammett at Hardscrabble Farm. "Dash wants this house if I do go away," she reported to Melby, "and I think I will let him have it." He was briefly on the wagon, and so "in a not very good humor." She wanted Melby to believe her feelings toward Hammett were remote. "Poor guy," she confided to Melby, "it's a tough pull, I guess."

While Lily was gone, Dash asked her secretary, now Edith Kean, to make a scrapbook of all the articles about him. "I've got to find out what all the to-do is about," he said coyly. He also busied himself scraping, bleaching, and refinishing her dining-room table. He bought a Zenith hearing aid the better to hear birds and flies and animals. Lily let him know the hearing aid frightened her. "Everybody knows she is a giddy type woman and it's likely as not she'll be wearing the hearing aid legitimately before long, thus saving herself $50," he wrote Nancy Bragdon. Her foibles continued to amuse him; her miserliness he had long suffered. He also learned she was now doing a rewrite of the second act of her new play.

Soon Lily was off to Paris for a UNESCO conference. Unaware that the Department of State, determined to exclude "Communists or near-Communists," had almost rescinded her invitation, Lily proclaimed herself "disgusted" with the arrangements. Afterward, she motored around the South of France with the Wylers, returning on the *Queen Mary*.

"For some people I guess life is just a round of pleasure," Dash wrote his daughter Jo. Hammett's New York branch of the Civil Rights Congress sponsored a petition calling for the abolition of the House Un-American Activities Committee, aiming for 100,000 signatures. It also opposed the outlawing of the Communist Party as a "direct assault on American democracy, on the American tradition of civil rights and liberties and of electoral freedom."

When Marjorie May went to Cuba, Dash wrote her from Hardscrabble Farm. "When are you coming home?" he inquired ardently, as he had once written Lily. "When are you going to tear your dwindling buttocks away from the traffic jams, the dancing caballeros, the morticians' bars and the circling buzzards . . . ?" He added, "There's nothing to hurry home to but me." He was writing, he said, a novel called *The Valley Sheep Are Fatter*.

*   *   *

Only when *Another Part of the Forest* was completed did Lily read it to Dash. He had "always been a tough critic for me," she reported to Melby. "He liked it very, very much. He had almost the same criticisms of it as I had, the main one being that the plot had not worked out correctly." The extended denouement in the third act was a mistake. Dash did like the title, as he always enjoyed using the obvious where no one had used it before. Once again, Lily had to report to Melby, Dash had "been very good to me." Their bargain was intact, a lifelong commitment, to be fulfilled now as he best could. Dash lent Max Hellman five thousand dollars in September 1945, which would form part of Max's investment in *Another Part of the Forest*, as his life continued to be intertwined with Lily's.

Kermit Bloomgarden's young assistant, Flora Roberts, on her first job, was assigned to analyze Lily's play. She agreed with Dash; the third act was a disaster. Now she must tell Lillian Hellman.

"Tell Mother what you think of her play," Miss Hellman said, sounding very tough. Flora told her.

"How much do you make a week?" Lillian demanded. It was $49.50.

"Give this girl a raise!" Lillian ordered Kermit Bloomgarden. "Unfortunately, she's right, and unfortunately, I don't think I can fix it." Lily wasn't always so generous, however. She was directing the play herself, with difficulty, and when the assistant director, Coby Ruskin, irritated her, she found a way to get rid of him. "You're suffering from money-pause," he told her drunkenly on the train to Detroit. Bloomgarden was too frightened even to pay him as he fired Ruskin at Lillian's insistence.

Sexual fidelity could not be expected of the she-Hammett, even as she genuinely loved Melby. Soon she had her eye on the young actor who was playing Oscar, Scott McKay. Meanwhile Dash showed up at the rehearsals sometimes drunk and sometimes sober. Once he remarked he would commit suicide if it weren't for the trouble it would cause Lily.

"Oh, don't let that stop you," she retorted. "I've had troubles before!" At that he laughed out of all proportion to the wit of the remark because it had the quality of understatement he so enjoyed.

Sometimes he sat by himself or at the end of the stage, or in the audience companionably with Dorothy Parker. Sometimes he came onto the stage, and Lily would run over to him and he would smile and laugh, as if he were giving her encouragement because she was so awful, so inept at directing the actors. He'd give her a gentle pat to overcome her obvious insecurity. Meanwhile the cast was terrified of her.

Soon he was coming to rehearsals not to offer writerly wisdom, but because he had become infatuated with the young star, Patricia Neal.

Lillian jealously called Pat "the starlet" behind her back. In public Lily flirted. "Oh, Dashiell," she would say, and become a little girl, hardly the woman who got Coby Ruskin fired with a snap of her fingers. No matter, Dash told Pat Neal he loved her. But he was capable now of only a kiss. He was a broken man, Pat observed, and she too pitied him. Lily, however, got revenge. In a minor dalliance with British writer Roald Dahl, Lily later arranged for him to meet Pat, and soon they were engaged. She had set Pat up.

Dash's work on *Another Part of the Forest* coincided with a year, "a long time," having passed since she had parted from John Melby. "One has to go on with a life in the place one is," she wrote him. "And that I have had to do." Little had changed, she wrote opaquely, "but that little has to be considered by me and treated by me with respect due those who were involved in it." If Melby wanted her to make a complete break with Dash, she was not about to do it. Nor, however, had Dash forgiven her for not being there for him upon his return from the Army. He did not go to Boston for the out-of-town tryouts of *Another Part of the Forest*.

They remained officially a couple. At a board meeting of the Independent Citizens Committee for the Arts, Sciences and Professions (ASP), formed to reelect Franklin Roosevelt, one day Lily slid a note across the table to young Walter Bernstein, who had interviewed Tito for *The New Yorker*. "Dash likes your work," it read. When Shumlin remarried, Lil and Dash together went to see him and his new wife, Carmen. They were together yet apart, just as she was with Melby. James Roosevelt spent a year working for ASP and began an affair with Lily. Later he pronounced her "the greatest lay I ever had." I would marry her if she wasn't who she is, Roosevelt said.

An independent woman outsmarting capitalist society, Lily grew richer. By October 1945 her royalties on *The Searching Wind* alone were $20,415.32. Her income in 1944 was a staggering $110,925. She collected on her trust income and got a salary of $50,000 from Hal Wallis. She purchased stock from Sears, Roebuck and Remington Rand and bought bonds. Her accountant, Bernard Reis, recommended conservative investment trusts. Her net worth in March 1946 was $306,323.59. To offset her taxes, she mortgaged Hardscrabble Farm. In her safe-deposit box at the Chase National Bank she continued to keep a power of attorney for Hammett as well as a signed blank check on his County Trust checking account.

Dash arrived at the November opening of *Another Part of the Forest* alone, although he was down on Lillian's list for two tickets for opening night. He had requested the last seats on the side, last aisle, and got them. From the consulate of the U.S.S.R. Lily invited Andrei Gromyko and Mrs. Gromyko and Mr. Molotov and Mr. Vyshinsky. An embarrassing moment came when Max Hellman yelled after the curtain came down on the first act, "My daughter wrote this play. It gets better!" When money was mentioned, Max removed money from his wallet and waved it maniacally

Dash was available to calm Kermit Bloomgarden, who was deeply upset over negative reviews of this, his first play as a producer. "These things happen and you can't do anything about them," Dash said. "You've got to live with them." Lily was to echo these words years later when another of her plays did not please all the critics. When the cast of *Another Part of the Forest* came to Hardscrabble Farm for dinner at Christmas, Lily and Dash ice-skated on the lake, hand in hand.

It was now clear that Melby would not be able to arrange even a visit and Lily would not be coming to Nanking or anywhere else in war-torn China. Nor, fearing career reprisals, had he taken any steps to divorce his wife. Finally Lily said Averell Harriman had informed her that Melby "did not want to come back." Outraged, Melby called it "pure malice" on his part.

Discouraged, Lily had extricated herself in her customary manner, with a dollop of mischief. By the end of 1946 she was writing to Melby less frequently. There was a world elsewhere.

18

Dash in Disarray

"Life is as difficult for those who can only think of one thing at a time as it is for those who try to do more than one."

DASHIELL HAMMETT

When in the winter of 1947 Dash wanted to move from Sixty-sixth Street, Lily urged him to take over Kober's lease. So she would keep everyone close. Dash was "a good tenant . . . good furniture and good about not breaking things," she encouraged a dubious Kober. "He never gives parties." She knew he was reliable "from his long occupancy at Pleasantville." It was as if he were a distant cousin.

Dash chose independence. Rejecting the idea of the Kober domicile, he rented an apartment on West Tenth Street in Greenwich Village. It was a duplex; the cellar level contained the bedroom; the living room was on the first floor. Working as his secretary, Marjorie May came in the morning and left at four. She claimed she wanted to be a writer; one day he tossed her a fragment of a story called "The Hunter" and challenged her to finish it.

The apartment was fully stocked with alcohol, Johnnie Walker Red, his favorite, but also cheaper brands. "Did I have money when you left here last night?" Dash inquired one day of Rose Evans. "A walletful," she told him as he stared at his empty wallet. Nights vanished into days.

Mary Jane Hammett, the daughter who was not his, who, blond and blue-eyed, bore no resemblance, of course, to him, had been addicted to pills since she was twelve years old. She had been expelled from parochial school for striking one of the nuns, and the family called her a pathological liar. "Something's wrong with her brain," Jose said. Unable to cope with her alcoholic and promiscuous daughter, now twenty-five years old, she encouraged Mary to go live with her father in New York, ostensibly to get orthodontal care.

Mary soon began to sleep with her orthodontist. Before long, with Lillian's assistance, Dash was arranging abortions for her. "The same thing that's wrong with your mother is wrong with Mary," Dash told Jo. "They both twist reality to suit their own purposes." Jose had never even told her relatives that she and Hammett were divorced.

Mary now entered the alcoholic violence of Hammett's life. Lily upbraided Dash for drinking in front of Mary. "It's terrible to drink around Mary when you know how badly alcoholic she is," Lily said. It was Lily who saw through Mary's lies, Lily whom Mary could neither control nor manipulate. Dash stood by, helpless in his guilt.

Mary and Dash would appear at Hardscrabble Farm and scream at each other, while even Lillian was at a loss, so fierce was the tension, so bizarre the interaction between the two. Lily called Mary "the child from hell." Sometimes she accused Mary of drinking so that Dash would drink. Some observers accused Lily of being jealous of Mary.

Lily was driving the two of them up to the farm one night. Both Dash and Mary were already drunk. So violent became their battle in the car that Hammett ordered Lily to stop. Then he got out. When she arrived at the farm, Lily put Mary into a guest room and locked the door, sending meals up to her.

Back on Tenth Street, Dash, drunk, hit Mary, battered her, as he had Elise De Viane, the young Lillian, and other impossible women. There developed between them what an outraged Lillian was to term "an almost incestuous love." In sadomasochistic byplay, Dash beat Mary up badly several times. Dark bruises appeared around her eyes, bruises she would not explain.

One drunken night there was also an episode of sexual fondling, as if Dash were testing himself to see if he could be sexually aroused by this woman who was not his natural daughter, but one of the bad women who could always excite him. He fondled and petted her. They were sexual together. Then it stopped. Dash could go no further, could not perform the sexual act.

Mary in turn could be sexually aroused only by being hurt.

Dash consulted Zilboorg. Lily intervened, insisting that Mary have an apartment of her own. She also had a message for Dash. "I never want to see you again," she told him.

The next day, in distress, Lily went to Zilboorg. "You mustn't do this," he advised. "It's a terrible thing about this girl. It's irrational." Zilboorg told her not to abandon Hammett entirely. But she increased her distance.

When Mary finally visited a psychiatrist back in Los Angeles, she confessed that she understood her father because she was just like him. She also told him that Dash was impotent, so whatever sexual act she had lured him to perform, he had been unable to accomplish it. It was obvious to the psychiatrist, Edward Teicher, that Mary was fixated on her father.

Lily managed her life with her customary competence. In April 1947 her problem was how to invest "the $120,000 *Searching Wind* money." The issue was whether the transfer of the motion picture rights to Hal Wallis could be considered a capital asset by the corporation, Dashiell Pictures, Inc.; this ploy would reduce the taxes to 25 percent. In 1947, Dashiell Pictures, Inc., was finally liquidated.

Peripatetic, she went to Cuba for two weeks. She remembered sadly how much of *Days to Come* was written in Havana. The sun, the vigor of Havana, did her spirit good. Less enjoyable was that she had to spend her last two days with Dorothy Parker and her "child beau," Ross Evans. Lillian would have preferred to be alone, she wrote John Melby, and to have met "some of the very interesting gents of the political part of the city."

Back in New York, Lily had to cope with Max's mental deterioration, the effects of syphilis, Lily now knew. Late in August 1947 Lily felt she had no choice but to have her father committed to a hospital as "an alleged mentally ill person." Furious, Max attacked her. "You are outrageously mean to me," he told her, begging for his freedom. "I beg your pardon for the many pains, aches & cursings that I done you. Never will I stop loving you." He wrote to enlist his sisters in New Orleans, pleading that Lillian had been vindictive. He begged them to set him free.

Bewildered, Aunts Jenny and Hannah sympathized. Lily defended herself. Hadn't she taken care of Max since her mother's death, giving him a tax-free $8,000 a year? Hadn't she urged him to marry Sally Morse, although she was appalled by "the cheap lying and vulgarity of the woman"? While Lily wrote of these troubles to Kober, Dash remained abstracted, in the next room reading *Fantastic Stories*.

*   *   *

It was in 1947 that Lily let Melby know it was finally over between them. "I want you to do what you want to do, and do whatever you have to do, or want to do," she wrote. "I do not want to trick you back here with promises I may not be able to fulfill." Her pride intact, she resumed being a woman with no man permanently in her life.

It was better in these years when Dash was absent. Norman Mailer, who entered Lily's circle when she optioned *The Naked and the Dead*, came to Hardscrabble Farm with his sister, Barbara, and Hammett, very drunk, pulled her down on his lap, pretending a prelude to the sexual act. Lily seemed not to notice. Drunk, he continued to ask every good-looking woman he met to fuck him. On other occasions Dash was a quiet presence, sitting there drinking. One night he fell asleep in the living room like an old man.

Hammett invited Mailer to lunch. In an hour they consumed four double scotches as Dash gave writerly advice. When Mailer began to show off, Hammett gave a jaunty wave and took off down the street, leaving Mailer, dead drunk, in his wake.

Meanwhile Lily tried her sexuality out on Mailer, inviting him up to her bedroom on Eighty-second Street to discuss the adaptation of *The Naked and the Dead*. Lily was lying, like Catherine of Russia, Mailer thought, in a huge bed wearing a sexy nightgown which exposed a "truly formidable bare breast." Suddenly Arthur Kober, downstairs, announced his presence. "Oh, Arthur, come on up," Lily called. "What did you think we were doing? Fucking?"

One night, when Lily and Dash attended a meeting of ASP, Dash took a fancy to an attractive, and married, activist named Helen Rosen. Lily went home, but Dash invited Rosen to the Copacabana. Drunk, he began to insult a woman at the next table. His language became so vile that he was asked to leave. Another night, as Lily was struggling to hold Dash upright in the street, an aspiring mystery writer named Michael Avallone recognized the pair. "Take care of him. He's worth the trouble," Avallone called out.

"Damn well told!" Hammett said, according to Avallone.

"Shut up and mind your own business," Lily sputtered as she tried to shepherd Dash into a cab. "Dash, get hold of yourself, for the love of God," Lily pleaded.

"Can't I do it without His help?" Dash waffled on, pleased with himself.

He took Ginny Bloomgarden to a Joe Louis fight, and later they went to the Stork Club, where Dash got drunk on one martini. Still he would disappear for ten days at a time; still Lily became frantic when she did not know where he was. He came to Hardscrabble Farm to dinner with the Kronenbergers, and fortified with "a little sugared Dubonnet or something," he confided to Emmy Kronenberger that "if she hadn't been so interested in money, Louis would have made a fine critic." Louis ignored it.

One day Lily remarked to Ginny, "One of the extraordinary things to me about Dash with his alcoholism is that he never has really gotten into trouble. In all the times he has disappeared, you never hear of his being picked up by the police or getting into a fight with anyone." To some friends she did complain. "Well, you know, you don't have to put up with this if you find it so difficult," Ruth Goetz finally told her. "After all, you can unload him. He's got his own little place downtown."

"You don't understand," Lily replied. "He gave me *The Little Foxes.*"

One weekend in April 1948 on Martha's Vineyard, as Lily struggled still with her adaptation of *The Naked and the Dead,* Leo Huberman introduced her to a longshoreman named Randall Smith. "Pete" Smith was a Communist, a veteran of the Abraham Lincoln Brigade, and was active in the Henry Wallace presidential campaign, as was Lillian. He was ten years her junior. Another romantic fantasy flared.

The Wallace campaign held no fascination, however, for Hammett. Soon he took to leaving a room whenever Henry Wallace entered it, and once he said, "He'd be better off leaving things alone and cross-breeding himself," a reference to Wallace's agricultural experiments. Whatever progressive ideas lurked in Wallace's consciousness were, for Hammett, undercut by his ineffectuality.

But Lily campaigned and, in an obvious lie, defended the Wallace campaign against the charge that it was controlled by the Communist Party. "These days a Communist is anybody who thinks maybe a dividend check should be higher," Lily said, speaking, of course, of herself. Only later would she admit how disgusted she had been with Wallace for professing ignorance that Communists had been prominent in his campaign; she had even gone to Earl Browder for counsel. Still she had her principles, and when a Colorado summer stock company wanted to use a white actor in blackface instead of a black actor in *Another Part of the Forest,* she withdrew her approval for the production.

Lily asked Pete Smith to look in on Dash. "You and Dash would get along fine. Dash would like you. You would like Dash," she told him. When Smith was reluctant to impose himself on the famous author, Lily insisted. "I'm worried about his health. He's not eating. When you're down at Dash's," Lily said in her peremptory tones, "will you please see to it that he eats something?" Pete Smith and Dash were never at Hardscrabble Farm at the same time.

Smith found Dash athletic, lean, and tan. He had a trim gray mustache, gray eyebrows, and twinkling brown eyes behind his rimless glasses. When he was not drunk and vomiting, which was often, he seemed healthy. But Smith could never get him to eat anything, nor did he ever see a piece of food enter Hammett's mouth. He did drink a quart of scotch a day.

Have you ever had roast beef hash at the Stork Club? Dash asked Pete one night. Off they went. Dash got so drunk he couldn't remain upright in his seat. They went on to "21," then to the King Cole Room of the St. Regis. Smith saw that Dash enjoyed testing people, using the word "nigger" to see if they would object, making a pass at a woman to see if she would tell him off. As for his politics, he seemed a dilettante.

Marjorie May tried to persuade Smith she was Dash's girlfriend, and indeed Hammett did try to have sex with her, although she was to reveal later that he was invariably unsuccessful. Smith did not like May. She seemed "a sort of intruder that you tolerated rather than welcomed." His views were influenced by Lily, who now spoke of May as "some sort of a gold digger . . . not a constructive influence on Dash."

One night Smith observed a blind-drunk Hammett take an umbrella and lift May's skirt as she came into the living room. On another night, he watched as May threw a glass of whiskey in Hammett's face, while Mary looked on. Smith made his share of passes at Mary, who had moved to an apartment in the East Fifties. But she was either drunk, getting drunk, or suffering from a hangover.

"We can get along without Marge here," Mary told her father one day, sexual jealousy always in the air. Nor did Rose Evans like May, accusing her of eavesdropping on her conversations with Mr. Hammett. Finally Hammett fired Marjorie May.

In the years to come, May put up for auction at Christie's many Hammett items, including the pages of "The Hunted," a two-page typed working outline for *The Thin Man,* a manuscript with carbons of an unpublished short story called "A Knife Will Cut for Anybody," and a page of the manuscript of a story called "Something Somewhere Else," with a page of notes in his handwriting. There were also photographs, a silver-plated Pocket Books "Gertrude" award for his having sold a million copies, and a wristwatch from Abercrombie & Fitch, which he wore in the Aleutians. After Lillian Hellman's death, May also put up for sale a volume of Hammett stories—which had been inscribed to Lillian herself. In explanation, she told writer Sally Richards she had been "executor of his estate at the time."

*   *   *

Dash and Mary went to California to attend Jo's wedding. Lily sent a blue cloisonné locket. But Jose objected. "The pearls will look better," she told her daughter, unwilling ever to criticize Lillian directly. Dash was as drunk in Los Angeles as he had been in New York, distressing Jo by making a pass at the wife of Mike Romanoff right at the dinner table. He was sober as he walked Jo, who had inherited his dark red hair, down the aisle. On the day of the wedding, Dash telephoned Hardscrabble Farm.

"What's new?" he asked Lily.

She told him that an editor named Herb Mays was ready to pay him $5,000 if he would write a short description of his favorite plays.

"Tell him I'll do it," Dash said. "But I won't write any paragraphs. I'm not a writer anymore."

Lily burst out laughing.

In California, he visited dying Maggie, whose paralysis was now entering her throat.

In August 1948, craving the sea, Lily rented Margaret Webster's house on Martha's Vineyard. One night she got into an argument about Oliver Cromwell with Ginny Bloomgarden and Ilo Wallace, Henry's wife, who had been invited to prevent her from saying "stupid things" to the press. "Dash is like an encyclopedia," Lily said as she telephoned California. "Dashie'll know. Dashie knows everything." Voracious reader Hammett had the answer to the question.

Working without Hammett's help, Lily failed to make Mailer's characters sound like soldiers. She still owed Mailer nearly $10,000. When he said, "Let's waive that," even as she gave up trying to turn his novel into a play, their friendship was sealed.

Fed up with Henry Wallace for his repudiation of the Communists who ran the Progressive movement, Lily went to Yugoslavia in the early autumn of 1948 for an opening of *The Little Foxes* and to interview Marshal Tito. She went in the wake of the first public rupture between Stalin's Russia and one of the Eastern European Stalinist leaders. Rather than see an independent Communist Yugoslavia outside his sphere of influence, Stalin after World War II preferred a restoration of the monarchy. But unlike the leaders of other Eastern European societies, Tito, having been a partisan during the war, had an independent base of power and his own bureaucracy. His plan was to play Stalin and the West off against each other, to outmaneuver his mirror image to the east. Against Stalin's accusations that he was a capitalist spy, Tito stood his ground.

Yugoslavia was now eager to win over the old intellectual apologists for Stalin. Lillian's invitation had been extended by Yugoslavia's Deputy

Foreign Minister, Srdja Prica, who had visited Hardscrabble Farm, where he debated with Hammett over Yugoslavia's widening split with Stalin. During Prica's visit to Pleasantville, Hammett and Leo Huberman had been recalcitrant: taking Moscow's line, as always, Hammett refused to believe that Yugoslavia had been abused by the Soviet Union; he thought Tito "resented not being treated as the favorite child of the Balkans."

Worried about leaving Dash, Lillian asked Ginny Bloomgarden to look after him. "Dash is very fond of you," Lily said, her eyes full of tears. Dash was drinking heavily. Would Ginny have dinner with him, play Ping-Pong?

One night Dash and Ginny sat up until four as he talked about his days as a Pinkerton on the case of someone who had stolen a Ferris wheel.

"You made that up!" Ginny accused.

"No, I didn't," Dash insisted. He also told her how he had too soon discovered the location of the plundered gold hidden on a ship and so lost a trip to Australia. What a fool he had been, he said now, although travel had never lured him. With Lily gone, he allowed the cook, Wilma, who usually wore a gray uniform with a white bow and an apron, to run around in a little pair of shorts.

"Lillian would kill you," Ginny said.

"Lillian doesn't have to know about it," Dash said. "She's comfortable. What difference does it make? When Lily's back, she'll put her uniform back on."

"Why don't you write?" Ginny summoned the courage to ask him one day. "That really upsets me."

"Oh, honey, I'll get around to it someday," Dash said.

Lillian was treated like royalty in Yugoslavia. She was met at the airport on October 5 by members of the Culture and Science Committee, by Milan Bogdanovic, representing the Yugoslav Authors Association, by Milan Djovovic, a director at the state opera house, and by many actors. A newspaper described her as a "progressive American authoress." Lillian attended the opening night of *The Little Foxes,* followed by a banquet. The next day she lectured at the USIS library, where she said that in the Soviet Union state backing made it possible to attain greater perfection in the theater because of a longer period of rehearsals. In New York financial reasons often limited rehearsal time to only four weeks. She did add that the Soviet Union had produced no really good plays for the past thirty years.

Lillian's secretary, Edith Kean, wrote her on October 7. She had let

Dash know of Lillian's safe arrival in Belgrade, but he did not respond. Edith telephoned the apartment on Tenth Street, but each time Mary answered. Edith asked to speak to Dash. "He's asleep," Mary said, putting her off.

Lillian met Marshal Tito, who only the previous June had declared his independence from Stalin, leaving the Soviet bloc. She was driven to his home, fifteen miles from the center of Belgrade, in a prewar upper-class neighborhood. In a large room overlooking a garden, alone except for Prica, they talked about the prospects for peace. Tito said he thought "the atom bomb did not scare as many people as America supposed it did. It still took armies to win wars and land for the armies to fight on."

Although it was the one question that interested her readers, Lillian amazingly did not raise the question of his split with Stalin. It was her old unwillingness to put herself outside acceptance by the higher-ups. She knew in advance her support would go to the Soviet Union no matter what Tito said, so she said nothing.

Tito himself broached the issue. "It was not a decision to abandon socialism," he explained to this most recalcitrant of Stalin's friends. By October 11, she was gone. On her way home she stopped in Paris, where she heard an actress read for a French version of *The Little Foxes*.

One night in the late autumn of 1948, shortly after Lillian's return from Yugoslavia, Hammett took to his bed. He wouldn't stop drinking; he could scarcely get to the bathroom, could no longer move. "Don't call Lillian!" he ordered Rose Evans. "I'll be all right."

Lily was in the throes of a brand-new romance, with Srdja Prica, whose partisan credentials impressed her. At forty-three, Lily was feeling old. "Soon the need must be fulfilled—it is getting late," she wrote in her diary. She felt incomplete, depressed, miserable without a man in her life. Perhaps she had found him in Prica, a man exactly her own age.

Prica was "sharp and handsome and aggressive," qualities Lillian liked in a man. He was also incapable of loving and accepting her. Indeed he viewed Lillian Hellman as a mere middle-class liberal who had not gone very deeply into things. Lily was, for Prica, a person to whom he could feel superior. She herself was troubled by their relationship. She had lied to Prica, as she remained a victim of her lifelong addiction to lying, of which Zilboorg, although he had tried, had failed to cure her.

Lies "must be told cold," Lily wrote after her meeting with Prica in Yugoslavia, "a moral approach cannot be used in telling because it becomes ridiculous in judging, and dangerous." She lied to hide her insecurity, her self-doubt, her longing for what she feared she might not ever have: to be loved for herself as a woman. From childhood, she had lied to hide her vulnerability; later she lied for an edge, to create a persona stronger than the frightened little girl she remained within. One of the actors in *Montserrat,* her 1949 adaptation of the French play by Emmanuel Roblès, was to say he would have liked to get to know her better, but "she was living under a self-constructed suit of armor," because she "felt more powerful that way." That persona was designed to hide her terror.

Lily was warned by her lover's compatriot Vladimir Dedijer, who liked Lily. Prica, Dedijer knew, was "a man who regarded women who were in love with him as just like an old newspaper." Unlike Melby, Prica neither wrote to Lily with any regularity nor acknowledged her letters. But to friends she spoke of him proudly as "His Excellency."

One night at dinner at Eighty-second Street Lily had entertained two young Yugoslav diplomats, who pleaded for understanding of why their country, for its survival, had to break with Stalin. "You believe them?" Lily demanded of playwright Arthur Miller after they departed. It will all blow over, Lily remarked. Besides, Tito might be an American agent. Her loyalty to Stalin remained intact. It was inextricably bound to her loyalty to Hammett, who was still doing the Party's bidding, signing and authoring (if not actually writing) its petitions. Whatever Prica's politics, or Dedijer's, Lily's remained those of Dashiell Hammett, or what she imagined them to be.

Are you or are you not a Communist? Dash's brother demanded over one of the dinners they shared regularly now that Richard had moved to New York with Standard Oil.

"I'm not a Communist. I'm a Marxist," Dash replied.

The telephone rang at Lillian's. Selma Wolfman, her new secretary, took the call. It was Rose Evans, who had a message for Lily: "Please come down here and see to Mr. Hammett because I think he's going to die." Ignoring Zilboorg's advice, Lillian hadn't spoken to Dash for two months; refusing to become his caretaker yet again, she said no. Only when Wolfman threatened to go down to Tenth Street herself did Lily relent and head downtown.

Hammett was shouting and shaking with the DTs. It was "heartbreaking," Lily thought when she saw his condition. Together Lily and Rose Evans dressed him, which was difficult because he could scarcely lift his arms and legs. The words she remembered speaking were those of a she-Hammett: "I've only come to get you because you're so sick. When you're well, I'll go back to not seeing you again."

They got him to Eighty-second Street, where Lily fixed a home remedy that only made matters worse. Later, when the crisis was over, laughing, she said, "You know, leave it to me, I could have killed him." But it was no small matter when at three or four in the morning she had to get him to Lenox Hill Hospital. There Hammett spent Christmas 1948.

Abe Abeloff, Lillian's doctor, went to see him. He would be dead in six weeks if he didn't stop drinking, Abeloff told Hammett. Hammett promised to stop drinking—forever. "It's my duty to have said it," Abeloff explained to Lily, "but it won't do any good. He can't and he won't."

In January, Hammett returned to Hardscrabble Farm. He didn't drink. Nor did his vitality return. "He couldn't have looked worse," Lily reported to Maggie. "I hope to God he stays on the wagon, but I am not sure I have much faith that he will." Six years later, Lily admitted to Hammett that Abeloff had doubted he would stop drinking. "But I gave my word," Hammett, ever the provincial, protested.

"Have you always kept your word?" Lily asked slyly. It was as far as she could go with him.

"Most of the time," Hammett replied, guileless, refusing to take the bait. "Maybe because I've so seldom given it."

Soon he seemed to bounce back with "that wonderful resiliency which could have been so valuable and important," Lily noted. Mourning the overwhelming waste of his life, she credited herself with—in this crisis at least—having been "gentle and understanding." She took to nagging him about his writing, sometimes in the presence of others.

"Leave me alone! Leave me alone!" Hammett told her, irritated. He was a used-up man now.

At the turn of the year 1949 little had changed. "I wish there was some happy, romantic news I could give you," Lily wrote Maggie. If Dash was a presence at Hardscrabble Farm, Lily was his "absentee hostess." She might drive to Pleasantville on a Wednesday night, then drive Dash to New York, where he would have dinner with his daughter, Mary, or show up at the Jefferson School. But he couldn't wait to return to Hardscrabble Farm for what he termed "another week of nothing much to do except deciding whether to let Salud [Lillian's poodle] into the house." Writing had become a sardonic joke. He signed one of his letters to Jo "Earle Stanley Gardner," with great John Hancock flourishes.

Still Dash and Lily made mischief, had fun together, entertaining portrait painter George Bergen and joking about a bar in St. Louis where the proprietor wanted a mirror and got a Miró instead. One Sunday afternoon, Lily and Dash and the Bloomgardens were driving back to New York.

"My head is hurting," Lily complained.

"Lily, you're on fire!" Dash said. With her cigarette she had set ablaze the mesh veil of her straw hat.

"If Dashie hadn't told me, I would have told the doctor I had a headache," Lily, the helpless female, insisted.

Dashiell Hammett was now, and would be for as long as she owned the place, a permanent houseguest at Hardscrabble Farm. His room, filled with butterfly nets and fishing rods, was messy. Although Lily was neat, she ignored the disarray. When he came in one day with ducks hanging from his belt loop, very proud, Lily cooked them herself. Dash had the lake stocked with trout. They went fishing together.

He spoke of Lily as if he were her father and she a precocious daughter of whom he was immensely fond but who was impossible. Or so Norman Mailer thought. "Oh, you know Lillian, she's a total hysteric on that," he would say, or "You know Lily, she never did have any sense." He laughed at her gardening. "Lily's a very interesting gardener," he said. "She's got four layers of flowers there. She doesn't trust what it says on the packet, so she puts in a layer, digs a little more, puts in another layer." The moral came finally: "She doesn't know what she's doing!" Lily laughed.

He also teased her in a parody of the old days. "What were you doing all morning, Lily baby?" Dash would say in front of others. "I thought you were going to write." When she protested that she was busy in the garden, he replied as of old.

"That's not going to get your play finished."

"After lunch, I want you to tell me, Dashie, to go in my workroom and shut the door and work."

"Lily, go in that room and shut the door and get to work," Dash said.

"Oh, you're a pain in the neck. Leave me alone," Lily answered.

"Honey, you told me to remind you, you told me to remind you," Dash said. "I wouldn't do it if you didn't tell me." Then, in an aside, he murmured, "Oh yes I would!"

Dash would say, "Just go in that library and shut the door and do your work, honey. You know, for a writer, I don't know how you write. You're always trying to do something else." Sometimes she brought him a page. He would read it and then say, "That's better."

He enjoyed spending time with children, particularly little Cathy Kober. Lily berated Cathy one day for leaving the door to the chicken coop open, so that the varieties of chickens got mixed up. "How could you do that!" Lily raged, blaming Cathy for the chicken pecks inflicted on the workers who put the chickens back. But Dash told her that the chicken pecks weren't that terrible, and he took little Cathy to see the new poodle puppies and then the robin's nest. His voice was quieting, soothing. It was a great comfort to the little girl who had to pretend that her mother wasn't dying. Dash wrote Maggie a note every day.

With the exception of children, he disapproved still of most of Lily's guests and wondered one day "what grotesques" she had "lined up for this weekend." When Howard Fast arrived, Dash fled to his room and shut the door. Upset, Lily tried to get him to come down—to no avail. "That Dash!" Lily said. "This is nothing new. If he doesn't like someone, he'll let you know it." It was apparent from her demeanor that no one must criticize him.

Life was not dull. Once Hammett set two acres on fire attempting to burn gypsy moth cocoons. Because the property was partly in Pleasantville and partly in Chappaqua, Lily had trouble getting either fire department to come. Dash laughed at Henry Wallace, with whom he now made a bet. They would meet at 165 pounds. Wallace was down from 199 to 182. Dash had ten pounds to gain. "Last year's election shows he's not too hard to beat," Hammett said in his sardonic way.

Politically they marched in step, both in February 1949 signing a National Council of the Arts, Sciences and Professions telegram to President Truman urging him to "accept Premier Stalin's bid to discuss the problems that are now blocking the path toward real peace." But it was Lily who was active that March in the Waldorf Conference as a vice-chairman; Dash gave his name, but decided not to attend. "There are few things I like less than sitting around listening to intellectuals," he said. But he would not have liked Norman Cousins' speech attacking the conference and the "small political group" behind it which owed its allegiance "not to America but to an outside government." Lily answered Cousins then, forcefully and yet irrelevantly, resorting, as Hammett often did, to style when a political argument was unanswerable. "I would recommend, Mr. Cousins, that when you are invited out to dinner you wait until you get home before you talk about your hosts."

Neither Lily nor Dash foresaw the political struggle looming before them. Dash accused Lily of lying in bed all day not because she had the "grippe," as she pretended. It was, rather, because "the newly published Congressional Committee on Un-American Activities pamphlet on the recent Peace Conference lists her in the group of sponsors who have been affiliated with 31 to 40 red-front organizations while I'm in the smaller and more elite 41 to 50 group, including something—where I seem to be alone—called the Crown Heights Committee for a Democratic Spain." They were living once more in symbiosis. "Providence punished me for writing lightly of Lillian's grippe in my last letter," he confessed to Jo. "The next day I came down with a dose of flu."

His Party activity continued throughout 1949. In February he signed a petition in which seventy cultural leaders urged President Truman to respond positively to Stalin's offer for a meeting on American-Soviet relations. In June he chaired a Conference for Civil and Human Rights at the City Center Casino. Another petition Hammett signed was sponsored by the American Committee for the Protection of the Foreign Born and asked Attorney General Tom Clark to protect noncitizens.

"Red-baiting's kind of rife these days in these parts," Dash observed idly. Lily couldn't help but notice; for political reasons she didn't get the job as screenwriter for her friend William Wyler's *Carrie*.

Although Hammett did not work with her on *Montserrat*, he followed its progress, whether it would be play or film, who would be cast. His horoscope read, he reported to Jo, "Romances could be affected by careless words, and would need time for recovery." As he waited impatiently for Lillian to arrive of an afternoon, he would write letters. "I had told her," he wrote Jo, "to feel free to drop in at any time while I was here as a guest—and maybe her petticoats will be dragging." Then he would bolster her confidence, as always. Even as Lily professed to long still for a romance worthy of Scarlett and Rhett, neither she nor Hammett were ready to let the other go.

In the summer of 1949, Max needed an emergency operation for a strangulated hernia. Wearily, Lily asked Dash to accompany her to the hospital, where Max chatted cheerfully. He survived the operation and was talking with a nurse when his heart gave out. Max Hellman died at the age of seventy-five on August 4, 1949. His profession on his death certificate was listed as "salesman" in the "clothing business." Among his assets was thirty thousand dollars, which included his share of the "distribution from *Another Part of the Forest*."

Lily could not forgive her aunts Jenny and Hannah for doubting her. "When I think of the years to come," she wrote Hannah, "I would be very glad to know that there would be somebody who loved me enough to take care of me as well as Daddy has been taken care of." There was no longer any question that Hammett would not be that man.

On a hot Saturday, Lily called Hammett in the Village and asked him to accompany her to Max's funeral. In the spring, he had ordered Rose to store his blue woolen suit. "I won't need it," he told her. "I'm not a businessman." Gratefully he found the blue suit hanging ready in his closet.

A few days after Max Hellman's death, Marjorie May asked Hammett to help her with a play she was writing. He declined, with little embellishment. "It's simply not my kind of theater," he wrote. "My kind—if I can be said to have any—is the playwright's theater." His letter was cold and unforgiving and he signed it "yours," which was most unusual for him. He also told May that he was off to Martha's Vineyard, an obvious euphemism for his having returned to Lillian at this moment of her loss. At the top his stationery bore the address of Hardscrabble Farm.

Together Lily and Dash went to Gay Head on Martha's Vineyard for a month. There Lily compiled a list of those who had sent messages upon her father's death—and those who had not. Among those who had not was Dorothy Parker.

19

Hammett Edits Hellman, Reprise

"I've frittered myself away."

THE AUTUMN GARDEN

"Wasn't it better when I drank?"

DASHIELL HAMMETT

In the autumn of 1949 Lily and Dash settled into a new shared understanding. They were to have nearly two years to revive and nurture their connection. Apart, they remained together. Together, they worked on one more of Lily's plays.

Hammett resumed a more active life. He attended conferences for a movie sale of "The Fat Man," and wrote a three-page single-spaced report to Kermit Bloomgarden about how to stage Sean O'Casey's *Purple Dust;* Hammett suggested having live animals, ducks, chickens, pigs, and maybe even a sheep on the stage. He scribbled a list of "Notes for 'How to Live in the United States.'" "It is suicidal to know only one thing well enough to make a living at it; it is safe to know three or four," Hammett wrote.

Meanwhile Lily readied *Montserrat,* to be one of her least successful adaptations, for an October opening and agreed to edit the letters of Anton Chekhov. She was not too busy to protest against Bernard Reis's charges for doing her and Hammett's accounting, enlisting Stanley M. Isaacs, her lawyer. Isaacs was appalled to discover that Hammett did not keep any records of his own, just a checkbook. Yet Reis had wanted $7,500 for assembling Hammett's records from 1942 to 1947 and for keeping his books for 1948 and 1949.

Resisting, as always, Lily's attempts to take over his life, Hammett now hired a secretary named Muriel Alexander, a beautiful red-haired young woman, who became part assistant, part confidante. At times he asked her to sit with him silently in his bedroom at the garden level. Even as he struggled to remain active, he settled back into idleness. When Jean Potter, now Chelnov, sent him a check repaying part of his loan to her and asked whether he was writing, he wrote back, "There's always plenty of time: nobody dies young anymore."

Lily retained her customary intimacies. It was Kober she told about the "small growth on the skin of my vagina"; in a letter to Maggie she referred to Arthur as "our husband." When Dash went to California at the turn of the year 1950 to work on a screenplay for Sidney Kingsley's *Detective Story,* which William Wyler was directing, Lily sent a letter and a telegram to await his arrival at the Beverly Wilshire.

At dinner one night with Kober, Dash compared a desk Lily bought him with one she had bought Kober; Dash's was an antique. "Lily thinks it's all in having the right desk," Hammett said. Not drinking at all, he reflected on reformed writing drunks who "should have stayed drunk, so that they don't wake up to find out they haven't any talent."

Hammett found himself "kind of jittery" out in California, knowing he wasn't "doing enough, good or bad." Willie is "more worried about it than I am," he wrote, which could not have surprised Lillian. Soon it was clear there would be no Hammett script for *Detective Story.* When reporters cornered him, demanding to know if he was up to anything in Hollywood, Dash's answer was a resounding "positively not."

At the close of every paragraph of his February 2 letter, Dash wrote Lily that he missed her. "I miss you," he said first, even as he announced that he was going to Pat Neal's for dinner. Whether the dinner turned out good or bad, he said next, "in either case I shall miss you." The third paragraph ended, "of course I shall miss you." Even as he mocked her insatiable need for reassurance, he complied. "I love you and miss you, cutie," he closed.

Most nights he did have dinner with Pat Neal. But at the expensive restaurants he chose he would sit silently, interpolating a funny remark only to lapse back into silence. Pat had to do most of the talking. Afterward they went back to the Beverly Wilshire and lay in bed together. Dash kissed Pat on the lips, but that was all. She was certain he wasn't capable of anything more.

If he asked Muriel Alexander to send Pat presents, to Lily he wrote of

Neal disparagingly. Pat was "not too entirely fascinating if you don't think her career the most important thing in the world," Dash wrote, trying to assuage Lily's jealousy. To Jo, he remarked of Pat, "She's a nice girl, but she's not the brightest kid you ever met." Lily had set a standard: smart, shrewd, quick, and bright; Lily made other women sound dull. Yet Dash loved Pat Neal and among his effects when he died was her photograph in a silver frame engraved with his name: Samuel Dashiell Hammett.

He saw Jose, who still adored him. He visited dying Maggie Kober as often as he could. She became dimply and young, like a schoolgirl, when she talked to others of his visits. He saw Lee Gershwin. "She hasn't yet mentioned your name," he informed Lily. He was "waiting her out."

When he was away from Lily, he wanted to know everything she was doing. A list of guests about to descend on Hardscrabble Farm led him to make a plea he knew would go unheeded: "It might be better all the way round if you tried to sort of stay by yourself as much as you can till I get back." Still he tried to set a standard for Lily; still he deplored her celebrity guests. "I love you," he closed one letter. "I love you very much, Lilipie," ended another. Yet when she gushed over a chair he bought her, he wrote jokingly to Muriel Alexander that he might now have to get Lily a desk. Always he kept his ironic distance.

Knowing how he could elude her, protestations of affection notwithstanding, knowing he could always be found with other women, occasionally Lily allowed her bitterness to surface. Should she ever sell Hardscrabble Farm, she said, there should be a wing "built for Mr. Hammett the permanent guest. This is the way the 18th Century treated writers." Lily did not conceal some irritation about his being her permanent guest, and later he described Hardscrabble Farm to Jo as "where I hope I'll be allowed to stay till I have to go in for the new school term next week."

With Hammett in Hollywood, in March 1950 Lily went to bed one last time with John Melby, en route to Indochina. She remembered 1945, their sexual love "a fever—such a fever almost physical." Now sex with Melby was neither pleasant nor unpleasant. What they had once was gone forever. Emotion remained, but not passion.

"Woman pursuing can be oppressive," she chastised herself in her diary for 1950. It had never been easy for her to win the devotion of men. It would be even more difficult from now on.

Hammett returned to Hardscrabble Farm, "where I belong," the place where "all sensible people are whenever possible." He watched Tennessee senator Estes Kefauver's Senate Crime Investigating Committee put former Mayor Bill O'Dwyer on the stand. Dash's prejudice against the man deepened. Still, it was the best television since *Howdy Doody*, Dash thought.

On April 28 Aunt Jenny died. Lily went to New Orleans to see Aunt Hannah, wondering who might nurture her at the end of her life. She made the journey, she joked, "in the hope that Cathy Kober will fly to help me when I am seventy-six. The Jewish God is a just God, they tell me."

Together and apart: In June, Hammett returned to California to see his new grandchild, baby Ann. Back at Hardscrabble Farm he and Lily cooked dinner down at the lake. He read volumes on theoretical physics and Stendhal's *The Green Huntsman*.

Lily was now at work on a new play, *The Autumn Garden*. Hammett again turned play doctor. Lily of course was in command. The title Hammett suggested, *Some of Us,* was weak and Lily rejected it. But grateful for his revived concern, she dedicated the work to him: "For Dash." (Her inscription to Zilboorg in the published version, however, was "For Gregory/Who is responsible for its existence.")

Lily and Dash spent an idyllic summer on Martha's Vineyard at Gay Head. It was beautiful even when, as Hammett put it, hurricanes romped up the Atlantic and the wind blew. By now Lily was in the middle of her second act. "The part I've read is nice," Dash reported to Jo, revealing none of the fits of temper Lily later described.

That summer of 1950 it was an old marriage revived. Dash thought he might go sailing for the first time since the summer of 1933. But idleness and his debilitated state weakened his resolve. He took to chewing tobacco; Lily, ever the fastidious housekeeper, was "a little uncooperative about spittoons in the house." One day when Lily went fishing, Dash mopped the floors, threw out the garbage, washed the dishes, and sprayed insecticide everywhere. Then he went out into the sun with a book. Lily went crabbing and cooked the crabs for dinner, then retired upstairs to work. Dash had new titles for books he was never to write; *Look for Something to Look For* now replaced *December First*.

Together they went to the movies, seeing Gene Kelly and Judy Garland in *Summer Stock*. Past physical passion, past expectation, they were comfortable together. Lily wrote later in her memoir *Pentimento* that it was "the best of our life together." She called it a "passionate affection," and it was.

In September, Dash noted, "Lillian's finished the second act of her new play and it reads awfully good." So contented were they both that they remained on the Vineyard until the middle of that month. Hammett joked, "There's no reason why this shouldn't be a nice place to spend Christmas, though I guess we've got to go back sometime."

They returned to Hardscrabble Farm, where by November Lily had a final version of her first act, which Dash found "kind of wonderful." So delighted was she with his new interest in her work that she proposed that he direct the play, enlisting several friends to endorse the idea. "I don't feel too sure that I should start a new career till I'm in my sixties," Dash demurred, "and I'm three years away from that." As always, he postponed.

He preferred the solitude of the farm. When a November storm knocked out the electricity, he remained in Pleasantville anyway. Lily, "who has a play to finish," he wrote Jo, "beat it back to the city." At Christmas, Lily gave Dash a television set. So companionate had they become that they began to talk of writing a farce together. It would be called *Millions, Millions* and be about the impossibility of stealing from the rich.

She enjoyed his sardonic humor, which sometimes took on the imagery of the long-ago Catholicism of his youth. One day in 1950, as they were strolling down the street, Lily and Dash ran into Howard Fast. Fast talked of the jail sentence he would soon have to serve. No more than in the Hardscrabble days did Dash like the man. As they moved away, Dash said, "It will be easier for you, Howard, if you first take off the crown of thorns."

Bernard Reis saw to it that Lily would not have to pay any taxes at all for 1950.

The Autumn Garden reflected Lily's mood at midlife. It revealed both her own and Hammett's emotional state, as many of the characters in this ensemble reflect the perspective of either one or the other. "Maybe lonely people are the only people who can't afford to cry," an alcoholic Hammett surrogate named Crossman says. He plays "a game called getting through the day while you wait for night," as Dash did. He remembers "there used to be a lot of things to do with" night, as Hammett knew. Crossman also goes on the wagon twice a year.

Among the women, Constance, a woman forced to live among her regrets, most resembles Lillian. "I don't like being alone, anymore," she says. "It's not a good way to live." Like the real-life Lillian, she insists that liver not be overcooked and stuffs crabs for dinner. In failing to reach out to each other, Crossman and Constance have killed the love that was once strong between them, Lily's searingly honest epitaph for herself and Dash. At the end of the play Crossman, speaking as Hammett, says, "I've never liked liars—least of all those who lie to themselves." But Lily lets Constance have the last word, insisting to Dash that she be forgiven for this foible: "Never mind. Most of us lie to ourselves, darling, most of us."

The Autumn Garden with its ensemble of characters is replete with autobiographical resonances. A mother is opposed to her son's marriage, as Hammett's was to his alliance with Jose. Rose Griggs, who cannot face the reality that her marriage has long been over, is Jose. An artist named Nick has not finished a portrait in twelve years, as Hammett had not written in just that time. There's a jealous dig at Hammett for being so successful in flirting with "women and men and children and animals" that he now includes "books-in-vellum and sirloin steaks, red squirrels and lamp shades." Mrs. Ellis berates Nick for being "a toucher," engaging in "little moments of sensuality. One should have sensuality whole or not at all. Don't you find pecking at it ungratifying?" There indeed was Hammett, who frequently gave Lily small pats on the back or the shoulder, mingy tokens of his affection.

According to Lillian, when she was finished, Hammett grinned, patted her hair with one more of those stingy tokens of his affection, and said, "It's the best play anybody's written in a long time. Maybe longer. It's a good day. A good day." There was, however, still a speech in the last act which "went sour." This was General Ben Griggs's moment of truth. Griggs, another Hammett surrogate, now realizes there will be for him no second chance, no starting over. Lily's first version of the speech was prosaic, cumbersome:

> "There comes a time in most lives when you can still move around—
> when there is still room within yourself, and enough in you to use it
> and go some other way. I don't know at what age other people under-
> stand that—but I have no excuse: I knew it ten, fifteen years ago—
> but I let it run past me, thinking that when I knew the way to go, of
> course I'd take it. [With great feeling.] Well I found out. There are no
> minutes of great decision. Only a series of little ones coming out of
> the past. You don't suddenly turn around—because it's too damn
> late, and you've let it go too long."

"Do it again," Dash said. Lily tried:

> "And so there are no minutes of big decision. No time when you can
> suddenly turn around. All those years when you promised yourself
> the day would come when you would wipe out the mistakes, or do
> the work you'd never done, or think the way you'd never thought or
> have what you've never had.
> [Shakes his head.]
> "No. That's not for people like me. I guess it has to be the sum
> of it all, of a whole life, and none can be thrown out as you tell your-
> self you can wait for the great day. Can't do it that way. Well, I let it

all run past me, all the wasted time, sure that when I knew the way to go, nothing would stop me. Then suddenly it gets too late."

"Go to bed and let me try," Dash said, still unsatisfied. Then he sat down and wrote the speech that would become the centerpiece of *The Autumn Garden*. It was a personal *cri de coeur* for the writer he had been:

"So at any given moment you're only the sum of your life up to then. There are no big moments you can reach unless you've a pile of smaller moments to stand on. That big hour of decision, the turning point in your life, the someday you've counted on when you'd suddenly wipe out your past mistakes, do the work you'd never done, think the way you'd never thought, have what you'd never had—it just doesn't come suddenly. You've trained yourself for it while you waited—or you've let it all run past you and frittered yourself away. I've frittered myself away, Crossman."

So Hammett knew. There would be no turning point for him either: "it just doesn't come suddenly." He had "frittered" himself away; he would not do the work he had never done. He had known what was happening even as he was powerless to alter it.

Dash spoke openly of the play as a collaborative effort. In January 1951 he said, "*We* finished the last—and I think practically final—revision of Lily's play yesterday afternoon." He spoke often of "we" and "us" in reference to *The Autumn Garden*. One night he told his Jefferson School class, "We got the Marches today, though Freddie doesn't know it yet. Florence [Eldridge] makes the decisions in that family." He relished this collaboration as he had not done with a Hellman work since *The Little Foxes*. (He was watching the film version with Jo when the opening lines came on: "Little foxes have lived in all times, in all places. This family happened to live in the deep South in the year 1900." Suddenly Dash had cried out excitedly, "I wrote that! I wrote that!")

Studiously, Dash attended rehearsals, smoking in the back of the theater. To the cast, they seemed like a married couple. Often Lily went back to ask his opinion. Afterward, they often went out for coffee with Kermit Bloomgarden and director Harold Clurman. Never letting the actors know how he felt, Dash believed "the acting still needs a lot of work and some of it needs a great deal." Both Dash and Lily now shared a distaste for actors: "I think all plays should be written for puppets who can be whittled out of pieces of pine by nances on Sullivan Street," Dash said.

Nor did he and Lily like Clurman's work. "I'm more of Madame's opinion," Dash said, "that when you take people's money—even if on the road—you ought to try to give them something for it." Finally he reconciled himself to Clurman's effort. "Without going so far as to call him a great director," Dash decided, "I think he's done well with the play, better, I dare say, than Lillian could have done if she'd directed it."

Dash called the previews "awful." In Philadelphia, where he accompanied Lily, he found "there's a lot of work still to be done on it, chiefly in the way of getting actors in shape." After a more satisfactory performance, he wrote Maggie that the cast "seemed very good to us, but that was largely because they had been so bad the couple of nights before." Then he returned to Hardscrabble Farm, leaving Lily to visit the Barnes collection of modern art by herself.

On opening night he pronounced the actors "very good." For the first time in years he behaved as if he had a stake in Lily's work. "It's as good as anything Chekhov ever wrote, maybe better," he concluded. It was Kober, a 1 percent investor, who was shrewd enough to warn Lily about the awkward melodrama of the third act, having Sophie demand blackmail money; he also thought all the characters should "take it for granted that Nick has seduced Sophie." Lily didn't agree. If Dash didn't say so, it must not be so. (On opening night, they returned to Hardscrabble Farm, where Lily, who often fell at key moments in her life, now tumbled down the cellar steps.)

Still, Dash had forebodings of failure. It would be a hit, he thought, but not a "smash hit." He wrote Jo he was "fortunate" not to be an investor in a show in which the actors were being paid so much. He did have a small piece, but his share came "out of royalties, which are paid before you start figuring out whether investors are making or losing their pennies."

As always, Lily had taken care of him well, giving him 15 percent of her share for his work with her on this play, and she sent him weekly statements which she signed personally. Through April, May, and June, he was to receive royalty checks from the production itself, from the out-of-town tour, and from both the Little, Brown book publication of the script and the foreign rights.

Once more Lily had been his pupil, he the mentor. He called *The Autumn Garden* "easily Lillian's best and—what's more important—points at better ones to come . . . if she'll keep her nose to the grindstone." His assessment reflects his mood at that moment, optimistic, higher on life than he had been for a long time.

As the weeks passed, Dash continued to take a close interest in how business went, whether reviewers who had given it mixed notices were willing to reconsider. When Norman Mailer, referring to the homosexual subtheme, the alliance between Frederick and Payson, which Lily drops, told her it would have been a great play had she not lost her nerve, Dash jumped to her defense. "Almost everybody loses their nerve," he said. "You almost didn't, and that's what counts, and what he should have said."

On the move, Lily agreed to give a lecture on playwriting at Swarthmore College. Then she told Dash she didn't know what to say, and was so "disagreeable" that, he wrote to Maggie, "if I had not been . . . raised in the racket I do not think I'd care to associate with writers."

In her lecture, Lily admitted that Dash had helped her with *The Little Foxes* and the "blackamoor chit-chat." Then, less honestly, she spoke of how writers stood alone. "So little" help and advice can be given, she said, "and you so dislike those honest enough to give it that often they cease to give it." Yet if Hammett had strayed, he had returned to help her extensively with *The Autumn Garden*, which remained their mutual favorite. Both were sorry when it closed in May after only two months. It lost $75,000.

The shared pleasure of their collaboration on *The Autumn Garden* was followed in the early spring of 1951 by a visit. A proud grandfather, Dash brought Jo's nine-month-old baby, Ann, to Hardscrabble Farm. On the plane from California, he managed to feed her and change her. In New York, Lily awaited them on Eighty-second Street. When she saw the baby's blond hair, Lily cried out, "That's the color! That's the color I want!" Dash was amused. "She looks like one of those babies you'd see on a Russian tractor," he said. On Saturday morning the three set out for Hardscrabble Farm, where Lily and Dash competed over who would do the feeding and changing. Meanwhile Lily quickly hired a nurse.

So Lily acted out the fantasy of their sharing a child, of being given a second chance, the aborted baby returning. She was "quite nuts" about the baby, Dash wrote Maggie, boring "the bejesus out of even me." One night the baby crawled up to the window where the curtain was moving and laughed. Lily, still trying to please him in she-Hammett style, said, "I think that kid's drunk."

Soon she took to inquiring of people whether they thought the baby was beautiful. Only an affirmative kept them off "her son-of-a-bitch list," Dash said. Before long, she was boring not only him but "a great many people."

Lily thanked Jo, telling her "you have given me great pleasure by allowing her to come." Dash, she said, seems younger now than when she first met him. He was "one of the few people in the world who has grown more interesting in time." Then Lily took off for New York. "The baby and I press on more or less bravely without her," Dash reported.

In September 1949, Lillian Hellman had signed an affidavit demanded by the Authors League of America of its union officers: "I am not a member of the Communist Party or affiliated with such party." She didn't like loyalty oaths, but, ever cautious, she complied. "If it must be done then it must be done, and that is all there is to it," she wrote Oscar Hammerstein II. She did not give her name when the National Council of the Arts, Sciences and Professions called for negotiations between the United States and the Soviet Union on the Korean crisis, although Dash gave his. When she did sign a statement, she scrutinized the bona fides of the sponsoring organization; the National Institute of Arts and Letters was acceptable, ASP now less so. Dash signed many statements against the House Un-American Activities Committee. Lily had grown careful.

In her memoir *Scoundrel Time,* she admitted obliquely that in the years prior to the fifties she had not taken a courageous stand against the coming witch hunt. She "worried," Lillian said, without saying exactly what she meant, "often about what didn't worry him, inhibited by what he ignored." What inhibited her was fear of being marginalized by her politics. Dash, however, continued to behave entirely according to his principles.

Jo arrived to pick up the baby and found Lily and Dash behaving like a married couple. Sometimes Lily took Jo to the theater; sometimes Dash did. They told Jo funny stories, zeroing in on people's foibles and weaknesses, like how Herman Shumlin, allergic to poison ivy, caught it from the dog. Together they listened to classical music.

As always between Lillian and Dash's daughter, however, there were awkward moments. Lily told Jo that Jose had once brought an alienation of affection suit against her. The notice had been printed in the New Orleans newspapers, embarrassing her before her aunts. "I have the clipping upstairs," she said. But somehow she never showed it to Jo.

Jo also made the mistake of remarking to Lillian that the Mexican divorce between her parents wasn't actually legal. "Oh yes it is," Lillian insisted.

Lily hadn't lost her ambition for Dash. When he was invited to Paris by the Comité National des Ecrivains, she tried to make him go. "Madame has a firm belief that one should go almost anywhere for almost any purpose if it's free, and of course she's been trying to get me to France for years," he said. But every day at Hardscrabble Farm was precious to him, and he felt "cheated" even if he was detained in New York. Dash also doubted whether in the present political climate he would be granted a passport.

He returned to California for his lawsuit against Warner Brothers over the rights to "The Fat Man." Lily complained of his coldness to her. "This is a love letter because I say it is," he wrote. "It has a great deal of warmth—enough to satisfy anybody—because I say it has, so don't let's have any arguments about it."

He enclosed new snapshots of baby Ann. "If you don't clearly recognize me in one of them," he teased, "it can only be because, not really loving me, you have never paid enough attention to me to recognize me by sight . . . and I'd hate to think that." Once more he revealed that whatever estrangement they had suffered had come because of her false sense of priorities, her not putting him first, her not loving *him* enough. As for his ties to "the Hammetts of Purdue Avenue," knowing how Lily was always jealous and alarmed when he visited Jose, he described an evening there as a "duty dinner."

There was a new warmth between them and it felt as if the tension had dissolved, allowing a real companionship that would mature and deepen in the years to come. Lily was working well; the whoring had receded. Dash was not drinking. The farm became their mutual refuge. Spring, then summer of 1951 arrived and Dash retired once more to Hardscrabble Farm.

Dash pruned the dogwood trees, planted gloxinias, cut sprays of forsythia for indoor forcing, and put out suet cakes for the birds. He enjoyed playing with a new puppy, who was named Gregory after the ubiquitous Zilboorg. He could fix his own dinners too: broiling lamb chops, baking potatoes, salting scallions and radishes, buttering bread, brewing tea. In June, Dash broke in the puppy Gregory to go fishing with him in his boat, and began his annual turtle-trapping campaign. Lily wondered whether to go to Europe to write a screenplay of Ibsen's *A Doll's House.*

Dash had withdrawn from political engagement, settling into a vague armchair philosophizing. "I'm not too appalled by the thoughts of a possible World War III," he intoned when the war in Korea threatened to be expanded into China, risking American nuclear attack. "We've had two of those World War things and both were silly and wicked, but not much more silly and wicked than most large-scale things we tackle in our present childish state. The way we live, I daresay war can be considered as normal as peace." He thought neither as a Marxist nor as someone with a serious commitment to socialism. His voice had been emptied of the impassioned sense of capitalism's relentless inhumanity which had so informed *Red Harvest.*

Yet Dash remained allied loyally with the American Communist

Party. In May 1950 he joined a group of Communist writers declaring themselves willing to discuss peace, as they responded to the American government's decision to refuse entrance visas to Picasso and the Dean of Canterbury. Among Hammett's fellow signatories were Albert Maltz, Michael Gold, John Howard Lawson, Howard Fast, and Herbert Aptheker. In August 1950, he signed a statement requesting the Department of Justice to continue bail for eleven Communist functionaries arrested under the infamous Smith Act, which had been enlisted against the Trotskyists a decade earlier. That summer he feared even that the Jefferson School might be closed down "as subversive under the Smith Act."

Years later Murray Kempton speculated in print what Hammett "might have said to Miss Hellman on the night he came home from the meeting of the board of the Civil Rights Congress which voted to refuse its support to the cause of James Kutcher, a paraplegic veteran who had been discharged as a government clerical worker because he belonged to the Trotskyite Socialist Workers Party." As they always had, the Communists ignored the troubles of their rivals on the left.

He continued as president of the New York State chapter of the Civil Rights Congress, but it was a titular role. In these postwar years Dashiell Hammett was not involved in the decisions concerning the policy and advocacy to which he continued to lend his name. It was a name that had become synonymous in the culture with official Communism. A reader had sent a poem to the New York *Times* in 1949 which included the following couplet:

> *Democracy is threatened by a host which runs the gamut*
> *From Marshal Joseph Stalin to subversive Dashiell Hammett.*

Indeed the government was now deploying the Communists' subservience to Stalin to launch a vast repression. The repugnancy of the Stalin regime enabled it to tar all dissidents with the Stalinist brush. Under siege in particular were the very Communists who had applauded when the Smith Act had been used against the Trotskyists and members of the CIO in Minneapolis who built the Teamsters and pioneered cross-industry union organizing.

In June 1951, seventeen Communists, among them V. J. Jerome, the Party's literary commissar, were arrested and charged with advocating and teaching the overthrow of the government of the United States by force and violence. Not only had they done nothing of the sort, but their views were of course protected by the First Amendment, as the Hollywood Ten had insisted.

Communist Party supporters who had justified the murder of dissidents in the Soviet Union, as well as the prosecution of Trotskyists in America, were not credible when they donned the mantle of martyrs once their own civil liberties were threatened. Yet they were, of course, no less entitled to be defended now that they were under attack. Unfortunately, their own lack of commitment to the civil liberties of others now played directly into the hands of the agents of repression abroad in the society.

On July 2, four of the defendants became fugitives, forfeiting $80,000 in bail money. In the U.S. District Court in New York, Judge Sylvester Ryan directed four trustees of the bail fund of the Civil Rights Congress, which had put up the bail, to appear in court the next day. Aided by Assistant U.S. Attorney Roy Cohn, he invoked an English law which decreed that a defendant remains, in essence, in the "friendly custody" of whomever puts up his bail; that party then assumes responsibility for the defendant's appearance in court. It was a legal means of intimidating anyone who helps or supports the accused, the better to isolate McCarthyism's victims.

Dash was both the president of the New York State branch of the Civil Rights Congress and a trustee of its bail fund, which had freed the Communists. It was a facet of McCarthyism, this absurdity that all five thousand contributors to the bail fund could be held responsible for the missing defendants. What the government sought with these tactics of intimidation were the names of the contributors, the better to proceed with the economic and social terror of the witch hunt.

FBI agents were dispatched to Tenth Street, where Muriel Alexander stood them off. When they appeared a second time, Alexander telephoned Dash at Hardscrabble Farm. He decided to return to New York to accept the summons immediately after the Fourth of July holiday.

Early in the morning on July 4, FBI agents drove to Hardscrabble Farm, in search, they said, of the missing Smith Act defendants. Lily showed them politely around the farm in her car. They found no lurking Communists.

Now Lily and Dash made plans to go to New York so that Dash could accept the government's subpoena. Lily's feelings were ambivalent. This was what she had always wanted, she thought, as she faced the government's harassment of Dashiell Hammett: a place where only she knew where he was, where only she could take care of him. Finally he would be hers. Then she caught herself, chastising herself for such ignoble thoughts. "You are a disgusting woman," she wrote in her diary.

"You don't drink anymore, so I can't give you a drink," she said out loud to Dash.

"Wasn't it better when I drank?" was the response.

2 0

The Man Alone

"It's an unpleasant, upsetting world these days, full of uneasiness."
                                                    LILLIAN HELLMAN

On Thursday morning, July 5, 1951, Lily and Dash drove back into New York. Accompanying them in the car were two turtles. One was a snapping turtle, destined for supper. The other had been spotted by Willie Wyler. It was a wood turtle, a she-turtle, whom Dash had named Wilhelmina, or Willy for short, and who became a favored pet.

That night they argued. Lillian was surprised that Dash permitted any discussion at all about what he planned to do about testifying in federal court about the Civil Rights Congress bail fund and the four missing Smith Act defendants, whose bail had been revoked once the Supreme Court affirmed the conviction of the leaders of the Communist Party. It was then, in defiance of what they considered a fascistic decision, that they refused to surrender and became fugitives.

Still she made her case. She was worried about him, she told Dash. She did not see why he had to go to jail, since he didn't know the names of the bail fund contributors. You're "nice," Dash replied. He called her "a nice woman." His decision he would not discuss with her at all. That as the figurehead leader of a branch of the Civil Rights Congress he didn't know the names of contributors to the bail fund, which numbered in the thousands, was entirely irrelevant to what he planned to do.

Hammett accepted his subpoena. He and Lily then returned on Friday afternoon, July 6, to Hardscrabble Farm. That same day Hammett's co-defendant, Frederick Vanderbilt Field, another bail fund trustee, who had already been to court, was granted bail by Judge Thomas W. Swan in Connecticut. But there were so many delays that he languished in jail all weekend. Field had long since sacrificed his Vanderbilt inheritance for his radical beliefs.

On Sunday, Lily and Dash returned New York. There was a meeting at Lillian's apartment with labor lawyer Victor Rabinowitz, who, as Frederick Field's lawyer, had been engaged to help represent the other bail fund trustees as well. Lily did most of the talking. They discussed how Roy Cohn, who was helping prosecutor Irving Saypol, had propounded the view that bail fund trustees, by English common law, could be held accountable for the appearance of the four missing defendants. To Rabinowitz, Dash seemed more an observer than the central figure in the event.

Dashiell Hammett's court appearance came the next day, Monday, July 9. He was represented by Mary Kaufman, the lawyer for the Civil Rights Congress, an attractive, dark-haired, vibrant thirty-six-year-old woman, who had been a young prosecutor at Nuremberg. Later she worked for the National Labor Relations Board in Washington. Her co-counsel was Rabinowitz, as each argued some of the points. Lillian herself did not come to court to stand by Dash, although she had never had any connection with the Civil Rights Congress.

Hammett was the final trustee to testify. There was never any doubt in either his own or his lawyers' minds about what he would do. As soon as Field and the others had answered some questions, they had jeopardized their ability to take the Fifth Amendment on others. So they made themselves vulnerable to contempt charges.

Questioned about the names, ordered to hand over the Civil Rights Congress bail fund checkbook and receipt book, Hammett pleaded that answering might tend to incriminate him. He would not even admit that he was a trustee of the bail fund, even as the court held documents of the Civil Rights Congress containing Dash's initials beside the minutes of meetings he had obviously attended. All he admitted to the court was on which days he had been present in New York.

Judge Sylvester Ryan decreed that since Hammett was a witness, and not accused of any crime, he was not entitled to invoke the Fifth Amendment in full, diminished, or any other form. Rabinowitz argued that since the Civil Rights Congress was on the list of subversive organizations issued by the Attorney General, even whether Hammett was a trustee of the bail fund was a privileged question. Mary Kaufman objected boldly that the judge had taken it upon himself, in violation of the Constitution, to act as a grand jury. Neither Kaufman nor Rabinowitz could prevail in that political environment, however brilliant their arguments.

In the early evening of that same Monday, Dashiell Hammett was sentenced to six months in prison. Judge Ryan denied him bail pending his appeal, a decision based "upon the entire conduct of the witness throughout his entire examination . . . his demeanor has been contumacious."

"Samuel Dashiell Hammett, have you anything to say as to why judgment should not be pronounced on you by this court?" Judge Ryan demanded angrily.

"Not a thing," Dash said.

It was all over. Slimy Roy Cohn then went up to Hammett with a question. "How could you have been so duped?" Hammett just looked at him.

Dash was transported to the West Street jail. The prospect of the six-month jail sentence left him unperturbed. His view was that neither the names of the bail fund contributors nor the whereabouts of the fugitive Communists were any of the government's business. He showed so little interest in the case that it was as if it were happening to someone else.

"You can do this much time with your socks on," Dash said.

Mary Kaufman went immediately to the U.S. Court of Appeals for the Second Circuit. She chose to address distinguished jurist Learned Hand, whose views were to prevail in the larger case, *United States of America v. Dennis,* in which he would reveal that, despite the constitutional issues involved, even he was submitting to McCarthyite hysteria. Kaufman argued forcefully that, pending his appeal, Hammett's particular case should be treated as an application for habeas corpus.

On July 12 Judge Hand issued an order setting temporary bail for Dashiell Hammett in the amount of $10,000, the figure which had been set for Fred Field. Final judgment would be rendered by the full court.

On this same day, the Treasury Department filed an income-tax lien against Dashiell Hammett for $100,629.03 for failing to pay his taxes between 1942 and 1945. Dash had been under the mistaken impression, as he had written Nancy Bragdon, that there was plenty of time to pay after the war. Then he had let the matter slide, relying on Lillian's accountant, Bernard Reis. An Internal Revenue Bureau agent had interviewed him, but Dash had not taken the man seriously; he had talked about his sick wife and starving children, so Dash suspected he might want a payoff. Dash had underestimated what was at stake. The government was clearly out to use Dashiell Hammett as a pawn in its Cold War ideology and as an example to further its reign of terror.

*　　　*　　　*

Dash and Lily's friends soon learned that bail had been set. Jerome Weidman read in the newspaper that Dash would remain in jail because he didn't have ten thousand dollars. His wife, Peggy, pointed out that no one wanted to be associated with paying bail for a Communist; everyone was terrified to put up the money.

Appalled, Weidman decided to contribute the $10,000, his life savings. He telephoned Lillian, but was unable to reach her. He tried Arthur Kober, but he wasn't answering his telephone either. Maggie had gone to school with Peggy Weidman, and so Weidman called Maggie and asked her to have Arthur call him.

"I cannot believe that his friends are going to let Dash go to jail," Weidman told Kober. At once Kober began to bluster.

"I'm not criticizing you, Arthur," Weidman quickly added. "I've got ten thousand dollars. I'm perfectly willing . . . "

"Are you out of your mind?" Kober demanded. "You're a married man! You have two children!" Kober also let Weidman know that both he and Lillian were keeping out of the whole affair. Lillian did not want to jeopardize her opportunity to write the screenplay for *War and Peace* for producer Alexander Korda. Kober himself was about to make a deal which would have actress Rita Hayworth play in a film version of *Wish You Were Here,* the musical adaptation of his one success, *Having Wonderful Time.* It meant too much personal jeopardy to put up bail for a Communist.

Lily did not see Weidman for eight more years, and when they met at a Tony Awards dinner, she behaved as if it were Weidman and not herself who had cowered under the threat of McCarthyism when Dash was in trouble.

"Let's get together," mild-mannered Weidman suggested.

"Yes, now that I'm politically clean at last," Lillian said nastily within earshot of a crowd. Later she told Weidman she had never been told that he had been willing to put up Dash's bail money.

At the time, Lillian disappeared. She refused to put up Dash's bail money herself—there was never a question of her doing so. Later she was to write that in an effort to raise $100,000, a ridiculous figure she invented, she pawned her jewelry since it would take too long to mortgage her house. In an elaborate invention, she wrote she had then rushed up to Martha's Vineyard, where Leo Huberman agreed to mortgage his little house and give the money to Dash. If later she rewrote history, at the time Dash could not turn to her.

Nor could Dash have written her a note which, according to Lillian, read: "Do not come into this courtroom. If you do, I will say I do not know you. Get out of 82nd Street and Pleasantville. Take one of the trips to Europe that you love so much. You do not have to prove to me that you love me at this late date." Lily wrote that one of Hammett's lawyers gave her that note. But neither Mary Kaufman, who never met Hellman, nor Rabinowitz, nor, later, Charles Haydon, ever delivered such a note from Dash to Lily. Its style is of course her own. It is obvious that she wrote it herself pretending that Dash had insisted she not be involved.

What actually happened was that at the moment of his hearing Lillian Hellman, in fear for her own career, the career for which she had bartered everything, abandoned Dashiell Hammett. Not only did she not stand beside him in court. She began to make plans to leave the country. She let him down.

Finally Dash telephoned Ruth and Gus Goetz temporarily out in California and asked them to put up the $10,000 for his bail. Ruth wanted to do it, but Gus said they couldn't afford it. They had already given money to Ring Lardner, Jr., who had gone heroically to jail as one of the Hollywood Ten.

On July 13, Muriel Alexander, walked into the U.S. District Court, Judge Ryan's court, with $10,000 in cash. A rich comrade had finally put up Dash's bail money, insisting on remaining anonymous. Alexander was brought before U.S. Commissioner McDonald, who immediately asked for the origin of the money. Alexander claimed that the money was her own. He did not believe her. He would not approve "the tender" without "justification."

Three days later, on July 16, Judge Ryan formally ruled that the bail money for Dash could not be accepted because Alexander would not discuss "when and from what sources said cash had been obtained." Mary Kaufman objected, then withdrew the offer.

Recognizing she would get no satisfaction from Judge Ryan, Kaufman decided to return to the Court of Appeals. She would request that the District Court be forced to accept the bail, without making Alexander justify where she got the money. It was a lost cause, as Dash had known.

With a heavy heart, Kaufman went down to the West Street jail, where Dash was being held. Weeping, she told him what had happened. He was the first client she represented who would be going to prison. Through the bars, Hammett reached out and patted Mary on the shoulder, trying to make her feel better. Soon he was laughing. He had never had any illusions about what would happen to him. Before long, unaware of the Treasury Department's action against him, he contacted accountant Reis to see if he could guarantee some money for his granddaughter Ann's future.

At the West Street jail he enjoyed the male camaraderie. Nor did he seem overly to mind when after a July 23 hearing before the New York State Banking Commission, he was subjected to a body search upon his return to jail. "You won't find the fugitives there," Fred Field told the examiner peering through his spread legs. Dash called the little jailhouse library "great" because they had a copy of *The Maltese Falcon*. A Catholic prisoner, learning Hammett had once been a Catholic, urged him to go to confession.

"I'd hate to pull the Fifth Amendment on the good father," Dash said.

Muriel Alexander visited him every opportunity she got, which was every Thursday. Although Lillian was on his list of visitors, she did not go to see Dash at West Street. Instead she gave Alexander a list of questions to ask. "Does he think of me?" Lillian wanted Alexander to inquire of Dash. But this Muriel would not do; it seemed so inappropriate. Meanwhile Lillian demanded to know everything, and was irritable, never satisfied with Alexander's accounts of her visits.

Mary Kaufman charged no fee to Dashiell Hammett. Neither did Victor Rabinowitz, although Hammett never thanked him. To Rabinowitz, who admired the stand Dash had taken, he seemed a cold, withdrawn person. Disapproving of both of these progressive and dedicated lawyers, left-wingers whom she did not consider respectable enough, Lillian Hellman fired them both.

For Dash's appeal, she wanted her own lawyers, Paul O'Dwyer and Oscar Bernstien, to represent Dash. But O'Dwyer's brother, William, remained under investigation by the Kefauver Commission for corruption during his tenure as New York City mayor; the red tinge of Paul's representing Hammett was not desirable in William's time of trouble.

On the same floor of their building at 40 Wall Street, however, was a thirty-four-year-old lawyer named Charles Haydon, who carried no left-wing taint and who worked for a distinguished firm. Having hired Haydon to file a brief with the Court of Appeals, Lily then turned and ran for her life.

In her diary, she admitted that she "lost her head." It was "a moral mess." Although Ring Lardner, Jr., did, she would not sign the "Open Letter to J. Howard McGrath, U.S. Attorney General," protesting the imprisonment of Hammett and his co-defendants without bail. Rather, she panicked. She reached for the telephone and called her travel agent. She escaped. "Those three weeks before I left were the worse [sic] I ever knew in my life," she was to write Jo. She had lost six pounds. On August 3, she left for Paris.

By August 9, Lily was in London, a resident at Claridges, one of the swankiest hotels. As if Dash's entire world had not collapsed, she became a tourist, traveling to Hampton Court with the Zilboorgs and to Cambridge. When Sam Spiegel expressed interest in making a film of Dash's story "The King Business," Lily wired her secretary to ask Muriel Alexander for a copy. Lily's means of keeping in touch with Dash now was having her secretary ask Muriel Alexander, who was still able to visit Dash in the West Street jail, whether Dash had left any messages for her. Invariably the same answer came. Dash had sent no message to Lillian.

She was so frightened that FBI agents might find her and subpoena her back to America that she mailed the letters she wrote to Dash to her secretary. Addressed to "Dashie," they were signed only with her first name. On the envelope would be her New York address. Before long Lillian Hellman had so entirely lost contact with Dashiell Hammett that she had no idea where he was.

Meanwhile, as if nothing was wrong, she went shopping. She had a list of sixteen recipients for whom she needed to purchase gifts; Dash was one of them. She bought him ties, prints, a scarf, and a cigar cutter. On the list next to a description of each present was how much she had spent. She told people Dash had reacted to going to prison "as if he had long expected it."

By August 16, Lily was in Antibes, where she boarded Alexander Korda's yacht. But they could not work out an agreement for a script of *War and Peace*.

From the West Street jail, Dash was sent to federal prison, first at a facility for juvenile offenders at Chillicothe, Ohio, then at Ashland, Kentucky. It was a low-security prison where many inmates were bootleggers, convicted of operating illegal stills in the hills of Kentucky and Tennessee and West Virginia. At night they played hillbilly music on their guitars. Hammett drew "light duty," sanitation detail with a mop and a broom. The young prisoners liked him because he had not ratted on his comrades, although they would sometimes mischievously throw extra dust around and then berate him for doing a poor job.

The company was hardly enlightened. One inmate told Dash, "It's not that I'm prejudiced, because I've got no reason to dislike niggers, but I just hate 'em!" Dash knew how to talk to inmates and guards alike. At lunchtime, a guard provided him with sandwiches in the "pen."

Aggrieved by Lily's cowardice and her having abandoned him, Dash did not put hers on his list of names of people with whom he wished to correspond. On his original list, only the names of his family and of Muriel Alexander appear. Nor would he write or send messages to Lillian. The government soon decided that since Dash was a political prisoner, he could write only to members of his immediate family. Although Jose continued to pretend they were still married, the government knew otherwise and she was not deemed an acceptable correspondent.

Then Dash relented. Lily was what she was. Early in October, testing the regulations, he asked that Lily "be added to his list." He described their relationship "as one of friendship only." At the same time he needed permission to write to Muriel Alexander, she and Lillian being "the only two who know anything at all about my affairs."

The director of the Bureau of Prisons consulted the FBI for "any information which you may have which would reflect upon Miss Hellman's suitability as a correspondent." The FBI replied with a document listing Lillian's political affiliations, headed by the notorious "National Council of the Arts, Sciences and Professions, one of the most important Communist front organizations in the country and a basic Communist front with a long record of succession from other Communist fronts."

Permission for Dash to write to Lily, or Lily to Dash, was denied. Nor would she be permitted to visit him. Because efficiency was not the Bureau of Prisons' strong suit, eventually a few of Jose's and even a few of Lillian's letters were to reach Dash in prison.

By mid-October, Dash didn't know whether Lily was in France or in England. Mildly, he said he believed she was "having a pretty good time in spite of her worrying about things." Even as she had behaved badly, Dash could not imagine life entirely without Lily. He requested of his daughter Jo that she intercede, "do some go-betweening between Lily and me. First-off I'd like to know if she's back from Europe yet and, if not, when she's due." But Lily was not to be the recipient of his sentimental feelings. On the romantic side, Jo was instructed to telephone Pat Neal and "give her my love and tell her sometimes I've found it awfully easy to be in love with her in jail."

Lily returned to the United States in October. At once she began to telephone Charles Haydon, demanding to know whether they could still try to get Hammett out on bail and whether she could get permission to visit him in Ashland. Haydon requested that Lillian be permitted to visit on the ground that she "was involved with some business transactions with Mr. Hammett." Her visit was not approved.

Lily immediately descended on Muriel Alexander. Taking over, as Dash learned and told Jo, she "finally managed to blackjack some sort of information out of Muriel (she's a real dope!) about my affairs." Alexander gave Jo such cryptic messages to include in her letters to Dash that he didn't understand them. One involved a friend with "pearls" who had turned out to be nicer than they had expected. Dash had no idea what this meant.

Armed with a résumé of his affairs which Lily had extracted from Muriel Alexander, Haydon visited Hammett alone on October 25. He took along six original and valuable Matisse postcards Lily had purchased in Paris. A guard remained in the room with them.

"They call him, euphemistically, an 'intelligence officer,'" Dash explained. "You've got to ask him for permission to give me the post-cards."

The guard examined the postcards. "Well, he can have them, but he can't use them to send a message or write. He's got to use a regular prison postcard."

Dash laughed. Accepting the postcards, he said laconically, "Tell her thanks." It seemed to Haydon as if he was merely tolerating Lillian. Nor had he any message for her. Haydon also asked Dash whether, his appeal having failed, he wanted to carry it up to the Supreme Court.

Upon his return to Manhattan, Haydon headed for Ruth and Gus Goetz's apartment. Waiting there were Lillian and her lawyer Oscar Bernstien. Bernstien impatiently interrupted Haydon's boring preface about a traffic jam. "Stop being so silly," he demanded. "She's not inter-ested in all that. Tell her about Dashiell. Tell her how he looked."

"How did he look? What did he have to say? What is he doing there?" Lily had questions. Haydon reported that Dash looked "relaxed," was serving very soft time, and was comfortable. At once Lily wrote Jo with the news: She did not "know enough of his business to take care of very much," but urged Jo to send more pictures of the baby.

On November 7, Dash finally agreed to permit Haydon to carry the case to the Supreme Court. Lillian at once deemed it "a wise decision." But when Haydon outlined the arguments he intended to make, Dash showed little interest. "Nothing is going to make any difference," he said.

As his months in jail passed, Dash's health began to give out. One day waiting in line for food, as Fred Field remembered, he "suddenly turned white as a sheet and staggered to a nearby bench." Hammett had very little energy now. Even with Fred Field, a special member of the Communist Party like himself, he did not discuss politics. When he talked about Lillian, it was in the context of how hard he had worked with her on her plays.

Lily wrote him gossipy letters. In one she revealed her fear that she was being blacklisted. Irving Lazar had come to explain "the Hollywood situation," that "many people were out of work for many reasons." She sent Lee Gershwin's regards: "My god you've had awful taste in women, and awful admirers among them," Lily could not resist the gibe. The

French were interested in publishing his short stories. Willy the turtle was surviving. The road tour of *The Autumn Garden* was doing well. In one letter Lily reminded Dash that he had "an anniversary on November 22nd and if you would like me to send the lady a present, I will be glad to do so." That November marked their having known each other for twenty-one years.

"The news from L. was very good," Dash wrote Jo, "in that it all sounded very Lillianesque and she doesn't always sound Lillianesque unless she's in good spirits." He talked of her as if she were another of his children who he hoped was doing well. He resumed sending her his love.

Lillian was indeed being "Lillianesque." On the night of October 31 she was at the opening of Maxwell Anderson's *Barefoot in Athens* at the Martin Beck Theater. As the audience applauded, Lillian Hellman was the first to charge up the aisle. At the back of the theater she encountered general manager Victor Samrock. "This play stinks!" Lily sputtered as she headed for the exit.

Some of Lillian's letters were returned to her in mid-November, marked: "Your name does not appear on his approved correspondence list." She was asked to "advise us fully regarding the necessity for corresponding."

Feeling shaky, his health broken, Dash lost fifteen pounds in prison. He expected Lillian to meet him in Ashland on the morning of his release, December 9. Lillian promised Jo she would fly down to Ashland and then fly back with him. Meanwhile Dash could imagine only the immediate future. He decided that as soon as he was released he would go to Hardscrabble Farm for two weeks of duck shooting.

Early in December, affirming the Court of Appeals, the Supreme Court denied Hammett's plea for bail. Justices Black and Douglas dissented. "Long may they live," Hammett murmured. It didn't matter, of course, since he had almost served his sentence. Haydon visited again, bearing two sets of clothes selected by Rose Evans, including a topcoat, since it was winter. He told Hammett that Lillian would not be coming to meet him upon his release from prison.

Dash treated this news with his customary sangfroid. He did not expect courage of her, even as there was no one else close enough to him to make the trip and he was so frail that he needed someone to accompany him. He was truly a man alone. Meanwhile Lily had an excuse ready. She was not going to Ashland to meet Dash, she said, because her lawyer had advised her not to go.

Anticipating his return, however, she went down to Tenth Street, where she ordered Rose Evans to get rid of any liquor that remained there. Evans refused. She wanted Hammett to find his apartment exactly as he had left it.

Dashiell Hammett served five months, having been granted one month off for good behavior. On December 9, he boarded a Greyhound bus for Charleston, West Virginia, and from there a plane to New York. It landed in a snowstorm. Dash immediately headed for the men's room and vomited.

Lily had come to La Guardia Airport in a limousine. When Dash did not emerge from the men's room, she sent the driver to check on him. It was a bad hamburger, Dash said.

Back on Eighty-second Street, Lily, at Hammett's request, had oysters on the half shell, quail, and sweetbreads waiting. But he was too sick to eat. The next morning Dash was ready to return to his own apartment in the Village, where Rose Evans—and Willy the turtle—awaited him.

"Please don't drink when you go back up there," Rose told him, referring to Lillian's. "She'll blame me."

Lily had bitter news for Dash now, the nastiest of surprises, and it may account in part for why she had not gone to Ashland to meet him. There would be no duck shooting. There would be no trips to Pleasantville at all. While Dash was in prison, Lily had sold Hardscrabble Farm.

In August 1951, with Dash already in jail, the Internal Revenue Service ruled that the sale of the movie rights to *The Searching Wind,* as well as her sale of the rights to *Watch on the Rhine,* could not be considered capital gains; both were subject to tax as ordinary income. Her accountants had outsmarted themselves, as McCarthyism extended its tentacles.

Simultaneously the government disallowed Hardscrabble as a working farm, arguing that it had lost money for eleven years. It was "gentleman farming," not a business for profit on which Lillian could claim major deductions on her property taxes. The auditor had even challenged Lily's claim that she used her Cadillac for business. Lily owed the government $110,000 in back property taxes and they demanded the entire sum right then and there.

Lily panicked again. She sold Hardscrabble Farm without even informing Dash. They had lost the scene of their common life. Things were so bad she had to sell the farm, Dash told Jo in his understated way. But he would never criticize her before others about serious matters.

Frail, weak, he accompanied Lily to dinner at the Bloomgardens'. Lily told Ginny it was all right to drink in front of Dash, but he should have milk. Her taffeta rustled; she talked animatedly at the dinner table, smoking furiously, occasionally erupting into a fit of coughing.

Dash would now begin sentences. "Well, when I was a writer. . . ." Life was behind him. His sardonic side alone remained. He took Pat Neal to the Stork Club only to be stopped at the door. You can't come in, he was told. "I think they may have a point," Dash said as he led Pat away.

If anyone praised his courage for having endured jail, he seemed embarrassed. Fearlessly he resumed his political endorsements. He agreed to be the chairman of the Committee to Defend V. J. Jerome, who had been indicted in June 1951 under the Smith Act and faced a five-year prison sentence ostensibly for having written an article entitled "Grasp the Weapon of Culture," published in *Political Affairs,* which he edited.

I. F. Stone refused to sponsor a rally-tribute to Jerome, however. "Politically he has tried to ride herd on the intellectuals in a way most offensive to anyone who believes in intellectual and cultural freedom," Stone said. "I'd feel like a stultified ass to speak at a meeting for Jerome without making clear my own sharp differences with the dogmatic, Talmudic, and dictatorial mentality he represents." Stone would defend Jerome as a Smith Act victim but could not pretend he was a libertarian. It didn't bother Hammett. Many cultural figures signed the petition for Jerome, including Lillian. ("If the Lawsons and Hellmans ever got into power I think no one would have any freedom," Budd Schulberg came to believe.)

Among Party initiatives in the spring of 1952 was a petition calling for a reversal of the vote by the U.S. representatives to allow the Tunisian question to be heard in the United Nations. Duly Dash signed.

As they had on Lily, so now the Internal Revenue Service and the state of New York closed in on Dashiell Hammett. The tax lien issued when he had been in jail meant that he couldn't afford now to keep his Village apartment. He attended a fund-raiser on behalf of New York people who had been arrested under the Smith Act. When his time to speak came, he was terse. While all this talk is going on, there are people having a time of it in prison, Dash said.

In April, Dash was back before a grand jury. "I have no special reason for supposing anything will happen in the immediate future," he tried to reassure Jo. Subpoenas kept him from traveling anywhere without permission from the District Attorney's office. "That saves me the trouble of having to go places I don't want to go," he told Jo.

That April, Lily left Pleasantville for good. "It's going to leave quite a hole in life," Dash said. Pleading that he was sick, he let Lily do all the packing herself. Lily "suspects me of having taken to bed to avoid the unpleasantness of helping her move," Dash reported to Jo. If a herd of deer came onto the lawn to bid anyone farewell, as Lillian Hellman was to write in *Scoundrel Time,* they did not find Dash at home. As she was packing, in a closet Lillian discovered an underwater harpoon. There were, as well, "many foolish books in the bookcase," evidence of Dashiell Hammett's deeply eclectic reading taste.

To calm herself as she awaited the public ordeal she was soon to face, Lily went to Jamaica for a week. Dash wrote of how he missed her, "missed the idea of phoning you all afternoon." He described himself as "a fairly spry old man." He hoped he had done "enough on the book to brag about in this space," as he continued to lie to himself about writing, recalling Lily's rebuke within the text of *The Autumn Garden,* Constance's reply to Crossman, who said he never liked liars.

"I'm looking forward to seeing you again," Dash wrote to Lily in Jamaica. "It seems like weeks and weeks."

PART SEVEN

The End of the Affair

21

McCarthy Aftermath

"Why in the world would he ask me about kissing John Melby?"

LILLIAN HELLMAN

"If you are tired you ought to rest, I think, and not try to fool yourself and your customers with colored bubbles."

DASHIELL HAMMETT, "TULIP."

I n 1947 the first group of Hollywood writers had received subpoenas from the House Un-American Activities Committee. In an article for *The Screenwriter*, a union publication, Lillian called those "friendly" witnesses like Gary Cooper, Ronald Reagan, Ayn Rand, and Walt Disney who cooperated "Judas goats." Ten of the nineteen "hostile" witnesses invoked the Fifth Amendment and refused to answer the committee's questions; they were sent to jail for contempt, and became known as the Hollywood Ten. It was at this time, Lillian reported, that Harry Cohn offered her a contract to write five pictures if she signed a "morals clause." That meant she had to be careful about whom she saw, where she was seen.

"What about Dashiell Hammett?" she asked.

"Can't you go to a quiet restaurant?" Cohn replied. When she burst out laughing, Cohn was insulted and the deal evaporated. But Lillian knew it would not have worked out. Cohn had underestimated the mood of the times.

Lillian Hellman was scheduled to testify before the House Un-American Activities Committee on May 21, 1952. She was terrified of going to jail, a terror she later attributed to Dash. It was he who feared for her, she would explain, because he knew how terrified she was of rats and mice. Lily could not possibly go to jail, she was to claim Dash insisted, because although she had strength, she lacked "stamina." So she justified her failure to stand up to McCarthy and his cohorts as he had done.

As she awaited her day before the McCarthy committee, Lillian spoke so much of her fear that Gregory Zilboorg finally told her, "Well, go to jail." These words, she said, were the ones that gave her the most courage. What she displayed in Washington, however, was endurance rather than courage. She named no names. Otherwise, her position was hardly worthy of the mantle of Joan of Arc she assumed after her ordeal was over.

As soon as Lily hired Joe Rauh, her second choice after Abe Fortas, he asked her to write a statement about her political history. In her draft Lily wrote: "I joined the Communist Party in 1938 with little thought as to the serious step I was taking." She had remained a member until 1940, she said, feeling "no bitterness towards the misguided lady who asked me to join." So she made it clear that, whoever had recruited her, it had not been Dashiell Hammett. "I am not a political person," Lily wrote, "and have no place in a political organization."

Rauh was appalled. Not only had she confessed to being a Party member but she was "so little critical of the Communist movement in America that it will be considered an acceptance of it." She had spoken of membership in the Party as if it were akin to joining a ladies' literary society or a good works club. Rumor had it that Rauh, head of Americans for Democratic Action, a group of New Deal democrats which excluded Communists, prided himself on never defending an actual Communist. Rauh went on to author her statement, except for one quotable sentence which was Lillian's.

On that spring day in Washington, Lily took a position certain to have landed her in jail had it not been for Joseph Rauh's canniness, her own reputation for feisty troublemaking, and the fact that she was a woman. For the occasion, she had dyed her hair freshly blond. In a black hat and a new brown-and-black-checked silk dress, a Pierre Balmain original, a handkerchief clutched in her clasped hands, she took the Fifth Amendment. Predictably, the committee, as it had with others attempting the same strategy, refused to allow Lily to speak about herself but not about others. Referring to the "letter" she had written to the committee which would explain everything, she alternated between answering innocuous questions and demanding the protection of the Fifth Amendment. Admitting she was not a Communist in the years 1950, 1951, and 1952, she pleaded constitutional protection for any earlier time.

Meanwhile Rauh had mimeographed her statement, which featured her one line: "I cannot and will not cut my conscience to fit this year's fashions even though I long ago came to the conclusion that I was not a political person and could have no political place in any political group." In the middle of the hearing, Lillian had asked that the committee consider what she said in her "letter." So she and Rauh whetted the appetite of the press. Quick on his feet, Rauh distributed the statement. Amid all this drama, the committee backed down. Lillian Hellman's reputation for speaking out, making trouble, made her seem a witness likely to do them more harm than good. "Why cite her for contempt?" Chairman John S. Wood was later quoted in *Time* magazine. "After all, she's a woman."

By taking the Fifth Amendment, she had been as vulnerable to a contempt citation, and jail, as Dash had been, and as Sidney Buchman, who had taken that very position before her and gone to jail. But as an opponent the committee deemed formidable, Lily escaped. Although she had not named names, neither was she in danger, Ring Lardner, Jr., thought, despite her subsequent self-dramatizations.

Later, in a taxi, Lily, still the she-Hammett, put her hand on Joe Rauh's thigh. John Melby, in Washington, joined her that day to celebrate. When less than a year later her passport was renewed, people wondered: only those who had named names got their passports renewed.

Lily quickly discovered that her picture-writing days in Hollywood were over. Arthur Miller suggested she ask Helen Harvey at the William Morris Agency to represent her. But the head of that firm, Abe Lastvogel, refused. Harvey called Lillian and admitted that the Morris agency objected to Lillian's politics.

"You're very decent to tell me that," Lillian said. Then she sent Harvey flowers.

In May 1952 all the money Dashiell Hammett had in the world was $2,760.44. In an attempt to save him from destitution, Lily went before the New York State Tax Commission and swore that he owed her $2,163.69. Lillian enlisted Oscar Bernstien to see if something could be done about the government's lien against Dash's property, to no avail.

Having become "a local heroine," Lily fell once more into depression. Without a man in her life, she felt "foolishly restless and frightened to be alone." She was "lost." Although it had long been over between them, she wrote John Melby that she wished he was with her. She wanted, she said, "to run away, but I don't know where, or how, or why."

In June 1952, John Melby faced a State Department Loyalty Security Board hearing. By July, Lily was in Washington consulting with Joe Rauh and Melby on whether she ought to testify on Melby's behalf. His entire career was in jeopardy, in part because he was one of those who brought the bad news from China, that Chiang Kai-shek lacked popular support and the corruption-ridden Kuomintang was certain to be defeated by Mao. What the State Department would use to bring him down was his friendship with Lillian Hellman.

Dash spent the summer of 1952 in New York City, rarely emerging from his apartment. "I still haven't got up to your neighborhood," he wrote his "dearest Lilipie." In July, he had Charles Haydon draw up his will.

Dash divided his estate into four equal parts. One part went to "my friend Lillian Hellman." A second part went to "my daughter Mary Jane Hammett." Josephine M. Marshall, his natural daughter, received two parts. The executrix and literary executrix would be Lillian, who was granted another power of attorney. "I've never written a play without him," Lillian had told Haydon. Haydon concluded that Lillian was the only person close to Dashiell Hammett.

Alone in his apartment, Dash read Proust. "I love you with the utmost extravagance," he wrote Lily, "even if I do set the 'expand' key so that not too many words will take up a great deal of room when I write, but it does not always seem to me that such words as run through my head are at their best when embalmed in black on white, and what are *your* problems as a writer, Miss Hellman?"

It was yet another plea for her understanding. Out of jail and out of prospects, he talked about writing, as if by rote, with no real conviction. "I'm having a mess of trouble with my book," he wrote Lily in August in an effort to make it sound as if it were the real thing, "having a hard time making it nearly as good as I want it in the way I want it." The new book would be called "Tulip." Lily was the writer now. Sounding like a beginner, Dash permitted himself his share of "solemn bellyaching."

In "Tulip" Dash attempted to be honest about why he had stopped writing. His pride notwithstanding, he had thought too much about it over the years, he concluded. "You've got to think everything comes through the mind, and of course things get dull when you reason the bejesus out of them that way," he summed up. He had thought too hard and too long about how to write outside of the detective story genre. "You whittle everything down to too sharp a point," he tells himself. He could no longer just "write things down the way they happen and let your reader get what he wants out of 'em." But what then remained? He shrugged, a Hammett habit. Of fame and fortune, he had his fill. Now he was tired.

Unable to afford his Greenwich Village apartment any longer, Dash moved in October 1952 to Katonah in Westchester County, about a half hour's distance from Hardscrabble Farm and an hour and twenty minutes from Manhattan. There was no question of his moving in with Lily on Eighty-second Street. He left behind on Tenth Street the scrapbooks attesting to his past fame as a writer.

Dash's new home was the small, four-room white clapboard guest cottage on the Orchard Hill Road property of Sam and Helen Rosen. He predicted it would "turn out to be one of the nicest homes I've had," and agreed to pay the Rosens fifty dollars a month in cash. Meanwhile Lily made an agreement with the Rosens that they would tell people Dash was living free so that government would not think he had any money. Indeed agents of the Internal Revenue Service turned up, wanting to know how Hammett paid the Rosens. He was living rent-free, the Rosens fibbed. The Rosens paid his telephone and electric bills.

There were no frills attached to the little bungalow with its screened-in porch, except for a wood-burning fireplace. Dash didn't mind. He would sit on his porch and survey the world of nature where alone he felt at peace.

Lily, however, was angry. She did not want Dash in the Rosens' cottage, out of her control, and she let him know it. She also wanted Rose Evans to work for her now. Rose declined. "I need Rose but you won't let me have her," Lily complained to Dash. He was not in favor of the idea. "You'd be fired in two or three minutes," Dash told Rose.

Within a year Lily had hired a new housekeeper, a feisty black woman named Helen Richardson. Dash did not like her, perhaps because he resented her zeal as a converted Catholic. But Helen suited Lillian, whose persona was now more emphatically than ever that of the Southern woman cared for by a black mammy as once Sophronia, whose photograph still adorned her parlor, had taken care of her. Lillian began to call Helen "Madame," what Dash often still called her.

Although there was no work for her in Hollywood, Lily was not idle. The New York theater remained free of the taint of political repression, of a blacklist. In October 1952, Lily went into rehearsal for a revival of *The Children's Hour* that would star Pat Neal and Kim Hunter.

Helen Rosen observed that Dash seemed not to want Lillian to visit and would make excuses to put her off. Helen easily fended off Dash's sexual overtures. But he came to the tennis courts on Sunday mornings to watch, calling Helen "Hebe," the bearer of drinks. Once a horsefly came and sat on his arm. Dash stroked its wings.

"You've got him hypnotized," Helen observed.

"Shush," Dash whispered.

He did not hang Luis Quintanilla's painting of Lily in the cottage. When she telephoned, he remained cold and unwelcoming.

"I thought it would be nice to say hello this time of year," Lillian began tentatively one cold winter day. As she had been from the beginning, she was afraid of him.

"What?" Dash asked. So she had to repeat herself.

Lily provided gossip. Dorothy Parker had remarried Alan Campbell, whom Lily had taken to calling a "fairy-shit." There had been a blizzard.

Things look bad, Dash said. There may be a big-scale war because the Russians now want it.

That makes it simple, Lily tried.

It doesn't seem simple, Dash contradicted her.

Why? Lily asked him.

She tried to keep the conversation going. When she remarked she felt sorry for the boys in Korea, Dash just said, "Sure, but there's going to be more of it." His tone remained cold, as recently it had often been. Lily decided it was to cover his embarrassment. It felt to her as if he were talking to somebody he wished would just hang up. There was not the slightest sign of friendliness or warmth.

Lily came to Katonah to visit him. The place wasn't good enough for him, Lily said, making no secret of her contempt for the rustic four-room cottage. He should find somewhere else, she insisted. "You don't belong in a place like this," Lily said. "You belong in a different setting."

Finally Dash lost his temper.

"Get out of my life!" he told Lily angrily. "Stop bothering me!" He liked the cottage and the Rosens, and she wasn't going to tell him what to do.

Before long Lily found an opportunity to go to war with the Rosens. At a dinner party, someone remarked how wonderful it was that the Rosens were giving Dash the cottage free of charge, and someone else, who knew, replied that he paid fifty dollars. This got back to Lily, who blamed Helen. It was supposed to be a secret.

It wasn't that Lily paid the fifty dollars herself. Hammett still had money coming in, and Lily managed to launder it through John Melby's bank at Yale University; he would then send untainted money back to her. Lily later wrote she made a list of the people who owed him money and even composed a letter asking for repayment. "Forget it," Dash told her, she wrote. "There is a very good reason for not sending the letters.

Nobody will answer them. They are all shits." Why, then, did he lend them the money? she asked. "Oh, Lily, because they needed it" was his reply. "Because they are shits doesn't mean I have to be."

In the winter of 1953 Lily testified for John Melby. Melby "never had anything to do with any political interest of any kind," she said. "I was not even very clear about what Mr. Melby's job was in Moscow." Gracefully she defined theirs as "a completely personal relationship of two people who, once past being in love, happen also to be very devoted to each other and very respectful of one another."

The idiocy of John W. Sipes, legal adviser to the State Department Loyalty-Security Board, and company in high gear, the committee demanded to know how it was that when she and Melby met even now they kissed each other. It was "a Southern custom," Lily allowed. Nor would Melby agree that he would never in his life meet her again. By the end of that day in February 1953, John Melby's career in the foreign service was over.

Depressed, aimless, Lily chose her customary cure. She went to the Virgin Islands this time, which she found "very beautiful but full of drunks and fags." Puerto Rico, "where the govt people seemed to me kind of nice New Deal, and at least people were trying for something," was better. Worst was her brief stay in Miami Beach. That its vulgarity was "Jewish vulgarity—and gangster—didn't make it better."

Dashiell Hammett became a virtual recluse in Katonah. When Lillian's name came up in conversation with the Rosens, he showed no enthusiasm. When he spoke of his daughters now, it was as though they didn't understand him. They had abandoned him because he had wronged their mother, so that everything he did was wrong, he felt.

Ring Lardner, who was visiting the Rosens, telephoned. "Ring, I really don't want to see anyone," Dash told him. He did see Barrows Dunham, who had been fired from Temple University for his beliefs, for being a Communist. As for Dunham's book, *Giant in Chains,* Dash pronounced it "philosophy if you want to call it that for Temple undergraduates if they want to call it that." His political sympathies never interfered with his judgment of what made good writing. But he was willing to participate in a forum, "Fiction Writing as a People's Art," with Howard Fast and V. J. Jerome. They could count on him still.

He met Irene Lee, now Diamond, and a Katonah neighbor, whom he taught how to coax a skunk from her empty swimming pool. He never mentioned Lillian. Hannah Weinstein, Lillian's friend and a mastermind of the Waldorf Conference, brought her three daughters. Hannah he found "a pleasant if dullish woman"; as always, he preferred the company of children. His favorite was Paula, whose middle name was Henry, so he called her Hank. When Helen Rosen's daughter Judy was about to marry, Dash took her to dinner in New York and over venison spoke of how difficult it was to be married to someone you didn't love.

He had a cleaning woman. A laundryman picked up his dirty clothes. But he cooked his own meals, watched baseball and the fights on television, and surrounded himself with books. A large Indian blanket covered his bed.

On an electric typewriter, he tried to work on "Tulip." In the fragment that remains, Hammett examines the waste of the fifteen years he had spent without writing. Hammett splits himself in two; there is a Hammett surrogate and his alter ego named Tulip; through their exchanges he offers his *apologia pro vita sua*. "I don't exist just to write," the Hammett persona replies to Tulip's question about why he has stopped writing.

He reveals a fear of intimacy that has kept him not only from writing, but from intimate connection with the people closest to him. "As soon as things or people threaten to involve you," he says, "you make up a fantasy you call the memory of some place else to drag you away from any sort of responsibility." Now, however, he had real excuses for not writing: "I'm just out of jail. The last of my radio shows went off the air while I was doing my time, and the state and federal people slapped heavy income tax liens on me. Hollywood's out during this red scare."

He admits to what was obvious even from his ragged screenplay for *Watch on the Rhine*. Not having written for so long, he feels compelled to say everything in one book, and so falls once more into paralysis. "You'd never get it all in one book," he knows. As for Lillian and her role in his life, Hammett revealed in "Tulip" that she had ceased to figure in his life emotionally. "I have been married as often as I chose and have had children and grandchildren," he says. Dreading the self-analysis that would have led him to new fiction, he stopped writing.

Yet, as always, he repaired his tattered relations with Lily. He began to meet her once a week in New York. Rarely would she come out to Katonah. When she did, they ate supper with the Rosens. Lily would spin one of her tales and Dash impatiently would demand, "Now, Lily, what really happened?" Then she might climb onto his lap and talk her old baby talk. Jealous of beautiful Helen, she made a show.

To assert her claim, she would chide him. "Put on your jacket if you're going for a walk," Lily ordered one day. "Fuck you," he replied. Once Dash added, "Get your coat shortened." So he was not beyond seizing an opportunity to put her in her place. Lily, of course, had long known how to retaliate. "This place looks dirty," she said. On parting they would kiss, but Dash remained sardonic.

One day Lillian discovered that the Rosens had a houseguest, Paul Robeson, who spent ten years under house arrest during these dark times. Lily went into the kitchen, ostensibly not wanting to drink in front of Dash. Then she cornered Helen.

"How could you do this to me? How could you have him here?" she demanded. "You know what I've just been through. I may be followed and I should be careful and you shouldn't have him in the house with me!" Unaffected by Robeson's troubles, she feared only that being in the same house with him would incite the FBI against her. Helen concealed from Dash what Lily had said. She believed he would have excused it anyway, so understanding was he of Lillian.

That Dash required her money irritated her. In May 1953 he bought Lily a panel of antique lace picturing Queen Isabella and King Ferdinand at the Court of Spain, an exquisite painting in lace eight feet long. Lily was furious; he had paid for the lace with her money, the money she kept in her safe in New York, which he dipped into as he needed it. She threw the lace panel at him. When she tried to return it, and the store refused to take it back, she flung it into a closet in disgust.

Lily held grudges, assumed moral self-righteousness, unlike Dash, who was tolerant even of those who had informed, named names. One day as he and the Rosens, along with Zilboorg, Henry Wallace, Irene Lee Diamond, and Clifford Odets, were chatting about the Korean War on the Rosen porch, filmmaker Robert Rossen, a government informant, appeared.

"Please leave!" Helen said at once. Later Dash laughed and teased her. "You're too emotional about it," he told her. "Don't take it so seriously. Some people can take harassment of that kind and some can't. If somebody would torture me physically, I couldn't take it." Even as he despised informing, he forgave the informers. Lily was no Hammett. At a party she ran into Budd Schulberg for the first time since he had been a cooperative witness.

"Lillian, I want to be your friend," he began.

"Don't touch me. You're dirty!" Lillian told him, moving away quickly.

As Dash lived on quietly in Katonah, the fifties became a restless decade for Lillian. She was forty-seven years old in 1952, an old forty-seven, relentless smoking and drinking having taken their toll. She had succumbed to overweight, was even a bit frumpy. She grew sharp with people, traveled, tried to work on a play. She had no common life with Dash now.

Dash went to Washington in March 1953 to testify before Senator McCarthy's subcommittee investigating the purchases of books by Communists for State Department libraries. "If I were fighting Communism," Hammett, looking frail and emaciated, told Roy Cohn, his old nemesis, "I don't think I would do it by giving people any books at all." When Cohn wondered whether the profits from his writing went to the Communist Party and whether he had been under its discipline, Dash invoked his Fifth Amendment privilege.

Knowing the mannerism irritated her, he joked with Lillian: "I was shrugging my shoulders just for you." A week later, he chaired a meeting called "Culture Fights Back, 1953," at which V. J. Jerome spoke. Two months later, his books were removed from two hundred United States Information Service libraries. *The Children's Hour* was also banned. "By paying not too much attention to what people do and none at all under any circumstances to what they say I keep myself pretty well convinced that nobody's having too tough a time of it," Dash said.

Carefully staying clear of the political shoals, Lily fled to Europe yet again. By June 1953 she was moving between London, Paris, and the South of France, hiding, she admitted. She settled in Rome, choosing two rooms at the Eden Hotel at 49 Via Ludovisi as her base. "I don't like Rome food," Lily decided on this, her first visit to that city. "It is entirely too middle class refined." She traveled to Milan to visit with Henry Sigerist. By the end of June she wrote her secretary, Lois Fritsch, that she was "sick of travel and sick of Europe and sick of hack work."

Dash sent a message to her in London at fashionable Claridges (despite Hollywood's being closed to her she was hardly impoverished). "It's nicer here and there's more loving and missing. Dash." Her bills that spring included one for over three hundred dollars for a black hat from John Frederick's and another for a white chiffon dress and fur jacket from Bergdorf's.

She was, Dash observed, "fluttering around in some sort of circle." But she "sounded all right." His habit of worrying about her lingered. "She now thinks of herself as representing me, the USA, and Flora the dog," he laughed.

Meanwhile her forty-eighth birthday brought her bad nights. "There are certain facts that must now be accepted," Lily thought, "I guess, as little as I like them and as much as I had always hoped they wouldn't be." Her Faustian bargain with Hammett had left her without a husband, without children, forced to depend only on herself. Alone in Europe, the consequences of her choice tormented her.

Fearing that Senator McCarthy was on her trail, Lily chose to remain in Europe until October, even as Dash was suffering from shortness of breath and had come down with pleurisy. But Lillian feared that should she return home for the *Children's Hour* rehearsals she "might run into trouble and that trouble might make it difficult or impossible to return with the script." Then all her work at "this lousy job at a disgraceful fee" would have gone for nothing. She occupied herself adapting a Jessica Mitford book, and a script for Alexander Korda for the British film *A Town Like Alice*, which never materialized because Korda didn't like her script, and the director "cut [her] throat." She told people she was being paid $5,000 for her script; in fact the figure was $60,000.

In Rome, Lillian suddenly scaled down. She moved into one room, and then into an apartment in Parioli at the Residence Palace Hotel, which she feared might be bugged. And she had an affair with a young painter named Stephen Greene, who was in Italy on a Prix de Rome. She had written to Greene, pleading that she knew no one, although the Wylers were there. Another of her lovers was in Rome too, mercurial, alcoholic theater producer Jed Harris. Lily slept with Harris that summer in Rome because, she said, he needed it. She also kept in touch with John Melby: "I went to High Mass, I am still a Jew," she wrote him.

At thirty-six, Greene was young, handsome, and talented. He was a Jew from the Lower East Side of New York, just coming into his own as a painter. Lily, her face ravaged at forty-eight, was a worldly woman, a Broadway celebrity. She smoked one cigarette after another; he rushed to light them. She made him feel as if she wanted him to succeed, and he allowed himself to be seduced.

Later someone told him, "The trouble with Lillian is that she wanted to be a beautiful woman and wasn't," and Greene concluded that it was true. Greene told her he had been involved with another woman for a year before he came to Rome and now missed her.

"Who was she?" Lily demanded. Greene told her the name: Anita Ellis, a fine singer.

"Well, she can't be anybody if I haven't heard of her," Lily said. In the sexual wars, Lily could never win. To demonstrate her sexual desirability, and to urge from him a response, she criticized Greene for his lack of ardor. "I'm used to having my men very romantic in the morning," she told him. She enumerated her many sexual conquests. But Greene found this approach less than attractive. She was aroused, she wanted him, but he could summon no great passion; he wanted to sleep with a young woman. And yet he loved her. (When Greene was seventy-five years old he discovered: "I still love her.")

Lily told him, "You know I can't have children." She seemed ill, was in fact suffering from a bleeding fibroid tumor, although to Greene she

admitted only that she was "just plain sick." He found her a touching figure, charming, intellectually exciting, with "the warmest, most welcome
smile of anyone he had ever known." She was never boring and she could
make of any small thing, even a cup of coffee, a special occasion. An air
of vulnerability accompanied her and added to her attractiveness. The
richness of her personality—warm, outgoing, caring—was apparent.

Soon they were declaring that they loved each other, and he took her
to the wedding of his friends Rose and Bill Styron. Using costume, as
always, to feel attractive, Lily wore a hat with a pouffed brown veil and
little birds all over it and a brown silk taffeta dress. Greene met her for
dinner one evening at the bottom of the Spanish Steps and he could not
help exclaiming: "Good God! What did you do to your hair?" The beauty
shop had not done well by her. Lillian, ever vain about her hair, was
upset.

She talked endlessly about Dash, how admired he was in France,
and how he had influenced many good writers. She spoke as if she were
in awe of him, as if he were her conscience. "Why didn't you marry Hammett?" Greene finally asked her one day.

"He was already married," Lily evaded the question. As for why she
had married Kober, Lily said, "It was the thing to do at the time." The
other man she spoke of a great deal was John Melby.

All summer she behaved as if she feared she would be arrested at
any time. Greene wondered whether Hammett had been a Communist.
"I don't know," Lily said. Then she added, "There are certain things you
should never tell anybody." Indeed, when Greene referred to a relative of
his who had been a Communist, Lily ordered him, "Be quiet!" She
thought the room was bugged. She sent Lois Fritsch to Washington to
see Joe Rauh, fearing she would be "slugged again." She had heard "indirectly that Rauh was convinced she might be hauled again into testifying."

One day Lily and Greene strolled down the Via Veneto, then settled
at Doney's bar, where they ran into Sam and Frances Goldwyn. "Italy—I
love it!" Goldwyn gushed. "It's all Romeo and Juliet." Spotting a wall of
cafeteria-style relief sculpture in imitation Greek art of boys and girls in
tunics, he exclaimed, "Look, just look at what this country has done. If I
wasn't so busy, I'd buy it and have it all sent to me in Hollywood!" Lillian
said nothing, and later Greene asked her, "Why were you so nice to
someone who blacklisted you?" When she was not in control, she could
be timid, indecisive, even weak.

When Dash didn't write to her, she had Lois Fritsch telephone him:
"Call Dash and tell him to continue to use this address as little as he has
been using it. Tell him I have written three times to his once, but that

today I went to see Cellini's jail cell out of deference to him." Her secretary should "find some excuse for calling once or twice a week." Lily found pretexts. Lois was to tell Dash "you still have money that belongs to him and how does he want it. Do this immediately," Lily ordered. "How much of Dash's money have we left, and has he drawn any of it?" she asked Lois. They were able to garner some of his earnings and conceal them from the government. Hearst owed him $572.10. It took some time before the government moved against the Amalgamated Bank, MCA, and Knopf as third parties to his debts, and Knopf had to send Hammett's royalties to the New York State Tax Commission.

Lily put Dash in charge of helping Kermit Bloomgarden with the casting of the road company of *The Children's Hour.* Nobody else would carry the weight with Kermit that Dash would, Lily thought. Dash, Lily sent instructions through her secretary, "should be as firm as he wishes to be, since he is now the only person who knows what the hell the play is all about or how it should be done." All decisions about cast or directing must be made by Dash. "If Dash feels that it would be better for me to write all this to Kermit before he sees him, then you tell me and I will do so," Lily wrote. Dash was to dispel Kermit's anger against Pat Neal because she had criticized Ginny's audition for the part of Karen.

Indeed, Dash went to New York in the middle of August to listen to actresses read and continued to travel to New York for rehearsals. He agreed to go to Wilmington for the opening. Sardonic as always, he noticed that the French postal employees went back to work at precisely the moment Lily arrived at Arles. He could not escape her. They were collaborators for life.

Almost daily that summer, beginning late in June when Lois reminded him of her birthday, she sent him messages. Dash was to turn on the motor of her car once a week, or have the Rosens' hired man do it. If the dog Flora, sick, had to be put to sleep, Dash should take charge of it before her return; indeed Dash arranged for the ten-year-old poodle to be "chloroformed." Lily lost a jeweled clip; Dash wrote that it had been purchased in the shop in the Ambassador Hotel. She detailed when and where he could call her.

Some of her messages were seductive, as she continued her lifelong habit of wooing him. "Tell him Florence is far more beautiful that [sic] his three goddamn actresses," Lily wrote Lois. In one message she attempted to awaken his interest by invoking an old rival: "Tell him that Prica is not as handsome as he is and I wish to apologize for all those years of argument." Lois was also to "tell him that I was solicited tonight by a very young man on the Champs-Elysées." She conducted the discourse of their relationship still on his terms, always on the surface.

Remaining twenties people, they eluded feeling with smart repartee; flip, careless, ironic remarks were enlisted to conceal their real feelings.

That summer Lily made certain that Dash knew of her every mood, her every debility. "Tell him," she wrote Lois, "I haven't written much because I feel a little weary . . . tell him, however, that I have his snapshot on the fireplace and that I think he's a fairly nice old boy who has a grandchild growing up to be a Goddamned actress and that if he hadn't been such a ham, holding on to that cane for pictures of *The Thin Man,* it would never have happened and I sure hope he's not going to have his picture taken peeping out of a tulip for this one." She participated with him in the illusion that "Tulip" would be his next book.

Meanwhile, back home, admitting to "stage fright," Hammett had put "Tulip" aside.

Immediately upon her return Lily went to Cleveland, then to Chicago to look at *The Children's Hour.* At Kirk Askew's gallery she purchased a painting by Stephen Greene called "The Wall," in which a man holds a woman's breast in his hand as if it were a piece of fruit. "I have finally found the man I want to marry," Lily announced to Kober, attempting to sustain a romantic fantasy about Greene. But soon Greene married someone else.

Lily renewed her pursuit of Jed Harris. She had tried to engage the married Arthur Miller with a crude overture that forced him to be openly ruthless in his rejection. So she had settled on the unpleasant Harris, as if she were an adolescent parading a conquest. "You mean she's sleeping with Jed!" People were incredulous.

Jed Harris was another of Lillian's wrong men, outrageous, zany, inaccessible. Harris was also particularly cruel. "He entered the room as noiselessly as a snake," Ben Hecht said. Harris had been out of work for three years. To many it seemed as if he was using Lillian to get to Kermit Bloomgarden in the hope he might be hired to direct Miller's *The Crucible.* "I have to close my eyes to fuck her," Jed said, sans chivalry. Meanwhile Lily told Jed Harris stories against herself, how he insisted the jewelry he gave her was expensive only for it to turn out to be fake.

Dash welcomed her return. She complained about her back, her ailments. "I like her," Dash admitted to Jo, "so her complaints often seem cute to me, but the truth is as I grow older I have less and less understanding—of which I never had much . . . of either the reason behind complaints or the reason for them. They seem to me just talk." Ever the stoic, he had even less patience than ever with self-indulgence, even Lily's.

22

Welcome Tory Soldiers

"You'll find plenty of girls who are prettier and will give more plea-sure—and will not ask as much. You don't want me."

The Lark

As the fifties dwindled down, Lily and Dash both suffered in full measure the consequences of their life choices. Dash became so fragile, so thin, that Judy Ruben, Helen's daughter, was afraid to leave her baby with him for fear the baby would kick him and break an arm. Having abandoned "Tulip," he was at loose ends and depressed. In January 1954 Lily suggested that Jo persuade him to visit her and his grandchildren, Ann and now Evan. "It would be wonderful if some time during the next year something could be arranged," Lily wrote. "Both children have meant an enormous amount to him."

That year Lily was working with Leonard Bernstein on an operetta version of *Candide*. She struggled ferociously not to allow herself to be marginalized as a former Communist or leftist; she sought the success only the mainstream, Broadway, and an association with Leonard Bernstein could provide. The experience was not a happy one.

The other facet of Lillian's response to McCarthyism was that conservative people began to enter her coterie, people whose friendship and support would grant her respectability, a bulwark against being discriminated against as a member of the left. Lily's guests were to include people like McGeorge Bundy, Kingman Brewster, and Joseph Alsop, who said, "I never discuss politics with Lillian."

She also relentlessly extended her hospitality to the dominant literary personalities of the day. Edmund Wilson joined her circle. Philip Rahv found her introductory notes to her collection of Chekhov's letters "engaging" and "perceptive" and soon he was seated at her table. Lionel and Diana Trilling, and younger critics like Norman Podhoretz, became frequent guests at her fabulous parties. Every New Year's Eve, Lily entertained lavishly.

Politics also took second place to financial security. The Chase Bank told her that they had a check for $10,000 from the Soviets. It wasn't enough, of course. "For goodness' sake, cash it first and complain later," Dash said. By 1958 she would empower the Authors League to negotiate with the Soviet authorities over her missing royalties, having called it "a deplorable state of affairs."

In this effort to join the established order, old political loyalties were erased. Systematically she severed her old left-wing connections. In April 1954, Lily wrote to the Spanish Refugee Appeal of the Joint Anti-Fascist Refugee Committee. "Many years ago," Lily said, she had written "explaining that I did not wish to be a sponsor of any organization where I had not enough time to attend the meetings." The group could discover no record of her having sent them such a letter. Now she did cut her conscience to suit the year's fashion.

If, unlike Lily, Hammett never altered in his commitment, he was weary. Testifying in February 1955 before a New York State legislative committee investigating philanthropic organizations, Dash explained as much as he ever would. "Communism to me is not a dirty word," he said. "When you are working for the advancement of mankind it never occurs to you whether a guy is a Communist." As to whether he had ever been a member of the Party, Dash hesitated. "Well, I, if you're going to ask that I'll have to fall back on the Fifth Amendment," he said.

In the course of his testimony, he revealed he had never known much about the Civil Rights Congress. "For all I know I may still be state chairman," he admitted, forgetting his title had been president, "although since I came out of jail I took it for granted maybe they'd leave the old man alone." He admitted too that he had been a "voluntary figurehead" all along.

The Army-McCarthy hearings came and went. Lillian prospered.

Lily loved salt water, fishing, and boating and swimming. In 1955 she bought an old yellow frame house with climbing roses dating from 1750 on Martha's Vineyard in Vineyard Haven. Carved into one of the windowpanes were the words "Welcome Tory soldiers." Lillian's large bedroom had a bay window looking out over oak trees to the harbor.

The house's many levels were connected by a circular tower formed by the shell of an old Cape Cod windmill dating from the late 1600s. This windmill-tower became Dash's retreat, the place where he could avoid Lily's noisy celebrity guests. Ever the hard trader, for this house on three acres with its own beach at the foot of the sloping lawn, she paid $21,000, a price that included family antiques. On the upper level of the property Lillian at once put in a vegetable garden of herbs, corn, beans, and tomatoes. Most of the furniture came from Hardscrabble Farm, and soon Lily had another warm, gracious home. Her new telephone number went to the inner circle: Dash, Arthur, Kermit, Jed, Dottie, Arthur Miller, Oscar Bernstien, her agent Kay Brown.

Clothes continued to preoccupy her. She now wore a size fourteen. Nothing bulky, she insisted. Nor would she wear stripes "running across me." Dash brought her "rubber girdle" when he came to stay. She continued to see Gregory Zilboorg.

In August 1955, Dash suffered a heart attack on the Vineyard. Although he was in great pain, he stubbornly refused to call a doctor. Only five weeks later did he allow himself to be examined. Now Dash could say he was no longer writing "for obvious reasons." He applied for his veteran's benefits on the ground that he was totally disabled. He lived on loans, he wrote on his application; his income for the coming year would be two to three hundred dollars. (The following year Kermit Bloomgarden was prevented from sending Hammett even twenty dollars due from his investment in *Montserrat* because of the court order of the New York State Tax Commission.)

Lillian became embroiled with Meyer Levin over the theatrical adaptation of *The Diary of Anne Frank*. Drawing on her association with Kermit Bloomgarden, Lillian saw to it that the Hacketts were given the assignment, despite Levin's long association with the project. Dash stayed out of this brouhaha except to remark sardonically of the Hacketts' dialogue, "It was no worse than if she'd gone to a girls' school." Meanwhile Lily, with the bravura she summoned in ambiguous circumstances, told Frances and Albert Hackett, who were deemphasizing the Jewish aspect of the story, with Lillian's full approval, how to face down their critics: "What you write will be true."

Dry of inspiration, Lily began to adapt Jean Anouilh's *L'Alouette (The Lark)*, because, she said, she "needed money." Then shrewdly she added: "which is a good way not to make any." When Anouilh's lawyer reported that the playwright objected to Lillian's taking on the project because of her politics, Lily seized the high moral ground. "I found that a bitter piece of comedy from the author of a play about Joan," she wrote Jan van Loewen. The subject did not appeal to Dash. "I don't think much of this St. Joan business," he told her.

Dash's heart attack prevented him from attending many rehearsals, but he did go often enough for Julie Harris, playing Joan, to find him a "saintly man." Mostly now he remained in bed, hoping to gather the energy to attend the opening in Boston. It was Lillian's friend Harry Levin, professor of comparative literature at Harvard, who offered advice. Although he abhorred academic criticism, Hammett liked Levin and enjoyed his *Context of Criticism.* "It's a good thing to find a literary man with some common sense once in a while," Dash said. Despite his early objections, he found it "all to the good" when in November 1955 *The Lark* received rave reviews, but for a retaliatory pan from Meyer Levin, who wrote, "I state flatly that Miss Hellman contributed nothing whatever to Anouilh's creative interpretation of Joan . . . she has only vulgarized and blunted the graceful French writing." No matter, Lily went out and bought herself a new mink coat.

Candide progressed at a crawl. When Lillian proved herself unable to work with John La Touche, about whom she was known to express homophobic objections, Harry Levin recommended a young poet named Richard Wilbur to write the lyrics. Collaboration was never a happy experience for Lillian, who attempted to tighten the plot in keeping with her approach to the well-made play, losing what she knew was "much of the wonderful chaos of the book." She chose a "non-active pastoral end" which obviously didn't work and she blamed others, even Richard Wilbur. His work, she decided, "is just plain bad, and it is bad because he is a real poet." She leaned on Harry Levin as once she had on Hammett. He advised her to treat the episodes more freely.

Late in January 1956, Dash drove to Martha's Vineyard with Lily to inspect her new house. Together they picked out wallpaper. They had, Dash said, "a good time." When Lily went to Florida that winter to recover from an operation to remove polyps from her vocal cords, Dash made the trip into New York from Katonah to see her off. So he listened to stories of how her gas range had blown up, how she had banged up one of her ankles, how her toe hurt. Revealing the details of her physical well-being was part of her gift for intimacy as she made fun of the mundane side of life. Meanwhile Richard Wilbur composed a poem about her polyps:

> *What! Shall our modern drama's Muse*
> *Be pestered by a Polyp?*
> *Come, Limber thy Olympian thews,*
> *And give DISEASE a wallop.*

*   *   *

In 1956 Dash came in to New York to have dinner with Lily once a week. He was so "worn out from the short journey" that they scarcely talked. Hating to be alone in these years, she penciled in an engagement for every evening of the week: the Hacketts, Rahv, Mailer, and Dash. On May 27, she wrote "D. Hammett (birthday?)." They talked on the phone, as he followed the casting of *Candide*. If some people chatted noisily in the back during a rehearsal, Lily might say, with her special dislike of the Jewish middle class, "Who are those Rappaports back there?"

Dash spent most of May 1956 at Lily's new Vineyard house. As soon as he was back in Katonah, he longed to return to the Vineyard. In June he experienced such shortness of breath that he entered a hospital for a week of tests. Doctors told him that his lungs didn't "manufacture enough oxygen for my great big muscles." But they were as concerned about his heart as about his battered lungs. Lily met him in New York and she recounted the troubles of *Candide* over dinner. But Dash was preoccupied now with his rapidly failing health. He spoke of "old age . . . catching up with me a little prematurely," as if he had been taken by surprise. Toward world affairs he was sanguine. The Cold War was "only a family quarrel"; the presence of a neutralist bloc of nations would help "maintain peace."

Together they returned to the Vineyard for the remainder of that summer. Now it took an effort for him even to turn the pages of the New York *Times*. Yet at dinner, seated at the head of the table, he could be sharp and tease Lily.

Her new hairdo was practical, Dash said, but bore no relation to actual human hair. He ridiculed her habit of using pronouns without antecedents, lines like "Well, he came again this morning." Impatiently Dash would demand, "Who the devil do you mean?" He pounced on her every time she did it, with joy at each new transgression. It was a habit she had given to Rose, the ditzy wife of General Griggs in *The Autumn Garden*. "There's nothing particularly genteel about pronouns, my dear," Mrs. Ellis, a Lillian alter ego, tells Rose, as Lillian had mocked herself.

One day Lily saw Hammett returning late from the beach. "Where have you been, Dashie!" she asked before their guests. "Weren't you worried about me?" They're like a couple of old dogs sniffing each other, William Styron said as he watched in disgust.

Lily's dog Gabrielle adored Hammett. Finding her too servile, needy, Dash did not like Gaby, who would sneak up to Hammett's room and stand in the doorway. He would then fix her with his eagle's eye. "SCRAM!" Dash said. Still he hid his feelings, hated need, primarily his own. He liked the line from the song "You Are My Destiny" that went

"You are what you are to me," because, he wrote Lily, "it's got that kind of nice ambiguity that I like." That was as far as he would go in revealing feeling which might be attributed to need. Need rendered him vulnerable to the power others might seize over him. It was a deformation of his otherwise generous sensibility which hurt Lily from the first. It would pain her until the end of his life.

Among the first guests Lily entertained at her Vineyard home were Stephen Greene and his new wife, Sigrid. Alone with Greene, Lily revealed that she experienced his marrying as a personal betrayal. "Sigrid has a beautiful face," Lily told him, "but doesn't she know that you can get a dress that looks nice for very little money?" Sigrid had in fact paid only nine dollars for her dress and it showed. Greene was mortified. It was as if she were saying: why are you with her and not with me? As if to compensate for Lily's barbs, Hammett was very nice to the Greenes.

Hammett had been very important to her work, Lily told the Wilburs on the Vineyard that summer of 1956. Anything else was long over. It was obvious she continued to be awed by him, to admire his probity, his strictness with himself, qualities she lacked.

Dash never discussed politics now. His favorite topic was baseball. Literature ran a distant second. He agreed with Wilbur that his best book was *Red Harvest*. He enjoyed the company of Wilbur's son Christopher because he knew almost as many baseball statistics as Dash himself did. He was willing to chat with Leonard Bernstein's brother Burton about the Army; it was an effort for him to talk.

Lily now considered him a semi-invalid. Yet Dash wrote Jo he hoped to live into the next century or at least to "die in my eighties." He wanted "to try to do at least a little better than my father, whom I'd like to beat at the longevity racket and who was about 83 when he popped off."

Most of the time the only signs of Hammett were the dents in the cushion of the chair where he had been sitting before he fled upon the appearance of one of Lillian's guests. Lily then explained; he was thinking, or he was tired, or he was busy. One afternoon a boat of ragtag theatrical people, men in black leather suits, arrived. Soon they were drinking bullshots. Lenny played the piano as delicate young men danced together. Dash fled to his tower.

If an uninvited guest were to catch him off guard, before he could escape, he would rise elegantly, and shake hands, his smile opaque and distancing. Then he would vanish. Should anyone ask his opinion on anything, from how to clean a meerschaum pipe to a matter of writing, Lily would convey his answer the next time the questioner visited. You might catch a glimpse of him of an afternoon walking slowly and silently to the library.

For the sweet people, the Levins, the Wilburs, playwright William Alfred, he would appear. One Sunday morning he teased Alfred as Alfred got ready for mass. It was close to Labor Day. The priest will say, Dash predicted, "You're all going home now after having a wonderful summer. I must tell you, we need a new furnace."

Lillian's talk seemed ever more outrageous in these years. Anarchically anti-Semitic, it seemed to some to be homophobic and racist as well. At a party given by a rich Jewish family she spied chicken à la king at the buffet. "Goy dreck in a rich Jewish house!" Lily said in horror. Those who didn't know about sailing but flamboyantly kept their craft in the Vineyard harbor had "Jewish cocktail boats." Dash had encouraged this view of middle-class Jewish vulgarity. "No amount of practice in shmalz-spreading will ever make your people a really tactful race," he had written Lily after reading an article about him in *PM* by Sam Hakam.

Lily's homophobic remarks, often directed against Leonard Bernstein, matched those against Jews. "I'm sick and tired of dealing with two collaborators," she said, referring to the producer of *Candide*, Ethel Reiner, and Bernstein, "one of whom claims she's having periods when she's not, the other who is probably having periods, but won't tell us."

Candide opened in November 1956 to an admiring New York *Times* review by Brooks Atkinson, who quietly proclaimed the production "admirable" and refused to step on the toes either of "the literary lady," Lillian Hellman, or of Leonard Bernstein, "the music man." The paying public was to be less charitable. At a performance of *Candide*, Dash ran into Ed Spitzer. "It's not a play, it's a pageant!" he said sarcastically, revealing his distaste for Lily's new associates. On opening night, Dash made his position clear. "I made no contribution to that," he said. Later Lillian would say she got nothing but pain out of *Candide*. It turned out to be a flop in England as well. "Had she read Christopher Logue, or even Shakespeare?" *Sunday Times* reviewer Harold Hobson wanted to know.

Lily's battles with Leonard Bernstein over *Candide* were to range over many years. Behind his back, she called him "the Maestro." He considered going ahead with productions without her approval. Years later he hung over his desk a composite from *National Lampoon* of Lily's head and a sexy young body in blue jeans, with the line "Lillian Hellman . . . For a *Hell* of a fit!"

In 1966 she had her name taken off the project except for a line reading "based on the original book by Lillian Hellman." Long afterward, Lillian continued to believe that the project had left her "with a neurosis that took a long time to solve," a "panic passivity." Her conclusion by

1971 was that it was a valuable property ruined out of vanity and ignorance. Her old friendships with Leonard Bernstein and agent Robert Lantz were ruined; it was all a "disgusting waste."

Indeed Lily acknowledged in the mid-fifties that a certain "passivity" had overtaken her. Once more she tried to write a short story. The fragment she began is narrated by a rich woman named Sarah Curtis; the characters include "a fag" and the husband of Sarah's friend Meg, who "seems to have some faggish background." Lily wrote, "Much of their servility is traced to people 'being good to them.'" Lily gave the pages to Dash for his reaction. "Well, it doesn't mean one damn thing," he told her.

Working on *Candide* she had found herself surrounded by seemingly happily married couples like the Levins and the Wilburs, and that depressed her anew. One day she even told Elena Levin she resented hearing about what fun the married couples had together. In defiance of her unattractiveness, demanding attention in spite of being now a plain woman in late middle age, she took to changing her bathing suit on the beach. Wrapping herself in a towel which concealed little, she would call out, "Don't peek! Don't peek!"

"Who wants to peek?" Bernstein muttered once. Sometimes she assumed a Baby Snooks voice and behaved like a demanding, horrid little child, talking baby talk, trying to control people by offering, then withholding her favor. Her figure had changed and she now had a tummy, large pendulous breasts, no buttocks at all, and a flat, razor-straight back. "Lillian, you don't have any ass at all!" Charlee Wilbur said as one day Lily emerged from the shower.

"Yes, it's been a big trial to me," Lily said. It was why she always used a dressmaker now.

"You're the best-looking person in a towel I've ever seen," Charlee told her. Lily was delighted. Perhaps she was not quite as plain as she had always feared.

Openly complaining of her loneliness, suffering from insomnia, she fed her emotional need with shopping. "Do you want to see a lot of dreck?" she asked Charlee one day, opening her bulging closets. The payment for the Faustian bargain she had made had come due. The person most consistently by her side now was her housekeeper, Helen, large, stiff, formal, rarely smiling, and standing up to Lillian in full measure.

She became demanding of her friends, sometimes in a meanspirited way. Felicia Bernstein was seized by abdominal pains and had to be rushed to the hospital, causing Lenny to miss Lillian's picnic. Angrily Lily dismissed his excuse: "There are social standards," she intoned heartlessly.

A cigarette dangling always from her lips, her face wreathed in smoke, she courted young men like novelist Herbert Gold, who, while appreciating the help she gave him in his career, would not succumb to sexual overtures. "You mustn't breathe a word, but you're going to get this prize!" Lily, who had nominated him before the National Institute of Arts and Letters, told him. When Gold sided with Meyer Levin, Lily accused him of ingratitude. Lily joined Burton Bernstein's poker game as the only woman, one who didn't play like a woman at all. She liked to have an attentive young man get her drink, and if there were several young men, so much the better.

As a she-Hammett, she was as predatory as ever. Harry Levin came to New York and Lily set up the dinner table in her bedroom. A faithful husband, Levin pretended not to notice." Lily, half in jest, wrote Richard Wilbur, "You can tell Charlee that I am already deeply in love with you," her intentions unmistakable. Well aware of Lillian's "mean desire," Charlee Wilbur took her aside and said, "Now, I want you to know this is not going to happen."

On the beach one day she pulled Archibald MacLeish's pants down, and they had their moment, which Lily reported in minute detail to her friends. He talked about roses; he demonstrated some peculiarities. She approached *Saturday Evening Post* editor Stuart Rose, and Telford Taylor, unsuccessfully. At a Vineyard picnic, S. J. Perelman spotted Kober "busily engaged in pawing La Hellman around the embers, a pursuit it was evident she was deliriously happy about."

Lily spoke to friends of how she wished she had gotten married, but no one married her. Yet in the fifties she took up with yet another of her wrong men, a flamboyant, self-invented Philadelphia lawyer named Arthur Wyndham Allen Cowan, né Abraham Cohen, who had made a considerable amount of money in Honolulu. Cowan was vigorous, masculine, athletic, blue-eyed with dark hair, nearly six feet tall, and built like a prizefighter with a tough-guy aspect that parodied Hammett's. Unlike Hammett, however, Cowan, a shallow man, was impressed with celebrities, particularly celebrity intellectuals.

He lived at Hammett's old haunt, the Hotel Madison, in a decorator-furnished apartment, all dark wood and leather as if he were an English gentleman. He owned three Rolls-Royces. Fancying himself a poet, he had published a volume of his own works, and was a benefactor of *Poetry* magazine. He was also excitable, given to a choleric temper, and often depressed despite a madcap sense of humor. Politically, he was a Republican.

With full energy, Lily courted Cowan, leaving a pair of tickets for *The*

Lark in his name for nine evenings in December 1955. Dash saw that Cowan was incapable of loving her, disapproved, and kept his distance.

Before long Lily asked Cowan to sleep with her, and then to marry her. Another of the men who needed a beautiful, much younger woman on his arm, Cowan resisted. No matter how importunate her advances, he would not take her to bed. "Please don't leave me alone with her," he pleaded with his sister Sadie one night when Lily was staying over at his Philadelphia apartment. "She wants my body." Sometimes he talked about how Lillian's age bothered him, although they were both born in 1905.

Yet Lily took this man seriously, devoted considerable time to pursuing him, and tried to plumb the depths of his superficiality. He gave a waitress a fifty-dollar bill at the old Oyster House in Boston for service beyond the closing hour. Obsessed, Lily pondered: "Was there any kindness in it? To whom was he showing off? Was it about power over the woman?" Out of balance, Lily for years found an essentially trivial man interesting.

Jokingly, unwilling to surrender the obsession, Lillian sent Cowan a list of possible reasons they might offer the world as to why they did not marry:

1. Mr. Cowan has syphilis.
2. Miss Hellman is married to a negro who will not give her a divorce.
3. Miss Hellman is joining the Church and Spellman forbids Mr. Cowan.
4. Miss Hellman is frigid.
5. Mr. Cowan has been castrated.
6. Mr. Cowan only likes women with money.
7. Miss Hellman hasn't enough and has refused demands made.
8. Mr. Cowan is secretly in love with Gertrude McBride [wife of his closest friend, Tom McBride] and the affair of long standing.
9. Mr. Cowan is secretly married to a French woman and has three children, all idiots in a chic asylum.

If wit could woo, Lily would have had her man. As it was, she had to resort to lying. Cowan had proposed to her, she told Charlee Wilbur. What should she do, since he had never made love to her? He had kissed her, but nothing more. Was he "queer"? He was friendly with actor Jon Hall, who had once played Tarzan. Was he sweet on Jon Hall? As with Greene, so with Cowan, it was simple; he wanted a young woman in his bed. Once one of his blond chippies, of which there was always a supply, asked Cowan whether he ever had sexual intercourse with Lillian. "No," he replied, "it would be like going to bed with Justice Frankfurter!" "Arthur, think of *The Little Foxes*," he quoted a friend of his as warning him.

In these years, Lily also proposed to distinguished critic and *Partisan Review* editor Philip Rahv. "Forget about her politics," said fiercely anti-Stalinist Rahv. "She's got guts!" In financial straits, Rahv pondered the proposal. She was a clean old woman, and rich. Then he pulled himself up short. "I'd have to sleep with her!" he realized. Rahv turned out to be another of the wrong, emotionally adolescent men whom Lily pursued out of her self-loathing. Dashiell Hammett's supposed intellectual superiors were unable to penetrate Lily's outer trappings to nurture the hidden child who craved acceptance.

By the turn of 1957, Dash had taken a turn for the worse. In his cottage he would sit for hours in an old leather chair by the cold fireplace smoking a cigarette. Catatonically he stared across the room.

Some days Dash remained in bed watching television, everything from the evangelists to *Oedipus Rex* on *Omnibus* to *Troilus and Cressida*. His taste elegant, he preferred Chaucer to Shakespeare. He gave an interview to an Englishman named James Cooper, who counted three typewriters in Hammett's cottage and wrote that at noon Hammett was still in his pajamas. "I'm living on money borrowed from friends," Hammett said. He did not utter Lillian's name.

Once more he addressed why he had stopped writing. "The thing that ruined me was the writing of the last third of 'The Glass Key' in one sitting of 30 hours," he told Cooper. "Ever since then I have told myself: 'I could do it again if I had to.'" There was no definitive explanation. "It is the beginning of the end when you discover you have style," Hammett added.

In February 1957, the United States, not done with him yet, filed a new judgment for taxes, including those supposedly owed from December 15, 1950, to February 28, 1957. Their bill came to $140,795.96. "So I'm broke!" he wrote Jo ironically. So that she wouldn't worry, he told her he was using Lily's money, taking taxis in New York, "and usually have a steak and some caviar and whatever I happen to think of in the ice-box."

Alarmed, Jo wrote to Lillian. She had consulted a doctor, Lillian reassured her. He believed there was "no danger to his living alone in the country." Jealous still of Jose, Lillian asked Jo not to tell her mother anything about his health. Meanwhile Lily paid the bills on his charge accounts from Tripler's, A. Sulka, Bloomingdale's, Abercrombie & Fitch, McCutcheon's, and Brentano's. Dashiell Hammett's habit of having the best of everything had not left him.

*   *   *

In New York, Lily left Monday nights open for Dash, should he be able to make it. She renewed her efforts to break the Sophie Newhouse Trust, whose assets belonged to her only during her lifetime. By 1957 she had made four unsuccessful attempts to replace her aunt Florence Newhouse as a trustee with her own lawyer, Paul O'Dwyer. She enlisted the aid of Arthur Cowan, who proved to be very useful to her after all.

Early in November, Dash saw Lily twice in one week in New York. But Thanksgiving Day found him alone in Katonah. It was a stark, gray, chilly day. The Rosens were in England. Dash, however, was not alone on the property. John Rosen, their son, was home from medical school. John knew Dash had to be telephoned before anyone went over to the cottage. That had been the arrangement.

But it was Thanksgiving. On an impulse, John put on a heavy overcoat and walked over to see if Dash needed anything. He knew it was four miles to the nearest store, and Dash didn't drive.

John rang the bell. Dash opened the door, wearing a tweed overcoat over his pajamas. In his hand was a pistol, half chrome silver, clearly the real thing. Unaware of who might be at his door and knowing the Rosens were away, Dash pointed his pistol at the intruder.

John never had a pistol pointed at him in his life. He was frightened, then shocked, then alarmed that Dash should on his parents' property feel so vulnerable that he would point a gun at a caller. It was completely out of character for this man who had always been mild-mannered and kind. It crossed John's mind that Dash had purchased that pistol because he might be contemplating suicide. John telephoned his parents in England, and the Rosens decided that Dash must not remain alone in Katonah any longer.

Knowing Lillian's animosity toward Helen, Sam Rosen made the call. Dash had a pistol, he told Lillian. He had been suffering from a "more or less progressive breathlessness and weakness" for two years now. He had grown increasingly depressed and lately had been falling down.

"He's not that sick!" Lillian said. "His doctor agrees with me." Mildly, Sam suggested that his daughter was returning from England and wanted the cottage. This explanation was designed to save Dash's pride; it need not seem as if he was being evicted.

"He's much happier in the country," Lillian insisted.

"He's too sick to remain out there alone," Sam told her. "He isn't eating and he has paper in the typewriter with nothing written on it." There was also the matter of the pistol.

"What is the implication, Sam?" Lillian demanded. "Suicide? Is that what you're saying?"

"Yes, I guess that's what I'm saying."

"It's outrageous!" Lillian answered angrily. "He's never owned a pistol. He would never use it on himself. He's fine. Leave him there."

Cherishing his independence, Dash was at first furious with Helen Rosen. He immediately saw through the subterfuge, the obvious excuse that Judy needed the cottage. He wanted to remain exactly where he was.

At Christmas, Dash visited Lillian in New York. On January 5, he saw her for lunch, then returned to Katonah. That she knew how ill he was is indubitable—because he told her. "Life ain't always good even to tall goys," he wrote her on January 14. Unable to breathe, he was experiencing "a kind of maximum discomfort." His tone was melancholy. "It's getting around to things before you die that counts, so you die human," he wrote her.

Nonetheless, the end of January 1958 found Lily in London for the opening of *Candide*. Then she went on to Dublin and Paris. Dash was uneasy. He needed news of what she was up to, "or when you're going to Paris or some such." One day he waited to finish a letter to see if there was one from her to him in the mail. "There was nothing from you, so I guess you don't know anything either," he closed.

Lily, the person closest to him in his life, did not return from Europe until the first week of February. "It'll be awful nice seeing you on the 6th or 7th," Dash wrote her from Katonah on January 28. On January 31, even as he knew she was about to return, he complained, "It seems like a long time since I've heard from you, though it was only last Sunday. Maybe there'll be a letter from you today before I go shopping, or maybe no. I guess not." It was a rare moment of self-pity.

In March, Dash was again in the hospital. Lily now knew something had to be done. She vented her anger in full measure on Helen Rosen. It went beyond her grievance that Helen had supposedly violated their secret agreement by telling people that Dash had paid rent. Lily was clearly angry that responsibility for the sick man should fall on her shoulders.

In retaliation, she made certain that Dash would never again set eyes on beautiful Helen Rosen. Lily insisted that Dash told her he didn't want to see Helen. Fifteen years later, Lillian was still contending it was Dash who had said he never wanted to see Helen again. "I am not a liar," she told Sam Rosen, "it was not I who had the strong feelings. It simply and plainly was Dash himself."

23

Their Last Years

"Women, of course, have regrets for certain delicate early minutes."
TOYS IN THE ATTIC

"I thought you got over that agitprop shit years ago."
DASHIELL HAMMETT

In May 1958, Dashiell Hammett moved to New York to live with Lillian. He said he wanted to move to a veterans' hospital. This, Lily told him, she could not abide. Too weak to argue, he relented, reluctantly. It would be the first time in their twenty-eight years that they would be living together. For Hammett, it was not a happy solution.

"All right," Dash said. "If you think you can stand it." He insisted it was not to be a permanent arrangement. He would go to New York for the month of May, then spend the summer on Martha's Vineyard. "After five years and a half I finally tore myself, or got torn, I'm not sure which, from Katonah," he wrote Jo. "After the summer I don't know."

In the mid-thirties, Dash had virtually asked Lily to take care of him; during World War II, he had fantasized coming home to her; after jail he also longed for the security of Hardscrabble Farm. Each time he had been disappointed. Now he did not invoke their old bargain which granted to him Lily's indulgence; he merely succumbed.

Nor was Lily glad to have him with her now. Even as she insisted that he live with her, she chafed, hating to disrupt her orderly routine at

Eighty-second Street. Her second-floor library-workroom now became Dash's bedroom.

Her housekeeper, Helen Richardson, whom Hammett had never liked, brought him his food, mail, and books. Soon Lillian remarked that although he never asked Helen for anything, she knocked herself out for him anyway. "Oh, Mr. Hammett," Helen said, "he's such a saint. He never asks for anything."

"He doesn't have to," Lillian told her dryly. "He's got you thinking about what he wants before he even names it." Yet although many of Lillian's friends saw Helen as a tragic woman, one whom Lillian herself did not treat at all well, Dash's heart did not soften toward her. Helen is like "a stone wall," Dash told Jo. Sometimes he was sardonic. Helen is "the only Negro who can't carry a tune, and you're the only Jew," Dash told Lily.

"Hammett's taken over the whole goddamn house!" Lily soon complained to Ruth Goetz. "He's impossible." It cramped her style, it seemed, with him upstairs while she entertained Arthur Cowan on the living-room couch below. Now that he's here, I can't travel, Lily dramatized.

"How is Dash?" Becky Bernstien asked one day.

"Oh, he's dying," Lily remarked. In the next breath she announced she was off for a weekend with Cowan. What if Dash dies while she's away? Becky wondered.

She was his caretaker now, not his lover, and she made no secret of the fact that it was a strain. Sometimes she tried to force him to leave the house because she thought it was good for him. But Dash preferred to stay inside reading. Lillian even asked her secretary, Selma Wolfman, to try. "Mr. Hammett, you ought to get out, go out to dinner," Selma ventured. Hammett got dressed then and took a taxi by himself to a nearby Longchamps.

"Please keep it down. There's a dying man upstairs!" Lily told her lively dinner guests one night. Norman Mailer thought there was now a Howard Hughes aura about Hammett. You would hear about him all the time, but you never saw him. In search of the toilet one evening Norman Podhoretz opened the wrong door and there was Hammett in bed in his pajamas reading a book. Hammett flashed Podhoretz a sweet smile; an embarrassed Podhoretz fled.

Lily guarded Dash like a lioness, carefully controlling his visitors. Helen Rosen, of course, was forbidden entry. Cathy Kober, Ginny Bloomgarden, and Pat Neal were permitted to visit. "You know he loves you and he loves Pat Neal," Lily told Bloomgarden. "If you'd just come and see him, it would mean something to him." During one of Cathy Kober's visits, she caught him looking at a photograph of his daughters. As he turned to her, he placed the picture facedown. He was completely in Lillian's hands, and Cathy realized that he would have preferred it were otherwise.

With Ginny, Dash continued to flirt. "Nah, she's got 'em all beat with the legs," he said. When Lily heard about this remark, she thought: everyone but me.

One evening Ginny came to sit with Dash. "If he wants a drink, give it to him," Lillian told her as she left for the evening. "You can offer him a little vodka." The doctor had told her it no longer mattered.

Whatever emotional pain he could still inflict on her, no one else was permitted to criticize him. Diana Trilling remarked that if Hammett's beliefs had landed him in jail, they had been his free choice. At least in this country you're not hauled out of bed in the middle of the night.

"How can you say that to me after everything Dash went through?" Lily retorted.

"He went to jail for a few months," Trilling persisted. The next day Trilling received a telephone call from Lillian.

"Never, never are you to speak that way about Dash to me," Lillian told her. Others admired the ferocity with which Lily protected Dash. "She can be a bitch on wheels," Ginny remarked to Kermit, "but the friendship and affection that she shows for this man. . . ."

Not everyone agreed. Jerome Weidman felt that whatever rapprochement they achieved at the end was based on a secret gladness on Dash's part that Lily was not doing as well as a writer as she once had. Meanwhile, Weidman believed, she didn't mind so much that he had long since stopped writing; now no one could suggest that she would not have made it without him.

Often in the late fifties, continuing to cultivate the useful rich, Lily sought refuge with Ruth and Marshall Field at Chelsea Plantation near Ridgefield, South Carolina. At Chelsea Plantation servants grabbed your clothes as soon as you stepped into the shower; before you knew it they would be returned freshly laundered. During the day, dress was casual. Lily, however, was always carefully made up. She spoke of how sorry she was for Hammett. But she could also be sarcastic, and once she made a joke about Dash and a wheelchair. No one doubted that she had come to the Fields' plantation to escape the burden of taking care of Dash.

That Lily was so anxious to have Dash come to live with her that spring of 1958 may in part be related to the fact that after nearly a decade Lily was at work on an original play. She attributed the idea for

Toys in the Attic to Dash, who had told her, "There's this man. Other people who say they love him, want him to make good, be rich. So he does it for them and finds they don't like him that way, so he fucks it up, and comes out worse than before."

Long gone were the days when Dash's ideas were better than her own. Lily admitted that she considered this theme. Then she decided she could not write a play that centers on a man, although, of course, she had done just that with *Watch on the Rhine.* She said she wanted the play to be more about the man's sisters, his wife, and her mother.

"Well," Dash said, "then my idea's out the window. Never mind. I'll use it myself someday." The character of Julian in the final version, however, was very much as Dash had conceived of him and was clearly based on Max Hellman.

Lily enlisted Dash once more to read her work, to help her. Later she admitted that Hammett "was absolutely bewildered by why I couldn't get down to the play. That I . . . up till half of the play I haven't let anything happen." Even as he did not contribute to this play significantly, she felt insecure without his presence and approval.

Together Lily and Dash went to the Vineyard for the summer of 1958. There Lily finished the second act, knowing at once it needed rewriting. Hammett was too weak to help her in the old ways, and his presence remained an irritant. Before long Lily had to feed Dash. When he went upstairs one day, she spoke resentfully. Hammett had so many friends. Yet now she could not get any of them on the telephone to ask them to give her time off. Sometimes she complained about the amount of money he was costing her.

"The cigarette smoking here is intense," she complained to Richard Wilbur. "I wish I had stayed in New Orleans," she wrote half regretfully, "and maybe married a nice, middle class fellow and at this minute was putting on a tacky dress to go to the country club annual and watch my daughter get stewed and my son smoke marijuana on the columned porch." Max Hellman's business failures had of course precluded their remaining in New Orleans. But Lily liked to embellish her Southern past. Often now she realized that the Faustian bargain she had made with Dashiell Hammett, one of her own devising and choice, had been costly indeed.

Weak as he was, Hammett did not let her down. As she struggled with that second act, she admitted, "My severest critic will read it soon. He's been good to me about the play, the way he used to be: patient, and sharp when needed." Dash even wrote a speech for a character named in an early version Julian N. Warkins: "I didn't say all that but I sure-god thought it, but I went along nice as you please just thinking things and not saying them and playing him along like a trout on a line." The joke was that the character was a cross between Julian, the Max Hellman character, and a character named Warkins, a man so overcome by the discovery that his wife is part black that he destroys Julian's chance of financial success. Dash's speech does not appear in the final version of the play.

As she had so many times before, when Lily thought the play was finished, she left it open for Dash to read. In a reprise of their old collaborations, he told her it was far from finished. In fact, he said, it was terrible. Rewrite it, was all he had the strength to advise.

Lily's writing of Toys in the Attic was marked by some very "sad" days between her and Hammett. Still he did not trust her. Always he resented her pity. If she offered him her hand, he would look away, as if he didn't see it. He was too weak to eat at the table, let alone to be interviewed for the Paris Review. He sent the message: "Lily will explain."

In these last years Dash often sent people messages through Lily. William Alfred had given him a volume of literary criticism, only to discover it on the hall table when he next visited New York. "Dash said, thanks so much, drop it on the table there . . . he's much too old to read shit," Lily reported. What she meant was that Alfred should take it back and leave it on one of the tables in a Common Room at Harvard for the academics to read.

With Helen remaining in charge, Lily lectured at Wesleyan. She traveled to Boston with Arthur Cowan. She visited New Orleans. In March 1959 she went to California, where she did some work for David O. Selznick as an adviser on Ivan Moffat's script for Tender Is the Night. Her critique lacked substance, Selznick complained. It wasn't enough for her to tell him that the script failed to achieve "the spirit of the times" or that it didn't have "a feeling for the people of the times." Lily offered to terminate the arrangement; in his reply Selznick requested actual help since Lillian Hellman came "high from a money standpoint."

Hardly housebound, Lily left for London on April 15 to see the British Candide, stopping at Claridges. She had rewritten and patched and tried to rescue her book for this play, never to her satisfaction. The end of the year 1959 would find Lillian again in London, this time at the Ritz supervising the casting of Toys in the Attic.

In April 1959, Dash reopened his claim for compensation payments from the Veterans Administration. He was "practically bedridden most of the time," he wrote. His nearest relative was his daughter, Josephine—in fact, of course, his only daughter.

Lily continued her flirtatious relationship with Cowan, from London writing she would "dream of you." She talked of an autobiographical play to be performed in the tiger cages of the Bronx Zoo in which "Miss Hellman is adored by five men." One of the men is her father, "the first to bring her pain." Some of her letters to Cowan were addressed to "Sam dearest," her college sweetheart whom she made "give up dope," as she had failed to persuade another Sam to give up alcohol. Her imagination transformed the psychic truths of her life into fantasy. "Truth, and only truth, and more truth," she scribbled.

In one of her many notes, she forgives one of his outbursts. "You are a weak man," she writes, as she might have written to Dash had she not feared his wrath and his temper. In still another letter addressed to Cowan as "Edwin," the police find a note proving that "you never were a Communist." Lily added, "I know that full well. But how else was I going to disguise you in the play except by making you a Party member?" So came the gibe at Cowan for lacking the convictions of Dashiell Hammett.

The ordeal of McCarthyism continued to consume her imagination. "What difference did it make whether you were or weren't?" she speculates. Of herself, she writes: "I was, as you know, one of the few people in those days who acted with courage, or almost." The methodology of the later memoirs is already present.

Sometimes Lily spoke of Hammett as her "critical guest." Hammett liked Wilbur's introduction to the poems of Edgar Allan Poe. No matter how many times Lily told him she had read it, she reported to Wilbur, Hammett insisted on describing it to her in detail. "He is a man of sense and there are not too many of those," Hammett said in praise of Wilbur. Lily reported this "trade last," or "TL," to Wilbur in the hope of extracting a similar encomium about herself.

With the help of her agent, she tried to sort out Hammett's tangled literary affairs. There were constant offers for the rights to the character of Sam Spade, which Hammett now owned after his victory in legal battle with Warner Brothers; the court had ruled that he had reserved character, series, and sequel rights to *The Maltese Falcon* as his "common law rights incident to authorship of a literary work." But until a deal could be made about his back taxes, the Internal Revenue Bureau would attach every dollar. He could not agree to a situation where the government would get all the money.

Lily had a plan. If someone offered a $200,000 guarantee for the rights to Sam Spade, Hammett would have enough capital to settle his taxes, with something left over. It never happened. Meanwhile, as Lillian later wrote, "the fact of breathing, just breathing, took up all the days and nights." His emphysema was progressive and excruciating.

At the turn of the New Year 1960, Lily dyed her hair the color of bronze. Weighing ten pounds more than usual, she gave "my party." Her social calendar as always was full: Telford Taylor, Shumlin, Melby, the Bloomgardens, Cowan, Lenny, Kober, Rahv, even Laura Perelman.

On January 11, *Toys in the Attic* went into rehearsal. Arthur Penn, who was directing, came to see Lillian at Eighty-second Street. Dash was in bed, exhausted. Tubes were connected to his nose; he could neither breathe nor talk.

Lillian herself proved difficult to deal with for Penn. At rehearsals, whenever she saw something she disliked, she would begin her immediately recognizable cough, which sent a chilling message to the actors. When she began to talk about firing some of the actors, Penn banned her from rehearsals for five days.

"Just tell everybody they were wonderful," Maureen Stapleton, who was playing Carrie, a character based on one of Lillian's Hellman aunts, advised her.

"Dash used to tell me that," Lillian replied.

"He was right," Maureen said. "You didn't do it for him. Start doing it now." But Lily, still the unfinished woman, replied, "I can't do it. I can't do it."

Frail as he was, Dash accompanied Lily to rehearsals in Boston, where they stayed at the best hotel in town, the Ritz-Carlton. Immediately Lily expressed her perplexity. Anne Revere had been so honorable during the McCarthy period. How could she now be giving so much trouble to Penn and to the other actors?

"I can't get over it," Lily told Dash. "She was absolutely flawless during all that bad period. She was heroic."

"What makes you think a hero can't also be a son of a bitch?" Dash retorted.

At rehearsal one afternoon Dash was in the theater. The sad, weak, destructive, and essentially selfish and stupid character named Lily, based on Lillian's mother, Julia, remarks, "It's awfully hot to go to work." Her husband's sister Carrie replies, "Yes. And sometimes it's awfully cold." Dash nudged Lily in the ribs then.

"I thought you got over that agitprop shit years ago," he said.

It was clear to director Arthur Penn that Dash did not like this play. "Oh, Dash, stop it!" Lily said loudly at one of the rehearsals. Kermit concurred; the opening, for one thing, was too slow. "You've got to speed up the opening," he told Penn.

"Lillian, everybody seems to feel that we're way too slow," Penn told the playwright.

"You know what we should do?" Lillian answered. "Slow it down even more." And Penn discovered that she was absolutely correct.

One night in Boston at the bar, Lily had a drink with Jason Robards, who was playing Julian. "Marry me!" he drunkenly proposed.

"I'll fuck you, but I won't marry you," she answered.

Just as with *The Thin Man* Dash seemed to have run out of material, so Lily had suffered the same fate. For *Toys in the Attic*'s characters she turned to the Hellman side of the family, her parents, and her maiden aunts with their frustrated longing for her father. Julian, the pampered male, with his failed shoe factory, a man who has been betrayed by his partner, repeats Max's experience. The character Lily is Julia Newhouse, as Lillian Hellman reveals that, far from having changed her mind about her mother after Julia's death in 1935, she despises her as much at the age of fifty-five as she did as a young woman. In an obvious Freudian projection, she gives the figure based on her mother her own name.

Lily, a weak, whining, idle woman uses sex to keep her husband. Pretty, as her daughter was not, she succeeds in ruining her husband's life. By lying to him, she turns his flash of success to failure. Lillian Hellman, of course, denied that the character Lily bore any autobiographical resonances. Yet they are unmistakable.

As if she were still locked in combat for Max, playwright Hellman has Lily quote Julian with a line taken from Hammett's "Tulip," as if Julian-Max were Hammett, the man she did make her lover, as she was unable actually to seduce her father. Julian has told his wife she "must learn to cook because he'd always believed that a woman who was good in the bedroom was good in the kitchen." In "Tulip," the line appears as advice from Hammett's mother and reads: "Don't waste your time on women who can't cook because they're not likely to be much fun in the other rooms either." So Lillian seized one more opportunity to best her mother, who was no cook, unlike her daughter. In the play's subtext Lillian Hellman argues that she herself would have made Max a better partner and wife and thus prevented him from the philandering which seems to have injured the adolescent Lily more than it did fey Julia Newhouse.

Toys in the Attic was written as Lillian knew Hammett was dying. She looks back with yearning to the excitement of their first heady days together. So Lillian's alter ego, named Albertine, reflects. "Marriages change from day to day and year to year. All relations between people. Women, of course, have regrets for certain delicate early minutes." In another autobiographical exchange, Lillian pays homage to her relationship with Dashiell Hammett. Albertine speaks of "so many people who make things too hard for too little reason, or none at all, or the pleasure, or stupidity. But we've never done that, you and I."

Albertine's black "fancy man," Henry, corrects her.

"Yes, we've done it," he says, a Hammett surrogate too honest to hide behind illusion. "But we've tried not to."

Toys in the Attic opened in New York on February 25, 1960. For the occasion Dash purchased new dinner clothes. Lily sat in a little sealed-off upper box at the Hudson Theater which the stage manager had equipped with table, chair, pad and pencil, a small bottle of brandy, a flashlight to minimize the hazards of the dark stairway, and a doll. Lily took the first tranquilizer of her life that night. Flowers came from her hairdresser, from the Wilburs, the Bernsteins, Joseph Kaufman, Bobbie Weinstein, Arthur Cowan, the Penns, Stephen Greene and his wife, Sigrid, the Kronenbergers, Elinor Gimbel, the Hacketts, Marc Blitzstein, Irene Lee, and many others. Her agent Kay Brown sent a bronze lily. Kermit sent gardenias. Letters gushing with admiration came from Lionel Trilling, Jason Epstein, and even from her old admirer St. Clair McKelway.

Afterward, Lily and Dash and a company that included editor Robert Giroux and Peg Zilboorg, now Gregory's widow, repaired to the Oak Room of the Plaza.

Hammett attacked Lily viciously: "After all I've been through with you, after all I've taught you, you turn out this piece of shit!" He named specific speeches, specific scenes. He liked none of it. Unconcerned that he was embarrassing their guests, he kept up his tirade for a long time. Nor had he had much to drink, only one drink or so.

It was as if he were venting years of suppressed anger, anger at her for still another success, anger at his complete dependence on her now, anger at her for doggedly writing through dry times, as he had been unable to do. Now he was not going to permit her to enjoy yet another triumph.

Giroux was horrified, so cruel was Hammett's attack. Giroux wanted to jump in. But, he thought, this is a sick man. Still it was awful. Hammett was mean. As if trying to provoke her, he kept it up, determined to give her a terrible time. Giroux had been looking forward to meeting Dashiell Hammett. Now he found his behavior just plain ugly as he kept repeating how awful her play was.

Lily did not permit herself to be provoked. She kept a poker face. She sat there pretending that she did not hear him. She did not utter a single word in defense of her play. Finally she turned to producer Robert Whitehead and began to discuss Anne Revere's performance.

Toys in the Attic ran for 556 performances. Among Lillian Hellman's plays it was her most successful after *The Children's Hour,* winning the 1960 Drama Critics Circle Award. For the published version of the text,

Lillian garnered blurbs from some "very fancy characters," as she called them: Harry Levin, Robert Lowell, Lionel Trilling, Philip Rahv, Norman Podhoretz. Others of the coterie who enjoyed her table, ate her gumbos, sent appropriately flattering letters. Editor Jason Epstein compared her to Jane Austen. Critic Alfred Kazin vowed to be her "knight." In fact, the play was far from her best. Heywood Hale Broun was amazed that the author of *Watch on the Rhine* should have written this.

Shortly after the opening of *Toys in the Attic*, Lily gave an interview to the New York *Post*. "I've lived alone the greater part of my life," Lily admitted, "and there have been times I haven't liked it. But I really don't mind being alone." She mentions Hammett as her "old and good friend" who years earlier used to accompany her and her father to Tarzan movies. She described herself as a woman who read poetry, went fishing, swam and cooked and smoked three packs of cigarettes a day. In March, she flew off to Jamaica, stopping at the Round Hill Hotel in Montego Bay, where she did her best to avoid what she called "this strange mixture of Dukes and Jews." Then she headed for Ann Arbor to lecture. She went where she was asked.

Lily now renewed the effort she had begun in 1957 to terminate the trust of her grandmother Sophie Newhouse. That she was the income beneficiary was hardly enough; in 1951 she had received only $1,537. Meanwhile the stock dividends were being added to the principal of the trust, a source of great exasperation.

As her mother's heir, and her father's, this money was hers under the "Lillian Hellman Trust/Florence F. Newhouse As Successor Trustee/ Under the L.W.&T. of Sophie Newhouse—Deceased." Since Sophie had left the trust fund to Julia for her lifetime, and then to Lillian for her lifetime, should Lillian die the money would go to distant relatives of Sophie Newhouse. Arthur Cowan was certain the distribution of the entire principal to Lillian could not be successfully challenged. "No one would have any standing in court to object."

Cowan was wrong to believe it would be easy. In May 1958, he had claimed, they had "crossed the Rubicon. The only thing we can do now is to follow the slogan, 'damn the torpedoes, full speed ahead!'" Cowan attempted first to get all beneficiaries, Florence and Miriam Newhouse, Jennie and Hannah Hellman, as well as Arthur Kober, to whom Julia Hellman had left $10,000 in her will, to surrender their rights to Lillian.

Kober at once wrote an assignment. Hannah Hellman died, leaving Lillian her residuary estate. Florence, Miriam, and Jennie remained; then only Lillian's aunt Florence remained as an obstacle. At first Florence's lawyer agreed; they would not oppose the distribution of the trust. But in 1960 Aunt Florence told Lillian that her lawyer had advised that she would be breaking the law "if I gave over the trust fund to you." She feared being sued. Lillian replied she felt "sad and bewildered." Being "bewildered" or "confused" was always a euphemism for Lily. It meant she was blood angry.

In 1960 Lily refurbished Hammett's room. Her new decorator, Mildred Loftus, arrived to measure the windows for curtains. Lily did not think Hammett had a proper desk; a work area was to be measured. Lily stuck her head in the door.

"Are you sleeping?" she asked Dash.

"No, come on in, Lillian," Hammett said. When she and Loftus entered, they found him lying on top of the covers in pajamas and a cotton robe, reading a book. He was pale as a ghost, all white, his skin white, his hair white, his bushy mustache snow white. Despite his illness, Loftus thought, he remained incredibly handsome, like a Christ on a cross. As Lillian began to introduce Mildred Loftus, Dash tried desperately to rise to his feet. But he could not. "Lie back," Lily and Mildred both said.

"Lily likes nothing better than to move furniture," Dash remarked pleasantly.

"Miss Loftus and I are going to have lunch. Helen will bring yours up shortly," Lily told him. She revealed what his lunch would be.

"You girls go off and have a good time," Dash said.

But he was often as meanspirited as he had been on that opening night. He caught a cold. Lily reported her frustration to the Wilburs. Dash "will do nothing about it except to be bad-natured," she confided. The success of *Toys in the Attic* meant that money was pouring in. Dash "says the food isn't nearly as good, or as much, since we got rich," she said. Still his words were sacrosanct.

Never satisfied, in June, Lily went to yet another performance of *Toys*. "Maureen has gained weight again," she complained to Kermit Bloomgarden, "and was hogwild from the start and Revere has gone back to the almost mournful quality she sometimes gets." Meanwhile the slowness of the pace was now Robards' fault: "This is either a sick man or a worn out man," Lily said.

The world of the New York theater was hardly glamorous. In June, Kermit had to send a harsh note to Robards: "I am shocked at your failure to appear at today's most important rehearsal. Your lack of responsibility to yourself, your fellow actors, Lillian and myself is most unprofessional." Lillian also kept up that New York social life, part literary, part theatrical, which half repelled, half titillated her. A party at Leonard

Bernstein's for Alberto Moravia left her wondering why she was there as she watched a girl make long-distance calls on Lenny's phone. In one of her notebooks she copied out a line: "There is something about Lillian Hellman that makes many men, and some women, want to throw whiskey at her."

That summer of 1960 they were once more on the Vineyard. In June, Jo came to visit her father, bringing her husband and children. Lillian now confided to Jo how harsh Dash had been about *Toys in the Attic*. He had told her it was terrible, and she had redone it, and still it wasn't good enough. She had been crushed. She did not describe that terrible scene at the Oak Room.

Dash asked Jo what she really thought of Lillian. "I've been with her so long I don't know what to think of her anymore," he confessed, his tone as light and forgiving as ever. He told Jo he wanted to write, but now his fingers wouldn't type out the words. Revealing she had never transcended her father's abandonment, Jo told him, "We all have our crosses to bear." Still the lapsed Catholic, Dash laughed. Then he said, generously, "Boy, how right you are!"

"You know, your father's dying," Lillian told Jo when they were alone.

"I know he's dying," Jo said.

"I wonder what's going to become of him," Lillian went on. It seemed that in an indirect way Lillian was asking Jo to take Dash back to California with her. "He says he'll go into the veterans' hospital," Lily added, revealing that she and Dash had talked it over.

"Well, I guess that's best," Jo replied. She now had three small children to raise, and was pregnant with her fourth. It was obvious that Lillian didn't want to take care of him any longer and had been saying: I don't want him, you take him.

Yet although she complained, neither was Lily about to allow Dash to enter a veterans' hospital now. She had tried to extricate herself from this burden. When she couldn't, she kept him. It wasn't saintly, Jo thought, but at least she did it.

In September, the doctor told Lillian that Dash had inoperable lung cancer. Lily decided there was no point in telling him and said nothing. Determined not to miss the London opening of *Toys in the Attic*, Lillian did consider putting him in a nursing home. Diana Trilling dissuaded her. "You'll feel very bad," Trilling warned. "You can't desert him like that." Lillian's guilt rose to the surface once more, and she abandoned the idea.

Before she left for London, she rounded up some friends to look in on Dash. "When I'm away, call Dash and go out for a drink with him," Lillian asked Maureen Stapleton.

"I never thought I'd live to see the day when you would tell me to take Dash out for a drink," Maureen said.

"I never thought I'd live to see the day either," Lily told her. "But it's here."

With the end of Dashiell Hammett's life in sight, Lillian seemed a woman in disarray. On the plane to London that October, Arthur Penn chatted with a male acquaintance, only for Lillian to be furious that he was paying so much attention to someone else. From Claridges, Lily wrote seductively to Lionel Trilling of her dream in which he was exposed as the lover of another Columbia professor's wife. Writing as if Trilling was a man who desired women other than his wife, she sent him a fine pipe and told him to "put that in the pipe and smoke it and tell me what it means." The she-Hammett always had to use subterfuge to win sexual favors, those Dashiell Hammett in palmier days gained with a mere twinkle of the eye.

2 4

The Death of Dashiell Hammett

"The love that started on that day was greater than all love anywhere, anytime, and all poetry cannot include it."

LILLIAN HELLMAN AND DASHIELL HAMMETT

"Why me?"

LILLIAN HELLMAN

From the day Dash arrived at Eighty-second Street, Lily longed for a final word of affirmation. Yet even as he never complained of his illness, he offered no words in which she might take comfort later. His silence, an implicit denial that what they had was meaningful, continued. Yet Lily remained at the center of his life. One day she telephoned, and when he learned it was she, he scrambled out of bed to the phone, so eager was he to talk to her. Knowing how Lillian longed for a sign from him, Selma Wolfman pondered why Dash couldn't express any affection when she was there.

One day, she dared venture, tentatively, "We've done fine, haven't we?"

"Fine's too big a word for me," Hammett insisted. "Why don't we just say we've done better than most people?" Lily remained frustrated, unable to lift the barrier between them which the years had wrought.

In the early morning of November 25, the day after Thanksgiving, Lily sat down at her old Remington typewriter and wrote a note to commemorate the thirtieth anniversary of their acquaintance:

On this thirtieth anniversary of the beginning of everything, I wish to state:

The love that started on that day was greater than all the love anywhere, anytime, and all poetry cannot include it.

I did not know what treasure I had, could not, and thus occasionally violated the grandeur of this bond.

For which I regret.

But I give deep thanks for the glorious day, and thus the name, "Thanks-giving."

What but an unknown force could have given me, a sinner, this woman?

Praise God.

Signed.

Dashiell Hammett

Lily handed the note to Dash. He was to read it, and then sign. His signature now was shaky; he could scarcely summon the effort for his customary emphatic "D." But he signed his name. Then he added in big, sloppy letters: "If this seems incomplete it is probably because I couldn't think of anything else at the time. DH."

It was something. Yet he continued to show her resentment, hostility. He couldn't stand Arthur Cowan, who he thought was a crazy man pretending he was crazy, and let her know it.

In her loneliness she chronicled his moods in a diary. One December day the poet Robert Lowell visited. "Dash was gasping in a bad attack," Lily wrote. But he refused to allow her to call a doctor and was "disagreeable." By eleven the next morning the doctor had been summoned; by two in the afternoon Dash was on his way to Lenox Hill hospital.

"Oh, are you coming?" he murmured as he looked up from the stretcher and saw that Lily had her coat on. Still he denied their closeness. So he revealed even now his resentment over all those times he had not been her priority, not least in these last two years when she had traveled, leaving him alone. Lily felt insulted; Lily said nothing.

If up to now Dash had acted the hard-boiled hero, suppressing his fear, now he became terrified of dying. "Fear is bad and obvious now," Lily wrote. By December 19, he was back on Eighty-second Street. There was nothing the doctors could do for him.

"I don't think I'll ever be better." Dash said what Lillian had long known. He developed a rash all over his body, which Lily thought must be shingles.

One evening he rejected his nightly martini. "I never thought I'd turn one down," he said.

The effort to walk was too great and his face grew sadder with each passing day. He did stagger out of bed to show Selma the new robe the Wylers had sent him. For a few days he seemed a little better. Then it was bad again.

Lily had accepted a teaching position at Harvard for the spring 1961 semester. Dash would be put in a nursing home. If he could not be moved to Cambridge, she would return to New York "at least once a week or every ten days." The doctor would decide "whether the loss of me at this time will do more damage than the trip to Boston."

Late in December 1960, Cathy Kober, now eighteen years old, visited. Lily watched as still Dash seemed excited, gladdened by her visit. Jealous as ever, Lily suspected that there might even be a "last sexual surge." The old fantasies, images of Dash making love to other women with which she had tortured herself in years past, returned.

His door was open. She saw him touch Cathy; there was "a little grabbing." Along with the old jealousy came moral judgment, how she had told him he could harm innocent young women with all that touching and seducing. Then Lily told herself she was being foolish. The women knew it was harmless. They were even pleased. It was only sad, a "last try" at life.

Even as, once more, she felt excluded by him, compassion overtook her.

During these last days he spoke of "Tulip," complaining that he couldn't work, as if writing remained somewhere close, just beyond his reach.

"I've never liked writers who don't know what they're doing and now I don't know what I'm doing," Dash said.

"Maybe because the book came from another period," Lily tried.

She was as afraid to talk as she had always been with him. She was "always afraid and hating it." She had always been "frightened of being hit, frightened of the humiliation, frightened of the superiority." He had always kept her on tenterhooks and as he lay dying he showed no sign of relenting.

Yet, she thought, he had done better than she; he at least had some kind of love in his life, "much of it, duty, maybe." She was thinking of his daughter, Josephine. "And I will not," Lily, lamenting, feeling sorry for herself, wrote; there would be no one to love her, no children, no one to care for her as she was caring for him.

He spoke of two other books he might write. Lily was "torn with pity and love and hate and so bored by the struggle."

In these last days, there was only his ill nature. When he looked at her, he seemed to hate her. He called her "hard-eyed." She longed for a scene, "tears that would have been good for me, gratitude, or admission of love." But he had closed himself off from her. She tried to tell herself it was the lack of oxygen going to his brain that made him turn on her. She became angry nonetheless; she was often angry with him now. "Why me?" she asked herself.

There was one difference now. A few minutes later he seemed to forget that he had just been angry at her. She thought he had become irrational. Was he angry or not? But maybe his forgetfulness, his ceasing to punish her, his forgetting his anger, were attempts to move closer to her. She could not bring herself to believe it.

One afternoon he came into her bedroom. "Why is it happening?" he demanded. "We must try . . . why is it happening?"

"It's because you were mean to me," she said quickly.

"That isn't what I'm talking about," he said, his anger flaring. Nothing more was said. It had been years since they had really talked, years since they had known each other. Now it was too late.

I've done my best, Lily told herself when she was alone. Then, sadly, she had to admit, "it wasn't a very good best." And still it rankled. With other women, he always expressed warmth, even need. In these last weeks, he had manifested sexual need, and a need for the consolation only a mother, a woman, could provide.

But never with her.

On New Year's Eve there would be no party on Eighty-second Street. Lily was going to spend the evening with the Trillings. She went in to see him before her departure. Now Dash cried, a solitary tear.

"Tough. It's been tough, been tough these last four or five years," he said.

"Tell me," Lily urged. "Do you want to talk about it?" Still she was afraid, as afraid as she had been since the day they met of invoking his scorn.

"No," he said with a touch of anger. "I'm trying not to think about it. My only chance is not to think about it."

Dinner proceeded at the Trillings until the telephone rang. It was Dash's nurse. She was alarmed. Mr. Hammett was irrational. "Do you want me to come and stay the night with you?" Lionel Trilling offered. Lily went home alone. She found Dash reading a book upside down.

"Look at it, darling, it's wonderful," he said. As Lily moved toward him, she realized he was speaking not to her, but to the nurse. In his old flirtatious way he caught the nurse's hand, and kissed it. It was only the nurse who was able to persuade him to take the ambulance.

Once Dash was in the hospital, Lily went to Cambridge and chose a nursing home housed in a big Greek Revival building on Kirkland Street. William Alfred thought the place seemed dirty; Elena Levin was upset when the proprietor, who showed them the room that would be Dash's, said, right in front of the present occupant, "His room will become available in. . . . " Should Dash live in such a place?

"He won't care; he doesn't listen anyway," Lily said. Nor did the absence of common rooms trouble her. "He won't come out of his room anyway," she said.

When she visited him at Lenox Hill on January 3, Lily decided he was coherent enough for her to tell him that she had accepted the position at Harvard. He could be brought in an ambulance. Dash expressed concern about the expense. Visting, Ginny Bloomgarden confessed to Dash her fear of nuclear war. Dash told her no one was going to use the bomb again.

"Honey, the world will change," he comforted her. He put no stock in Jack Kennedy, however. "One President isn't much different from another," Dash said. With Ginny, with Pat Neal, there was none of the sharpness he reserved for Lillian. Pat revealed that her son had been hit by an automobile and was in this very hospital. Dash summoned the strength to be deeply concerned. Charlee Wilbur sent him a message: "Tell Dash I love him only for his BODY."

On January 8, at four in the morning, Lily received a call from the hospital. Dash had taken a turn for the worse. It was not only emphysema and lung cancer and heart disease which were wracking his body, but now pneumonia too. Lily got dressed and hailed a cab.

Believing he was dying, the nurse ordered Lily, "Run quickly to the bed and shout into his ear as loud as you can." Lily shouted.

Startled, Dash opened his eyes in "shocked surprise." Dash looked at her, an expression of profound terror on his face. He tried to raise his head, then fell back. He was never conscious again. When Lily went home, among the people she telephoned was Rose Evans. "I didn't want you to read about it in the newspaper," she said.

Dashiell Hammett died at seven in the morning on January 10, 1961. Lillian and Helen got to the hospital at seven-thirty. At nine, Lillian telephoned Josephine. She assumed Jo would call Mary. Then Lily called her best friend, Hannah Weinstein, who was living on Cadogan Square in London. Selma called Rose Evans, who at once wept. By two-thirty in the afternoon, Lily was deep in session with her psychiatrist, George Gero. The next day at eleven in the morning, Lily was seated at her hairdresser's. Hair was something she could control, alter, fix, contain.

*   *   *

Dashiell Hammett's funeral was held on January 12 at Frank Campbell's. The tiny chapel was packed mostly with Lily's friends, like Kermit Bloomgarden and Arthur Kober, Leonard Bernstein, Lionel and Diana Trilling, Emmy and Louis Kronenberger, even St. Clair McKelway. But Rose Evans, Muriel Alexander, Pat Neal, and Lee Brown Spitzer were there. Jerome Weidman had been a friend to them both. Louis Weinstock, the general manager of *The Daily Worker,* who had known Dash in prison, attended, and later offered a quotation for the paper's obituary: "He was a good man."

Neither Mary, who was not his daughter, nor Jo, whom he loved more than anyone else, came East. Nor did Jose, who soon would claim to be his widow and ask the government for widow's benefits, insisting, falsely, that they had lived together for six months in 1950. On the Hammett side, Dash's nephew Richard T. Hammett attended.

The body lay in an open casket, dressed in the evening clothes Dash had purchased for the opening of *Toys in the Attic.* Pat Neal walked up to it, and Dash seemed to her like a stranger. He didn't resemble himself at all. Whose funeral am I at? Pat wondered, temporarily disoriented. But there was Lillian, so it must be Dash.

Lillian mounted the podium to deliver his eulogy with a sure step.

She began with an anecdote. A few weeks before, on a night when he was having a rough time, Lily had told him, "You're a brave man." Hammett had smiled. "Better keep words like that for the end," he had told her.

"He would not have wanted words today," Lillian told their friends. The funeral, she added truthfully, was for her sake. Calmly, with forcefulness, and elegant understatement, she spoke of Hammett as a hero who "had contempt for heroics." Beginning a mythology she would continue to the end of her life, she said Hammett was not a Communist, but a man who had gone to jail for a principle. As always in the fabulations to come, there would be the half-truth, for Hammett indeed had gone to jail for his beliefs.

"The night before he went to jail," Lillian said, "he told me that no matter what anybody thought he had no political reason for the stand he took, that he had simply come to the conclusion that a man should keep his word." From the day of his funeral, she became the interpreter of his opinions, the arbiter of his views. "He is dead and there is nobody to tell the truth about him except me," Lily would say. She spoke now as if his political activity had been about style, more Sam Spade than V. J. Jerome. There could not have been a "night before he went to jail," because on July 8 he had not known this would be his last night of freedom for half a year, could not have known that Judge Ryan would clap him into jail the very day he testified and that there would be no bail.

"He didn't think well of the society we live in," Lillian said, "and yet when it punished him he made no complaint against it, and had no anger about the punishment." This indeed had been true. She smoothed away all the hard edges. "He was a gay man, funny, witty," she remembered for their friends. "Most of his life was wide open and adventurous, and most of it he enjoyed." His generosity, which had so often exasperated her, she now affirmed: he "gave away anything he had to anybody who needed it, or even wanted it"; he "accepted everybody with tolerance."

Best and most noble was his honesty. "In the thirty years I knew him I never heard him tell a lie of any kind," Lily said, "and that sometimes made me angry when I wasn't envying the courage it takes."

The dramatist Lillian Hellman moved toward catharsis. People needed to weep for Dash and Lily knew how to elicit the sentiment for this man his friends knew as gentle, kind, honest, even saintly:

Blessed are they, I hope, who leave good work behind. And who leave behind a life that is so worthy of respect. Whoever runs the blessing department, may they have sense enough to bless a good man this last day he is on earth.

Lillian played very well, Pat Neal judged. Standing there before that full room, she managed to keep her emotions in check. John Marquand thought there was something theatrical about it, as if Lillian were talking *to* Dash there in his casket. Back at the house, Emmy Kronenberger looked around for Hammett's daughters. But they weren't there. Nor had Lillian in her eulogy made a single reference to either Jo or Mary, to Dash as father and grandfather.

The next day was bitterly cold. Accompanied by Kermit Bloomgarden and Howard Bay, sheltered in a reddish, long-haired fur coat, Lillian took the train for Arlington for Dash's burial. It had been Dash's idea, he who had served in two wars, that he be buried in Arlington National Cemetery.

It was a simple military funeral. Attending were Hammett's first cousin once removed, Jane Fish Yowaiski, who had read about the event in the newspaper, her father William Fish, Charles and Agnes Mattingly (Agnes was another Hammett cousin), and Dash's sister, Reba. Dash's brother Richard had been expected but failed to show up. He was moving down South and gave the excuse that he had to be at his new house when the movers arrived.

The cousins were not admitted to the chapel service, although Dash's sister Reba was inside with Lily. Afterward, Lily, Kermit, Howard, and Reba drove in a limousine to the burial site. A little Volkswagen followed them. Later the driver introduced himself as one of the soldiers who had been with Dash in the Aleutians.

At the graveside taps was played. Lily and Reba sat in chairs; the others stood behind them. The honor guard shot off the guns and at each of the twenty-one volleys Lillian shivered, her shoulders shaking. She covered her face with her hands, as if to shield herself. She's an actor too, Jane Fish Yowaiski thought, noting how Lily's hair matched her coat.

There was no religious service at the graveside. The pallbearers simply handed Lily the flag which had covered Dash's casket. Nor did Lily speak to Dash's relatives. Quickly the mourners went their separate ways.

The FBI had schemed to prevent Dashiell Hammett's burial at Arlington by enlisting one of their "press contacts" who would expose the "incongruous situation . . . wherein one who has been a member of an organization which believes in the overthrow of our government by force and violence receives a hero's burial among those who gave their lives to support this government." If the FBI had its way, the Smith Act would follow Dash to his grave. Fortunately, before this scheme could be implemented, Dash was safely in the ground.

In February, Lily went to Cambridge to teach her Harvard course. It was about "stealing," she said provocatively, how a writer can make use of what he reads. "Great writers steal," Lily told her class in what they could not have known was a justification of her appropriation of Hammett's style. "Mediocre writers imitate." She did tell her students that by teaching she was trying to replace what she had lost with Hammett's death. Lily and Helen lived in Archibald MacLeish's tenth-floor apartment at Leverett Towers with its yellow satin-upholstered chairs. It overlooked the Charles River and, on a clear day, Boston.

Lonely in Cambridge, Lillian took dinner once a week with Bill Alfred, then made him stay up with her until six in the morning. She talked of Hammett, telling that story of how her straw hat had caught fire and she thought she had a headache and he had called her "a silly son of a bitch." Certain that she too had emphysema, she consulted a doctor. For years, she was to complain of this imaginary illness.

"I'll never be in bed with a man again," she told Herbert Gold, although, of course, she had not been in bed with Hammett for two decades. It felt as if she was asking him to feel sorry for her, contradict her, and invite her to his bed.

After his death, Lillian Hellman did not always picture Dashiell

Hammett as a saint. One of his fellow soldiers from the Aleutians told her of how Dash had held forth around a campfire one night. "Oh yes, I know that period," Lillian said. "He never was without a drink in his hand. Of course he was loquacious. He could talk forever."

But soon she began to preface her sentences with "as Dash would say." She would pack for a trip and, uncertain of her arrangements, would declare, "I know what Dash would say. Get packing and get going." More than ever now she emphasized the she-Hammett, tough-talking-twenties-moll aspect of her personality. The day her new secretary, Rita Wade, met her for the first time, she was being interviewed by a man from the New York *Times,* who asked about the difference between male and female playwrights.

"Well, one thing is that their sex organs are different," the she-Hammett told him.

Disoriented and yet compulsively organized, she sat down and made a list of loans she had made to people, dating back to Lois Jacoby's 1946 loan of $1,050. Melby owed her a balance of $500. "To Dash Hammett in 1948," she wrote, "$1,059.30."

At the end of 1961, Lily sold the house on Martha's Vineyard. "I missed your father too much to stay in it any longer," she told Jo. Then she began the construction of a new house with a design by Howard Bay. As always, she made her meticulous lists: the plantings she wanted included seven Japanese black pines, fourteen red cedars, and sixty grandiflora roses, Queen Elizabeth variety. The new property was on an acre of ground with one hundred feet of beach. She hung her Picasso lithographs and resumed her life at the place she most loved.

In his will, dating from 1952, Hammett left a quarter of his assets to Lillian, a quarter to Mary, and half to Jo, his natural daughter. Lillian was the executor. Since the government owned all his property at his death against their lien, the will was null and void. The copyrights to most of his works belonged to the federal government, which claimed it owned everything. Hammett had never contested this fact, never litigated this issue on the ground that his copyrights were more valuable than what he owed the government.

Lillian paid the hospital bill at Lenox Hill, which for two weeks amounted to $490.78. Dash's electric razor was missing, and Lillian demanded that the hospital reimburse her. She paid his doctors, and she paid $282.53 for the funeral. "Should this be charged against the estate?" she asked Hammett's lawyer, Charles Haydon. "My reason for wanting to know is that my accountant thinks there may be some way of deducting it from my income tax." Jo contributed $150 to help pay her father's expenses, and Lillian placed this sum in her own account. Uncertain of the time of Hammett's divorce, she had Haydon approach the Social Security Administration, which produced the date: 1937. It was Lillian who collected the lump-sum death payment from the Social Security Administration. Discovering among his effects a Treasury Department check for fourteen dollars dating from 1954, she cashed it. By February, she had set to work compiling lists of all of Hammett's stories.

In April, the state of New York claimed $10,455.81 against Dashiell Hammett's estate. The federal government's final bill was $163,286.46. Lillian turned to Oscar Bernstien now in an effort to free Hammett's copyrights.

Bernstien told the Internal Revenue Service the estate had tried unsuccessfully to sell the rights to Hammett's unexpired copyrights for a sum that would allow them to pay the government and get rid of the lien. "In essence, the Estate is hopelessly insolvent," he claimed. Bernstien offered the government $5,000 "in compromise of all claims and release its liens against such rights." Meanwhile, Lillian wrote to Jo. "MCA is NOT convinced that your father's work will ultimately be of great value," she said.

In April 1962, Lillian requested that Josephine participate financially in the settlement she planned to make with the government. "I have the hope," she wrote, "that maybe you and Mary can contribute to this final possible settlement with the government." Unless they made the deal, Lillian warned, "the Government has the right to demand all the written material for themselves."

How much should she send? Jo immediately asked. Lillian said that she needed $5,000. Jo replied, "Let us know when you want the check and we'll send it." On June 18, 1962, Lillian wrote back: "As no sum has yet been mentioned, I will not need anything until I let you know."

Meanwhile Lily's attack was two-pronged. With Arthur Cowan's legal help, she determined which rights to Hammett's works were free, which not. In November she renewed the copyrights for "His Brother's Keeper," "Two Sharp Knives," *The Maltese Falcon,* "Secret Agent X-9," and "This Little Pig." Simultaneously she swore to the state of New York that she had tried to find a purchaser for his literary works and unexpired copyrights, but had failed; even MCA (Music Corporation of America) had turned her down.

Always on the offensive, Lily insisted that she had been approached to "write a book about the deceased or his works." For the purpose of writing his biography, it would be "of some interest or benefit to her to obtain all rights and interests" in his literary works and copyrights, "free and clear of all claims, and especially all claims and liens of the United States Government."

She offered the Internal Revenue Service two thousand dollars, plus any Knopf royalties owing, less Hammett's final expenses. The government replied by demanding an appraisal of the value of Dash's copyrights. Now all Lily needed was documentation attesting to the fact that the rights to Hammett's works weren't worth very much. By September, she had in her hands a letter from Kermit Bloomgarden stating that should he and Joseph Weinstein, a lawyer and Lily's good friend Bobbie's husband, were to make an offer themselves for the Hammett rights, it would be between $2,000 and $3,000. Kay Brown, Lillian's agent, wrote a similar letter. This part had been easy.

Meanwhile, Howard N. Meyer, from Bernstien's firm, told the government that Dash's assets were "pitifully small." He had died with no insurance, no real estate, no stocks or bonds, no cash or bank accounts but for $131.64 in the Emigrant Savings Bank, and a pension check for $78.25. His liabilities included a sum of more that $40,000 which he owed Lillian. Future royalties were problematic, and, indeed, who could prove otherwise? Lily produced an MCA report dating from 1961 which stated that "the field of publication seems to be a diminishing one rather than an upbeat one. The television market is limited as to compensation."

Once the government began to quibble over whether Dash's copyrights were worth $4,000, $5,000, or $6,000, victory was in sight. Now Lily brought to bear her long-standing poker-playing skill. She was going to withdraw her offer of $5,000, she said, "since I had been very nervous about never recovering it." There "would be a revival of Dash some day," no doubt, but "the day would probably be very far off." Should they not act quickly, they might not even obtain the $5,000.

Simultaneously, she took her customary moral high road. Her "primary job in this whole affair was to honor a writer and a man that I admired," she said, "and to make sure that the proper work was published in the proper places and the bad work ploughed under." Nor would she allow the government to go on collecting Dash's royalties while making use of her services as his literary executor. She would not permit the government or anyone "to stand over my shoulder when it came to literary work."

PART EIGHT

Lily Alone

25

"Shyster Clever"

> "For many years it has been for all practical purposes impossible to steal from the rich."
> DASHIELL HAMMETT, NOTES FOR "HOW TO LIVE IN THE UNITED STATES."

> "Don't you think people often say other people are tough when they do not know how to cheat them?"
> THE AUTUMN GARDEN

> "I bought the estate. I'll leave them something when I die."
> LILLIAN HELLMAN

Before long Lillian changed her mind about sharing the Hammett copyrights with Josephine. Instead of supplying a figure Jo was to send to complete the purchase, she remained silent. So Lillian turned her back on the moral imperatives of her role as Dashiell Hammett's literary executor, which would have decreed that she divide the copyrights in keeping with the wishes he expressed in his will. Legally she was not required to honor the terms of the null and void document. And she didn't.

Like a child, she grabbed what she wanted. A fierce competitor all her life, she had a new battlefield, a new arena in which to exert her will. For years money had been her obsession and the means to retaining an edge over detractors. Now she would seize Hammett's works. As age exaggerates the worst of our foibles, so Lillian became obsessed with financial security. The sale of Hammett's works was one means she used to secure the advantages only a perpetually well-stocked bank account could provide.

Yet it wasn't primarily about money. Hammett's reputation was at its lowest ebb following the McCarthy period. It wasn't apparent that he would enjoy a new vogue or that one could be manufactured. Rather, Lillian's seizing for herself the rights to his work followed another emotional trajectory.

As soon as Hammett died, she was angrier than she had ever been with him—for not loving her enough, for that week with Laura Perelman which she obsessively relived—for not affirming what they had, except when she made him do it. That she had supported him for years while he had not loved her made her capture of his work all the more psychically justifiable. At last she had discovered the appropriate revenge.

Even now this unfinished woman with her avowed childish nature remained jealous of the person she perceived Hammett loved more than her, his daughter Jo. In denying Jo a claim to Hammett's work, she would be denying the closeness of their connection as well. If she could not control Hammett in his lifetime, she could control the best of him after his death, which was his work. She could possess him as she never had before and free him at last of them all: the clinging Jose and her awful brat Mary, no less than Jo, his primary heir.

At once her lawyer sent waivers for Josephine, Mary, and even Jose to sign. They were to renounce any claim to the Hammett copyrights. Meanwhile Jo was told not that Lillian was negotiating with the government for a sale, but that she was trying to "clear your father's name." Should she not sign the waiver, she and her sister would be liable for Hammett's debts. Jo and Mary both signed.

Realizing that Lillian's estimate of the value of Hammett's works had been "grossly understated," reluctant to accept $5,000, yet unable to figure out what figure to set, the government insisted on a public auction. Still in her role as Hammett's executor, even as she was about to betray that role, Lillian placed advertisements for the auction. The *Publishers Weekly* ad was buried under "Special Notices," sandwiched between "Business Opportunities" and "Remainders." In *The Saturday Review of Literature* the ad appeared under "Personals," amid advertisements for shoes and wallpaper, earrings and "authentic Scottish tartans":

> The undersigned will sell at auction all the right, title and interest of the estate of Samuel Dashiell Hammett late of New York County, to all copyright interests which had not expired at the time of his

death, on November 18, 1963, at offices of O'Dwyer & Bernstien, 50 Broad Street, at 9:30 a.m. Terms of sale on file in Surrogates Court New York County, p. 419/1961 and at said attorneys' office. Minimum bid—$5,000.00. L. Hellman, Executrix.

The auction took place on that morning of November 18; the auctioneer was O'Dwyer and Bernstien employee Howard N. Meyer. The only bidders were Lillian and Arthur Cowan. Out in California, Jo Marshall had no idea her father's copyrights were being auctioned off.

Seated beside Cowan, Lillian seemed self-important, expressing no graciousness to those she deemed her inferiors. Later she would call herself "shyster clever." Never had she masterminded a greater coup than she did on this day.

"How much am I bid?" Meyer began.

"Five thousand dollars," Lillian said.

Once, twice, three times, and it was done. Lillian and Cowan each contributed $2,500; the fee to O'Dwyer and Bernstien came out of the $5,000 since Hammett's estate was "insolvent." The Internal Revenue Service received a check for $3,615.93 for the rights to all the Hammett novels, and many of his stories.

Lillian acted as if her behavior had been in Jo's best interest. "It is time to say bluntly that I will do whatever I will do only in honor, and in love, of your father," she wrote Jo. "Therefore you will owe me no thanks." Although she had kept silent, and never told Jo how much money to send, now she claimed she was "surprised . . . that we heard nothing from you because you had once written to me that you would contribute to the settlement asked by the Internal Revenue Department."

Since she had heard nothing, Lillian said disingenuously, she had been forced to ask "help from an old friend, Arthur W. A. Cowan." Now she and Cowan owned "what was the estate." It was Jo's own fault that she was left with nothing.

As if this wasn't bad enough, having learned that Jo and Mary still owned the rights to stories whose copyright renewal date came after Hammett's death ("This Little Pig," "His Brother's Keeper," "Two Sharp Knives," and "Secret Agent X-9"), Lillian asked Jo to hand over "the disposition of these stories to me, as your father would have wished, and so stated in his will about all the work." Even as she was violating its terms, Lillian invoked Hammett's will. In return, she promised ambiguously, she would send Jo and Mary "your proper share of any money received in the future from these stories."

Putting her far weaker adversary on the defensive, Lillian now told Jo she found it "strange and chilling that I never hear from you." Having no knowledge of copyrights, viewing Lillian as having been her "father's wife," Jo acquiesced. Whatever money would be sent to her from the sale of Hammett works would be at Lillian's discretion, dependent on her whim. In practice, Jo would be lucky to receive 3 percent, rather than the 50 percent Hammett had intended she receive from the rights to his work.

From the beginning Lillian revealed she had no intention of honoring the terms of the will: "only when in my sole judgment I feel it is equitable that I do so, after provision for other moral obligations," she wrote, would Jo receive anything at all. The moral obligation was what Dash owed Lillian in exchange for not having loved her enough. The financial obligation was itself ambiguous; he had supported her for years before *The Children's Hour;* he lived with her for two and a half years until his death.

By 1963 Lillian was a rich woman. Yet she allowed Cowan to put up money. "I didn't think I could afford it," she later told Nora Ephron, although this was not true. But if someone else could foot a bill, so much the better. She also felt she owed Cowan something for having masterminded the sale with Oscar Bernstien. In June 1964 the government offered her back Hammett's rights to half of 1 percent of *Death of a Salesman* for $150. "Tell them to have it for a present from me," Lillian answered haughtily. In victory, she was arrogant.

As Lillian and Cowan quickly renewed Hammett copyrights, thirty-eight stories, some of his finest, passed into her hands. These included "The House in Turk Street," "The Girl with the Silver Eyes," "The Big Knockover," and "$106,000 Blood Money," as well as the novels and *The Continental Op, The Return of the Continental Op,* and *Adventures of Sam Spade and Other Stories.* Lillian hired Robert Lantz, an elegant, Old World Berlin-born agent, to market the Hammett properties. At once they planned an edition of Hammett's stories with Lillian's own introduction, to be called *The Big Knockover.*

Nervous about Hammett's children having been eliminated from all rights to his work, Lantz asked Lillian to write to Jo and Mary and get them to agree to assign their copyright and all rights in perpetuity to the particular stories in the forthcoming collection. No matter how many waivers they signed, no matter that on her 1964 tax return Lillian deducted a $40,000 "non-business bad debt" she claimed Hammett owed her, as Hammett's children they had copyright claims. In the decade to come, hundreds of thousands of dollars would be earned by Hammett's literary works, and it would all go to Lillian Hellman.

Lillian and Cowan agreed that should either of them die, the other would inherit their half of the Hammett rights. Lillian spoke vaguely of putting a clause in her will leaving Cowan "part of my share," since she wanted "most of my share . . . to go to his grandchildren." Cowan put his agreement in a letter to Oscar Bernstien which Lillian witnessed and signed: "If I die I want all my rights in the property to go to Lillian Hellman absolutely." He told Bernstien he would give all his rights to Lillian "when I die before her," something of a joke since they were the same age. And yet Cowan's prediction came true. He died in an automobile accident in Spain on November 10, 1964.

Although there was no will leaving to Lillian Arthur Cowan's 50 percent of the Hammett rights, she behaved as if his share now belonged entirely to her. When even Oscar Bernstien was skeptical, Lillian copied out a letter from Cowan to her suggesting that they use "the money from DH's works to start a portfolio of stock and land investments in our names with my half going to you if I die before you, and your half going to anyone you name in your will if you die before me." Lillian and her lawyers and her agents went on to behave as if this was legally binding.

A few years earlier Lillian had befriended Random House editor Joe Fox, a collector of Hammett's *Black Mask* stories. One day on the Vineyard as he sat at lunch with Lillian and Dorothy Parker, Fox had spotted a shadow from the second floor of her house peering down. When the shadow perceived it had been observed, it disappeared. It was Fox's only sighting of Dashiell Hammett.

Now Fox became the editor of the collection of Hammett stories called *The Big Knockover*. Lillian wrote a reminiscing Introduction. Throughout the manuscript she called him "Hammett," only in her final revision of January 1965 to change most of the "Hammetts" to "Dash." So officially began her romanticization of their relationship.

So also began the systematic marketing of Hammett's works even as the copyright situation remained murky, if legally unchallenged by Hammett's daughters. In November 1965 Lillian wrote to Oscar Bernstien: "I have never understood which copyrights belong to me and which copyrights belong to Hammett's daughters." In December, she sent Howard Meyer a new list of stories, asking him to figure out "whether any of these stories are owned by the daughters." Acknowledging the ambiguity of her ownership, she struggled to capture all the rights for herself.

Movie studios were more nervous than publishers about Lillian's claim to sole ownership of the Hammett copyrights. In optioning Hammett stories, most demanded a quitclaim from the Cowan estate. *The Big Knockover* was published in 1966 without a problem. But in 1967 M-G-M, about to option "The Big Knockover" and "$106,000 Blood

Money," demanded that Arthur Cowan's sister Sadie sign a quitclaim renouncing "all claim, right or interest" in the stories.

Sadie hesitated when Lillian told her about the agreement she had with Arthur. But never liking Lillian, who had claimed that Cowan had promised her money when he died, who had demanded that the gifts she had given him be returned to her, Sadie wanted to be rid of her now. She signed the quitclaim warranting that Arthur Cowan's estate had no claim of ownership to those two stories. When in 1974 Lillian was ready to market another anthology, *The Continental Op,* Raab had to sign another declaration, this time for Random House.

Stimulated by the classy publication of *The Big Knockover,* aided by the radicalization of the 1960s, which shed the stigma of McCarthyism at last, a Hammett revival erupted. Enormous amounts of money were earned from movie options and electronic rights and foreign rights to Hammett's stories and novels in the next decade. In May 1967 Columbia Pictures sent Lillian a check for $2,500 for a television pilot.

This was only the beginning. Between 1975 and 1977, the option money for "The Big Knockover" and "$106,000 Blood Money" alone totaled $100,000. Lillian argued she needed "a fairly large amount of money" for these options because "Mr. Hammett felt very strong against giving away material on options." Occasionally she would turn down an offer on the ground that "Dash himself felt very strongly about things not being done on speculation, and I have tried to follow his interests." He never would have justified abandoning a principle for the sake of a larger dollar figure.

Yet this is what she did, and in his name. Having assumed his style in her work, she now spoke for him in his absence, taking positions he never would have taken. Lillian treated low offers with scorn. When Patrick O'Neill, who owned the Ginger Man restaurant in New York, offered $500 for a one-year option on "Corkscrew," Lillian's reply was sarcastic: "Why don't you call him and say that I'll give him an option on the story for $500 if he'll give me an option on his restaurant for $500."

Lillian broke with Robert Lantz over *Candide,* as she accused him of favoring Leonard Bernstein, whom he also represented, over her. Bernstein's $25,000 fee for "supervising" a California production cut into her royalties, she raged. "I feel as if I am sitting on Kafka's head." Ever the gentleman, Lantz stepped aside and Don Congdon took over representation of both Lillian and the Hammett estate. From the first she lied: Congdon was told she had purchased the rights to the Hammett copyrights for $40,000, the figure she claimed Hammett owed her.

*   *   *

Soon Congdon was busy marketing the Hammett rights. Vintage republished the novels, excluding stage dramatizations. "That is a right that Hammett, and thus I, still own," Lillian asserted. European producer Albert Grimaldi paid Lillian $25,000 just for the exclusive film right to use the title *Continental Op*. By the mid-seventies the Hammett books, Congdon reported to Lillian, were "on a rising curve." Between 1972 and 1978 *The Dain Curse* alone sold over 70,000 copies and was optioned for television by Martin Poll. Poll paid Lillian $125,000 for what would be CBS's first miniseries, aired in May 1977. First, however, he asked to see "the pertinent papers to confirm the transfer of the Hammett estate to you and Cowan and from Cowan to you." There was, of course, no such document of transfer.

Congdon attempted to use the quitclaim they had obtained for *The Big Knockover*. But this did not mention *The Dain Curse*. Sadie Raab had to sign a document agreeing that the Cowan estate "has and makes no claim, right, or interest in or to a story written by Dashiell Hammett, to wit 'The Dain Curse.'" When Congdon tried to put an end to the copyright ambiguity, however, he failed. In September 1974, he told Raab that since "there is a lot of interest in motion picture rights to Hammett stories . . . it would be practical if you could provide us with a blanket quitclaim on all the Hammett stories in the event of any new deals." Raab refused. A year later Grimaldi paid Lillian $150,000 for the rights to "The Big Knockover," "$106,000 Blood Money," "The Golden Horseshoe," "The House in Turk Street," and "The Girl with the Silver Eyes."

Occasionally, when small sums were involved, Lillian exercised her power over Hammett and his work by refusing offers. The English publishers of the *Dashiell Hammett Omnibus* could not sell book club rights to any club "devoted to crime stories." Hammett transcended the crime genre, she insisted. He was better than that. NBC could not quote from a 1924 Hammett story called "One Hour" on a program called "Violence in America" unless they informed her "how they intend to use the quotation, what they are out to prove and certainly will want to be paid."

"Fly Paper" was dramatized at the John Drew Playhouse in East Hampton, Robert Brustein having obtained Lillian's permission. When Arthur Kober reported that actors were dying onstage only to get up and play other parts, when Lillian did not like the name of one of the characters, no matter that it was Hammett's original name, she exploded. "I can't have it!" she raged, demanding that Brustein close down the production. "It's a new form," he pleaded, unwilling to do her bidding.

"Don't talk to me about form," Lillian retorted. "I invented form."

Even as she continued to violate the terms of his will, Lillian invoked not her ownership of the rights, but her role as literary executor of Hammett's estate. A musical version of *The Maltese Falcon* was stopped because "it is my job as literary executor to do what I believe Hammett would wish me to do." So occasionally she rejected offers even seemingly against her financial interest, as if as literary executor she was preserving Hammett's reputation. Only she could speak for him now, and no one knew him as well as she.

"Ellery Queen" and *Ellery Queen's Mystery Magazine* were granted rights to "Too Many Have Lived" and "One Hour" because "Hammett liked Queen," who had published him in the forties when "no one else seemed interested." "I guard what he wrote as carefully as I can," Lillian insisted, "but I'm really violating what Hammett wanted. He didn't want to see the short stories published again." At such times she seemed still to fear him, to be wary of incurring his disapproval.

Hollywood money alone makes writers rich, as it had Hammett and Hellman both in the thirties. In the mid-seventies Lillian attempted to sell the rights to the story of her relationship with Dashiell Hammett to Universal for $450,000 plus 6 percent of the gross. Lillian's close friend Mike Nichols would direct.

Knowing full well that Hammett would never have permitted any film about them to be made, she wrote five pages of stipulations. The depiction of their relationship must not be critical, could contain no "approval or disapproval by other people of the way that Hammett and Hellman . . . conducted their personal lives or managed their beliefs." The source must be Lillian's own memoirs; any film must ignore what she had ignored so that her views could not be questioned as mythology or lies or half-truths. She had not shown Hammett to be a Communist and so neither could a film. ("Was he a Communist?" Congdon couldn't resist asking her. Once she said Hammett had a Party card. But on another day she said he didn't have a Party card.)

The film could not "treat either one of them as lost or loose people, or redeemed, or sad, or comic." In any representation of her visit to the Soviet Union under Stalin, it had to be clear that "the author saw and heard nothing about prison camps." The film was to make "no adverse comment . . . on his political beliefs, and his beliefs must be taken as the convictions of a serious, honest man who deeply believed in democracy." So contractually she ruled out the possibility of an honest depiction of his politics.

Hammett at the end of his life was not to be presented as "in any sense a charity case," as Lillian revealed a source of dissension between them in those last years. Rather, the film had to reveal her gratitude to him: "He gave a great deal more than he accepted and no change may be made in this situation." Thus she undermined her frequent argument that she had the right to complete ownership of his work because he was so deeply in her debt. But like a Renaissance overreacher, she never imagined the contradiction would be exposed.

Uneasy still, she insisted on "final cut" and seemed to believe Nichols had agreed. If a director could have final approval, "why then is a writer less to be trusted?" she argued. Nichols gave her "script approval," only for the deal to collapse. In 1976 the rights were sold to Warner Brothers for $400,000. Pocketing $75,000 on signing, Lillian added a new stipulation. Now Hammett was not even to be depicted as "a left-wing character." Lillian insisted that "politics had nothing to do with the relationship." Her written consent was required should the names "Lillian Hellman" and "Dashiell Hammett" be used. After a decade, the project languished.

All along Lillian kept writing to Jo promising her "rightful share" of the Hammett royalties. For a childish fantasist, it was as if stating a moral obligation was tantamount to fulfilling it. There was never an accounting, never an attempt to send Josephine half of the proceeds of any of these deals, as Hammett's literary executor was morally compelled to do. In a year when tens of thousands of dollars were earned, Jo would receive, always at Christmas, a check for $3,000.

With one letter in the late seventies Lillian send $500 for Mary and $1,000 for Jo. "I would, of course, be glad to send you my $500," Lillian wrote, suggesting that she did not wish to profit from Hammett's work, "but it would cause some extra difficulty particularly in the light of what I hope to do in the future." Through the years she promised Jo that one day she would be rich. Meanwhile Jo struggled to educate the children Lillian had told Cowan would be her heirs to the Hammett copyrights.

Often Lillian, in her typical manner, invoked complexities she pretended she could not understand. When *The Continental Op* was published in 1974, she wrote Jo: "I have told my lawyer and accountant that, depending on your father's debt to me, and, of course, the possible future income, I would like to send you part of the money." By now Hammett's "debt" was what she declared it to be. It was a "far more involved situation than I knew about," Lillian insisted. Income tax was involved. Who was to pay it? Only when it was sorted out would she send "a check." Jo should write if she had questions.

Seven months later, in July 1975, Lillian had "bad news" for Jo. The lawyer and the accountant had forbidden her from "giving you the proceeds of any one piece. They believe it will even endanger the sale of one story and perhaps others." She had cost herself "a great deal of money for the investigation of this whole mess," she wrote, as if Jo should be grateful. She was writing at the height of the Hammett renaissance, when thousands of dollars were pouring into the Hammett account. Now, she said, she had "to return to my Christmas gifts to you and Mary."

Sending his daughters Hammett copyright money as gifts, let alone at Christmas, meant, of course, that Lillian was offering beneficence; the legal implication was that she owed them nothing, but was extending charity. Jo should be grateful and remember "not to pay income taxes" on the gifts since Lillian, out of her great kindness, had already done it. In December 1975, Lillian sent a check with a new stipulation, one different from what Hammett had written in his will, thus again negating his wishes. Now Jo was to "keep two-thirds for yourself and your children, and divide the other one-third between your mother and Mary," no matter that Jose was not in the will at all. "It comes with affection from your father," Lillian declared, once more the undisputed arbiter of Hammett's feelings.

Another Christmas in the late seventies Lillian remarked to Congdon: "I've been thinking about giving them each five thousand dollars." Guilt feelings must have surfaced, Congdon thought. She had appropriated everything, yet she couldn't avoid the occasional twinge. In 1977 Jo received a small check from what Lillian called an option on one of Hammett's stories to a movie company. This she should keep all for herself and her family. If she wanted to share it with Mary and her mother, "then I would prefer that you keep at least $1,500 for yourself."

That March Lillian again invoked "the legal tax people," who had to weigh in before she could give her and Mary "a piece of one of the properties of your father's movie sales." Three months later, Lillian wrote Jo that it could not be done. Throughout Jo remained entirely in the dark about the extent of the Hammett earnings.

The Christmas when Lillian had been enriched by the sale of the Hammett-Hellman story to Warners she sent Jo $4,000—$3,000 for herself, $1,000 for her children. She was sending a smaller check to Mary. "In computing the checks," she wrote, with her customary tones of conviction, as if it were true, "I have followed the terms of your father's will." Jo had no idea of where the money came from.

When Jean Potter Chelnov paid the final $2,000 of the loan Hammett had made to her in the forties, Lillian sent a thousand to Jo, five hundred for Mary, and kept her own five hundred, although this money had nothing to do with Hammett's copyrights. Lillian even admitted she had no claim to any of it. But she was taking her share because "it would cause extra difficulty, particularly in the light of what I hope to do in the future." That future, of course, was never to dawn. When she spoke of her rights to his estate, there crept into her talk, Diane Johnson, Hammett's biographer, thought, an element of revenge that lasted well into the 1980s. The legalities be damned, it was about possession.

Into the seventies and early eighties the earnings from Hammett's stories and novels continued to grow. Lillian received $86,500 from *The Dain Curse* book royalties alone. A single reading of *The Glass Key* by Canadian Broadcasting brought $2,000 dollars in 1978. A German publisher paid $3,200 for another collection, combining *The Big Knockover* and *Continental Op.* Typically, in 1984 Lillian turned down $300 for a collection from *Black Mask:* "bodies piled up by d.h."

For the remaining Christmases of her life, Lillian pretended she was abiding by Hammett's will, "which is one part to Mary, one part to me, and two parts to you," she wrote Jo in 1979. Again there was no accounting. The check at Christmas 1980, Lillian said, "should be divided the usual way." Only now she had "ceased to care how much Mary gets." But, Lillian admitted, "I guess your father in some way did care." It was all up to Jo. In 1981 the "Christmas present" was late owing to "Mr. Reagan's new tax law." The check was for $3,000, now to be divided "as usual: one third for Mary and two-thirds for yourself."

That December, the mass-circulation Sunday magazine *Parade* printed the following question: "I've been told that Dashiell Hammett— her lover and mentor, who wrote 'The Thin Man'—left [Lillian Hellman] all his money. How much was it?" *Parade* replied cautiously, mentioning Hellman's purchase of the copyrights: "The story is that she, in turn, distributes the money to Hammett's two daughters, Mary and Josephine."

Four thousand dollars went to Jo at Christmas of 1982. She was "tired of Mary," Lillian repeated. "If she is not in need I would advise you not to give her anything." Lillian suddenly tacitly admitted she was not sending Jo all she was owed under the terms of the will. "If you need any more," she wrote, "most certainly you can have it. I carry a separate account for your father's books and it usually has some money in it." Jo would have to ask, as if she were a supplicant.

Christmas 1983 was Lillian's last. Long tired of the charade that Mary was Hammett's natural daughter, she wrote to Jo: "I suppose she should get a small sum in any case."

In her will Lillian left the revenues of Dashiell Hammett's works, but not the copyrights, to Jo and Mary according to the terms of his will. These would be processed by her estate, keeping her in control of the elusive Hammett even after her own death. As the copyrights expired, the ambiguity of their ownership once more surfaced.

Mary died on February 21, 1992, without ever learning that she was not Dashiell Hammett's biological child. Did Lillian's estate, or did Jo, have the right to renew licenses awarded during Hammett's lifetime? In an effort to recapture at least the American rights to her father's writing, Jo hired a lawyer, Robert Montgomery, of the prestigious New York law firm Paul, Weiss, Rifkind, Wharton & Garrison. By the mid-1990s the rights to Hammett's novels finally reverted to Josephine Marshall, who planned to use whatever money was still to be earned to educate Hammett's two great-granddaughters. Ann, the baby Dash had brought to Hardscrabble Farm, and his first grandchild, was married but had no children.

2 6

Hammett's Successor

"I love you very, very much."

LILLIAN HELLMAN

"I've never been betrayed by a man."

LILLIAN HELLMAN

In 1962, a year after Hammett's death, Lillian committed herself to another major romantic fantasy. Dash's death had released in her the old hunger for a man who was hers alone. Arthur Cowan had made his sexual indifference clear. Now Lillian recapitulated yet again her old struggle to win a man who could not possibly want her.

She chose Blair Clark, tall and dark, slim, handsome, rich, and a goy. Better, if Hammett had been born "of early settlers" who had not distinguished themselves, among Clark's ancestors were railroad magnate John I. Blair and U.S. senator Simon Cameron, who had served as Abraham Lincoln's Secretary of War. If Lillian of the two was indubitably the celebrity, Clark numbered among his connections his Harvard classmate and friend, John F. Kennedy.

It seemed that Blair Clark, gentle and unaggressive, would be more pliant than Hammett. Lillian believed she was choosing a man with whom she could at last be open; she need not fear his sarcasm or his fists. Nor would Clark have power over her by virtue of his being older. Lillian was fifty-six, Clark forty-four. Hammett had been eleven years

older than she and he had made the rules. Might not she now reverse
that equation?

They had met in the late fifties on the Vineyard through a mutual
friend, another Clark classmate, Robert Lowell. In April 1962 they
encountered each other again. He was divorced and free, seemingly
available. Still following her lifelong pattern, Lillian was quickly cast in
the role of the pursuer, Clark as the pursued.

She enlisted her considerable wit, her sense of fun. She sent him
$160. In return, he must promise to be her "feudal knight forever." That
letter closed as one of Hammett's might: "in fealty." She offered herself
for what she was—with some editing, presenting him with a photograph
of herself taken in Rome during the summer of 1953 and telling him it
dated from 1961. Her birth date, she said, was 1907. Two more years
were all she dared claim.

That year her new play, which would be her last, an adaptation called
My Mother, My Father and Me, was an abysmal failure. "The whole year
has been dreary," Lillian wrote Louis Kronenberger, "maybe because I
was never before really without Dash some place on earth." Dash's existence had been a reminder of her youth, of what they had once believed.
Now Lily felt a chasm yawn beneath her. "I don't feel I know anything,"
she told Kronenberger, "or can rest on all that dogma I once liked so
much and rather regret losing."

A month into the connection, Lily's romantic fantasy was deeply in
jeopardy. Lillian wrote in her diary: "Blair? Did not call." From the start,
she did most of the telephoning. "*Mauvais,*" she wrote beside a record of
their meeting. "Party at Blair house," she wrote on March 20, 1963, "bad."
If Hammett had been unable to open himself to a woman, Lillian had chosen a pale version, equally "remote," as Jack Kennedy had described Clark.
Then she tortured herself for being rejected. Made uneasy by her pressure,
Clark pleaded he was "dissatisfied with self and things but not totally discouraged about some big prospect of the mind, the soul, the essence." On
May 1, 1963, she wrote: "Blair—broken: bad." A painful evening was
redeemed by a call at ten the next morning with an "explanation." In her
presence he left a party with Elizabeth Hardwick Lowell. That stung.

They traveled in November to San Juan. But when he called on
December 1, he seemed vague, busy. In retaliation she went to Israel to
write about the Pope's visit, then to a conference in Mexico. Always she
made checklists for her maid to pack:

> moisture cream; cold cream; conceal stick; Dr. Baer cream; eight
> hour cream; eyebrow pencil; eye liner; brush eye liner paste; eye

shadow; extra face lotions; face brush; cover fluid; foundation cream, light; foundation cream, dark; hair spray; small kleenex; lipsticks; lipstick brush; liquid face stuff; mascara; nail file; perfume; small power puffs; pumice; rouge; deodorant; talcum power; extra tooth bridge; tooth brush; Klenite; fixodent; tweezer; oil; toilet water; mirror; bobby pins; corn knife; curlers; combs for back of hair; hair brush & comb; hairnet; hairpins (bone); rollers; razor or Neet; toenail clipper; Brillantine for hair; hair spray (small); wig. . . .

The plain little girl who was perpetually insecure was made more insecure, even as Blair Clark's name was always on her lips. Rose Styron noticed that she was crazy about him and jealous of his other women. Indeed her competition was formidable and ranged from a famous sculptress to the newly widowed Jacqueline Kennedy, whom ever after she dubbed "the widow Kennedy." Lillian hated Jackie so much that when she gave a blurb later to her friend Richard de Combray for his Doubleday book it was with the stipulation: "I will not have that woman edit my quote." Yet Lillian gave a dinner on the Vineyard for Jackie and allowed her guest of honor to edit the guest list, disinviting at Jackie's request even the Styrons, who had accepted the invitation weeks earlier. "I'm sorry, but I have no room for you," Lillian said, pretending that Rose had not replied at all.

When she felt in danger of losing Clark to the sculptress, Lillian organized a campaign. The Lowells must dissuade him from following her to Venice and proposing marriage; they were to let him know how awful this woman was. As she held her grudge against Jackie, years later, in her memoir *Scoundrel Time,* Lillian implied that the sculptress and her husband were agents of the Central Intelligence Agency, almost bringing a lawsuit down on her head.

She wooed Clark with glittering entertainments and with juicy gossip. "Kermit's wife is holding out for vast sums," she reported. "Shumlin's wife is holding out for vast sums. I would love to hold out for a vast sum but I don't know how." She met Carlos Fuentes in Mexico and reported: "I'd lay bets the radical would turn up in a Conservative government someday."

She also declared an abiding love. She was "frightened of the strength of what I felt," she told him. He argued that were they to make love, their relationship would end. It was friendship of the highest order, but not romantic love. She pretended to be satisfied, then told her friends sometimes sadly, sometimes joking, "We necked and necked and necked and necked and never went to bed."

Meanwhile he told her about his troubles with other women. She listened, and concealed her pain, confiding only to her diary how she detested the "litany of love, how much, more than other people, etc." She was giving so much. Surely soon their relationship would "shut off all others." Longing for affirmation as a woman, she struggled impatiently.

She had never held her tongue. Now she went on the verbal attack. Her handwriting shaky, she wrote: "Blair thought I had been harsh. Was in panic of losing & jealous." Yet even as she knew he did not see her as a sexual partner, she would not retreat: "Loved more than ever."

In late middle age Lillian Hellman suffered the masochism of a woman born in post-Victorian times. Lacking in the self-esteem she believed only beauty could have granted her, she allowed herself to be vulnerable to a man who was incapable of accepting so self-sufficient a woman. Remote as Hammett, Clark demonstrated to her that as a woman she did not measure up. She rebelled and she raged even as at some level she expected her men to have other women, as her father and Hammett had.

She became obsessed by Clark's involvements. "Had parted from Mrs. X after eve with Mrs. K. on the basis of what he felt," she recorded, "but now had new appointment with Mme. X and had written letter. Had told Mme. that I had made things possible short of total possession of her." So he used their friendship to hold other women at a distance even as he was not giving himself to her. One night at his town house the telephone rang. It was Mme. X, Lily knew. She was "mad."

Another day she decided he had "edited the story of his meeting with Mrs. K." She dispensed advice. "No further eves such as Mrs. K. could happen—respect had to be paid," she told Clark. Meanwhile he must "tell Mrs. S. she was monster." Her rivals, she proclaimed, "were bitchy." Alone, she gave way to greater honesty. No, she wrote, "cord running through was they all wanted him more than he wanted them," like her.

He kept her dangling, as Hammett had. He revealed he was not truly available to the other women because "his feeling for me had stood in the way." She allowed herself to believe that their relationship prevented him from truly caring for Mrs. P. or Mme. X or Mrs. K. or Mrs. S. He told her she was "the most important person in his life." "That was what she had been for Hammett," she wrote in her diary, "and what she really wanted more than anything else, and got." He would be Hammett's successor.

To Clark, she recounted the more flamboyant episodes with Hammett. She had thrown things at him when he was drunk. Yet even as she admitted she wanted to own Hammett, she credited him with her success: if Hammett hadn't made me sit down and write *The Children's Hour,* it wouldn't have happened, she said. When Clark told her he wasn't interested in her and Hammett, she stopped.

The sexual rejection was like a running sore. They referred to it as their "famous secret," a dilemma they discussed at length. She admitted there was no law that said someone had to sleep with someone else. He still believed their friendship would vanish. She urged him to visit her psychiatrist, George Gero, to break down the sexual barrier between them, and he went, once, to no avail. She simply did not appeal to him in this way. Meanwhile they met nearly every day, talked on the telephone, presented themselves to the world as lovers. At dinner parties she sat on his lap and talked baby talk. "How I would love to make love to Blair in that," she said as it rained one day on Martha's Vineyard.

As the years passed, she persisted, admitting to her secretary, Rita Wade, that her goal was marriage. "I love you very much," she wrote Clark in April 1964 when he was in Paris for CBS. "And having written those words I realize how seldom I have ever written them before." No matter, on that trip he began another long involvement. Persisting in her self-deception, Lily was taken by surprise. Then it tortured her as Clark recounted how the woman's husband had discovered the affair, the turmoil. Only later did she tell him that conversation was one of the most painful experiences of her life.

She tried to make him jealous with Harvard chemistry professor William Doering, with Philip Rahv. For a while things got "quieter," with "the shoe more on the other foot." It was a Pyrrhic victory. "You and I are in a kind of limbo," she soon wrote, "between a past I do not want and a future I do not know."

The blacklist behind her, she went to Hollywood in 1964 to write *The Chase* for Sam Spiegel, only to fall into "the longest and meanest depression of my life." In Los Angeles memories of Hammett surfaced. "I have very happy memories of it because of nice times with Dash, and the first times we had money, and books and days spent reading and drinking, and talking, and all I learned in those days because I was so anxious to learn," she wrote Clark. Meanwhile director Arthur Penn concluded she was "dysfunctional" and Horton Foote completed the film.

"You have become my life," she wrote Clark two years into their connection. "Maybe we've always been in a kind of suspension between what you call my delicacies, and I call your withdrawals." Obsessed, she wrote: "I love you very much, and miss you so hard that I can see you come in the door." In chaos, after a Bernstein dinner, she drunkenly disrupted the household with the accusation that Jacqueline Kennedy had walked off with her mink coat. The next morning she called Felicia. I "never *took* my mink coat to your party last night," she said, as if it were an accusation. There was no apology. "I hope you didn't ask Mrs. Kennedy to return the fur coat," Robbie Lantz told Felicia later.

Lillian couldn't bring herself to attend Arthur Cowan's funeral. "It took me a year to cry for Dash," she said, "and not much then, but this time I guess I was crying for myself." In her new version of the truth Cowan had "bought the Hammett copyrights for me when I couldn't afford to."

For years she pleaded with Clark. If only they could be together she would abandon "the pressures of the past." The other women didn't matter; she was "convinced that we are not at the mercy of other women—or other men." He was her life. When he was gone, she "felt in space . . . very sad without your sturdiness, without the possibility of laughing at some nice thing you've said."

She had always wanted Dash to write her poems. On Valentine's Day 1965, Clark wrote one dedicated to "Lilly Pie, Baby":

> *I love my Lillian*
> *What a gal is she.*
> *She's a real live woman*
> *She belongs to me . . .*
>
> *That is, she was my woman*
> *Till she tired of me*
> *But I broke her spirit*
> *Now she's still with me . . .*

That Christmas she headed for the island of St. John. "The last weeks have not been easy for us, alone or together, or with other people," she wrote. The sexual rejection continued to rankle until mischief in the form of a face-saving tale assuaged her ravaged spirit. For Blair Clark alone, Lillian concocted a story, "one thousand percent for him," she might have said. She was not the rejected woman whom no man wanted, but a normal one who had even borne a child—to her Yugoslav lover Srdja Prica. Now she was not only a mother but a grandmother.

Only on Clark did she bestow the extraordinary fabrication that she had given birth to a child in the late forties at the Yugoslav embassy in Paris, where "His Excellency," the name by which she referred to Prica, was ambassador to France. Details were abundant. It was a boy. She had taken him to Pleasantville, where he hunted turtles with Hammett. Hammett, of course, was not told the boy was her son. Prica visited, played with the boy, then took him back to Yugoslavia. He was educated at Cambridge, studied physics, married a Chinese girl; they had two children. Then he died of leukemia, at Massachusetts General. A woman could not be feminine without motherhood; Lily made herself a mother. She told the fable with such elaborate detail in tones of such conviction that Clark believed her.

Still she would not let go. When Clark told her the "Jackie-B. stuff had been over a year ago," her hopes were renewed. "Without you I will be diminished," she pleaded. Even without sex the relationship made her "happy and I thank you for it." They sat together at the Y listening to Norman Mailer, Irving Howe, Norman Podhoretz, and Steven Marcus discuss "politics and literature," and scribbled notes to each other about Valentine presents. "Is ten thousand dollars enough?" Clark joked about how much he planned to spend. "Too much," Lillian decreed. "A Clark new bracelet" soon joined her collection containing the "Clark other gold bracelet" and the "gold leaf Hammett pin" and an "18kt. gold cluster pin with 18 diamonds (Cowan)."

He was a liberal, and would manage Eugene McCarthy's 1968 campaign for the presidency. Keeping the works of Karl Marx prominent, she remained loyal to the politics she shared with Hammett. "I can't get it out of my head that Stalin was right," she said.

"You're a political idiot!" Clark told her at two in the morning at a house he had rented in the Hamptons. Lillian demanded a taxi and returned to New York. She went to Berlin in 1966 to see Brecht plays, still thinking of Clark. "You float above and around me awake and asleep and most of the time I have happy feelings of resting in security," she wrote, only to pull herself up short. "What a word to slip out! When have I ever used it?" Hammett had taught her never to expect security. Yet she longed for the romantic ideal.

She dreamed Gero told her to leave Clark, that if she felt better, she would find it easier to break with him. Awake, she chronicled more bad times. "*Très mal dans l'auto et après*," she wrote in her diary. Clark visited her on the Vineyard, quickly departed. "*Mal, mais triste*," she wrote in her schoolgirl French. She took her estrogen to maintain her vitality. "*Les Révélations?*" she wrote next to a dinner date with Clark at the Four Seasons. One night she vilified Mme. X, then threw Clark's rubbers into the street after him. "*Après demi-heure*," he had not telephoned. "Three ladies in two months," she wrote sadly. She didn't stand a chance.

In 1967 Blair Clark went to Salzburg to teach at the annual festival. "A little lone ceiling staring would do me good," he wrote Lily. "It's not a question of missing you," she wrote back. "It's as if a part of me got mislaid and I am bewildered without. Please love me because I love you."

They were "both dependent," he admitted. Knowing she was being "immodest," she tucked into a letter a description Henry Sigerist had written of how handsome she looked in a Roman toga at Hardscrabble Farm.

With Clark in Austria, she lunched with his mother at the Colony Club. "I had hoped you would want it," she wrote him. One of her teasing jokes involved his incestuous feelings toward his mother, a variation on the "everyone but me" theme of her life with Hammett. "Maybe I could sprinkle the weak soup with a little talk of incest," she threatened playfully before the event.

"Blair is very devoted to you," Mrs. Clark told her.

"And I to him," Lillian replied. "I love Blair."

"I know," his mother said. "You take care of each other."

She pictured herself as "being on a long line of ladies who wait for a letter," recapitulating again early rejection, the self-contempt of the enraged little girl who would never be pretty. She was writing her memoirs now, she confided to "Blairsie Pieburger," and her relationships with men were coming out "fake and foolish." There was a level at which she knew she had never loved a man for himself, but to satisfy her emotional agenda. As poet Pearl London was to observe, Lillian, narcissistically, wanted not a real relationship with a man, but homage, a man to be devoted to her. The better to compete with the beauties, she needed a tall, remote goy as a flattering appendage to her, a short, plain Jewish woman.

Jealous as ever, she teased Clark about one of her beautiful rivals, socialite Marietta Tree, who had praised his "high ideals." He was "the beautiful beloved of the beloved beauty, with her high ideals." To Diana Trilling, Lillian spoke spitefully of how awful it was that Tree was being unfaithful to her husband, no matter that Ronald Tree was openly homosexual.

She tortured herself with images of Clark "waltzing beautifully with three swooning ladies." Alas for Lillian, there were not "three swooning ladies," but one, a beautiful, blond young woman from Warsaw. In appearance she was all Lillian wished herself to have been, as Lillian had drawn herself for a volume of self-portraits. On the side of the page she wrote in self-mockery: "blonde curls, natural," and "deep blue eyes, natural": the nose on her caricature was turned up and short, with two dots for nostrils.

On her way to the Soviet Union, she flew to Paris to meet Clark. On the telephone she perceived a "sense of sharpness," a new distance. Over dinner she forced the issue. "When are we going to stop this and talk?"

she demanded when she could tolerate inane conversation no longer.

He had "fallen hard," Clark told her. This was worse even than Mme. Y. Reeling, Lily fell into "buzzy talk" of Dash, of William Doering, anything to save face. Once more Clark confided to Lily his romantic travails, the "panic" he had felt when the girl left Vienna. Worse, Mme. Y. had found photographs of this girl and they had fought. Then he had sex with Mme. Y. Lily felt as if the world had come crashing down around her.

Lily went shopping. Then she went to Moscow as planned, where she offered a toast before the Writers' Union on behalf of intellectuals who "seldom like to drop bombs and almost never wish to imprison men for speaking words they do not like . . . freedom is the essence of thought, the blood on the paper."

Even when Clark revealed he planned to marry the Polish woman he met at Salzburg, Lillian would not give him up. "I do not tell the truth when I say it is over," she admitted to herself, "and that is recognized—it is only lesser, less surprised masochism." Obstacles to the marriage calmed her. She watched for new competition. "English girl of last year," she wrote in her diary of Deborah Rogers, the literary agent with whom she suspected Clark had a fling.

"I want to find a way, an altered way, for us to keep each other forever," Lillian wrote Blair Clark now. "I hope with all my heart we will survive, not in a barren corner of memory but in full life, despite all others. I love you more than I can ever say. That has been one of the troubles. I cannot say the measure because I grew up in a generation that did not believe the words, but did believe the actions, and in between, maybe, depended upon angry or critical or teasing talk." That had been her mode with Hammett. It had "caused trouble" between her and Dash, she now admitted. Her love for him, Lillian told Blair Clark, "starts up at the sight of you and always will, I hope." Even if he married, they would retain what they had.

"We could never say goodbye," he told her gently.

Yet even now Lillian did not leave the field gracefully. Obstacles resurfaced. Lillian resumed her role as adviser, now with spite and concealed anger. The Polish woman had "ambitious motives," Lillian was convinced. She would be marrying Clark for his money. When he visited her on the Vineyard, she then accused him of injustice, of his "old fear that I stand in the way of marriage or permanent alliance," as of course she did.

By no means reconciled to his making his life with another woman, she said she was "sick, sad and puzzled." He was a man who would "go on leaving rooms with somebody somewhere, and I will go on resenting it with somebody somewhere, feeling snubbed and cheated, right or wrong." She accused him of fearing self-examination, one more trait he had in common with Hammett.

As after his last Thanksgiving she had extracted from Hammett an affirmation of what they had meant to each other, so now she wanted the same from Clark. "You and I have been deep in some kind of love for a long time," she wrote him. "We have been good and mostly kind to each other; there is an iron bond somewhere, not made of stinging little neuroses, but of whatever was the best of us both." It had been "everything," and yet "not enough." She acknowledged that it was "absolutely understandable" that he should desire "another life." Proudly, she asserted, "And so do I." She hoped still for a man who would want her.

"I have accepted it with better grace than you are willing to credit me with," she added. She pleaded for a "solution" which "does not stand in your way, and is good for me, too." She would accept the other woman if only she could remain a dominant presence in his life.

Meanwhile as the marriage was delayed she kept up her old terms of endearment. He was "Blairsie," she was "Lilly-pie." From Guadeloupe, she wrote from the volcano: "If I teeter on the edge, your name will be my last word." He was "God or The Devil, and either frightens me." So she pictured herself as helpless, overwhelmed, in need of rescue. From London she wrote: "A weary woman loves Blair Clark."

In 1969 he was on the Vineyard for her birthday: "Blair alone . . . Blair left . . . Blair arrived . . . Blair wrote . . . Blair called," she wrote. Only in 1971 did she grow close to writer Peter Feibleman, whose parents she had known in New Orleans, whom she first met when he was a child. Now her calendar could read: "Blair called me. Peter called me" (February 8), and "Blair called. I called Peter" (February 10).

In 1970 she sold her house on Eighty-second Street and purchased a co-op at 630 Park Avenue. Blair Clark wrote a recommendation to the building committee: "She is a lady of great distinction, as everyone knows, and of the finest character." A mock letter, never of course sent, called her "a shouter and a furniture smasher" who had been "turned down for membership in the Colony Club," which in fact had occurred, not for her "highly irregular habits (dopetaking, men at all hours, etc.)," as Clark pretended, but out of anti-Semitism.

Clark married the woman he loved at last. Lillian promised her farewell present would come "in a glass tube and be, as they say, a little dangerous." Despite all her protestations, she was deeply hurt. "My thanks for certain good minutes in the past; my hopes that you will have a decent future without me," she wrote, signing: "L. F. Hellman."

*　　　*　　　*

When the marriage faltered, she gave more advice, not meaning him well. And as she predicted, they did continue the kind of joking relationship, "teasing talk," she had recalled from her youth with Hammett, the only kind of relationship she could sustain. So in 1973 she wrote his horoscope, depicting him as a "handsome smiling baby, who sleeps with Jocasta, thinks it's his mother, but we know is not." His life ends in 1962 when he "meets Lillian Hellman, the Rebecca West of her day. Finale." He in turn wrote an imaginary paragraph into his former boss William Paley's memoirs, referring to Lillian: "I have always regretted that we couldn't make sweet music together. I would have been happy in those days to have played even second fiddle in the orchestra of Lillian's admirers."

Clark separated from his wife in 1979, and, despite a nasty custody battle, Lillian, like a child, complained that in his preoccupation he was rejecting her. Accusing Clark of not being "a good friend to me," she said his distance left her "in my present bad state with your making me feel unwanted and unloved." It was how Hammett had made her feel with his many chippies, and what her father had done. It was, of course, her view of Clark's earlier behavior as well.

Now she also accused him of "your anger against women like me." It was her independence, her self-sufficiency, those qualities with which Hammett too had been uneasy, which kept him at a distance. Clark, Lillian pointed out, was able to "stand a great deal from one kind of woman and almost nothing from another." So Hammett had been comfortable with Pat Neal and Ginny Bloomgarden and Helen Rosen, but not with her. Clark said he would have preferred to forget his own problems by identifying with a woman he loved who also had problems. But he could not.

Even her friends were not entirely sympathetic with this obsession as it stretched over the years. Clark had delivered to her the public illusion that she was having an affair with a handsome and distinguished man, not a bad bargain. "He's not Hammett; Hammett's dead, Lillian," another said. "You're trying to replace Hammett with an understudy."

"I looked up and here was a good-looking goy, upper class, a rich man, with the shadow of Hammett," she admitted. "Was Blair always this silly?" she finally asked Mike Nichols. The relationship allowed her to relive Hammett's sexual rejection, her old pain. Any man would have done.

Into the 1980s, her jealousy surged. A friend had reported Clark had been seen with a woman she didn't know. As if he was a husband, she confronted him angrily. It was, he defended himself, a mere "little adventure," with a woman for whom he felt nothing. Yet Lillian raged, releasing what he called her "accumulated resentment."

How did that "little adventure affect you and me?" he pleaded. "You talk of your 'nature' as if it were a chain around your neck dragging you down," he wrote in a letter he did not mail, "but somehow authorizing behavior which you would otherwise condemn." He reminded her that in 1962 he had told her it would be fatal to their friendship had they taken "the other course" and made love.

Now she remained "my dearest friend who has taught me so much." But as Lillian had never forgiven Hammett for betraying her with Laura Perelman, among other transgressions, so she never forgave Blair Clark. In her will she left him the highboy from *The Children's Hour,* which had stood in her bedroom. It was a reminder of Hammett, and a last cry of outrage at the sexual rejection in that room. As he had not been Hammett, so the highboy was a reproduction. Without a word, for he never criticized her to others, he offered the highboy to the woman with whom he had the "little adventure." Lillian also left Blair Clark any photographs of her he might choose, so that he might remember her.

A decade after Lillian Hellman's death, as he recalled how sick and frail she had been at the end, how she had required help for even the simplest physical acts, Blair Clark's eyes filled with tears. When it came to his feeling for Lillian, he was not remote. As she had been the most important person in Dashiell Hammett's life, so Blair Clark did love her. He had loved her from the start, and he loved her still.

PART NINE

Dash Said

27

Fabulations: The Memoirs

> "I've kept myself busy looking into other people's hearts so I wouldn't have to look into my own."
>
> THE AUTUMN GARDEN

> "I tried in these books to tell the truth."
>
> "ON READING AGAIN," THREE

> "It's no news that each of us has our reasons for pretending, denying, affirming what was there and never there."
>
> MAYBE

Whatever hopes she nurtured of a relationship with Blair Clark, Lillian knew full well that she was perceived as a woman alone. Soon after Hammett's death she began her project of creating a written and spoken legend of their relationship. Far from having been stranded in late middle age without a devoted and loving companion, she created the myth of herself as a woman who had been adored by the most brilliant, the most principled, the most sexually attractive of men, one who had suffered for his beliefs, one who had stoically resisted cant, self-pity, or any of the blandishments to which lesser men succumb. No matter the reality, the world must not find her wanting. From the ashes of her defeat, her failure wholly to possess this man, who hated lying, she chose in her depictions of their connection the psychic strategy of the lie.

Hammett appears in the memoirs and in her commentary to *Three*, her collected memoirs published in 1979, as a bitter opponent of all lying. He tells her "a lie is an annihilation of dignity," that "lies are boring." Retaliating, she accuses him, despite "all the past drinking and wild ladies, and foolish spending, and messy junk Bohemia," of being "a conventional man with rigid ideas of what is right and wrong." Her need to have lived a life other than the one she did overwhelmed her anxiety over his disapproval. In print she allowed him to voice his opposition to her fabricating even as she went on to do it.

In four volumes of memoirs, as in public interviews and private conversations, she conveyed the impression of a romance with Hammett charged with such vitality that it rendered pale and inadequate domestic arrangements which bore the legal imprimatur of marriage. She might be alone now, but she had a great love once, a love greater than any woman had known. With Hammett dead, Lillian chose to reinvent their life together. For the first time now she could openly speak of their love. He wasn't there to turn away, withhold himself, prefer others, or no one at all. He wasn't there to disapprove of the entire enterprise.

Her sentences often now began: "Dash said." More than once she declared, "I'm not brave. I just think about what Dash would have wanted me to do and then I just do it." Lillian's telling their story in her memoirs, Hammett's daughter Jo thought, made a comic strip of their relationship. When Lillian asked Jo to cooperate with Alvin Sargent on the Hammett-Hellman Warner Brothers screenplay, she told her misleadingly that it was a dramatization of her memoirs, not of their relationship. "He wouldn't want their story told," Jo believed. "He would have throttled her if she had done it in his lifetime."

Hammett became the companion in death he had not been in life. It was at last a way of making him hers. She spoke as if they had lived together as man and wife at Hardscrabble Farm, which had not been so. She needed, her close friend critic Richard Poirier thought, to have on the record a deep human attachment, one essential to her imagination of herself. In fact, of course, for years before his final illness they had gone their separate ways.

After his death she read his unfinished autobiographical novel "Tulip," which is set at Hardscrabble Farm. Lily was "a little insulted" to discover he made no reference to her. "You call everybody honey," a girl who might be speaking for Lillian accurately accuses him in "Tulip." Hammett evades her, as he did anyone who offered any challenge to him whatsoever. "I used to call everybody darling," he retorts, "but now I think honey's more refined." There is a reference to "the daughter you liked so much," to which Hammett answers generously, "I liked both of my children." In fact, it was Jo he adored, to whom he once wrote, "I love you, darling, deeply and completely."

Now Lillian set out to make a very different record. She spoke so often of Hammett as the abiding presence in her life that Philip Rahv, increasingly disgusted, dubbed it "Tristan and Isolde." No matter, on her ancient Remington typewriter Lillian chronicled their unconventional yet magical relationship, first in *An Unfinished Woman* (1969), then in *Pentimento* (1973), in *Scoundrel Time* (1976), and finally in the fantastic "story" *Maybe* (1980).

Each was told in the language of the she-Hammett, hard-boiled, no-nonsense prose with a voice moral in origin, authoritative in tone. "Tell her I like what money buys, but I don't like handling it, and won't, and that's that," Hammett says in *An Unfinished Woman*. "I refuse to preside over violations against myself, and to hell with justice," says Lillian, imitating Hammett. Writers should steal from each other, she had told her Harvard class. In her memoirs, she admitted to her friend Richard de Combray, she stole her style from Hammett. As she worked on that first memoir, she knew it was "a strange book, full of holes."

On publication she supervised the party list, orchestrating a grand social event at the Four Seasons restaurant. The guests included Blair Clark, William Doering, the Marcuses, Richard Goodwin, Kay Graham, John Hersey, Mr. and Mrs. Aristotle Onassis. There was a list of those who received autographed copies of the book: Edmund Wilson, Fred Gardner, Leonard Bernstein, Mrs. Aristotle Onassis, the Herseys, Mrs. Marshall Field, George Gero, Kober, Loftus, Mr. Bay, William Alfred, Norman Mailer, and those whose copies were not autographed, such as St. Clair McKelway.

The glittering party for *Pentimento* was held in October 1973 at "21." The guests were her circle: Warren Beatty, Mike Nichols, John Hersey, Jules Feiffer, Renata Adler, Blair Clark, Peter Feibleman, Albert Hackett, Robert Penn Warren, Harry Levin, McGeorge Bundy, Kingman Brewster, Ruth Field, Norman Mailer, Don Congdon, Robert Brustein, Senator Charles Goodell, George Gero, Steven Marcus. Forgetting for the moment the traumas over *Candide*, Leonard Bernstein embraced her. Lillian then stared straight into the eyes of photographer Martha Holmes. "If you keep photographing me, I'll leave," she said in her most severe tones.

Later Lillian requested a copy of the photograph Holmes took and mailed it to Bernstein. "I hope you will notice that I am leaning on you for support," Lillian wrote Bernstein, half in jest. "Where is the money?" The San Francisco reception for *Pentimento* was held at the elegant

Mark Hopkins. Little, Brown inaugurated the publication of *Scoundrel Time* in 1976 with a dinner at the Four Seasons.

That the reviewers of *An Unfinished Woman* bought the legend encouraged her to perpetuate it. "The love of her life was Dashiell Hammett," *The Atlantic* wrote, "he was generous, ironic, acute in his understanding of Lillian." In *Life,* V. S. Pritchett, whom she supported later with the help of her friend Max Palevsky, wrote that "her relationship with Hammett was a relationship of Puritan master and of recalcitrant but adoring pupil. She tried but unsuccessfully to shake his socialism and admits now she only did it to provoke." As she had told the Hacketts, nervous about their adaptation of *The Diary of Anne Frank,* "what you write will be true."

If many reviewers conspired in her project of immortalizing their love, her friends knew better. "There's not a word of truth in this," Louis Kronenberger said after reading *An Unfinished Woman.* Herman Shumlin echoed the sentiment. "She keeps building him up," S. J. Perelman noticed, "and promising wisdom that doesn't come forth." William Doering concluded, "Whenever you read anything that Lillian wrote you have to ask yourself to what extent it corresponds to any reality at all." It wasn't a good idea to speak such words in her presence. When Richard Wilbur remarked that her memoirs were in essence fiction, she became furious. "Maybe this all has something to do with why two former good friends don't see each other anymore," she told him.

She was an influential woman, a hostess of legendary parties, a charming friend one chose not to offend. Letters of adulation poured in. "If Hammett lives again," Bernard Malamud wrote her after the publication of *An Unfinished Woman,* "it is because you as an artist have recreated him." Jean Kerr decided that she probably "love[d] him because he was (maybe) the only man in the world who was more rigidly honest than you were." Hammett became a fictional character to whose quasi-biography others now contributed. "Are you aware," William Redfield, who had replaced Steven Hill as Montserrat, wrote her, "that Hammett used to visit my dressing room and just stand there and smile charmingly and never say anything—not even hello?"

In her life as in her prose, Lillian invoked him at every opportunity. Always the implication was that they had been perpetually together, he always at her side to offer wisdom, so that an irritated Gore Vidal couldn't resist asking whether anyone had actually ever seen them together. "He told the truth," Lillian said to Barbara Walters on a *Not for Women Only* show. "When I did something he didn't like, he said it very bluntly and very sharply and he didn't really give one damn whether I liked it or didn't like it."

Above all, he was always right about her. "Dashiell Hammett always said I was the only Jew he knew who was also a Puritan," she said. Now every aspect of her character was a consequence of her relationship with him. "Part of my anger used to be anger at Dash because he was such an un-angry man," she said. "Dash always said I had two bay horses in every play. I never tried to avoid repeating things," she revealed. The common denominator remained; he was always there. It was as if her validation as a human being depended on the ubiquitous role he played in her life as the man who had truly loved her.

Having appropriated him as her own, Lillian now became the final arbiter of Dashiell Hammett's likes and dislikes. "He very much disliked Arthur Miller," she insisted, although it was she who could not forgive Miller for being her rival on the American stage, as well as for his sexual rejection. She insisted Hammett disliked Dorothy Parker, although when he visited California in the late forties, he introduced Parker to Jo. Later he asked Jo her impressions of Dotty.

"She seems like someone who always walks around with a wet hanky," Jo replied. Dash became angry then, hardly the Parker adversary Lily made him in her memoirs.

"Dash would have liked you," Lillian told Poirier.

"Would I have liked him?" Poirier returned. Lily did not much like that. Nor would Norman Mailer succumb to the idolatry Lillian encouraged. "I had considerable respect for Dash," he wrote her in the late seventies, "but not because he would often refuse to face into knotty problems and would instead dismiss them by an exercise of his personal style."

But Lillian used Hammett as the measure of the value of other people. She told her brilliant Harvard student Fred Gardner that he reminded her of Hammett. When he listened to a baseball game on the radio instead of talking to her about one of his stories, that was like Hammett. Once she said, "Dashiell Hammett was the only other man that was rude to me in that way." How could she then not forgive young Gardner, who was only doing what Hammett had done?

Self-dramatizing, she spoke as if his ghost hovered about, interfering with her, endlessly caring, making the rules. So Lillian told Marilyn Berger, who interviewed her in 1979 for the five-part series for public television: "I'll find myself doing something and hearing a voice behind me telling me what to do, or make fun of me, or tease me and I'll get very angry about it, and actually have conversations with it."

*　　　*　　　*

Her politics, her apologies for Stalin, were about Dash too. In a cir-
cuitous piece of circumlocution and fabrication she told Peter Feibleman
she would not say she never joined the Communist Party, not because
she had joined, which she did, but because "I wouldn't want them to
think I got mad at Dash and finked out." When she visited the Soviet
Union the second time, in 1967, her old friend and translator Raya
Orlova asked her how Dashiell Hammett had reacted to the 1956 Twentieth Party Congress, the Khrushchev revelations of Stalin's iniquity.

"Raya, you always think that the world is revolving around your country. Nobody gives a damn about your Congress," Lillian snapped. Hammett had not criticized the Soviet Union even then; neither would she.
That readers might uncover the contradictions, as in her statement in *An
Unfinished Woman* that "Hammett and I had not shared the same convictions," was left for readers to ponder, if they dared. In *Scoundrel Time* Lillian Hellman never gets around to saying exactly what she and Hammett
did believe in the thirties and forties. It was as if, as Martin Peretz and
others have remarked, because they and their fellow Communists became
victims, that fact conferred virtue upon them and validated their politics.

As part of Hammett's omnipresence in her life, she endlessly
recounted how he had worked on her plays with her. She told Rose Styron, she told many, how as she finished a few pages of a play, she would
push them under his door and wait to find out whether he approved or
disapproved. On writing problems he was a seer, and she used his words
before the classes she taught at various universities. She told her 1966
Yale class they had gone on vacation to a Caribbean island (which they
never did) and she had talked so much about a story that he finally told
her to just shut up: "You've already solved the problem five times. If you
find a solution, will you for Christ's sake just use it." He dubbed "laziness" her unwillingness to reread anything after finishing it. When she
helped young Peter Feibleman with his novel *The Columbus Tree,* she
told him, "I'm not like Dash. I'm too easy."

Lillian did not, however, fabricate stories of the depth of their physical passion for each other, did not lie about the force of their sexual love.
Yet despite Hammett's sexual infidelity, Lillian suggested they had an
appetite for life, and an energy unmatched in other people's relationships
which was underlyingly sexual. In one scene in *An Unfinished Woman*
she bets him she can spit right in his eye if she so determines. Her prize
will be a set of "Jap prints," which is how World War II veteran Dash
would have described *ukiyoe.* When Lily succeeds, spits in his eye, Dash
is proud of the she-Hammett. "That's my girl," he says. "Some of the time
the kid kicks through."

* * *

Part of the fabrication involved the omission of crucial moments. The memoirs omit vast reaches of their life together. There is no reference to her having been pregnant with his child or that she had insisted that he get a divorce; we do not learn she aborted his child. She revealed the "secret" that Mary was not his child to Gregory Zilboorg, to Josephine Marshall, to Fred Gardner, to Steven Marcus, to his biographer Diane Johnson. But, as if he might strike her down from beyond, she never said so in print.

Most of the episodes Lillian invented are designed to demonstrate Hammett's deep attachment to her. Although the title *Pentimento* suggests the simultaneity of the imaginary or remembered life with the actual, in her depictions of her life with Dashiell Hammett, Lillian fictionalized, not because memory was ineffable, but because reality did not measure up. Or it required alteration, as in Lillian's transforming Hammett's discovering her with John Melby in 1945 into his disappearing and her discovering *him* ensconced in the apartment of some wayward socialite. Her memoirs are peppered with fabricated scenes between her and Hammett which never could have taken place.

In *An Unfinished Woman* Lillian placed herself, Hammett, Ernest Hemingway, and Gustav Regler, a former Communist, at the Stork Club in New York in 1939. Hemingway is sanctimonious, demanding of Hammett, "So you're against saving the intellectuals." Hammett replies, "I said there were other people in the world," a transposition of Lillian Hellman's peculiar and repeated insistence about the Nazi camps that others besides Jews perished. Hemingway then challenges Hammett to crush a tablespoon between the muscles of his upper and lower arm, which he has just done. Hammett refuses to play along, telling Hemingway, "Why don't you go back to bullying Fitzgerald? Too bad he doesn't know how good he is. The best." His parting line is "Why don't you go roll a hoop in the park?" Neither Regler nor Hemingway was in New York at the time.

In another invented episode, Lily and Dash, alone together at Hardscrabble Farm, solve the riddle of the turtle that wouldn't die. The turtle seems a symbol of their love, which survived even her abortion of their child. That Lillian invented the "Turtle" chapter of *Pentimento* may be discerned from the constantly rewritten dialogue in her drafts of the story. At first, when she grabs the poodle Salud's collar and throws him too hard against a rock, Hammett says, "Don't do that." Later she changes Hammett's response to "Hey, the turtle can't bite him." She replies, "I don't like killers." That becomes "How do you know?"

Hammett did help her with *The Autumn Garden*. Yet in her memoirs Lillian went on to describe their lives in 1950 in images from the time of

The Little Foxes. Once more he speaks as if by writing badly she has betrayed him; once more she is "shocked" and "pained." In *An Unfinished Woman* she depicts in a midwinter scene the two of them fighting and her storming back to New York. Before she departs, she tears up the play, puts "the scraps in a briefcase," and leaves the briefcase outside his door. In fact, it was not winter at Hardscrabble Farm as Hammett read that first draft of *The Autumn Garden,* since he spent January, February, and part of March that year in California. Nor could it have been the winter of 1951, since by then the play was almost finished; it opened in March 1951.

In fact, as Hammett read her first pages of *The Autumn Garden* on Martha's Vineyard, he was neither angry nor passionate, but complacent. In the middle of that July, far from having had "glaring" bouts with her, he had "seen none of it since the first few pages which were pretty good." Lillian wrote that she tore up the first draft of that manuscript, but Hammett biographer Richard Layman discovered at the University of Texas among her papers a revised typescript of *The Autumn Garden* marked by Lillian "first draft." It was not torn.

In each of the volumes of her memoirs, Lillian gave Dashiell Hammett a more active role in her life than he ever had, and both of them a level of domesticity which in fact had been rare. He did not accompany her to New Orleans early in 1950 to visit her aunt Hannah after the death of her aunt Jenny, as she wrote in *Pentimento.* He was in California working on *Detective Story.* Yet Lillian spins out the story, describing how Hannah had never met Hammett, how Lily "had not told her he was coming with me," and how nervous Lily herself was because she knew Hannah "had never, could never approve a relationship outside of marriage." Not surprisingly, the week turns "into a series of fine, gay dinners." Hannah and Hammett have in common their dislike of docile women who "were often ninnies with oatmeal in the head," Lily's own dislike of pretty women who need say nothing. "Ninnies are easier women to be unfaithful to," Hammett says, as Lillian Hellman implicitly exhibits pride in the trouble she made for Hammett on account of his infidelities. If he was unfaithful, she explains, her pride intact, she did not make it easy for him.

In the fraudulent autobiographical enterprise Lillian persistently returned to her common denominator: whenever she turned around, there he was. She even told Alvin Sargent, the cadence of her voice even with scrupulosity, as if she were recounting events rooted in historical reality, that in the fifties she and Hammett had lived for two years—all year round—on Martha's Vineyard. "We spent two years here," she confided, "two quite happy years, happier I think for him than for me because he was crazy about this kind of terrible weather."

The thread of truth remained: Hammett did enjoy wind and damp, as he had on the Aleutians. The lie was amplified. Lillian, hating the damp, departed during the second January, leaving Hammett with her housekeeper, Helen. So Lillian was able to erase from history those years when he lived in Katonah and was close to the Rosens, and she was left to fend for herself. So she used her imaginative enterprise to alter what her life had been, to deny that Hammett had been angry at her and had felt betrayed.

Often she maintained that their romantic connection continued long after it was gone. She even invented a fictitious letter from an imaginary woman Dash had known in Alaska and to whom he speaks words of love for Lillian he never spoke in their life together. This letter appears in the manuscript for her Introduction to *The Big Knockover,* and was deleted as, perhaps, too preposterous, for the final version.

The woman, unnamed, worked in a store in Fairbanks selling shoes to Russians, although Miriam Dickey, who knew everyone in Fairbanks then, is positive no such person existed. This woman, who supposedly met Hammett through someone named Marion, wrote to Lillian that "every time he got drunk he told the story" of how she wired him to meet her as she made her way to Russia that autumn of 1944. So threads of truth are woven into the fantasy, for this was accurate. Hammett laughingly told many people how Lillian sent a wire supposing that he could traverse thousands of miles of the Aleutian chain to meet her for a day in Fairbanks.

Then the fiction begins. "One night," Lillian has the woman write, "I made the touch and told all about why and in between I was nervous I guess and asked about you, saying you like Miss Hellman, don't you. Love her, what chance would anybody else have." Hammett remains silent, in character. The woman repeats: "You do love her, don't you?" Finally Hammett answers angrily: "Do I love my left arm? Do you think about your left arm?" It's a passionate declaration and one drawn from the story Jean Potter Chelnov told Lillian in the 1970s about how Hammett had once remarked to her that Lillian was his left hand and he was her right foot. In the imaginary letter Hammett makes the woman a large loan, as he had Chelnov. At the end of the fabricated story, he departs angry but quiet, saying, "I don't let people ask questions like that." The woman never saw him again. It was Lillian, after all, who was the constant in his life.

So from the fibers of history, his meeting Jean Potter Chelnov in Alaska, his making her a loan, his remarks about Lillian later in New York, she wove a more dramatic, more self-serving version of him and her. Hammett had told Chelnov that Lillian *was* his left hand; in the new version she added the word "love." She had waited by his deathbed for an assertion of his love for her; as it had not come, she created it, as she had written that last testament for him to sign on the day after the final Thanksgiving of his life.

Overwhelmingly, Lillian's fabrications are designed to demonstrate how much Hammett cared about her. In one story she told Alvin Sargent late in her life she had broken her leg and been forced to sleep downstairs, only to be enraged when Hammett goes off early to bed. Then she awakens at four in the morning to find him sitting beside her in a chair reading. "Lily," this Hammett says, "you're the greatest sucker for those who talk of anybody I know in the world. I went to bed to get an hour or two of sleep so I could sit up with you the rest of the night." It was a typical example, Lillian added, of his "un-showoffy care." The moral is clear; the feelings of the silent man run deepest.

The realities of their relationship during the McCarthy period above all required invention. There was fabricating to be done to justify Lillian's failure to appear by Dash's side in court in July 1951, her unwillingness to put up his bail money, and her panic and flight to Europe. So Lily invented that message supposedly delivered by his lawyer, and worded differently for *An Unfinished Woman* and for Hammett biographer Diane Johnson. "Tell Lily to go away. Tell her I don't need proof she loves me and don't want it," she wrote. It was a line drawn from *The Thin Man*. "I don't need proof," Nora says. In fact, it was Lily who needed proof, and invented it when it did not come. As always, fictions were sheathed in specificity. The message, Lillian wrote authoritatively, had been scrawled "on the back of an old envelope."

In life as in her memoirs she lied about that time. Hammett had been represented by two outstanding radical lawyers, Mary Kaufman and Victor Rabinowitz, until she fired them. But she told Alvin Sargent, "I called eleven radical liberal lawyers in New York City. No one would touch his case." In fact, not wanting a "radical" or Communist lawyer at all, she had hired Charles Haydon. She also insisted that she had tried to pawn her jewelry to raise $100,000 for bail money, a ludicrous figure, and then flown to the Vineyard, where Leo Huberman offered to mortgage his property.

To affirm Hammett's devotion, when she receives her HUAC subpoena, she has him taking "the next train" from Katonah. But this was April, and Hammett did not move to Katonah until the following October. Uneasy about having taken the Fifth Amendment, she also devoted considerable time to Hammett's evoking images of rats in jail, as if it were his choice that she do anything to avoid prison. It was his responsibility that her position, taking the Fifth Amendment, was something less than heroic.

"I don't give a damn what Mr. Fortas thinks," Dash supposedly says. "I do give a damn that you are ass enough to believe that those stinkers are going to pay attention to your high class morals." It was he who feared the "rats in jail, and tough dikes," he who feared the "food you can't eat and unless you do eat it they'll put you in solitary." She was headed for a "breakdown, if not worse." As if they were living together, she told Marilyn Berger, "every single night of his life I got a little talk about rats in jail." In fact, as Joseph Rauh, her lawyer, told one of her biographers, William Wright, "there was never the slightest danger of her going to jail . . . and Hellman knew it."

Where she felt guilty, and found her own behavior reprehensible, she reversed the truth. In that same scene where Dash expresses his fear for her, she tells him she will have to sell Hardscrabble Farm. The scene occurs a good six months after she had sold the place. "We made the decision," she writes, although in fact she made it alone, while he was in jail. She pictures herself wondering whether to subdivide the land, until Hammett tells her, "Let everybody else mess up the land. Why don't you and I leave it alone," as if they were a couple, making joint decisions. She wrote as well that he wanted to accompany her to Washington, but it was she who told him not to come. He is pictured back home eating a lamb chop, indeed his favorite.

Enlisting Hammett in a far more significant fabrication, she has him tell her she had once sat at a lunch table of sixteen or seventeen people with Martin Berkeley, the screenwriter who accused her and Hammett of appearing at a Communist cell meeting at his house. It was as if her not having been at that meeting, but having met Berkeley under other circumstances, demonstrated the falsity of the accusation that she had been a Communist. It was a piece of extraordinary sophistry, and one in which this time she enlisted her fictionalized Hammett. By the 1970s it was no longer dangerous, but clearly not fashionable to have been a Communist, and so Lillian wrote that she had not been.

After she testified, she wrote in Scoundrel Time, she "called Hammett and left a message I'd be home for dinner," again as if they were living together. She wrote in both An Unfinished Woman and Scoundrel Time that she feared for Hammett, although her behavior indicated fear for herself. That reality hovers near the surface in the episode in An Unfinished Woman in which "a few steps from Sixth Avenue"—always the concrete detail—Dash tells her, "Lilly, when we reach the corner you are going to make up your mind that I must go my way. You've been more than, more than, well, more than something-or-other good to me, but now I'm trouble and a nuisance to you. I won't ever blame you if you say goodbye to me now. But if you don't, then we must never have this conversation again."

The episode concludes with Hammett turning away, only for Lily to run and catch up with him. Set in 1953, the story is an exorcism for what she actually did, which was to go her own way. The clues are there: her habitual verbal tic, that something must never be spoken of again, and the physical act of running, which she never did.

To make her relationship with Hammett the defining one of her life, she wrote almost nothing about other men, not her former husband, Arthur Kober, not John Melby, let alone Stephen Greene. "I was married to that woman for seven years and she writes a book about her life and she gives me one line," Kober remarked. Stephen Greene winced to read that she had no one in Rome. Nor, years after he could have been in political jeopardy, does John Melby make an appearance in her autobiographical books. For Hammett to assume the dominant role in her life, others had to be erased.

In all the fabrications, of course, Hammett never emerges as anything less than a hero, as he does when, waiting for an elevator, he meets Roy Cohn.

"Well, Mr. Hammett, we meet again," Cohn remarks.

"I've never met you, Mr. Cohn," Hammett replies. When Cohn tries to enter the elevator, Hammett, in a gesture most unlike him, puts up his arm and says, "No, I don't want you in here, Mr. Cohn." The incident is purported to have occurred in the late fifties when Hammett was a dying man.

Hammett's abiding moral sense surfaces as well in another fabrication, this one set only a year before his death, when he was already mortally ill. Lillian presented it to author Peter Manso for his oral history of the life of Normal Mailer. It is January 1960, and in the aftermath of having stabbed his wife, Adele, Mailer is in Bellevue Hospital. From a phone booth, he calls Lillian, tells her he is broke, and asks her to bring him $5,000. Lillian then takes a "very large pin" of her mother's to a pawnshop on Fifty-seventh Street, where "I got $1,500 and got the other $3,500 from my bank account." Pawning her jewelry, indeed, figures in several fabrications.

Hammett is weak with emphysema and lung cancer, is drifting in and out of coherence. Yet when Lillian enters his room to say goodbye, and confesses her purpose, Hammett stops her.

"Lillian, you're not going to do any such thing," he supposedly says. "You're a sucker and often a goddamned fool, and you're not going out of this room." Weak as he is, Hammett drags himself out of bed, locks the door with a big brass key, puts the key in his robe, and gets back into bed. "You're just not going to meddle in this business," Hammett decrees.

"Now, take your hat and coat off and sit yourself down," Hammett orders. Lillian heads for the bed in an effort to obtain the key, but Hammett remains the dominant male. "I'm strong enough to break your arm if you try it," he tells her, tough guy to the end. The next day, Lillian told Manso, she had "a terrible fight with Dash, and I felt so hideously guilty about fighting with a man who was so sick that I literally ran from my apartment on 82nd Street up to 92nd Street to the psychiatrist. I was going to a psychiatrist in those days because I couldn't handle myself with Hammett, and he's the only other person who knows the full story."

Anticipating being exposed, she insists, as she did frequently with her fabrications, that there is an independent source to the story, George Gero, who did indeed practice on Ninety-second Street. But, as Rita Wade was to remark after watching Zoë Caldwell's Broadway performance as Lillian, Miss Hellman never ran, never, not a day in her life. In many fabrications Lillian mischievously added just such a clue for those who knew her best, an admission that a story was invented. The need to tell the truth, to expose the truth about herself, was of course reflected as well in the guilt that surfaced intermittently over her handling of the Hammett earnings and the claims of Josephine and Mary.

Adding further mystery, Lillian told Peter Manso that a "very anti-Norman sentence" explained why Hammett was so adamant about her not going, but this she would never repeat. Lillian's story ends with her revealing that when she told Mailer the story, he denied ever having telephoned her. "Lillian," he supposedly said, "that is a totally invented story," to which she replied, "Norman, you know I don't lie well. You've just forgotten it." This, she insists, was a demonstration of "Norman's good nature and sweetness." Sometimes as she lied, indeed, she anticipated and incorporated into the fabrication her being found out, as if to the very end of her life she remained little Mary of The Children's Hour.

Although Lillian had insisted, "When I remember, I remember exactly. I don't fake about it," she had agreed to be interviewed by Manso only if she could review and edit the transcribed text. Immediately she changed the amount of money she was bringing Mailer from $5,000 to $500. She also altered Hammett's dialogue. Where she had him say, "You're just not going to meddle in this business," she wrote: "You're not going to give it to him." None of it rings true. (Although Mailer denies he ever called and asked her for money, Peter Manso insists that Mailer read the final manuscript of his book precisely to ferret out untruths, and yet did not object to Lillian's story.)

Mailer observes another pattern to Lillian's fabrications: didn't she also write that Frank Costello gave her $5,000, for Spain? "I think Lillian's tic may have been five thousand dollars," Mailer laughs. Hammett had "brought out the best in her." Once he was gone, all things were possible.

Considerable invention was also required in her depiction of Hammett's coming to live with her on Eighty-second Street. It was not "the last five years of his life," as she told Marilyn Berger. Hammett arrived in May 1958 and died in early January 1961. Nor did Lillian welcome the assignment. "You people haven't been any help to me at all," she had told Jo Marshall angrily.

Suspecting that Hammett had slept with Helen Rosen, she invented his telling her when Helen called to visit him, "Not only will I never see her again, but she's the dirtiest little piece I ever met." Sexual jealousy appears in the fabulations of the last years of her life. So obsessed was Lillian with Helen Rosen that in an interview with Alvin Sargent she extended the story. She was walking down Madison Avenue a year before Hammett's death, only for the Rosens to hail her from their car. Helen calls out, "Lillian, you must solve for me why Hammett doesn't want to see me."

"All right," Lillian says. "I'll tell you why. You did a very dirty little job on me. You didn't tell him the truth, and you should have known this was not a man you lie to. You went around saying he lived on your charity and you knew it was a lie because you knew I gave you seventy-five dollars every single month. It's all right for you to cheat the government. But it's not all right for you to make him a charity case because you know the pride of this man and it's a terrible thing to have done to anybody!" Again there was the thread of truth: Lillian and Helen had agreed that no one would know Hammett was paying rent; Lillian had been upset when a Rosen acquaintance blurted out at a dinner party the truth that he was paying rent.

In the story, Lillian adds that she didn't go to Sam Rosen's funeral because "Dash wouldn't have liked it," as great a distortion of his character as the line calling Helen "a dirty little piece." When sexuality was involved, Lillian made Hammett a harsher person than he had been. But he had done the unforgivable, had not loved her enough. It was Lillian, of course, whom Hammett accused of making him feel like a charity case.

To confound the reader, to confound herself, there are also true moments in these memoirs and in her interviews. "Hammett guessed it once," she told playwright Marsha Norman, admitting she was a "total coward." Even more telling was the moment in *Pentimento* when Lillian supposedly goes out late at night in Cambridge to stand in front of the seedy nursing home Hammett was to have inhabited. When she returns home, her housekeeper, Helen, chides her: "Maybe he don't want to come back, and maybe you don't."

Until the last year of her life she continued to fuel the Hammett-Hellman legend. In her interview with Norman, Dash is again omnipresent. "I once had a beau who went to Hammett for advice," she confided. "This particular beau wanted to marry me for money, of course, but can you imagine going to Dash for advice?" There could be only one answer. Even in her fantasy the masochism she acknowledged in her letter to Blair Clark surfaces; Lily is loved not for herself, but for her money.

Lily's suitor tells Hammett he is disturbed that Lillian "seems to leave the room every now and then." He wonders what to do. Hammett advises: "If I were you I would do nothing. If she's thinking anything at all, it's not very profound. Maybe she's thinking how to move the sofa up against the chair. The only other thing it could be is she's trying hard to find out how to leave you." The story is absurd, as Hammett stepped away always from Lily's romances. Now he intervened, keeping her free for himself.

In one of the last pieces Lillian wrote, the unpublished memoir-like story called "Meg," about one of her poodles, which was rejected by *Vanity Fair*, Hammett appears yet again as the purveyor of wisdom. He is there to stop her from entering the whelping box, there to take turns with her feeding puppies, there to save one of the puppies from its hostile mother. Hammett kicks Meg "very hard" and chases her out of the house. He hates this dog, as in reality he hated poor Gaby, the dog who had loved him so much. "An Indian once tried to kill me outside of Sioux City and I could've easily killed him," says this mythological Hammett. "But there was no temptation. I must tell you I have a great temptation to kill Meg."

"When you hate, you hate; when you love, you love," the Hammett of "Meg" tells Lillian. "The wear and tear must be terrible." He knew her and was forever there to approve or disapprove. "Meg," set in 1951, ends with Hammett's return to New York to await the FBI's subpoena, the moment of the moral break they would never make right.

The "uncontrollable" little girl, that "rebel" and "nuisance" and "cut-up," remained into her seventies a woman with the same "childish nature" she had observed in herself when she was a very young woman. Feeling, as she had when she was a spoiled child, that she never had enough of what she craved, starting with love, in her memoirs she set out symbolically to offer herself what life had denied. In her memoirs, as in her life, she behaved as if she had suffered so profound a betrayal that she was justified in behaving without restraint, still the little girl for whom no one had ever set any limits.

Inventing her autobiography, in old age she remained that little girl doubly betrayed: by her father, who had first preferred her mother and then his chippies, and by her mother, who had not been woman enough to hold Max. It had been Julia who defined Lily's fate: that of being a woman whom men abandoned.

In four volumes of memoirs Lillian Hellman supplied to herself what she had been denied: a lifelong emotional attachment with a man, not the actual one she had with Hammett, but one more romantic. She would not be outdone by women who had secured the unending devotion of their men. With her connection to Dashiell Hammett, the fabulating was finally unnecessary. The relationship they had, while far from being a made-in-Hollywood paradigm of conventional domesticity, had for many years been strong; she had been his closest friend. But, in her writing as in her consciousness, Lily remained a conventional woman, as she had accused Dash of being a conventional man.

The realities of her relationship with Hammett were not, in the eyes of the commonplace world, validating. Nor had Lillian Hellman ever resolved the contradiction between her having become an independent, achieving, self-sufficient woman and her need to be protected, vulnerable, and adored by a man whose chilly Anglo-Saxon repression fed her lifelong masochism. So to the end she subscribed to the culture's demeaning view of women she had in her life long ago transcended. She presented herself as the small weak woman who required nurture from a protective male.

The fantasy of her relationship with Hammett pays homage to middle-class respectability, a value he did not share with her. It relies on convention. Hammett rises from his sickbed to protect her—a weak-minded woman—from her own worst impulses. He is more macho than Hemingway. He sends her to London to retrieve the body of the fictional Julia.

Her plays appealed to a middle-class audience and to the common taste. Her memoirs rewrote her life in an effort to do the same. Hammett emerges as sexy and tough, but only superficially unconventional. He is not a Communist. Mildly, he shocks the bourgeoisie. It was as if Lillian, the "unfinished woman," did not trust the life she had made, just as she was never to forgive Hammett for refusing to allow her wholly to possess him as a clinging wife might do.

The one truth she could not face, the one which might have comforted her, was that Hammett, for all his recalcitrance, remained deeply dependent on her. As she continued to believe, long after it was so, that she needed him to read and edit her work, it was she who nurtured him, taking charge of his financial life as of his physical well-being. For years, as he acknowledged, his emotional stability seemed possible only at Hardscrabble Farm.

Lillian did admit to Marilyn Berger that she had realized Hammett was "very dependent upon me, but equally capable of walking out at any minute of the day and night and not returning." It was simply not enough. She said also that Hammett had allowed her to believe she needed him more than he did her and so sold her "a bill of goods." This was not so. From 1942 on Hammett consistently told her she no longer needed his advice as a writer.

In her memoirs Lillian also awarded herself heroism on other fronts: in Russia, in Spain, in Nazi Germany. Let art substitute for life literally, she declares implicitly. The inventions were presented as gospel with an air of conviction, her self-confident tone one more act of defiance. Let history sort it out, Hellman dared, as she interwove fantasy with reality. Literary history, she wagered, would have no choice but to take her word. Out of psychic pain never resolved, not by Zilboorg, by Gero, by anyone, she embellished her joke on the world. To the end she remained the same fierce competitor whose greed for worldly success was boundless. Yet the lies suggest some unconscious doubt about the authenticity of her achievement as a playwright, as if it had all been undeserved, a fraud no less than the fables she now concocted.

As were most of her plays, the memoirs were enormously popular. Some perceived the inventions and viewed them as the imaginings of art. Others objected, however, to a falseness of tone. Clive James accused her of a "garrulous pseudo-taciturnity," and many agreed that her attempts at hard-boiled prose were arch and mannered, "a solid course of bastardized Hemingwayese," the "Hem-Dash dialogue" indeed "of a windiness," as James put it. But enough of the interstices of the story had been true for the enterprise to succeed nicely: she did go to Spain and to Russia; she did testify before HUAC, writing that line about refusing to cut her conscience.

Rarely would Lillian Hellman admit that any of the events in her memoirs had been invented. But one day, sitting on her living-room sofa, she opened one of her memoirs to a page describing her relationship with Hammett. An old lady now, Lily pointed to the text and told Richard Poirier, "That's all a lie." Most of the time she recounted the anecdotes written into her memoirs to friends as if they had actually taken place. It was crucial to her that other people believe that he had loved her. And yet she needn't have lied. He did.

Lillian Hellman was a woman rich in personality, with an acute intelligence, a ready wit. She knew how to savor life: cooking, gardening, entertaining, travel. As a playwright, she made her mark on her era. She had many devoted friends willing, as Norman Mailer put it, to forgive "the bad Lillian." Poirier says "she was tremendous fun and generous and spirited and deeply intelligent and loyal, was one of the nicest innocent people I've ever known."

Yet she who outwardly believed in moral integrity went on to sabotage her own. Out of the insecurity inflicted on little girls in this culture, she remained rooted in the view that a woman's looks contain her value; her weakness and vulnerability make her lovable. The pain she felt over those looks often made her unable to want a man at all.

After his death, angry at Hammett for his deathbed silence, she dwelled on what she considered his disloyalties, like a child forgetting her own. Bill Doering, who met her a year after Dash died, concluded that she hadn't liked Hammett very much at all. As she had made her Faustian bargain, the memoirs compensated for Hammett's failings by rewriting their common history.

"Your love affair with Dashiell Hammett sounds so wonderful, Lillian," Carol Matthau told her one day. "It must have been terrific."

"It was terrific in some ways, I suppose," Lillian, in an honest mood, granted. This, however, was not what Matthau, representing Lillian's audience, wanted to hear.

"It was so romantic!" she said. Lillian looked at her hard then.

"It does sound romantic, doesn't it?" she agreed. "That's the fun of being a writer. That's what writing is for."

Lillian Hellman at home.

Lillian at Hardscrabble Farm:
(*left*) "You mean you did that outside? It's disgusting!"
(*below*) She kept cows and killed their calves for the meat, savoring the livers.

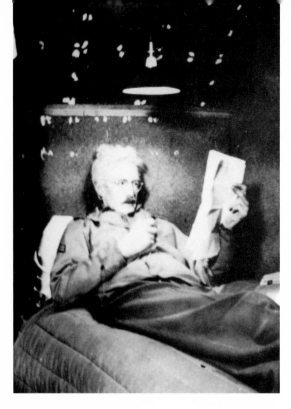

Dash in the Aleutians: "I tell you, sister, the gentry can be trusted to save our world." (*Photography Collections, Humanities Research Center, University of Texas*)

Dash in the Aleutians, 1944: for his birthday tribute his Adakian staff listed as his most famous work, written when he was seventeen, "The Gefulte Fish." (*Photography Collections, Humanities Research Center, University of Texas*)

Lillian Hellman painted by Luis Quintanilla:
"You are to have Luis Quintanilla paint you for me.
I have spoken." (*Courtesy of Peter Feibleman*)

Lillian at Dzerazhinsky
Children's Hospital, Moscow
December 15, 1944.

Lillian in London,
February 1945: "The deep
reverence & respect that even
intellectuals have for Stalin."

John Melby: "I am in
love with you and
always will be."

Dash in California for the wedding of Josephine, 1948. He was sober as he walked Jo down the aisle. (*Photography Collections, Humanities Research Center, University of Texas*)

Augustus Goetz, Willie Wyler, and Ruth Goetz on the set of *The Heiress*, 1949. Dash telephoned Gus and Ruth Goetz out in California.... (*Courtesy of Judith Firth Sanger*)

Dash's lawyer, Mary Kaufman: Through the bars, Hammett reached out and patted Mary on the shoulder. (*Courtesy of the late Mary Kaufman*)

Dash and Lily, c. 1950. John Zilboorg, the son of Gregory and Margaret Zilboorg, is in Lily's lap. Dash entertains Button Kuhn, the son of Parker Kuhn: "This is a love letter because I say it is." (*Courtesy of Margaret Zilboorg*)

Painter Stephen Greene in Rome in 1953 in a white silk dressing gown from Gucci's that Lillian said she had bought for herself. "I got it for me and it doesn't fit me." (*Courtesy of Stephen Greene*)

Lillian in Rome in 1953 in a photograph she sent Blair Clark eight years later: "This comes with love that I didn't feel when this picture was taken only because it was a year before I knew you...." (*Courtesy of Blair Clark*)

Lillian at middle age: "Does he think of me?"

Dash at Katonah with Judy Rosen Ruben's baby, David: Judy Ruben was afraid to leave her baby with Dash for fear the baby would kick him and break an arm." *(Courtesy of Judy Ruben)*

Farley Granger, Shelley Winters, Lillian, Arthur W. A. Cowan. "To whom was he showing off? Was it about power over the woman?" *(Courtesy of Marilyn Raab)*

Dash on the Vineyard, c. 1960:
"Who the devil do you mean?"
(*Courtesy of Josephine Marshall*)

Lily on the Vineyard
at the Mill House:
"There are social
standards!"

Charlee Wilbur with Dash: "Tell Dash
I love him only for his BODY." (*Photography
Collections, Humanities Research Center, University of Texas*)

Jo and Lloyd Marshall and their children visit
Lily and Dash on the Vineyard, summer
1960: "You know your father's dying...."
(below) Baby Ann is to Lillian's left:
"I've been with her so long I don't know
what to think of her anymore."
(Courtesy of Josephine Marshall)

"Dashiell Hammett Is Dead":
(*Photography Collections, Humanities
Research Center, University of Texas*)

Left to right,
Joe McQuaid,
Blair Clark,
B. J. McQuaid,
putting out the
New Hampshire
Sunday News:
"I love you very
much, and miss
you so hard that I
can see you come
in the door."
*(Courtesy of
Blair Clark)*

Blair Clark: "Blair? Did not call."
"You have become my life."

Scrabble on the Vineyard.

Lillian photographed by
Richard de Combray:
"I think you look like a whore."
(*Courtesy of Richard de Combray*)

Lillian on the Vineyard: "Who wants to peek!"

Lillian with Leonard Bernstein at the party for *Pentimento* at "21": "If you keep photographing me, I'll leave!" (*Photograph by Martha Holmes,* Time *magazine*)

Lillian with Chinese guests. John Hersey is at far right: "Dear Lillian, you are a finished woman, now."

Lillian Hellman with Peter Feibleman in Egypt, 1976: nearly blind, she points to a detail she cannot possibly see.

Lillian with
Richard de Combray
"I wish I looked like
you." (*Courtesy of
Richard de Combray*)

Lillian with Dr. Jonathan La Pook: "Leave
it to the Jews to steal the songs of the
Negroes!" (*Courtesy of Jonathan La Pook*)

Lillian at work on
the Vineyard.

Lillian with Milton Wexler: "Anybody who has a head that cannot be bought even in a ten cent store must and should have some kind of permanent sadness."

Lillian with Kay Boyle (*left*) and her friend, professor and critic Richard Poirier, at Rutgers conference on women in the arts in the twenties, 1979: "Should I have a facelift?"

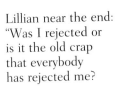

Lillian near the end:
"Was I rejected or
is it the old crap
that everybody
has rejected me?

Miss Hellman at War

2 8

Biographical Warfare:
The Hammett Biographers

"In the end, you can't stop biographies, and maybe the best thing is to leave as little as possible. I hope I can bring myself to destroy all of it."

LILLIAN HELLMAN

"I do not want my ex-beau played around with in this fashion."

LILLIAN HELLMAN

She had invented their relationship, erased the reality to substitute imaginary events occurring at times when he was elsewhere in places he had not been. In the process she created a new persona for herself, the moll to her sexy tough-guy lover. When biographers turned up shortly after Dashiell Hammett's death, they became Lillian's natural enemies. Hammett's biographers threatened to undermine the entire edifice of what she had asserted they had been for each other. Yet, although she could gain script approval from Warners, biographers were not easily controllable. Passivity was never her mode. Lillian would not sit back as biographers, scrutinizing her memoirs and researching Hammett's life, rendered her a liar.

Both Lily and Dash abhorred the idea of others writing about them.

In their early days, she had questioned him about his past until he could take no more.

"I want to get everything straight for the days after your death when I'll write your biography," she defended herself.

"You're not to bother writing my biography," he answered, as Lillian relates in her Introduction to *The Big Knockover,* "because it will turn out to be the history of Lillian Hellman with an occasional reference to a friend called Hammett." Whether he feared her habitual lying might come into it, she does not reveal.

Hammett wanted neither Lillian nor anyone else to define him. When Pru Whitfield threatened to write a memoir of their friendship, gently he discouraged her. He "would prefer that you did not write a book about you and me," he told her, "just paint a picture of it or something."

When Hammett died in 1961 and biographers appeared, Lily did her best to swat them away. She termed it her "moral obligation" to deny them her help. If in 1965 she had decided she was "going to have to forget what he wanted" and reprint the stories, including a long biographical introduction of her own, she remained determined to thwart any and all strangers and interlopers.

Biography, Lily told William Maxwell in her best Hammettese, was "a sort of modern racket: a man dies and a publisher immediately subsidizes the biggest researcher he can find, or the biggest magazine hack, to do a biography which will be closest to what he thinks the public taste is that year." There were "serious biographers, but not many." She doubted whether "anybody's life shows us much about their work."

In a 1974 review she wrote for the New York *Times* of the letters of H. G. Wells and Rebecca West, she remained vehement in her opposition to biography. "It is not to my taste to make available the revealing letters of a lover," she wrote, "and I refuse right now to read those protests from academics and Docs and post-Docs who believe in the preservation of all material about the famous. To hell with what can only come down to who slept with whom, when and how." Already she had requested that John Melby return the letters she wrote to him, in exchange for his to her. She vowed to destroy them all. Hammett had never saved anything, which was to the good.

At first she believed that her refusals to cooperate with Hammett biographers would solve the problem. Random House editor Joe Fox consulted her about giving William Nolan permission to quote from Hammett's books. "Under no circumstances," she told Nolan, would she "turn over Hammett's letters or private papers." Meanwhile Don Congdon must require a fee from all scholars quoting from Hammett's works: "Never mind the good of society." She might yet frighten them all away.

In 1973 a British writer named Jonathan Green approached her; she told him she had "several times before refused such offers and therefore the books were not published." Moreover, it was "ill-advised that a biography of so American a character as Hammett be written by an Englishman who is too young to know the background."

She herself had stimulated the Hammett revival and the requests kept coming. In 1974, Otto Penzler, later a leading publisher of mysteries, sent Lillian a copy of his entry about Hammett for the *Encyclopedia of Mystery and Detection*. Lillian wanted a distinction drawn between Hammett's "leaving" his wife and children and "separating from them," as she sought to protect his reputation no less than their legend. Penzler also had written that Hammett was "working with his mistress on her plays." Lillian underlined the word "mistress" and put a question mark in the margin. She also bracketed the line: "A great deal about Communism worried him."

One morning Penzler received a telephone call from an angry Lillian Hellman. His article bore "no relation to the truth," she told him. She would sue him if he printed it as it was. "I was never his mistress," she said. "I object to the word mistress."

"What was your relation to him?" Penzler had the temerity to ask, blind to the pejorative.

"It's none of your business," Lillian replied, exasperated. Penzler changed the line to "began a love affair that lasted until his death three decades later." She was, she wrote him later, "the only person on earth who has any true knowledge of Hammett." This would be her stance ever after.

Before Lillian could catch her breath, a professor from the University of Cincinnati named William Godshalk declared himself a Hammett biographer. At first Knopf granted him permission to quote from the five Hammett novels they had published, and he began. Hammett's San Francisco admirers, like novelist Joe Gores, who was completing his novel about Hammett, tried to help. The publisher would be Twayne, whose academic nature destined Godshalk's biography for scant distribution.

Lillian knew now that she must seize the offensive. She decided to appoint her own Hammett biographer. Her choice was a friend, critic Steven Marcus, a Columbia professor and protégé of Lionel Trilling. Marcus would both edit a *Continental Op* collection and write the biography. The contract, drawn between Lillian, Random House, and Marcus, was signed in March 1974, with the *Op* Introduction due in August. The Hammett biography would be due on April 1, 1977. Marcus had three years. In the contract it was described as "Untitled Biography of Dashiell Hammett and Lillian Hellman."

Trilling warned Marcus that he would have absolutely no independence. But Marcus signed an agreement with Lillian granting her a "right of exclusion." If she believed that any material should not be included, the decision rested with her. So she would control the facts of what had occurred between her and Hammett. Marcus would have "complete and unlimited access to all relevant documents and information in her possession." At the end she would review the manuscript and destroy all the material she excluded, preserving no copies.

Lillian gave Marcus a huge stack of letters from Hammett to her and allowed him to tape her on the terrace at Martha's Vineyard and by her account also at the Vineyard Haven Yacht Club. She seemed to have solved her problem. Now she wrote Jo that she should feel "perfectly safe" in talking with Marcus, "since I will have the final approval of the book." It was, Lillian said, "the first time I would trust anybody to write about your father, and I assure you that whatever you tell him will be used with the greatest discretion." She admitted she had "been squashing all other books." Hiring Marcus, she said, was her "way of keeping them squashed."

Meanwhile in San Francisco, Joe Gores informed Godshalk that "a friend of la Hellman's" was working on a Hammett book and garnering the cooperation of Knopf, which Godshalk was now being denied at Hellman's request. The Hammett San Francisco–based coterie believed that Lillian Hellman was responsible for Hammett's having stopped writing, that she had destroyed his career and damaged his life.

An inexperienced biographer, Godshalk wrote to Bill Nolan, who, despite Lillian's opposition, had published his *Dashiell Hammett: A Casebook* in 1969, and to Marcus suggesting that they exchange information. When Marcus politely declined ("there are certain matters and documents which I could not possibly release"), Godshalk sought sympathy from Gores and wrote petulantly to Marcus about adversary parties and enemy clubs. The Hammett cult had immediately concluded that if Marcus had Hellman's cooperation, he must be wrong for the job. His book was destined to be flawed.

Recognizing that he could not handle the research, Marcus then hired San Francisco detective David Fechheimer to penetrate the secrets of Hammett's life from his Pinkerton exploits to the complexities of his relationship with the Veterans Administration. In 1975 he contributed to the special issue of *City* magazine devoted to Hammett, which featured an interview with Mary Hammett, now Miller, and Jose Hammett conducted by Fechheimer and a fellow detective.

As soon as Lillian discovered that Mary had consented to the interview, she wrote a chastising letter. "I never said that the young men who called upon you about Dash were O.K.," she wrote. "The only person I ever said was O.K. was Steven Marcus." As her control of the Hammett biographical enterprise seemed threatened, Lillian now had advice for Mary. "It would be very unwise, at this point," she wrote, "for you to be quoted again about your father; you must take great care to see that your mother is not quoted, either." She told Mary she had "every intention of trying to stop various projects about your father." Mary's financial circumstances made her heed Lillian's warning.

Meanwhile Fechheimer sent one of his operatives, a former university professor named Josiah Thompson, who had written a book about the John Kennedy assassination, to Baltimore to unravel the threads of Hammett's early life. By 1976, Fechheimer was sharing his material with Godshalk. Fechheimer also had a man checking on Hammett's divorce records in Nogales (he found nothing) and was on the trail of the VA records. That summer of 1976, Bill Nolan, Joe Gores, and David Fechheimer shared a Berkeley platform discussing Dashiell Hammett.

Marcus began with a chapter on Hammett's court appearance. It took him a year. Lillian sent corrections. To Marcus' statement that the Civil Rights Congress supplied bail money for Communists, she added "not only." Hammett's biographers must do as she did, obfuscate about Dashiell Hammett's relationship to the Communist Party. Another of her corrections was that Leo Huberman "was not a fellow traveler." Although her implication is that he was not a Communist either, the reverse might well have been true.

Marcus next wrote a chapter about Hammett in prison. Lillian read it with some irritation. "The reason must be given why I did not go to Ashland to meet Hammett," she told Marcus, uneasy with her vulnerability on this matter. Her lawyer had told her not to be there, Lillian insisted. But now she had a deeper quarrel with Marcus.

"Where am I in all this?" she demanded. So far Marcus had granted her only a peripheral role in Hammett's life. Three and a half years had passed, and there were only these two chapters. Exasperated, Lillian complained to editor Jason Epstein.

In addition to Godshalk, other interlopers had appeared, including one James Nashold. "The publisher did not accept the idea of a biographer who is not known to him or me," she wrote, "so I am afraid, for the minute, you will have to drop the project." She dispatched a documentary filmmaker named Peter Packer; Jo wrote Packer that "under no circumstances will my mother grant you an interview or consent to use of material regarding her in a movie script about my father, Dashiell Hammett." Then, just as the Packer problem was resolved with a legal threat, Lillian learned that Fechheimer himself was planning to write his own book. At once Lillian wrote that Jo must be "absolutely sure" neither Jose nor Mary would speak again to him.

Lillian's relationship with Steven Marcus ended badly. Three years is an unreasonably short deadline for a biography, and most publishers agree to extend such contracts. Random House, succumbing to Lillian's pressure, and uneasy that she had ended her cooperation, chose not to do so. In April 1978, a year after his book was due, Random House attorney J. J. Sheehan wrote to Marcus requesting that he repay the $20,000 advanced to him. Lillian herself wrote Marcus: "Please do not go on making yourself miserable with this problem. It will only end up making victims of you, me and Hammett."

Now Lillian became obsessed with Marcus' returning the materials she and others had given him. More specifically, Marcus had in his possession an interview he had done with Mary and Jose, as well as one with Lillian in which she had revealed that Mary was not Hammett's biological daughter. In danger of losing control over Hammett's life story, she was determined to prevent Marcus from writing anything about Dashiell Hammett at all.

Her method was to convert Marcus into an enemy. Lillian wrote Jo she regretted "that you ever saw him, or that anybody else ever did." She accused Marcus of not having returned to Hannah Weinstein a carbon copy of the minutes of the Waldorf Conference. Sometimes it was minutes, sometimes a scrapbook, sometimes a "press book . . . the only press book that exists."

"A marriage is at stake regarding the scrapbook," Lillian said mysteriously.

Marcus was perplexed. He says he called Hannah, who told him to leave the materials with her doorman, which he did. Hannah says she didn't get it back, Lillian insisted. Since Hammett had not even taken part in the Waldorf Conference, the whole brouhaha was perplexing. Perhaps the package had been sent to Hannah, Lillian at one point speculated, in a tacit admission known only to herself that Hannah had indeed received Marcus' package.

Lillian went to war with Marcus. In a memo to John Sheehan at Random House she demanded "to be paid, and paid highly, for the time that I spent recording with him, or helping him put the book together." There was no one more adept than Lillian at mystifying, troublemaking.

"I had to force Miss Alexander into a legal threat to make him give back the scrapbook," Lillian wrote Sheehan, although Muriel Alexander did no such thing. Lillian had called Alexander and asked her to get the materials back from Marcus; he had delivered them with no problem; Alexander had never threatened to sue Marcus. Then, Alexander noted with bitterness that came of three decades of difficult acquaintance with Lillian, it took three weeks before Lillian sent her secretary to collect the clipping scrapbook.

Lillian also accused Marcus of not returning all the tapes they had recorded together, although she had to admit: "I cannot prove this." She was further stymied because she did not know the names of all the people Marcus interviewed, or which he had taped. "Your guess of why he has kept this material to which he has no right is as good as mine," she wrote Sheehan. But she wanted papers served on Marcus "which will require him to divulge information about his activities in connection with the Hammett book from 1974 to the present." She wrote as if he had committed a crime. When Random House refused to sue Marcus, Lillian had her own lawyer, Ephraim London, write to him.

London was now performing the role for her that Oscar Bernstien had once played. London wrote Marcus he was indebted to Lillian for $10,000 "for work done and material furnished." If he did not pay her within five weeks, she would "consider legal measures." A "cause of action" would be instituted if he did not "immediately return to Hannah Weinstein the stenographic transcript of The World Peace Conference you borrowed and promised faithfully to return," a document which "has considerable intrinsic value."

Marcus had to hire lawyer Cy Rembar, a cousin of his friend Norman Mailer, to extricate him. Meanwhile Lillian had Hannah Weinstein write Marcus to say she agreed with Lillian: Marcus was "confusing the World Peace Conference book with a scrapbook of newspaper clippings given him by Muriel Alexander."

It was all so bizarre that some wondered whether in Lillian's extreme reactions there might not be an element of sexual betrayal, her jealousy over Marcus' new marriage. It was a triangle of her own imagination; Marcus had not been her lover. But her behavior recapitulated her extreme reaction when Blair Clark told her he was marrying. In November 1979, Lillian was still insisting that Marcus had retained two tapes. Meanwhile "the woman who owns the transcript," who remained nameless, was pondering taking action against Hannah. Marcus had involved them all "in a very ugly situation." He had treated her "so badly" that Lillian had no choice but to inform the president of Columbia University about "the history of you and the Hammett book."

On this threat, Lillian made good. On January 28, 1980, William McGill appeared in her apartment and she told him about a missing tape of Jose and Mary Hammett and about the missing World Peace Conference book. McGill promised to speak to Marcus. "She wants to hurt you; she wants to injure you," McGill told Marcus.

Late in February, Marcus wrote Lillian again, denying he had taped meetings with her at the Vineyard Haven Yacht Club, denying he had confused the scrapbook with the black spring binder that contained a copy of the Waldorf Conference transcript, which he had left with Hannah's doorman. He offered to copy all his research and turn it over to Lillian for her use. She remained intransigent. The loss of the Waldorf Conference book had caused "the possible breakup of a marriage." One of the tapes had contained their "secret conversation" in which she had revealed that Mary was not Hammett's natural daughter. This so "frightened" her that she had to reveal the secret to Josephine Marshall.

Nothing could anger her more than the sense of losing control over Hammett's life. So she wrote an exceptionally vicious letter to Marcus. Included was her outrageous claim "that the day we sat on the plane together, and you told me that you had named your child for a former SS colonel, and allowed his mother, a speaking radical, to return him to the Catholic church, made me so nervously sick that I wanted really to have no further look into what was happening." Carbons went to Dr. McGill at Columbia and to Jason Epstein. In her covering letter to McGill she called Marcus "a very, very sick man, or a calculating one."

Marcus never wrote another word about either Hammett or Lillian Hellman. If her motive had been to prevent him from writing anything outside of her control, she accomplished her purpose. Marcus concluded she had wanted a "manufactured biography" of Hammett. That she had scarcely figured in the two chapters he had written had alarmed her sufficiently to enact this nastiest of campaigns against him.

Meanwhile more would-be Hammett biographers were surfacing. In 1978 a writer named Hugh Eames published a book which contained a section on Hammett. It was "extremely inaccurate," Lillian told him. "The truth is that any piece about Hammett cannot and should not be written without my aid. And I do not wish to give it."

Indefatigable Bill Nolan announced he was planning a full-scale Hammett biography. Scholar Richard Layman, who had compiled the definitive Hammett bibliography, was also working on a Hammett book. In February 1978, Layman wrote to Lillian inquiring whether Marcus was still at work on his biography of Hammett. In his research he had "found no evidence that he is." Indeed that had been one of Lillian's complaints, that Marcus had not been working energetically enough. In March, Lillian wrote Layman informing him that Marcus was no longer writing the biography; he should send a sample of his work for her and Jason Epstein to evaluate. This Layman did. When Lillian hesitated, Layman requested the opportunity to provide more material "before a final decision about Hammett's biographer is made."

In July, Lillian was able to write Layman: "A book is already contracted for and is being presently written." She "squashed" one more documentary about Hammett, this one by George H. Wolfe. Meanwhile her secretary, Rita Wade, was instructed: all future biographers were to be told: "Biography already commissioned."

In January 1979, William Godshalk gave up his biography, turning his materials over to Richard Layman. Bill Nolan generously allowed Layman to use his archival material since his own book would be more popular than scholarly. Nolan decided to help Layman not only because he was "a damned nice guy" but because he would "love to see Hellman outsmarted . . . there is a dire need for a *non*-official much-more objective DH biog." Muriel Alexander and Marjorie May rallied to Layman's side. David Fechheimer, calling himself "not a writer," relinquished the idea of his own book and opened a trunk of materials for Layman's use. His publisher would be Harcourt Brace Jovanovich co-publishing with Layman's own firm, Bruccoli Clark.

With continuing unselfishness Nolan read Layman's galleys. "It is amazing how much you kept her *out* of your book!" he told Layman, speaking of Lillian. "Which is all to the good." If Lillian insisted that she was the dominant personage in Hammett's life, those deprived of her assistance were writing as if she had not been all that significant to Dashiell Hammett, that her role in his life was far more minimal than her memoirs claimed.

Lillian's new official biographer of Dashiell Hammett was distinguished novelist Diane Johnson. Lillian signed an agreement with Johnson in September 1978. Lillian would provide the research; Diane would do the writing. At Don Congdon's suggestion, and to his later regret, Lillian would retain "sole absolute and arbitrary right of approval of the manuscript." The publisher would, again, be Random House, the editor Jason Epstein. Lillian would own 20 percent of the book. Motion picture and television rights went 75 percent to Lillian and 25 to Diane. The advance was a respectable one for a biography at that time, $60,000.

Lillian was more careful than she had been with Marcus. She told Jo that Mary was not to be interviewed by Diane Johnson unless Jo herself was present; Diane was not to see Jose, who Lillian had decided was senile. There is "a small army of books coming out about your father," Lillian warned Jo, "and we will all have to face the pain that they will probably cause."

With her now failing eyesight, Lillian attempted to cull through Hammett's letters in order to decide which to show Johnson. Some "deeply pleased and amused me," she said. Others "pained me very deeply." "I felt great pride in this gent, and bewilderment about myself and the past: there was so much that I didn't see," Lillian confessed.

There was yet another thorn in Lillian's side as Diane Johnson began. Lillian was already involved in a protracted campaign to stop Francis Ford Coppola from producing a film version of Joe Gores's novel *Hammett*. This time her quarrel was not with the depiction of her own role, since Gores's novel, set in 1928, focused on Hammett as an ex-Pinkerton writer who becomes involved in an adventure in San Francisco. Rather, as if she owned Hammett's life, she needed to control any and all projects even mentioning him. In December 1975 she had spotted an item in the New York *Times* reporting that Coppola had bought the novel for the movies.

"I knew how painful such a book would have been to him," she began, in an effort to persuade Coppola to desist. She pleaded that he "not . . . make an intensely private man, a man who became almost a hermit, into a character," although, of course, she had done the same thing. "Hammett would have been contemptuous of such a book," she said. Taking the high moral road, she asserted that his children and grandchildren didn't "like this half-hero worship, half-jesting with a serious man." Worse, many of the "facts" in Gores's novel, she said, were "incorrect."

When Coppola did not respond, Lillian mailed him another copy of her letter. Finally Coppola invoked a moral argument of his own: wouldn't it be best if he did the movie rather than have it bought by someone else who would do a bad job? He had proven his cinematic artistry with the first two *Godfather* movies. She could do worse. Unappeased, Lillian then asked Jo for permission to tell Coppola that Jo was considering an invasion of privacy lawsuit on the family's behalf.

A lawyer wrote to Coppola invoking the protection of Mrs. Josephine Hammett and calling the projected film an "outright attack." That it portrayed Hammett's wife as dead alone must render it painful to Jose. A few days later Lillian wrote again to Coppola, announcing that although she could not sue him since she did not appear in the book, Josephine had consulted a lawyer. Lillian would "help her in any way I can."

Matters seemed to rest until March 1977, when Lillian discovered that Nicholas Roeg had agreed to direct the film. She called to tell him she "was disapproving," as was Jo, and that Jo was "going to take legal action about the script." Roeg bowed out, ostensibly because a star couldn't be found to play Hammett. François Truffaut turned down the project. In 1978 when Lillian heard that Orion Pictures might distribute the film, she wrote to Arthur Krim: "I have no objection whatsoever to Hammett being the subject of a motion picture, as long as the truth is told."

"Just keep saying no," Lillian instructed Jo. When her lawyers conceded that Coppola's company, Zoetrope, had the right to make the film, Lillian sought a new strategy. "Our only weapon now are [sic] interviews right before or after the picture comes out." Jo must be certain "that neither your mother nor Mary speaks to anybody *ever*."

German director Wim Wenders was eventually hired. He wrote Lillian he wished to come "to talk to [her] about the Hammett film." She must be "counted out of the picture as long as Hammett's name is used in any form," Lillian replied. She would "never have to do with any fiction about Hammett, and, when the fiction appears," she threatened, "I will say so as loudly and as strongly and as often as I am able to." She hated the novel, "a thoroughly cheapjack-cash in job." Wenders promised to make a statement that he was not "representing" the "real" Dashiell Hammett in 1928, but only his imagination, the myth of the private detective that he had created in the city of San Francisco. His wife and daughter would not appear in the film.

But even the Hammett who lived before they met belonged to her. "If there is no desire to cash in on Hammett's name," she demanded, "why use it at all?" It was only she, ironically the woman he had not married, who could use his name. Wenders' invocation of Hammett's imagination inflamed her too. That was "high class talk with nothing to back it up: you know nothing of his 'imagination,'" she told Wenders, "because I don't." Again she threatened: "So long as people dare to invent a life for Hammett, I will do my best to protect his real life."

Lillian became angry when she learned that Diane Johnson had met with Wenders. Her anger again erupted when she discovered that David Fechheimer had stolen some of Hammett's hospital and other records and the Coppola-Wenders crew had access to them. Then Zoetrope ran out of money. By 1981 Coppola was calling the film "unreleaseable," and the script, "the stuff nightmares are made of," in a play on a line from *The Maltese Falcon*. Finally *Hammett* opened in a small way, created a woozy San Francisco mood, and sank without a trace. Lillian, it appeared, had worn out them all.

When Jose died in November 1980, Lillian wrote Jo wondering whether she should now reveal to Mary that she was not Hammett's daughter. He had "never told anybody but me, and one other person—an analyst," Lillian said, mistakenly. Surely it would give Jo herself "a great sense of relief that she is only half related to you." Since Lillian had lied to Jo about so many other things, in particular that alienation of affection suit she insisted Jose had brought against her in New Orleans, Jo could not believe her now.

Lillian was furious to discover an acknowledgment to Muriel Alexander in Richard Layman's biography of Hammett, which appeared in 1981. (The Los Angeles *Times* called *Shadow Man* "a fine, comprehending and engrossing work of research.") This book could get them all into a lot of trouble, Lillian said angrily, accusing Alexander of showing Layman stolen material: copyright records from Hammett's files, a scrapbook of condolences. Lillian threatened to sue. In fact, Layman had seen neither. When John Leonard in his New York *Times* review mentioned that Steven Marcus "had already been dismissed," and hoped Diane Johnson "will not be so obliging," Lillian wrote an angry letter to Leonard. Had she wished to own Hammett, "I'd have written his biography myself instead of offering what you call 'enigmatic spoonfuls.'" Leonard had said Hammett's face "wants to love itself more than it thinks is justifiable," that Hammett had contempt for himself. "Hasn't everybody got contempt for themselves?" Lillian demanded.

At first Lillian was so pleased with Diane Johnson that she recommended her to write the Hellman-Hammett film screenplay for Warners; when Johnson's tall, thin, white-haired husband, John, visited her in a San Francisco Hospital, Lillian reacted dramatically. "Oh, stand there!" she called out. "I thought it was Hammett!" Meanwhile David Fechheimer refused to help Johnson because he believed she was in the pocket of Lillian, the person who had ruined Dashiell Hammett's life. According to Johnson, he even asked a researcher, in exchange for his help, to sign a paper saying she would not talk to Johnson.

Lillian soon made it clear that Johnson was to assume her point of view on all major issues. She was to write that Lillian had managed the Hammett copyrights so well that Jo and Mary both would one day be wealthy women, and to explain "why the estate will make his children and grandchildren rich." She was not to portray Hammett's marriage as a "love affair," because there was an "awful secret" behind it—namely, that Mary was not Hammett's natural child.

Johnson's book was to reflect that Dash "was never in love with his wife," but "married her out of pity." Johnson was to take the position Lillian had suggested to Blair Clark in that horoscope: his biography began and ended with his meeting her. To Johnson's astonishment, Lillian even quoted Pascal: "I came into it long before I came into it."

Johnson must write that Lillian was the only woman Hammett had ever loved, never once contradicting what Lillian in her memoirs had written. Lillian insisted that she had "no need personally or in public to prove Hammett's love for me or my love for him." She did "have a need to stand by what I have written about him in all the books." Attempting to obliterate the existence of other women, she complained of "too many references to Elise De Viane. "I do not think Hammett ever thought of her again," Lillian decreed. "I do not want my ex-beau played around with in this fashion," Lillian closed one set of her comments.

"Hammett joined the Communist party," Johnson wrote. Lillian objected because she had not said so in her memoirs. "Since I never had any proof that he did I'd like to know where she got her proof," Lillian said. It was one more "possibly dangerous situation." At stake was Lillian's self-invented persona as a person who told the truth, a persona now jeopardized by the biographer she herself had hired.

Lillian attempted to subject Johnson's research to her need for people to believe, as Jason Epstein concluded, that Hammett "was madly in love with her." Lillian's corrections placed Hammett with her more frequently than he had been: on Tavern Island, even in the ambulance when he was taken to Lenox Hill with gonorrhea. If Lillian did not know a Hammett acquaintance, he must not exist. Another sore point was Hammett's drinking. He was a "stylish drunk," Lillian insisted.

The most deplorably dishonest of her emendations had to do with the issue of who put up his bail money in 1951. Johnson had written that it was his family and friends and left it at that. "It was I who put it up!" Lillian told Johnson, an outright lie. When Johnson held firm, unable to discover any evidence that Lillian had put up his bail money, Lillian went to war. Johnson knew that her work would never appear if she did not yield. Confronting that ugly moment known only to authorized biographers, when truth gives way to the demands of self-serving mythology, she succumbed.

With Jason Epstein's help, Lillian wrote four and a half manuscript pages concocting the story of how she had tried to pawn her jewelry to raise $100,000 for Hammett's bail, how she tried to raise money from Leo Huberman, how Hammett had sent her that note about how she must stay away from court, not having "to prove to me that you love me at this late date." These pages were inserted into Johnson's text.

By the end pathology poisoned Lillian's relationship with Diane Johnson. Johnson "didn't like me," she said. Why else would she so underestimate the number of presents Hammett had given her? Lillian enumerated:

one mink coat, one even more expensive broad-tailed coat, one enormous broad tail stole, one Beau [sic] Martin jacket of enormous cost, a necklace that I immediately took back and had the money credited to him, and an endless amount of jewelry which I still have.

Lillian now treated the biographer as a rival for Hammett's affection. Hammett "might have fallen in love with you and that would certainly have made me very jealous," Lillian said. Johnson had committed "that very nice and almost obligatory act from a biographer of falling in love with his subject." "If he were alive," Lillian feared, "he would be in love with you." It had been awful for her to deal with Johnson, Lillian insisted, because Johnson was "in some kind of competition with her."

Lillian reminded herself Hammett wouldn't have wanted any biography. She felt "an unpleasant guilt that I did what I knew he wouldn't have wanted me to do and got punished for it." If Johnson had "missed the man," how could she not? Only Lillian knew him. She insisted she did not "give one damn" whether Johnson portrayed her as "beloved by Hammett," only that she had written that she was, and that she "loved greatly." "The word love has increasingly through the years made me almost sick," Lillian confessed.

Admitting Johnson's biography was "moving" and "a fine job," Lillian consented to its publication. If it was "unexciting," that was "because it was written by a woman." Then she had Johnson replaced by Alvin Sargent as the Hammett-Hellman screenwriter. He understood Hammett as Johnson did not, "perhaps because he is a man."

On October 16, 1983, the New York *Times* reviewer, George Stade, sensed that Johnson "does not tell us all she knows." Reading Johnson's admission that she had "seldom ventured" into the preserve of Hammett's relationship with Hellman," Stade wrote: "I wish she had." Mistakenly, Stade attributed Johnson's reticence to her employing the novelist's method. Out in California, weighing in for the Hammett cult, Bill Nolan gleefully noted that Johnson's biography, despite Hellman's "official blessing" and "a ton of letters," was "a colossal disappointment . . . the runt of the litter—sick, weak and ugly."

A year after Lillian's death, Diane Johnson wrote a coda to her biography for *Vanity Fair*. Had Lillian not been alive, she wrote, she could have written "an intriguing story of a powerful woman's struggle to possess and command at last the elusive ghost of a man about whom she was insecure in life." If "love" was a motif of their story, so were "control, revenge, hate and money."

Johnson revealed Lillian had viewed her biography as a means to "get back at" Hammett for his sexual coldness, "or to believe finally in his love, or to come to some view which would enable her at last to bury him." Johnson had been ordered to tell the story of Hammett as a "hero who had been waiting for her all the years until he met her," and who "despite his cruelties, loved her underneath all along." Meanwhile Lillian had come to hate her as if she were an actual sexual rival.

Now that Lillian was dead, both Muriel Alexander and Marjorie May announced they would be writing their own books about Hammett. May said she had waited so long because she did not wish to hurt his daughter Mary.

29

Me Alone

"Now, don't be a naughty girl, Lily."

BLAIR CLARK

"No, Warren, there's only one part in the play that you would be right for and Elizabeth Taylor is playing it."

LILLIAN HELLMAN TO WARREN BEATTY

Hammett had always disapproved of her thirst for celebrity, had disappeared when the powerful appeared at her door. Now in the last decade and a half of her life, with Hammett gone, Lily was free to act out all manner of impulses of which Hammett would have disapproved. Not least was her posing as a "legend" in a Blackglama mink advertisement. "Dash would have laughed at it," Howard Bay was certain. Jo thought he would just have told her to cut out all that "legend in her own time" nonsense.

Her behavior in these years ranged from generosity to meanness, exhibitionism to aggression. The habit of retaliation had remained with her. Unimpeded, she could indulge in baby talk without more than a memory of Hammett's raised eyebrow. Often she was gracious and polite. She was never rude unintentionally, her friend novelist Shirley Hazzard noted. Her taste remained impeccable. She chose as her fee not the Blackglama mink, but a $5,000 credit toward a magnificent brown Swakara broadtail with a "theater piece" which zipped on to make the coat ankle-length.

Restless, she traveled, always choosing the finest hotels. In 1973 she stayed at the Hotel Cipriani in Venice. From London at Claridges, she went down to Kent to visit Robert Lowell and his new wife, Lady Caroline Blackwood, a Guinness heiress whom Lillian dubbed another of her "Lady Gigglewitzes."

She despised the Caribbean, yet when Caskie Stinnett got her an assignment for *Travel & Leisure,* off she went to Martinique. On that trip she visited Mike Nichols, who was shooting *The Day of the Dolphin.* She told fellow houseguest, translator Albert Todd, that she had been watching his body in the water, and it was apparent that she experienced the erotic pleasure of a man swimming. Still she enjoyed a sexual imagination.

"Tired of the tourist joints in the Caribbean," in the winter of 1974 she rented a house in Sarasota with Sid Perelman and Frances Goodrich and Albert Hackett. One day Frances told her, "You're destroying my personality! You make me feel as if I don't exist."

"What could she have meant by that?" Lily later asked Richard Poirier.

"You know exactly what she meant," Poirier said. "You made her feel like a cipher."

"That's a terrible thing to say," Lily responded. The following year Lillian was back in the Caribbean, in Barbados in a pink cottage rented from her old nemesis Marietta Tree. In 1976 she sailed down the Nile on a cruise as the guest of Max Palevsky. By 1979 she couldn't travel alone and Peter Feibleman accompanied her to Martinique.

Her apartment at 630 Park lacked the charm of the house on Eighty-second Street with its spectacular stairway and artifacts from her plays. Now she lived in a rather small apartment, a dining area at the far end of the living room. The colors were muted: cream on the walls, green chairs. There were still the photos, and some of the props, the highboy in her bedroom from *The Children's Hour,* the birdcage from *The Autumn Garden.* It was life scaled down; her heart remained on the Vineyard.

After the film *Julia* appeared in 1977, with Jane Fonda playing Lillian to Jason Robards' stoical Hammett, her celebrity was further renewed. One day she entered a San Francisco restaurant and the waiter addressed her diminutive, if gray-haired, companion as "Mr. Hammett." He was, in fact, her editor William Abrahams.

For all her notoriety, however, alone in late middle age Lillian was deeply unhappy. "Me alone" she wrote into her diary for those rare evenings when she was not engaged. She put on her lipstick and tea rose scent and went where she was asked. One night in 1978 at the home of

ACLU president Norman and publishing lawyer Harriette Dorsen she broke down. "My whole life is fucked up," she wept. Drunk, she allowed self-pity to overtake her.

Most of the time she kept her head up. "I hope you won't think of me as sad," she wrote Vlado Dedijer. "It seems to me that anybody who has a head that cannot be bought even in a ten cent store, must and should have some kind of permanent sadness." But hers, she hoped, was "basically a hopeful and cheerful nature."

That same year the BBC did a documentary about her. Scenes were filmed at Hardscrabble Farm. Not well enough to travel to Westchester, she telephoned the farm during the filming. "You're all there and I'm here," she told the current owner, Ellen Hodor. Then she broke down and wept.

She remained a woman of contradictions, always with a finer sensibility than many gave her credit for. If her life had been shadowed by her astonishment at being plain, unlike most women in her place she had, at one level, accepted herself. Her friend Claudette Colbert had three face-lifts. Lily abstained. Claudette has the body of a teenager, Lily pointed out. A new face would not go with her body. "I still have the same old heart, the same old liver," she laughed. "What good would it do to have another face?" She laughed at her worn body and indulged childishly in exhibitionist self-mockery.

So at a Lord & Taylor gala, she wore a gauzy dress omitting any underwear. Embarrassed, her escort, Richard de Combray, suggested she put something on. "What do you mean?" she demanded. "You can see my cunt?" One night, standing before him stark naked, she insisted that Richard Poirier sit and talk to her while she dressed for dinner. On that cruise down the Nile she slept nude with the shades up and flirted with a greasy sailor offering sexual favors.

Whenever a man visited, she put on makeup, had her hair done. What you write will be true, she had told the Hacketts. So she behaved as if the image she presented of herself would be accepted as the reality. Because she believed she was attractive, she became attractive, and even in her old age men were happy to be in her company. With a caressing voice one night at Kitty Hart's she charmed a handsome Welshman named Richard Llewellyn Davis. She made a forward motion with her body as she talked; she smiled. You forgot what she looked like, an amused Mrs. Hart observed. On other occasions, honesty surfaced. At the party for *Pentimento* Norman Mailer came up to praise the book. He took her hands in his and told her she looked beautiful. Lillian did look beautiful that night, regal in ice blue.

"Don't lie, Norman," Lily said. "I don't look beautiful. I look terrible. I look old."

"Lillian, you look just like Baby Snooks," Mailer told her affectionately. Then he paused. "A mean Baby Snooks!" Lily laughed. Attention was what she craved.

A woman must always make the best of herself. In double mockery at the 1975 memorial service for Lionel Trilling, when mourners were urged to bow their heads, Lily took the opportunity to take out her compact and repair her makeup. "You are much too young to let your hair turn gray," she told her decorator Mildred Loftus. Then she gave Loftus an expensive navy blue taffeta dress with a big organdy collar which she had kept for years. When she had bought it, she modeled it for her father. Max had looked up from his newspaper and said, "You look like a bridesmaid." Lily never wore the dress.

Despite all the unresolved contradictions, not least about her father, she was wise about being a woman. "Serious considerations," she told the Barnard graduating women in 1976, included "gaiety, pleasure for yourself and others." In a piece she wrote in these last years for *Rolling Stone* about Rosalynn Carter, Lillian saw the President's wife as an intelligent woman who tried to conceal her intelligence as unfeminine and unattractive. "It is a losing game," Lily knew. "Intelligence pops out in speech or voice and cannot be withdrawn at will because it will reappear against the will." Yet young women of her acquaintance like Max Palevsky's wife, Lynda, observed that Lillian believed a woman should put up with a lot from a man, as she had done from Hammett; savoring her role as the dispenser of advice, larding her honest concern with mischief, Lillian urged Lynda to remain in her deteriorating marriage.

She cultivated the available pleasures. She cooked wearing a blue painter's smock with a shirred back and a Peter Pan collar; it invariably became messy with chocolate stains splattered down the front. Worthy friends were sent recipes. Nora Ephron received one for ham signed "The Jewish Ham Expert." Summers, she grew vegetables and roses, puttering outside in her Vineyard garden among her Chinese pea pods wearing a straw hat and thick glasses.

Fishing delighted her to the end. Weighing less than a hundred pounds, barely able to see, and traveling at five knots an hour with one hundred yards of line out, with John Hersey as her companion, she pulled in more bluefish than anyone. Then once more she would take out her compact and attempt to put on lipstick and powder her face.

Her housekeeping remained impeccable. Written instructions went to her staff. The linen on her bed was to be changed twice a week, the ice bucket filled each day at four, or at noon if there were guests for lunch. Under "serving" she enumerated: the platter should be passed to her as the first person to be served; "the next person to be served should be to your left." One day a few years after Hammett's death she flew into a rage over not having enough fish forks of the same pattern.

"Miss Hellman, I sure wish I had your problems!" Helen told her.

Helen died in 1965 and some thought Lily had been stingy, unkind to her. There were times when in full view of others she was abusive to defenseless women, which included her servants. Annabel Davis-Goff, then married to Mike Nichols, felt the way Lillian talked to her household help was pre-Civil War. Fred Zinnemann, the director of *Julia*, was appalled as he perceived the contrast between her professed concerns for mankind and the way she reduced his obliging assistant to tears.

Powerless people seemed fair game. "I'll finish you on this island," Lily was heard shouting at the man who put in her Jacuzzi. "I won't pay the bill. You'll have to go to court." She became enraged at airline reservations clerks, at the set designer for the 1980 production of *The Little Foxes*. Part of it was her old Hammettesque determination to outsmart the world. "You've got to understand that I'm a great actress," she explained one of her rages to Richard de Combray.

Indeed she put on a show at a screening of *Julia*. She had read the script and knew exactly what was in it. Yet when Lily asks Dash, "Am I preventing you from doing your work?" Lillian raised her voice in the darkened theater.

"That's deplorable!" she cried out. An old guilt had surfaced.

Being effective also meant exercising power over one's own work, and in 1981, half blind, she wrote the actress playing Alexandra in *The Little Foxes* that she should speak the line "Are you afraid, Mama?" "with greater meaning and thus greater force."

With Linda Anderson, who worked for her, Lily could be cozy, as she laughed about how Pat Neal had gone after Hammett. Claudette Colbert had asked, incredulously, "You don't give the servants the same food you eat?" Lily did.

Young women inspired the childlike old woman's unresolved anger about her looks. When at a party a young woman approached, gushing that she had read everything Miss Hellman had written, Lillian snapped, "What have you read?" She did not relent. "You haven't read anything. You're just making that up for cocktail talk," Lillian snapped again. Her escort that day, Bob Towbin, believed that had it been a man who approached her, she would have enjoyed just that cocktail talk.

Lily also became angry at other reminders of what life had denied her. As she had destroyed the possibility of sharing a child with Hammett, the presence of children enraged her. One evening in her last years she asked Lynda Palevsky not to bring her child to a Vineyard dinner, although the only other guest was Robert Brustein. Believing Lillian could not see, uneasy about leaving her little boy with strangers, Lynda brought him to the table. Lillian sensed at once that the child was there. "Get that child away from this table!" she demanded.

As if to deny this emotional deficiency, she insisted on being named the godmother of friends' children: Susanna Styron, Nina Bernstein, James Marquand, Molly Penn, and also little Jonathan Palevsky, whose presence at her table she had forbidden. She involved herself little in these children's lives. One day she did tell five-year-old Nina Bernstein, "When the plane goes down, I'll get you!" and the child was terrified at the prospect. She seemed bitter and scary, like a witch, and the Bernstein family dachshund, the fierce, sausage-shaped Henry, responding to the children's discomfort, would bark and bite her ankles whenever she visited.

When he was four or five, Lillian told James Marquand she was not sending him a gift that year for his birthday because he had not sent her a thank-you note for last year's gift. There were, even for children, "standards."

Children, however, were inconvenient because she needed to be the center of attention. As she had termed herself an unfinished woman, she remained to the end the spoiled only child, as if she were her friends' child who never had grown up sufficiently to have children of her own. So she fussed over her birthday parties and birthday presents. "This has been a terrible birthday," she told Mildred Loftus one year. "All I've gotten is dreck."

Nonetheless she urged Bob Towbin's daughter, Mina: "The one thing you should do is have children. It's the one thing I regret." To others, she said, "I would have loved to have a child." But she was not nurturing, as her own mother had not been. There was nothing maternal in her, Pearl London observed, no dimension of leniency. It remained difficult for her to accept another person's autonomy; this alone would have made motherhood excruciating.

Fulfilling her image as Southern belle, she could be charmingly gracious. "It obviously is a measure of your great affection for Hammett," she wrote Jean Potter Chelnov as she repaid Hammett's loan. "If I have a right to speak in his name, and of course I haven't, then I must tell you that I think your undoubted sacrifice in sending it is the kind of thing Hammett would have most liked and admired. Stick to Dash's belief that the writing will go well for you." She enjoyed playing the great lady, the aristocrat. Of course, for years she had indeed spoken in Hammett's name.

To protect herself from rejection, she would invoke Hammett. Bishop Paul Moore, handsome and seemingly eligible, came for a weekend to the Vineyard with his daughter, Honor. Lily peppered her conversation with references to Dash. "You pronounce his name 'Da-shiel,'" she instructed. Moore father and daughter learned how Dash liked his eggs.

When they were about to attend a Styron party, Honor had trepidations; she had not been Robert Brustein's favorite student at Yale and he was certain to be there. "You'll walk in on my arm," Lillian said, dressed like an empress in a coral floor-length gown. That weekend Lily's efforts did not pay off. The bishop later told his daughter that Lillian was not attractive enough for him.

Into 1979 when she was in New York she wanted to be out every night: Lady Keith, Jean vanden Heuvel, a dinner Kitty Hart gave for Claudette Colbert, a Marietta Tree dinner, it seemed not to matter with whom. If she didn't like who her dinner partner was, surreptitiously she switched place cards. She bought her meat still at Schaller & Weber and entertained at small dinners on Park Avenue. But being out meant forestalling the demons, and having fun.

Lily became more parsimonious than ever. Howard Bay had worked hard designing her new Vineyard house. "How much do I owe you?" Lillian asked. "I leave it up to you," Bay told her graciously. To his astonishment, Lillian paid him $500. She sent her old clothes to the thrift shops, making long lists for tax purposes. Hats, wigs, books, girdles, all went. In 1963 she had sent Hammett's clothes: six men's evening shirts and four pairs of gloves. She recycled gifts and sent people cheap candlestick holders and to Becky Bernstien a piece of old kitchen iron.

"Money makes you laugh," Kitty Carlisle Hart told her. Lily asked Maureen Stapleton what she wanted as her opening-night present for *The Little Foxes* in 1980. "I want diamonds," Stapleton, capable of mischief herself, replied.

"Oh, you'd lose them," Lillian told her. Maureen got a red satin stole with a note: "This is as expensive as diamonds."

On the eve of Reagan's election, November 4, 1980, Lily gave Bob Towbin, who was managing her money, a commission. "I want to buy a fur coat for twenty thousand dollars," she told him. "I'll give you ten thousand dollars. You have a month to double it."

At the end of the month Towbin had earned for her $18,500. He told his secretary to draw the check.

"That's not twenty thousand dollars!" Lily balked. But she was not about to offend a man who had made her a fortune.

To the end, she remained ambivalent about the rich. At dinner at

Peggy Guggenheim's Venice palazzo in July 1974 she watched as a dirty-looking servant entered the dining room in a filthy apron with a pot and ladle under his arm. Then he dumped a serving of some undefinable mess onto each hand-painted porcelain dinner plate.

"Now I know how the rich stay rich," Lillian whispered, sotto voce, to her dinner partner, biographer Deirdre Bair. "They eat dog food!"

Lily could be down-to-earth, and funny as well. Passover at the La Pook family abode in Great Neck culminated in the singing of "Let My People Go." "Leave it to the Jews to steal the songs of the Negroes," Lillian laughed. One June, Roger Straus, publisher of her edition of Chekhov's letters, appeared at her birthday celebration, predictably without a gift.

"You're the only one who didn't bring me a present," Lily told him. Straus promptly handed her a ten-dollar bill, which Lily tucked into her bosom.

"That's ten dollars more than you offered me for an advance," Lily told him. It was too good a joke. Straus took to telling it on himself.

Near the end of her life, Lily became obsessed with not having enough money. Her staff now included round-the-clock nurses. She asked Max Palevsky, a brilliant mathematician-cum-businessman, who had sold his company, Scientific Data Systems, to Xerox, and was very rich, to help her. "She was always hustling me for money," he was to remember. Yet he gave her $100,000 over a period of time, solely to ease her mind as hospital and nursing bills mounted. It didn't matter to him that she could afford them herself, because he cared about her. "We had a contract," he says modestly, finding it a fair exchange, her company on his cruises unique. When she asked him to help her support V. S. Pritchett, he contributed money to the Pritchetts every month until Lily died. He blanched only when he took her on his yacht to visit Ruth Field in South Carolina and had to contend with an anti-Semitic close family member. Palevsky at once pulled up anchor.

Yet Lily sent her emissary, young doctor Jonathan La Pook, with $10,000 for Christina Stead. Her note was gracious: "It gives me enormous pleasure that you have accepted it from me because I feel you must have some faith in me for accepting it."

As her closest friend Peter Feibleman was to reveal in his memoir, *Lilly,* mischief freed her in these last years from boredom and self-examination. Small mischief included claiming a turkey Bill Styron had stored in her refrigerator was in fact hers. Darker mischief involved the fake love letters she wrote to Bill, asking him to have sex with her. It was the she-Hammett, not as Hammett was in essence, but how he behaved during the worst of his drunks when all things were permissible. Rose was a terrible mistake, Lily told herself. It was she who should have been with Bill, not Rose. "I won't fuck you anymore," she told Styron nastily when he took Diane Johnson off to show her the sights of Martha's Vineyard.

She also told people Norman Mailer had almost raped her, an obvious inversion of her unfulfilled desire for him. The story went to a woman she considered a rival for Mailer's friendship, Diana Trilling. Mailer had pounded on her door. He had almost gained entry. "Oh, come on, Lillian," Trilling said. Renata Adler was told various versions of the story, in one of which Mailer had torn off her dress and carried her to her room, only for her to break a lamp over his head. In another version she told Adler, Lillian had honestly revealed her deepest masochism. Mailer had her in bed while she held the lamp over his head. Then he had said the cruelest thing a man could say to a woman: "You disgust me."

Money and mischief went hand in hand. Lily took to making false claims to insurance companies. She reported the loss of a gold man's Patek Philippe watch when she was swimming on the Vineyard. "There is also the possibility of a dog having passed by and picked up the watch as a toy," she wrote on her report. One evening she went with Blair Clark to the theater. The next day her insurance company heard from her. "I felt somebody bump against me very hard and as soon as it was possible in the incredible jam I looked down to find that my purse was open," she wrote. An envelope containing $682 was gone, along with a small gold comb. Clark remembers no such incident.

There came at the end ugly moments which would have made Hammett shudder. Driving home from a concert in Los Angeles, she remarked of the black conductor: "Is he fucking Lenny or is Lenny fucking him?"

"I'm in the car, Miss Hellman," the conductor said from the back seat.

"There's no point in taking it back because I said it," Lillian told him. "If I hurt your feelings, I'm truly sorry." She admired his music. He invited her to lunch.

"He's not a fag," she reported her revised opinion to Feibleman. "Oh, because he takes you out he's not a fag?" Feibleman was one of the few in her life able to put her in her place.

Often she yielded to meanness which, unprovoked, originated in unresolved childhood anger. Suddenly at dinner one night she turned to her friend John Marquand and said, "It's too bad. You're a good writer. You would have been a really good writer if your father hadn't been such a son of a bitch." Marquand was devastated.

Worse, on a miserably hot and humid Washington day at a benefit concert for Leonard Bernstein's sixtieth birthday, she got up and asked why no one had talked that night about Felicia, his wife, who had died in June. His children felt her words cast a pall over the occasion. Others thought you could measure her friendships by how deeply she fought with people. One night, she insisted, conjuring up an anecdote, she had told Lenny at a restaurant, "Get your penis out of my pasta."

Yet she could not bear to be neglected and in 1982, after she had been ill and Bernstein had been silent, she sent him birthday wishes along with a plaintive demand for attention: "It is more than possible that your life no longer has room for me." By the end of the year he received an angry, threatening letter from her regarding the most recent production of *Candide*.

Hammett had joked about "your people," but he had also prided himself on the number of Yiddish words he knew, and he larded his conversation with them. Lily shocked many during these years with what seemed like outright anti-Semitism. One night in the crowded elevator of her Park Avenue building, she remarked to Bob Towbin, "There are an awful lot of kikes in this building." It was one thing to insist on being the center of attraction, but ugly to use anti-Semitic remarks as a means of attaining it.

At a party hosted by the Strauses, she suddenly launched into an attack on a fellow guest, S. I. Newhouse.

"I do declare," she said, affecting the persona of the Southern belle in one of her ugliest moments, "I never thought I'd meet a kike nigger."

Then she had climbed onto Blair Clark's lap. "Now, don't be a naughty girl, Lily," he cajoled. She was the little girl being horrid, the spoiled child, who, still a child, would surely be forgiven. The next day she defended herself outrageously to her outraged hostess. "Don't you know my mother's name was 'Neuhouse,'" she said, unregenerate. "What right had the Newhouses to take my name?" The Jews of the 1840s migration, she insisted, were superior to the Eastern European Jews of the later vintage. Surely Mrs. Straus, who, like herself, was a German Jew, would understand. There was no apology for the scene.

"I myself make very anti-Semitic remarks but I get very upset if anybody else does," Lily told an interviewer. She had decided, she said to another reporter, "a long time ago that I was very glad I was born a Jew." Some who knew her were not persuaded as the word "kike" invaded her talk. It also called into question her political criticisms of Israel, which in themselves need not have been viewed as anti-Semitic.

Being Jewish even in these last years was a muddle in her mind, and tied up with her ambivalence toward Max Hellman, short, fat, vulgar, and yet unattainable. Vacationing in the Virgin Islands in the seventies, Lily wrote Mildred Loftus: "The food is not to be eaten and it is hard to tell Jews from Goys and I find, for some reason, that I don't like that. Maybe because it makes everybody too well bred." Her friends knew as well how she coveted the Anglo-Saxon male, tall, lean, and self-contained—the Hammett and not the Arthur Kober model—and it seemed like a response of the self-hating Jew.

Along with "kike," the word "nigger" cropped up in her talk, shocking Alvin Sargent, who otherwise admired her. On other occasions her stance was different. In a taxi in Washington she listened to a taxi driver indulging in racial slurs. Lillian then demanded that he turn around.

"Driver, look at me!" Lillian insisted. "I'm a Negro. I may be very white, but I'm a Negro." The man at once apologized. She lived amid a myriad of contradictions.

As her health failed, Lillian seemed to be restored only by conflict, which required a constant fresh supply of enemies. Richard Goodwin had been part of her Vineyard coterie. When he defected, moving to Maine, she accused him of stealing the little boat they had in common, the same boat she was to sell in 1973 because, she told Nora Ephron, she "could no longer manage it alone." She yelled at her closest woman friend, Hannah Weinstein, so ferociously that people thought she used Hannah as a scapegoat and wondered why poor Hannah put up with it. She created those imaginary sexual triangles. By the end everyone was ambivalent about her. Those who loved her the most seemed the most angry.

Needing to be thought a sexual woman, in defiance of Hammett's rejection still, she surrounded herself with accomplished men: Mike Nichols, Max Palevksy, Richard Poirier. She required a handsome movie star and found him in Warren Beatty.

She never lost her ability to make herself seductive, to transform herself into the soft, feminine Southern belle. She was virtually blind, but when a good-looking man entered the room, Lily's head went up, Max Palevksy noticed. It was Hammett's response to women in his drunken heyday. "Her whole manner is strictly below the belt," Truman Capote wrote in *Playboy*, naming her one of the sexiest women he knew: "the way she moves her hips, her arms, her hands . . . the funny thing about it is, it works." Of one thing he was certain: "The LAST thing on Hellman's mind is literature or art." She was seventy-five years old.

Lily practiced. She flirted with a taxi driver, with an intern taking her blood pressure. "Am I going to be all right?" she asked as her head went down in a flirtatious move. Nothing pleased her more than being thought a sexy woman still. "I think you look like a whore," Maureen Stapleton had told her, eyeing Lillian's picture on the jacket of *An Unfinished Woman*.

"Oh, you're so right," Lily crooned.

She flirted with women as well, so that one night Sue Marquand told her husband, John, "You know, I'm afraid Miss Hellman is a lesbian." Was it a reprise of Hammett's offer that she make love to another woman while he watched, so that, Lily had confided to Peter Feibleman, she turned him down only because she feared she might enjoy it too much? Even as she made slurs about "fags," she liked to suggest that she had a lesbian past. She told Richard Poirier how at a political meeting at Carnegie Hall she had gone up to the table where women were selling tickets "and there was a woman that I had been to bed with and I just couldn't face it, I had to turn around and leave." She spoke as if in a reverie. Was it so?

Diana Trilling, before she was rendered an enemy, had the same experience as Sue Marquand. Lillian invited her to a tête-à-tête, an intimate lunch on a cold winter day. The scene was set for a seduction. The curtains were drawn. A table was set with exquisite linen before a blazing fireplace. Lillian appeared in a velvet hostess gown. Delicious food was brought. Lillian got up and closed the doors in a theatrical gesture. Trilling concluded that "there was a real homosexual something between her and me." It was as if Lillian, having failed to capture Lionel, chose Diana to "replace him in the sexual sphere."

Lillian Hellman was "the most charming person" she had ever known, Trilling says. Her gift for intimacy was large; she possessed the ability to turn the simplest event into an amusing story; it was an enormous pleasure to be in her company. "Guess what the doctor found?" Lillian told Trilling one day as she lay in a sickbed. "I have a big mark under my left breast. And you know what it is? It's a bite. Now, how in the world could I have bitten myself under my left breast?" Lily roared with laughter. "I haven't been with a man making love to me for years," she admitted. On another occasion she joked: she "hadn't seen a man undressed for a century" and so she had forgotten: "did men also have belly buttons?"

Yet jealousy might surface at any time. Lily invited Trilling to a rehearsal of *Toys in the Attic*. When Trilling didn't immediately praise the play, hardly one of Lillian's best, she was angry. "You've been analyzed, Diana," Lillian said. "You know what lies behind that kind of thing." The implication was that Diana must be jealous of her.

During these years, as he reports in his memoir, she had a brief sexual relationship with Peter Feibleman. It was gentlemanly, short in duration, and of the oral variety. She did not accept its demise gracefully. Mike Nichols had to write to her: "You must get over the idea that you are going to have further sexual relations with Peter."

She did not go gentle. Until the last year or so of her life Lillian Hellman could on a good day make someone believe she was the sexiest older woman they had ever encountered. She threw her head back and in heroic self-dramatization tried to live as if her best years were not behind her.

3 0

Woman in Command

"Norman, I have to talk to you."

LILLIAN HELLMAN

It wasn't all Blackglama mink and exhibitionism on the beach at Martha's Vineyard during Lillian's last two decades. The memoirs restored her to literary celebrity. "I have publishing offers for an autobiography," she had told Arthur Cowan, "but that I couldn't write ever; who the hell would care and nothing that much happened." *An Unfinished Woman* was a best-seller. So successful was *Pentimento* that Don Congdon sold every chapter to a magazine before publication.

In the seventies she became a feminist heroine, filling the house wherever she spoke, no matter her expressed disdain for the excesses of the women's movement, like bra burning. She didn't care who took out the garbage, Lillian insisted. Yet feminists thought: here was a woman who had not married the great love of her life, had not bought into the motherhood myth, who was too shrewd not to know a woman can't have it all, and who had produced meaningful work.

The social life Lillian had begun in the late fifties, she reinforced with a vengeance now. Well connected on the highest levels of American life, she would never again be a marginalized person, a Hammett-like victim. She safeguarded her literary reputation fiercely. Men of genius like Edmund Wilson, Rahv, Trilling, Cal Lowell, and Robert Silvers continued to accept the myth she and Joe Rauh had created about how valiantly she had stood up to the McCarthy committee. If they remembered, as Rahv did, that she was "at bottom" an old Stalinist, they didn't care. She was a lion hunter, as Dorothy Straus observed, and the lions came meekly.

When she was attacked in print, these friends were expected to defend her. In 1967 on the occasion of a revival, Elizabeth Hardwick shredded *The Little Foxes* in the pages of *The New York Review of Books*. It was "our American version of Socialist Realism," she claimed, "the deluxe conventional." At once Richard Goodwin wrote an open letter in Lillian's defense, calling Hardwick's piece "a hatchet job." He behaved as if he were rallying people around a political candidate as he accused editor Robert Silvers of having deliberately sought "an unfavorable review from other sources" before he settled on Miss Hardwick. "I would really love to know who said that," Silvers told Lillian. It wasn't so.

"My lips are sealed," Lillian said. She was convinced Hardwick's piece was vindictive, based on jealousy of her friendship with Robert Lowell and on the demise of their marriage. She remembered a night when Hardwick had telephoned her at three in the morning "in tears and in liquor" to denounce Blair Clark and accuse him of helping Lowell take an apartment with another woman.

Lillian marshaled her forces. By the turn of the New Year 1968, Edmund Wilson had defended her in the pages of the same *New York Review* in "An Open Letter to Mike Nichols." *The Little Foxes* was redeemed, Wilson thought, by Miss Hellman's refusal to write "a tragedy with a happy ending." The modesty of his nonpolemical approach, unlike the shrill tones of Hardwick's article, carried the day.

Renata Adler performed the same function as Goodwin and Wilson when Charles Thomas Samuels attacked the *Collected Plays* in the New York *Times*. Hellman's plays were, Samuels thought, "contrived without compensating stylization; realistic in style but lacking reality; mechanically tooled but noisily clanking; engaging evil only to reduce it melodramatically." Adler accused Samuels of "critical ineptitude," hardly the case. Meanwhile Lillian attributed Samuels' malice to his having been a disciple of John Simon, with whom she had wrangled over his helping her with a translation at Harvard.

She taught at Harvard, at Yale, at MIT, and shrewdly assessed the deterioration of literary education in this country. She urged that MIT president Jerome Wiesner demand required courses in the history of literature. The redesign of the curriculum in the sixties had made it possible for students to avoid the major works of cultural history and Lillian was appalled. The present courses, she wrote Wiesner, "are nonsense examples of ten-cent store tie-dyed this year's chic," and she was right. In Hammettesque language she registered her complaint against the political correctness curriculum exalting slave narratives, women's studies, gay texts. Students needed, Lillian saw, "some basic knowledge of what literature means." Nor should it be "a choice of the young; it must be a demand from the rest of us." She did not cut her conscience to suit sixties political fashion.

It wasn't only to the Hammett estate that she brought her "shyster" cleverness. She remained determined to break the Sophie Newhouse Trust. Just because she had no children, Lillian reasoned, she should not be prevented from willing the capital of the trust upon her death. In August 1972 her aunt Florence Newhouse at last resigned as successor trustee; Lillian had her replaced with her own lawyer, Paul O'Dwyer. To free the trust for liquidation, Lillian sent Cathy Kober the $10,000 her mother had willed Arthur Kober.

"What is this ten thousand dollars?" Cathy asked.

"I owed it to your father," Lillian said vaguely. By 1977 she achieved her goal, netting $132,000. "It was not only the money that has bugged me all these years," Lillian said. "It was a disgrace that after my death the money would have gone to 5th and 6th cousins I had never seen and never want to see." It was a long-sought victory over the Newhouses.

My father told me a terrible thing, Lillian revealed one day to Alvin Sargent. He admitted he had married her mother for her money. The Newhouses had been right to distrust him. As soon as Max spoke those words, Lillian said, she had told herself, "I'll do everything I can for you, but I won't love you anymore. We have come to an end." Was it another of her fabulating reversals? As Max had accused her of not loving him anymore by committing him to a hospital for syphilitic dementia, so she admitted that she did reject him, but for a different, a justifiable reason.

If *An Unfinished Woman* and *Pentimento* had brought her new acclaim, the publication of *Scoundrel Time* in 1976 rained upon Lillian Hellman torrents of incredulity. In this account of her travail under McCarthyism she seemed unregenerate in her Stalinism. Nor would she even now admit that she and Hammett were Communists. Fighting back, she accused liberal anti-Communists of attacking "radicals" rather than capitalists and imperialists. But she was at last being held accountable and it stung.

Scoundrel Time had its defenders, among them Murray Kempton, who wrote, without having done his homework, that Lillian would be remembered as "someone who knew how to act when there was nothing harder on earth than knowing how to act." She had written that "radicals" like herself had done no harm. To those for whom the fate of democratic socialism mattered, she was not forgiven.

For having discredited the ideal of socialism, Irving Howe took her to task most eloquently in the pages of *Dissent.* "Dear Lillian Hellman," he wrote passionately, "you could not be more mistaken. Those who supported Stalinism and its political enterprises, either here or abroad, helped befoul the cultural atmosphere, helped bring totalitarian methods into trade unions, helped perpetuate one of the great lies of our century, helped destroy what possibilities there might have been for a resurgence of serious radicalism in America. Isn't that harm enough?" (Surprisingly, Lillian termed Howe's "the review of a gentleman.") Equally passionate was Phyllis Jacobson's piece in *New Politics,* which accused Hellman of "political amnesia" and termed *Scoundrel Time* "an exercise in self-justification."

Lillian was ready to quarrel with those who pointed out the hypocrisies latent in *Scoundrel Time.* Over a glancing reference to the Trillings as people who had "different political and social views from my own," over the accusation that the Trillings kept company with Whittaker Chambers, and the dark hint that in the antiradical camp were "men who turned down a dark road for dark reasons," a typical Lillian obfuscation, her friendship with Diana Trilling came to an end.

Lillian suggested that the anti-Communists had not sufficiently opposed McCarthy, which was true. Indeed many anti-Communists behaved as if the victims of McCarthyism were not worth defending because their views were reprehensible, an odd, antidemocratic position. It was as if the principle of freedom of expression did not demand the defense even of the indefensible, or, as Martin Peretz puts it, the "morally contemptible." So in their attacks on her Stalinist politics, Lillian's enemies played into her hands.

Diana Trilling replied to Lillian's references to her and her husband in a collection of essays which were under contract to Lillian's own publisher, Little, Brown. At once the publisher, as Roger Donald, the editor-in-chief, put it, "lost our enthusiasm" over Trilling's work. Trilling was to agree to have her remarks about Lillian edited or find another publisher. It appeared that none of them opposed censoring the disagreeable, the inconvenient, or the reprehensible. Certainly Little, Brown feared Lillian's wrath. Seizing upon Trilling's assertion that she didn't need them— that Harcourt was willing to publish her—they quickly bowed out.

At a lunch at Tavern on the Green, a nasty quarrel had erupted between Donald and Trilling. Trilling raised her voice; Donald fled. At once he telephoned Lillian, reporting that Trilling had been "hysterical." Lillian heard him say there had been a "hysterical attack on her in Trilling's manuscript." It was Trilling who gave the story to the New York *Times*, insisting her book had been censored. Asked to reply, Lillian referred to the "hysterical attack" in Trilling's book.

The quarrel of the lady writers made the front page of the New York *Times*, their pictures appearing side by side. When Lillian read a line about her "diminishing intellectual force," she laughed. "I don't give a damn," she said, still the she-Hammett. She stopped laughing when she saw that Donald had corrected her with respect to the "hysterical attack." If there was anything she could not abide, she the lifetime liar, it was being made to appear inaccurate. Fiercely, she upbraided Donald.

"Do you know who the last person was who called me names like this?" Donald asked her. Lillian again laughed. By the end, none of the parties emerged unscathed. Little, Brown seemed cowardly, breaking a contract to avoid an author's anger. Lillian seemed petty, a woman whose publisher so feared her they broke a contract for a book in which she was mildly criticized. Trilling also seemed unreasonable, with her demand of a public correction of the intent behind Lillian's mentions of the Trillings in *Scoundrel Time*.

Not to be left out, their mutual friend Norman Mailer weighed in, accusing Lillian of doing what Hammett had so often done, dismissing serious issues with an "exercise of his personal style." Lillian demurred. "Hammett's influence, there or not, doesn't matter much," she told Mailer, "because I have long ago found attacks painful and hard to recover from." Trilling had engaged in "the weary old Red-baiting style," nothing more. By the way, Lillian asked, "what were *you* doing there adjudicating, in the name of God?"

Soon Lillian discovered that Mailer had written an enthusiastic blurb for Trilling's forthcoming volume of essays. Not long after, he came for dinner. "Norman, I have to talk to you!" Lillian said severely as soon as the meal was over. She ushered him from the table to her study. Lillian shut the door and they sat down on the couch. What was involved, she said, was "some decent loyalty." She began reasonably: "If you like the book, and believe I'm guilty, you had a right to give the blurb."

By the end of the conversation she was furious: "Why didn't you call me before you gave the blurb?" she demanded. "I wouldn't have done this to you in a thousand years." Mailer was to go home. "I don't want anybody in my house who decides to endorse a book that attacks me."

When they emerged from the study, Mailer seemed pale, chastened. He remained for an hour, then left. There will be no blurb, Lillian confided in Renata Adler. Indeed, Mailer telephoned Harcourt and so edited his blurb that it became unusable.

The following summer, 1977, Diana Trilling complained she was not being invited out to dinner on the Vineyard as she had been in the past. "This ought to be called Lillian's island," she told the New York *Times*. Once more on the moral high road, Lillian had the last word. "It is remarkable to think of yourself as so important to an island that contains 40,000 summer residents and to worry so much about who is invited where. I do not live my life in quite so high a fashion, but then I do not stand in front of a mirror all day."

Always in quest of a fresh supply of adversaries, Lillian quarreled with movie star Jane Fonda over a casual remark Fonda made to *Newsweek*. In *Julia*, she had played Lillian Hellman as more ascetic than she actually was, Fonda said, to counteract her own sexy Barbarella image. "Why you wished to make me into a kind of other-generation whorish woman and yourself into an ascetic," she could not understand, Lillian said. As for her wearing sexy underwear, her underpants came from "the Vineyard Haven Dry Goods Store" and ran in price "from $2.95 to $3.95." When it was convenient, Lillian claimed the mantle of feminism. "The falling out of women offends me and always has, in my old-fashioned women's-personal-liberation way," Lillian said. As for Fonda's apology, it was "not acceptable."

The price of her bloomers or the pumpkin papers and the guilt of Alger Hiss: it was all the same. Life was adversarial. Politics remained supporting Dashiell Hammett's never disavowed Stalinism. In 1969 Lillian attacked Anatoly Kuznetsov for cowardice because he waited until he was abroad before protesting against Soviet censorship, a strange form of justifying her own public blindness to Stalin's atrocities over the years. In her foreword to Lev Kopelev's *To Be Preserved Forever*, written as a favor to his wife, her old friend Raya Orlova, Lillian managed to call the Kopelevs brave patriots, because, unlike Solzhenitsyn, they did not wish to leave their country.

Roger Straus, Lillian told his wife, Dorothea, was a "malefactor," because he published Solzhenitsyn. "If you knew what I know about American prisons," she claimed, "you would be a Stalinist too." American injustice allowed her now to maintain good faith with the tyrant, who had, despite his methods, industrialized the "first Socialist state." George Orwell's *Homage to Catalonia*, which exposes Stalin's betrayal of the Spanish revolution, was, Lillian insisted in the late seventies, "a load of crap." Meanwhile, even as her Communism had once brought the imprimatur of state power, so now, mainstream acceptability her goal, her table was peopled by conservatives like Joe Alsop and McGeorge Bundy or Kennedy acolytes like Richard Goodwin.

The Alsops and the Bundys held their tongues. But *New Republic* publisher Martin Peretz, a weekend guest on the Vineyard, did not feel that eating her gumbos meant suppressing his views. "Lillian, Communism has hurt two of the people you cared most about in your life," Peretz remarked, referring to Otto Katz, murdered in the Slansky show trials in Czechoslovakia in the early fifties, and, of course, Hammett.

"Dash was not hurt by the Communists," Lillian insisted. When Peretz held his ground, Lillian left the table. Her friendship with Peretz ended when she attacked him for participating with Roy Cohn in a fund-raiser for a Jewish cause.

"I did socialize with Roy Cohn," Peretz said, "but at least I never socialized with Stalin!" Lillian hung up on him.

Friends like Peretz were alienated by Lillian's constant, personalized attacks on Israel. "Zionism has sapped the dissident juices, the creative juices from the Jews," she insisted. "The Jews had to find a way to survive," even Hannah Weinstein argued softly. Lillian's attacks seemed more an unresolved anti-Semitism, a projected self-loathing, than a political position about Israeli politics. Even her secretary, Selma Wolfman, had to conclude that Lillian did not like being Jewish, would have been happier not being Jewish.

Any political overtures which threatened her need to be part of the mainstream were now rejected. "Who the hell gave you my number?" Lillian demanded when organizer Lynn Chaleff requested that she sponsor a dinner on behalf of the Veterans of the Abraham Lincoln Brigade. Civil rights meant little to her. "Black people are much better off in New Orleans than in the rest of the South," she told her friend writer Blair Fuller, and it seemed like a defense of the status quo. Fred Gardner requested her support for his coffeehouse movement against the Vietnam War, but dissident politics held no appeal and the antiwar movement passed her by. Lyndon Johnson's role in Vietnam did not trouble her, and by 1981 she was making Vineyard real estate suggestions to Lady Bird Johnson. Now she had two First Ladies in her camp.

Life was a "cakewalk," as Peter Feibleman was later to title his play about their friendship. Her choices remained contradictory, capricious. Having ceased to be a political woman, in 1970 Lillian founded a valuable political group, the Committee for Public Justice, to defend the Constitution and the Bill of Rights. Now connected on the highest levels of American life, Lillian enlisted her friends in a defense of civil liberties.

Even as she attacked the government, as Robert Silvers noted, it would not be from a leftist ghetto. She invited to join her Nuremberg prosecutor Telford Taylor, Harvard chemist William Doering, Martin Peretz, Robert Coles, Jerome Wiesner, John Hersey, and Norman Dorsen, then general counsel for the ACLU.

"Lillian, I'm a civil libertarian, not a person of the left," Dorsen told her, mistaking her intention.

"That's why we want you," Lillian answered.

Lawyer Stephen Gillers, for a time the committee's director, noted she sounded like "a progressive civil libertarian hostile to Nixonian Republicanism and willing to characterize it as 'fascism,'" but hardly a radical. The issues were free speech, privacy, and the abuse of the criminal justice system. Yet the committee's focus on the FBI's and the CIA's encroachments on the rights of Americans who had committed no crime but to dissent echoed Hammett's travail in the fifties when he had been persecuted for his beliefs.

Among the committee's accomplishments was a Princeton conference on the abuses of the FBI. In response to their invitation, J. Edgar Hoover had replied in an angry nine-page single-spaced letter, which was leaked and appeared on the front page of the New York *Times*. To challenge him then required great courage, as the conference produced the first major exposure of the FBI's violations of the civil rights of American citizens. Another conference was called "Watergate as Symbol." Lillian toured Trenton State Prison, a notorious hellhole, favoring the committee's prison work because Hammett had been in prison. He had called the people who ran Ashland "two-faced," she said.

Lillian attended every meeting, sitting with a burning cigarette in her hand beside a table which held a small photograph of Dashiell Hammett. Rita Wade would hand her a glass filled with a colorless fluid. It looked like water; it was vodka. The room was rich with chatter. Lillian waited until the moment felt right.

"Well!" she began. Silence fell. She picked up another cigarette, held it out in front of her, then met it halfway. She inhaled, exhaled, gathered her thoughts, then continued. Had there been a "swing to the right"? She proposed a conference on the subject. One of her favorite words was "behave." There was a correct way for the government to behave, and an incorrect way. "That is not acceptable," she might say with her combination, as Robert Silvers saw it, of self-centeredness, toughness, and coquetry. By the end of the meeting, her eyes would be glassier, her words slurred.

She favored mass rallies in Madison Square Garden, mobilizing people as in the old days. "One thing I'm really fed up with is this talk of lawyers," she complained. They were concentrating too much on lawyers. Yet they had no mass base, in the unions or elsewhere, nor a program appropriate to create one. "It's all just for lawyers," Lillian balked. "I don't see why I should go to all this trouble." She threatened to pull out.

"Let us concentrate on what we can do," Robert Silvers suggested. He was the intellectual bridge between the show business and the academic factions.

Hammett had always been appalled at Lillian's lion hunting. Now she rejected old friends like Martin Gabel and Arlene Francis. They were no longer important enough to be sponsors of a committee fund-raiser at the opening of *Julia*. "She's a little nobody," Lillian might say, shocking the idealistic young people who ran the committee. With the men, like Gillers, Lillian flirted. When one defected, as did Ray Calamaro, paranoically she accused him of being a spy. How could he have risen so high in the Carter Justice Department? she insisted.

Lillian was so tough on Calamaro that he finally called her the worst person he had ever known, only to correct himself and call Hannah Weinstein the worst, and Lillian the second worst. Of the young women lawyers, she was condescendingly dismissive. Dorothy Samuels, who headed the committee from 1977 to 1979, took to writing down her remarks and reading them back to her, lest Lillian deny what she had said moments before, as was her wont. "You're turning this into a lawyers' group," she attacked Samuels. She complained about how much the *Justice Department Watch* newsletter cost, although under the supervision of Gillers and edited by Silvers, it was an important achievement of the committee. Finally Samuels complained to Silvers. During her tirades, no one stood up to Lillian, Samuels said. Why didn't they stop her? You can't let her run me into the ground like this, Samuels appealed to Silvers.

When Silvers approached her on Samuels' behalf, Lillian was intractable. The women were not hardworking enough, she insisted. Yet she backed off and Samuels suffered no further abuse. After she resigned, she never wanted to see Lillian Hellman again. The heroine feminists had welcomed seemed to look down on women and be unable to acknowledge their achievements. Dorothy Samuels was a graduate of Bryn Mawr and Northeastern Law School. Her successor, Nancy Kramer, a graduate of Columbia Law, had already published a book when she began in 1979. No matter, Lillian humiliated her publicly at a fund-raiser held at Leonard Bernstein's.

"You're a liar!" Lillian shouted before a crowd of people, unjustly accusing Kramer of not doing a task she had in fact done. Someday she will die and her biographers will come to you and you'll have a chance to talk about this, Gillers consoled Kramer. Nancy Kramer pitied Lillian, growing old and frail, lashing out with anger at her fate. But she did not forgive her.

Meanwhile, her hair dyed as blond as ever, Lillian greeted Warren Beatty at a committee event held in honor of her seventieth birthday. Jackie Onassis was there. But it was when Warren Beatty embraced her that Lillian feigned ecstasy. "Warren, I can't TELL you what it means to be kissed by you," she mocked herself.

As the years passed, the anecdotes she told at meetings grew less credible. People were dubious, even as Lillian seemed unaware of their skepticism. One evening she recounted how a baggage handler at JFK Airport had informed her he was instructed to search certain people's luggage without a warrant on direct orders from the United States government. There was polite silence.

In the wake of the attacks on *Scoundrel Time,* Lillian grew more litigious than ever. No longer merely "shyster clever," she was now a full-blown Renaissance overreacher. Revenge had become her sword and shield as in the late 1970s she began to threaten people with lawsuits. "I ask you as a friend to make certain of your research," she wrote Diana Trilling in October 1976. "Otherwise we are going to be in legal trouble and God knows I do not ever want that." Trilling escaped with that broken book contract. Others would be less fortunate.

At the 1977 Academy Awards, Lillian presented the award for documentary short subject. She invoked the Spanish Civil war and Joe McCarthy, declaring she "had no regrets for that period." The owners of the motion picture industry, she said, had confronted the "wild charges of Joe McCarthy with the force and courage of a bowl of mashed potatoes." A standing ovation was her reward. But on the CBS news in his commentary on the event, Eric Sevareid remarked that Jane Fonda "did not know, apparently, that Miss Hellman was a systematic supporter of Stalinism, in spite of its mass horrors."

Lillian wrote at once to Richard Salant at CBS demanding time for herself or someone else to reply. When Salant declined, indicating she had already stated her political case on *Who's Who,* Lillian had her lawyer, Ephraim London, intervene. Sevareid's remarks had been "a malicious personal attack," London wrote. When CBS lawyers invoked the FCC personal attack rule, which exempted commentary like Sevareid's, London wrote to the FCC himself, complaining that CBS had refused to allow Lillian to answer an attack which was "malicious, premeditated and had nothing whatever to do with the news."

Nothing came of that skirmish. Lillian lost another when James

Wechsler threatened her with a lawsuit for calling him a "friendly witness" in *Scoundrel Time*. Later editions were altered. But Lillian was ever more vigilant of her honor now. In April 1978, reading an account of her contretemps with Diana Trilling in *Esquire,* an article in which Alfred Kazin referred to the quarrel as a "brouhaha among the literary teacups," Lillian asked London to "have a look at" this "despicable" article. Should they proceed to law?

That spring George Will attacked her in a *Newsweek* piece called "The Myth of Alger Hiss," calling *Scoundrel Time* "a celebration and misrepresentation of herself and her politics." Will's article was "dirty stuff," Lillian wrote her Vineyard acquaintance *Newsweek* publisher Kay Graham. Lillian also wrote to Will, demanding that he tell her "where in my book I misrepresented myself. Perhaps we could manage a nice law-suit." Undaunted, Will urged her to "feel free." He did not have "the right to say that I lied without saying where I lied," Lillian answered. Inevitably, accusations that she had not told the truth elicited her wrath. So she revealed that whenever anyone suggested her persona had been built on lies, she was prepared to fight to the death. Her honor, and Hammett's, her entire invented identity, were in jeopardy.

Lillian did not sue George Will. She was tempted to go to court once more in 1979 when she considered suing *National Lampoon* over that fake advertisement in which her face was pasted over a sexy body in blue jeans, the page that Leonard Bernstein had tacked up gleefully on his bulletin board.

Then, two years after she vowed "to stay away from all legal matters," Lillian set in motion the biggest lawsuit of her life.

31

The McCarthy Suit and Julia

"What is true should not be obscured by the fear of lawsuits."

LILLIAN HELLMAN

"My days are now off and on: one day better and one day worse. I sure wish we could move our trial ahead so that you would not have a piece of rag when it takes place."

LILLIAN HELLMAN

By 1980 Lily was unable to walk in the street by herself. A decade earlier, when she had met Stephen Gillers, she had seemed a robust woman in late middle age. Now she was a very old seventy-five. Coughing uncontrollably, and frail, she was rapidly losing her eyesight to glaucoma. The writing in her appointment book had to be in block letters made by a thick black Magic Marker. Her heart faltered. High blood pressure sometimes caused her to fall into a strange, almost comatose state. Although she did not suffer from Hammett's emphysema, she found it difficult to breathe. Yet she kept on smoking, ashes scattering everywhere. She set papers on fire because she couldn't see.

Death seemed to be overtaking her. One day she told Dr. Jay Meltzer that she wanted to put in her will that she didn't want to be kept alive by machines. Meltzer laughed. If it's in your will, it won't be read until after you're dead, he reminded her. Lillian renewed her prescription for nitroglycerin and tried to maintain her social life. To cheer herself up she went out and bought herself a new nutria coat and a mink hat.

In the wake of the attacks on *Scoundrel Time,* Mary McCarthy, living in Paris, began a series of attacks on Lillian, as if she were fresh from the battles of the 1949 Waldorf Conference when Lillian had stood firm in her support of the peace-loving Soviet Union and McCarthy was in the opposition as an anti-Stalinist. "I can't stand her," McCarthy told *Paris Metro* in 1978. "I think every word she writes is false, including 'and' and 'but.'" With that witticism, the interviewer noted, McCarthy's steady smile grew into a full grin.

McCarthy went on to describe Lillian Hellman at their 1948 meeting: "she had rather aging wrinkled arms, bare, and on them were a lot of gold and silver bracelets—and all the bracelets started to jangle." The attack was obviously personal; Lillian's style did not include dangling bracelets at that or any other period of her life.

On the subject of Mary McCarthy, Lillian had been more measured. In her 1968 *Paris Review* interview, she called McCarthy "often brilliant and sometimes even sound." Then she added that McCarthy's fiction placed her as "a lady writer, a lady magazine writer."

Soon the two American women writers were at war. Although some saw their quarrel as forming part of the political debate about socialism, this was not so. For years both McCarthy and Hellman had stood far from the arena of socialist discourse. A Cold War liberal, McCarthy could no longer be defined as an anti-Stalinist or a Trotskyist of any stripe.

Rather, she seemed a hard, bitter woman no less obsessed by her place in American literary history than Lillian was by hers. McCarthy's renewed interest in Lillian seemed a direct consequence of Lillian's iconic success with her memoirs, and the ensuing admiration she garnered from the women's movement, as well as from her having been portrayed in a major motion picture by Jane Fonda as a beautiful and courageous political heroine. Suddenly the attacks on *Scoundrel Time* had rendered Lillian Hellman vulnerable, easy prey at last.

It was one of those winter nights when Lillian might have described herself as "me alone." On the cold evening of January 24, 1980, she was at home on Park Avenue watching *The Dick Cavett Show.* His guest was a vituperative sixty-seven-year-old Mary McCarthy, whom Cavett, in an attempt to supply for the acerbic writer some audience appeal, had introduced as "a born truth-teller."

In response to Cavett's question about "overpraised" writers,

McCarthy replied: "The only one I can think of is a holdover like Lillian Hellman, who I think is terribly overrated, a bad writer and a dishonest writer." Lillian belonged "to the past," McCarthy claimed. When Cavett followed up, asking what was dishonest about her, McCarthy paused to chuckle: "heh, heh."

"Everything," she then added. "I said in some interview that every word she writes is a lie including 'and' and 'the.'" Laughter erupted among a studio audience comprised of McCarthy's friends.

Lillian watched and saw the rewards of her Faustian bargain crumble. Cold comfort as it had been to sacrifice family and love, the support of a devoted partner for celebrity, she perceived an ultimate challenge to her very existence. Lillian had invented and lied repeatedly in her work as in her life. At times her lying had repelled her; at times she had been scrupulously honest, in keeping with what she imagined Hammett expected of her.

More often, she had been a consummate, highly crafted liar. She had lied in print, in one chapter alone of *Pentimento* pretending that she never wanted to marry Arthur W. A. Cowan, that he was two years older than she, that he died in the company of some nineteen-year-old German girl, all fabrications. She had lied on television, telling Dan Rather, "I happen never to have been a Communist." Lying had been her strategy against the raw deal nature had dealt her, her means of maintaining power, and her tool to maintain an edge over life's inevitable stew of adversaries.

As Robert Silvers observes, her whole persona had long depended on none of these lies being acknowledged, none catching up with her. McCarthy threatened her very identity, that of the gruff, courageous, direct, outspoken woman who never lied. Her myth had been nourished by her supposed heroism under the HUAC siege, and even as Julia's brave friend. Calling her a liar was the worst thing you could say to a woman who had constructed her persona on lies. McCarthy had menaced her, and Lillian responded as if not only her literary reputation but her deepest self was in jeopardy.

Feeling old, calling herself a "piece of rag," still shaken by the public skepticism which had greeted the self-justifications of *Scoundrel Time,* Lillian remained a driven woman. Numbed by pain, she was revived by anger. Never one to retreat, she seized the offensive. Ephraim London, her lawyer, and so close a friend that at meetings of the Committee for Public Justice they appeared like brother and sister, was a telephone call away.

Lillian first wrote to Dick Cavett: "It seems to me I have a right to expect any reporter to ask where is the lie, and about what." Whether

McCarthy's attack was protected by the First Amendment was up to the courts to decide. "However, let us all see what we will now all see, after my lawyer listens to the tape." Her plan was to sue not only McCarthy but also Cavett and the Educational Broadcasting Corporation, which sponsored his program. Since the interview had been taped on October 18, they had had plenty of time to consider whether issues of defamation rendered it unsuitable to air.

"You're going to lose," London, a distinguished civil libertarian, warned in an effort to dissuade her.

"I don't care if I win or lose," Lillian said. "I hate that woman. I'll bleed her and impoverish her." To a friend, she said, "I'll break her. I can't lose. I win because I'm punishing her."

Even as her stature as a writer in the public perception had far out-stripped McCarthy's, Lillian was a far richer woman, and one with rich friends. Her net worth was officially $1,934,947, but for tax purposes everything had been undervalued, not least her jewelry, at a mere $10,425, and her Park Avenue apartment, listed at $116,681; it sold for close to a million dollars four years later. Her safe-deposit box was crammed with stocks, blue chips from AT&T to Xerox. McCarthy was living on her husband James West's government pension and from what she could earn from her writing. Her primary magazine outlet was *The New York Review of Books*.

Lillian seized her financial advantage. In addition to the resources of her own fortune, she would be represented by so devoted a friend that he could not bear to send her a bill for his services. It became a blood feud, a question of metaphoric vindication. Nor did the issue of how Hammett would have felt worry her. "I think Hammett would have thought she was not worth the trouble," Lillian granted. "He had great contempt for that whole group. He had great contempt for people who call other people names."

On some level she was fighting for the truth of what Hammett had believed too. She would be challenging the Mary McCarthy–Dwight Macdonald–Jim Farrell political nexus, and their view that Stalinism had destroyed the socialist ideal. She was no doubt correct that, ever evasive, Hammett would have converted the whole problem to one of style, to the unpleasantness of people who call other people names. Hammett had never been a man to answer his critics on the substance of his positions. The she-Hammett in *Scoundrel Time* had been his double.

On April 21, 1980, at 8:55 in the morning, a young lawyer named Terence R. Dellecker, who lived in Paris but was a member of the New York bar, rang the doorbell at a fifth-floor apartment at 141 rue de

Rennes. A short woman, whom he described as "about sixty years old with gray hair and fair skin," opened the door. When she identified herself as Mary McCarthy, he handed her a Summons and Complaint. Her statements about Lillian Hellman had been, it said, "false and . . . made with ill-will, with malice, with knowledge of its falsity, or with careless disregard of its truth or falsity, and with intent to injure the Plaintiff personally and in her profession." Lillian asked for $1,750,000 in damages and $500,000 in punitive damages.

Within the year, McCarthy was replying to Hellman's interrogatories, arguing that her statements had been opinion protected by the First Amendment. "Plaintiff is a bad writer and an intellectually dishonest writer," she insisted. Lillian's memoirs "distort events which are part of the history of plaintiff's time, distort and aggrandize her relationship to those events, and are harshly unfair to many individuals." If it was unseemly for McCarthy to be raising these issues in such a venue, it was Lillian who had put her there.

When she was asked to offer statements of Lillian's she knew to be untrue, McCarthy pleaded that her files were in Paris. It would be "unduly burdensome" for her to assemble this information. All she could come up with was that Lillian had pretended to be the first person willing to discuss her own activities with HUAC while being unwilling to divulge the names of others. Sidney Buchman had preceded her.

Another Hellman distortion was her characterization of James Wechsler as a "friendly witness" in *Scoundrel Time,* a moot point since Wechsler had been at least cooperative. But Lillian had to change her text. McCarthy soon began to speculate. Hellman *must have* known about Stalin's purges in 1937, although she denied it. Hadn't she signed a letter in 1938 to *New Masses* indicating that the signers at least knew about the trials, if not "the real facts about the situation in the Soviet Union"?

McCarthy then played her trump. She called "Julia," the chapter in *Pentimento* about how Lillian had carried money into Nazi Germany for her socialist-activist friend, a "dishonest work." It was all "incredible," McCarthy said. Lillian had in fact referred to a woman named "Alice" in *An Unfinished Woman* whose story was identical to that of "Julia." Could she have known "two women, both with medical careers, both Marxists, both Americans killed in Vienna?"

Lillian wrote for London a reply to McCarthy's answers. On the purge trials, she remained unregenerate. She had been in the Soviet Union for only ten days in 1937, she pointed out, ignoring the fact that the trials were international news on the front pages of all the newspapers. "When the purge trials did come," she insisted, "I disliked them as much as anybody else, although there was certainly a period when I thought mistakenly that many of the people might be traitors." Nothing had changed. "Certainly the purge trials were being used by the anti-red forces in America, and elsewhere, for their own purposes. Some of those purposes were good, and some of them were not so good."

The most flagrant of her lies would take some fancy explaining. Should she name them, Lillian told London, she would be "in very large danger from Julia's very unpleasant family." One of the "larger benefactors," she hinted darkly, "lives in Boston." This woman had almost guessed that Julia was her relative. Lillian had denied it for legal reasons "and because the lady herself is in terrible personal difficulty." It was the same argument she had used when she had accused Steven Marcus of not returning the Waldorf Conference minutes. In the service of her defense of her persona, Lillian lied even to Ephraim London. As he listened to these arguments, as he wondered how she could possibly be in danger over events which had occurred forty years earlier, he disbelieved her and he forgave her.

Lillian well knew that she would be criticized by the literary community for suing a fellow writer. In the press, she took the high road. "I am not a liar," she told the Los Angeles *Times* that summer, "and I do not believe it is anybody's right to call me a liar . . . without proving it." Feeling a need to explain herself to her acquaintances, she wrote to McCarthy's close friend Barbara Epstein. "Nobody can ever say they told the complete truth, nor do I think I did," she granted. But McCarthy, whose statement was "brutally damaging," had to "designate where I have lied." "What a disgusting messy business it all is, full of envy, malice, and women's hatred of women," Lillian added.

Some friends at once rallied to her defense. Kay Boyle, George de Trow, and Alger Hiss sent endorsements of the suit. John Hersey wrote Dick Cavett that for him not to have challenged McCarthy's statement was "truly shameful." Most were uneasy with a lawsuit initiated by a writer which attempted to stifle another writer's freedom of thought and speech. William Styron wrote Lillian that while he found McCarthy's statements "vicious, mendacious and . . . appallingly tasteless," he could not defend the suit which was "unfortunate," and as "loathsome" as McCarthy's words had been. Norman Mailer blamed Richard Poirier for encouraging Lillian in the suit and published "An Appeal to Lillian Hellman and Mary McCarthy" in *The New York Times Book Review*, in which he remarked that it was "natural for them to detest each other." Weren't all writers "dishonest" anyway? Mailer rambled. Mary had gone "too far," but Lillian should have walked away. That saner voice, Robert Silvers, told her he thought the suit was "deeply wrong."

"Lillian, I don't think it right for one writer to sue another over some expression of opinion," he said.

"I want to hear in court someone try to prove that I lied," she answered. "I want to know wherever, whenever I lied. I want someone to show me that." Over and over she repeated: "I want her either to show publicly where I lied or to say I didn't."

If she could accept these words from Robert Silvers, she was furious when William Alfred told her the suit was "mistaken," that her honor needed no defense. She wrote back demanding to know who had prompted him to write such a letter. "You call Miss McCarthy and you tell her that if she gives me an apology, I'll drop the suit," she said. It was her anger which was her downfall, Alfred concluded, causing her to waste so much of her life. That anger had led her to abort Hammett's baby, the child who died which had not been "Julia's baby," but her own.

Lillian's enemies, of course, were elated. Mary McCarthy had not cut "her conscience to fit the whims of Joseph Stalin," William F. Buckley, Jr., noted. Diana Trilling was happy to tell the New York *Post* that Miss Hellman was "greatly gifted in the writing of fictions both for the stage and in her books of memoir."

Now a former member of Lillian's coterie, Renata Adler, devoted to the suit a paragraph of her novel *Pitch Dark,* in which Lillian enjoys a walk-on part as one Viola Teagarden. Ezra Paris, she wrote, referring obviously to London, had taken a suit "of no legal merit," justifying it to himself on the ground that "she was sad, hurt, pitiable, distraught." Martin Pix, Adler speculated incorrectly, had paid for it. In fact, Max Palevsky opposed the suit and believed Mary McCarthy had been exercising her hyperbolic privileges as a writer.

"Viola Teagarden has no memory of doing you any harm except sending you a book bag for Christmas," Lillian wrote Adler, "which you told Mike Nichols the maid put in an ice box." Her letter was addressed to "Miss Brett Daniels, A Goy Princess." Adler was, of course, Jewish. No Jew could have so hurt her, Lillian implied. Adler went further than the roman à clef. A graduate of the Yale School of Law, she did research for Mary McCarthy, compiling "lies" from Lillian's works.

"I am sick of asking for a bill," Lillian had written Ephraim London in September 1980. She sent him a check in the hope that "this will buy you one serge suit." In a postscript she added, "Does serge exist anymore?" In October 1981 she sent him a check for $3,000, which had to represent a tiny fraction of what he would have been owed.

Virtually blind and lame, beset by many small strokes, Lillian had all New York talking. By 1981 her sight was entirely gone in one eye. She fractured her pelvis. In the early morning of November 22, her heart stopped, and she was rushed to intensive care. "Fell off the toilet," she wrote in her diary on December 6. On the eleventh she attended the opening of Jules Feiffer's *Grown Ups*. She dyed her hair with L'Oréal and peroxide and kept on going.

Part of the suit involved her compiling a list of people who would vouch for her honesty and integrity. Lillian chose: Ambassador Kingman Brewster, John Hersey, Mrs. Marshall Field, head of the Field Foundation, Joseph Rauh, Joseph Alsop, Lord Victor Pritchett, Richard Locke, Edward Said, Richard Poirier, Judge Benjamin Kaplan, Mrs. Katharine Graham, Mike Nichols, Jason Epstein, Roger Straus, Arthur Thornhill, publisher and president of Little, Brown, and Milton Wexler, a California psychoanalyst. She named the communities in which she had a "reputation for honesty and integrity": Pleasantville, New York, Los Angeles, Martha's Vineyard, London, and Paris, and "other places in which my books have been sold." It was December 1981. Her signature was scarcely legible.

The strain of the suit took its toll on Mary McCarthy, and in the deposition she made after her first interrogatories, she blinked. "It may well be that the plaintiff has persuaded herself of her version of the truth and is deaf to any other," McCarthy added, unable to prove that Lillian had consciously lied. Now she denied she was speaking of "prevarication per se," which would "require a conscious intent to state an untruth." The result, in any case, was "pervasive falsity."

McCarthy was asked to define "pervasive falsity." It "does not mean that her writing is made up of literal lies," McCarthy retreated, "and I don't mean literally nothing when I say 'nothing in her writing rings true,' I don't mean of course, say perhaps 70 percent of factual statements are probably true . . . I mean the general tone of unconvincingness and falseness." Did she mean that all of Lillian Hellman's writing was in fact lies?

"I would say 'no,'" McCarthy had to admit.

The McCarthy side was helped substantially by the publication of an article by Martha Gellhorn, called "On Apocryphism," in the Spring 1981 *Paris Review*. Gellhorn systematically shattered Lillian's version of her trip to Spain, and questioned most of what she ever had to say about her encounters with Ernest Hemingway. "It might not be a bad idea," London wrote Lillian gently in August, "to prepare to answer McCarthy's and Gellhorn's statements about the lies you told." But she should answer only "those questions that you can answer without difficulty." Meanwhile he saw to it that there were delays. She was in Los Angeles, he told the court; she was on a yachting trip with Max Palevsky. London himself would be out of town when she returned.

In March 1982, John G. Koeltl, representing Educational Broadcasting, was told by London that if he wanted to review "specific documents" he had better do it right away. Lillian would be leaving town by the middle of April. Lillian left a note with the material: "It is all that I have saved and have nothing else to show you."

The assistant went to Lillian's apartment four times, sifting through her boxes. There were 1,725 items dating from 1934 to 1982. There were also 1,426 clippings in which she was mentioned. Typewritten lists were compiled identifying all her writings, all writings in which she was the subject or was mentioned by name, all radio and television programs in which she appeared, all press releases she had ever issued, all lectures, speeches, and public appearances she had ever made before audiences of twenty-five or more, whether she participated "in the advertising, promotion or endorsement of any product." Part of the purpose of the McCarthy side was to argue that she was a public figure, the most public of celebrities, the most recognizable of personalities, which would then have required her to prove "actual malice" on McCarthy's part.

In April, Rita Wade was asked to copy *The Ladies' Home Journal's* retraction dating from Lillian's piece on the 1963 March on Washington. Lillian had accused the police of Etowah County, Alabama, of putting cow prodders to a boy and had to apologize to the sheriff. But even in her apology she insisted that her article told "the truth." She dissociated herself from *The Ladies' Home Journal's* own retraction: "What is true should not be obscured by the fear of lawsuits."

The McCarthy researchers compiled articles where Lillian was accused of fabricating: they found a scant few. But there was a *New Republic* review of *The Children's Hour* in which Lillian de la Torre pointed to "the danger of using historical sources, and bowdlerizing them," an accusation that might have been made equally against Shakespeare. A squib from a 1944 *New Yorker* focused on the title *The Searching Wind.* There were two quotes about the origin of the title. In one, published in *The Sun,* Lillian said she took the title from *Bleak House* by Charles Dickens. In the other, from the *Herald Tribune,* she said she got the title "from a colored maid who used to work for me. Some mornings when she came she'd say, 'It's a searching wind today.'" The *New Yorker* headline read: "What Paper D'Ya Read?"

Time was on Lillian's side because she had money to spend; time was on McCarthy's side because Lillian was older and in frail health. But McCarthy too increasingly felt the strain. Her lawyers finally threatened Lillian with "an appropriate court order" to demand that she reply to their interrogatories. As late as January 1983 the McCarthy side was complaining about "the inadequacy of plaintiff's interrogatory answers." Lillian placed herself firmly on the offensive and stood there, intractable.

Her health took turns for the worse. She felt control slip from her, and lashed out. She was horrified over a new production of *Candide,* she wrote Robert Lantz. "That piece of shit that appeared . . . was as if Mr. Prince had taken out his penis and waved it at a gaggle of fags and Mr. Wheeler stood right behind him doing the same thing." Only a dream about Felicia Bernstein restrained her from a lawsuit. She didn't want to "harm anybody or anything that Felicia had loved."

By 1982 hallucinations caused by her medications beset her. She had a stroke. Her leg collapsed. She was told that without surgery she might be confined to a wheelchair. That summer of 1982, because she fell often, her doctor forbade her to go to the bathroom alone. "You know, it's not easy to defecate with people in the bathroom," she said with wry humor. Angry, terrified, she went to see her psychoanalyst, George Gero, just as she had when Dash was dying. She didn't want to think about it, she said. Gero agreed that it was bad for her to talk about how she felt, about all that was going wrong.

"Yesterday I felt, and I guess today, that nothing is ever going to be right again," she told Dr. Meltzer. "I had better get that out of my head, right?" The last five years had been "a major decline of everything." Despite sleeping pills, she could sleep only in the daytime. Nights were for brooding. She could no longer read. In July 1982 she entered Massachusetts General Hospital for tests. "I am a kind of mess, but I love you," she wrote London. There was a seventeen-week stay at Massachusetts General Hospital in 1983 during which her carotid arteries were repaired.

London knew that the McCarthy side would focus on the obvious fabrication of the story "Julia," since by now it was apparent that Lillian had appropriated the life of Muriel Gardiner and turned it into the life of a personal friend, one in which she had played a courageous part. Lillian, of course, had heard Gardiner's story from their mutual friend and lawyer Wolf Schwabacher, into whose Pennington farmhouse Gardiner had moved in 1940. The publication of Gardiner's memoirs, *Code Name Mary,* in the spring of 1983 did not bode well for her case.

Fearing that the "Julia" fabrication might destroy the entire lawsuit, London told Lillian he needed the name of the real Julia in order to defend her. Out of a labyrinth of regret, revenge, and yearning, Lillian came up with the answer; the real name of Julia's family was Clark! But it wasn't a member of Blair Clark's family—that would have been too easy to verify, too obvious a self-exposure. No, it was a Singer Sewing Machine Clark, the family of her enemy Martin Peretz's wife, Anne, whose grandfather was Stephen Clark. So she could toy with, mock both Peretz and Blair Clark at the same time, even as she lied to kindly Ephraim London.

"It's a complete fabrication," Martin Peretz says. His wife, Anne, agrees. Anne had no relation remotely resembling either Muriel Gardiner or Julia. But Lillian would not retreat from this claim.

She decided that George Gero must telephone Muriel Gardiner and extract a statement that she was not Julia and that Julia could have existed without her knowing it. Lillian had never actually used the words "Austrian underground." Perhaps that might help. She also said she was willing to apologize for not answering Gardiner's letter, of which she had no memory. "And for that I am deeply sorry," she told Gero, using her familiar locution.

In fact, Rita Wade had placed Gardiner's letter neatly in the *Pentimento* folder marked "fan mail." On October 26, 1976, Gardiner had written to Lillian, gently pointing out the similarities between herself and Julia. Her friends had often asked her, "Are you Julia?" As for the actual plot of the story, Gardiner later remarked, "It was perfectly impossible." Although she had never met Lillian, Gardiner wrote she had "heard of you often from our good friend Wolf Schwabacher." In her memoir Gardiner revealed that she had gone to Vienna to ask Dr. Herbert Steiner, director of the Documentation Archives of the Austrian Resistance, what other American women had been deeply involved in the Austrian underground. The answer was always "only Mary," Gardiner's code name.

After the publication of *Code Name Mary*, in May 1983 Lillian planned a trip out to Pennington, New Jersey, to confront Muriel Gardiner, and get her to say she was not Julia. She would be accompanied by her lawyer, London, and Blair Clark. Lillian told Gero that London was "very frightened" of Muriel Gardiner, "and so indeed am I." But when she learned that Lillian planned to bring her lawyer, Gardiner canceled the meeting; her own attorney was not available.

Instead of journeying to Pennington, London, Clark, and Lillian had lunch that Saturday afternoon at Le Cirque. London and Clark planned to convince Lillian that she had nothing to fear legally if she named Julia. But Lillian resisted. "They" would sue her, she said. Hadn't she represented them as "awful" to Julia and her child? She had suggested that the child might be alive. Wouldn't some part of the Clark fortune belong to her? Wouldn't Martin Peretz try to get revenge?

When London pleaded with her, Lillian claimed she didn't "understand" what he was saying. Clark asked suddenly for the first name of

Julia's father as well as the name of the grandfather, neither of which Lillian could now remember. Julia "left me quite a lot of money because she had told me so," Lillian claimed, explaining why naming Julia would still cause her legal difficulty.

That same money had been inherited by Martin Peretz's wife, Anne, who, one day as she was driving her in Boston after Lillian had lectured at Radcliffe, had admitted it to her. And Lillian had told her she "thought it was disgraceful that her money—Julia's money—was going to support a fascist magazine." Cornered, about to be unmasked, she struck now at the Peretzes. Anne had "looked very near tears," Lillian reported, "and said very sadly, 'But, Lillian, I can't break him.'" Lillian then added she herself was "scared to death of crossing" Peretz; this was her reason for being unable to mention Julia's proper name. It was a story akin to the Norman Mailer rape fantasy, and more insidious. Her slanders far outdistanced McCarthy's original meanspirited hyperbole.

Lillian also claimed she had a letter from a lawyer named "Wolf" telling her to "lay off the Julia-and-child story," echoing the part Wolf Schwabacher had played in the real event, he who told her the story of Muriel Gardiner's life. Her lies contained always clues to the reality. That letter supposedly also said that if she didn't stop the calls to Julia's grandmother and grandfather, they would sue her for defaming their characters.

Where is that letter? London asked her. She had looked for it "desperately," Lillian answered, but it had disappeared. She had put it in a bag, which had gotten lost. "I guess I tore it up," she said when London pressed her to look for the letter or letters.

Both London and Clark were deeply sympathetic to the frail Lillian Hellman. In an effort to ease her mind, Clark wrote a letter, which Harper's published that same May 1983. "Poor Mary McCarthy!" it began. "The only recourse after Miss McCarthy's vulgar and outrageous statement, other than to grin and bear it, was to ask a court of law to find it false, malicious and defamatory." Harper's deleted "vulgar and outrageous."

Now she sounded so certain of her facts, they tried to grant some credibility to her inventions. Julia's mother must be dead by now, Clark remarked. Since Julia was Lillian's contemporary, that would put the mother in her mid-nineties. Suddenly Lillian told them that Julia was ten years younger than she, in clear contradiction of everything written in Pentimento.

After that lunch at Le Cirque, London and Clark escorted her back to her Park Avenue apartment. Then they walked several blocks together. McCarthy's lawyers will "destroy" her on the witness stand, London feared, if all she had was what they heard at lunch. Her mind was not clear. "The case will never go to trial," London speculated, and it was clear to Clark that he hoped it would not.

Clark went home feeling depressed. What was the statute of limitations should Lillian reveal Julia's name? he wondered. Would money actually have to be redistributed were a child alive? Who of that family was still alive? Did Lillian actually possess any letters from Julia, as she suggested? Did Julia, as Lillian had claimed, really send her the Toulouse-Lautrec drawing which "hangs today" in her house? (That year Lillian told Alvin Sargent that Dorothy Parker had given her the same drawing in repayment of a loan.) Unable to accept that it was all fantasy, Clark found it excruciating not to believe her.

Five days after their lunch at Le Cirque, he brought a Chinese dinner to Lillian's apartment. Sitting on the living-room sofa with a drink, he pressed her again about Julia's identity. Returning to the motif of Julia's age, he reminded her that she had told him that Julia's mother was just a little older than Lillian herself, that Julia would be younger than Blair, who was twelve years younger than Lillian. Yet in *Pentimento* she had depicted them as adolescents together.

Lillian's mind wandered. Soon she changed into one of her pink shorty nightgowns and asked him to join her in the bedroom. As she did so often with male guests, she exposed her matchstick-thin, now ulcerated legs. It was a last defiance of the moment when she had discovered that beauty meant power and she didn't have it.

Lillian confided that she had many dreams and for ten minutes afterward she was unable to convince herself that the dream people were not still there with her. He pressed again for the exact name of Julia.

Julia was, in fact, the middle name, Lillian now revealed. The first name was either Dorothy or Doris, so that she was often called DJ. Lillian again expressed her fear that Martin Peretz would sue her. Hadn't she said very harsh things about him? Hadn't he a motive? Suddenly she remembered something more. Her former decorator, Eleanor Merrill, "knew them all." These Clarks had a place in "Clarksville" which Merrill had decorated.

"Cooperstown," Clark corrected her. Lillian said nothing.

"I hope I'll be well enough to testify," she said. Clark told her an hour in the library with *Who's Who* would establish everyone's identity. No, Lillian demurred. Nothing must be done to "suggest that London had not done the necessary."

There were many bad days. In a Madison Avenue boutique a young man accidentally bumped her. Lillian raised her cane and brought it down on his arm. "How dare you push me!" she cried. When her assistant Robin Hogan pleaded that the store was crowded, Lillian turned on her: "How dare you defend this man against me!" The many drugs she was taking made Lillian dream that the people taking care of her were trying to kill her. It was guilt over how she treated them, her friend Milton Wexler thought.

The drugs also blocked normal censoring impulses, impaired her judgment. A taxi driver said something she thought was insulting and she got out of the cab and began wildly swinging her cane in an effort to smash his headlights. Another driver she managed to hit on the head with her pocketbook, a tiny old lady weighing less than a hundred pounds doing battle for her honor in a parody of Hammett in the old speakeasies of San Francisco. Lillian said she felt as if she were standing "in a closet facing death all the time."

She fired three nurses in one night alone, furious because they had tried to take away her cigarettes. She called the agency and more troops were dispatched. It was, Alvin Sargent observed, like MacArthur requesting reinforcements, and you knew they would not survive. She fired Dr. Meltzer. She needed an ambulance and was enraged that her doctor didn't follow the ambulance in his own car. "We each . . . have a right to our standards of conduct," she told him, exactly what she had said when Lenny Bernstein had not attended her picnic after Felicia fell ill. Still she wanted the New York *Times* read to her every day. Huge boxes of shrimp and crawfish arrived and she masterminded a cooking spree. Still she wore makeup, but not on her poor, weakened eyes.

In 1984 the court was ready to hear Mary McCarthy's motion for a summary judgment dismissing Lillian's original complaint. This motion focused on the argument that McCarthy's attack had been constitutionally protected opinion even if it was expressed "in an exaggerated and rhetorical manner." More, it had been directed toward a public figure who had presented no proof of "actual malice." Hellman would have to prove McCarthy had spoken in reckless disregard of the truth, or with the knowledge that her statement was false. As Doubleday chief counsel Harriette Dorsen suggests, there is no precedent for a prominent writer not being considered a public figure in connection with a discussion of her work. McCarthy was not, after all, talking about Lillian's sex life, but about her writing.

Ephraim London argued, however, that since McCarthy's statement had not been made in a review, it could not be considered a literary opinion exempt from the charge of defamation. It should be treated, rather, as a statement of "alleged fact." Nor was Lillian Hellman a public figure "within the special meaning of that term in the law governing causes for libel and slander." London urged that a jury hear the case.

In an attached affidavit, Lillian denied she was a public figure in the sense of one who "assumes roles of special prominence in the affairs of society" or who occupies a position of "persuasive power and influence." She had not been that for years. As the case proceeded, Robert Silvers had noticed, there was a definite slackening-off of the activities of the Committee for Public Justice. Lillian, of course, was not well. But she did seem to find something difficult or wrong with every project suggested. The committee finally disbanded in 1982.

And might not one argue that McCarthy had acted in reckless disregard of the truth? She knew so absolute a statement could not be true, and had offered no foundation on which she had based such an opinion. By the standard of *Times* v. *Sullivan*, Lillian even as a public figure had a right to sue her. McCarthy had acted out of the legal definition of malice, she the woman Katherine Anne Porter had once called "in some ways the worst tempered woman in American letters."

In May 1984, State Supreme Court justice Harold Baer, Jr., accepted Ephraim London's argument and denied Mary McCarthy's motion to dismiss the suit. Lillian Hellman was not an "unlimited and voluntary public figure," which he defined as being not only a person of "general notoriety" but also someone involved in a "public issue, question or controversy." He based his view on the "total" public figure defined in the 1974 landmark *Gertz* v. *Robert Welch, Inc.,* case. "To call someone dishonest, to say to a national television audience that every word she writes is a lie, seems to fall on the actionable side of the line—outside what has come to be known as the 'marketplace of ideas,'" he ruled.

Since Mary McCarthy had obviously made a "false statement of fact," Baer went on, she enjoyed no constitutional protection or privilege unless the plaintiff was held to be a public figure. It was that line— "every word she writes is a lie"—which had distressed the court. That McCarthy had made virtually the same statement to *Paris Métro* not only negated innocent error but provided some proof of "actual malice." In calling Lillian Hellman a liar, McCarthy had crossed the boundary between opinion and fact. She was guilty of "reckless disregard of the truth." The case would go forward.

It was May 10, 1984. "The power of L.H.—a puzzlement, even when one knows how concentrated she has been in its service," Elizabeth Hardwick had written to her friend Mary McCarthy in 1977. Her distraught husband, Robert Lowell, had immediately gone to Lillian. "This is the worst moment of my life," he all but wept.

So once again had Lillian's power been demonstrated.

It was a stupendous victory for Lily, her last. She died a month later. Her suit against Mary McCarthy expired with her.

Yet even after her enemy's death, Mary McCarthy was not done. "There's no satisfaction in having an enemy die," McCarthy crowed. "You have to beat them." Lillian Hellman's depiction of her relationship with Dashiell Hammett, McCarthy added, striking where she knew her enemy had been most vulnerable, had been "a kind of awful way of giving yourself loveability."

32

Requiescat in Pace

"I wish I had stayed in New Orleans and married out of that good German Jewish county club set and had an affair with the same man my cousin now sleeps with, or did, if he hadn't died on her."

LILLIAN HELLMAN

As medication obliterated her censoring impulses, no contradiction surfaced more sharply than that the feisty, independent woman felt life was unbearable without a husband, a man of her own. Lillian in her last years behaved as if she must have a distinguished, good-looking man, one younger than she, to complete herself; it was more important to her in her seventies than ever. As Shirley Hazzard noticed, quoting biographer Gordon Haight's observation about the novelist George Eliot, another artist who was not a beauty, she was "not fitted to stand alone." Since Arthur Kober, there had been no man entirely hers.

Prematurely aged, wrinkled, coughing, all but blind, Lily laughed with Hannah Weinstein for indulging in what she called the "Mrs. Schwartz syndrome." All the while she knew she could never have been satisfied with being a wife, spending her days shopping, having a nice boring husband take care of her. Yet Hannah had three daughters; Lillian had none. "I always guessed," Lillian Hellman wrote five years before her death, "and certainly I now clearly know, that somewhere along the line I could and maybe should have chosen another way, a safer way. On winter Sundays I am sorry that I didn't."

From the fifties on, her male friends fended off her half-mocking sexual appeals, the most recent being Bill Styron, who told Carlos Fuentes he wound up hating her. "If you were ten years younger, I would have married you," Mike Nichols gently had told her; she seemed grateful at how graciously he had let her know it would never be romantic between them. Still, she was difficult at his 1976 wedding to Annabel Davis-Goff. Only when Warren Beatty devoted himself to her did she cheer up. That year too, in jest as in despair, she told Alvin Sargent, who had just written *Julia,* "I've hired Rabbi Nussbaum." Then in mock conspiracy she asked producer Richard Roth to plead her case. It would "give him a chance for a third or even a fourth bride," she argued. "Do point this out to him."

One middle of the night on the Vineyard when Sargent was visiting, Lillian suddenly walked into his room stark naked. In her hand she held a mirror. "I've never seen my clitoris," she told him. Would he hold the mirror so that she could see her clitoris? Sargent complied.

She was the most insecure woman Dorothea Straus had ever known. If Lillian Hellman had modeled herself on the tough, hard-boiled persona popularized by Dashiell Hammett, in her last years it was clear that the role had worn thin. More than ever she affected the Southern belle needing protection, the woman who would have married again, like a shot. She remained a sexy woman. How about a kiss? a taxi driver asked after a ride when she sat up front because it was easier with her crutches.

"A quarter!" Lillian bargained. He gave her the quarter; she kissed him. She made it her business for men to think she was sexy until the day of her death.

Now she sometimes proposed to male friends like Richard de Combray, and mischievously told people they were close to an erotic relationship. She insisted to Blair Clark that de Combray had promised to consummate their relationship, do what he had never done. "I wish I looked like you," she told the tall, blond, slender de Combray, who was so handsome that he had once been a model.

They had been friends for a decade. It was a nonsexual relationship, of course, and as Hammett had written her love letters when they were no longer lovers, so Lillian used the same cadences in her letters to de Combray. When he was traveling in 1975 she addressed him in her letters as "Prof," just as Hammett had called himself "the old professor" in his letters to her. "It seems to me, in the face of my fidelity, a letter from you should arrive very soon," Lily wrote, as Hammett had from the Aleutians so often declared his celibacy to her. Another letter closed with a cacophony of "I miss yous," just as one of Hammett's to her had done:

4. I hope you will miss me when you get home.
5. I will miss you.
6. I hope you will miss me.
7. I will miss you.

In 1960 she had told Jason Robards, "I'll fuck you, but I won't marry you." Two decades later as they were looking to replace an actor in the 1980 revival of *The Little Foxes,* she told director Austin Pendleton, "Why don't you call up Jason and say I've changed my mind. I will marry him!"

Above all, she wanted to marry the person on whom she depended most, Peter Feibleman. When they became lovers, she had even announced the fact to his mother. "I hear Lillian has you in her net," Feibleman's mother told him. He was twenty-five years her junior.

She said Hammett had liked the portrait Luis Quintanilla had painted of her. After Hammett's death she tossed it into a closet. When Feibleman admired it, she laughed. "It makes me look like a three-times-divorced editor of *Vogue,*" she said. "Fuck both of you." She gave the painting to Peter, along with the exquisite lace panel depicting the Court of King Ferdinand and Queen Isabella which Hammett had bought in 1953 with what had to be her money. When Feibleman displayed it in his Los Angeles house, Lillian made a show of turning her back whenever she entered its proximity.

She was a mother figure, mentor, friend, lover, but he could not marry her; his motive would have seemed to be her money. Lillian did not give up easily. One day she even told him she had bought wedding rings, and indeed Rita Wade had gone down to Lillian's favorite jeweler, Gold Art, and picked them up. "I got two for the price of one. They were on sale," Lily said. She wanted a safe, established relationship, the certainty he would be there for a while. When she fell ill in 1983 Peter was there—not as a husband but now, in the final reversal of roles, as the parent.

At Massachusetts General, Feibleman saw to the hospital and the doctors, forgiving her for the jealousy that led to her hiring a private detective to spy on him. "Hammett used to hurt me in the same sense you believe that I did," she told him, justifying her behavior, although Hammett would have been incapable of violating another person's privacy, dignity, and rights. Feibleman arranged for them to write a book together, a collection of "Recollections & Recipes."

In gratitude, Lillian told Feibleman, "I've only taken seriously two men in my life," smoothing out the edges. "One was too young and one was too old." This was not quite the Hammett problem, since only eleven years separated them. The trajectory she had gone through in her acquaintance with Hammett was repeated with Feibleman and in other connections: when the blush of romance, of fantasy died away, she hung on and never let go. "Lillian has a way of binding people to her," Selma Wolfman had remarked. "Unless she wants you to get away, you're not going to get away."

When she talked of Hammett in these last years, it was to say she regretted the fighting; rather than letting her temper flare, she should have forgiven him everything. She recounted dreams about Hammett. In one "he was lying on his back in the earth." The ground was "soggy," and he "was sinking back into it." Hammett, she said, "kept smiling and beckoning to me with his hand." Then he stared at her, and she didn't like the way he was staring. It was the stare she could never penetrate and she remembered it to the end.

In a dream she relayed to Jonathan La Pook, a young Hammett yelled at her, "Forgive me. Forgive me. I didn't mean to die! I'm sorry that I died. It's not my fault." She was angry at him still, for the Laura Perelman betrayal, for dying and leaving her.

She wanted Linda Anderson, her last surrogate Sophronia, to cook her favorites: pigs' feet, cow tripe, roast pork, corned beef hash, hog brains. To Linda, she talked often about Hammett's infidelities and how his venereal diseases had prevented them from making love for a long time.

"He satisfy your soul," Linda told her, and Lillian laughed her deep, throaty laugh.

"Linda, be very careful, because men can ruin your life," Lillian warned. "Men can be bastards." Then she paused, and added, "And they can be motherfuckers too."

Into her last year she maintained her social life: New Year's Day drinks at Hannah Weinstein's, a dinner party complete with bartender in February out in Los Angeles, more dinners out in New York, with a nurse nearby.

For some years now she had faced for herself what she had for Hammett: the invasion of biographers. In the early sixties, she thought her Harvard student Fred Gardner might make a good biographer and he set to work. He interviewed John Melby, Arthur Kober, Blair Clark, Helen Rosen, and others, and composed a draft, but then Lillian told him she was going to write her own story. "You can write a book later," she said.

Knowing how much work he had done, she offered him a share in the Vineyard beach house she owned with Leo Huberman.

Gardner was relieved to abandon the project as he perceived the disparity between her version of events and the facts garnered in his research. It had disturbed him as well that she was not forthcoming when he asked questions about the purchase of the Hammett estate. He had been disappointed to discover that money, not Marxist politics, or even a sense of class, consumed her thoughts.

In 1970 Lillian asked Gardner to write Hammett's biography, informing him that Mary was not his natural daughter. When she told him that she and Hammett had never discussed whether he was a member of the Communist Party and had no real criticism of their politics, Gardner knew he could not put his name to such a collaboration. The history of the left in America was too important an issue for him not to treat it with full honesty.

In the intervening years a writer named Katherine Lederer and a professor named Richard Moody published books about her work. Lillian read their manuscripts carefully but contributed little about her life. With these diligent researchers she had trouble sorting the truth from the fabrications she had written in her memoirs. "I don't know where the story of briefcase torn-up-play came from but it is not true," she wrote Lederer, who had taken the incident from *An Unfinished Woman*. When Lederer wrote that Lillian had compared her father's conversation with Hammett's, Lillian had to tell her, "I don't think this was ever true."

Her annotations to Moody's manuscript, made in April 1971, corrected his accurate research, so that he was left with no alternative but to print her fabrications. Moody had her date of birth correct: 1905. Lillian insisted it was 1906. Many corrections had to do with Hammett. Beside a Hammett quotation about writers writing for money, she wrote, "No, never said this," as if she knew everything he had ever said. Moody quoted a newspaper story datelined Havana which said that Lillian was finishing a new play and that when she returned Dashiell Hammett might help in "doctoring" it. "No!" she wrote in the margin. Moody had to add that the notion of Hammett as "doctor" was a reporter's invention.

When Moody wrote that after the failure of *Days to Come*, Lillian had reminded Hammett that he had said it was the best he had ever read, and then quoted her own published words, Lillian denied them. "No. Just that it was good." Moody placed her in Paris finding a letter from Hammett: "how remote and inconsequential all of this seemed, even Hammett's divorce, as she departed for the front." Lillian blanched, even as she told Moody nothing about why Hammett got his divorce at that moment. "Oh, *no!*" she wrote. Moody deleted "even Hammett's divorce."

She guarded the myth. Where Moody wrote that her friendship with Hammett "had survived many stormy periods," Lillian underlined the word "stormy" and wrote "never." He wrote that Lillian was "unable to cope with [Hammett's] periods of depression; Lillian changed the text to "insobriety."

Moody wrote that "one of her friends once chided her for restricting herself to successful people, thus missing a lot of her fellow creatures whom she might have found more fascinating." This was "almost comically untrue," Lillian insisted. Moody then revealed his source, one very close to her indeed. "Bay told me this. Said Dash told her same thing." No matter that Moody had impeccable sources, Lillian sought to protect her myth about herself and Hammett. When after all this Moody requested a blurb for the jacket of his book, Lillian declined. There was "something very wrong about an author being quoted about a book about herself," as, of course, there was.

She requested that both Moody and Lederer remove any thanks to her or mention of their collaboration. "I hope you will remember," Lillian wrote Lederer, "that I told you I wanted no book written about me during my lifetime, and that I had previously stopped two books, one by a very close and dear friend." That, of course, was Fred.

Lillian felt safe from biographers as she retrieved many of her letters from their recipients and destroyed them. Luckily, Hammett hadn't saved her letters. But David Cort, with whom she had betrayed Kober and who had been her lover when she met Hammett, had. Noticing that he had not been mentioned in Lillian Hellman's memoirs, Cort told Lois Jacoby in 1976 that he was planning to set the record straight. He would publish their letters, having in his possession both her letters to him and his to her, which he had once asked her to return. Signing his letter "the false Abelard," Cort wrote Lillian he would tell theirs as a classic love story.

Alarmed, she made an effort to charm him, revive their old feeling, and so stop publication. "I haven't been in love very often and I'm willing to forgive in its name," Lillian wrote Cort. Refusing to accept his chronology, that he was seventy-two and she seventy-five, she added, "I was never as old as you."

Unappeased, Cort told her he was amazed she did not know how upset he had been at their breakup, which had been caused by the advent of Hammett in her life. "The last time we met you asked me whether I had wanted to kill you," he reminded her. Cort had told the young Lillian Hellman, "Hammett perhaps but not you, the love object."

Lillian made her case. "If I gave you back your letters, then why do you think it proper that you give mine to somebody else? Why not give them to me, as I to you?" She invoked the law: only she had the right to publish her own words, whoever owned the physical property. She also invoked morality: "Please do not revenge yourself on me at this late date." If she had rejected him, hadn't he also rejected her at times?

Cort's reply was nasty. He offered to postpone the project until after her death. He added a parting shot: "I hear you smoke too much." Indeed, to her death Lillian smoked four packs of cigarettes a day.

The next letter went from Ephraim London, who told Cort her literary executor would see that he did not publish the letters even after Lillian's death. The letters ultimately perished in a fire. The antibiography gods remained on Lillian's side.

She was safe almost to the end. There was that brief picture of her as Viola Teagarden in Renata Adler's *Pitch Dark*, a picture of Lillian who says "my *back* went up," and speaks of her anger "as though it were a living, prized possession, a thoroughbred bull, for instance." Lillian contacted the man in Adler's life. "You must know that I will not sue Renata," she wrote. "I have very little interest in her malice because her malice, although it is growing in size and frequency, will never reach importance."

William Luce, who had written *The Belle of Amherst,* a one-woman show about Emily Dickinson, wrote *Lillian.* But he was permitted to use only material from her own memoirs. It would be, Luce realized, "carpentry," but he went along. Lillian wanted to be played by a movie star; her first choice was Faye Dunaway. But it was Zoë Caldwell who played her on Broadway after her death, wearing Lillian's tea rose scent.

Near the end real biographers at last appeared: Hilary Mills and William Wright. Learning of their projects, Lillian wrote a form letter and sent it to her friends requesting that they not cooperate with these "unauthorized biographies of me." Mills backed off. But Wright went ahead.

On May 2, 1984, in a final effort to stop him, she added a clause to her will naming her editor and friend William Abrahams as "my one and only official biographer." "Having an official biographer seems to make me into a Queen Victoria," she wrote Richard Wilbur, "but it had to be done." Even after her death, her closest friends obeyed her wishes. "I think I know what she wanted and didn't want," Blair Clark, declining to be interviewed, wrote to Wright. "I feel bound by that."

She altered her will continually, changed the dollar amounts she was leaving friends, threatened to omit people entirely. There was always an intrigue. In June 1980 she asked Ephraim London whether she could add "a very private clause" without any lawyer seeing it, "even somebody as close to me as you." Rita Wade thought it was not mysterious; it had to do with Miss Hellman's not wanting to pay a lawyer to do more work on the will. She wrote a separate paper decreeing that Richard Poirier receive income from the collection of her memoirs, *Three*.

The final will was drawn up by Hannah's attorney, Isidore Englander. As soon as he read the document, Englander saw there would be problems. "I'll be dead. You're the one who's going to have the problems, not me," Lillian told him.

Only later was Englander to discover she was a secretive person. When she acquired her Park Avenue apartment in 1970, in exchange for a low purchase price she had signed an agreement that the sellers would receive 25 percent of whatever price she received upon selling it above what she paid for it. A team of lawyers approached Englander bearing her signed statement, and part of the difference between the few hundred thousand she paid and the $900,000 for which it was sold had to be returned.

Her first impulse was always generous, as when she gave her secretary, Selma Wolfman, a signed blank check when her son needed medical treatment. As time passed, she would whittle down her gifts. When all else failed, blackmail and bribery might suffice. Robin Hogan quit her job as Lillian's assistant, and Lillian called out to Rita in Hogan's hearing, "We have to call and change the will!" She promised Kitty Hart she would leave her the birdcage which had appeared in *The Autumn Garden* if Kitty would leave her first one and then a more elaborate ruby pin. Then, feeling that Hart had stopped being attentive to her, Lillian left the birdcage to Howard Bay.

She offered people jewelry and asked them to come and choose what they wanted. Annabel Nichols-Goff pleased her by choosing a diamond necklace made from a watch fob which had belonged to her mother, one of her less showy pieces. People who thought they would surely be mentioned in the will were not. The will was an excellent instrument of mischief, exposing the follies of courtiers, the greed of the high-minded. She fiddled with it until May 25, 1984, a month before her death.

Lillian left Selma Wolfman "the pallet pin which Dashiell Hammett gave me." To Fred Gardner's dismay, in what had to be interpreted as a rebuke, she left him the same amount as Jason Epstein, his sixties adversary. She also left money to the Pritchetts, to John Melby, to Ruth Field, to Abrahams.

Her principal heir would be Peter Feibleman, who had taken care of her. She had considered making Jason Epstein a literary executor, then changed her mind and chose Feibleman, Richard Poirier, and William Abrahams.

The estate was valued at $4,420,357. Lillian left $35,000 to each of the four grandchildren of Dashiell Hammett, "to be designated as a gift from Dashiell Hammett." There was no separate bequest to Josephine Marshall. She bequeathed her title to the works of Hammett in trust to her own literary fiduciaries, Feibleman, Poirier, and Abrahams, for them to divide in shares—one to Mary Miller, two to Josephine Marshall, and one to themselves—in keeping at last with Hammett's original wishes and her role as the literary executor of his will. Upon Jo's death, her share would be divided among her children. This trust would be terminated after the deaths of the children of Jo Marshall.

The trust would remain to be administered by her own literary executors, who were authorized to make all decisions concerning "the use, disposition, retention and control of the works of Dashiell Hammett, both published and unpublished." The copyrights of Dashiell Hammett would be registered in the names of the Trustees of her own Literary Property. It was they who would renew Hammett copyrights when they expired. Among their other rights was "the decision as to what correspondence, if any, should be made public, and the destruction of any of my correspondence."

Lillian attempted to control, to possess Dashiell Hammett even after her own death. She wrote her will so that all his royalties would pass through her estate. The fiduciaries would also be paid 10 percent of the gross proceeds from the literary works of both Hellman and Hammett, divided annually and equally, and each Fiduciary would be paid as well an additional 10 percent of the balance of the gross receipts. Hence 40 percent of the Hammett income went to the fiduciaries off the top. Each time a Hammett work sold, the literary executors would collect their percentage first. The lawyer and the accountant would be paid. Only then would the Hammett heirs receive anything.

Lillian Hellman's residuary estate went in equal parts to "The Lillian Hellman Fund" and "The Dashiell Hammett Fund," which would be administered by the Fund for Free Expression, which later became the Free Expression project of Human Rights Watch. Award selections for the Hammett fund were to be guided by Hammett's perspective, he "who was a believer in the doctrines of Karl Marx." It was one of the rare times when Lillian publicly distinguished her views from his. In 1989 the two funds were merged into "The Hellman-Hammett Fund." Awards totaling $200,000 a year were offered, mostly to recipients from abroad. "Dash would be furious," Judy Ruben, now an editor at the Monthly Review

Press Foundation, thought. She had applied for a grant to publish out-of-print political novels, like Mike Gold's *Jews Without Money* and Ruth McKenney's *Industrial Valley,* only to be turned down. Few Americans would benefit from the money left by this most American of writers.

Knowing she was being ridiculous about her will, Lillian, the consummate anecdotist, invented a story against herself shortly before her death.

Following the success of *The Children's Hour,* she had decided to make her will. She was sitting with her father and Hammett. "Which of you would like what?" she asked, the same question she put to friends in the eighties.

Hammett turns to Max Hellman and says, "Isn't this boredom awful?"

"You and your will can go fuck yourself," her father says, "if you don't stop boring both of us. All rich women turn into blackmailers. Here you have two people who can't be blackmailed. Why don't you take that goddamned will upstairs and tear it up, go to bed with it, get out of the room!"

Hammett applauds enthusiastically. Lily grabs a vase and throws it in his general direction. The truth lurks within the fabrication. Lillian Hellman saw Dashiell Hammett still as the one honorable person in her history, the single individual who could not be corrupted, blackmailed, bribed, and on whom in his lifetime she dared make no mischief.

By April 1984 Lillian could go out only seldom. She had agreed to appear at a tribute to Claudette Colbert at Lincoln Center, then was too ill. Richard de Combray went in her place and read her playful remarks: "I have been introduced as Lillian Hellman," they began. "But I am really Claudette Colbert's grandmother. The facts say that I am two years younger than Miss Colbert, which shows you what rot facts are." So the ambiguity of truth, the charge that she had lied, remained in her consciousness.

As she did every year, in June 1984 Lillian went to the Vineyard to prepare for her birthday party. Her love for the island, for the sea, remained. "Sea-pie," she had said one day, patting the water. Then she had to laugh at herself.

This year she arrived on June 8, accompanied by her nurse. The Jacuzzi had been readied. Life proceeded as usual. Max Palevsky had put $10,000 in her account, which she arranged to go in English pounds to V. S. Pritchett. The bills from her winter stay in Los Angeles had to be paid, many from Mickey's Fine Pharmacy in Beverly Hills. "Do you ever get to New York?" Lillian had asked Jo Marshall during this last visit. "You must. We'll go to the theater."

Now she wanted a local hotel inspected so that she could put up some of the guests for her birthday party. They would include Jerome Wiesner of MIT, the Jules Feiffers, the Styrons, the Herseys, Richard de Combray. Pearl London's birthday present arrived: an apricot silk caftan which matched the reddish cast of her hair. She dictated gracious thank-you notes for her birthday presents.

Then Lillian was too ill, too frail. The birthday party had to be canceled. She did have dinner on June 28 at the Herseys's, the people who loved her most, who forgave her everything. Refusing to be undone, Lillian was soon negotiating for her next fishing trip on Hersey's boat.

Her dinner partner that night was Gilbert Harrison, the former publisher of *The New Republic*, whom she had seen out West during the winter.

"Let's meet privately," Lillian whispered to Harrison as soon as the Herseys were out of the room. Harrison presented her with a bag of sourballs, which she tucked away as the evening's trophy. Still she sought validation as a woman in the form of one more romantic fantasy.

She was alone with her nurse, however. There was no man, no surrogate child those last days of June. Once she had told Renata Adler, "I'm trusting when I'm old you'll be the one wheeling me around in my wheelchair." Lillian often told Rita Wade she wanted her to be there when she died to hold her hand. On what she was to call the "nonfatal weekend," Rita had pinned a medal of the Blessed Virgin inside Miss Hellman's pillow.

Now neither Rita nor Peter Feibleman was on the Vineyard.

On June 29, the day after the Hersey dinner, Lillian spoke with Hannah's daughter Dina on the telephone. In this last year after Hannah's death she grew angry if the girls didn't call her. Three days earlier she had screamed at Lisa, "You haven't called me for a week! I'm sick and I'm alone and I can't stand this nurse. Your mother's dead and you're not paying attention to me!" Still she tested people, almost the way a child would, Lisa thought, as if to say: how horrible can I be and still have you love me? Hannah had never been in her will. Yet she had demanded, when Hannah herself left no will, that the girls give her a large set of Royal Crown Derby china.

"I'll see you when you come back to town," Dina promised.

After midnight her breathing changed. The German nurse massaged her neck where she had her surgery. Lillian, grateful, took her hand and squeezed it. "I think you and I are going to get along just fine," she told her.

Then Lily's heart stopped.

Efforts to revive her in the ambulance were futile. She was pronounced dead at 2:30 a.m. The official cause of death was cardiac arrest, arteriosclerotic heart disease, a myocardial infarction of one hour's duration.

The last words in her diary were written by a Rita Wade beset by guilt, believing that Miss Hellman had given up because she had not been with her: "1:15 a.m. June 30th: departed—R.I.P."

Lily would have been amused had she known that on the night before her funeral Warren Beatty arrived on the Vineyard and accepted the best bed in the house, slept in her bed. "It's your house now," Rita Wade told Peter Feibleman, uneasy at this impropriety on the night before the burial. As Hammett had rolled his eyes at her consorting with celebrities, Peter gave way.

The first sentence of the New York *Times* obituary on July 1 declared her to be "one of the most important playwrights of the American theater." Two days later a *Times* editorial called her "a major figure during a vibrant period of the American theater." In his eulogy John Hersey addressed her: "Dear Lillian, you are a finished woman, now."

That she had never been.

It is a cold and gloomy March day in 1961, two months after Dashiell Hammett's death. Lillian thinks of him today and feels depressed. All these weeks, given a few drinks, she has been trying to say, to too many people, that somewhere there was something to be learned. I don't know what, she tells herself.

It tortures her still that she had not been taken into the last secrets, and it makes her angry at him yet again. Was I rejected or is it the old crap that everybody has rejected me? she wonders.

He wanted to be good friends, more than that, she thinks. And often I know, she admits to herself, that he didn't. Didn't trust me, didn't believe in my final kindness. His credo had been to explain nothing to anyone and that had included her. Beneath her feisty independence, beneath her persona as rebel, there had been neediness, hunger, an enslavement to Hammett, an imprisonment in her Faustian bargain.

She longs still for the admission of love Hammett never granted her. He at least had not died in the company of strangers. She fears that will be her fate, and it frightens her.

She tortures herself for what she lost and for what she has never had.

Worried that she has been breathing too hard, she thinks she should see a doctor. Aimlessly, she wanders about. He could read. She can't read much. She wishes the sun would come out. She eats too much.

It will be a long twenty-three years.

Notes

Sources

Works frequently cited appear as follows:

HRHRC: The papers of Lillian Hellman and Dashiell Hammett are housed at the Harry Ransom Humanities Research Center of the University of Texas at Austin.

The letters of Dashiell Hammett to his daughter, Josephine Marshall, appear courtesy of Josephine Marshall.

LAY: Many documents relating to the life of Dashiell Hammett are quoted courtesy of the private Dashiell Hammett archive of Hammett biographer Richard Layman.

Correspondence between Lillian Hellman and Richard Wilbur is housed at Amherst College.

Letters between Lillian Hellman and Arthur W. A. Cowan appear courtesy of Cowan's niece, Marilyn Raab.

Butler Library of Columbia University houses the papers of Random House, as well as those of the Harold Matson literary agency.

WIS: The diaries, papers, and correspondence of Arthur Kober are housed at the Wisconsin State Historical Society, University of Wisconsin, Madison. Some papers of Herman Shumlin and Kermit Bloomgarden are available at Wisconsin as well.

The letters of John Melby to Lillian Hellman were made available courtesy of the late John Melby.

In addition, correspondence between Lillian Hellman and Leonard Bernstein was made available by Jamie Bernstein-Thomas and Nina Bernstein. The letters of Dashiell Hammett to Lillian Hellman, including but not limited to those from the Aleutian Islands during World War II, and not designated HRHRC, appear courtesy of Mr. William Abrahams. Letters of Lillian Hellman to Blair Clark appear courtesy of Mr. Clark.

Preface

xiv "He had an absolute contempt for lies": Lillian Hellman interview with Alvin Sargent, June 13, 1982. Courtesy of Alvin Sargent. See also Lillian Hellman, *Three: An Unfinished Woman, Pentimento, Scoundrel Time,* with new commentaries by the author (Little, Brown: Boston, 1979), commentary for *An Unfinished Woman,* 303. See also "He had such enormous contempt for lying—Dash wouldn't lie about anything. He didn't always tell the truth but he wouldn't lie." Peter Feibleman, *Lilly: Reminiscences of Lillian Hellman* (William Morrow: New York, 1988), 167.

xv "Tomorrow, if there's no more news": Dashiell Hammett to Lillian Hellman, October 2, 1944.

Prologue

1 "In spite of her chic": Jerome Weidman, *The Sound of Bow Bells* (Random House: New York, 1962).

1 "It's tough, been tough": All dialogue as well as Lillian Hellman's thoughts in this prologue are based upon unnumbered pages tucked into her *Diaries,* HRHRC.

2 He has few visitors: Catherine Kober, December 4, 1992, and January 20, 1993; Virginia Bloomgarden Chilewich, December 7, 1992, and January 15, 1993; Helen Rosen, January 17, 1992, and October 14, 1992, interviews with JM.

1. "Who's That Man?"

1 "I wanted blond curls": Dan Rather, "A Portrait of Lillian Hellman/1977," in *Conversations with Lillian Hellman,* ed. Jackson R. Bryer (University Press of Mississippi: Jackson and London, 1986), 210.

7 The scene of Lillian Hellman's first meeting with Dashiell Hammett was described by Lee Gershwin to Carl Rollyson. Interview tape courtesy of Mr. Rollyson.

7 queen bee herself: Lucy Strunsky interview with JM, 1993.

8 On their first date: Lillian Hellman described her first date with Arthur Kober in an interview with Fred Gardner. Typescript courtesy of Mr. Gardner.

8 Louis Kronenberger, said made him think: Emmy Kronenberger interview with JM, May 10, 1993.

8 she wore very good gloves: Kitty Carlisle Hart interview with JM, October 21, 1992.

9 preferred that she marry Kronenberger: Lillian Hellman interview with Fred Gardner.

9   "cutting each other's throats": Ibid.

9   "on the fringe of the Garden district": William Wright, *Lillian Hellman: The Image, The Woman* (Simon and Schuster: New York, 1986), p. 15.

9   1718 Prytania Street: I am indebted for this discussion of New Orleans to Pat Sims, "Looking for Lillian Hellman," *Figaro*, September 27, 1978. Available at HRHRC.

10   "I'm a friend of your niece's": See papers of Lillian Hellman. HRHRC.

10   bruised by having had to live in the aunts' tawdry boardinghouse: JM interview with Pearl London, January 6, 1994.

10   The shabby lower-middle-class surroundings: Ibid.

10   "I was uncontrollable": Lillian Hellman interviewed by Marilyn Berger, *Profile: Lillian Hellman*, Program No. Four. KERA, Public Communication Foundation for North Texas, 1979. Reprinted in *Conversations with Lillian Hellman*.

10   Lillian looked in the mirror. Feibleman interview. See also Feibleman, *Lilly*, 223–24.

10   rosebud mouth: Dan Rather, "A Profile of Lillian Hellman," in *Conversations*, 210.

10   Can it be repaired?: Peter Feibleman interview with JM, November 24, 1992.

11   "She was a very naive woman": Christine Doudna, "A Still Unfinished Woman: A Conversation with Lillian Hellman," in *Conversations*, 197.

11   "I didn't have a mother": William Doering interview with JM, June 4, 1993.

11   "I was mean to her": JM interview with Emmy Kronenberger, May 10, 1993.

11   "I was desperately in love with her": Lillian Hellman interviewed by Marilyn Berger, Program No. Four.

11   "I was a cutup": Lillian Hellman interviewed by Fred Gardner. Courtesy of Fred Gardner.

11   "Don't go through life": Lillian Hellman, *An Unfinished Woman: A Memoir* (Bantam Books: New York, 1969), 12.

11   nuisance: Bill Moyers, "Lillian Hellman: The Great Playwright Candidly Reflects on a Long, Rich Life," in *Conversations with Lillian Hellman*, 149.

12   Filled "with pity and contempt": *Unfinished Woman*, 9.

12   She compared her mother to a feather: Mina Towbin Pingar interview with JM, July 20, 1993.

12   "often angry when I was most like him": Ibid., 16.

12   "As an only child you never have enough": Lillian Hellman interviewed by Jerry Tallmer, New York *Post*, October 13, 1973.

12   "a handsome man, witty, high-tempered": *Unfinished Woman*, 6.

12   "You're jealous of your mama": Lillian Hellman, *Pentimento: A Book of Portraits* (New American Library: New York, 1973), 47.

12   "a schmeer of that and a schmeer of this": Arthur Kober *Diary*, April 2, 1936. WIS.

12   "since the day he was in his cradle": Lillian Hellman, *Maybe: A Story* (Little, Brown: Boston, 1980), 82.

12   "been in love with him since the day she first laid eyes": Ibid.

12   "interesting things to say": *Pentimento*, 24.

13   The root of her neurosis: John Melby to Lillian Hellman, May 10, 1946. Courtesy of the late John Melby.

13   "No, I cannot forgive you": Undated letter, Lillian Hellman to Arthur W. A. Cowan. Courtesy of Marilyn Raab.

13   "Shut up, you stinker": Ibid.

14   "worry about yourself": *Pentimento*, 48.

14   "dull": Annotations by Lillian Hellman to Richard Moody's manuscript for *Lillian Hellman: Playwright* (Pegasus: New York, 1972). The annotated manuscript is available at the Lilly Library, Indiana University, Bloomington, Indiana.

14   "left home": Margaret Case Harriman, "Miss Lily of New Orleans," *The New Yorker*, November 8, 1941, 22.

14   Wadleigh grades: Carl Rollyson, *Lillian Hellman: Her Legend and her Legacy* (St. Martin's Press: New York 1988), p. 27.

14   *Miss Gorringe's Necklace*: Harriman, p. 24.

14   "rather weak": Adolescent musings of Lillian Hellman are to be found in her notebooks for 1922, 1923, and 1924. HRHRC.

15   "My mind is not well-ordered": Ibid.

15   "Always—always when I write": Ibid.

16   "childish nature": Ibid.

16   The ink wasn't dry: From unpublished memoir of Samuel Marx. Courtesy of Carl Rollyson.

16   "She could have had him for breakfast": Talli Wyler interview with Carl Rollyson, Rollyson, p. 167.

16   "great future": Leo Friedman unpublished interview with Hilary Mills. Courtesy of Carl Rollyson.

16   "she thought he had a promising future": Rollyson, 35.

16   "going down" episode: Kober *Diary*, December 20, 1940.

16   "wondered if he was gay": Fred Gardner interview with Lillian Hellman.

16   "Things seem so unarranged": Lillian Hellman to Helen Berlin Schneider ["Monday"]. Butler Library, Columbia University.

17   Kober mailed: Arthur Kober to Mrs. Kober [Friday]. WIS.

17   "I think if she can be kept busy": Arthur Kober to Mrs. Kober [Wed 1930]. WIS.

17   "If I don't find something": Hilary Mills interview with Samuel Marx.

17   "flattery": Arthur Kober, "Dear Ma and Sa," Saturday [1930]. WIS.

17   "gaped at Gary Cooper": Ibid.

17   "a thin, bony slip": Private papers of Sam Marx. Courtesy of Carl Rollyson.

17   She was like a child: Ibid.

18   "the flatness of his chest": Dashiell Hammett, *The Glass Key*.

18   "development of the American tongue": *Town & Country*, March 9, 1930.

18   "His vogue is on the rise": Richard Layman, "Dashiell Hammett," in

Dictionary of Literary Biography: Documentary Series. Vol. 6: *Hardboiled Mystery Writers Raymond Chandler, Dashiell Hammett, Ross MacDonald,* ed. Matthew J. Bruccoli and Richard Layman. A Bruccoli Clark Layman Book. Gale Research, Inc. Book Tower: Detroit, 1989), 125.

19 Treatment for "The Ungallant" is available at HRHRC.

20 he changed his affiliation: JM interview with Jane Fish Yowaiski, October 30–31, 1993. See also Layman, 6–7.

20 "more or less on a rail": Richard T. Hammett, "Mystery Writer Was Enigmatic Throughout Life," Baltimore *News-American,* August 19, 1973.

20 For this description of turn-of-the-century West Baltimore, I am indebted to Fred Worden, "Gooseberries and Dashiell Hammett," Baltimore *Sunday Sun Magazine,* June 11, 1978, pp. 26–27.

20 The jobs of Richard Hammett: Diane Johnson, *Dashiell Hammett: A Life* (Random House: New York, 1983), 15.

20 "The Hammetts were an interesting family": Marshall interview.

20 Hockey incident reported in Layman, 7.

21 fiercely proud: Marshall interview.

21 Dashiell even once upbraided: Layman, 8.

21 "the ugliest boy": Layman, 9.

21 "fraction of a year": "Three Favorites," *Black Mask,* 7 (November 1924), 128.

21 "was elected to pick up": Richard Thomas Hammett to William Godshalk, April 1, 1974. LAY.

21 "Arabs": Layman, 8.

21 did not wish him to quit school: Yowaiski interview.

21 "I was kind of excited": Marshall interview.

22 "all men are no good": Richard Layman, *Shadow Man: The Life of Dashiell Hammett* (Harcourt Brace Jovanovich: New York, 1981), 5.

22 "I can loaf longer and better": Joseph Harrington, "Hammett Solves Big Crime; Finds Ferris Wheel," New York *Evening Journal,* January 28, 1934. See Layman, *Dictionary of Literary Biography.*

22 "Dashiell was a wild one": James H. Bready, "Books and Authors," Baltimore *Sun,* May 8, 1966.

22 Annie smelled: Yowaiski interview.

22 Tipped his hat: JM interview with Jo Marshall, June 20, 1995.

23 "I don't like his friends": Yowaiski interview.

23 "quite unspoiled": Frank MacShane, *The Life of Raymond Chandler* (E. P. Dutton: New York, 1976), 76.

23 "in trying to convict him": Marguerite Tazelaar, "Film Personalities: A Private Detective Does His Stuff in Hollywood," New York *Herald Tribune,* November 12, 1933, Section V, 3.

24 "In 1917, in Washington, D.C.": Layman, *Shadow Man,* 32.

24 "so hard-boiled": Dorothy Parker, "Oh, Look—Two Good Books!" *The New Yorker,* April 25, 1931, 91.

24 He never overtly asked: Josephine Marshall interview with JM, April 15, 1993, and many subsequent telephone conversations, 1993–95.

24 "I should like to have them": Dashiell Hammett to Mr. Block, July 14, 1929. Knopf Collection. HRHRC.

24 "a bit boiled": Letter to William Godshalk, March 27, 1974. LAY.

25 "assumption that he had no expectation": Nunnally Johnson to Julian Symons, January 16, 1961. LAY.

25 "monster ... without any human": Dashiell Hammett, *The Dain Curse.*

25 Description of Jose Hammett comes courtesy of her daughter, Josephine Marshall.

25 "merry": Dashiell Hammett, "Women Are a Lot of Fun Too." HRHRC.

26 "It seemed as if one of us had said": Dashiell Hammett, "Seven Pages" (unpublished story). HRHRC.

26 The child was not his: That Mary Miller was not Dashiell Hammett's natural daughter was told by Lillian Hellman to Fred Gardner, Josephine Marshall, and others. But Hammett himself revealed this information to Rose Evans as well. Rose Evans interview with JM, November 11, 1993. A handwritten note by Lillian Hellman reads: "The whole story of Josephine Dolan and the marriage could possibly have to be told although I have never told it . . . it cannot be told without the permission of Josephine Marshall and was obviously not told to Diane Johnson although I must read the footnotes to find out if she has any glimmer." HRHRC.

26 "This is going to kill me": Marshall interview.

26 "fine lady . . . bad women": Yowaiski interview.

27 lunch with Samuels: Courtesy of Richard Layman.

27 just sat in a chair: David Fechheimer, "Interview with Mrs. Hammett," *City of San Francisco* magazine, 9, No. 17 (November 4, 1975), 38. Souvenir Edition: Dashiell Hammett's San Francisco.

27 put her in a great big bed: Marshall interviews.

28 "rumpled": *Unfinished Woman,* 226.

28 rubbed red pepper: Marshall interviews.

2. Better Than Pretty

31 "Better than pretty": Lillian Hellman used this phrase in two of her plays, *Days to Come* (1936) and *The Autumn Garden* (1951).

31 "As a little girl": BBC Omnibus "Portrait of Lillian Hellman," 1978.

31 told him she was psychic: Dashiell Hammett to Nancy Bragdon, January 1, 1944. HRHRC.

32 "born of early settlers": *Unfinished Woman,* 227.

32 "elegant to look at": Lillian Hellman, Introduction to *The Big Knockover* (Vintage Books: New York, 1989), ix.

32 "the anger under the calm": Lillian Hellman, *Scoundrel Time* (Little, Brown: Boston, 1976), 47.

33 "a grand passion": Feibleman, 299.

33 "one of the most beautiful Renaissance faces": Ibid., 167.

33 "It was responsible": Ibid., 300.

33 "meant you wouldn't ever get married": *Pentimento,* 20.

33 "I'm the kind of woman": Karl Menninger to Lillian Hellman, August 12, 1970. HRHRC.

33   "It is not easy to convince": Lillian Hellman remarks at Janet Flanner's Memorial Service. HRHRC.

33   avoiding the mistake: Feibleman interview.

34   "Doesn't it remind you": Wright, 70–71.

34   a cruel man: Feibleman interview.

34   "You don't know the half": Emily Hahn interview with JM, 1993.

34   eyes blacked and face battered: Diane Johnson, "Obsessed," *Vanity Fair,* May 1985, 118.

34   "You can tell me if you have to": *Pentimento,* 33.

34   "fun-loving couple": Wright, 45.

35   "We'll take 'em on": Howard Benedict interview with JM, April 10, 1993.

35   "Lily! Let's do our trick": Wright, 45.

35   pathetic English accent: Jerome Weidman interview with JM, February 24, 1993.

35   "chance" meetings: Edward M. Zwick, *Life in Art: A Study of Lillian Hellman and Watch on the Rhine.* Unpublished senior thesis, Harvard University.

35   He threatened to kill himself: Rollyson, 45.

35   "I think I'd rather live with Hammett": Feibleman interview.

36   "the worst thing that has ever happened": David Cort to Lillian Hellman, July 6, 1976. Courtesy of Pearl London.

36   "the classic 'love story'": David Cort to Lillian Hellman, July 6, 1976.

36   "lost kids": Lillian Hellman to David Cort, July 16, 1976. Courtesy of Pearl London.

36   "I don't want a sweet man": Rollyson, 45.

36   "it was not Lillian's nature": Wright, 60.

36   "If you take care of the children": Marshall interview.

37   "did not learn the suspicion of such talk": *Three,* 302.

37   "He expected nothing": *Three,* 301.

37   "Sweetheart—I love you!": Dashiell Hammett to Lillian Hellman, undated, scribbled on undated menu [1932].

37   "You weren't made to be a liar": Lillian Hellman interview with Alvin Sargent, June 13, 1982.

38   "Can you stop juggling oranges?": *Unfinished Woman,* 166.

39   "Don't tell Mama": Marshall interview.

40   he got her into a taxi: Renata Adler interview with JM, December 7, 1992.

40   for fear of liking them too much: Feibleman interview.

40   "Independent natures aren't worried": Doudna, 206.

40   "He fed me": Feibleman interview.

40   "If you have worked": *Scoundrel Time,* 42.

41   "Let's hit the Trocadero": Lillian Hellman to Alvin Sargent, April 15, 1982. Courtesy of Alvin Sargent.

41   "a good, true drunk": Ibid.

41   "Open the window, James": *Unfinished Woman,* 52.

41   "Isn't it sad": Lillian Hellman interview with Fred Gardner.

41   "How much do you want?": *Unfinished Woman,* 55.

42   "I'm not going to sit there!" Marshall interview.

42   "Josephine, you're very religious": Ibid.

42   "She lived across the hall in [sic] Pine": Hellman, Introduction to *The Big Knockover*, v.

43   "mean" jealousy: Nora Ephron, "Lillian Hellman Walking, Cooking, Writing, Talking," in *Conversations*, 136.

43   "jealous of women who took advantage": Doudna, 203.

43   "half in plea": Unpaginated draft of Hellman, Introduction to *The Big Knockover*. HRHRC.

43   "How do I smell": *Maybe*, 27.

44   "what he did or spoiled": *Unfinished Woman*, 165.

44   "In every relationship there's a winner": Feibleman interview.

44   "All I ever wanted was a docile": *Unfinished Woman*, 238.

3. She-Hammett

46   She-Hammett: Hammett used this term in a letter to Lillian Hellman: "suspected you of the loosest sort of conduct even if I hadn't previously received reports about you. Ts! Ts! Just a she-Hammett!" A place called Hollywood on what's known as the thirtieth of April. HRHRC.

46   "I had found somebody": *Three*, 304.

46   he steered salesmen: Marshall interview.

46   "It bothered other people": Shirley Hazzard interview with JM, January 13, 1993.

47   "capable of walking out": Marilyn Berger, Program No. Two. *Profile: Lillian Hellman*, Program No. One. KERA, Public Communication Foundation for North Texas, 1979. Reprinted in *Conversations*.

47   "thousand-stanza narrative verse": Dashiell Hammett to Lillian Hellman, March 5, 1931. HRHRC.

48   "were no unusual idiocies": Dashiell Hammett to Lillian Hellman, March 4, 1931. HRHRC.

48–49   "the curse . . . cried like hell": Lillian Hellman to "Dear Baby" [1931]. WIS.

49   "I love you very much": "Kober, you are a liar and fake" [1931]. WIS.

49   For scene of Jose's visit to Arthur Kober, Marshall interview. See also Kober *Diary*, July 1, 1940.

49   "respectable a tint": Dashiell Hammett to Lillian Hellman, April 30, 1931. HRHRC.

50   "God knows I'm doing my best to keep celibacy": "a Tuesday" [1931]. HRHRC.

50   An unknown man called: Marshall interview.

50   "Why, for heaven's sake?": Johnson, 103.

50   "the fights": Dashiell Hammett to Lillian Hellman, March 6, 1931. HRHRC.

51   "Too many have lived": Dashiell Hammett to Lillian Hellman, February 23, 1932. HRHRC.

51   "Hemingway sees himself as Hercules": Lillian Hellman interviewed by Richard L. Coe on National Public Radio, 1977.

51 "simpered": *Unfinished Woman,* 185.

52 "She cries": Wright, 80.

52 "Did you ever meet such a shit": Marion Meade, *Dorothy Parker: What Fresh Hell Is This* (Villard Books: New York, 1988), 248.

52 "If you'd like to settle this thing": Rollyson, 51.

53 "You don't have to rise to greet me": *Unfinished Woman,* 41.

53 "straight" novels: Elizabeth Sanderson, "Ex-Detective Hammett," *Bookman,* January and February 1932, 518.

53 "a silly story . . . too manufactured": Ibid., 518.

54 "letting her go": Kober to Ma [1931]. WIS.

54 "I guess it's a pretty silly thing": Ibid.

54 "Lillian is all cut up": Ibid.

54 "emotionally upset": Ibid.

54 "Lillian wanted children": Ibid.

54 "her restlessness, her personal satisfactions": Kober, end notes to *Diary* for 1940. WIS.

54 "thoughtless, restless, idle": Kober *Diary,* 1942.

54 "passionately" fond: Kober to "Dear Ma" [1931]. WIS.

54 "cuckold": Kober *Diary,* October 22, 1940. WIS.

54 "Her success as a playwright": The fragmentary unpublished memoir of Arthur Kober is housed at Wisconsin. Quote is from p. 4.

55 "What is she going to do when she comes home": Kitty Carlisle Hart interview with JM.

55 "If he noticed that I had divorced him": Feibleman interview.

55 "I want you to meet Lily": Hilary Mills interview with Albert Hackett. Courtesy of Carl Rollyson.

55 Louis would write his joke: Fred Gardner interview with Lillian Hellman.

55 "with dollar bills between the pages": Courtesy of Emmy Kronenberger.

55 "bruised and battered in resisting": Johnson, 107.

55 "next week": Blanche Knopf to Dashiell Hammett, April 2, 1932. HRHRC.

55 "to find some such message": Dashiell Hammett to Lillian Hellman, May 4, 1932.

55 "There wasn't anything here": Ibid.

56 "Mr. Hammett when interviewed": Dashiell Hammett to Lillian Hellman, May 5, 1932, the second day of the hegira.

56 "I feel as though he is not getting my letters": Johnson, 106.

57 "those of us who grew up in the twenties": quoted in Jay Martin to Joan Mellen, March 12, 1993.

57 "lustrous hair": Dorothy Herrman, *S. J. Perelman: A Life* (Simon and Schuster: New York, 1986), 54.

58 "Leave him alone": Johnson, 122.

58 "I haven't any money": Ibid.

58 Laura disliked Lillian: Ruth Goetz interview with JM, December 12, 1991.

4. The Literary Grift

59   "I haven't had a dry shoulder": Dashiell Hammett to Lillian Hellman, January 4, 1943.

60   Always she would fear him: See the *Diaries* of Lillian Hellman. HRHRC.

61   A lifelong romantic: Feibleman interview.

61   As good a poker player: Howard Benedict, Burton Bernstein, and Frederick Fields interviews with JM.

61   "the toughness of his criticism": *Pentimento,* 142.

61   "I worked better if Hammett": *Unfinished Woman,* 233.

62   "the deep pleasure of continuing interest": *Unfinished Woman,* 242.

62   Hammett continued to publish sporadically in the early thirties. "Woman in the Dark," subtitled "a novel of dangerous romance," for example, appeared in *Liberty* magazine in the spring of 1933.

62   "an affectionate pair of people": Doudna, 207.

63   "Nightshade" was published in *Mystery League Magazine* on October 1, 1933.

63   "Nick's wife . . . is real": New York *Evening Journal.*

63   "one of the few marriages in modern literature": *Unfinished Woman,* 236.

63   "there isn't anything more to write": JM interview with Heywood Hale Broun, October 20, 1993.

64   a woman drops her fork on her plate: Feibleman interview.

64   "was not going to be any good": Marilyn Berger, Program No. Two.

64   "annoyed me back into writing": Ibid.

64   "a teacher, a cool teacher": *Unfinished Woman,* 44.

65   Hammett would even type them up: Howard Benedict interview.

65   "as if one lie would muck up": *Pentimento,* 142.

65   "Now you've begun to write": Fred Gardner interview with Lillian Hellman. Courtesy of Fred Gardner.

66   he ordered her to stop writing about herself: Feibleman interview. See also Lewis Funke, "Interview with Lillian Hellman," in *Conversations,* 96.

66   "he was chancing the whole relationship": Berger, Program No. Two.

66   "good enough to fix things": Berger, Program No. Two.

67   "he spared me nothing": Hellman, Introduction to *Four Plays* (Random House: New York, 1942), xiii.

67   "If this isn't any good": Ibid.

67   "If you never write again": Ibid.

67   "would be all right some day": Ibid.

67–68   he had read only the fourth draft: "The Films Now Know Miss Hellman," New York *Herald Tribune,* July 1, 1935, Section V, 3.

68   Hammett suggested that Lillian remove Judge Potter from *The Children's Hour.* Ibid.

69   "Oh don't let's have any more of this": See draft of *The Children's Hour.* HRHRC. Hammett's handwriting with its circles dotting the *i*'s is apparent.

69   "Feed the lettuce to the cow": Marshall interview.

69   "What's the point?": Marshall interview.

69   "not a mystery story": Marguerite Tazelaar, "Film Personalities, New York *Herald Tribune,* November 12, 1933, Section V, 3.

70   reviews of *The Thin Man:* Isaac Anderson, "New Mystery Stories," New York *Times Book Review,* January 7, 1934, 18; John Chamberlain, Review of *The Thin Man,* New York *Times,* January 9, 1934; Will Cuppy, Review of *The Thin Man,* New York *Herald Tribune,* January 7, 1934, 11; T. S. Matthews, "Mr. Hammett Goes Coasting," *New Republic* January 24, 1934, 316; Edwin Balmer, "Our Literary Nudism," *Esquire,* 30, (September 1934), 89.

70   "to finish my next book": Dashiell Hammett to Jose Hammett, January 22, 1934.

70   "sick": Lillian Hellman to Arthur Kober, "Dear Babe" [June 1934]. WIS.

70   "work steadily on the play": Ibid.

70   "screamed at each other": Ibid.

71   "quite free to move around": Ibid.

71   Lillian did not go to Europe in 1934: Evelyn Teichmann interview with JM, December 12, 1993. Herman Shumlin told Teichmann it was not possible, so consistently had he been aware in 1934 of Lillian Hellman's whereabouts.

71   "The play is grand": Alfred A. Knopf to Dashiell Hammett, undated. HRHRC.

71   didn't like beautiful women: JM interview with Carole Klein, author of *Aline,* the biography of Aline Bernstein.

5. The Tops off Bottles: 1934–35

75   "There's never been a time in my life": Feibleman, 195.

75   "SO FAR SO GOOD": Dashiell Hammett to Lillian Hellman, October 26, 1934.

75   "HAVE NOT GOT USED": Dashiell Hammett to Lillian Hellman, October 27, 1934.

76   "pleasantly . . . picture-galleries": Dashiell Hammett to Lillian Hellman, "Tuesday" [1934]. HRHRC.

76   "I think it's going to be all right": Ibid.

76   "awfully . . . . it would be so thoroughly": Ibid.

76   "a very quiet and reserved presence": Wright, 95.

76   "a bewildering kind of person": Albert Hackett interview with JM, November 25, 1992.

76   "Well, I don't know": Ibid.

76   "It just cluttered up the thing": Ibid.

77   "awful drunks": Ibid.

77   "but still loving and missing you": Dashiell Hammett to Lillian Hellman, October 31, 1934. HRHRC.

77   "back on the booze pretty heavily": Dashiell Hammett to Lillian Hellman, November 5, 1934. HRHRC.

77   "I've been faithful enough": Ibid.

77   "my pay-check is sewed up": Ibid.

77   "I love you something awful": Ibid.

77   "I love you and miss you": Ibid.

78   "Too hangovery to go out to the studio": Dashiell Hammett to Lillian Hellman, November 1, 1934.

78   Laura Perelman was often drunk: See Kober *Diary*, November 26, 1934, for example. WIS.

79   "It is really a swell play": Telegrams Lillian Hellman received are part of the archive at the HRHRC.

79   sent the wardrobe woman out: Hellman interview with Richard L. Coe. She told this story as well to the BBC, 1978: "I sent the wardrobe woman out for a bottle of brandy and began to drink a bottle of brandy. And I think I was as drunk, I was as sick drunk as I've ever been in my life."

79   patted her arm: Lillian Hellman to Gerald Nachman, November 13, 1979. HRHRC.

79   could be found lying passed out: Philip D'Arcy Hart interview with JM, December 20, 1993.

79   "She's the kind of girl who can take the tops": Margaret Case Harriman, "Miss Lily of New Orleans," 22.

79   "should have telephoned Hammett": *Pentimento*, 131–32.

80   "Dear, sweet, gorgeous, lovely": Herman Shumlin to Lillian Hellman, December 27, 1934. HRHRC.

80   "woman playwright": "Miss Lily of New Orleans," 22.

80   Richard Maney, *Fanfare: The Confessions of a Press Agent* (Harper & Brothers: New York, 1957), p. 334.

80   "Lillian Hellman would be sore as hell": Howard Lindsay to Roy Temple House, July 10, 1947. Western History Collections, University of Oklahoma at Norman. World Literature Today Collection, Box 1.

80   consciously set out to write: Lillian Hellman, "People and Places: Notes from a Journal," III. Courtesy of Fred Gardner.

81   "nice, well born people": Lillian Hellman interview with John Phillips and Anne Hollander, *Conversations*, 66.

81   "awkward, embarrassing and unyielding," Moody, *Lillian Hellman: Playwright*, 43.

81   "astringent," Harold Clurman, Introduction, to *Lillian Hellman: Playwright*, xii.

81   "harmed . . . by many sentimental minutes": Lillian Hellman, "People and Plays: Notes from a Journal," II.

81   "I see things happening in a room": Lillian Hellman interviewed by Fred Gardner.

82   "whose effects are contrived": Lillian Hellman, Introduction to *Six Plays*, x.

82   "her work is constructed": Robert Brustein, *New Republic*, March 14, 1960.

82   "limited by their realism": JM interview with Robert Brustein, June 4, 1993.

82   "complete worldliness": Ibid.

82   "corrupted modern meaning": Lillian Hellman, "Back of Those Foxes," New York *Times*, February 26, 1939.

82   "I think we should do something": Lillian Hellman to Kermit Bloomgarden, July 18, 1960. HRHRC.

83   "I am a moral writer": Introduction to *Six Plays*, viii.

83   "bold efforts": Clive James, "It Is of a Windiness: Lillian Hellman," *First Reactions: Critical Essays 1968–1979* (Alfred A. Knopf: New York, 1980), 226.

83   "I do miss Lillian": Kober *Diary*, November 26, 1934. WIS.

83   "Perhaps it's Lil's success": Kober *Diary*, November 27, 1934. WIS.

83   "Oh, who gives a shit!": Austin Pendleton interview with JM, June 20, 1993.

84   "her gratitude toward Dash": Kober *Diary*, December 11, 1934. WIS.

84   "how I'm completely and entirely": Ibid.

84   "Miss Moss Heart": Dashiell Hammett to Lillian Hellman, September 9, 1937.

84   Hammett on homosexuality: See Feibleman, p. 25.

84   "the vast army of hacks": Arthur Kober to Lillian Hellman [1934]. Wis.

84   "her success with Goldwyn": "Miss Lily of New Orleans."

85   "gay & animated": Kober *Diary*, December 19, 1934. WIS.

85   "how silly it is for me to make": Kober *Diary*, December 20, 1934. WIS.

85   "Because she is author": Available in *Vanity Fair: Selections from America's Most Memorable Magazine; A Cavalcade of the 1920s and 1930s*, ed. Cleveland Amory and Frederic Bradlee (Viking Press: New York, 1960), 315.

85   "strong tie between her and Ham": Ibid.

85   "awful people present": Kober *Diary*, February 7, 1935. WIS.

85   Lillian never picked up a check: Kober *Diary*, May 15, 1935. WIS.

85   "Most enjoyable": Kober *Diary*, December 26, 1934. WIS.

85   "Something had gone wrong": *Diaries* of Lillian Hellman. HRHRC.

86   "frightened of being hit": Ibid. Also Irene Diamond interview with JM, June 9, 1994. When Hammett was drunk, he was invariably mean.

86   accuse him of flirting with the waitress: Marshall interview.

86   Hammett did manage to produce: See Richard Layman, *Dashiell Hammett: A Descriptive Bibliography* (University of Pittsburgh Press: Pittsburgh, 1979), 159.

87   "ask her to describe the chandelier": Johnson, 123.

87   "her vigorous green-blonde mother": *Unfinished Woman*, 54.

87   "very unhappy these days": Kober *Diary*.

87   grinding a burning cigarette: *Unfinished Woman*, 167.

87   "I don't think anything in the world goes faster": Berger, Program No. Four.

87   "still very upset with Hammett": *Maybe*, 56.

87   "of status of her arrangement with Dash": Kober *Diary*, February 22, 1935. WIS.

87   "No, it shouldn't be like that": Ruth Goetz interview.

88   "was very excited about it": Lillian Hellman to Arthur Kober [1935]. WIS.

88   "strong or weak or mysterious": Gertrude Stein, *Everybody's Autobiography* (Cooper Square Publishers: New York, 1971), 4–5.

6. Retaliations

89   *A Cincher:* Poem published by Dashiell Hammett in *Argosy All-Story Weekly,* 1923. LAY.

89   "Certain older people": "Plain Speaking with Mrs. Carter," *Rolling Stone,* No. 226 (November 18, 1976), 43–45.

90   "arrogant": quoted in Dashiell Hammett to Lillian Hellman, June 25, 1944.

90   She wanted to be unattached: Kober *Diary,* February 22, 1935.

90   "quite far away from me": Kober *Diary,* March 7, 1935. WIS.

90   "Hammett-Hellman-Perelman-Kober": John O'Hara, *Selected Letters of John O'Hara,* ed. Matthew J. Bruccoli (Random House: New York, 1978), 109.

90   "horse's ass": Kober *Diary,* May 23, 1935. WIS.

90   "I went to a whorehouse": Hilary Mills interview with Ralph Ingersoll. Courtesy of Carl Rollyson.

91   She asked their mutual friend: Hilary Mills interview with Bobbie Weinstein. Courtesy of Carl Rollyson.

91   "She was very handsome": Hilary Mills interview with Ralph Ingersoll.

91   "Come, darling": The meeting of Lillian Hellman and Ralph Ingersoll is described in Ingersoll's roman à clef, *The Great Ones: The Love Story of Two Very Important People* (Harcourt, Brace: New York, 1948), 197.

92   "The gayest [adventure]," Ibid.

92   "the least little gesture": Ibid.

92   Lillian Hellman knew how to make love: Hilary Mills interview with Ralph Ingersoll.

92   "Such Hammett *mishigos*": Kober *Diary,* June 23, 1935. WIS.

93   For the Hammett-Perelman liaison: Interviews with Ruth Goetz, Irene Diamond, Dorothy Herrmann. According to Mrs. Goetz, August 25, 1994, Laura Perelman, her own closest friend, was in love with Dashiell Hammett.

93   Had Lillian heard anything?: Feibleman, 167.

93–94   "absolutely cheap and despicable": Kober *Diary,* July 9, 1935. WIS.

94   "If you love him as much": Laura Perelman to Lillian Hellman [July 1935]. Courtesy of William Abrahams.

94   "the Hammett influence": Kober *Diary,* July 23, 1935. WIS.

94   "foolish arguments": Kober *Diary,* August 5, 1935. WIS.

94   "started and torn up": Laura Perelman to Dashiell Hammett, July 27 [1935]. Courtesy of William Abrahams.

94   Why hadn't he told her?: Feibleman, 167.

94   "because he'd given Laura his word": Ibid.

95   "hooked": Hilary Mills interview with Ralph Ingersoll.

95   "I could kill him": Feibleman, *Lilly.* See also "I wish he were alive so I could kill him": Albert Hackett interview with JM.

95   "new boyfriend": Kober *Diary,* September 9, 1935. WIS.

95   "into which she could be worked": Roy Hoopes, *Ralph Ingersoll: A Biography* (Atheneum: New York, 1985), 131.

96   whose illness had always repelled him. Dorothea Straus interview with JM, August 16, 1993.

96	"He's not like other people": Ibid.
96	"tremendous beaks": Kober *Diary,* December 2, 1935. WIS.
96	She was no longer in love with her father: Lillian Hellman interview with Alvin Sargent, June 13, 1982. Courtesy of Alvin Sargent.
96	wear her mother's wedding ring: John Melby interview with JM, December 14, 1992.
96	default judgments: Layman, *Shadow Man,* 162.
96	"the service is too lousy": Dashiell Hammett to Josephine Hammett, undated from Private Pavilion, Lenox Hill Hospital, New York. Courtesy of Josephine Marshall.
96	walnut-paneled lobby: For a description of the Madison Hotel in 1936, see Moss Hart, *Act One: An Autobiography,* 1959 (St. Martin's Press: New York, 1987), 248.
97	"Because I don't think writers who cry": *Scoundrel Time,* 65. See also, Thomas Meehan, "Q: Miss Hellman, What's Wrong with Broadway?" "A: It's a Bore," *Esquire,* 58 (December 1952), 140, 142, 235–36.
97	"an anti-Semitic son of a bitch": Hoopes, 133.
97	"could be a very cruel man": Hilary Mills interview with Ralph Ingersoll.
97	"He was too totally detached": Hoopes, 132.
97	"Anxious to know how the book goes": Blanche Knopf to Dashiell Hammett, May 5, 1936. LAY.
97	"you must be about finishing": Knopf to Dashiell Hammett, July 20, 1936. LAY.
98	"looks . . . quite a bit like you": Dashiell Hammett to Josephine Hammett, March 14, 1936. Courtesy of Josephine Marshall.
98	"I had a drink downstairs": Scenes between Dashiell Hammett and Eleanor Wolff come courtesy of Miss Wolff, who kept a daily diary during the months she worked for Dashiell Hammett. Wolff saved as well the library slips she made for her research at the New York Public Library. This account has been supplemented by Eleanor Wolff interview with JM, September 16, 1993.
101	"not very cheerful with her": Kober *Diary,* May 16, 1936.
101	"to get away from it all": Kober *Diary,* May 30, 1936.
101	"a horrible banana-eating crowd": Kober *Diary,* June 4, 1936.
101	"I'm missing you terribly": Johnson, 131.
101	"Well, where else am I going to get news": Dashiell Hammett to Lillian Hellman, June 11, 1936. HRHRC.
101	"I've been practicing looking like Corey Ford": Ibid.

7. Roosevelt Bohemians

102	"Roosevelt Bohemians": Benjamin Gitlow, *I Confess: The Truth about American Communism* (E. P. Dutton: New York, 1940), 485.
103	To behave as if they were enthusiastic members: Irving Howe and Lewis Coser, *The American Communist Party: A Critical History* (Frederick A. Praeger: New York, 1962), 319.
103	"colonial and pioneer stock": Eugene Lyons, *The Red Decade: The Stalin-*

ist Penetration of America (Bobbs-Merrill: Indianapolis and New York, 1941), p. 65.

103 "These writers are united": "American Writers: 1935 to 1929," *New Masses,* June 20, 1939.

104–105 For a discussion of the detective story genre as it existed when Hammett began to write, see Layman, *Shadow Man,* 65.

105 "The Advertisement IS Literature," *Western Advertising,* October 1926, 35–36.

105 "American naturalism but cranked up": Larry McCaffery, "An Interview with William Gibson," in *Storming the Reality Studio,* ed. Larry McCaffery (Duke University Press: Durham and London, 1991), 269.

105 "murder out of the Venetian vase": MacShane, 47–48. James M. Cain, however, denied that he was influenced by Dashiell Hammett: "I am often bracketed with him, and Clifton Fadiman once spoke of my 'Hammett & tongs style'—as though there was some relationship. I have to say there wasn't, though if there were I think I would admit it." James M. Cain to William Godshalk, March 4, 1974. Courtesy of Richard Layman.

106 "chiefly from reading Henry James": Lillian Hellman to Diane Johnson, December 12, 1979. HRHRC.

106 Herbert Asbury, Review of *Red Harvest, Bookman,* March 29, 1929, 62.

106 William Curtis, "Some Recent Books," *Town & Country,* February 15, 1930.

106 Donald Douglas, "Not One Hoot for the Law," *New Republic,* 62 April 9, 1930, 226.

106 "a little man going forward day after day": Ibid., 47.

106 Richard Layman has put it best: Layman, *Shadow Man,* 85.

107 Lily joined him: See Lillian Hellman draft of statement for Joseph Rauh, 1952, in preparation for her appearance before HUAC. HRHRC.

107 a special group of the Communist Party: Interviews with Maurice Rapf, October 25, 1993, Alice Hunter, April 28, 1993, Frederick V. Field, January 17, 1994. The FBI file for Lillian Hellman, 100-28760, puts it this way: "It was a group . . . which required extra protection from exposure." Office Memorandum. To: Director, December 19, 1951. From: SAC, Los Angeles (100-22366).

108 Dorothy Parker . . . did openly send a check: Goldie Kleiner interview with JM, February 10, 1994.

108 she too joined the Party: Lillian Hellman, draft of statement written in 1952 for her lawyer, Joe Rauh, April 14, 1952. HRHRC.

108 Mike Gold: See Lyons, 179.

108 "Radical" was the term Hellman used in *Scoundrel Time* (see p. 47, for example) and elsewhere when she was referring to Communists.

108 an "establishmentarian": Norman Mailer interview with JM, May 24, 1993.

109 Lillian's 1936 dinner is described in James T. Farrell to William Godshalk, September 5, 1974. LAY.

109 a "Red": Johnson, 117.

109	"Hammett's belief that he was living in a corrupt society": *Scoundrel Time*, 48.
109	"a world that was rosy": *Red Harvest*, 160.
110	in "an ugly Spanish house": *Scoundrel Time*, 43.
110	"a blackface Cliff Odets": Johnson, 202.
110	"on the right side, but": Ibid.
111	"Oh, this is very temporary": Lillian Hellman interviewed by Diane Johnson, courtesy of Diane Johnson, and elsewhere.
112	"a gift . . . from the rich Mr. Ham": Kober *Diary*, January 2, 1935. WIS.
112	"Lil who has just found the cause": Rollyson, 91.
113	never entirely "reliable": Howard Fast interview with JM, October 21, 1992.
113	"For many years . . . you've thought it cowardice": Dashiell Hammett to Lillian Hellman, May 23, 1944.
113	"Whose side was it on?" Wright, 136.
113	it wasn't always easy: Marshall interview.
113	"turning toward radical political solutions": *Scoundrel Time*, 43.
114	Lillian played only a public role. Ruth Goetz and Becky Bernstien interviews with JM, July 6, 1993.
114	"'Li'l Abner' . . . a fascist comic strip": Bill Moyers, "Lillian Hellman: The Great Playwright Candidly Reflects on a Long, Rich Life," in *Conversations*, 152.
114	He gave her Engels: Rollyson, 274.
114	Spanish Communists: For a discussion of the role of the Communist Party and the Soviet Union in Spain, see, for example, Felix Morrow, *Revolution and Counter-Revolution in Spain* (London: New Park Publications, 1963; first published in 1938), 34ff.

8. The Baby Years

116	"I drank a lot": "Tulip" appears in *The Big Knockover*, 342.
116	"Caution to Travelers": *The Lariat*, November 1925, 507.
116	"Woman waiting": HRHRC.
116	to do battle: It was Lillian Hellman who urged Earl Browder to go to Hollywood to raise funds and to see Hollywood as fertile ground for Communist activity. See Kober *Diary*, June 2, 1936. WIS.
116	Sexy: Rapf interview.
117	I have no reason to condemn him. Albert Hackett interview with Hilary Mills. Courtesy of Carl Rollyson.
117	"I've done it again!": Lee Gershwin interview with Carl Rollyson.
117	"had to be loveable or hateful": Dashiell Hammett to Lillian Hellman, May 23, 1944.
117	"I feel blue and lousy": Lillian Hellman to Arthur Kober ("Dearest Art") (undated). WIS.
117	"a beggar on horseback": Ibid.
117	For scene at Lenox Hill Hospital, see Johnson, 131. See also Kober *Diary*, August 29, 1936. WIS. "She describes heating process to cure him & I'm damned if I could stand the pain."

117   "Stop it!": Hilary Mills interview with Albert Hackett. Courtesy of Carl Rollyson.

117   "contrary activities of both parties": "Miss Hellman Again," *New York Times*, December 13, 1936, IE, 4.

118   the image of Hammett for Lily that summer: *Unfinished Woman*, 226–27.

118   "the handsomest sight I ever saw": Ibid.

118   "good": See Lillian Hellman annotations (p. 68) to the manuscript for Richard Moody's *Lillian Hellman: Playwright*.

118   "the most silent man": Hilary Mills interview with Ralph Ingersoll.

118   "gay, witty, and relaxed": Hoopes, 6.

118–119 "to take the best of capitalism": Hilary Mills interview with Ingersoll. See also Hoopes, 133.

119   "awful": Kober *Diary*, October 3, 1936. WIS.

119   "how much she leans on Dash": Ibid.

119   incident of Dash grabbing the policeman's gun: A. Robert Towbin interview with JM, July 14, 1993.

119   "Here is collaboration!": Kober *Diary*, October 9, 1936. WIS.

119   For scenes of Hammett in Princeton: "Dashiel [sic] Hammett Flees Night Club Round Succumbing to Rustication in New Jersey," *Daily Princetonian*, November 11, 1936, 1, 4. See also Dan Piper to William Godshalk, May 2, 1974, and July 16, 1974. LAY.

119–120 For Hammett's changes to the script of *Days to Come*: Text available HRHRC. Manuscript is dated November 9, 1936, brown folder.

120   "pretty body in fine silks": Dashiell Hammett to Pru Whitfield, September 9, 1944. Courtesy of Peter Stern.

120   "pre-Hammett past": Dashiell Hammett to Pru Whitfield, October 24, 1944. Courtesy of Peter Stern.

120   "Oh, Pru . . . So she always wants": Rollyson, 97.

120   "You who are such an attractive man": Flora Roberts interview with JM, March 30, 1994.

121   had "to be fixed": Kober *Diary*, December 6, 1936. WIS.

121   "fall to & tear the Perelmans": Kober *Diary*, December 13, 1936. WIS.

121   "weeping hysterically on Herman's": Kober *Diary*, December 15, 1936. WIS.

121   For the scene of the opening-night party of *Days to Come*: Hoopes, 135, Rollyson, 100ff, and Margaret Case Harriman, "Miss Lily of New Orleans." See also Kober *Diary*, December 15, 1936: "A pall is over it and we try to be gay. Max is there bewildered, not knowing what to make of the play, James Farrell too."

121   "very happy": Fred Gardner interview with Lillian Helman.

121   declared POUM: George Orwell, *Homage to Catalonia* (Beacon Press: Boston, 1952), 64.

122   "I'll have to go to work": Dashiell Hammett to Lillian Hellman, December 28, 1936. HRHRC.

122   "Lilushka": Dashiell Hammett to Lillian Hellman, Late at night late in December late in 1936 A.D. Courtesy of Fred Gardner.

122   "You're so little and the boat's so big": Ibid.

122   "a phone call from Prue": Dashiell Hammett to Lillian Hellman, late at night late in December late in 1936.

122   "I'm not going to continue": For this scene of Lillian Hellman speaking at the New School, I am indebted to Sydney Schiffer. Sydney Schiffer to JM, May 5, 1993.

122   "leaned heavily on Dash": Kober *Diary,* January 27, 1937. WIS.

122   "A sweet guy, but dull": Dashiell Hammett to Lillian Hellman [1937]. Courtesy of Fred Gardner.

122   "thoughts of a middle-aged and slightly tight": Dashiell Hammett to Lillian Hellman (undated). Courtesy of Fred Gardner.

122   "like a soft hawk": Dashiell Hammett to Lillian Hellman, March 13, 1937. Courtesy of Fred Gardner.

122   "Open Letter to American Liberals": *Western Worker,* February 1937.

122   "They're dopes!": Hilary Mills interview with Sam Marx. Courtesy of Carl Rollyson.

123   "All right": Franklin Folsom interview with JM, March 6, 1994. See also Folsom, *Days of Anger, Days of Hope: A Memoir of the League of American Writers 1937–42* (University Press of Colorado: Niwot, 1994).

123   gloomily: Dashiell Hammett to Lillian Hellman, March 13, 1937.

123   "wonder[ed] at Lillian": Kober *Diary,* March 28, 1937. WIS.

123   suing him: William M. Sloane interview with JM, January 13, 1994.

123   "gloom and sordidness of the background": Scott A. Berg, *Goldwyn: A Biography* (Alfred A. Knopf: New York, 1989), 316.

123   "I've decided to live flamboyantly!": Layman, *Shadow Man,* 161.

123   "I should be more than pleased": Dashiell Hammett to Lillian Hellman (undated). Courtesy of Fred Gardner.

124   "They're thinking of sending me to Spain": Marshall interview.

124   "Lil & Dash very domestic": Kober *Diary,* June 17, 1937. WIS.

124   Lily became pregnant: Philip D'Arcy Hart interview. See also Marilyn Berger, Program No. Two.

124   "She'll never divorce you": Marshall interview.

124   Dash ordered the girls out of the room: Marshall interview.

124   "ladies": Janet Chusmir, "Lillian Hellman on Lillian Hellman," in *Conversations,* 160.

124   Even her being pregnant did not bind Hammett: Alvin Sargent interview with JM, April 16, 1993.

124   "How was I going to support them?": Dan Rather, "A Profile of Lillian Hellman," 215.

125   "Dash's change of feelings": Kober *Diary,* July 19, 1937.

125   "very much like quarreling married people": Kober *Diary,* July 28, 1937. WIS.

125   "No, you don't": *Unfinished Woman,* 61.

125   flirted so outrageously: Martha Gellhorn interview with JM, April 9, 1994.

125   who adored her: JM interview with Irene Diamond.

125   These scenes with Hemingway described by Gellhorn. See also Gell-

horn, "On Apocryphism," *Paris Review,* No. 79 (Spring 1981), 280–301, and *Unfinished Woman,* 66–67.

126   "It never happened": Sargent interview.

127   "worried over his fragile lungs": Dashiell Hammett to Lillian Hellman, September 9, 1937. Courtesy of Fred Gardner.

127   "mix in politics": See "Writers and Politics," *Variety,* December 15, 1937.

127   "I was divorced in Nogales": Dashiell Hammett to Lillian Hellman, September 9, 1937.

127   "very bitter over him": Kober *Diary,* November 20, 1937. WIS.

127   "grew heated": Mary McCarthy, *Intellectual Memoirs: New York 1936–1938* (Harcourt Brace Jovanovich: New York, 1992), 61.

127   "My Lilly is a postage stamp miser": Johnson, 141.

127   "new fable of how Nick loved Nora": Dashiell Hammett to Lillian Hellman, December 26, 1937. Courtesy of Fred Gardner.

127   "brooding over nothing": Ibid.

127   "Did I forget to tell you": Dashiell Hammett to Lillian Hellman, January 15, 1938.

127   "the international class struggle": Philip Rahv, "Two Years of Progress: From Waldo Frank to Donald Ogden Stewart," *Partisan Review,* 4, No. 3 (February 1938).

128   "tea-party": Kober *Diary,* January 4, 1938. WIS.

128   "great weight makers": Kober *Diary,* February 5, 1938. WIS.

128   "well-spoken, direct and honest": Kober *Diary,* February 13, 1938. WIS.

128   "The ideal democratic state": Kober *Diary,* January 7, 1938. WIS.

128   "childish as far as style": Kober *Diary.* January 12, 1938. WIS.

128   "Very depressed": Kober *Diary,* January 28, 1938. WIS.

128   "It is raining here": Dashiell Hammett to Lillian Hellman, February 19, 1938. Courtesy of Fred Gardner.

128   "immersed in the minutiae": Nancy Lynn Schwartz, *The Hollywood Writers' Wars* (Alfred A. Knopf: New York, 1982), 116.

128   "Well, if I get Talbot Jennings": Schwartz, 124.

129   "Trotskyite-Buckharnite [sic] traitors": "Leading Artists, Educators Support Soviet Trial Verdict," *Daily Worker,* April 28, 1938.

129   "no mere figurehead": "Hammett Featured in New Art Exhibit," *Hollywood Now,* April 23, 1938, 2.

129   "Did it cost more than five hundred": Dashiell Hammett to Lillian Hellman, June 25, 1944.

129   "Hammett is in his room": Sidney Skolsky, "Hollywood," New York *Mirror,* March 14, 1938.

129   "carries brass knuckles": "The Lyons Den" New York *Evening Post,* March 14, 1938.

129   "weak, frightened and panicky": Lenox Hill Hospital report. Johnson, 152.

129   "the first I'd had since when": Dashiell Hammett to Lillian Hellman, May 14, 1938. HRHRC.

129   "Just about what little imagination I've got": Dashiell Hammett to Lillian Hellman, "Darling" (undated). HRHRC.

130   "Hammett's feeble blue eyelids": Rollyson, 132.
130   "He can die here as quickly": Johnson, 151.
130   "terrified": Rollyson, 132.
130   "Dash business": Kober *Diary,* June 3, 1938. WIS.

9. Hammett and *The Little Foxes*

131   "Often I hated him": Marilyn Berger, Program No. Two.
131   "partly about her family": Kober *Diary,* May 12, 1938. WIS.
132   Lily suggested to Kober that they remarry: Kober *Diary,* May 15, 1938. WIS.
132   "like the old days": Kober *Diary,* December 11, 1938. WIS.
132   "Both of us want help": Ibid.
132   Elbow Room: Irene Kuhn, "My Word!" *Motion Picture Daily,* June 3, 1938.
132   "Churlishly": Lillian Hellman, "Back of Those Foxes," New York *Times,* February 26, 1939.
132   "It's too hot to return to the city": Ibid.
132   "If only Miss Lillian could write 'em": Ibid.
133   "Missy write blackamoor chit-chat": Margaret Case Harriman, "Miss Lily of New Orleans."
133   "The script is getting warmer": Lillian Hellman, "People and Plays: Notes from a Journal" (manuscript), 7. Courtesy of Fred Gardner.
133   "It really happened": Incident related in Feibleman interview.
133   "I hope *this* satisfies you": John Phillips and Anne Hollander, "The Art of the Theater: Lillian Hellman—An Interview," in *Conversations,* 69.
133   "Well, you're on your way": Eve Merriam, "Living Playwrights in the Living Theatre," *Dramatus,* May 1982.
134   "It took bravery and great affection": Marilyn Berger, Program No. Two.
134   "Get it": See drafts of *The Little Foxes.* HRHRC. The notebook of Hammett's suggestions is also available. HRHRC. See in particular long yellow legal sheets, under "Dash."
138   "Dash thinks it should": Richard Moody discovered this marginalia, *Lillian Hellman: Playwright,* 108.
138   they are demonstrations against the Soviet Union": Howe and Coser, 226.
138   "poor Rose . . . the lady with the broken heart": Kober *Diary,* December 3, 1938.
138   Lily had perched on Shumlin's lap: Irene Diamond interview with JM.
139   "something cheap about Lil": Rollyson, 136.
139   "The cultural heritage does not transmit": Quoted in Malcolm Cowley, *The Dream of the Golden Mountains: Remembering the 1930s* (Viking Press: New York, 1980), 282.
139   "contrived and shabby rationale": Irving Howe, *Politics and the Novel* (Meridian Books: New York, 1957), 213.
139   "meretricious": Ibid., 212.
139   "There is none whose conversational": "The Voice of New York," New York *Evening Journal,* June 9, 1938.

139   "very silly and loose in his talk": Kober *Diary,* November 30, 1938. WIS.

139   "deplorable": Ibid.

140   brought them to Dash: Kober *Diary,* December 10, 1938. WIS.

140   "ought to do it at a high moment": Kober *Diary,* December 6, 1938. WIS.

140   chiding Edla Benjamin: Kober *Diary,* December 23, 1938. WIS.

140   Lily carried the mink skins: Doudna, 192.

140   she felt herself grow more awkward: Mrs. Howard E. Sternau to Lillian Hellman, October 30, 1973. HRHRC.

141   "Let's go home and mix a pitcher of martinis": Johnson, 170–71.

141   the social engagement . . . seemed more useful: Annabel Davis-Goff interview with JM, January 5, 1993.

141   a limited capacity for happiness: Max Palevsky interview with JM, April 21, 1993.

141   "Do you really think you are doing right" Johnson, 207.

142   would happily have gone to bed with him again: Charlee Wilbur interview with JM, May 12, 1993.

142   "Thank God the sex had stopped": Renata Adler interview with JM.

142   "miserable and drunk": Berger, Program No. Two.

142   he did cure her of heavy drinking: Blair Clark interviews with JM.

142   her chronic lying: Peg Zilboorg interview with JM, June 10, 1993.

142   the deprecatory way with a curling lip: Ibid.

142   he rolled his eyes skyward: Rollyson, 198.

143   he learned more about himself: Doudna, 201.

143   "a good deal of her money": Milton Wexler interview with JM, April 17, 1993.

143   The relationship with Hammett could bring her only pain: Alvin Sargent interview with Lillian Hellman. Courtesy of Alvin Sargent.

10. Hardscrabble Days: 1939–42

147   "Lily, I'm too old for that stuff": *Pentimento,* 230.

147   Lily bought Hardscrabble Farm: See New York *Times,* June 7, 1939, IE, 9: "Lillian Hellman Buys Estate of 130 Acres."

148   "I was running a boarding house": "(I was speaking of Hannah Weinstein)" (manuscript). HRHRC.

148   "We are now in a theatre": Poems of Lillian Hellman to Herman Shumlin (manuscript). HRHRC.

148   the "jimjams": Victor Samrock interview with JM, March 30, 1994.

148   in "a riot of colors": Kober *Diary,* June 8, 1940. WIS.

149   "blue trim and pink sheets": These instructions remain in the cedar closet at Hardscrabble Farm. I am indebted to Ellen Hodor for her generosity in inviting me to visit.

149   "I," not "we": Dashiell Hammett to Josephine Hammett, June 14, 1939.

149   "It's beginning to look as if I'm not going": Ibid.

149   "Mr. Samuel Dashiell Hammett, former eccentric": Margaret Case Harriman, "Miss Lily of New Orleans," 29.

149   guests saw him come into her workroom: Helen Rosen interview with JM, July 18, 1994.

149   listened to a baseball game: Dashiell Hammett to Lillian Hellman, October 3, 1943.

149   she tore open the mail: Dashiell Hammett to Lillian Hellman, October 2, 1943.

150   crawled into his bed: Feibleman, 168.

150   "hated" Alan Campbell: Lillian Hellman to Arthur and Maggie Kober ("Darling Maggie, darling you know who") (1941?). WIS.

150   "very refined dinner": *Autobiographical Writings of Henry E. Sigerist.* Wednesday, April 30. HRHRC.

150   On a typical Saturday: This scenario is outlined in Dashiell Hammett to Lillian Hellman, October 9, 1943.

150   walked in on Dash having sexual intercourse: James Weinstein interview with JM, October 6, 1993.

150   "perpetual fear of failure": Kober *Diary.*

150   Shumlin would look right into a woman's eyes: Flora Roberts interview.

150   far better lover than Hammett: Feibleman interview.

151   Herman-Sherman, this hymn I cast: Poems of Lillian Hellman to Herman Shumlin. HRHRC.

151   "*Marry? You* decided?": *Pentimento,* 141.

151   report her to the income-tax people: Flora Roberts interview. Also Jerome Weidman interview with JM, February 24, 1993.

151   "I'm thinking of writing a play": Quoted in Dashiell Hammett to Lillian Hellman, February 1, 1944.

152   "It should be easy to remember a name like Dashiell": "All of Us," *Montana Standard,* May 13, 1938, reprinted in many papers.

152   They did not touch each other: Marshall interview.

152   "Come back in an hour": Feibleman, 167.

152   "carrying books": *Unfinished Woman,* 239.

152   "I was almost raped by a hummingbird": Marshall interview.

152   sucker for the Irish: Lillian Hellman and Peter Feibleman, *Eating Together: Recollections & Recipes* (Little, Brown: Boston, 1984), 73.

152   "Now let's get in there and use": Lillian Hellman interviewed by Fred Gardner.

152   "Please sit down": Doudna, 209.

153   "She hasn't got a train of thought": Feibleman interview.

153   "ragging tone": *Unfinished Woman,* 101–2.

153   "Now, Lily, what really happened?": Helen Rosen interview with JM, July 18, 1994.

153   "Lily, grow up!": Ibid.

153   "Keep your damn TLs to yourself": Wright, 403.

153   "I was mean to her": Emmy Kronenberger interview with JM, May 10, 1993.

153   "unhappy nature": Lillian Hellman, BBC Omnibus "Portrait of Lillian Hellman," 1978.

153   "always on point of tears": Kober *Diary,* January 18, 1940. WIS.

153   "too difficult and irrational": Kober *Diary,* January 14, 1940. WIS.

153   "too weak and too tortured": Ibid.
153   "the quarrel between Dash & Lil": Kober *Diary*, January 2, 1940. WIS.
153   "jittery with Dash's high spirits": Kober *Diary*, January 9, 1940. WIS.
153   "apparent he has been drinking again": Kober *Diary*, January 12, 1940. WIS.
153   "out of sorts": Kober *Diary*, February 1, 1940. WIS.
154   "an extraordinarily good-looking Virginian": Hoopes, 85–86.
154   "a blow to her pride": Kober *Diary*, March 1, 1940. WIS.
154   "a louse, stinker & finally a shit": Kober *Diary*, May 14, 1940. WIS.
154   his politics were considerably less liberal: Hoopes, 235.
154   unrequited passion for Bennett Cerf: Irene Diamond interview.
154   "very bad tho puts up a bold front": Kober *Diary*, August 14, 1940.
154   "just hopeless": Albert Hackett interview with JM.
154   "As handsome as Dash?": Jerome Weidman, *Praying for Rain*, (Harper and Row: New York, 1986), 387.
155   Leane Zugsmith came: Lillian Hellman, "Yes, I knew Leane very well." April 15, 1974. Beinecke Library, Yale University. No salutation.
155   "smuck": For these incidents which follow, see Weidman, *Praying for Rain*, 381ff.
155   "If you had a hat": Jerome Weidman interview.
155   See Weidman, *The Sound of Bow Bells*.
156   "badly . . . beer binge is doing him no good": Kober *Diary*, September 7, 1940. WIS.
156   "If I can't be maid of honor": Kober *Diary*, October 21, 1940. WIS.
156   Lillian's picture would be displayed: Catherine Kober interview with JM, December 4, 1992.
156   to "my own erotic dreams again": Kober *Diary*, January 27, 1941. WIS.
156   "I preach to her to go away": Max Hellman to Arthur Kober, April 24, 1941. WIS.
156   For the visit of Hammett's daughters: Marshall interview.
156   "gentle apology": Peg Zilboorg interview.
156   "What are you doing here?" Marshall interview.
157   "the hottest of the uptown sepian spots": *Swing* (Detroit), June 1939.
157   "He couldn't get it up!": Emmy Kronenberger interview.
157   a nurturing Lillian: Burton Bernstein interview with JM, April 1, 1994.
157   "My feeling is that McKelway has wandered": Kober *Diary*, February 25, 1942. WIS.
158   "very unhappy": Ibid.
157–158   "crabs": Kober *Diary*, February 26, 1942. WIS.
158   "Lil so envious": Kober *Diary*, March 24, 1942. WIS.
158   it was Lillian who was the patriarch: Catherine Kober interview with JM.
158   For "Turtle," see *Pentimento*, 219–34.

11. The Communist Couple

159   "Maybe you had to be a socialist": Judith Firth Sanger interview with JM, June 28, 1993.

160 "He had the politics of a baby": William Phillips interview with JM, March 8, 1993.

160 Eddie came home drunker: Mary Rolfe interview with JM, November 20, 1993.

160 "Now I'm going to get up and type": Dashiell Hammett to Lillian Hellman, March 10, 1939. Courtesy of Fred Gardner.

160 "Hammett and I had not shared": *Unfinished Woman,* 145.

160 hard-boiled egg, lettuce, and tea: Helen Rosen interview.

161 "Lillian's a wunnerful woman": Folsom, 64.

161 "I haven't got it": Ibid., 52–54.

161 "a kind of platonic affiliation": Irving Howe interview with JM, February 23, 1993.

161 Dashiell Hammett file, Department of State: "We, the undersigned Artists of Hollywood, joining the overwhelming majority of the American people appreciate your efforts to preserve the peace of the world and urge the immediate repeal of the embargo on Spain, so that the principles of freedom and democracy shall not perish from the earth." Dashiell Hammett, Chairman of the Motion Picture Artists Committee.

161 "Isn't that true, Lillian?": Margaret Case Harriman, "Miss Lily of New Orleans," 24.

161 "All the Communists I know would be very glad to have you": Dashiell Hammett to Josephine Hammett, August 1, 1938.

161 "aristocracy and the middle class": Gardner, "Politics/PM" (unpublished manuscript). Courtesy of Fred Gardner.

161 "You don't trust Stalin": Hoopes, 223. See also Laura Z. Hobson, *Laura Z: A Life* (Arbor House: New York, 1983), 235.

162 invented the charge that Tallulah refused: Margaret Case Harriman, "Miss Lily of New Orleans," 24. See also *Not for Women Only: Women Who Have Changed Our Lives,* Show #877, interview by Barbara Walters. Transcript at HRHRC.

162 "I don't believe in that fine, lovable little Republic": Harriman, 24.

162 "cutting up about giving benefit": Kober *Diary,* January 20, 1940. WIS.

162 "I feel enraged at this drunken, foul-mouthed": Kober *Diary,* January 23, 1940. WIS.

162 "an attempt to spike Tallulah's": Kober *Diary,* January 26, 1940. WIS.

162 "Theatrical benefits for Finnish relief": "See Finnish Aid Imperilling Peace," New York *Times,* January 21, 1940, L, 27.

162 "new kind of newspaper": Hoopes, 187.

163 "challenged all my ideas": Gardner, "Politics/PM." See also Hoopes, 133.

163 "He never opened his mouth": Gardner, "Politics/PM."

163 "the financial set-up of movie companies": Ibid.

163 "broken promises": Lillian Hellman interview with Fred Gardner.

163 "You can't bring this out": Ibid.

163 "The man is already a hysteric": Ibid.

164 "son of a bitch": Hilary Mills interview with Ralph Ingersoll.

164 "Incidentally, Dash . . . things are pretty hot": Hoopes, 232.

164 "at friends to hide his terror": Kober *Diary,* July 27, 1940.

164   "a real fingering job": Fred Gardner interview with Lillian Hellman.

165   "net-full of zanies": Dashiell Hammett to Lillian Hellman, January 16, 1944.

165   "sending back a fortune": Jerome Weidman interview with JM.

165   he was sorry he hadn't gone to Spain: Jack Bjoze interview with JM, July 19, 1993.

165   "not tolerate the active participation": Rahv, "Two Years of Progress," 27.

165   "It is among the writers particularly": Folsom, 101.

165   a "fantastic falsehood that the USSR": Lyons, *The Red Decade,* 342. See also Howe and Coser, 341.

166   a tactical maneuver: Ring Lardner interview with JM.

166   "the greatest meeting-goer in the country": Gardner, "Politics/PM."

166   "lash out at Roosevelt's": Kober *Diary,* May 23, 1940. WIS.

166   "whether or not you will become Nazi slaves": Ettie Stettheimer, "American Writers' Congress Hit as Camouflage for Anti-Defense Forces," *New Leader* (undated, 1941). Yale University Library.

166   "Before the Hitler-Stalin pact they were": Suzanne La Follette to Ettie Stettheimer, May 25, 1941. Columbia University.

167   supporters of Communist longshoreman: Donald Congdon interview with JM, October 14, 1993.

167   "I am a writer and I am also a Jew": "Lin Yutang Holds 'Gods' Favor China," New York *Times,* January 10, 1940.

167   "You don't know what you're talking about": Marshall interview with JM.

168   "The Communist Party protests the denial of civil rights": FBI file, Dashiell Hammett: 100-14499, New York: 100-9118.

168   a "blacklist" of people on the left: See William Phillips, *A Partisan View: Five Decades of the Literary Life* (Stein & Day: New York, 1983), 174. See also Gitlow, 400: "We in America sank so low in our ethical standards that we resorted to gangster tactics against fellow-Communists because they disagreed with us. That confronts me with the horrible speculation: had we Communists attained power in America, myself included, would we hesitate to go through with blood purges?"

168   a "truly literary conference": "American Writers: 1935 to 1939," *New Masses,* June 20, 1939.

168   "deeply shocked . . . I do not ask the politics": Lillian Hellman to Herbert H. Lehman, November 3, 1941. See also September 10, 1941, and October 1, 1941. Butler Library, Columbia University.

169   "a partner of the Axis powers": Herbert H. Lehman to Lillian Hellman, November 25, 1941. See also September 16, 1941, and September 30, 1941.

169   "from the money coming in from the Congress": Lillian Hellman to Franklin Folsom, May 10, 1941. HRHRC.

169   "the new and greater American national defense": Folsom, 201.

169   "The Motherland has been attacked!": Schwartz, 173.

169   "for the Soviet fight against the Nazi invasion": Dashiell Hammett to "dear fellow writer," September 15, 1941. Columbia University.

171   so "un-angry" a man: Lillian Hellman interview with Fred Gardner.

12. Hellman Edits Hammett

172   Both Dashiell Hammett's script, dated April 23, 1942, and Lillian Hellman's typewritten version of *Watch on the Rhine* are available at HRHRC.

173   For Communist responses to *Watch on the Rhine: Daily Worker,* April 4, 1941; Alvah Bessie, "Watch on the Rhine," *New Masses,* April 15, 1941; Albert Maltz, "What Shall We Ask of Writers?" *New Masses,* February 12, 1946; Howard Fast, "Art and Politics," *New Masses,* February 26, 1946; Joseph North, "No Retreat for the Writer," *New Masses,* February 26, 1946; Albert Maltz, "Moving Forward," *New Masses,* April 9, 1946.

173   Hammett told Kober he liked the play: Kober *Diary,* September 27, 1940. WIS.

173   he did not come to rehearsals; Lucy Ruskin interview with JM, April 6, 1994.

173   massaging Lily's sore foot: Abe Abeloff to Lillian Hellman, May 25, 1944. HRHRC.

174   Nor . . . was Dash at Sardi's: Diana Fuller interview with JM, April 13, 1993.

174   "You ruined a great play": Lillian Hellman interview with Fred Gardner.

174   "sufficiently desirable": Lillian Hellman, FBI file: 100-22366:

174   "too long and involved a story": Robert Van Gelder, "Of Lillian Hellman," New York *Times,* April 20, 1941, Section 1, 4. See also "Being a Conversation with the Author of *Watch on the Rhine,*" in *Conversations,* 12.

174   "Only eleven months have gone by": Lillian Hellman, Introduction to *Six Plays,* xii.

174   "A birthday present for Lillian Hellman": Margaret Case Harriman, "Miss Lily of New Orleans, 30.

175   "uh, huh": LH interview with Fred Gardner.

175   Hal Wallis wanted Lillian to write it herself: Hal Wallis to Jack Warner, January 6, 1942. Warner Brothers Archive.

175   "slowness": Hal Wallis to Jake Wilk: January 16, 1942.

175   Wallis nervously insisted: Memo: Wallis to [Jake] Wilk: January 14, 1942. Warner Brothers Archive. See also Hal Wallis to Jake Wilk, February 14, 1942. The following citations from the correspondence between Wallis, Wilk, Shumlin, and Hammett are from documents housed at the Warner Brothers Archive.

175   He paid her $11,500: budget, June 6, 1942. #412. *Watch on the Rhine.* Warner Brothers Archive. Doheny Library. University of Southern California. The largest salary went to Bette Davis: $73,333. Shumlin got $35,000 for directing, Hal Wallis, $25,000 for producing.

175   "some work" that needed to be finished: Telegram from Jake Wilk to Hal Wallis, January 17, 1942.

175   "get script out in record time": Telegram Jake Wilk to Hal Wallis, January 17, 1942.

175   Dashiell Hammett's treatment for *Watch on the Rhine* is part of the Warner Brothers Archive.

176   "Shumlin agrees with you and Hellman with me": Dashiell Hammett to Hal Wallis, February 23, 1942.

176   Wallis considered hiring another writer: Hal Wallis to Jake Wilk, March 13, 1942.

176   "a gentle goosing": Hal Wallis to Jake Wilk, March 6, 1942.

176   "the complete job will be in your hands on schedule": Hal Wallis to Jake Wilk, March 26, 1942.

176   "set him back a couple of days": Herman Shumlin to Hal Wallis, March 26, 1942.

176–177   "I know that Dash has kept steadily": Ibid.

177   "If I don't break a leg": Dashiell Hammett to Hal Wallis, April 13, 1942.

177   "Don't indicate that we expect to pay": Telegram from Hal Wallis to Jake Wilk, April 7, 1942.

177   "unacceptable": Joseph I. Breen to Jack Warner, May 29, 1942. Library of the Academy of Motion Picture Arts and Sciences, Los Angeles.

177   "suggestive" dialogue: Ibid.

177   "go off scot-free": Ibid.

177   "scandalous": Lillian Hellman to Joseph Breen, July 13, 1942. Library of the Academy of Motion Picture Arts and Sciences, Los Angeles. Wallis backed her up by writing himself to Breen: Hal Wallis to Joseph I. Breen, July 20, 1942.

178   "Miss Hellman . . . will attempt": Joseph Breen to Will Hays, July 21, 1942. Library of the Academy of Motion Picture Arts and Sciences, Los Angeles.

178   "I suspect that Lil has changed": Kober *Diary,* May 31, 1942. WIS.

178   "He did it as a favor to me": Jan Albert, "Sweetest Smelling Baby in New Orleans," in *Conversations,* 171.

179   believes he has all the time in the world: Berger, Program No. Two.

181   organdie: Margaret Case Harriman, "Miss Lily of New Orleans," 22.

183   "He's put in one scene that I'd have given anything to have written": Rollyson, 191. Source is newspaper clipping in the files of the Billy Rose Theatre Collection, New York Public Library.

185   "artistic expression of the ideals": "Watch on the Rhine," *New Masses,* September 14, 1943.

13. The Woman Alone

189   "Woman pursuing can be oppressive": Lillian Hellman *Diary* for 1950. HRHRC.

189   "plugging away at": Dashiell Hammett to Bennett Cerf, January 14, 1939. Columbia University.

189   "A. No, I'm not drunk": Dashiell Hammett to Bennett Cerf, undated. Columbia.

189   "cold, hard, impersonal": Weidman, *Praying for Rain,* 383–84.

190 "Dash never lies about Orson Welles": Ibid.

191 "You can't go": Weidman interview with JM. See also *Unfinished Woman*, 224.

191 her personal deprivation: Weidman interview with JM.

191 "almost sick with milk and pudding and potatoes": Lillian Hellman to Dearest both of you (undated). WIS.

191 "I hope to God they take him": Ibid.

191 "the tall, spare American type": Dashiell Hammett to Lillian Hellman, July 13, 1944.

191 "We'll let you in this time": Dashiell Hammett to Lillian Hellman, January 6, 1943.

191 "Hammett's yellow! Hammett's yellow!": Dashiell Hammett to Lillian Hellman, October 1, 1942.

192 "low brown shoes . . . the size is ten and one-half": Dashiell Hammett to Dear Missie (undated).

192 "I've had so many X-rays": Franklin Folsom interview with JM, March 6, 1994. This incident is also described in Folsom, 227.

192 "like a wolf": Dashiell Hammett to Lillian Hellman, September 28, 1942.

192 "given him back his self-respect": Dashiell Hammett to Lillian Hellman, October 1, 1942.

192 A soldier named Robert Boltwood: Robert Boltwood to Lillian Hellman, September 13, 1973. HRHRC.

192 "in the African landing force": Lillian Hellman to Darling (Arthur Kober) (undated). WIS.

193 "bundle up in great coat": Dashiell Hammett to Lillian Hellman, December 14, 1942.

193 "I've been lonely here": Lillian Hellman to Arthur Kober (undated). WIS.

193 "I have five cows": Lillian Hellman to Darling (undated).

193 "no longer manage it": Lillian Hellman to Maggie and Arthur Kober (undated). HRHRC.

193 "never be happy with anyone else": Arthur Kober to Darling (Maggie) (undated). WIS.

193 "I know it isn't right now": Lillian Hellman to Dearest both of you [the Kobers] (undated, 1940s). WIS.

193 "as a pair . . . a closed book": Dashiell Hammett to Lillian Hellman, February 29, 1944.

193 "You never made any recognizable pattern": Ibid.

193 "I know you're gone": Dashiell Hammett to Lillian Hellman, December 14, 1942.

193 "I love a girl like you": Dashiell Hammett to Lillian Hellman, October 1, 1942.

193 "I liked him, liked the show": Lillian Hellman to Dearest both of you [Arthur and Maggie Kober] (undated). WIS.

193 "It has been brought to my attention": Irene Diamond interview with JM.

194 "You're a low character": Dashiell Hammett to Lillian Hellman [January 1943].

194   "Haven't you been out in that place": Dashiell Hammett to Lillian Hellman, January 8, 1943.

194   "It is nice waking up there Sunday mornings": Dashiell Hammett to Lillian Hellman, January 12, 1943.

194   "awfully nice . . . more comfortable than the barracks": Ibid.

194   "disrespect": Lillian Hellman to Lewis Milestone, February 19, 1943. HRHRC.

194   "What I have to say will not be altered": Ibid.

194   "I LOVE YOU TOO MUCH": quoted in Berg, 375.

194   "AND I LOVE YOU TOO MUCH": Ibid.

194   "Dear cutie and good writer . . . last night I read": Dashiell Hammett to Lillian Hellman, January 7, 1943.

195   "Shut up, shut up, shut up": For Lillian Hellman's travail over *The North Star,* see Berg, 375–76.

195   "No people in the world were ever as happy": Lillian Hellman to Lowell Mellett [chief of the Bureau of Motion Pictures for the Office of War Information], November 17, 1943. HRHRC.

195   "what they've done to *The North Star*": Dashiell Hammett to Lillian Hellman, October 17, 1943.

195   "When Stalin got depressed": Berg, 378.

195   "Graybeard": Dashiell Hammett to Lillian Hellman, January 22, 1943.

195   "Whitey": Dashiell Hammett to Lillian Hellman, January 23, 1943.

196   "to trick me and to injure me": Lillian Hellman to Samuel Goldwyn, June 25, 1943. HRHRC.

196   "junk . . . I hope you paid for it in Confederate": Lillian Hellman to Samuel Goldwyn, June 25, 1943.

196   "I can't afford much more than that": Notes on Mulvey-Hellman telephone conversation. June 21, 1943. HRHRC.

196   "There was no letter from you at noon": Dashiell Hammett to Lillian Hellman, January 13, 1943.

196   "I'll put coins in phones": Dashiell Hammett to Lillian Hellman, January 25, 1943.

196   "more radiant": Dashiell Hammett to Lillian Hellman, January 25, 1943.

196   "Keep some of that radiance": January 29, 1943.

196   "so kindly . . . have a little just-you-and-me": Dashiell Hammett to Lillian Hellman, January 25, 1943.

196   old friends had daughters: Dashiell Hammett to Lillian Hellman, July 15, 1943.

196–197 For this description of George Backer, I am indebted to his daughter. Sarah Jane (Sally) Kramarsky interview with JM, February 2, 1994.

197   "of whom I am very fond": Lillian Hellman to Darling Arthur, darling Maggie [1940s]. WIS.

197   Backer noticed that Lillian: A. Robert Towbin and Judith Firth Sanger interviews with JM.

197   Why not marry George Backer?: Kitty Carlisle Hart interview.

197 "Where did you meet that cunt?" Blair Clark interview.

197 "I'm sick of all writing": Lillian Hellman to Dearest Artda, Megda, and Catherine [1940s]. WIS.

197 "I hate like hell to write anything": Lillian Hellman to Dear Madame and Mister [1943?]. WIS.

198 "If you had any memory": Dashiell Hammett to Lillian Hellman, January 4, 1943.

198 Lilishka: See, for example, Dashiell Hammett to Lillian Hellman, September 28, 1942.

198 "What's News": Dashiell Hammett to Lillian Hellman, January 30, 1943.

198 "prick": Dashiell Hammett to Lillian Hellman, December 15, 1942.

199 "The only way a playwright has of earning a living:" Lillian Hellman to Rabbi Feibelman, November 13, 1941. HRHRC.

199 "ordinary income": Stanley M. Isaacs to Arthur O. Ernst, December 1943. HRHRC.

199 "Please buy bonds": Dashiell Hammett to Lillian Hellman, June 28, 1943. HRHRC.

199 "well and cheerful": Lillian Hellman to Darling Arthur, Darling Maggie (undated). WIS.

199 she cried out: Johnson, 177.

200 "very horrible": Lillian Hellman to Dearest Maggie, dearest Kobe, and darling Cathy (undated). WIS.

200 "He goes straight along in an incredible fashion": Ibid.

200 "I love you . . . The Cold Corporal": Dashiell Hammett to Lillian Hellman, February 1943.

14. Love Letters from the Front

201 "Do you want me to tell you": Dashiell Hammett to Lillian Hellman, October 25, 1943. Letters from Hammett to Hellman from the Aleutian Islands appear courtesy of William Abrahams.

201 "Do you suppose I'm in love": Dashiell Hammett to Lillian Hellman, September 21, 1943.

201 hairdresser: Dashiell Hammett to Lillian Hellman, September 28, 1943.

201–202 "a long time since I have seen you": Dashiell Hammett to Lillian Hellman, May 9, 1943.

202 "What do you look like?": Ibid.

202 "now have presentable grown daughters": Dashiell Hammett to Lillian Hellman, July 15, 1943.

202 "a lot of letters": Dashiell Hammett to Lillian Hellman, July 24, 1943.

202 he had not had a drink: Dashiell Hammett to Lillian Hellman, July 22, 1943.

202 "So I'm an alcoholic": Ibid.

202 "I felt better after talking to you": Dashiell Hammett to Lillian Hellman, July 18, 1943.

202 "elderly": Dashiell Hammett to Lillian Hellman, July 28, 1943.

202   "I am a dull old man": Dashiell Hammett to Lillian Hellman, July 27, 1943.

202   "Just as every woman thinks any woman": Dashiell Hammett to Lillian Hellman, July 28, 1943.

202   "and I've still got at least one more": Dashiell Hammett to Lillian Hellman, July 22, 1943.

203   "very intelligent and mean": Dashiell Hammett to Lillian Hellman, July 20, 1943.

203   "an aging tulip tree": Dashiell Hammett to Lillian Hellman, September 28, 1943.

203   "I imagine Bonwit Teller were pretty surprised": Dashiell Hammett to Lillian Hellman, October 11, 1943.

203   "for the press, for foyer display": Dashiell Hammett to Lillian Hellman, May 25, 1944.

203   "very cooperative": Dashiell Hammett to Nancy Bragdon, September 30, 1943.

203   "Men were going places": Dashiell Hammett to Lillian Hellman, July 29, 1943.

203   "Dash has landed somewhere": Lillian Hellman to Maggie Kober, August 20, 1943. WIS.

203   "That's a part of my life that's all over": Eliot Asinof interview with JM, April 1, 1994.

204   "It'll teach you patience": Dashiell Hammett to Lillian Hellman, October 13, 1943.

204   "If it weren't for you there wouldn't": Dashiell Hammett to Lillian Hellman, September 28, 1943.

204   "Cliff Odets": Dashiell Hammett to Lillian Hellman, October 2, 1943.

204   "nothing's too good for the little woman": Dashiell Hammett to Lillian Hellman, October 15, 1943.

204   "Or do you want to make out you're different?": Dashiell Hammett to Lillian Hellman, August 11, 1943.

204   "to send the ex-wife and youngsters": Dashiell Hammett to Lillian Hellman, July 14, 1943.

204   "small and dark and elfin-pixyish": Dashiell Hammett to Lillian Hellman, August 3, 1943.

204   "Madame Helsinki": Dashiell Hammett to Maggie Kober, September 22, 1943. WIS.

204   "Whether and what I should invest": Dashiell Hammett to Lillian Hellman, October 5, 1943.

204   "editing little tasties out of Ellery Queen": Dashiell Hammett to Lillian Hellman, November 28, 1943.

204   "borrowing" money from his account: Dashiell Hammett to Lillian Hellman, October 5, 1943.

205   "light, strong, and naturally expensive": Dashiell Hammett to Lillian Hellman, October 7, 1943.

205   "light weight wool-mixture socks": Dashiell Hammett to Lillian Hellman, October 13, 1943.

205   "Thank you, darling, you are kind": Dashiell Hammett to Lillian Hellman, December 19, 1943.

205   "You are a generous girl as well as a good one": Dashiell Hammett to Lillian Hellman, October 12, 1943.

205   Lillian was now writing the social commentary: Robert Colodny interview with JM, July 20, 1993.

205   "a simple, compact, neat and moving": Dashiell Hammett to Lillian Hellman, December 20, 1943.

205   "2 × $78.20": Dashiell Hammett to Lillian Hellman, October 13, 1943.

205   "What goes on?": Dashiell Hammett to Lillian Hellman, October 13, 1943.

205   "a firm stand on money matters": Ibid.

205   "Lady . . . I didn't join the Army to get rich": Ibid.

205   "secretary": William Glackin interview with Richard Layman, and confirmed in interview with JM, July 11, 1994.

206   "trying to make a miser of me": Dashiell Hammett to Lillian Hellman, October 25, 1943.

206   "to get the proper erotic reaction out of it": Ibid.

206   "Does that mean I should try some of those other pompous": Dashiell Hammett to Lillian Hellman, October 29, 1943.

206   "I'm not sure the book isn't a rather shameful": Dashiell Hammett to Lillian Hellman, October 31, 1943.

206   "Crawl back in your kennel, Proust": Ibid.

206   Das Kapital: Glackin interview with Richard Layman.

206   "You are a very rich woman": Dashiell Hammett to Lillian Hellman, September 23, 1943.

206   "I want a ring": Dashiell Hammett to Lillian Hellman, September 23, 1943.

206   "I'm glad you're glad I asked for the ring": Dashiell Hammett to Lillian Hellman, October 17, 1943.

206   "I keep looking at the ring": Dashiell Hammett to Lillian Hellman, November 16, 1943.

207   "Aleut squaw": Dashiell Hammett to Lillian Hellman, October 23, 1943.

207   "I hope his health is on the upgrade": Dashiell Hammett to Lillian Hellman [1944].

207   "The Variety Man liked 'Watch'": Dashiell Hammett to Lillian Hellman, August 22, 1943.

207   "Write it now and begin to worry": Ibid.

207   "hot stuff": Dashiell Hammett to Lillian Hellman, Thanksgiving Day, 1943.

207   "Ideologies don't win wars": Colodny interview.

208   "It's nice that your old man should like": Dashiell Hammett to Lillian Hellman, October 17, 1943.

208   He had never forgiven his father: Marshall interview.

208   "with Annabella the Movie Star": Dashiell Hammett to Lillian Hellman, October 19, 1943.

208   "what's left of yourself": Dashiell Hammett to Lillian Hellman, July 24, 1943.

208   "You've always been healthy as a horse": Dashiell Hammett to Lillian Hellman, October 25, 1943.

208 "as healthy as so many Hellmans": Ibid.
208 "that tittying around is no fun": Dashiell Hammett to Lillian Hellman, November 19, 1943.
208 "I don't like it and won't like anything": Dashiell Hammett to Lillian Hellman, November 28, 1943.
208 not to conclude Mary had forged his signature: Dashiell Hammett to Lillian Hellman, September 21, 1943.
209 "entitled to years of complete rest": Dashiell Hammett to Lillian Hellman, August 22, 1943.
209 "starting with not helping you rearrange": Ibid.
209 "fat and edible gray squirrels": Dashiell Hammett to Lillian Hellman, October 3, 1943.
209 "I'd like to be eating one of your gumbos": Dashiell Hammett to Lillian Hellman, October 5, 1943.
209 "He didn't have you": Dashiell Hammett to Lillian Hellman, November 4, 1943.
209 "extra-special double-portion triple-ply": Dashiell Hammett to Lillian Hellman, October 31, 1943.
209 "It's obvious that I'm writing this": Dashiell Hammett to Lillian Hellman, November 6, 1943.
209 "God's older brother": Dashiell Hammett to Lillian Hellman, November 6, 1943.
209 "So even if I love you and miss you": Ibid.
209 "No temper now!": Ibid.
210 "LOVE POEM": Ibid.
210 "Now all you've got to do is get home": Dashiell Hammett to Lillian Hellman, Thanksgiving Day, 1943.
210 Hammett got more radiograms: E. E. Spitzer interview with JM, September 16, 1993.
210 "Yes, Ma'am, it's thirteen years": Ibid.
210 "I think, however, it would be better all around": Dashiell Hammett to Lillian Hellman, February 22, 1944.
210 "the first time I've had any excuse": Dashiell Hammett to Lillian Hellman, September 21, 1943.
210 "whatever takes the Hellman eye": Dashiell Hammett to Lillian Hellman, Thanksgiving Day.
210 "what I'm giving you for Christmas": Dashiell Hammett to Lillian Hellman, December 19, 1943.
210 "now do you want to tell me what I gave you": Dashiell Hammett to Lillian Hellman, December 28, 1943.
210 "buy an extravagant one": Dashiell Hammett to Lillian Hellman, January 8, 1944.
211 "It seems a long, long time since I've heard": Dashiell Hammett to Lillian Hellman, December 18, 1943.
211 "This will be the second Christmas in a row": Dashiell Hammett to Lillian Hellman, December 22, 1943.
211 "six months ago tonight": Dashiell Hammett to Lillian Hellman, December 28, 1943.

15. Hammett of the North, Big Brother of Nanook

212   "So it must be love": Dashiell Hammett to Lillian Hellman, January 14, 1944.

212   "without Hammett's having uttered: Bill Glackin interview with Richard Layman.

212   "north country insular Ingersoll": Dashiell Hammett to Lillian Hellman, February 17, 1944.

212   "A woman would be nice": Lillian Hellman, draft of the Introduction to *The Big Knockover.* HRHRC.

213   "He seemed pleased. Bill Glackin to Lillian Hellman, March 1980. HRHRC.

213   "Lillian will no doubt be unpleasant": Dashiell Hammett to Nancy Bragdon, September 30, 1943.

213   "involve Lily heavily": Dashiell Hammett to Nancy Bragdon, January 1, 1944.

213   "stick your pretty little nose": Dashiell Hammett to Lillian Hellman, December 31, 1943.

213   "what's cooking in the national mind": See Dashiell Hammett to Lillian Hellman, January 2, 1944.

213   "remote": Dashiell Hammett to Lillian Hellman, December 31, 1943.

213   "a worthy effort though probably propaganda": Dashiell Hammett to Lillian Hellman, January 8, 1944.

213   "not to sit up late in smoky rooms": Dashiell Hammett to Lillian Hellman, January 11, 1944.

213   "clumsy ox": Dashiell Hammett to Lillian Hellman, February 14, 1944.

213   "I don't love nobody no better": Dashiell Hammett to Lillian Hellman, May 19, 1944.

213   "I love you to the extent": Dashiell Hammett to Lillian Hellman, January 8, 1944.

213   "My instinct was always right": Dashiell Hammett to Lillian Hellman, January 8, 1944.

214   "be cut off with a phrase": Dashiell Hammett to Lillian Hellman, February 6, 1944.

214   "After all, what are money and fame": Dashiell Hammett to Lillian Hellman, February 6, 1944.

214   "one of your admirers": Dashiell Hammett to Lillian Hellman, February 22, 1944.

214   "It is only money": Dashiell Hammett to Lillian Hellman, January 8, 1944.

214   "not to sulk": Dashiell Hammett to Lillian Hellman, February 22, 1944.

214   "not to mislead the bank with hints": Ibid.

214   "Maybe it didn't fit his dancing": Dashiell Hammett to Lillian Hellman, January 24, 1944.

214   "His mental processes are those of the true Hammett": Dashiell Hammett to Lillian Hellman, March 5, 1944.

214   "how much love in a romantic sense": Quoted in Dashiell Hammett to Lillian Hellman, May 27, 1944.

214   "the western Hammett family allowance": Dashiell Hammett to Lillian Hellman, March 5, 1944.

214   "Now, emboldened by your silence, I clear": Dashiell Hammett to Lillian Hellman, April 5, 1944.

214   "I hope the play is coming along better": Dashiell Hammett to Lillian Hellman, February 3, 1944.

215   "writing a lot of dull shit": Lillian Hellman to Arthur Kober [1940s]. WIS.

215   "You give it what you've got": Dashiell Hammett to Lillian Hellman, February 9, 1944.

215   "Does it go forward with running?": Dashiell Hammett to Lillian Hellman, February 18, 1944.

215   "If it can't go on till September": Dashiell Hammett to Lillian Hellman, February 20, 1944.

215   "America's foremost playwright": Dashiell Hammett to Lillian Hellman, February 21, 1944.

215   "You're practically breaking my heart with your letters": Dashiell Hammett to Lillian Hellman, March 10, 1944.

215   "Your instinct is right": Dashiell Hammett to Lillian Hellman, January 16, 1944.

215   "Until it gets here": Dashiell Hammett to Lillian Hellman, January 21, 1944.

215   "polite comedy": Dashiell Hammett to Lillian Hellman, March 15, 1944.

215   "a defter touch than in any of your other": Ibid.

216   "Catching these characters now here": Ibid.

216   "still a cluck": Dashiell Hammett to Lillian Hellman, March 21, 1944.

216   "a blood-flecked froth of casting": Dashiell Hammett to Herman Shumlin, February 14, 1944.

217   "I suppose the die is more or less cast": Dashiell Hammett to Maggie Kober, March 5, 1944. WIS.

217   "That's a bad play": Austin Pendleton interview with JM.

217   a picnic of two salamis: Virginia Bloomgarden Chilewich interview with JM, December 7, 1992.

217   "It's not very flattering of you": Dashiell Hammett to Lillian Hellman, March 28, 1944.

217   "I'm walking the floor": Dashiell Hammett to Lillian Hellman, April 1, 1944.

217   "The news about the play is marvelous": Dashiell Hammett to Lillian Hellman, April 25, 1944.

217   "I just go around muttering": Dashiell Hammett to Lillian Hellman, April 17, 1944.

217   "You are a big girl now": Ibid.

218   "What are you going to do now?": Dashiell Hammett to Lillian Hellman, April 22, 1944.

218   "make good your threat to write a novel": Dashiell Hammett to Lillian Hellman, April 23, 1944.

218   "That gives you no exclusive right": Dashiell Hammett to Lillian Hellman, March 25, 1944.

218   "Sleep, write, sleep, write": Dashiell Hammett to Lillian Hellman, April 20, 1944.

218   "out of sorts": Dashiell Hammett to Lillian Hellman, June 12, 1944.

218   "that the strong of heart never remember": Dashiell Hammett to Lillian Hellman, June 12, 1944. See also Dashiell Hammett to Lillian Hellman, April 28, 1944: "I'm inclined to think you're about ripe to go on ahead and play your string out in your own way and to hell with the no-matter-how-well-meaning-or-even-shrewd counsel of no-matter-whom."

218   "I may not be able to do you much good": Dashiell Hammett to Lillian Hellman, April 28, 1944.

218   "Should I do anything about my income tax?": Dashiell Hammett to Nancy Bragdon, February 12, 1944.

219   "continue to love you until your negligence": Dashiell Hammett to Lillian Hellman, February 25, 1944.

219   "queer": quoted in Dashiell Hammett to Lillian Hellman, March 21, 1944.

219   "Of course there's a great deal of good": Dashiell Hammett to Lillian Hellman, August 13, 1944.

219   "bored": Dashiell Hammett to Lillian Hellman, March 5, 1944.

219   "something like gold paper": Dashiell Hammett to Lillian Hellman, March 6, 1944.

219   "The Gefulte Fish": *The Adakian,* 1, No. 50 (May 27, 1944), 2.

219   "I guess I'll go around clicking like a dice": Dashiell Hammett to Lillian Hellman, March 23, 1944.

219   "If I had any sense, I'd stay away": Dashiell Hammett to Lillian Hellman, May 10, 1944.

219   "What did Caligula have?": Dashiell Hammett to Pru Whitfield, July 23, 1944.

219   "Tonight I need a soothing hand": Dashiell Hammett to Pru Whitfield, September 6, 1944. Courtesy of Otto Penzler.

219   "very exciting—and annoying": Dashiell Hammett to Pru Whitfield, March 5, 1944.

219   "I would like to see more of the poetry": Ibid.

219   "That does not mean that I do not love": Dashiell Hammett to Maggie Kober, March 5, 1944.

220   "I do not like your friend André Gide's": Dashiell Hammett to Lillian Hellman, March 12, 1944.

220   "Writing people besides you": Dashiell Hammett to Lillian Hellman, March 27, 1944.

220   "I guess the smaller your world": Dashiell Hammett to Lillian Hellman, July 30, 1944.

220   "be an intellectual": Dashiell Hammett to Lillian Hellman, July 30, 1944.

220   "It has been a long time since": Dashiell Hammett to Lillian Hellman, September 9, 1944.

220   "what I say is, Lily is a cutie": Dashiell Hammett to Lillian Hellman, August 21, 1944.

220   "It's likely a good idea": Dashiell Hammett to Lillian Hellman, September 5, 1944.

220   "I guess I'd like you to live": Dashiell Hammett to Lillian Hellman, September 7, 1944.

220   "In cold weather you sleep": Dashiell Hammett to Lillian Hellman, September 13, 1944.

220   "office-holding": Dashiell Hammett to Lillian Hellman, March 27, 1944.

220   "Joe McCarthy's regards": Dashiell Hammett to Lillian Hellman, July 9, 1944.

220   "Would Madam speak to me": Dashiell Hammett to Lillian Hellman, March 27, 1944.

221   "best pickings . . . an earnest left winger": Ibid.

221   "loaf—and I mean really loaf": Dashiell Hammett to Lillian Hellman, April 17, 1944.

221   "I've probably only got fifteen or twenty": Dashiell Hammett to Lillian Hellman, Ibid.

221   "populated by people I don't understand": Dashiell Hammett to Lillian Hellman, April 28, 1944.

221   "I'm trusting you to put your mind": Dashiell Hammett to Lillian Hellman, April 28, 1944.

221   "bales of flowers": Dashiell Hammett to Nancy Bragdon, April 1, 1944.

221   "EASTER VERSE": Dashiell Hammett to Lillian Hellman, April 9, 1944.

221   "could give in to a temptation": Dashiell Hammett to Lillian Hellman, May 16, 1944.

221   "begun turning out a new crop": Dashiell Hammett to Pru Whitfield, June 27, 1944. Courtesy of Peter Stern.

221   "saloons and whorehouses": Dashiell Hammett to Lillian Hellman, June 28, 1944.

221   "Go easy on those plans": Dashiell Hammett to Lillian Hellman, April 28, 1944.

222   "I trust you're going ahead": Dashiell Hammett to Lillian Hellman, May 27, 1944.

222   "And I don't like its being referred to": Dashiell Hammett to Lillian Hellman, August 21, 1944.

222   "but if you can't trust the Shumlin books": Dashiell Hammett to Lillian Hellman, February 14, 1944.

222   "I was quite proud": Dashiell Hammett to Lillian Hellman, May 25, 1944.

222   "a very gaudy": Dashiell Hammett to Lillian Hellman, June 7, 1944.

222   "across the lake by the hook": Dashiell Hammett to Lillian Hellman, June 26, 1944.

222   "I love him as much as you do": Dashiell Hammett to Lillian Hellman, July 27, 1944.

222   "glad for you and glad for him": Dashiell Hammett to Lillian Hellman, October 11, 1944.

223   "that the high rent area wouldn't be a good buy": Dashiell Hammett to Lillian Hellman, September 5, 1944.

223   "one long year": Dashiell Hammett to Lillian Hellman, June 25, 1944.

223   "Try to be worthy of the love": Dashiell Hammett to Lillian Hellman, June 16, 1944.

223   "could have used a little more Hellman in it": Dashiell Hammett to Lillian Hellman, July 4, 1944.

223   "to me, of course, it's absrud": Dashiell Hammett to Lillian Hellman, July 31, 1944.

223   "handsome Russian colonel": Dashiell Hammett to Lillian Hellman, July 2, 1944.

223   "I'm sure I don't approve": Ibid.

223   "a very satisfactory dream": Dashiell Hammett to Lillian Hellman, July 27, 1944.

223   he dreamed of a yellow cat: Dashiell Hammett to Lillian Hellman, July 30, 1944.

223   "I'm interested in the details of your inner": Dashiell Hammett to Lillian Hellman, April 3, 1944.

223   "Darling, just put these in the archives": Dashiell Hammett to Lillian Hellman, August 18, 1944.

223   "You would be an idiot": Dashiell Hammett to Lillian Hellman, July 22, 1944.

223   "You've got no right to classify all trips": Dashiell Hammett to Lillian Hellman, July 22, 1944.

224   "one of the key figures": Rollyson, 216.

224   "I'm tickled to death": Dashiell Hammett to Lillian Hellman, July 27, 1944.

224   "Strict orders, to be carried out": Dashiell Hammett to Lillian Hellman, August 13, 1944.

224   "I should like to find you the same simple": Dashiell Hammett to Lillian Hellman, August 18, 1944.

16. Lily Is Loved

225   "I am in love with you": John Melby to Lillian Hellman, January 21, 1945. The letters from John Melby are quoted here courtesy of the late John Melby.

225   "It's awful nice to hear your voice": Dashiell Hammett to Lillian Hellman, March 10, 1945.

225   "Thank God I've always led a sheltered life": Dashiell Hammett to Pru Whitfield, October 4, 1944.

225   "You don't remember me, but I met you": Dashiell Hammett to Lillian Hellman, October 4, 1944.

225   "against the local fleshpots": Quoted in Dashiell Hammett to Pru Whitfield, September 3, 1944.

225   "It's nice to think of something belonging to me": Dashiell Hammett to Pru Whitfield, September 30, 1944.

225   "saloons, stores, restaurants, taxis": Dashiell Hammett to Josephine Hammett, August 23, 1944.

226   "Mix baby a Dashiell Hammett special!": Clara Browne to Lillian Hellman, December 12, 1969. HRHRC.

226   "he was shacked up with a native woman": Dashiell Hammett to Lillian Hellman, September 3, 1944.

226   "You know me and actresses": Dashiell Hammett to Lillian Hellman, October 16, 1944.

226   "You could have talked to any of the other thousands": Lee Brown interview with JM, September 16, 1993.

226   "where you go and what you wear and eat": Dashiell Hammett to Pru Whitfield, October 24, 1944.

226   "so I'll have my fingers on your past": Ibid.

226   "I'm worrying about your worrying": Dashiell Hammett to Lillian Hellman, September 7, 1944.

226   "how to be snippy": Dashiell Hammett to Lillian Hellman, October 5, 1944.

226   "a silly little woman to whom nobody": Dashiell Hammett to Lillian Hellman, September 5, 1944.

227   "It would be nice to think you were far to the north": Dashiell Hammett to Lillian Hellman, October 11, 1944.

227   "see much sense in trying to get back home": Dashiell Hammett to Lillian Hellman, October 5, 1944.

227   She flirted with Cap: Miriam Dickey interview with JM, July 8, 1994.

227   He showed her wire: Leslie Hansom interview with JM, October 28, 1992.

227   "if everything went like clock work": Dashiell Hammett to Lillian Hellman, October 5, 1944.

227   "probably go stark raving mad": Dashiell Hammett to Lillian Hellman, October 1944: "You may go blind trying to read this, and it won't be worth it . . . I won't be up that way for at least another month, and it's likely to be later than that—and you would probably go stark raving mad if you had to hang around that long."

227   "your Russian bomber has already picked you up": Dashiell Hammett to Lillian Hellman, October 26, 1944.

228   "he who wishes he were with you": Dashiell Hammett to Lillian Hellman, November 5, 1944.

228   "give him a hint of her possible return": Dashiell Hammett to Lillian Hellman, November 3, 1944.

228   "for which I'm thanking the appropriate": Dashiell Hammett to Lillian Hellman, November 24, 1944.

228   "fine": Jean Potter Chelnov interview with JM, April 13, 1993. See also Jean Potter to Stephen Talbot, March 8, 1982, printed in Johnson, 322.

228   notes on 3-by-5 cards: Bill Glackin interview with JM.

229   "the pre-writing period when all is grand": Dashiell Hammett to Pru Whitfield, March 13, 1945.

229   "anybody's actually panting": Dashiell Hammett to Pru Whitfield, March 25, 1945.

229   "in terms of *if* I stayed": Dashiell Hammett to Lillian Hellman, May 3, 1945.

229   "Maybe I'm lucky in love": Dashiell Hammett to Lillian Hellman, October 29, 1944.

229   fell into each other's arms: For this story of Lillian Hellman in Siberia, I am indebted to Yevgeny Yevtushenko's translator and friend Albert Todd.

230   warmth and wit of Eisenstein: Lillian Hellman, "Notes on Eisenstein." HRHRC.

230   "Let's heckle Lillian": Robert Meiklejohn interview with JM, July 26, 1993.

230   "I think I'm dining with more generals": Hellman *Diary.*

230   "very attractive quality": Ibid.

231   "Russian diplomats in black uniforms": Lillian Hellman *Diary* of her trip to the U.S.S.R. HRHRC.

231   "the deep reverence & respect": Ibid.

231   The man disapproved of her mockery: scenes with John Melby from John Melby interview with JM, December 14–15, 1992.

232   "Los Cuatro Generales": unpublished diary of Robert Meiklejohn. Courtesy of Mr. Meiklejohn.

232   "went down on": John Melby to Lillian Hellman, December 10, 1945.

232   "the strange and exciting odor": Ibid.

232   "always be life and creation": Ibid.

232   "You're safe!" Kathleen Harriman Mortimer interview with JM, February 23, 1993.

232   "the Great Thinker": Lillian Hellman to John Melby (undated).

232   "pleased": Hellman *Diary.*

232   "all of security and pleasantness and warmth": John Melby to Lillian Hellman, January 31, 1945.

233   "bitter doubts and discouragements": John Melby to Lillian Hellman, February 8, 1945.

233   "My beauteous one, I love you": John Melby to Lillian Hellman, March 6, 1945.

233   "a piece of canned crap": John Melby to Lillian Hellman, November 3, 1945.

233   "It looked like a scene from War & Peace": Hellman *Diary,* January 2, 1945. HRHRC.

233   "out of our Aleutian stagnancy": Bernard Kalb, "Remembering the Dashiell Hammett of 'Julia,'" New York *Times,* September 25, 1977, Section D, 15–16.

233   "If I stay here for any length of time": Melby interview. On MacLeish's offer, see Robert P. Newman, *The Cold War Romance of Lillian Hellman and John Melby* (University of North Carolina Press: Chapel Hill, 1989), 70–71.

234   "a nice man, a dignified man": Hellman *Diary.* HRHRC.

234   "I guess it's about time that I started seeing": Dashiell Hammett to Lillian Hellman, January 10, 1945.

234   "snapped up . . . gamble on my chance": Ibid.

234   "surprised to find I can have a good time": Ibid.

235   "I tell you, sister": Dashiell Hammett to Lillian Hellman, February 25, 1945.

235   "it would be wonderful": John Melby to Lillian Hellman, January 31, 1945.

235   "Baby, God made your cunt": John Melby to Lillian Hellman, December 4, 1945.

235   "a bastard": Dashiell Hammett to Maggie Kober, March 10, 1945.

235   "She's been gone so long I have no clear": Dashiell Hammett to Nancy Bragdon, February 25, 1945.

235   "conventional, strait-laced stuffed shirt": Dashiell Hammett to Pru Whitfield, April 9, 1945.

235   "mighty glad of it even if": Dashiell Hammett to Lillian Hellman, February 27, 1945.

236   "I'm still without a letter": Dashiell Hammett to Lillian Hellman, March 10, 1945.

236   "I guess I'll never understand women": Dashiell Hammett to Maggie Kober, March 10, 1945.

236   "I know what you mean about Potter": Dashiell Hammett to Lillian Hellman, March 15, 1945.

236   "second father": William Glackin to Mr. Godshalk, August 9, 1974. LAY.

236   "I don't especially like him": Dashiell Hammett to Lillian Hellman, May 4, 1945.

236   "the frayed ends": Dashiell Hammett to Nancy Bragdon, February 25, 1945.

236   "mildly disapproved": Dashiell Hammett to Lillian Hellman, February 27, 1945.

236   "for which I've got a kind of feel": Dashiell Hammett to Lillian Hellman, March 4, 1945.

236   "utterly . . . as often as a Spaso": John Melby to Lillian Hellman, May 10, 1945.

237   "our children": John Melby to Lillian Hellman, June 14, 1945.

237   "Right now, I think it would be nice": Lillian Hellman to John Melby. [Monday night] Harry S. Truman Library.

237   "bad; dried and older": Lillian Hellman to John Melby. [Monday night] Harry S. Truman Library.

237   "pretty pickle": Dashiell Hammett to Lillian Hellman, April 23, 1945.

237   "That bank account shall be treated as sacred": Dashiell Hammett to Lillian Hellman, April 10, 1945.

237   "encouraged Maggie a little": Dashiell Hammett to Lillian Hellman, May 6, 1945.

237   "what days of the week are best": Dashiell Hammett to Lillian Hellman, May 3, 1945.

237   "The Little Foxes folk back": Dashiell Hammett to Lillian Hellman, May 4, 1945.

237   "I do not pay much attention to your complaints": Dashiell Hammett to Lillian Hellman, May 4, 1945.

238   "a good little piece on your emotions": Harold Ross to Lillian Hellman, March 2, 1945.

238   "feathers were completely plucked": for an account of this weekend, Arthur Kober to Pooks (Cathy Kober), June 25, 1945. WIS.

238   "still represent the heart and guts": Dashiell Hammett to Lillian Hellman, May 6, 1945.

238   "Try to pretend you're not sorry": Dashiell Hammett to Lillian Hellman, June 3, 1945.

17. The Postwar

241   "Lillian is my right foot": Jean Potter Chelnov interview with JM.

241   "lovely Sammy's beach": Lillian Hellman to John Melby [July 1946].

241   "So you're the young mystery man": Peg Zilboorg interview. See also Wright, 202.

241   "I can't begin to tell you the terrible": Herman Shumlin to Lillian Hellman, July 24, 1945. HRHRC.

242   "You don't really love me": John Melby to Lillian Hellman, November 19, 1945.

242   "a silly woman": John Melby to Lillian Hellman, March 5, 1946.

242   in the hallway he encountered: Melby interview with JM.

242   as she spun the tale: Alvin Sargent interview with JM, April 16, 1993.

243   a reference to "Lillian Hellman": Lee Brown interview with JM.

243   "You know, you're really okay": Ibid.

243   Would you like to be president: E. E. Spitzer interview with JM, September 16, 1993.

243   "a fat $160,000": Dashiell Hammett to Josephine Hammett, October 10, 1946.

243   "When something is finished": John Melby to Lillian Hellman, December 4, 1945.

244   a large hunting knife: Jean Potter Chelnov interview.

244   "Give it to Ethel": Ibid.

244   "I'll go with you": Melby interview with JM.

245   "Who am I to be able to get you into China?": Philip D'Arcy Hart interview.

245   "a true art theatre": Lillian Hellman, "Outline for a plan for a national American Repertory Theatre." WIS. See also memo of Lillian Hellman to Spyros Skouras, November 19, 1945. WIS.

245   "full of hidden nastiness and resentments": Lillian Hellman to John Melby, "Friday." See also Lillian Hellman to John Melby, Tuesday, 28th: "I feel sad and depressed and angry and resentful, and I wish you were here." Letters of Lillian Hellman to John Melby. Courtesy of the Swann Gallery and HRHRC.

245   "not even sure that you really want to": Ibid.

245   "were happy together and would be": Quoted in John Melby to Lillian Hellman, January 20, 1946.

245   "You never told me whether Dash": John Melby to Lillian Hellman, April 2, 1946.

245   "all the strain is gone": Lillian Hellman to John Melby, "Sunday, 9."

245   She was able to approve of Max's: John Melby to Lillian Hellman, May 10, 1946.

246   pleased her when she didn't bore her: Lillian Hellman to John Melby [c. March 1946].

246   "pleasant lady club manner": Lillian Hellman to John Melby (undated).

246   "She's colored": Rose Evans interview with JM, November 11, 1993.

246   "Oh, I see you got that chair fixed": Ibid.

247   "obviously been on a long and debilitating": Lillian Hellman to John Melby, "Tuesday."

247   "I would like to think it would be to do him good": Lillian Hellman to John Melby, "Tuesday."

247   "talked Dash into riding back": Lillian Hellman to John Melby, "Wednesday" [1946].

247   "No three drunks were going to keep me up": Lillian Hellman to John Melby (undated).

247   "quite drunk and sad": Lillian Hellman to John Melby, April 17.

247   "pleasant . . . except for the times": Ibid.

248   "the best plays written since Ibsen": Lillian Hellman to John Melby, "Sunday."

248   "monthly lecture . . . as worthless": Lillian Hellman to John Melby, April 17th.

248   "very devoted to Dash": Ibid.

248   "heartbreaking": Ibid.

248   "more sad that so much that is wonderful": Lillian Hellman to John Melby, "Sunday."

248   "It makes me sad to know it": Ibid.

248   his hero was an artist named Helm: Dashiell Hammett to Josephine Hammett, December 27, 1945.

248   "You're crazy . . . ladies' lunches": Kitty Carlisle Hart, Kitty: An Autobiography (St. Martin's Press: New York, 1988), 147.

249   At Cornell: Jim Weinstein interview with JM.

249   "Take what you want": Belle Moldevan interview with JM, April 24, 1993.

249   "Hey, you with the knockers": Goldie Kleiner interview with JM, February 10, 1994.

249   "a dispirited guy holding himself up": Samm Baker Sinclair to Joe Gores, October 9, 1975. LAY.

249   "with a supercilious grin": Arthur Miller, Timebends (Grove Press: New York, 1987), 391.

250   "my secretary": Morris Hershman to Richard Layman, March 9, 1986. LAY.

250   May was not worth her attention: Helen Rosen interview with JM. Also interview with Miriam Procter, April 29, 1993, and Joan Cook, August 12, 1993.

250   "I want to be with you": Lillian Hellman to John Melby, December 1945. Harry S. Truman Library.

250   "plot-muddled and far too talky": Lillian Hellman to John Melby, April 17th.

250   "come back and make me better": Ibid.

250   "Marx ever wrote about revolution": Lillian Hellman to John Melby, April 17th.

250   "slightly tight": Lillian Hellman to John Melby, "Sunday."

250   "To be thought well of by him": John Melby to Lillian Hellman, June 3, 1946.

250   Herman took them on an all-night cruise: Jerome Weidman interview with JM.

250   "a gent who is now her lover": Lillian Hellman to John Melby [1946].

251   "Dash wants this house": Lillian Hellman to John Melby, "Thursday."

251   "Poor guy, it's a tough pull": Lillian Hellman to John Melby [June 1946].

251   "I've got to find out what all the to-do": Dashiell Hammett to Nancy Bragdon, August 16 or 17, 1946. HRHRC.

251   "Everybody knows she is a giddy type woman": Dashiell Hammett to Nancy Bragdon, September 10, 1946. HRHRC.

251   "disgusted" with the arrangements: See Solomon V. Arnaldo to Maurice Kurtz, July 9, 1947. Lilly Library. "Her complaints: Her desires and travel preferences had been misunderstood all along. The amount she had advanced for her travel had not been refunded. Outside of a cable from Dr. Huxley, she had not heard of anything else from Paris. She does not know where the meeting will be held, nor whether she had hotel accommodations on arrival in Paris. She is disgusted with almost everything concerning arrangements for the meeting, particularly transportation, about all of which she is still very much in the dark, she said."

251   "For some people I guess life is just": Dashiell Hammett to Josephine Hammett, July 29, 1947.

251   "direct assault on American democracy": *Daily Worker,* March 12, 1947.

251   "When are you coming home?": Dashiell Hammett to Marjorie May, September 10, 1946. Courtesy of Otto Penzler.

252   "always been a tough critic for me": Lillian Hellman to John Melby (undated).

252   he always enjoyed using the obvious: Marshall interview with JM.

252   "been very good to me": Lillian Hellman to John Melby, Saturday, 5 [1946].

252   "Tell Mother what you think of her play": Flora Roberts interview with JM.

252   "You're suffering from money-pause": Lucy Ruskin interview with JM.

252   he would commit suicide: Lillian Hellman interview with Fred Gardner.

253   he was capable now of only a kiss: Patricia Neal interview with JM, January 13, 1993.

253   "One has to go on with a life in the place": Lillian Hellman to John Melby, Saturday, 5.

253   "Dash likes your work": Walter Bernstein interview with JM, March 30, 1994.

253   "the greatest lay I ever had": Helen Rosen interview with JM.

254   "My daughter wrote this play": Richard Moody annotated manuscript. Lilly Library, Indiana University, Bloomington. His source was Kermit Bloomgarden.

254   "These things happen and you can't": Virginia Bloomgarden Chilewich interview.

254   ice-skating on the lake: Flora Roberts interview.

254   "did not want to come back": quoted in John Melby to Lillian Hellman, December 10, 1946. Melby wrote that this was "pure malice" on Harriman's part: "I suppose one can deceive oneself, but I don't think I am doing that when I say that I do want to come back . . . when I left the States I really did think I would be back before this time . . . it may sound feeble, but I think it is true that this game here has to be played out."

18. Dash in Disarray

255   "Life is as difficult for those": Notes for "How to Live in the United States," unpublished manuscript. LAY.

255   "a good tenant . . . good furniture": Lillian Hellman to Arthur Kober, June 5, 1947. WIS.

255   "Did I have money": Rose Evans interview with JM.

256   "Something's wrong with her brain": Marshall interview with JM.

256   "It's terrible to drink around Mary": Marshall interview.

256   Lillian was driving the two of them: Lillian Hellman interview with Diane Johnson. Tape courtesy of Diane Johnson.

256   "an almost incestuous love": Diane Johnson interview with JM, April 9, 1993.

256   Dark bruises appeared: Johnson, 222.

256   He fondled: Diane Johnson interview with JM.

256   sexually aroused only by being hurt: Randall Smith interview with Richard Layman.

257   "I never want to see you again": Johnson, 222.

257   Dash was impotent: Diane Johnson interview with JM.

257   "You are outrageously mean to me": Max Hellman to Lillian Hellman, March 27, 1949. See also March 5, 1949. HRHRC.

257   "the cheap lying and vulgarity of the woman": Lillian Hellman to Jenny and Hannah Hellman, October 1, 1947. HRHRC.

258   "I want you to do what you want to do": Lillian Hellman to John Melby [1947].

258   pulled her down on his lap: Lillian Hellman interviewed by Peter Manso in Mailer: His Life and Times (Simon and Schuster: New York, 1985), 129.

258   Hammett gave a jaunty wave: Norman Mailer interview with JM.

258   "a truly formidable bare breast": Ibid.

258   "Take care of him": Michael Avallone, "The Noseless One," from Reflections in a Fleshless Eye, unpublished manuscript. Courtesy of Mr. Avallone.

259   "One of the extraordinary things to me about Dash": Virginia Bloomgarden Chilewich interview with JM.

259   "you can unload him": Ruth Goetz interview with JM.

259   "He'd be better off leaving things alone": *Scoundrel Time,* 124.

259   "These days a Communist is anybody who thinks": Speech made by Lillian Hellman at a "Women for Wallace" lunch, February 10, 1948.

259   "You and Dash would get along fine": Rollyson, 269.

260   he was invariably unsuccessful: Richard Layman interview with JM.

260   "some sort of a gold digger": Randall Smith interview with Richard Layman.

260   "We can get along without Marge here": Johnson, 221.

260   Christie's materials courtesy of Otto Penzler.

260   "executor of his estate": Sally Richards conversation with JM, June 2, 1994.

261   "The pearls will look better": Marshall interview.

261   "What's new?": Jerome Weidman interview with JM.

261   "Dash is like an encyclopedia": Virginia Bloomgarden Chilewich interview with JM.

261   "Let's waive that": Norman Mailer interview.

262   refused to believe that Yugoslavia": "The Blacklist, Jug. Trip," unpublished manuscript of Fred Gardner.

262   "You made that up": Scenes courtesy of Mrs. Chilewich.

262   "progressive American authoress": Document of the Foreign Service of the United States of America, No. 792, dated October 12, 1948, from the American Embassy, Belgrade, Yugoslavia.

263   "Don't call Lillian!" Rose Evans interview. See also Johnson, 223.

263   "Soon the need must be fulfilled": *Diary.* HRHRC.

263   "sharp and handsome and aggressive": Description of Prica in Lillian Hellman, notes from trip to Yugoslavia in a brown notebook. HRHRC.

263   "must be told cold . . . a moral": Ibid.

264   "she was living under a self-constructed": Rollyson, 280.

264   "a man who regarded women who were in love": Vladimir Dedijer, "The Sad Heart of Lillian Hellman," unpublished manuscript, June 3, 1985. Bentley Historical Library, University of Michigan.

264   "You believe them?" Miller, *Timebends,* 257.

264   "I'm not a Communist": Richard Layman interview with Bill Glackin. LAY.

264   "Please come down here": Rose Evans interview.

264   she said no: Lillian Hellman to Selma Wolfman, November 4, 1980. HRHRC.

264   "heartbreaking": Lillian Hellman to Philippe Soupault, December 28, 1948. HRHRC.

264   "I've only come to get you because": Lillian Hellman interview with Diane Johnson.

265   "You know, leave it to me": Lillian Hellman to Philip D'Arcy Hart, (undated). Courtesy of Dr. D'Arcy Hart.

265   "It's my duty to have said it": Introduction to *The Big Knockover,* ix.

265   "He couldn't have looked worse": Lillian Hellman to Maggie Kober [1948]. WIS.

265   "But I gave my word": Introduction to *The Big Knockover,* ix.

265   "that wonderful resiliency": Lillian Hellman to Philippe Soupault, December 28, 1948.

265   "Leave me alone!": Virginia Bloomgarden Chilewich interview with JM.

265   "I wish there was some happy, romantic news": Lillian Hellman to Maggie Kober [1948]. WIS.

265   "absentee hostess": Dashiell Hammett to Josephine Hammett, January 12, 1949.

265   "another week of nothing much to do": Dashiell Hammett to Josephine Hammett Marshall, January 25, 1949.

265   "Earle Stanley Gardner": Dashiell Hammett to Josephine Hammett Marshall, February 13, 1949.

265   "My head is hurting": William Alfred interview with JM, June 3, 1993.

266   "Oh, you know Lillian": Norman Mailer interview with JM.

266   "Lily's a very interesting gardener": Virginia Bloomgarden Chilewich interview.

266   "What were you doing all morning?": Virginia Bloomgarden Chilewich interview.

266   "How could you do that?": Catherine Kober interview with JM.

267   "what grotesques": Dashiell Hammett to Nancy Bragdon, September 4, 1946. Courtesy of Fred Gardner.

267   "Last year's election shows he's not too hard": Dashiell Hammett to Josephine Hammett Marshall, March 14, 1949.

267   "There are few things I like less": Ibid.

267   "grippe . . . the newly published Congressional": Dashiell Hammett to Josephine Hammett Marshall, April 25, 1949.

267   "Providence punished me for writing": Dashiell Hammett to Josephine Hammett Marshall, May 2, 1949.

268   "Red-baiting's kind of rife": Dashiell Hammett to Josephine Hammett Marshall, April 18, 1949.

268   "Romances could be affected by careless": Dashiell Hammett to Josephine Hammett Marshall, January 25, 1949.

268   "I had told her to feel free": Ibid.

268   "When I think of the years to come": Lillian Hellman to Hannah Hellman, June 10, 1949.

268   "I won't need it": Rose Evans interview.

268   "It's simply not my kind of theater": Dashiell Hammett to Marjorie May, August 10, 1949. Courtesy of Otto Penzler.

19. Hammett Edits Hellman, Reprise

270   Wasn't it better when I drank?": *Diary* fragment of Lillian Hellman marked "Notes." HRHRC.

270   three-page single-spaced report: Dashiell Hammett to Kermit Bloomgarden, October 2, 1949. Courtesy of Fred Gardner.

271   sit with him silently: Layman, 216.

271   "There's always plenty of time": Dashiell Hammett to Jean Potter Chelnov, January 23, 1950.

271   "small growth on the skin": Lillian Hellman to Arthur Kober [1948 or 1949]. WIS.

271   "Lily thinks it's all in having the right desk": Scene described in William Nolan, *Hammett: A Life at the Edge* (Congdon & Weed: New York, 1983), 210–11.

271   "kind of jittery": Dashiell Hammett to Lillian Hellman, February 2, 1950.

271   "more worried about it than I am": Ibid.

271   "positively not": "Dashiell Hammett Has Hard Words for Tough Stuff He Used to Write," Los Angeles *Times,* January 7, 1950.

271   "I miss you," Dashiell Hammett to Lillian Hellman, February 2, 1950.

271   Pat had to do most of the talking: Patricia Neal interview with JM.

272   "not too entirely fascinating if you don't think": Dashiell Hammett to Lillian Hellman, January 31, 1950.

272   "She's a nice girl": Marshall interview with JM.

272   "She hasn't yet mentioned your name": Dashiell Hammett to Lillian Hellman, January 27, 1950. HRHRC.

272   "It might be better all the way round": Dashiell Hammett to Lillian Hellman, February 8, 1950.

272   "Lilipie": Dashiell Hammett to Lillian Hellman, January 27, 1950. HRHRC.

272   he might now have to get Lily a desk: Dashiell Hammett to Muriel Alexander, February 8, 1950. Courtesy of Richard Layman.

272   "built for Mr. Hammett the permanent guest": Lillian Hellman to Maggie Kober, May 10, 1950. WIS.

272   "where I hope I'll be allowed to stay": Dashiell Hammett to Josephine Hammett Marshall, January 11, 1951.

272   "a fever—such a fever": Hellman *Diary.* HRHRC.

272   "where I belong": Dashiell Hammett to Josephine Hammett Marshall, February 2, 1951.

273   "in the hope that Cathy Kober": Lillian Hellman to Maggie Kober, May 10, 1950.

273   *Some of Us:* Dashiell Hammett to Josephine Hammett Marshall, January 11, 1951.

273   "The part I've read is nice": Dashiell Hammett to Josephine Hammett Marshall, August 20, 1950.

273   "a little uncooperative about spittoons": Dashiell Hammett to Josephine Hammett Marshall, September 3, 1950.

273   mopped the floors: Dashiell Hammett to Josephine Hammett Marshall, August 9, 1950.

273   "the best of our life together": *Pentimento,* 164–65.

273   "Lillian's finished the second act of her new play": Dashiell Hammett to Josephine Hammett Marshall, September 9, 1950.

273   "There's no reason why this shouldn't be a nice place": Ibid.

274   "kind of wonderful": Dashiell Hammett to Josephine Hammett Marshall, November 19, 1950.

274   "I don't feel too sure that I should start": Ibid.

274   "who has a play to finish": Dashiell Hammett to Josephine Hammett Marshall, November 26, 1950.

274   writing a farce together: Dashiell Hammett to Josephine Hammett Marshall, January 15, 1951.

274   "It will be easier for you, Howard": *Unfinished Woman*, 230. Although the source of this Hammett remark is the often unreliable Hellman memoir, Josephine Marshall says Lillian quoted her father saying this to her, and that it sounded very much like Dashiell Hammett, whose humor often reflected irony toward his long-ago Catholicism.

274   any taxes at all for 1950: Sidney Shainwald to Lillian Hellman, April 12, 1951. HRHRC.

275   "It's the best play anybody's written": *Unfinished Woman*, 234.

275   "went sour": Ibid.

275   For the texts of General Ben Griggs's speech, HRHRC.

276   "Go to bed and let me try": Lillian Hellman interviewed by John Phillips and Anne Hollander, *Conversations*, 81.

276   "We finished the last—and I think": Dashiell Hammett to Josephine Hammett Marshall, January 11, 1951.

276   "We got the Marches today": quoted in Bernard Drew to Lynn Caine, March 12, 1972. HRHRC.

276   "I wrote that! I wrote that": Marshall interview.

276   married couple: Gaby Rodgers interview with JM, October 16, 1993.

276   "the acting still needs a lot of work": Dashiell Hammett to Maggie Kober, February 18, 1951. HRHRC.

276   "I think all plays should be written for puppets": Dashiell Hammett to Josephine Hammett Marshall, January 1, 1951.

277   "I'm more of Madame's opinion": Dashiell Hammett to Maggie Kober, February 18, 1951.

277   "Without going so far as to call him a great": Dashiell Hammett to Maggie Kober, February 24, 1951. HRHRC.

277   "awful": See Dashiell Hammett to Maggie Kober, March 11, 1951: "After stinking up 49th Street with a couple of preview performances that had us seriously thinking of postponing the opening the cast came through fairly well on the big night." HRHRC.

277   "there's a lot of work still to be done": Dashiell Hammett to Josephine Hammett Marshall, February 24, 1951.

277   "seemed very good to us, but": Dashiell Hammett to Maggie Kober, March 11, 1951. WIS.

277   "very good": Ibid.

277   "It's as good as anything Chekhov ever wrote": Lillian Hellman interview with Fred Gardner.

277   "take it for granted that Nick has seduced": Arthur Kober to Lillian Hellman, January 6, 1951.

277   didn't agree: Lillian Hellman to Arthur Kober, cable, January 13, 1951.

277   "smash hit": Dashiell Hammett to Josephine Hammett Marshall, February 24, 1951.

277   "out of royalties, which are paid": Dashiell Hammett to Josephine Hammett Marshall, January 15, 1951.

277   "easily Lillian's best and": Dashiell Hammett to Josephine Hammett Marshall, February 24, 1951.

278   "Almost everybody loses their nerve": *Pentimento,* 165.

278   "disagreeable . . . if I had not been": Dashiell Hammett to Maggie Kober, March 19, 1951. HRHRC.

278   "So little . . . and you so dislike": Talk delivered at Swarthmore College, April 6, 1950. HRHRC.

278   It lost $75,000: *Variety,* March 19, 1952.

278   "That's the color!": Marshall interview.

278   "She looks like one of those babies you'd see": Marshall interview.

278   "quite nuts . . . the bejesus": Dashiell Hammett to Maggie Kober, April 16, 1951.

278   "I think that kid's drunk": Marshall interview.

278   "her son-of-a-bitch list": Dashiell Hammett to Josephine Hammett Marshall, April 23, 1951.

278   "you have given me great pleasure": Lillian Hellman to Josephine Hammett Marshall.

279   "The baby and I press on more or less": Dashiell Hammett to Maggie Kober, April 23, 1951.

279   "If it must be done": Lillian Hellman to Oscar Hammerstein II, April 26, 1950. HRHRC.

279   "worried . . . often about what didn't worry": *Scoundrel Time,* p. 43.

279   "I have the clipping upstairs": Marshall interview.

279   "Madame has a firm belief that one should go": Dashiell Hammett to Maggie Kober, April 16, 1951.

280   "This is a love letter because": Dashiell Hammett to Lillian Hellman, May 20, 1951.

280   "I'm not too appalled by the thoughts": Dashiell Hammett to Josephine Hammett Marshall, June 27, 1950.

281   "subversive under the Smith Act": Dashiell Hammett to Josephine Hammett Marshall, August 9, 1950.

281   "might have said to Miss Hellman on the night": Murray Kempton review of *Scoundrel Time* in *New York Review of Books,* June 10, 1976.

282   he invoked an English law: Victor Rabinowitz interview with JM, August 25, 1993.

282   This was what she had always wanted: Lillian Hellman, unpublished manuscript, "Meg." Courtesy of Don Congdon and *Diary.* HRHRC.

282   "You don't drink anymore": Ibid.

20. The Man Alone

283   For the story of Dashiell Hammett in jail and Lillian Hellman's responses, I have relied on conversations with Hammett's lawyers, Mary Kaufman, Victor Rabinowitz, and Charles Haydon, on two conversations with his secretary, Muriel Alexander, on interviews with his daughter, Josephine Hammett Marshall, Ruth Goetz, Frederick V. Field, Si Gerson, Howard N. Meyer, and on efforts of the Bureau of Prisons to supplement Hammett's FBI file. I am also grateful to the Tamiment Library at New York University, and to the Schomberg Collection

of Negro Literature and History of the New York Public Library, which houses the papers of the Civil Rights Congress.

283   "It's an unpleasant, upsetting": Lillian Hellman to Maggie Kober, June 29, 1950. WIS.

283   "nice . . . a nice woman": Hellman *Diary*, 1951, Thursday, Friday, Saturday, Sunday afternoon. HRHRC.

284   he languished in jail all weekend: Frederick V. Field interview with JM, January 17, 1994, and subsequent follow-up.

284   There was a meeting at Lillian's apartment: Victor Rabinowitz interview with JM.

284   See transcript of the hearing in Layman, 248–62. See also United States Court of Appeals for the Second Circuit, *United States of America* v. *Frederick V. Field, Dashiell Hammett, and W. Alpheus Hunton.* Appendix to Appellants' Brief. On Appeal from the United States District Court for the Southern District of New York.

285   "How could you have been so duped?": Peter Manso interview with JM, August 3, 1994.

285   "You can do this much time with your socks on": Marshall interview.

285   Dash suspected he might want a payoff: Marshall interview.

286   "I cannot believe that his friends": Jerome Weidman interview with JM.

286   "Let's get together": Ibid.

286   She refused to put up Dash's bail money: Conversation with Muriel Alexander. According to Lillian Hellman's *Diary* for 1951, Gregory Zilboorg had advised her not to put up any bail money herself: "then came the moral mess—should I, could I, wise, unwise, Gregory advised not. The day with Ruth & the borrowing. The loss of head and too many consultations."

286   she was to write: Lillian Hellman wrote about her efforts to obtain bail money for Hammett in Johnson, 245–47. Johnson had failed to corroborate that Hellman had made these efforts. Under their agreement, Hellman then seized the right to add her own version of events to the biography.

286   Nor could Dash have written her a note: Neither Rabinowitz nor Kaufman nor Haydon, the only lawyers involved, delivered such a note from Hammett to Hellman. Text for this "note" appears in Johnson, *Dashiell Hammett: A Life*, p. 247.

287   Dash telephoned Ruth and Gus Goetz. Ruth Goetz interview. "She had no good jewelry anyway," Goetz says.

287   A rich comrade: This person insisted on anonymity and Muriel Alexander has honored that request even after the person's death.

287   Weeping, she told him what had happened: Mary Kaufman interview with JM, August 19, 1994.

288   "You won't find the fugitives": Frederick V. Field interview with JM.

288   "great": Si Gerson interview with JM, December 18, 1993.

288   "I'd hate to pull the Fifth Amendment": Quoted in Irving Weissman to Lillian Hellman, November 15, 1976. HRHRC.

288   "Does he think of me?": Muriel Alexander conversation, February 6, 1995.

288   "lost her head . . . moral mess": Hellman *Diary*. HRHRC.

288   "Those three weeks before I left": Lillian Hellman to Josephine Hammett Marshall (undated).

289 she went shopping: Letters to her secretary Sophia Lange and shopping lists. HRHRC.

289 "as if he had long expected it": Lillian Hellman to Henry Sigerist (undated). HRHRC.

289 "light duty": E. E. Thompson to Loveland, August 27, 1951. National Archives.

289 Nor would he write or send messages to Lillian: See D. R. Large, Acting Warden to Mr. Frank Loveland, Assistant Director, United States Bureau of Prisons, re: Field, Frederick Vanderbilt, 8415-AK, Hammett, Samuel Dashiell, 8416-AK, September 28, 1951.

290 "be added to his list": G. C. Rexroad, Warden to Mr. Frank Loveland, Assistant Director, Bureau of Prisons, October 3, 1951. National Archives, Washington, D.C.

290 "as one of friendship only": Ibid.

290 "the only two who know anything": Dashiell Hammett to Josephine Hammett Marshall, October 18, 1951.

290 The FBI replied: See "Concerning Miss Lillian Hellman," October 13, 1951. FBI file, Dashiell Hammett.

290 "having a pretty good time": Dashiell Hammett to Josephine Hammett Marshall, October 12, 1951. HRHRC.

290 "do some go-betweening between Lily": Dashiell Hammett to Josephine Hammett Marshall, October 18, 1951.

290 "give her my love": Ibid.

290 "was involved with some business transactions": Charles Haydon interview with JM, October 1, 1993. See also G. C. Rexroad to Mr. Frank Loveland, October 24, 1951. National Archives.

290 "finally managed to blackjack": Dashiell Hammett to Josephine Hammett Marshall (date illegible).

291 "They call him, euphemistically": Haydon interview.

291 "know enough of his business": Lillian Hellman to Josephine Hammett Marshall, October 26, 1951.

291 "a wise decision": Lillian Hellman to Josephine Hammett Marshall, November 8, 1951.

291 "white as a sheet": Frederick V. Field, *From Right to Left: An Autobiography* (Lawrence Hill & Company: Westport, Conn., 1983), 250.

291 "the Hollywood situation": Lillian Hellman to Dashiell Hammett, 1951. Courtesy of Peter Feibleman.

292 "an anniversary on November 22nd": Ibid.

292 "The news from L. was very good": Dashiell Hammett to Josephine Hammett Marshall, November 27, 1951.

292 "This play stinks!" Victor Samrock interview with JM.

292 "Long may they live": Dashiell Hammett to Josephine Hammett Marshall, December 4, 1951.

292 her lawyer had advised her not to go: Steven Marcus interview with JM, May 18, 1993.

292 she ordered Rose Evans to get rid: Rose Evans interview with JM.

293 It was a bad hamburger: Johnson, 254.

293 the Internal Revenue Service ruled that the sale of the movie rights: See

Herman Shumlin to Lillian Hellman, September 17, 1951. WIS. See also Document dated March 24, 1951, describing Lillian Hellman's tax situation. HRHRC. The Internal Revenue had audited Lillian Hellman's tax returns for the years 1944 through 1947, even disallowing the deduction of payment for research work performed by Margaret Stone because it was "an ordinary business expense of the taxpayer." Lillian also wrote: "Reis claims, and Mr. Shumlin seems to agree with him, that nothing has been lost by the claim of capital gains because even if I have to pay an extra $35,000, my tax rates were so high during the year of the Warner settlement that I would have paid more than the $35,000 in regular taxes. I do not understand this: without the claim of capital gains I would have been spared the five-six year interest due on the $35,000. But it is possible I am wrong and I would like this explained to me."

293   he should have milk: Virginia Bloomgarden Chilewich interview with JM.

293   her taffeta rustled: Judith Firth Sanger interview with JM.

294   "I think they may have a point": Patricia Neal interview with JM.

294   Stone quoted in Victor S. Navasky, *Naming Names* (Viking Press: New York, 1980), 287–88.

294   "If the Lawsons and Hellmans ever got into power": Ibid., 244.

294   "I have no special reason for supposing anything": Dashiell Hammett to Josephine Hammett Marshall, April 16, 1952.

294   "It's going to leave quite a hole in life": Dashiell Hammett to Josephine Hammett Marshall, April 10, 1952.

294   "suspects me of having taken to bed": Ibid.

295   "many foolish books in the bookcase": Lillian Hellman to Philip D'Arcy Hart (undated). Courtesy of Dr. D'Arcy Hart.

295   "missed the idea of phoning you": Dashiell Hammett to Lillian Hellman, April 27, 1952.

295   "I'm looking forward to seeing you again": Dashiell Hammett to Lillian Hellman, April 29, 1952.

21. McCarthy Aftermath

299   "Why in the world would he ask me": Newman, 252.

299   "What about Dashiell Hammett?": Lillian Hellman interview with Fred Gardner.

300   "stamina": Feibleman, 121.

300   "Well, go to jail": The late Harry and Elena Levin interview with JM, June 5, 1993.

300   mantle of Joan of Arc: Irene Diamond interview with JM.

300   "I joined the Communist Party in 1938": Lillian Hellman draft statement, April 14, 1952. HRHRC.

300   "so little critical of the Communist movement": Joseph Rauh to Lillian Hellman, April 30, 1952.

300   never defending an actual Communist: Renata Adler interview with JM.

300   she took the Fifth Amendment: See Communist Infiltration of the Hollywood Motion-Picture Industry—Part 8. Wednesday, May 21, 1952.

United States House of Representatives, Committee on Un-American Activities, Washington, D.C., public hearing: Testimony of Miss Lillian Hellman, accompanied by her counsel, Joseph L. Rauh, Jr.

301 "Why cite her for contempt?": "Meeting-Goer," *Time,* June 2, 1952.

301 neither was she in danger: Ring Lardner, Jr., interview with JM.

301 put her hand on Joe Rauh's thigh: Rollyson, 329.

301 "You're very decent to tell me that": Helen Harvey interview with JM, April 8, 1994.

301 Tax Commission. See Lillian Hellman's sworn statement, March 14, 1952. HRHRC.

301 "a local heroine": Lillian Hellman to John Melby [1952]. HRHRC.

302 "to run away, but I don't know": Ibid.

302 "I still haven't got up to your neighborhood": Dashiell Hammett to Lillian Hellman, August 20, 1952. HRHRC.

302 The will of Dashiell Hammett, dated July 1, 1952, available at HRHRC.

302 "I've never written a play without him": Haydon interview.

302 Lillian was the only person: Haydon interview with JM.

302 "I love you with the utmost extravagance": Dashiell Hammett to Lillian Hellman, August 21, 1952.

302 "I'm having a mess of trouble with my book": Dashiell Hammett to Lillian Hellman, August 24, 1952.

302 "bellyaching": Ibid.

303 "turn out to be one of the nicest homes": Dashiell Hammett to Josephine Hammett Marshall, October 20, 1952.

303 Lily made an agreement: Helen Rosen interview.

303 "I need Rose": Rose Evans interview.

303 "You'd be fired in two or three": Ibid.

304 He did not hang Luis Quintanilla's: Rosen interview.

304 "I thought it would be nice to say hello": Hellman *Diary.* HRHRC.

304 "fairy-shit": Lillian Hellman to John Melby, Sunday [1946].

304 The place wasn't good enough for him: Helen Rosen interview with JM.

304 "Get out of my life!": Judy Ruben interview with JM.

304 Lillian managed to launder it: John Melby interview with JM.

304 "Forget it": *Three,* 302.

305 "never had anything to do with any political": Newman, 242.

305 "a Southern custom": Newman, 246.

305 "very beautiful but full of drunks and fags": Lillian Hellman to John Melby [c. March 1953].

305 "Ring, I really don't want": Ring Lardner, Jr., interview.

305 "philosophy if you want to call it that": Dashiell Hammett to Judy Ruben, July 29, 1953.

306 "a pleasant if dullish woman": Ibid.

306 how difficult it was to be married: Judy Ruben interview with JM, January 15, 1993.

306 "Tulip" appears in the collection *The Big Knockover.*

306 "Now, Lily, what really happened?": Helen Rosen interview with JM.

306   "Put on your jacket": Judy Ruben interview with JM.

307   "How could you do this to me?": Helen Rosen interview with JM.

307   He bought Lily a panel of antique lace: Feibleman, 124, and Feibleman interview with JM.

307   "Please leave!": Helen Rosen and Irene Diamond interviews with JM.

307   "Lillian, I want to be . . . you're dirty": Herbert Gold interview with JM, December 29, 1992.

308   "I was shrugging my shoulders just for you": Phillips and Hollander interview with Lillian Hellman, in *Conversations,* 87.

308   "Culture Fights Back," held at Manhattan Center, April 24, 1952. Participants included Howard Fast, Elizabeth Gurley Flynn, and Paul Robeson, but not Lillian Hellman.

308   "By not paying too much attention to what people do": Dashiell Hammett to Judy Ruben, July 7, 1953. The letters of Hammett to Judy Ruben quoted in this chapter appear courtesy of Judy Ruben.

308   "I don't like Rome food": Lillian Hellman to Henry Sigerist, "Thursday." HRHRC.

308   "It's nicer here and there's more loving": Western Union cablegram, Dashiell Hammett to Lillian Hellman. Courtesy of Fred Gardner.

308   "fluttering around in some sort of circle": Dashiell Hammett to Judy Ruben, July 29, 1953.

308   "She now thinks of herself as representing me": Ibid.

308   "There are certain facts that must now be accepted": Lillian Hellman to Lois R. Fritsch, "Tuesday" [1953]. HRHRC.

309   "might run into trouble": Lillian Hellman to Lois R. Fritsch [1953]. HRHRC.

309   "cut [her] throat": Lillian Hellman to Lois R. Fritsch, July 31, 1953. HRHRC.

309   "The trouble with Lillian is that she wanted": Stephen Greene interview with JM, April 29, 1993. The scenes with Stephen Greene derive from this interview.

310   Lily wore a hat with a pouffed: Rose Styron interview with JM, March 29, 1993.

310   "Call Dash and tell him to continue to use": Lillian Hellman to Lois R. Fritsch [1953]. HRHRC.

311   "you still have money that belongs to him": Lillian Hellman to Lois R. Fritsch [1953]. HRHRC.

311   Nobody else would carry the weight with Kermit: Lillian Hellman to Lois R. Fritsch, July 31, 1953. HRHRC.

311   "should be as firm as he wishes to be": Ibid.

311   "chloroformed": Dashiell Hammett to Josephine Hammett Marshall, July 30, 1953.

311   "Florence is far more beautiful": Lillian Hellman to Lois R. Fritsch, "Thursday" [1953]. HRHRC.

311   "Tell him that Prica is not as handsome": The following messages are from Lillian Hellman to Lois R. Fritsch. HRHRC.

311   "Tell him that I was solicited": Ibid.

312   "Tell him that I haven't written much because": Ibid.

312   "stage fright": Dashiell Hammett to Josephine Hammett Marshall, June 14, 1953.

312   "I have finally found the man": Stephen Greene interview with JM.

312   a crude overture: Honor Moore interview, 1995.

312   "You mean she's sleeping with Jed!": Ruth Goetz interview with JM.

312   "He entered the room as noiselessly": Quoted in Martin Gottfried, *Jed Harris: The Curse of Genius* (Little, Brown: Boston and Toronto, 1984), 90.

312   "I have to close my eyes to fuck her": Martin Gottfried interview with JM, December 13, 1993.

312   only for it to turn out to be fake: Flora Roberts interview with JM. According to Barbara Epstein (interview with JM, March 2, 1993), Lillian liked to tell Jed Harris stories against herself.

312   "I like her": Dashiell Hammett to Josephine Hammett Marshall, November 23, 1953.

22. Welcome Tory Soldiers

313   afraid to leave her baby: Judy Ruben interview with JM.

313   "It would be wonderful if some time": Lillian Hellman to Josephine Hammett Marshall, January 29, 1954.

314   "I never discuss politics with Lillian": John Marquand interview with JM.

314   "engaging" and "perceptive": "The Education of Anton Chekhov, *New Republic,* July 19, 1955, 18–19.

314   "a deplorable state of affairs": Lillian Hellman to Yuri I. Gouk (cultural attaché of the embassy of the U.S.S.R.), October 11, 1957. HRHRC. It was Gouk who had sent her a check for $10,000 in May 1956 but with no statement of what it represented, which plays were produced, etc.

314   "Many years ago": Lillian Hellman to the Spanish Refugee Appeal, April 6, 1954. HRHRC.

314   "Communism to me is not a dirty word": "Got 300G, but only 6G to Defend 6," New York *Daily News,* February 24, 1955. See also "Rogge Says 'Trenton Six' Got $6,000 of $300,000," New York *Herald Tribune,* February 24, 1955, and "Hammett Won't Say If He's Red," New York *Journal American,* February 23, 1955.

315   "for obvious reasons": Dashiell Hammett to Josephine Hammett Marshall, October 14, 1955.

315   "It was no worse than if she'd gone": Hilary Mills interview with Albert Hackett.

315   "What you write will be true": Ibid.

315   "needed money": Lillian Hellman to Henry Sigerist [September–October 1955]. Yale University Library.

315   "I found that a bitter piece of comedy": Correspondence between Lillian Hellman and Jan van Loewen, 1955. HRHRC.

316   "I don't think much of this St. Joan": Lillian Hellman interview with Fred Gardner.

316   "saintly man": Rollyson, 391.

316   "It's a good thing to find a literary man": Lillian Hellman to Harry Levin [1957]. Courtesy of the late Harry Levin.

316   "all to the good": Dashiell Hammett to Josephine Hammett Marshall, November 28, 1955.

316   "I state flatly": Meyer Levin, "'Lark' Translation Tacks On a Little," Newark *Star-Ledger*, February 7, 1956.

316   "much of the wonderful chaos": Lillian Hellman to Harry Levin, January 31, 1955. Courtesy of the late Harry Levin.

316   "a good time": Dashiell Hammett to Josephine Hammett Marshall, February 5, 1956.

316   "What! Shall our modern drama's": "Sent to Lillian on the occasion of an operation, January 1956": "The Poet Calleth on the Goddess of Health to Awaken," Papers of Richard Wilbur, Amherst College. Courtesy of Richard Wilbur.

317   "worn out from the short journey": Johnson, 291.

317   she penciled in: See appointment books of Lillian Hellman. HRHRC.

317   "Who are those Rappaports?": Shirley Hazzard interview with JM.

317   "manufacture enough oxygen for my great": Dashiell Hammett to Josephine Hammett Marshall, April 24, 1956.

317   "old age . . . catching up": Dashiell Hammett to Josephine Hammett Marshall, June 5, 1956.

317   "only a family quarrel": Herbert Geller, "Hemingway Talks Too Much, Says Creator of 'Thin Man,'" *Patent Trader* (Mount Kisco, N.Y.), July 29, 1956.

317   turn the pages: Charlee and Richard Wilbur interview with JM.

317   hairdo was practical: Charlee Wilbur interview with JM.

317   "Well, he came again this morning": Ibid.

317   "Where have you been, Dashie?": John Marquand interview with JM.

317   "SCRAM!" William Alfred interview with JM.

318   "You are what you are": Marshall interview.

318   "Sigrid has a beautiful face": Stephen Greene interview with JM.

318   he knew almost as many baseball statistics: Richard Wilbur interview with JM.

318   "die in my eighties": Dashiell Hammett to Josephine Hammett Marshall, February 5, 1956.

318   Dash fled to his tower: William Alfred interview.

318   You might catch a glimpse of him: Phillips and Hollander interview, in *Conversations*, 66.

319   "Goy dreck in a Jewish house!": Burton Bernstein interview with JM, April 1, 1994.

319   "No amount of practice in shmalz-spreading": Dashiell Hammett to Lillian Hellman, March 25, 1944.

319   "I'm sick and tired of dealing": Charlee and Richard Wilbur interview with JM.

319   "It's not a play": E. E. Spitzer interview with JM.

319   he hung a composite: Nina Bernstein interview with JM, March 10, 1994. See *National Lampoon*, Fantasy Issue, January 1980.

319   "neurosis that took a long time": Lillian Hellman, "The History for the Record" (manuscript). HRHRC.

320   "disgusting waste": Lillian Hellman to Robert Lantz, November 5, 1971. HRHRC.

320   "passivity": Lillian Hellman interview with Fred Gardner. Courtesy of Fred Gardner.

320   "seems to have some faggish background": Start of 1h\s long story, early 50s: "told in first person by a woman named Sarah Curtis, daughter of an extremely wealthy man. She is visiting the friend of her dead sister, Elinore, Meg and Carl Ryan. A Colonel Palmer, who loves Meg, is there. A trio comes over for a drink: Mr. and Mrs. Sam Howard and Daffie [sic], a fag. Carl seems to have some faggish background. Palmer was in love with Meg; leaves when he learns that she has been the mistress of a wealthy neighbor named Diamond. Much of their servility is traced to people 'being good to them.'" Courtesy of Fred Gardner.

320   "Well, it doesn't mean one damn thing": Lillian Hellman interview with Fred Gardner.

320   "Don't peek!": John Marquand interview with JM, December 11, 1992.

320   Scenes with Charlee Wilbur: Interview with JM.

320   "There are social standards": Jamie Bernstein-Thomas interview with JM, February 2, 1994.

321   "you mustn't breathe a word": Herbert Gold interview with JM.

321   "busily engaged in pawing La Hellman": S. J. Perelman to Leila Hadley, August 25, 1956, in Don't Tread on Me: The Selected Letters of S. J. Perelman, ed. Prudence Crowther (Penguin Books: New York, 1988), 187.

321   For this description of Cowan, I am indebted to Edgar Dannenberg, interview with JM, November 6, 1993.

322   and then to marry her: Sadie Raab interview with JM, September 17, 1993.

322   "Please don't leave me alone with her": Ibid.

322   "Was there any kindness in it?": Hellman Diary. HRHRC.

322   "1). Mr. Cowan has syphilis": The letters of Lillian Hellman to Arthur Cowan appear courtesy of his niece, Marilyn Raab.

323   "Forget about her politics!": Dorothea Straus interview with JM.

323   "I'm living on money": James Cooper, "Lean Years for the Thin Man," Washington Daily News, March 11, 1957. As Richard Layman reports in his Dictionary of Literary Biography essay about Dashiell Hammett, this was Hammett's last public interview.

323   "So I'm broke!": Dashiell Hammett to Josephine Hammett Marshall, August 7, 1956.

323   "no danger to his living alone": Lillian Hellman to Josephine Hammett Marshall, February 21, 1957.

324   John knew Dash had to be telephoned: Dr. John Rosen interview with JM, July 1994. The following episode derives from this conversation.

324   "more or less progressive breathlessness": Dashiell Hammett to Josephine Hammett Marshall, August 7, 1956.

324   "He's not that sick!": Helen Rosen interview with JM.

325   "What is the implication, Sam?": Lillian Hellman tape with Diane Johnson. Courtesy of Diane Johnson.

325   "Life ain't always good even to tall goys": Dashiell Hammett to Lillian Hellman, January 14, 1958.

325   "or when you're going to Paris or some such": Dashiell Hammett to Lillian Hellman, January 24, 1958.

325   "It'll be awful nice seeing you": Dashiell Hammett to Lillian Hellman, January 28, 1958.

325   "It seems like a long time since I've heard from you": Dashiell Hammett to Lillian Hellman, January 31, 1958.

325   Dash told her he didn't want to see Helen: Helen Rosen interview.

325   "I am not a liar": Lillian Hellman to Sam Rosen, October 2, 1973. HRHRC.

23. Their Last Years

326   "I thought you got over that agitprop": William Alfred interview with JM.

326   "All right. If you think you can stand it": Lillian Hellman interview with Alvin Sargent.

326   "After five years and a half": Dashiell Hammett to Josephine Hammett Marshall, May 17, 1958.

326   she chafed: Ruth Goetz and Becky Bernstien interviews with JM.

327   "Oh, Mr. Hammett, he's such a saint": Marshall interview.

327   "a stone wall": Marshall interview.

327   "the only Negro who can't carry a tune": Feibleman interview.

327   entertained Arthur Cowan on the living-room couch: Dorothea Straus interview with JM.

327   "Mr. Hammett, you ought to get out": Johnson, 293.

327   "Please keep it down": Norman Mailer interview with JM.

327   Norman Podhoretz opened the wrong door: Norman Podhoretz interview with JM, April 27, 1993.

327   Lily guarded Dash like a lioness: Rollyson, 389.

328   a photograph of his daughters: Cathy Kober interview with JM.

328   everyone but me: Hellman, notes tucked into one of her appointment books. HRHRC.

328   "If he wants a drink": Scene courtesy of Virginia Bloomgarden Chilewich.

328   they had been his free choice: Diana Trilling interview with JM, January 17, 1993.

328   "She can be a bitch on wheels": Virginia Bloomgarden Chilewich interview with JM.

328   Jerome Weidman felt: Jerome Weidman interview with JM.

328   For scenes at Chelsea Plantation: Inge Dean interview with JM, May 12, 1993.

328   she made a joke about Dash: Ibid.

329   "There's this man": *Pentimento,* 170.

329   "was absolutely bewildered by why I couldn't": Richard G. Stern, "An Interview with Lillian Hellman," conducted May 21, 1958, in *Conversations,* 30.

329 she could not get any of them on the telephone: Burton Bernstein interview with JM.

329 "The cigarette smoking here is intense . . . I wish I had stayed in New Orleans": Lillian Hellman to Richard Wilbur [1958]. Amherst College.

329 "My severest critic will read it soon": Lillian Hellman to Charlee Wilbur [1958]. Amherst College.

329 Dash even wrote a speech: Text available at HRHRC.

330 "sad": Lillian Hellman to Richard Wilbur [1958]. Amherst College.

330 "Lily will explain": Phillips and Hollander interview with Lillian Hellman, in *Conversations*, 54.

330 "Dash said, thanks so much": William Alfred interview with JM.

330 "the spirit of the times": David O. Selznick to Lillian Hellman, March 17, 1959. HRHRC.

330 "practically bedridden": Dashiell Hammett to the Veterans Administration, April 29, 1959. LAY.

330 "dream of you": Letter to Cowan courtesy of Marilyn Raab.

331 "Miss Hellman is adored by five men": These quotations come from undated letters of Lillian Hellman to Arthur Cowan. Courtesy of Marilyn Raab.

331 "critical guest": Lillian Hellman to Richard Wilbur, April 15, 1959. Amherst College.

331 "He is a man of sense": Ibid.

331 For Lillian Hellman's efforts on behalf of the rights of Sam Spade, see papers at HRHRC, in particular memo by HIR dated February 2, 1959: "Kay Brown and I took a meeting with Lillian Hellman, at whose home the very ill Dashiell Hammett is now living and who is trying to handle his affairs. As I advised you, many people are trying to obtain the rights to SAM SPADE, but Miss Hellman does not feel it will be possible for the immediate future for us or anyone else to make any real progress. Among the complications is the fact that a title search is being made on all his properties. Also, every dollar Hammett makes is being attached by the Internal Revenue Bureau and unless and until a deal can be made covering back taxes, there is no chance he would agree to a deal where the Government got all the money. On that basis, the work of approaching the Government must be done and Miss Hellman thinks this cannot be accomplished until someone steps forward and offers somewhere around $200,000 guarantee for the rights to SAM SPADE, which would give him enough capital to settle his taxes and have something left over. . . ."

331 "the fact of breathing, just breathing": *Unfinished Woman*, 224.

332 Dash was in bed, exhausted: Arthur Penn interview with JM, May 17, 1994.

332 "Just tell everybody they were wonderful": Maureen Stapleton interview with JM, May 11, 1993.

332 "I can't get over it": Alfred interview with JM.

333 "Marry me!" Austin Pendleton interview with JM.

333 denied that the character Lily: Arthur Penn interview with JM.

334 "After all I've been through with you": This scene between Hellman and Hammett at the Plaza, Robert Giroux interview with JM, June 28, 1993.

335   "very fancy characters": Lillian Hellman to Kermit Bloomgarden, March 7, 1960. HRHRC.

335   Jane Austen: Jason Epstein to Lillian Hellman, May 12, 1960. HRHRC.

335   "knight": Alfred Kazin to Lillian Hellman, March 9, 1960. HRHRC.

335   "I've lived alone": Fern Marja, "A Clearing in the Forest," *New York Post Magazine,* March 6, 1960, 2.

335   "this strange mixture of Dukes and Jews": Lillian Hellman to Lionel Trilling [c. 1960]. Columbia University.

335   Papers connected with Lillian Hellman's efforts to break the Sophie Newhouse Trust, available at HRHRC.

335   "No one would have any standing in court to object": Arthur W. A. Cowan to Lillian Hellman, December 23, 1957. HRHRC.

335   "crossed the Rubicon": Arthur W. A. Cowan to Lillian Hellman, May 21, 1958. HRHRC.

336   "if I gave over the trust fund to you": Florence Newhouse to Lillian Hellman, May 27, 1960.

336   "sad and bewildered": Lillian Hellman to Florence Newhouse, June 13, 1960. HRHRC.

336   you sleeping?": Mildred Loftus interview with JM, March 9, 1993.

336   "will do nothing about it except to be bad-natured": Lillian Hellman to Charlee and Richard Wilbur [1960]. Amherst College.

336   "Maureen has gained weight": Lillian Hellman to Kermit Bloomgarden, June 27, 1960. HRHRC.

336   "I am shocked at your failure": Kermit Bloomgarden to Jason Robards, June 13, 1960. WIS.

337   For this scene of Josephine Marshall's visit to Martha's Vineyard, Marshall interviews.

337   "You'll feel very bad": Trilling interview with JM.

338   about a dream: Lillian Hellman to Lionel Trilling [c. November 1960]. Columbia University.

24. The Death of Dashiell Hammett

339   "The love that started on that day": Lillian Hellman to Dashiell Hammett, November 25, 1960.

339   "Why me?": Hellman, notes tucked inside a *Diary,* series from March 4, 1961.

339   he scrambled out of bed to the phone: Johnson, 294.

339   "We've done fine, haven't we?": *Unfinished Woman,* 242.

340   crazy man pretending he was crazy: *Pentimento,* 206.

340   "Dash was gasping in a bad attack": Hellman *Diary* for 1960. HRHRC.

340   "Oh, are you coming?": Berger, Program No. Two.

340   "Fear is bad and obvious now": Hellman *Diary* for 1960. Notes for December 1: "Dr. Fein or Feur called at 9, came at 11. Took Dash to Lenox Hill about 2 p.m. Fear is bad and obvious now." HRHRC.

340   "I don't think I'll ever be better": Hellman *Diary* for Tuesday, December 20: "Day fairly good, agreeable. Yesterday saw he would now be

bedridden. Today said he didn't think he would ever be better. Rash—shingles? discovered.

340   "I never thought I'd turn one down": *Unfinished Woman,* 226.

341   stagger out of bed: Lillian Hellman to Talli Wyler, December 5, 1960. HRHRC.

341   "at least once a week or every ten days": Lillian Hellman to Elena Levin, December 13, 1960. HRHRC.

341   "last sexual surge": Hellman, notes tucked into a *Diary.* HRHRC.

341   "a little grabbing": Ibid.

341   "I've never liked writers who don't know what they're doing": Hellman, notes tucked into a *Diary,* December 29 or 28. HRHRC.

341   "always afraid and hating it": Hellman, notes tucked into a *Diary,* Ibid.

341   "hard-eyed": Hellman, notes tucked into a *Diary,* from series March 4, 1961. HRHRC.

342   "Why is it happening?" Ibid.

342   a solitary tear: Hellman, notes tucked into a *Diary,* December 31, 1960, 8 p.m. HRHRC.

342   "Do you want me to come": Diana Trilling interview with JM.

342   reading a book upside down: *Unfinished Woman,* 243.

342   Scene of Lillian discussing the Cambridge nursing home, Elena Levin interview with JM.

343   No one was going to use the bomb: Virginia Bloomgarden Chilewich interview with JM.

343   "Tell Dash I love him only": Charlee Wilbur to Lillian Hellman, January 4, 1961. Amherst College.

343   "Run quickly to the bed and shout": Johnson, 298.

343   "I didn't want you to read about it": Rose Evans interview with JM.

344   "He was a good man": "A Gentle Man Who Wrote About the Underworld," *Daily Worker,* January 29, 1961, 4.

344   ask the government for widow's benefits: See Josephine Hammett to the VA, March 13, 1963: "My husband and I first separated around 1929. He left me, through no fault of mine. He would come back at different times for about a dozen times until the last time we were together in 1950. We stayed together about six months. He would leave me and go away. He was a writer and wanted to live by himself. I had to go to work as he would not contribute to my support. We were never legally separated. There is no court order." LAY. In fact, the divorce decree was entered in Nogales, August 26, 1937.

344   Whose funeral am I at?: Patricia Neal interview with JM.

344   Lillian Hellman's eulogy for Dashiell Hammett: See Johnson, 333–34.

344   "He is dead": Lillian Hellman to Mike Nichols, undated memo, p. 3. HRHRC.

345   For this scene at Arlington, I am indebted to Jane Fish Yowaiski.

346   prevent Dashiell Hammett's burial: The FBI attempted to prevent this from happening by stirring up opposition in the press. But by the time they organized their effort, Dashiell Hammett had been laid to his final rest: "incongruous situation": FBI memo to: Mr. A. H. Belmont, from: Mr. F. J. Baumgardner, January 17, 1961. FBI file of Dashiell

Hammett. See also Anthony Summers, *The Secret Life of J. Edgar Hoover,* (G. P. Putnam's and Sons: New York, 1993), 162.

346   "stealing": Fred Gardner interview with JM. See also Fred Gardner, "Harvard": Asked if she really meant stealing, Hellman replied, "Yes, but not copying. Copying is a dangerous pattern for a young writer, though we've all done it. It is not morally bad, but cramping and self-defeating. Your view of life is your own, after all, and not Beckett's or anybody else's. . . . there's every difference between copying and doing exercises along the lines of someone else's style . . . a style can be learned from other people, but then it must be your own."

346   It felt as if she were asking him to feel sorry: Herbert Gold interview with JM.

347   "Oh yes, I know that period": Mildred Loftus interview with JM.

347   "Well, one thing is that their sex organs": Rita Wade interview with JM, October 26, 1992.

347   list of loans: See HRHRC.

347   "I missed your father too much to stay in it": Lillian Hellman to Josephine Hammett Marshall, April 20, 1962.

347   "Should this be charged against the estate?": Lillian Hellman to Charles Haydon, February 23, 1961. HRHRC.

348   she cashed it: Selma Wolfman to Charles Haydon, April 6, 1961. HRHRC.

348   "In essence, the Estate is hopelessly insolvent": Oscar Bernstien to the Internal Revenue Service, April 24, 1962. HRHRC.

348   "MCA is NOT convinced that your father's": Lillian Hellman to Josephine Hammett Marshall, April 20, 1962.

348   "I have the hope that maybe you and Mary can contribute": Lillian Hellman to Josephine Hammett Marshall, April 20, 1962.

348   How much should she send?: Marshall interview with JM.

348   "write a book about the deceased or his works": Affidavit of Lillian Hellman, June 25, 1962. HRHRC.

348   Documents connected with Lillian Hellman's early attempts to purchase the rights to Hammett's works from the United States government are available at HRHRC.

349   "pitifully small": Howard N. Meyer to Vincent Broderick, October 1, 1962: "the assets of the Estate of Dashiell Hammett are so pitifully small compared to the Federal Government Tax Claim that there will be no residue for the state or for any other creditor."

349   "the field of publication seems to be a diminishing": Lillian Hellman to Howard N. Meyer, September 12, 1962: "On their way to you are three letters, one from Kay Brown, one from Kermit Bloomgarden and one from an old friend of mine, Mr. Joseph Weinstein whom Oscar knows. I quote here a paragraph from a report from MCA dated November 20, 1961: 'Our estimate on the situation as a whole is that the field of publication seems to be a diminishing one rather than an upbeat one. The television market is limited as to compensation.'"

349   "since I had been very nervous about never recovering": Lillian Hellman to Howard N. Meyer, October 4, 1962.

349   "stand over my shoulder": Ibid.

25. "Shyster Clever"

353   "shyster clever": Feibleman interview.

353   "I bought the estate": Lillian Hellman interview with Fred Gardner. See document of the Surrogate's Court: County of New York. In the Matter of the Judicial Settlement of the Account of Proceedings of Lillian Hellman, Executrix of Samuel Dashiell Hammett, Deceased. P. 419/1961.

353   she remained silent: Marshall interview with JM.

354   her lawyer sent waivers: Howard N. Meyer to Josephine Marshall, March 19, 1963. HRHRC.

354   Jo was not told: Marshall interview with JM.

354   "clear your father's name": Meyer to Marshall, March 19, 1963.

354   would be liable for Hammett's debts: Marshall interview with JM. Josephine Marshall returned the waiver of citation on March 24, 1963. HRHRC. See also "Objections to Account": Document August 12, 1963. Available, HRHRC.

355   "It is time to say bluntly that I will do": Lillian Hellman to Josephine Marshall [1963]. HRHRC.

356   her "father's wife": Marshall interview.

356   "only when in my sole judgment I feel it is equitable": Lillian Hellman to Josephine Marshall [1963]. HRHRC.

356   "I didn't think I could afford it": Nora Ephron, "Lillian Hellman Walking, Cooking, Writing, Talking," in *Conversations,* 135.

356   "Tell them to have it for a present": Lillian Hellman to Howard N. Meyer, June 1964. HRHRC.

357   "the money from DH's works": Arthur W. A. Cowan to Lillian Hellman, quoted in Lillian Hellman to Oscar Bernstien, May 24, 1965. HRHRC. See also the reply: Lillian Hellman to Arthur W. A. Cowan [1964].

357   "If I die I want all my rights": Arthur W. A. Cowan to Oscar Bernstien (undated). HRHRC.

357   Throughout the manuscript: The draft of Lillian Hellman's Introduction to *The Big Knockover* is available at Columbia University.

357   "I have never understood which copyrights belong to me": Lillian Hellman to Oscar Bernstien, November 22, 1965. HRHRC.

357   "whether any of these stories are owned by the daughters": Lillian Hellman to Howard N. Meyer, December 9, 1965.

358   "claim, right or interest": I am indebted to Ben Camardi of the Harold Matson Agency for showing me the quitclaims and other copyright materials and contracts connected with the Dashiell Hammett estate.

358   Cowan had promised her money: Sadie Raab interview with JM.

358   foreign rights: Between 1975 and 1982 foreign rights to *The Continental Op* collection were sold to Spain, Italy, Japan, Brazil, France, Germany, Sweden, Czechoslovakia, and Finland. Lillian haggled over every sale. When in 1975 Diogenes in Germany wanted to pay 2,000 Swiss francs for *The Continental Op,* the same price they had paid for *The Big Knockover,* Lillian demanded 2,500: "that's small enough." A decade after *The Big Knockover* was published, rights to the stories in that collection were resold in France, Norway, Portugal, and Holland. Yet when the French

wanted to add other Hammett stories to their edition of *The Big Knock-over,* Lillian refused. Those were his best. She refused to dilute the volume. Hammett had become enormously popular in France, and Carré Noir editions published *The Glass Key* in 1972, *The Maltese Falcon* in 1973, and *The Dain Curse* and *Red Harvest* in 1974. The biggest seller was *The Maltese Falcon,* which by 1975 had sold 121,343 copies.

358   "a fairly large amount of money . . . Mr. Hammett felt very strong": Lillian Hellman to Donald Congdon, June 7, 1971. HRHRC.

358   "Dash himself felt very strongly about things not being done": Lillian Hellman to Adrian Scott, February 11, 1972. HRHRC.

358   "Why don't you call him and say": Lillian Hellman to Ronald Bernstein, August 29, 1969. HRHRC.

358   accused him of favoring: Robert Lantz interview with JM, December 1, 1993.

358   "I feel as if I am sitting on Kafka's head": Lillian Hellman to Robert Lantz, April 5, 1971. HRHRC. For the story of Lillian Hellman's relationship with the Lantz agency, Robert Lantz interview.

359   "That is a right that Hammett, and thus I": Lillian Hellman to Donald Congdon, June 1, 1972. Courtesy of the Harold Matson Agency.

359   "on a rising curve": Donald Congdon to Lillian Hellman, January 8, 1975. Columbia University.

359   "pertinent papers to confirm the transfer": Donald Congdon to Lillian Hellman, August 14, 1974. Columbia University.

359   "there is a lot of interest in motion picture rights": Congdon interview with JM.

359   "how they intend to use the quotation": In pencil on a letter from NBC, 1976, asking permission to use a quotation from "One Hour" by Dashiell Hammett, written in 1924, which read: "the blow that came from behind didn't hit me fairly, but I got enough of it to fold up my legs as if the knees were hinged with paper—and I slammed into a heap on the floor. Something dark crashed toward me. I caught it with both hands. It may have been a foot kicking at my face. I wrung it as a washerman wrings a towel . . . As I twisted about to hurl a foot into a soft body, something that was like a burn, but wasn't a burn, ran down one leg . . . a knife. The sting of it brought consciousness back into me with a rush." The program was scheduled for January 3, 1977. HRHRC.

359   "I can't have it!" Robert Brustein interview with JM, June 4, 1993.

360   "Hammett liked Queen": Lillian Hellman scrawled on letter of Donald Congdon to Lillian Hellman, July 24, 1975: "I guess so. Hammett liked Queen. L.H." Columbia University.

360   "I guard what he wrote as carefully": Ephron, *Conversations,* 135.

360   "approval or disapproval by other people": Memo of Lillian Hellman to Mike Nichols (undated). Courtesy of Pearl London.

360   "Was he a Communist?": Congdon interview with JM.

360   "treat either one of them as lost": Lillian Hellman memo to Mike Nichols.

361   "final cut": Congdon interview with JM.

361   "a left-wing character": Contract between Lillian Hellman and Warner Brothers. Courtesy of the Harold Matson Agency.

361   "I would, of course, be glad to send you my $500": Lillian Hellman to Josephine Marshall, May 17, 1977.

361   "I have told my lawyer and accountant": Lillian Hellman to Josephine Marshall, December 18, 1974.

361   "far more involved situation": Ibid.

361   "bad news": Lillian Hellman to Josephine Marshall, July 3, 1975.

362   "keep two-thirds for yourself": Lillian Hellman to Josephine Marshall, December 1975.

362   I've been thinking about giving them each five thousand dollars": Donald Congdon interview with JM.

362   "then I would prefer": Lillian Hellman to Josephine Marshall, January 25, 1977.

362   "a piece of one": Lillian Hellman to Josephine Marshall, March 31, 1977.

362   "In computing the checks": Lillian Hellman to Josephine Marshall, December 2, 1977.

362   "it would cause extra difficulty": Lillian Hellman to Josephine Marshall, May 17, 1977.

363   continued to grow: In 1980 Knopf reprinted the *Hammett Omnibus.* "Corkscrew" was optioned for $7,500 in 1981. Lillian needed to know what films Alsa Productions had done; whom did Leslie Linder have in mind to play the detective? Robert Duvall, she was told. A year later the rights to "Corkscrew" reverted back to her. Foreign rights continued to be sold, the stories to Spain in illustrated juvenile editions in 1982, a Dutch edition of *The Big Knockover.* German radio adapted "The Girl with the Silver Eyes." Italian television contacted Congdon about several Hammett stories. In 1983 Knopf printed a special handset, limited edition of *The Maltese Falcon.* Each of four hundred copies would sell for $150. The Brazilians bought *The Continental Op* for $1,500. In 1988 Knopf published in a single volume *Woman in the Dark,* which had appeared in three installments in *Liberty* magazine in April 1933.

363   "bodies piled up by d.h.": Lillian Hellman to Joy Harris, February 22, 1984.

363   "one part to Mary": Lillian Hellman to Josephine Marshall, January 10, 1979.

363   "should be divided the usual way": Lillian Hellman to Josephine Marshall, December 19, 1980.

363   "Christmas present . . . Mr. Reagan's new tax law": Lillian Hellman to Josephine Marshall, December 17, 1981.

363   "I've been told that Dashiell Hammett": *Parade,* December 6, 1981.

363   "tired of Mary": Lillian Hellman to Josephine Marshall, December 29, 1982.

363   "I suppose she should get a small sum": Lillian Hellman to Josephine Marshall, December 19, 1983.

363   In her will: The will of Lillian Hellman is available at HRHRC.

26. Hammett's Successor

365   "I love you very, very much": The materials for this chapter derive primarily from the following sources: the letters of Lillian Hellman to Blair Clark, 1963–81, most of which, as was the case with her per-

sonal letters, are undated, *Diaries* of Lillian Hellman available at HRHRC, memos of his relationship with Lillian Hellman in the papers of Blair Clark, interviews with Blair Clark, as well as interviews with other of Lillian Hellman's friends: John Marquand, Peter Feibleman, Rose Styron, William Alfred, Rita Wade, and others.

365   "I've never been betrayed by a man": 1971 interview. HRHRC.

365   Cameron: Lillian would use the name Cameron in her final "story," or memoir, *Maybe,* as the name of the mysterious Sarah's first husband.

366   "The whole year has been dreary": Lillian Hellman to Louis Kronenberger, to "Louis dear" [1963]. Copley Library.

366   "moisture cream; cold cream; conceal stick": Document available HRHRC.

367   "I will not have that woman edit my quote": Richard de Combray interview with JM, February 12, 1993.

367   disinviting at Jackie's request: Linda Anderson interview with JM, August 12, 1993.

367   "I'm sorry, but I have no room": Rose Styron interview with JM.

367   "We necked and necked and necked": Diana Trilling interview with JM.

369   "How I would love to make love to Blair": John Marquand interview with JM.

369   "the longest and meanest depression of my life": Lillian Hellman to Arthur W. A. Cowan (undated).

369   "dysfunctional": Arthur Penn interview with JM.

369   "I never *took* my mink coat": Robert Lantz interview with JM.

370   "It took me a year": Lillian Hellman to Blair Clark, November 14, 1964. Courtesy of Blair Clark.

371   "I can't get it out of my head": Feibleman interview.

372   "blonde curls, natural": Elia Kazan, *A Life* (Anchor Books/Doubleday: New York, 1989), 324.

373   "seldom like to drop bombs": May 1967. Text of her toast is among Lillian Hellman's papers. HRHRC.

375   Clark had delivered to her the public illusion: Richard Poirier interview with JM.

27. Fabulations: The Memoirs

For this chapter I am indebted to interviews with Shirley Hazzard, Fred Gardner, Richard Poirier, Dorothea Straus, Blair Clark, Josephine Marshall, Peter Feibleman, Martha Gellhorn, William Doering, Alvin Sargent, Miriam Dickey, Jean Potter Chelnov, Helen Rosen, Diane Johnson, Annabel Davis-Goff, Martin Peretz. I have also drawn on Lillian Hellman's interviews with Marilyn Berger, Christine Doudna, Barbara Walters, and Marsha Norman, transcripts available at HRHRC.

379   "I tried in these books": *Three,* 9.

379   "It's no news": *Maybe,* 64.

380   "annihilation of dignity": *Three,* Commentary for *An Unfinished Woman,* 303.

380   she had a great love once: Annabel Davis-Goff interview with JM.

380   "I'm not brave": Dorothea Straus interview with JM.

380   as if they had lived together as man and wife: Dorothea Straus interview with JM, July 26, 1994.

380   "a little insulted": Lillian Hellman interviewed by Fred Gardner, October 11, 1963.

381   "I love you, darling, deeply and completely": Dashiell Hammett to Josephine Hammett, April 30, 1947.

381   "Tristan and Isolde": Dorothea Straus, "The Heraldist," *Virgins and other Endangered Species* (Moyer Bell: Wakefield, R.I., 1993), 186.

381   "a strange book": Lillian Hellman to Helena Golisheva, July 15, 1968. CIA file of Lillian Hellman.

381   "I hope you will notice": Lillian Hellman to Leonard Bernstein (undated). Courtesy of Nina Bernstein.

382   "The love of her life": *The Atlantic,* July 1969, 106.

382   "her relationship with Hammett," V. S. Pritchett, "Stern Self-Portrait of a Lady," *Life,* June 27, 1969.

382   "There's not a word of truth in this": Emmy Kronenberger interview.

382   "She keeps building him up": Sid Perelman to Pat Kavanagh, August 15, 1969, in Crowther, ed., 248–49.

382   "Whenever you read anything that Lillian wrote": William Doering interview with JM, June 4, 1993.

382   "Maybe this all has something to do with why": Lillian Hellman to Richard Wilbur, May 23, 1975. Amherst College.

382   "If Hammett lives again": Bernard Malamud to Lillian Hellman, June 22, 1969. HRHRC.

382   "love[d] him because he was (maybe)": Jean Kerr to Lillian Hellman [1969]. HRHRC.

382   "Are you aware that Hammett used to visit?": William Redfield to Lillian Hellman, July 9, 1969. HRHRC.

383   "Dashiell Hammett always said I was the only Jew": Rex Reed, "Lillian Hellman," Baltimore *Sun,* November 9, 1975, D3.

383   "Part of my anger used to be anger": Lillian Hellman interview with Fred Gardner.

383   bay horses: Ibid.

383   "He very much disliked Arthur Miller": Lillian Hellman interviewed by Diane Johnson. Tape courtesy of Diane Johnson.

383   "She seems like someone": Marshall interview.

383   "I had considerable respect for Dash": Norman Mailer to Lillian Hellman, June 8, 1977. HRHRC.

384   "Raya, you always think the world is revolving": Rollyson, 432.

384   "Hammett and I had not shared the same convictions": *Unfinished Woman,* 145.

384   they and their fellow Communists: Martin Peretz interview with JM.

384   "You've already solved the problem five times": Rollyson, 427.

384   did not lie about the force of their sexual love: Poirier interview with JM.

384   "Jap prints": *Unfinished Woman,* 171.

385   The scene at the Stork Club has been challenged by Martha Gellhorn in "On Apocryphism," 288. The scene is described in *Unfinished Woman,* 59.

385 Drafts of the "Turtle" chapter of *Pentimento* are available at Columbia University.

386 "seen none of it since the first": Dashiell Hammett to Josephine Hammett Marshall, July 12, 1950.

386 It was not torn: Layman, 218.

386 For the visit to New Orleans: *Pentimento,* 10–11.

386 "We spent two years here": Lillian Hellman interviewed by Alvin Sargent, June 13, 1982. Tape courtesy of Alvin Sargent.

387 worked in a store in Fairbanks: Miriam Dickey interview with JM. Draft manuscript for the Introduction to *The Big Knockover,* marked "Early Version," available at HRHRC.

388 she had broken her leg: Alvin Sargent tape with Lillian Hellman.

388 "Tell Lily to go away": *Unfinished Woman,* 229.

389 "I don't give a damn what Mr. Fortas thinks": *Scoundrel Time,* 56.

389 "there was never the slightest danger": Wright, 248–49.

389 "We made the decision": *Scoundrel Time,* 62.

389 lamb chop: Dashiell Hammett to Lillian Hellman, April 27, 1952.

389 "a few steps from Sixth Avenue": *Unfinished Woman,* 102.

390 the physical act of running: Feibleman interview.

390 "I was married to that woman": JM interview with Stephen Greene, to whom Kober made this remark.

390 Stephen Greene winced: Greene interview with JM.

390 "I've never met you, Mr. Cohn": Fragment recounting this incident available at HRHRC.

390 "Lillian, you're not going to do any such thing": Manso, 332–33.

391 "When I remember, I remember exactly": Revisions of her interview with Peter Manso are available at HRHRC.

392 "I think Lillian's tic may have been": Norman Mailer interview with JM.

392 "You people haven't been any help": Marshall interview with JM.

392 "Not only will I never see her again": Alvin Sargent tape with Lillian Hellman.

393 "total coward": Marsha Norma, "Articles of Faith: A Conversation with Lillian Hellman," *American Theatre,* May 1984.

393 rejected by *Vanity Fair:* Interview with Donald Congdon, to whom I am indebted as well for the manuscript of "Meg."

395 James, "It Is of a Windiness: Lillian Hellman," 221.

395 "That's all a lie": Poirier interview with JM.

396 "Your love affair with Dashiell Hammett sounds so wonderful": Carol Matthau, *Among the Porcupines* (Random House: New York, 1992), 189.

28. Biographical Warfare: The Hammett Biographers

  For this chapter, I am indebted to Richard Layman, Diane Johnson, Josephine Marshall, Otto Penzler, Steven Marcus, and Jason Epstein, as well as to brief conversations with Muriel Alexander, David Fechheimer, and William Nolan.

399 "In the end, you can't stop biographies": Lillian Hellman interview with Nora Ephron, in *Conversations,* 137.

399   "I do not want my ex-beau played around with": Lillian Hellman, "Notes" for Diane Johnson's biography of Dashiell Hammett, September 14, 1982. HRHRC.

400   "I want to get everything straight": Lillian Hellman, Introduction to *The Big Knockover*, v.

400   "You're not to bother": Ibid.

400   "would prefer that you did not write": Dashiell Hammett to Pru Whitfield, October 16, 1944. Courtesy of Peter Stern.

400   "moral obligation": Lillian Hellman to Arthur Kober, April 3, 1968. WIS.

400   "going to have to forget what he wanted": Lillian Hellman interview with John Phillips and Anne Hollander, in *Conversations*, 72.

400   "a sort of modern racket": Lillian Hellman, "Given to William Maxwell, 1971." HRHRC.

400   "It is not to my taste to make available": Lillian Hellman, "H. G. Wells and Rebecca West," *New York Times Book Review*, October 13, 1974.

400   she had requested that John Melby return: Melby interview with JM.

400   "Under no circumstances . . . turn over Hammett's letters": Lillian Hellman to Joseph Fox, November 3, 1967. Columbia University.

401   "Never mind the good of society": Lillian Hellman to Donald Congdon, December 30, 1976. Columbia University.

401   "ill-advised that a biography of so American": Lillian Hellman to Jonathan Green, April 10, 1973. HRHRC.

401   "leaving" his wife and children: Otto Penzler interview with JM, July 23, 1993. See also Lillian Hellman to Otto Penzler, June 5, 1974. HRHRC.

401   Contract materials for the Marcus biography "Untitled Biography of Dashiell Hammett and Lillian Hellman" are available at Columbia University.

402   Trilling warned Marcus: Diana Trilling interview with JM.

402   "perfectly safe . . . since I will have the final approval": Lillian Hellman to Josephine Marshall, March 21, 1974.

402   "a friend of la Hellman's": Joe Gores to William Godshalk, April 28, 1974. LAY.

402   she had destroyed his career: Richard Layman interviews with JM.

402   "there are certain matters and documents": Steven Marcus to William Godshalk, July 10, 1974. LAY.

402   adversary parties and enemy clubs: Steven Marcus to William Godshalk, July 22, 1974. LAY.

403   "I never said that the young men who called upon you": Lillian Hellman to Mary Hammett Miller, December 29, 1975.

403   "not only": Steven Marcus interview with JM, May 18, 1993.

403   "The reason must be given why I did not go": Ibid.

403   "The publisher did not accept the idea of a biographer": Lillian Hellman to James Nashold, December 1, 1977. HRHRC.

403   "under no circumstances will my mother grant you an interview": Josephine Marshall to Peter Packer, December 16, 1976. See also on the Peter Packer problem: Lillian Hellman to Josephine Marshall, November 19, 1976.

404   "absolutely sure": Lillian Hellman to Josephine Marshall, April 7, 1977.

404 requesting that he repay: J. J. Sheehan to Steven Marcus, May 12, 1978. Columbia University.

404 "Please do not go on making yourself miserable": Lillian Hellman to Steven Marcus, June 6, 1977. HRHRC.

404 "that you ever saw him": Lillian Hellman to Josephine Marshall, April 19, 1978.

404 "press book . . . the only press book": Lillian Hellman, "Re: Hammett Biography, December 15, 1978." HRHRC.

404 In 1978 Lillian accused someone else of an almost identical crime, suggesting that Marcus was telling the truth: Dorothy Samuels, heading the Committee for Public Justice, was supposed to have sent her a package of materials, only for the package not to arrive and Lillian to make accusations. "It's a great puzzlement," Lillian insisted. Unlike Marcus, however, Samuels, a lawyer and one who had grown to know Lillian well, had a receipt from the messenger. Dorothy Samuels interview with JM, March 2, 1995.

404 "to be paid, and paid highly": Lillian Hellman to John Sheehan, November 17, 1978. HRHRC.

405 "I had to force Miss Alexander": Ibid.

405 it took three weeks before Lillian sent her secretary: Muriel Alexander conversation with JM, October 1, 1994.

405 "I cannot prove this": Lillian Hellman, "Re: Hammett Biography, December 15, 1978": "I cannot prove this, but I am sure by remembering the things I said on them that all the tapes were not returned to me" HRHRC.

405 "Your guess of why he has kept this material": Lillian Hellman to J. J. Sheehan, November 17, 1978. HRHRC.

405 "for work done and material furnished": Ephraim London to Steven Marcus, June 19, 1979. Courtesy of Pearl London.

405 "confusing the World Peace Conference book with a scrapbook": Hannah Weinstein to Steven Marcus, October 25, 1979. HRHRC.

405 "woman who owns the transcript": Lillian Hellman to Steven Marcus, November 30, 1979. HRHRC.

406 "She wants to hurt you": Marcus interview. See also Lillian Hellman, "Re: Steven Marcus, January 28, 1980." HRHRC.

406 "possible breakup of a marriage": Lillian Hellman to Steven Marcus, March 13, 1980. HRHRC.

406 "that the day we sat on the plane": Lillian Hellman to Steven Marcus, March 13, 1980. HRHRC.

406 "a very, very sick man, or a calculating": Lillian Hellman to President William J. McGill, March 13, 1980. HRHRC.

406 "extremely inaccurate": Lillian Hellman to Hugh Eames, October 27, 1978. HRHRC.

406 "found no evidence that he is": Richard Layman to Lillian Hellman, February 27, 1978. HRHRC.

407 "before a final decision about Hammett's biographer": Lillian Hellman to Richard Layman, March 28, 1978. HRHRC.

407 "A book is already contracted for": Lillian Hellman to Richard Layman, July 19, 1978. HRHRC.

407 "squashed": Lillian Hellman to Josephine Marshall, March 21, 1974.

407 "Biography already commissioned": Lillian Hellman note to Rita Wade, affixed to letter of George H. Wolfe, August 2, 1978.

407 "damned nice guy . . . love to see Hellman": William Nolan to Richard Layman, February 17, 1979. LAY.

407 "not a writer": David Fechheimer conversation with JM.

407 "It is amazing how much you kept her *out*": William Nolan to Richard Layman [July 4?]. LAY.

407 "sole absolute and arbitrary right": Donald Congdon interview with JM.

408 "a small army of books coming out": Lillian Hellman to Josephine Marshall, November 8, 1978.

408 "deeply pleased and amused me": Lillian Hellman to Diane Johnson, October 11, 1978. HRHRC.

408 "I felt great pride in this gent": Lillian Hellman to Diane Johnson, November 27, 1978. HRHRC.

408 "I knew how painful such a book would have been to him": Lillian Hellman to Francis Ford Coppola, December 5, 1975. HRHRC.

408 "outright attack": Richard L. Paul to Francis Ford Coppola, January 21, 1976. Courtesy of Josephine Marshall.

408 "help her in any way I can": Lillian Hellman to Francis Ford Coppola, January 26, 1976. HRHRC.

408 "was disapproving": Lillian Hellman to Josephine Marshall, March 31, 1977.

409 "I have no objection whatsoever to Hammett being the subject": Lillian Hellman to Arthur Krim, May 23, 1978. HRHRC.

409 "Just keep saying no": Lillian Hellman to Josephine Marshall, August 18, 1978.

409 "Our only weapon now are [sic] interviews": Ibid.

409 "to talk to [her] about the Hammett film": Lillian Hellman to Wim Wenders, November 28, 1978. HRHRC.

409 "counted out of the picture as long as": Lillian Hellman to Wim Wenders, January 31, 1979. HRHRC.

409 not "representing" the "real" Dashiell Hammett: Wim Wenders to Lillian Hellman, February 7, 1979. HRHRC.

409 "If there is no desire to cash in on": Lillian Hellman to Wim Wenders, February 20, 1979. HRHRC.

409 "unreleaseable": Dale Pollock, "LA Story: Creativity Meets Crunch," Los Angeles *Times,* February 6, 1981, Part VI, 1.

409 "the stuff nightmares are made of": Erik Jendresen, "The Stuff Nightmares Are Made Of: A Hammett Update," *Mystery,* 3, No. 2 (September 1981), 45.

409 "never told anybody but me": Lillian Hellman to Josephine Marshall, November 25, 1980.

410 Jo could not believe her now: Marshall interview with JM.

410 Los Angeles *Times* called *Shadow Man:* Charles Champlain, "Life of Hammett: Some Spadework and Frustrations," *Los Angeles Times Book Review,* July 12, 1981, 1.

410 "already been dismissed": Lillian Hellman to John Leonard, July 11, 1981. HRHRC. John Leonard's review of *The Shadow Man* appeared in the New York *Times* on July 8, 1981.

410   "I'd have written his biography myself": Lillian Hellman to John Leonard, July 11, 1981.

410   "Oh, stand there!": Diane Johnson interview with JM.

410   "awful secret": Diane Johnson to Josephine Marshall, March 28, 1980.

410   "was never in love with his wife": Lillian Hellman's notes addressing Diane Johnson's manuscript of her biography of Dashiell Hammett are available at HRHRC.

411   "I came into it long before I came into it": Lillian Hellman to Diane Johnson, transcribed from a tape dated September 9, 1982. HRHRC.

411   never once contradicting: Diane Johnson interview.

411   "no need personally or in public to prove": Lillian Hellman to Diane Johnson, transcribed from a tape dated September 9, 1982.

411   "Since I never had any proof . . . a possibly dangerous situation": Lillian Hellman, handwritten responses to Diane Johnson's manuscript, p. 1. HRHRC.

411   madly in love with her: Jason Epstein interview with JM, November 16, 1992.

411   "a stylish drunk": Diane Johnson interview with JM. See also Lillian Hellman to Jason Epstein, September 15, 1982, HRHRC: "His drunks, which at least had style and flair and horror, had been cut into nothing more than a good many whores."

411   "didn't like me": Lillian Hellman to Diane Johnson, June 14, 1982. HRHRC.

411   underestimate the number: Lillian Hellman, handwritten responses to Diane Johnson's manuscript, p. 4. HRHRC.

412   "might have fallen in love with you": Lillian Hellman to Diane Johnson, transcribed from a tape dated September 9, 1982. See also Diane Johnson, "Obsessed," Vanity Fair, May 1985, 79–81 and 116–19.

412   "give one damn": Lillian Hellman to Jason Epstein, September 9, 1982. HRHRC.

412   "word love has increasingly through the years": Lillian Hellman to Jason Epstein, September 9, 1982. HRHRC.

412   "moving . . . a fine job": Lillian Hellman to Jason Epstein, September 15, 1982. HRHRC.

412   understood Hammett: Lillian Hellman to Jason Epstein, September 9, 1982.

412   "official blessing . . . ton of letters": William Nolan, "Setting the Record Straight on Dashiell Hammett: A Life," manuscript made available by Richard Layman.

413   Marjorie May spoke of writing: For example, Marjorie May to Richard Layman, November 23, 1985: "I have a good idea of how the book should go on." In a 1988 letter to Layman, May writes: "I don't want to hurt daughter, compris." Muriel Alexander, in conversation with JM.

29. Me Alone

414   "Me Alone": See for example Lillian Hellman's appointment book for 1968.

414   "Now, don't be a naughty girl": Dorothea Straus interview with JM.

414   "No, Warren, there's only one part": Austin Pendleton interview with JM.
414   "Dash would have laughed at it": Rollyson, 5.
414   just have told her to cut out: Marshall interview with JM.
414   never rude unintentionally: Shirley Hazzard interview with JM.
414   with a "theater piece": Rita Wade in one of many telephone conversations with JM, subsequent to interview.
415   she still enjoyed a sexual imagination: Albert Todd conversation with JM, December 14, 1994.
415   "Tired of the tourist joints": Lillian Hellman to Alan Maclean, January 14, 1974. HRHRC.
415   "You're destroying my personality": Richard Poirier interview.
415   "Mr. Hammett": William Abrahams conversation with JM, April 1993.
416   "My whole life is fucked up": Harriette Dorsen conversation with JM, June 15, 1994.
416   "I hope you won't think of me as sad": Lillian Hellman to Vladimir Dedijer, April 22, 1970. Michigan Historical Collections, Bentley Historical Library, University of Michigan.
416   "You're all there and I'm here": Ellen Hodor conversation with JM at Hardscrabble Farm, June 7, 1994.
416   "I still have the same old heart": Rita Wade interview with JM.
416   "What do you mean?": Richard de Combray interview with JM.
416   stark naked: Richard Poirier interview with JM.
416   flirted with a greasy sailor: Max Palevsky interview with JM, April 21, 1993.
416   she charmed a handsome Welshman: Kitty Carlisle Hart interview with JM.
416   "Don't lie, Norman": Roger Donald interview with JM, April 29, 1993.
417   Lily took the opportunity: Fred Hills conversation with JM, November 14, 1994.
417   "You are much too young . . . You look like a bridesmaid": Mildred Loftus interview with JM.
417   "Serious considerations": Barnard College Commencement Address, May 30, 1976. Text available at HRHRC.
417   "It is a losing game," Lillian Hellman, "Plain Speaking with Mrs. Carter," Rolling Stone, No. 226 (November 18, 1976), 43–45.
417   a woman should put up with a lot: Lynda Palevsky interview with JM, April 19, 1993.
418   the next person to be served": Lillian Hellman's instructions to her staff, memo dated April 10, 1973. HRHRC.
418   "Miss Hellman, I sure wish I had": Jamie Bernstein-Thomas interview with JM, February 2, 1994.
418   pre-Civil War: Annabel Davis-Goff interview with JM. Diana Trilling made the same observation.
418   Zinnemann was appalled: Fred Zinnemann interview with JM, December 20, 1993.
418   "I'll finish you on this island": Richard de Combray interview.
418   "with greater meaning": Lillian Hellman to Ann Talman, June 2, 1981. HRHRC.

418   "That's deplorable": Richard Roth interview with JM, April 21, 1993.

418   "You don't give the servants": Linda Anderson interview with JM.

418   "What have you read?": A. Robert Towbin interview with JM.

419   "Get that child away": Scene reported by both Lynda Palevsky and Robert Brustein.

419   "When the plane goes down": Nina Bernstein interview with JM, March 10, 1994.

419   She was not sending him a gift: John Marquand interview with JM.

419   "This has been a terrible birthday": Lillian Hellman to Mildred Loftus (undated). Courtesy of Mildred Loftus.

419   "The one thing you should do": Mina Towbin Pingar interview with JM, July 20, 1993.

419   nothing maternal: Pearl London interview with JM.

419   "It obviously is a measure of your great affection": Lillian Hellman to Jean Chelnov, May 25, 1977. HRHRC.

420   "You pronounce his name 'Da-shiel'": Honor Moore conversation with JM, October 3, 1994.

420   a piece of old kitchen iron: Becky Bernstien interview with JM.

420   "Money makes you laugh": Hart interview.

420   "I want diamonds": Maureen Stapleton interview with JM, May 11, 1993.

420   "I want to buy a fur coat": A. Robert Towbin interview with JM.

421   "Now I know how the rich stay rich": Deirdre Bair conversation with JM.

421   "Leave it to the Jews": Jonathan La Pook interview with JM, April 28, 1993.

421   "You're the only one who didn't bring me a present": Roger Straus conversation with JM.

421   "We had a contract": Max Palevsky interview.

421   "It gives me enormous pleasure": Lillian Hellman to Christina Stead, November 11, 1982. Courtesy of Jonathan La Pook.

421   fake love letters: See Feibleman, *Lilly.*

422   Rose was a terrible mistake: Jules Feiffer interview with JM, February 11, 1994.

422   "I won't fuck you anymore": Diane Johnson interview with JM.

422   raped her: Diana Trilling and Renata Adler interviews with JM, among others.

422   "There is also the possibility of a dog": See Lillian Hellman to Kurtis Sameth Hill, Inc., July 29, 1968. HRHRC.

422   "I felt somebody bump against me": Lillian Hellman to Calvin Siegel of N. W. Sameth, Inc., February 27, 1964. HRHRC.

422   Clark remembers: Blair Clark conversation with JM.

422   "Is he fucking Lenny?": Peter Feibleman interview with JM.

422   "It's too bad. You're a good writer": John Marquand interview with JM.

423   His children felt her words: Jamie Bernstein-Thomas interview with JM.

423   "get your penis out of my pasta": Robin Hogan interview with JM, June 15, 1993.

423   an angry, threatening letter: See Lillian Hellman to Leonard Bernstein, January 11, 1982, November 18, 1982, December 21, 1982. Also Lillian Hellman to Robert Lantz, December 9, 1982, and Lillian Hellman to Leonard Bernstein, March 3, 1983, June 28, 1983, October 6, 1983, and October 28, 1983. On October 6, she wrote: "I must now once again beg you to keep your word and not have this version of 'Candide' performed again. If you do not withdraw it, then I have no way to defend *my* 'Candide' except publicly to state what is in this letter." Beside her line "this letter will end the correspondence," (October 28), Bernstein wrote in the word "Hurray." Courtesy of Jamie Bernstein-Thomas and Nina Bernstein.

423   "There are an awful lot of kikes": Towbin interview.

423   "I myself make very anti-Semitic remarks": Sylvie Drake, "Writer Still Reluctant to Define Self at 74," Los Angeles *Times,* October 18, 1981, Calendar, 1, 6.

423   "a long time ago that I was very glad": Ibid. See also Doudna interview: "I just know that I would rather be a Jew," in *Conversations,* 197.

424   "The food is not to be eaten": Lillian Hellman to Mildred Loftus (undated). Courtesy of Mildred Loftus.

424   "Driver, look at me!": Howard Fast interview with JM.

424   "could no longer manage it alone": Lillian Hellman interviewed by Nora Ephron, in *Conversations,* 132.

424   Those who loved her the most seemed the most angry: Feibleman interview.

424   "Her whole manner is strictly below the belt": Truman Capote responding to the question: who are the sexiest women you know? *Playboy,* December 1980, 259.

424   "Am I going to be all right?": Robin Hogan interview with JM, June 15, 1993.

425   "I think you look like a whore": Stapleton interview with JM.

425   "You know, I'm afraid Miss Hellman is a lesbian": John Marquand interview with JM.

425   "and there was a woman I had been to bed: Richard Poirier interview.

425   "there was a real homosexual something": Diana Trilling interview with JM.

425   "You've been analyzed, Diana": Ibid.

426   "You must get over the idea": Feibleman interview.

30. Woman in Command

427   "Norman, I have to talk to you": Renata Adler interview with JM.

427   "I have publishing offers": Lillian Hellman to Arthur W. A. Cowan (undated). Courtesy of Marilyn Raab.

427   filling the house: Stephen Gillers interview with JM, March 8, 1993.

427   She didn't care who took out the garbage: See, for example, Sylvie Drake, "Lillian Hellman as Herself," Los Angeles *Times,* October 18, 1981, Calendar, 6.

428   "at bottom": Robert Silvers interview with JM, December 16, 1994.

428   "a hatchet job": For the story of Goodwin's defense, interviews with Richard Goodwin, June 3, 1993, and with Robert Silvers.

428   "My lips are sealed": Silvers interview with JM.

428   "in tears and in liquor": Lillian Hellman to Elizabeth Hardwick (undated). HRHRC.

428   Edmund Wilson, "An Open Letter to Mike Nichols," *New York Review of Books,* January 4, 1968.

428   "contrived without compensating": *New York Times Book Review,* June 18, 1972. See also Renata Adler, "A Review Reviewed," *New York Times Book Review,* July 9, 1972.

428   Lillian attributed Samuels' malice: See Lillian Hellman to Richard Moody, July 6, 1972. Moody mss., Manuscripts Department, Lilly Library, Indiana University, Bloomington.

429   "are nonsense examples of ten-cent store": Lillian Hellman to Jerome Wiesner, May 14, 1971. HRHRC.

429   "What is this ten thousand dollars?": Cathy Kober interview with JM.

429   "It was not only the money": Lillian Hellman to Donald Oresman, September 14, 1977. HRHRC.

429   My father told me: Alvin Sargent interview with Lillian Hellman. Tape courtesy of Alvin Sargent.

430   "someone who knew how to act": Murray Kempton, "Witnesses," *New York Review of Books,* June 10, 1976, 25.

430   "Dear Lillian Hellman, you could not be more mistaken": Irving Howe, "Lillian Hellman and the McCarthy Years," *Dissent,* Fall 1976, 382.

430   "the review of a gentleman": Lillian Hellman to Lee Clark, April 10, 1979. HRHRC.

430   "political amnesia": Phyllis Jacobson, "A Time of Assorted Scoundrels," *New Politics,* 11, No. 4 (Fall 1976), 14–24.

430   "different political and social views": *Scoundrel Time,* 84.

430   "men who turned down": Ibid., 85.

430   "morally contemptible": Martin Peretz interview with JM.

430   "lost our enthusiasm": Roger Donald interview with JM.

430   For this discussion of Little, Brown's decision not to publish Diana Trilling's essays: Roger Donald and Diana Trilling interviews with JM.

431   "hysterical": See, for example, Lillian Hellman to Diana Trilling, September 30, 1976: "*I* never said, nor did the New York Times story print, that *I* said you were 'hysterical.' I quoted Donald: your attacks on me were personal and you were hysterical about them. Indignation leads you to misunderstandings."

431   the front page of the New York *Times:* "Diana Trilling Book Is Canceled; Reply to Lillian Hellman Is Cited," September 28, 1976.

431   "diminishing intellectual force . . . I don't give a damn": Deirdre Carmody, "Trilling Case Sparks Publisher-Loyalty Debate," New York *Times,* September 30, 1976. See also Roger Donald interview.

431   "Hammett's influence, there or not": See Norman Mailer to Lillian Hellman, June 8, 1977, and Hellman to Mailer, June 13, 1977. HRHRC.

431   "what were you doing there adjudicating": Lillian Hellman to Norman Mailer, July 22, 1977. HRHRC.

431   Lillian shut the door: For the scene of Lillian Hellman's discussion with Mailer over his blurb, Renata Adler and Norman Mailer interviews with JM.

432   "This ought to be called Lillian's island": See in particular Michiko Kakutani, "Diana Trilling, Pathfinder in Morality," New York *Times,* November 16, 1981: "The social repercussions have been endless. I spend my summers on Martha's Vineyard where anyone who entertains me is never again invited to Lillian Hellman's house."

432   "It is remarkable to think of yourself": "Trilling Charge Denied by Lillian Hellman," New York *Times,* November 17, 1981.

432   "Why you wished to make me into a kind of": Lillian Hellman to Jane Fonda, November 7, 1977.

432   "malefactor": Straus, "The Heraldist," 187.

432   "a load of crap": Roger Donald interview with JM.

433   "Lillian, Communism has hurt": Martin Peretz interview with JM.

433   "Zionism has sapped the dissident juices": Ibid.

433   "Who the hell gave you my number?": Chaleff conversation with JM.

433   "Black people are much better off in New Orleans": Blair Fuller interview with JM.

433   requested her support for his coffeehouse: Fred Gardner interview with JM.

433   For the discussion of the Committee for Public Justice, I am indebted to Blair Clark, Norman Dorsen, Nancy Kramer, Stephen Gillers, Dorothy Samuels, and Robert Silvers.

434   "Lillian, I'm a civil libertarian": Norman Dorsen interview with JM, November 11, 1994.

434   "a progressive civil libertarian": Stephen Gillers interview.

434   For the picture of Lillian Hellman holding forth at a committee meeting, Stephen Gillers and Dorothy Samuels interviews.

435   "Let us concentrate on what we can do": Silvers interview with JM.

435   She complained about how much: Samuels interviews with JM, February 28 and March 2, 1995.

435   Why didn't they stop her? Ibid.

435   Lillian was intractable: Silvers interview.

435   "You're a liar": Nancy Kramer interview with JM, February 27, 1995.

436   a baggage handler: Stephen Gillers interview.

436   "I ask you as a friend to make certain": Lillian Hellman to Diana Trilling, October 14, 1976. HRHRC.

436   "malicious personal attack": Ephraim London to FCC, June 28, 1977. Courtesy of Pearl London.

437   "have a look at . . . despicable": Lillian Hellman to Ephraim London, April 26, 1978. Courtesy of Pearl London.

437   "dirty stuff": Lillian Hellman to Katharine Graham, March 22, 1978. HRHRC.

437   "where in my book I misrepresented myself": Lillian Hellman to George Will, March 22, 1978. See also Hellman to Will, April 18, 1978. Courtesy of Pearl London.

437   "to stay away from all legal matters": Rita Wade to Ephraim London, January 30, 1978. Courtesy of Pearl London.

31. The McCarthy Suit and Julia

I am indebted to Pearl London for making available to me the files of Ephraim London, who represented Lillian Hellman in her lawsuit against Mary McCarthy. Also helpful to me in this chapter were the papers and memos of Blair Clark, as well as conversations with Stephen Gillers, Harriette Dorsen, Norman Dorsen, and Renata Adler.

438   "What is true should not be obscured": "Retraction" by Lillian Hellman, *Ladies' Home Journal,* March 1964, 82.

438   "My days are now off and on": Lillian Hellman to Ephraim London, August 4, 1983.

438   strange, almost comatose: Lillian Hellman to Dr. Russell Hoxsie, February 5, 1979. HRHRC.

438   she set papers on fire: Palevsky interview.

438   If it's in your will: Rita Wade interview with JM.

439   "I can't stand her": Juan Dupont interview with Mary McCarthy, *Paris Metro,* February 15, 1978.

439   "often brilliant and sometimes even sound": Phillips and Hollander interview with Lillian Hellman, in *Conversations,* 60.

439   "a born truth-teller": Transcript of videotape of Dick Cavett interview with Mary McCarthy and audiotape: Ace Sound Studies, February 1, 1980. Courtesy of Pearl London.

440   her whole persona had long depended: Robert Silvers interview with JM.

440   "a piece of rag": Lillian Hellman note to Ephraim London, August 4, 1983. HRHRC.

440   brother and sister: Stephen Gillers interview with JM.

440   "It seems to me I have a right to expect": Lillian Hellman to Dick Cavett, January 28, 1980. HRHRC.

441   "You're going to lose": Quoted in Dorothea Straus interview with JM.

441   "I'll break her": Ibid.

441   sold for close to a million: Isidore Englander interview with JM, April 28, 1993.

441   he could not bear to send her a bill: Pearl London interview with JM.

441   "I think Hammett would have thought she was not": Wayne Warga, "Hellman at 75: Fragile but Furious," in *Conversations,* 277.

442   "about sixty years old": Affidavit of Terence R. Dellecker to Alan F. Dahl, Vice-Consul, Embassy of the United States of America, April 22, 1980.

442   "false and . . . made with ill-will": Summons and Complaint, courtesy of Pearl London. It reads: "The Statement is and was false and was made with ill-will, with malice, with knowledge of its falsity, or with careless disregard of its truth or falsity, and with intent to injure the Plaintiff personally and in her profession . . . the making and broadcast of the Statement was with intent to, and it did, damage the name, reputation and standing of the Plaintiff, and the Plaintiff has been exposed to shame, ridicule and obloquy. By reason of the foregoing Plaintiff suffered and still suffers great mental pain and anguish, and the Plaintiff has been injured in her profession and the numbers of

people who buy her books and attend her lectures and plays will be greatly diminished, and the Plaintiff is deterred from again writing autobiographical works or material, all to the Plaintiff's loss and damage in the sum of $1,750,000." The date is February 14, 1980.

442   "Plaintiff is a bad writer and an intellectually dishonest": Index No. 16834/80: Defendant Mary McCarthy's Answers to Plaintiff's First Interrogatories.

442   "When the purge trials did come": Lillian Hellman's Comments on Mary McCarthy's Answers to Plaintiff's First Interrogatories.

443   "in very large danger from Julia's very unpleasant family": Ibid.

443   he disbelieved her: Blair Clark interviews with JM.

443   "I am not a liar": Wayne Warga interview with Lillian Hellman, *Conversations*, 276.

443   "Nobody can ever say they told the complete truth": Lillian Hellman to Barbara Epstein, November 18, 1980. HRHRC.

443   Kay Boyle: Telegram dated February 28, 1980: "I love you and hope you win." George de Trow: "Dear Lillie-pie, here's hoping you get every nickel she's got. Love, George." Both at HRHRC. Alger Hiss to Ephraim London, February 23, 1980. Courtesy of Pearl London.

443   "truly shameful": John Hersey to Dick Cavett, January 26, 1980. Courtesy of Pearl London.

443   "vicious, mendacious and . . . appallingly": William Styron to Lillian Hellman, April 2, 1980. HRHRC.

443   "natural for them to detest each other": Norman Mailer, "An Appeal to Lillian Hellman and Mary McCarthy," *New York Times Book Review*, May 11, 1980, 3, 33.

443   "deeply wrong": Robert Silvers interview with JM.

444   "mistaken": William Alfred interview with JM.

444   "You call Miss McCarthy and you tell her": Ibid.

444   "her conscience to fit the whims": "The Honor of Lillian Hellman," New York *Post*, May 22, 1980, 25.

444   "greatly gifted in the writing of fictions": New York *Post*, February 16, 1980.

444   "of no legal merit": Renata Adler, *Pitch Dark* (Alfred A. Knopf: New York, 1983), 9.

444   Adler speculated incorrectly: Max Palevsky conversation with JM, 1994.

444   "Viola Teagarden has no memory of doing": Lillian Hellman to Renata Adler, May 19, 1983.

444   "I am sick of asking for a bill": Lillian Hellman to Ephraim London, September 29, 1980.

445   "reputation for honesty and integrity": Statement by Lillian Hellman, December 9, 1981: "It is impossible to identify every person who has knowledge of my reputation for honesty and integrity, and it is not possible to identify the dates when I obtained knowledge of my reputation. The communities in which I have a reputation for honesty and integrity are, Pleasantville, New York, Los Angeles, Martha's Vineyard, London and Paris, and other places in which my books have been sold." The signature is barely legible.

445   "It may well be that the plaintiff has persuaded herself": Defendant Mary McCarthy's Answers to Plaintiff's First Interrogatories, August 12, 1981.

445   "It might not be a bad idea": Ephraim London to Lillian Hellman, August 5, 1981.

446   "It is all that I have saved": Lillian Hellman to Dear Sir, April 9, 1982.

446   "the danger of using historical sources": *New Republic,* February 23, 1954.

446   "What Paper D'Ya Read?": *The New Yorker,* May 27, 1944.

446   "an appropriate court order": John G. Koeltl to Ephraim London, July 14, 1982.

446   "the inadequacy of plaintiff's interrogatory answers": John G. Koeltl to Ephraim London, October 4, 1982. See also Koeltl to London, November 17, 1982, and January 27, 1983.

447   "That piece of shit": Lillian Hellman to Robert Lantz, December 9, 1982. HRHRC.

447   "You know, it's not easy to defecate": Lillian Hellman interview with Alvin Sargent.

447   "Yesterday I felt, and I guess today": Conversation between Lillian Hellman and Dr. Jay Meltzer, transcribed March 5, 1982. HRHRC.

447   "I am a kind of mess": Lillian Hellman to Ephraim London, July 27, 1982.

447   the real name of Julia's family was Clark!: Blair Clark conversation with JM.

448   "It's a complete fabrication": Martin Peretz interview with JM, and Anne Peretz interview with JM, January 19, 1994.

448   "Austrian underground . . . and for that I am deeply sorry": Lillian Hellman to George Gero, May 27, 1983. HRHRC.

448   "very frightened": Ibid.

448   Gardiner canceled the meeting: Ibid.

448   "They" would sue her: For the account of the lunch at Le Cirque and its aftermath, I am indebted to a memo about the occasion by Blair Clark.

449   "left me quite a lot of money": Lillian Hellman to Ephraim London, May 27, 1983. HRHRC.

449   "But, Lillian, I can't break him": Ibid.

449   Draft of Blair Clark's original letter to *Harper's* is by courtesy of Mr. Clark.

450   he hoped it would not: Blair Clark conversation with JM, November 9, 1994.

450   Dorothy Parker had given her the same drawing: Alvin Sargent interview with Lillian Hellman.

450   a young man accidentally bumped her: Robin Hogan interview with JM.

451   it was guilt: Milton Wexler interview with JM, April 17, 1993.

451   drugs also blocked normal censoring: Jay I. Meltzer to Lillian Hellman, April 26, 1983. See also Annabel Davis-Goff interview with JM.

451   "in a closet facing death": Lillian Hellman to Leonard Bernstein, June 28, 1983. Courtesy of the Leonard Bernstein estate.

451   "We each . . . have a right to our standards": Lillian Hellman to Dr. G. H. McCormack, December 9, 1981. In his reply Dr. McCormack wrote her that with regard to his "standards of conduct," he would "match them up with yours or anyone's, any time, any day." HRHRC.

451   "in an exaggerated and rhetorical manner": Memorandum of Law of Defendant Mary McCarthy in Support of Motion for Summary Judgment.

451   "alleged fact . . . within the special meaning": Index 16834, May 18, 1983. Affidavits in Opposition to Motions for Summary Judgment in Lillian Hellman, Plaintiff, against Mary McCarthy, Dick Cavett, Educational Broadcasting Corp., and Daphne Productions, Inc., Defendants.

452   she did seem to find something difficult: Dorothy Samuels interview with JM.

452   "worst tempered woman in American letters," "Mary McCarthy," Vogue, November 1981, 292.

452   "unlimited and voluntary public figure . . . general notoriety": Court Decisions, New York Law Journal, May 29, 1984: Justice Baer: Hellman v. McCarthy. "This is a motion by defendants for summary judgment . . ."

452   "The power of L.H.—a puzzlement": quoted in Carol Brightman, Writing Dangerously: Mary McCarthy and Her World (Clarkson Potter: New York, 1992), 611.

452   "This is the worst moment of my life": Blair Clark interview with JM, February 15, 1995. Also Diana Trilling interview.

453   "There's no satisfaction in having an enemy die": Quoted in Brightman, 597.

453   "a kind of awful way of giving yourself loveability": Ibid., 619–20.

32. Requiescat in Pace

454   "I wish I had stayed in New Orleans": Lillian Hellman to Theodore Roethke (undated). University of Washington Libraries Manuscript Collection.

454   "not fitted to stand alone": Shirley Hazzard interview with JM.

454   "Mrs. Schwartz syndrome": Lisa Weinstein interview with JM, April 19, 1993.

454   "I always guessed and certainly I now clearly know": Three, commentary for An Unfinished Woman, 305.

455   "If you were ten years younger": Annabel Davis-Goff interview with JM.

455   "I've hired Rabbi Nussbaum": Alvin Sargent interview with JM.

455   "give him a chance for a third": Lillian Hellman to Richard Roth, May 20, 1976. HRHRC.

455   "I've never seen my clitoris": Conversation with Alvin Sargent, April 19, 1995.

455   How about a kiss?: Peter Feibleman interview with JM.

455   "I wish I looked like you": Rita Wade interview with JM.

455   She addressed him in her letters as "Prof": "the old professor": Dashiell Hammett to Lillian Hellman, May 23, 1944. See also Dashiell Hammett to Lillian Hellman, February 29, 1944: "The professor's store of knowledge is . . . not limitless." Lillian Hellman sometimes wrote to Arthur W. A. Cowan as "Professor." She also addressed Peter Feibleman that way.

455   "It seems to me in the face of my fidelity": Letters of Lillian Hellman to Richard de Combray, dating from 1975, appear courtesy of Richard de Combray.

456   "I hear Lillian has you in her net": Feibleman interview with JM.

456   "It makes me look like a three-times-divorced": Peter Feibleman interview with JM, July 20, 1994.

456   "I got two for the price of one": Feibleman interview with JM.

456   "Hammett used to hurt me in the same sense": Feibleman, *Lilly*, 318.

456   "I've only taken seriously two men": Feibleman interview with JM.

457   "Lillian has a way of binding people to her": Selma Wolfman to Mrs. Paul K. Sauer, October 18, 1963. HRHRC.

457   "he was lying on his back in the earth": Feibleman, 289.

457   angry at him still: Ibid., 167.

457   "He satisfy your soul": Linda Anderson interview with JM.

457   "You can write a book later": Fred Gardner interview with JM.

458   Gardner knew he could not put his name: Ibid.

458   "I don't know where the story of briefcase": Lillian Hellman to Katherine Lederer, April 12, 1977. HRHRC.

458   Annotations to Moody's manuscript are available at the Lily Library, Indiana University, Bloomington.

459   "something very wrong about an author being quoted": Lillian Hellman to Richard Moody, July 12, 1971. Lilly Library.

459   "I hope you will remember": Lillian Hellman to Katherine Lederer, April 4, 1977. HRHRC.

459   "the false Abelard": David Cort to Lillian Hellman, July 6, 1976. The letters of David Cort to Lillian Hellman and hers to him appear courtesy of Pearl London.

459   "I haven't been in love very often": Lillian Hellman to David Cort, July 16, 1976.

459   "The last time we met you asked me whether": David Cort to Lillian Hellman (undated).

459   "If I gave you back your letters": Lillian Hellman to David Cort, August 3, 1976.

460   "I hear you smoke too much": David Cort to Lillian Hellman (undated).

460   "my *back* went up": *Pitch Dark*, 3–4.

460   "You must know that I will not sue Renata": Lillian Hellman to Burke Marshall, August 30, 1983. HRHRC.

460   "carpentry": William Luce interview with JM, May 8, 1993.

460   "Having an official biographer seems to make me": Lillian Hellman to Richard Wilbur, April 30, 1984. Amherst College.

460   "I think I know what she wanted": Blair Clark to William Wright,
       September 7, 1984. Courtesy of Blair Clark.

461   "private clause": Lillian Hellman to Ephraim London, June 10, 1980.

461   not wanting to pay a lawyer: Rita Wade interviews with JM.

461   "I'll be dead": Isidore Englander interview with JM.

461   "We have to call and change the will!": Robin Hogan interview with
       JM.

461   she would leave her the birdcage: Kitty Carlisle Hart interview with
       JM.

461   pleased her by choosing: Annabel Davis-Goff interview.

461   To Fred Gardner's dismay: Gardner interview with JM.

462   Only then would the Hammett heirs: Josephine Marshall interview
       with JM.

462   "Dash would be furious": Judy Ruben interview with JM.

463   "Which of you would like what?": Lillian Hellman interview with Alvin
       Sargent, 1982.

463   "I have been introduced as Lillian Hellman": Speech courtesy of
       Richard de Combray.

463   "Sea-pie": Feibleman interview with JM.

464   "Let's meet privately": Feibleman interview with JM.

464   "I'm trusting when I'm old you'll be the one": Renata Adler interview
       with JM.

464   "nonfatal weekend": Rita Wade interview with JM.

464   "You haven't called me for a week": Lisa Weinstein interview with JM,
       April 19, 1993.

464   "I'll see you when you come back to town": Dina Weinstein interview
       with JM, April 21, 1993.

464   "I think you and I are going to get along": *Feibleman,* 333.

465   "1:15 a.m. June 30th": Rita Wade interview.

465   Eulogies for Lillian Hellman appear in Peter Feibleman's *Lilly.*

465   It is a cold and gloomy March day: The following scenes are derived
       from undated notes tucked inside one of Lillian Hellman's *Diaries.*
       HRHRC.

Selected Bibliography

Adler, Renata. *Pitch Dark*. Alfred A. Knopf: New York, 1983.

Berg, A. Scott. *Goldwyn: A Biography*. Alfred A. Knopf: New York, 1989.

Dick, Bernard F. *Hellman in Hollywood*. Fairleigh Dickinson University Press: Rutherford, Madison, Teaneck, 1982.

Dictionary of Literary Biography: Documentary Series. Volume 6: Hardboiled Mystery Writers Raymond Chandler, Dashiell Hammett, Ross MacDonald, ed. Matthew J. Bruccoli and Richard Layman. A Bruccoli Clark Layman Book. Gale Research Inc. Book Tower. Detroit, 1989. pp. 85–242.

Easton, Carol. *The Search for Sam Goldwyn*. William Morrow and Company, Inc.: New York, 1976.

Fast, Howard. *The Naked God: The Writer And The Communist Party*. Frederick A. Praeger: New York, 1957.

———. *Being Red: A Memoir*. Boston: Houghton Mifflin, 1990.

Feibleman, Peter. *Lilly: Reminiscences of Lillian Hellman*. William Morrow and Company: New York, 1988.

Field, Frederick Vanderbilt. *From Right to Left: An Autobiography*. Westport, Connecticut: Lawrence Hill & Company, 1983.

Folsom, Franklin. *Days of Anger, Days of Hope: A Memoir of the League of American Writers 1937–1942*. University Press of Colorado: Niwot, 1994.

Freeman, Joseph. *An American Testament: A Narrative of Rebels and Romantics*. Octagon Books: New York, 1973.

Gardiner, Muriel. *Code Name "Mary"*. Yale University Press: New Haven and London, 1983.

Gilmer, Walker. *Horace Liveright: Publisher Of The Twenties*. David Lewis: New York, 1970.

Gitlow, Benjamin. *I Confess: The Truth About American Communism*. E. P. Dutton & Co., Inc.: New York, 1940.

Gores, Joe. *Hammett: A Novel.* G. P. Putnam's Sons: New York, 1975.

Gottfried, Martin. *Jed Harris: The Curse Of Genius.* Little, Brown and Company: Boston and Toronto, 1984.

Graver, Lawrence. *An Obsession with Anne Frank: Meyer Levin and the Diary.* University of California Press: Berkeley, 1995.

Ingersoll, Ralph. *The Great Ones: The Love Story of Two Very Important People.* Harcourt, Brace and Company: New York, 1948.

Hammett, Dashiell. "On The Way." *Harper's Bazaar.* March 1932, pp. 44–45.

———. *Woman In The Dark: A Novel of Dangerous Romance.* Alfred A. Knopf: New York, 1988.

———. *The Big Knockover,* ed. Lillian Hellman. Vintage Books: New York, 1989.

———. *Red Harvest.* Alfred A. Knopf: New York, 1929.

———. *The Dain Curse.* Alfred A. Knopf: New York, 1930.

———. *The Maltese Falcon.* Alfred A. Knopf: New York, 1930.

———. *The Glass Key.* Alfred A. Knopf: New York, 1931.

———. *The Thin Man.* Alfred A. Knopf: New York, 1934.

Hart, Moss. *Act One: An Autobiography.* St. Martin's Press: New York, 1959, 1987.

Hellman, Lillian. *The Searching Wind.* New York: The Viking Press, 1944.

———. *Six Plays by Lillian Hellman: The Children's Hour, Days To Come, The Little Foxes, Watch On The Rhine, Another Part Of The Forest, The Autumn Garden.* The Modern Library: New York, 1960.

———. *An Unfinished Woman: A Memoir.* Bantam Books: New York, 1969.

———. *Pentimento: A Book Of Portraits.* New American Library: New York, 1973.

———. *Scoundrel Time.* Little Brown and Company: Boston, 1976.

———. *Three: An Unfinished Woman, Pentimento, Scoundrel Time,* with new commentaries by the author. Little Brown and Company: Boston, 1979.

———. *Maybe: A Story.* Little Brown and Company: Boston, 1980.

Hellman, Lillian and Feibleman, Peter. *Eating Together: Recollections & Recipes.* Little Brown and Company: Boston, 1984.

———. *Conversations With Lillian Hellman,* ed. Jackson R. Bryer. University Press of Mississippi: Jackson, 1986.

Howe, Irving and Coser, Lewis. *The American Communist Party: A Critical History.* Frederick A. Praeger: New York, 1957, 1962.

Johnson, Diane. *Dashiell Hammett: A Life.* Random House: New York, 1983.

Johnson, Paul. *The Intellectuals.* Harper and Row: New York, 1988.

Kanfer, Stefan. *A Journal Of The Plague Years.* Atheneum: New York, 1973.

Lardner, Jr., Ring. *The Lardners: My Family Remembered.* Harper and Row: New York, 1976.

Layman, Richard. *Dashiell Hammett: A Descriptive Bibliography.* University of Pittsburgh Press: Pittsburgh, 1979.

———. *Shadow Man: The Life of Dashiell Hammett.* Harcourt Brace Jovanovich: New York, 1981.

Levin, Meyer. *The Obsession.* Simon and Schuster: New York, 1973.

Lyons, Eugene. *The Red Decade: The Stalinist Penetration of America.* The Bobbs-Merrill Company: Indianapolis and New York, 1941.

Maney, Richard. *Fanfare: The Confessions of a Press Agent.* Harper & Brothers Publishers: New York, 1957.

Manso, Peter. *Mailer: His Life and Times.* Simon and Schuster: New York, 1985.

Martin, Jay. *Nathanael West: The Art Of His Life.* Farrar, Straus and Giroux: New York, 1970.

Meade, Marion. *Dorothy Parker: What Fresh Hell Is This?* Villard Books: New York, 1988.

Miller, Arthur. *Timebends: A Life.* Grove Press: New York, 1987.

Moody, Richard. *Lillian Hellman: Playwright.* Pegasus: New York, 1972.

Morrow, Felix. *Revolution and Counter-Revolution in Spain.* New Park Publications, Limited: London, 1963. First published in 1938.

Navasky, Victor S. *Naming Names.* The Viking Press: New York, 1980.

Newman, Robert P. *The Cold War Romance Of Lillian Hellman & John Melby.* The University of North Carolina Press: Chapel Hill, 1989.

Nolan, William F. *Hammett: A Life At The Edge.* Congdon & Weed: New York, 1983.

O'Hara, John. *Selected Letters of John O'Hara,* ed. Matthew J. Bruccoli. Random House: New York, 1978.

Orlova, Raisa. *Memoirs.* Random House: New York, 1983.

Orwell, George. *Homage to Catalonia.* The Beacon Press: Boston, 1952.

Perelman, S. J. *Don't Tread On Me: The Selected Letters Of S. J. Perelman.* Edited by Prudence Crowther. Penguin Books: New York, 1988.

Phillips, William. *A Partisan View: Five Decades Of The Literary Life.* Stein and Day: New York, 1983.

Podhoretz, Norman. *Breaking Ranks: A Political Memoir.* Harper & Row: New York, 1979.

Rollyson, Carl. *Lillian Hellman: Her Legend and Her Legacy.* St. Martin's Press: New York, 1988.

Schwartz, Nancy Lynn. *The Hollywood Writers' Wars.* Alfred A. Knopf: New York, 1982.

Stein, Gertrude. *Everybody's Autobiography.* Cooper Square Publishers, Inc.: New York, 1971.

Straus, Dorothea. *Virgins And Other Endangered Species: A Memoir.* Moyer Bell: Wakefield, Rhode Island, 1993.

Trilling, Diana. *We Must March My Darlings: A Critical Decade.* Harcourt Brace Jovanovich: New York, 1977.

Weidman, Jerome. *The Sound Of Bow Bells.* Random House: New York, 1962.

———. *Praying For Rain.* Harper and Row: New York, 1986.

Wright, William. *Lillian Hellman: The Image, The Woman.* Simon and Schuster: New York, 1986.

Zwick, Edward M. *Life In Art: A Study Of Lillian Hellman and Watch On The Rhine.* Senior Thesis, Harvard University.

Index

JUN 1996

DATE DUE

The Joint Free Public Library
of
Morristown and Morris Township
1 Miller Road
Morristown, New Jersey 07960